Virginia Slavery
and
King Salt
in
Booker T. Washington's Boyhood Home

by

Larry Linwell Rowe

Companion Book about his Boyhood Years:
Booker T. Washington's Boyhood American Dream:
The Climb of the Black Middle Class Up from Slavery

Book One of Two-Book Set

———————

4200 Malden Drive

Charleston, West Virginia 25306

larrylrowe1@gmail.com

Website Orders: larrylrowe.com

ISBN: 978-1-7339297-1-4

Library of Congress Control Number: 2019904299

Printed by

West Virginia State University

Institute, Kanawha County,
West Virginia

Cover Design: James A. Hale

Table of Contents

The Author's Viewpoint: **11**
   Inspiration: Alma Lee Davis Rowe 11
   Validation: Minnie Wayne Cooper 13

Acknowledgments **17**
   Help Getting on with the Project.. 17

Preface: **23**
   Ruffner Salt, Virginia Slavery and Booker T. Washington.................. 23

Introduction: **33**
   The Climb Up From Virginia Slavery Over The Idea
   of White Superiority and on to the American Middle Class 33

The Wilderness Of Western Virginia **45**
   Frontier Values in the Mountains 45
   Nature's Division of Virginia: East and West............................ 49
   German and Scot-Irish Pioneers in Western Virginia...................... 53
   Virginia Aristocrats Versus Mountain Pioneers.......................... 58

Settlers Push West Into
Native Hunting Grounds **63**
   Virginia Settlers Defy King George's Ban on Western Settlements..... 63
   George Washington Explores the Kanawha Valley 65
   Capture and Torture of William Crawford 68
   Massacre of Mingo Village Starts All-Out War........................... 70
   Settler Militia is Ready for Long Campaign 71
   Militia Marches to Point Pleasant 74
   Passing by Salt and Gas Springs 74
   Settlers' Militia Secures Western Border of America..................... 77

Virginia Leads In Revolution
For A Unified Slave Nation **83**
   Militiamen Lead Continental Army and Expansion West.................. 83
   Virginians Lead the Nation to a New Federal Government 85
   Sovereignty in "We The People" is Established............................ 89
   Slavery is Approved in Constitution by Implication...................... 91
   Virginia's Ratification Needed for a Unified Nation 96
   Constitution Wins Close Vote in Virginia Convention.................... 98

**Joseph Ruffner Moves His Family
To Western Frontier Of Virginia
Along The Great Kanawha River**......................................**105**
  Clendenin Settlement on "Great Kennawa" River............................. 105
  Joseph Ruffner Envisions an Iron Industry
  for Growing Markets on the Western Frontier 108
  Virginia Iron and Coal Industries Have Only East Coast Markets...... 110
  Salt Factories at the Beginning of the Industrial Revolution 111
  Joseph Ruffner Buys Kanawha Salt Spring
  and Explores Western Virginia Frontier.. 115
  Ruffner Family Moves to the Kanawha Valley 117
  Ruffners Purchase a Village and Fort at Charleston........................... 118

**Ruffner Dream Of A Major Industry
Becomes A Rich Reality**...**119**
  Rough Start to a Major New Industry 119
  Ruffner Brothers Drill First Deep Well in America 120
  History of True Pioneers Does Not Repeat Itself............................... 123
  Drilling Success Starts Golden Salt Rush 124
  Western Virginia Coal Industry Begins as Fuel for Salt Furnaces 125
  State Inspectors and Tariffs Protect Kanawha Salt Brand.................. 126
  Industry Expands on Salt Monopoly in War of 1812 129

**Attorneys As "Shock Troops Of Capitalism"
Rewrite Legal Doctrines At The Beginning
Of The American Industrial Revolution** **133**
  Salt Industrialists Create the First Business Trusts 133
  Attorneys Secure Industrial Investments
  with New Legal Doctrines... 136
  Business Trusts Have Limited Success in Malden.............................. 138

**Ruffners Bring Civic Improvements,
Education, And Religion To
The Western Frontier** **141**
  New Town is Established Named "Saltborough"................................ 141
  David Ruffner is The "Father Of Presbyterianism" 144
  Ruffners Support Free Public Education.. 146
  Ruffners Help Establish Mercer Academy in Charleston................... 149
  Ruffners are State Leaders for Higher Education.............................. 151
  Mercer Academy Closes With Damage in the Civil War 152

The Salt Aristocracy Of Malden **155**
Success of "Salt Kings" Creates an Aristocracy 155
Dickinson-Lewis Family 155
Shrewsbury Family... 159
Craik-Shrewsbury Family 163
Ruffner Family 164
David Ruffner:
Inventor and One of America's First Industrialists....................... 169
Henry Ruffner:
Antebellum Virginia's Leading Educator 170
Lewis Ruffner:
Salt and Coal Industrialist and State Maker................................. 173

**Lewis Ruffner Rebuilds His Life
After The Deaths Of
His Beloved Wife And Father**... **177**
Fateful Days in 1843 Change Lewis Ruffner's Life 177
Marriage of Lewis Ruffner and Viola Knapp, a "Yankee" Lady 178
Lewis Ruffner's Talented Nephew, William H. Ruffner 178
Lewis Ruffner in Louisville as Sales Agent for Kanawha Salt 181
Viola and Lewis Ruffner Return to Malden with New Ideas............. 181

The Horror Of Slavery **183**
People Adapt to Slavery by Building Families and Kin Networks 183
Thousands of Virginians Separated from
Their Slave Families and Friends... 192
Hundreds of Thousands of Virginians
are sent to the Deep South... 193
Demographic Changes in Virginia's Slave Population...................... 202
Slaves Submit to Protect Loved Ones from Forced Separation 203
Manhood Challenges in Protecting Families from Separations 205
Investments in Slaves Protected by Virginia Law,
but Not Slave Families 207
Court-Approved Maiming and Mutilations
of People with Free Spirits 209
People in Chains Walk Trails of Tears.. 217
Advertised Brand for Sales of "Virginia Negroes" 220
People in Slavery Sing More for a "Voice" Than for Joy 221
Official State Songs about People "Stolen"
Away from Their Homes 224

Cotton Booms And Virginia Prospers
With Slave Selling Livestock Industry 229
Economic Impact of the Cotton and Slavery Industry 229
Cotton Gin Starts the Cotton Boom 230
Cotton Creates Mass Migration of Slaves to Deep South 232

The Evolving History Of Slavery 235
Early Faux History: Slavery as Kind Help to Barbarians 235
History from the Southern View:
Reconstruction was "Criminally Stupid" 236
Slavery was a Profitable and Viable Industry
Before the Civil War 237
Families and Their Infants in Slavery 239
King Cotton Drives the American Economy 240
Work Gangs, High Picking Rates, and "Whip Torture" 242

Salt And Slavery Industry
Is Built In The Kanawha Valley 249
Virginians Held in Slavery Build an Industry
on the Western Frontier 249
Leased and Resident Slaves in Salt Production Industry 251
Free Blacks and Virginia Slavery 254
Industrial Danger at Salt Furnaces and Coal Mines 256
Wage Incentives Paid for Extra Work on Sabbath 258
People Held in Slavery by Lewis Ruffner 259

Opposition To Slavery Silenced In South
After The Nat Turner Rebellion 263
Ruffners use Slavery to Build Salt Industry 263
Frederick Douglass Speech: No Slave Celebrates July 4 264
Last Chance to End Slavery in Virginia Without War 265
Debate over Slavery Ends in Virginia
after Nat Turner's Rebellion 267
Professor Thomas Dew Claims that Slavery
Created a "Chivalrous" Aristocracy 269
America is Out of Step with the World 271

Americans Move West And
The Malden Salt Industry Declines
With New Competition 273
New Canals Bring Competition to Kanawha Salt 273

Women Salt Industrialists in Malden 276
Kanawha Salt Remains Popular for Good Taste
and Wins Awards in Europe 278

John Brown Attacks Virginia Slavery 281
Harpers Ferry Raid Sparks a Violent End to Slavery 281
Panic In The South And A Legendary Hero In The North 281
Robert E. Lee Predicts "The Last of John Brown" 284
VMI Cadets Led by Thomas Jackson--Later "Stonewall" Jackson ... 285
John Wilkes Booth Attends the Hanging of a Hero............................ 291
John Brown's Fort is Saved by His Wife's Attorney.......................... 293
Violence for Social Justice 295

Virginia Joins The Confcdcracy
And Protects Its Markets For Slaves............................. 301
Seven Agricultural States Start the Confederacy 301
Virginia's Capital Becomes Capital of the Confederacy.................... 304
Names for War and Its Battles Vary in North and South.................... 307

War-Time Dilemma Over Emancipation 309
Emancipation Dilemma for President Lincoln and Loyal Slavers 309
Quakers Urge Emancipation to be the Purpose of the War 310
Emancipation Brings Best Hope for Equality 316

Success And Criticism
Of Emancipation Proclamation 319
Emancipation Proclamation Wins the War.. 319
450,000 People in Border States are Left in Slavery 323
Father Abraham Stops the Whip Torture--Forever............................ 324

Statehood For Western Virginia 327
Lewis Ruffner's Dilemma over Compensation for Emancipation 327
Delegate Lewis Ruffner and the Wheeling Conventions 328
Jeopardy of Lewis Ruffner as Major General of Militia 332
Kanawha Industries and Population Base
Move State Boundaries South 335
Constitution for a New Slave State Sent to Washington 336
Statehood Bill Complicates Emancipation Issue
for President Lincoln.. 338
Lewis Ruffner Seeks Compensation for Loyal Slavers.................... 339

Civil War Ends Slavery But The Idea Of White Superiority Lives On With Segregation And White Supremacy 343

Southern View: The War was a War of Aggression Against Virginia . 343

Malden Spared Devastation Of War 345

Booker's Family are Courageous Social Pioneers
for Equality and Community Respect 347

Television Journalists Upend White Supremacy 354

A Glorious Celebration Of Freedom in a Slave Market 356

Conclusion 357

America's Story Of People Coming Up From Slavery
Continues In Book II With Jane Ferguson
Bringing Her Three Young Children To Malden 357

Appendix 373

Ruffner Family Tree 374

Henry Ruffner Pamphlet 1847: 375

West Virginia Statute Abolishing Slavery 1865 413

Preliminary Emancipation Proclamation 414

Final Emancipation Proclamation 416

Thirteenth Amendment 418

Fourteenth Amendment 419

Endnotes 421

Bibliography 467

Index 499

Young Booker at Hampton Institute, age 16-19 years – *Image Permission from Hampton University Archives*

This book is dedicated to the families of Malden who helped launch the career of Booker T. Washington and the black middle class in America.

Anderson, Austin, Bell, Bradford, Brown, Burk, Bush, Carpenter, Chandler, Crouch, Dehaven, Ervan, Fobbs, Garland, Haskins, Hawkins, Hick, Hughes, Irvin, Isaac, James, Johnson, Johnston, Jones, Kent, Lewis, Liggens, Lovely, Meadows, Moore, Page, Patton, Price, Rice, Roberts, Rollins, Scotts, Shrewsbury, Smith, Stanton, Steptoe, Straughter, Strawder, Strudwick, Teal, Wain, Waine, Wanser, Wadkins, Watkins, Wayne, Weaver, Webster, Wolfe, Woods, Wright

The Author's Viewpoint:
Inspiration: Alma Lee Davis Rowe

This work is written in a southern storytelling style. It is fundamentally about two families who changed their worlds and our worlds today. Book One sets the stage for the action in Book Two after Jane Ferguson brings her small children to Malden at the end of the Civil War. It is not a collection of facts set out in date, event and hero time lines in the style of most history writings. It is fact-based and presents the author's view of America, the South, slavery, Jim Crow and the American people from his experience growing up on the state's southern border with Old Virginia during the years of struggle for civil and human rights in a nation scarred by racism and white supremacy but recovering to a new day for more and more of its peoples. As such, it is appropriate to explain the inspiration and some validation of the work in detail.

Claude L. Rowe, Alma Lee Davis Rowe and her sister, Bertha Davis, Baltimore C. 1935 – *Author's Collection*

The inspiration for this work is my grandmother, Alma Lee Davis Rowe, a genteel southern woman who gave me a confident sense of self, defined by books, history, mountains and rural southern culture. Her family members were "good people" on southern farms in Monroe County. Her ancestors were German and Scot-Irish stock. The latter is a name she would prefer over "Scotch-Irish," since she did not favor any possible link to strong drink, ever, at all. I refer lovingly to her now as "Alma Lee" because the two words mean nurturing mother and a place that shelters in a storm, and she has been all that in my life.

Years later, I was compelled to do this project by the very brief but important time I enjoyed with Minnie Wayne Cooper when I purchased her home in Malden. She was a twentieth-century contemporary of Alma Lee, and, as a little girl, she fondly remembered her family's friend, Booker T. Washington. Both ladies were born at the "turn of the last century," in West Virginia. Both women cared deeply about tradition, social codes and social graces. They lived by standards of conduct they expected of themselves and others.

They were romantics with classic beauty defined by the four qualities of True Beauty: (1) an intentional grace in all matters, (2) a recognized presence in any social setting, (3) a distinct, individual sense of style, manner and dress, and (4) most of all, outstanding, unforgettable character. They were stylish dressers and ladies with modest homes and small formal dining rooms to set a "proper" table. Their long lives stretched across the twentieth century, with similar experiences but on opposite sides of the wall of segregation.

As gender roles progressed in the 1960s and 1970s, both women continued as elegant ladies rather than feminists, but they were both strong women who knew who they were. They were commanding in their domains of influence and respect.

Alma Lee was a warm, charming lady with a twinkle in her eye, who carried gloves to church that she did not need, because, simply, "that is what ladies do." She instructed me that all women deserve to be treated like ladies until they might prove themselves to be otherwise. The loss of her older son, First Lieutenant Claude Linwell Rowe, Jr., a pilot who was my father's only sibling, on Christmas Eve 1944 in the Battle of the Bulge in Fraiture, Belgium, marked her life and that holiday with life-changing sadness.

Alma Lee's special joys were her grandchildren and quilting and cooking. Our family lived with her and Granddad until my sister, Lynne, was born when I was seven, and we moved across the street. Her quilts were precious in the family, never slept under or sat upon. Bibles were honored by never placing anything on top of them, and quilts were given almost the same reverence. She wore "house dresses" in colorful patterns of cotton fabric she selected to eventually be used in her quilts. They were in pastel colors popular after synthetic dyes were perfected in the Depression years. She left the family 21 quilts, and she left me the memory of looking up as a small boy at her in the fabrics I now see in our family quilts.[1]

She was well known at church socials for her southern cooking: fried chicken, macaroni and cheese and other casseroles, congealed fruit salads popular at the time, cobblers of the season, her own home canned green beans that had to be of the Half Runner variety, and moist fresh coconut cakes. She had three home meals each day with meats served dutifully each time. She would stop her busy days anytime to play "Old Maid" cards with us. I liked her brown beans and cornbread and fried green tomatoes. She would remind me that while such food was tasty, it would not be a proper meal for guests, of course.

Importantly, she encouraged a passion for history, helping me win a state education award for proficiency in West Virginia history, granted each year, then, to four eighth grade students in each county, known as the Golden Horseshoe Award. In 1716, the royal governor of Virginia, Alexander Spotswood, led an exploration party of fifty gentlemen into today's West Virginia and gave each explorer a small golden horseshoe and the informal title of knight.[2] I was a proud young Knight of the Golden Horseshoe, so titled along with about 219 other Knights, with the touch of a sword on each shoulder in a ceremony at the State Capitol with the Governor and State Superintendent of Schools.

Alma Lee and my parents instilled in me a family duty to help people, and for myself a duty to never be shy about what I may be able to offer as help to the world. She was always kind and encouraging and made me feel special and worthy of explorations for excellence. At times, I thought loving and kind family members were wrong about me, but I proudly wore the family's love and admiration, like a new suit I had just outgrown. The ultimate self-confidence came when I could see myself reflected in the approving eyes of Alma Lee--as a perfect being. I felt perfect in her eyes, because, in her eyes, I was perfect. That is a childhood treasure for many fortunate grandchildren.

In my happy childhood in a small southern town, I observed my family, including Alma Lee, my mother as a homemaker, Rosaline Santolla Rowe, and my father, Eldridge Eugene Rowe, Sr., a factory supervisor, and my grandfather, Claude Linwell Rowe, Sr., an electrical worker, living simple, dutiful, Christian lives, much like Booker observed with his own family as a boy. But his family was in turbulent times, while my times were quiet. His family was fighting against all odds to build new life as social pioneers in their town, and my family was living in our town the prosperity of post-World War II white America. His family was fighting for entitlement and we were enjoying ours and not realizing it. For young Booker, it was a jarring, uncertain, and frightening time. For me, it was a time for good neighbors. It was easy living on the white side of the wall of separation.

Validation: Minnie Wayne Cooper

Mrs. Cooper provided validation for the viewpoint and purpose of this work. She was a beautiful African American lady of grace and esteem who helped me see Malden as a special place that had welcomed its freed people to succeed without the outward limitations of race prejudice.

She was a renowned elementary teacher who was a leader in the integration of Kanawha County Schools after it was ordered in 1954 by the United States Supreme Court in *Brown v. Board of Education*. Governor John D. Rockefeller, IV-- her "friend" as she would say--years later gave her a Washington-Carver state leadership award for outstanding community service as an African American. She was named by the Charleston newspapers as "Club Woman of the Year." She was active in Delta Sigma Theta Sorority, Phi Delta Kappa Inc., the Booker T. Washington Memorial Association, the National Association for the Advancement of Colored People, the NAACP, the League of Women Voters, the American Association of University Women, and other organizations.[3] The primary goal of her elder years was to save her family's quaint church in Malden, the African Zion Baptist Church.

She took great pride in her paternal grandmother, Caroline Wayne, who was one of the first enslaved Christian believers who courageously started the community of the African Zion Baptist Church in secret in 1852, nine years before the Civil War. In the southern Appalachian region, participation in illegal nighttime religious and singing meetings was one of the primary reasons for whippings. For such secret night time activity, slaves coined the phrase "stealin' the meetin.'" They also had night meetings in the woods at places they called "brush arbor" churches. Women were three times more likely to be punished than men for religious activity in the Appalachian South.[4]

Mrs. Cooper worked to save the African Zion Baptist Church in the 1980s after regular church services were no longer conducted. Mrs. Cooper wanted me to understand how important her family's church was in the life of the town, state and nation. The church had a distinct legacy as a community of Christian leaders for the uplift of freed people, including her "Uncle" Booker and others. She told me that she was not related to the great man but she had him in her kin network of respected and beloved persons.

Minnie Wayne Cooper was an elderly woman when I met her in 1990. She shared memories of "Uncle" Booker coming to visit her "Aunt" Amanda, who was his sister, Amanda Ferguson Johnson. His sister lived three blocks away, and she was the best friend of Mrs. Cooper's mother, Martha Wayne. Mrs. Wayne was prim and proper and she expected Little Minnie to be a lady. Doctor Washington gave Little Minnie dolls, toys and trinkets when he visited, about one time each year. She was eleven when he died in 1915. Historian Louis R. Harlan acknowledged in his book, *Booker T. Washington: The Making of a Black Leader, 1856-1901,* that Mrs. Cooper's memories enhanced the biography.[5]

Mrs. Cooper, in conversations as a lifelong elementary school teacher, would speak by describing action and things visually. She would put everyone in the scene so they could better understand what she was saying. In 1960, Mrs. Cooper taught my wife's older brother, Robert Beury, at Mercer School.

She forever marked my life in Malden when I asked her what Segregation Days were like for her. She put her right hand slowly on her chest, breathed deeply, smiled and said, "I have had a very romantic life." The answer was a surprise. She became animated, and told me about her seeing the last game the Dodgers played in Brooklyn and late-night, elegant rooftop dancing with her husband, Robert Cooper, when they stayed in the apartments of friends in New York, who were usually away on vacation each August. They could attend shows and events there when segregation at the time barred them in Charleston. She attended colleges out of state and graduated from West Virginia State University. She greatly enjoyed travel. She connected with sorority sisters across the nation for travel when segregation limited public accommodations. She sailed on the Queen Mary for a conference of university women in Helsinki, Finland. The Coopers, as members of the black middle class, turned the limitations of segregation into positive times with an extensive network of friends and accommodating acquaintances that spread nationwide.

She finished her answer by saying carefully, "Mr. Rowe, do you know the n-word?" She always called me Mr. Rowe. I bowed my head a bit, and said as respectfully as was humanly possible in a room without breath movements from me, "Yes, Mrs. Cooper, I do." She spoke intently, "Well, I never heard that word in Malden. I was always treated with the utmost respect."

The words ring in my head today. She was so refined and dignified, it was impossible to think of her as ever being disrespected by anyone. On reflection, it is striking that the memory of a romantic life she wanted me to see through her eyes of experience can be such a contrast to the lives of others in the South, where the scars of slavery were so painfully pressed with segregation. I can never know the pain, confusion or hopelessness that she

Minnie Wayne Cooper, African-American Teacher and Community Leader on her way to Helsinki, Finland. *Image: Arthur B. Hodges Center Brochure, C. 1990*

felt at times, or that other blacks have felt, or who may now feel for the scars of this history. But she convinced me that no one of any background, race, or religion has ever had as satisfying and romantic a life as she did in her beloved Malden. That was her point and purpose. Mrs. Cooper handed to me a baton of hope in her family's history of Malden, to pass on to the next generations. I learned from her and my grandmother that hope is an essential ingredient to success, and to happiness.

Alma Lee Davis Rowe and Minnie Wayne Cooper living as they did in the twentieth century have provided foundation ideas for this work. These ladies shared an earlier time of roles, fashion, propriety, and standards, in a race-directed culture, that have provided to me a somewhat special perspective on southern culture and its racial divide during and after the Horror of Slavery.

Their lives present a century-long experience of old-fashioned values and display how the idea of white superiority affected black America and white America in the twentieth century. I saw that idea, as a young person, to be so contrary to the values that surrounded me as a child, overthrown--at least in law and social propriety--by television reports of parents and students being abused because they just wanted to be treated fairly. I learned that positive things can happen when people believe in the good of their neighbors and are empowered to display that belief, a belief that invigorates us to believe in the happy futures of our youth.

The lives of these grand ladies are a connecting fabric for many subjects of this work. It is my intent here to honor Minnie Wayne Cooper and the romantic life she was able to enjoy in Malden and to honor Alma Lee Davis Rowe and her belief in a family talent for service which she thought should be the value of my life.

Acknowledgments

Help Getting on with the Project

There have been many people to encourage and help on the longtime writing of this work in two books. My family has carried me to the finish line, including my wife, Julia Beury, and, son, Christian Rowe, and, daughter, Hattie Rowe, who have patiently read early manuscripts and guided the flow and focus of the work. My mother, Rosaline Virginia Santolla Rowe, has always encouraged me to be a good person and do my best. My wife's mother, Harriett Smith Beury, read and proofed the work at the beginning and the end, eagerly and kindly, as is her way in life. My sister, Lynne Rowe, in Chicago has helped and encouraged it from day one, which was over twenty years ago. My brother, Eldridge Eugene Rowe, and his wife, Jean Quesenberry Rowe, have provided good wishes and prayers for us all.

Gerald Ratliff, a photographer and retired journalist whose home is in Malden, has gathered and generously shared extensive research of all topics on Malden, at the West Virginia Archives and History Library in the Culture Center and other research locations. He has unselfishly developed sources for the origin of the name of Malden, the 1869 race riot, the killing of Allen Belcher, the town marshal, who was his great-great uncle, the businesses in Malden, joint lynchings by a white mob and a black mob, possible dates that the African Zion Baptist Church was fire-threatened and when today's church building was constructed, and other sources which have greatly enhanced the richness and quality of this work. He is the best friend of this work and a very kind friend to me. His help cannot be overstated. Thank you, Gerald.

Blake Taylor, a gifted history graduate at West Virginia State University, has made the work possible with editing, original and secondary research and writing, computer design and skills, photographs, vision to divide the work into two books, proofreading, and ever good cheer and genuine interest. I grew up with his grandparents, Rick and Linda Miller. As early readers, they gave a helpful review and suggested more information on Dr. Washington's family in book II. Blake's skills and interest reflect his family's qualities of excellence. Without Blake, this book would not have been completed in this century.

Two other West Virginia State University graduates, Nicholas Stavrakis and Portia Smith, helped as research assistants for shorter periods, along with Matthew Kinder, a student at West Virginia University. They all made important contributions to the work and demonstrated that graduates of their schools are talented and very well prepared for their careers.

Martha Darneal Cole and Llewellyn Shrewsbury Cole were single sisters and renowned high school teachers, who were the last resident members of the old salt families in Malden. In 1980, Marty was State Teacher of the Year. Sister Llewellyn was in charge of the county science curriculum, and liked to tell of the summer fun she had staying in a dormitory and sharing a cafeteria with the Miami Dolphins of the National Football League. She helped a struggling young student named Gaston Caperton overcome a reading difficulty. He became West Virginia's 31st Governor in 1989. The "Cole Sisters" were the great-great granddaughters of Joel Shrewsbury, the leading salt industrialist who helped organize St. John's Episcopal Church in Charleston, where they attended for over 90 years. They lived on land owned by the Shrewsbury family since the early 1800s. They were great-nieces of the 26-year-old-man, Jacob Darneal Shrewsbury, who sold the house to Booker's family in 1869. The "Cole Sisters" organized the Malden Historic Society and, with help from James Thibeault, they had the town designated a National Historical District on July 18, 1980. The designation was based on 122 buildings of which 19 were pivotal structures and 56 were major contributing structures. Their father, John Slack Cole, was an important land surveyor and his father, John L. Cole, was state librarian when the state capital was moved to Charleston in the 1870s. Their mother, Llewellyn Norton Shrewsbury Cole, was a friend of Booker T. Washington's sister in town, Amanda Ferguson Johnson. Portia Washington Pittman telephoned their mother and visited in their home.

The "Cole Sisters" delighted in visitors, and their visitors always delighted in them. Visitors were tucked under broad wings of love and fun and flown to earlier times in the story of Malden. With joyous, endless storytelling, they stretched Malden across two fascinating centuries of history. But they never bragged on their ancestors because they said their mother told them if they did then the "better part of your lives would be dead." When they were both gone in 2014, it was said that losing them was like the library in town had burned to the ground. It did. They are missed.[6]

My closest friend, James Thibeault, has encouraged, questioned, and encouraged over and over since 1990 for me to get on with the project. As a Volunteer in Service to America, VISTA, he organized Cabin Creek Quilts. He has been recognized as the "Father of Historic Preservation in West Virginia" for his work to save the nineteenth-century village buildings in Malden. He put me in contact with Minnie Wayne Cooper, and then in contact with the good life of Malden on the river, and then with my beautiful wife, Julia, who was a VISTA worker at Cabin Creek Quilts. Our close friend and his dear wife, Karen Glazier, was lost to us in 2018. She touched all in her life with wit, charm and true caring. She was selected as the first State Social Worker of the Year, recognized as a pioneer in assisted elderly living. She is remembered in town for her special events like the spontaneous come-one-come-all, Malden Fourth of July Dog and Bike Parade. "Miss Karen" and her faithful encouragement are missed.

Cynthia Pendleberry in the law office has provided perspective, composition, ideas, cautions, and timely encouragement to finish the work. For the three Malden walking tours printed in 2000, 2002, and 2014, which ultimately turned into this broad work, Carol Hundley helped with great patience and skill. Colleen Anderson, a friend since 1973, helped with design services at Mother Wit for the walking tours and with political materials since I first ran for office decades ago. Her consultations on this project have been invaluable. Tina Sonis Holmes has provided excellent reading and revision services that have smoothed out the many wrinkles of the work. Friends all, they have given me friendships that honor my life.

Library assistance has been generous, helpful, and kind. The Kanawha County Library and the State Archives and History Library have enabled the research and production for this work. They have guided and encouraged my specialized research, with materials in their substantial collections and in the collections of other libraries that will loan materials. Elizabeth Frasure, head of the reference department at the Kanawha County Library, generously searched topics and discovered old hard-to-find articles on the salt industry, industry competition with canals, and black history in Virginia and West Virginia. Patience and special encouragement by all at these fine libraries have kept me going for years of work with local and national sources. It is a privilege to live in Kanawha County and have such great library resources and people "just down the road." I thank our voters in county levy elections for knowing the value of our county library's service and being willing to support it for the good of all. Thank you.

Ray and Connie Lewis and Carolyn Schade were the earliest to read and comment on an early draft of the book, giving me direction, some needed hand holding, kicks in the seat, and a wider vision that I could finish a three-and-one-half century history of how our folks got to the mountains that nurture us today. Ray Lewis provided important information and maps on the location of Booker's family home and about the relocation of African American cemeteries in Malden. He is related to the nineteenth-century state historian, Virgil Lewis. Close behind the Lewises is Henry Battle, the legendary head of the Kanawha Valley Historical and Preservation Society, whose friendship and model work for historic preservation are encouragement to all. Our friend Anthony Kinser continues tireless work of success for black history in Charleston's Block District and the mountain valley we love.

West Virginia State University, where I served two terms as Chair of the Board of Governors, has many friends who have helped me to understand young Booker and how his boyhood in Malden set his national leadership. The Carters, President Dr. Hazo Carter and First Lady Phyllis Carter, shared with me their special dream for the University's role in preserving Malden's salt village and its legacy for leadership. Phyllis Carter established the Booker T. Washington Institute for that purpose. Friends and neighbors known at the University include Dr. Jack Magan, Dr. Charles Byers, Millie Booker, Marvin Smith, Dr. Trevellya Ford-Ahmed, Coach Oree Banks, Patricia J. Schumann, Printer and Designer James A. Hale, William Lipscomb, Dr. Barbara Ladner, Dr. Timothy R. Ruhnke, Dr. Tom Guetzloff, Dr. Mickey Blackwell, Dr. Emily Waugh, Chief Joseph Saunders, Crystal Walker, L. Vincent Williams, Esquire, Melvin Jones, and many others. These friends have been there when needed, so many times on so many projects. Their community heritage as a leading historic black college or university (HBCU) is outstanding, and the university's institutional commitment to welcome and help all students is unusual, remarkable and inspirational.

Like Booker, my boyhood heroes and friends have given me the will and hope to write a book about the evil and separating idea of white superiority and how freed people in Malden climbed up and over the slavery that was born in Virginia with such an idea. His heroes were a community of leaders who nourished him and empowered his national leadership with their example. I am fortunate and honored to study and live in the place of his inspirational all-American story.

Thank you to all who have encouraged me over the years in my work, notably Professor John E. Stealey, III, a kind gentleman and a giant in West Virginia history, who twenty years ago told me to get on with a Malden history. Thank you also to the hundreds of people who have taken my church and cabin tours with its friendly telling of the nineteenth-century village story of Malden. Many have helped, and I thank all, especially those I have failed here to specifically name and acknowledge. I also regret to all readers in advance if I misstate any information in the books, and I ask for advice about such problem material. Assembling almost four centuries of American history is not easy and never perfect.

Finally, about viewpoint, I may be in the right place at the right time to ponder and share thoughts about what happened in Malden after the Civil War. First, my training as an attorney encourages me to see historic events like reported cases which are important only as they connect to affirm or reject an underlying idea of justice applicable to most other cases. Events in history then produce threads of ideas that connect and may sweep us to new theories on how life in society exists and how changes did or can occur in social history.

Second, connecting historic events like reported cases turns study into discovery and the limitations of traditional niche professional history fall away as exciting possibilities swirl and spin into many new truths and perspectives. In this work, the new ideas studied and proposed include the running thread of white supremacy empowered by a majority belief in white superiority; the unparalleled leadership of eastern Virginian slavers in the major events of our republic in 1776, 1787 and 1861; the past and current pain of a race of people who just now are assuming their rightful place in the world's economy, society and culture; the realization that separation is the foundation sin and evil that divides people and leads them to lawless conflict, violence and mayhem, and to limiting self righteous judgments of others; and how goodness flows easily from the connections of good neighbors living their lives, not in regret for lost glory and the "good ole days," but for the benefit of future generations.

Third, living in the boyhood home of Booker T. Washington, I have been able to visualize his life here among his family and their friends who were boyhood heroes, as he would rush to work, carry produce to sell for Miss Viola, run to school, dress for church, date his childhood sweetheart and future wife, and kick the same rocks we kick in a white community that changed to welcome freed people as neighbors, but only after conflict and injury to a respected community leader, Lewis Ruffner. In light of Dr. Washington's career of service, I can see young Booker's life unfurl like a flag of hope in the South and in his hometown—my hometown and the hometown of all middle class blacks who can rejoice at what happened here and see it as a beacon for change for a new day of freedom and equality, now—and with constant vigilance—forever.

Here, a freed people seeking their own foundation stone in Zion accepted a covenant with God, as directed by Bible Scripture, to create a "royal priesthood" of leaders to build a "holy nation."[7] They did it for their families, and we all have benefitted from their success. They lived The Golden Rule, and "did it" by being good neighbors—a simple, successful creed today, for us and our children in the world.

But, the value of the work will be told by the tale. As a skeptical southerner might say, "The proof, my friend, is in the puddin.'" Please read on.

Martha Wayne mother of Minnie Wayne Copper. *Image Courtesy of Mr. James Isaac*

Preface:

Ruffner Salt, Virginia Slavery and Booker T. Washington

The first story of American history for millions of Americans today is the story of slavery. The Anglo-Saxon majority's belief in their superiority over the people of other racial or ethnic groups and their cultures was unchallenged for centuries after slavery started in Virginia for the tobacco industry at Jamestown. It was the foundation idea for slavery which is the nation's original sin.

The idea of white superiority dominated the new nation's revolutionary ideas of freedom and equality limiting both to the white majority. These ideas were the inspiration for establishment of a national republic, the first to succeed in two thousand years since Julius Caesar ended the Roman Republic. The founding ideas survived for centuries, but only as subordinate ideas to an almost universal white majority belief in white superiority. This racist idea controlled the life and destiny of the nation into the late twentieth century, well beyond the Civil War and the end of slavery.

History is often organized and taught to future generations as a sequence of selected "major" events with leaders set in time lines often identifying a progression of humankind relevant to ideas affecting current events, people and their leaders. Although people generally oppose change, most people, especially Americans, like progress. History becomes rich and exciting when organized as ideas connecting times, events and leaders. If linked by ideas that are relevant today, history is more instructive and enlightening. It can be more fun as well because, for American history, it becomes a warts-and-all discovery of the glories and shame of a new nation of diverse peoples struggling majestically but imperfectly to secure for all citizens the nation's founding ideas for liberty, equality, and social justice. It is a bumpy but rewarding ride over the fabric of events and leaders from the nation's first settlements to present day.

The competition between foundational ideas creates a history that is lively and often written, explained, rewritten, explained again, revised, and explained again and again written. This work may be an extension of that sequence, but it attempts to present history from a different viewpoint with the study of two pioneering families in separate times of leadership who changed history by simply being good neighbors who worked hard and courageously for better futures for their families.

The story focuses on what freed people did for themselves to adapt to new roles of freedom and equality. It is not intended to focus only on the headlines of history about what horrors were done by white racists in a national system that empowered them to rule by will and whim over the lives and communities of people who were not white. A dominant thread of American history has been the idea of white superiority until recent generations. That idea led to the creation of slavery and supported vast expansion into the West against other civilizations. The expressed purpose of "Manifest Destiny" was to spread American civilization and democratic values to the west and to the world, but, as Historian Arthur Schlesinger, Jr. wrote, "No doubt it served in part as a mask for speculation in land and Texas scrip; but in part too it expressed an honest idealism about the future of the world."[8] The recent official rejection of the idea of white superiority has affirmed the best of America's culture and ideas, and it has established an identity for America as a unified nation of different peoples joining with each other to make an open society for all, again without perfection but with a unified direction and good evidence of progress.

Before and after the Civil War and into modern times, there have been many limitations on America's founding ideas when extended to people other than those of the dominant white majority. Acceptance of new groups who appear different from the dominant middle class, by race, ethnicity, religion or culture, have required a progression of integration into American life. The hope to share America's opportunity for all has brought many diverse peoples to the nation, some under the umbrella of the nation's founding ideas and some not. Most all European minorities have been accepted, much sooner than African Americans or persons of other races, religions, or cultures. Africans were never immigrants. They were peoples kidnapped away from their families, lands, and civilizations. Presumptions of inferiority were applied to them across the board as a race. Skin color made African Americans different and ultimately slaves of the white majority. But the belief in white superiority was not limited to persons of African descent.

Asians were barred entry into the United States by a series of race-based immigration laws in 1882, 1917 and 1924 that remained in effect until after the Second World War. These laws severely restricted immigration from most all countries in Asia and the Pacific Islands, ranging from Turkey to India, China, Japan and the Polynesian Islands. People with disabilities and "subversive" political beliefs were barred entry into the country. A literacy test was required for immigrants older than 16 and a head tax was charged. This work does not reach the many discrimination issues of immigrant groups, women, and diverse cultures, but the ideas of white superiority and racial exclusion were prominent in the nation's rejection of different peoples seeking to immigrate to America.[9]

Different ethnic, racial, and religious groups had to wait generations for acceptance into the white American middle class.[10] Acceptance came with slow integration of immigrant groups into regular relationships with white middle class neighbors. Prejudice by the majority against immigrants, especially those before and during Booker T. Washington's leadership, melted away only one generation at a time, first, in separate neighborhoods, and then in mainstream America. Segregation barriers for early immigrants were largely by custom not law, unlike for African and Asian descendants. After new ethnic and religious groups joined the white middle class, they experienced different levels of discrimination so long as they were perceived as in some way different from the white majority. For the groups who were accepted more slowly, the prejudice might have been skin or hair color, religion, or other cultural differences, facial features, and even ethnic last names or first names identifying pride in their separate family heritages. The children and grandchildren of these immigrants, including your author with an Italian immigrant grandfather, became more and more accepted as new generations of whites came to see them as equals when the neighborhood walls of separation became porous hedges and then garden paths for many immigrant groups.

The approach of this work is to trace the idea of white superiority in light of slavery and separation of African Americans, from the first use of slavery in Jamestown to its full bloom as white supremacy in 1963 attacks in Birmingham, Alabama, where students and parents were beaten, bitten by dogs, and hosed with water cannons. They were willing to die in order to have the founding ideas of the nation apply fully to themselves and to all African Americans. Television journalists displayed race terror on family televisions across the nation and convinced a young generation that white domination was "un-American" and had to be overcome by integration of the races and fair treatment to all. Many mature adults needed a long time to adjust to integration and the idea of equality of African Americans. Fundamental changes in a social order often require a new generation to give full uplift to change.

Change was needed for many discriminations that were obvious to blacks but unrealized to whites. As Dr. Henry Louis Gates, Jr. wrote, television made the battle for civil rights in the 1960s seem like a foreign war, when local area whites and blacks "seemed" to get along "pretty well."

All things considered, white and colored Piedmont got along pretty well in those years, the fifties and early sixties. At least as long as colored people didn't try to sit down in the Cut-Rate or at the Rendezvous Bar, or eat pizza at Eddie's, or buy property, or move into the white neighborhoods, or dance with, date, or dilate upon white people. Not to mention to try to get a job in the craft unions at the paper mill. Or have a drink at the white VFW, or join the white American Legion, or get loans at the bank, or just generally get out of line. Other than that, colored and white got on pretty well.[11]

America's greatest ideas now apply institutionally to all citizens without racial, gender, or ethnic exceptions, almost. But discrimination continues for those who are seen as different or outside middle American for their race, ethnicity, religion, life styles or even their geographic-based culture, like for those who live in the Appalachian region and are ridiculed "as hillbillies" by many people in urban coastal areas, even by the Vice President of the United States who told an incest joke on June 2, 2008 referring to West Virginians. Dick Cheney later apologized for his sad remarks, others do not. It is a common slur in coastal urban areas. Hillbillies are one of the few groups in American life that can be openly subjected to prejudice.[12] But equal treatment is generally considered to be "fair play" and "good sport" to include all people and peoples in the fullness of American life. Such ideas include everyone in the "American Dream," for those people who have the work ethic and talent to pursue the dreams of their youth for happiness and perhaps glory, for themselves and most especially for future generations. The term "American Dream" was not known to Booker T. Washington in his day. He knew the concept of full opportunity for all. The term "American Dream" was not popularized until a generation after his death.[13] The dreams of youth can propel the nation toward better ideas of innovation, social justice, balanced society, and a better life, when grounded in a fair view of the history of the nation's good and bad ideas.

This book and its companion, *Booker T. Washington's Boyhood American Dream: The Climb of the Black Middle Class Up from Slavery,* are about the ideas of a freed young boy in Malden named Booker, and the ideas he observed, tested and adopted from the courage and hard work of his boyhood heroes as they struggled to build a black middle class. He observed their ideas of equal opportunity, work, integration, and self-determination and turned them into a gospel for what today we would call the "American Dream." He wanted that concept to apply to and to be adopted by the ten million African Americans he led from 1895 until his death at age 59 in 1915--primarily through the inspiration of his example in coming up from slavery. He saw his heroes integrate their town and to work, not for their own benefit, but to elevate their children and their children's children into the American middle class. He would identify middle class and its opportunity for the American Dream not by financial success but by a family's struggle to succeed for future generations. The original idea of an American middle class of self -made men was popularized by Henry

Clay in the antebellum period.[14] His idea was more about recognizing individual success by rising up from humble beginnings than it was for the family-focused success touted by Booker T. Washington, who saw family success as the best goal for freed people who had first to prove their worthiness to succeed in order to launch better lives for future generations.

In 1844, an Episcopalian writer, Calvin Colton, wrote about the concept of American success. He wrote that in America "a comfortable degree of wealth is within the reach of every honest, industrious, and enterprising man." He wrote about the opportunity in America for self-made men.

> Ours is a country, where men start from an humble origin, and from small beginnings rise gradually in the world, as the reward of merit and industry, and where they can attain to the most elevated positions, or acquire a large amount of wealth, according to the pursuits they elect for themselves. No exclusive privilege of birth, no entailment of estate, no civil or political disqualifications, stand in the path; but one has as good a chance as another, according to his talents, prudence, and personal exertions. This is a country of self-made men, than which nothing better could be said of any state of society.[15]

A word about hindsight is appropriate. The work is intended overall to avoid the low perch of hindsight because it flattens the fabric of history into a succession of key events, usually wars, and fails to explain the ups and downs, hills, valleys and mountains of real people in the real time of their own lives. Hindsight can often be blind to their day-to-day struggles for social change and new ideas and values. They often had to make pragmatic compromises to survive under a power structure with contrary ideas and the will to violently crush all opposition.[16] Booker T. Washington and his national leadership deserve more than flat hindsight. He deserves review of the ups and downs, hills, valleys and mountains of his life and service. The Founding Fathers deserve the same review as we today evaluate their pragmatic compromises made to create a world of liberty and equality that they enabled but did not set up for all peoples in their time in history.

Leaders in any age, whether creating a new, first ever, constitutional republic as Founding Fathers, or leading a people forward toward the Promised Land of liberty and equality, or perhaps in trying to solve local problems in city council or church meetings, should be fairly commended for stepping forward and serving the public good in trying to improve their communities. The leaders of the nation throughout its history should be saluted in all generations if they worked to improve an inclusive, moral purpose for institutions in America, public and private.

Civil rights leaders deserve special commendation for working to end racism and other elitism, and while they could not change all hearts and minds, they have shifted the theoretical and political debate from individual to institutional morality.[17] With a new institutional morality for America leading to a new rubric for social discourse and interaction, they changed the ideas that are taught to next generations as the true sustaining ideas of the nation.

For Malden and Charleston in the Kanawha Valley, the story of Booker T. Washington is local history. His boyhood years have remained a mystery for over a century since his death in 1915. His early life in Malden is the lead story for the Kanawha Valley. It was much more favorable and nurturing than he would admit. In his early years, the city became a major population center and state capital, surrounded by mineral resource industries of salt, coal, natural gas, and later chemicals. Charleston became a city with the innovations and community service of one remarkable family of pioneers, industrialists, and educators. The Ruffner family invented modern deep well drilling, started two major industries--salt and coal, laid out their own town, helped establish some of the area's first churches and first academy school, supported universal free public education, and helped make a new state. But all of their business and social accomplishments were made possible only by the ready exploitation of the forced labor of enslaved Virginians. Without Booker T. Washington's story, the short title of Charleston's local history could be "Ruffner Salt and Virginia Slavery." The salt and slavery industry is why Booker's mother and stepfather came to Malden to live. It is the back drop of their lives in Freedom and their special connection to the Ruffner family. They changed the ideas of the Ruffners and made them champions for all freed people in their community.

Booker T. Washington is a favorite son of West Virginia. Nationwide, he is one of the most controversial figures in African American history. He is respected and berated. His leadership was complicated. It is celebrated and criticized. This work in two books tells the story of his boyhood heroes and how he observed them start a black middle class community in Malden in the first generation after slavery. They created a legacy of national leadership beginning with young Booker and continuing with three twentieth-century giants of the modern civil rights movement sent into national leadership from Charleston's First Baptist Church: Reverend Dr. Mordecai Johnson, as President of Howard University, Reverend Vernon Johns, an early activist and inspirational leader for civil rights, and Reverend Leon Sullivan, who led the international boycott of South Africa to end its modern slavery.

Booker T. Washington's gospel for the "American Dream" is legendary. He knew and promoted the concept without the benefit of its modern name. He believed that future generations of African Americans could only be equal in America and share in the American Dream if they adopted middle class values for self-sacrifice and self-determination to improve the lives of their children and grandchildren. He thought people became middle class when they were dedicated to helping future generations. He believed their sacrifice would open the door for all people to achieve their dreams in life, when they had the will, work ethic and talent to make their dreams come true. His leadership and boyhood roots deserve attention because they defined him as a man and leader with an illustrious career, and, candidly, because there are surprises, disappointments, and delights to be explored and explained.

Mr. Washington in characteristic pose addressing an audience   Mr. Washington silhouetted against the crowd upon one of his educational tours.   Mr. Washington in typical pose speaking to an audience at Shreveport, La.

Booker T. Washington Addressing Crowd – *Image Courtesy of West Virginia State Archives*

For some, the study of Booker T. Washington's leadership may put a different perspective on how change can be made at a community level by common people identifying a problem and finding a solution that can be generalized to other communities. Observing local heroes gave young Booker his path in life to a career of national prominence. Leadership is the key to social change in today's fast-changing world. Local leadership can inspire the young to assume their own roles of leadership in the "major" events of their generation. Booker T. Washington urged people after Reconstruction to stay in the South and be good neighbors to all. He encouraged community development at the grass roots. He wanted his students to carry their educations and middle class lifestyles back to their homes in the south to improve the lives of all freed people. His words, "cast down your bucket where you are" became a universal reference to local community development. They became popular in 1895 after his so-called "Atlanta Compromise" speech for the Cotton States and International Exposition in Atlanta, which began his national career of leadership. He told a story of two ships going from salt water to fresh water. When one ship captain desperate for fresh water asked the other for help, the reply was to cast down his bucket where he was. After several requests, the desperate ship captain put down his bucket and found that he was in fresh water and did not need help.[18]

A word about "local history" is appropriate. Local history tells a story, and it is a personal one. It enlivens local people, especially the curious young, who become interested and perhaps intrigued by their family history or by common questions that come to mind outside the world of books, such as "Why is this city here?" or "Why is it so important to have a monument or a street name here?" or, more fundamentally, "Why does my family live and work here?" The answers are sometimes confused or disregarded when not readily answered in a formal history text. Sometimes, questions may be dismissed as mere "local history," but the inquiry of local history takes interested people to the ideas of their generation and to the lives of real people such as their families and their ancestors.

Local history weaves information into a fabric for understanding "major" events and leaders in history and connects dots beyond "major events" that professional history often misses, and, therefore, should be studied carefully. It avoids the categorization boundaries of niche professional history. When a family leader is a pioneer or a family archivist, or a local historian, history for new learners explodes and passions are nourished for a new generation. Their energy and new inquires become relevant because they concern real people in real time, and they stress a social history rather than the recitation of events. Local history enriches the flow of "major" events and leaders in national and world history. The flow of those "major" events and leaders provides Christmas trees for the young, and the new to history, to decorate with local ornaments that connect them and their families across the fabric of history to the "major" events and leaders in history. More importantly, it connects them to their core beings and their ideas of life as it should be for them and their families and for others.

A history that studies ideas may encourage greater individual commitments to make insightful social changes as needed from time to time to assure that our communities and our nation will lead in the world through its best ideas, for equality, liberty, democracy and social justice, one neighborhood at a time, rather than through any claims of superiority or military or economic might. Ideas matter and the world is watching. Local history provides adults a more meaningful community life. For the young, it can lead them into futures that often follow childhood heroes they observed making needed changes in their world. This process connects learners, future leaders, and historians to a broader, richer and more valuable view of history and community life. Leaders and historians are born when they learn and share histories that are personal to them.

This work, somewhat ambitiously, seeks to reveal the essential dynamics of the nation's founding, through ideas and purposes that reflect a past belief in white superiority, that trumped the best ideas that should have sustained early America. It reviews the brutal system of slavery at its core and extremes to determine just how it was that "The power of the master must be absolute to render the submission of the slave perfect."[19] For that, the work rolls up and down, and over a fabric of information that become hills, mountains and valleys, and then the wrinkles, creases, knots, checkerboard and quilt patterns, cotton, damask, state songs and poems, mob lynchings, and many events and leaders from Jamestown's slavery for a lucrative tobacco industry to present day. Most of the weaving of that fascinating fabric was performed in Virginia, until it was separated from its western mountains to make a new state during the eastern part of the state's leadership for a second war of rebellion--one which Virginia made possible and lost. The legacy of Virginia's history has endowed the state's tourism industry with rich and popular stories of both rebellions, producing billions of revenue dollars and thousands of jobs across the state. The interpretation of its tourism history should continue to evolve with more about slavery, the Reconstruction era and Segregation Days.

Readers of this work, it is hoped, will put themselves in the time gardens of real people and events, spreading them all out fairly across the checkered and winkled fabric of America's history of ideas, enjoying every weed and morsel they can discover by asking how and when and why, bringing each to the table for examination and, for what your author hopes will become at least on occasion, a moment of delight.

H. G. Wells - *Image Courtesy of the Library of Congress*

Introduction:

The Climb Up From Virginia Slavery Over The Idea
of White Superiority and on to the American Middle Class

Historian H. G. Wells wrote that history is the history of ideas. It is said that there is nothing more powerful than an idea whose time has come. This work in two books acknowledges these statements as predictable truths for all ages and generations. The books are intended to focus on important events and leaders using the ideas that connect them to time and place, to create a better understanding of the full fabric of American culture and life. The key ideas to be reviewed include the long held traditional belief by the white majority in their own superiority to all other peoples, and the ideas challenging that belief upon which America was founded for liberty, equality, and social justice. The essential foundation of American slavery was racism. People who were not considered white became a pariah class, allowing a white master class to en-slave people who were not white.[20]

The belief in white superiority has dominated the political and social af-fairs of the nation since the first permanent English settlement at Jamestown.[21] This idea limited the morality of all institutions, public and private, and en-couraged individual morality to be prejudiced. To understand the remarkable success of Booker's family and friends in creating a black middle class during the swirling social and economic changes following the Civil War, it is import-ant to study the interplay of these competing ideas.

The ideas for the founding of the republic were identified and proclaimed most eloquently in 1776 by Virginian Thomas Jefferson in the Declaration of Independence. This declaration of human rights is one of the most glorious and enduring statements for basic human rights in history. For many proud Americans, it is the nation's flag flying over the history of the world. Thomas Jefferson's words ring in a truth much greater than the meanings of the words. To American ears, they ring like the bells of Eternity and cannot be repeated too often:

> We hold these Truths to be self-evident, that all Men are created equal, that they are endowed by their Creator with certain unalienable Rights, that among these are Life, Liberty, and the pursuit of Happiness.[22]

This proclamation states the purpose for the early colonial rebellion in terms of concepts and standards. But those ideas were subject to the more dominant and universal prejudice for claims of white superiority. Thomas Jefferson embodied the contradictions in American values in his time. He declared the words just cited, which some call the "American Creed," while he had hundreds of enslaved people, very few of whom he freed in his life time, or in his will, apparently because he was deeply in debt at his death. He saw himself as a humanist and scientist in the Enlightenment. More than any other of the revolutionaries, Thomas Jefferson's ideas and life present the nation's enduring difficulty with its founding ideas.[23]

The complexity of the problem is seen in Thomas Jefferson's writings made soon after he wrote the Declaration of Independence. In 1781, he thought slavery was an ill in Virginia to be corrected by gradual emancipation. He thought slavers should train, equip, and send freed people to colonies outside the country. He did not want emancipated people to remain in America, because he thought they could not be good neighbors, since he believed they were inferior to all whites.[24]

It is noted here that the term "slaver" is used in this work rather than the traditional terms, "slave owner" and "slaveholder," since those terms signify acceptance of the idea that a human being can be owned or held as the property of another. Slavers are formally defined as "dealers in or owners of slaves."[25] The term "slave," is used primarily as an adjective and occasionally as a noun because it projects the harsh reality of people who are bonded to an inhuman life without spirit, hope or relations and are required to use every breath they take for forced service to others. The terms, "enslaved people," "people held in slavery," and "freed people" are used intermittently to remind us of the humanity suffering under the label "slave." The term, "Horror of Slavery" is used to capture in sum all the terrors imposed by slavery first as a social institution and later for sales of people to the Deep South and West as part of a Virginia slave livestock industry. Slavery should be called "The Horror."

The future president, Thomas Jefferson, in his *Notes on the State of Virginia,* written as a young man late in the Revolutionary War era and published widely in 1853 by J. W. Randolph, studied and accepted the idea of white superiority as his personal belief in the inferiority of black people. Thomas Jefferson wrote from the perspective of an observant scientist, typical in the Age of Reason:

[B]lacks, whether originally a distinct race, or made distinct by time and circumstances, are inferior to the whites in the endowment both of body and mind. It is not against experience to suppose that different species of the same genus, or varieties of the same species, may possess different qualifications.... This unfortunate difference of color, and perhaps of faculty, is a powerful obstacle to the emancipation of these people.[26]

One historian has written that there is little substance to the supposed antislavery beliefs of Thomas Jefferson. Instead, Paul Finkelman asserts harshly that Thomas Jefferson was the "intellectual godfather of the racist pseudoscience of the American school of anthropology."[27]

Africans were brought to the Caribbean in 1562 by Sir John Hawkins aboard a tragically named ship, the *Jesus of Lubek* or "The Good Ship Jesus." Sir John Hawkins is acknowledged for pioneering the British slave trade to the Americas. He made several voyages and even added to his family coat of arms the drawing of a bound African woman with no blouse, in order to brag about his trade in kidnapping people from their homes in Africa. It was an evil business which in its early years was fully acceptable as proper and valuable. For him it was a source of pride. Africans were brought to Jamestown in 1619 by privateer ships under a Dutch flag, the *White Lion* and the *Treasurer*. The royal governor of Virginia and others purchased twenty negroes to work at forced labor as indentured servants. American slavery was based on skin color and race to create a controlled underclass to boost the colony's tobacco industry in the 1600s. The tobacco and slavery industry made Virginia the nation's most influential colony with a lucrative economy and English aristocratic social structure founded on the forced labor of African people.[28]

This book explores how eastern Virginians became dependent on slavery for their economic prosperity and aristocratic lifestyles. The idea of white superiority allowed slavery to flourish in eastern Virginia. The English elite who controlled Virginia were aristocrats who had no problem believing in their own superiority. Few were nobility but many were striving to be nobility in a new land with new estates. They were of a different type from New England settlers, who were religious and democratic and who gave high social status to good educations and community service. English planters first tried to force Native Americans to be the primary workforce for their tobacco-based economy.[29] The first Africans brought to Jamestown were freed after a number of years to pay for their passage. Virginians transformed the status of Africans to slavery as a race two generations later, if they had any part of African blood. A baby's status was determined by the mother's status. If she were a slave, her children were slaves and owned by her slaver. This began the livestock nature of slavery.

After two centuries, slavery became a major livestock commodity industry in Virginia from 1820 to the 1860 with high profit commodity sales of Virginians "sold south" to booming cotton, sugar and tobacco plantations. In the Deep South, the prices of people were sometimes double those in Virginia and the Upper South where excess populations of enslaved people reduced their value for work production. As a livestock commodity industry, slavery became too lucrative to end. It must be noted that the tobacco industry has survived its slave roots and is booming today as the supplier of a legalized addiction that kills almost 500,000 Americans a year. It is estimated that the annual health care costs in West Virginia alone for treatment of tobacco-related diseases exceeds one *billion* dollars.[30]

Slavery and the system of segregation after the Civil War degraded people of African descent by separating them from the mainstream of American society. By their separation and deprivations as slaves, they were labeled universally with traits of inferiority, which pseudoscientists of the day, such as Thomas Jefferson, could claim to be proof of inferiority. These deprivations were used to show that people of African descent were either a lower order of human beings or not human beings at all. At best, whites believed that enslaved people should be treated as children and never as equals. This was true for many abolitionists who vehemently opposed slavery. They, like other whites, had trouble accepting blacks as equal neighbors. Many northerners wanted slaves to be set free but not to live next door. Colonization to Africa was a popular solution.

Virginian planters led the colonies and the new nation for its first two and a half centuries. Virginia was the most influential state, being the largest colony and state by population and area. Virginia had gifted men who were influenced by the Enlightenment and the Age of Reason. They studied the new ideas of Jean-Jacques Rousseau for the sovereignty of people who were to be governed, and Montesquieu about the separate functions of government, and John Locke for social contracts and empirical knowledge. They would know Greek ideas of democracy and equality. They were wary of absolute democracy where equal votes may be granted to men who owned no property. They would have agreed with Socrates that:

> [Democracy]...is a charming form of government, full of variety and disorder, and dispensing a sort of equality to equals and unequals alike.[31]

Virginian leaders like James Madison believed they could create a "more perfect union" with a central government and limited governmental powers, that would be separated and balanced in a republican form of government. James Madison brilliantly envisioned a judicial branch of government that would protect minority rights guaranteed in the Federal Constitution from overreaching state or federal majority rule. By 1790, Virginia had over forty percent of the nation's people held in slavery in its eastern and coastal areas. Western Virginia had few settlers living on small farms with very few enslaved workers.[32]

With vast resources seventy years later, Virginia led the nation into a four-year, bloody civil war. The rebellion was in no small part to protect Virginia's lucrative markets for sales of Virginians to Deep South states. Those states were organized as agricultural slave societies, and they formed the Confederacy following the lead of South Carolina. They were rural states. Mississippi, Texas, Arkansas, Florida, and North Carolina had no cities with populations of 10,000 or more.[33] Virginia slavery had been transformed from a work production social institution into a slave livestock commodity industry to supply essential labor to lucrative cotton, sugar cane, and tobacco plantations. At the start of the Civil War, about one-third of the population in eastern Virginia was enslaved--or almost half a million people. By comparison, the number of people held in slavery in the western mountains was small, perhaps the smallest concentration of people held in slavery of any major region. There, the only large concentration of enslaved people was in the Kanawha Valley, because of the salt and coal industries. Without eastern Virginia in the Confederacy, a war with the Union by Deep South agricultural states would have been lost after a few skirmishes.

Under Virginian leadership and ideas, slavery remained the controlling social and political issue in America for four generations after the revolutionary founding ideas were presented in the Declaration of Independence. Blacks were not included in ideas of brotherhood or "We the People" in the Federal Constitution. The white majority held dear the idea that whites were "real" humans and a superior race with a superior European-style civilization to spread across the continent as the nation's "Manifest Destiny." That term was coined by John L. O'Sullivan in the *Democratic Review* to describe what he saw as "the white US citizens' God-given right to take the remainder of North America from Indians and mixed-race Mexicans."[34] For blacks, this meant whites would relegate them to being neither fully human nor civilized other than through the benefit of their forced work in slave societies that white Americans called "civilization."

The full story of Booker T. Washington's boyhood years requires a detailed account of the Ruffner family in the Kanawha Valley and the slavery system in Virginia that provided people held in slavery for exploitation by the Ruffners and other entrepreneurs to build a new industry. Young Booker spent formative years living with Viola and Lewis Ruffner. The time he was in their home is not known. Viola Ruffner thought it started in 1865, soon after young Booker came to Malden with his mother who became a chambermaid and cook at the Ruffner's home. Booker T. Washington could not recall how long he lived at the Ruffners. He wrote, "I think it must have been a year and a half." It likely was much, much longer, before and after he went to Hampton Institute in 1872.[35]

The Ruffners and others in the town they created in Malden, respected hard work and fair opportunity for all. Young Booker's stepfather, Washington Ferguson, was a valued worker in the Ruffners' salt factory and coal mines. His work ethic was respected. Booker's mother, Jane Ferguson, was a remarkable woman who should be heralded for her leadership in the Malden community. She was remembered by children in the Ruffner family to be an intelligent and clever woman. She held great ambitions for her children, John, Booker and Amanda. The Ruffners supported those ambitions knowing that Jane Ferguson's children and other promising freed youth would need education and fair opportunities to succeed in life. It was obvious to the Ruffners that a racist system of oppression and submission would deny those opportunities to able freed youth.

As Young Booker matured, he showed unusual promise with talent, character and a work ethic as great or better than the brilliant son of Viola and Lewis Ruffner, Ernest Howard Ruffner. He would finish first in his class at West Point in 1867. The Ruffners could see in young Booker the potential for outstanding success perhaps greater than the achievements of other talented family members, who had been national leaders in drilling, salt manufacturing, coal mining, education, religion and state making. Lewis and Viola Ruffner rejected the idea of white superiority and became champions for equality and civic justice for freed people after the war while living closely with the Fergusons and young Booker.

The Ruffners had a profound effect on young Booker who was only nine years old when he met them. He worked as a child in their home and garden for a number of years, most likely starting soon after he and his family arrived in Malden. He enjoyed a warm relationship with Viola Ruffner. Upper class whites in the South were generally paternalistic to freed blacks, but the relationship of young Booker and Viola Ruffner became familial and rose above race and class distinctions.[36] She delighted in his talents and strict dedication to duty. For her, like with a favorite grandchild, Booker could do no wrong.

From that familial bond with Viola Ruffner, young Booker would adopt the Ruffner sense of duty to improve the human condition of others around him. Later, he would preach local community improvement by urging all persons simply to "cast down your bucket where you are."[37] That sense of place and community kept young Booker in the Deep South with a career that was limited by severe racist social codes put in place and enforced with extreme terror after Reconstruction.

The Ruffner family should be remembered and studied today for its success in many ventures before the Civil War. They invented modern deep well drilling for the western world. They established a new industry for salt production years before major factory systems were producing cloth in New England to start the American Industrial Revolution. The Ruffners also established the coal industry in western Virginia. They were renowned as drilling, geology and river engineers. They established the first Presbyterian churches and the first school academy in the Kanawha Valley. The Ruffners were the leading state educators in Virginia before and after the Civil War. They believed that all citizens in a democracy needed a basic education. They fought for free public schools funded by property taxes, a radical idea for their day. Henry Ruffner, in a widely published 1847 pamphlet, proposed gradual abolition of slavery and a requirement that slavers teach enslaved people "reading, writing and arithmetic," so they would be ready for independence after emancipation. He believed that all men should be "free and equal" because that was their nature. He thought colonies in Africa would be good for emancipated people to settle because they were inferior to whites. The Ruffners were early supporters of co-education for women and non-discrimination for religious groups. They helped build Virginia's first public school system and its higher education system. College campuses in Virginia have buildings named for W. H. Ruffner to honor his work for higher education as state superintendent of schools after the civil war. He helped establish Virginia Tech and Longwood University. In 1976, Virginia Tech made its highest service honor the "William H. Ruffner Medal" acknowledging his early service and guidance to the University.[38]

The city of Charleston, which the Ruffners' salt industry made possible, provided a large population base later used by state makers, including Lewis Ruffner, to extend the borders of the new state to include all of today's southern West Virginia counties. The expanded southern border would make Charleston the capital of the new state, and, in the twentieth century, the center of the national coal industry and later the world chemical industry. But the principal Ruffner achievement for humankind is their rejection of white supremacy after the Civil War, and their encouragement and guidance to the talented young Booker, and his respected family and their friends, who built a black middle class in Malden.

This favorable view of Lewis Ruffner's social commitment to helping others is consistent with a commitment shared by the Ruffner family since moving to the Kanawha Valley. One commentator who knew Lewis Ruffner wrote of his charitable nature.

He freely did to the extent of his means the inauguration and prosecution of every public enterprise that had for its object the development of the resources of his country and state. No charity that was brought to his notice went unblessed by his contribution. In a word, General Ruffner indulged, as much as anyone within the knowledge of the writer, in the "Luxury of doing good."[39]

Young Booker's story is the story of his freed heroes, led by his family, as they climbed up from slavery to be role models to launch his career of national leadership. The Fergusons were leaders in the black community. They were respected and influential as hard working, good citizens. Notably, they purchased a home only four years after they were in slavery in direct defiance of an order by a secret band of night riders, like the Ku Klux Klan, proclaiming that blacks could not live in Malden. The Fergusons had been living in the safety of the former Ruffner slave quarters in Tinkersville, near the Ruffner home, factory and coal mines. The home the Fergusons purchased was located among white landowners and a mile away from work, school and church. It was impressive that the Fergusons were able to pay their $500.00 home purchase price by combining the wages of the parents and their young sons. As freed people struggling to survive in Freedom, they lived their lives to prove that the dominant white belief in the inferiority of the black race, simply was wrong.

A race riot broke out near their new Malden home six weeks after the Fergusons entered into the land contract to purchase the property. In the melee, Lewis Ruffner became permanently disabled when he was hit with a brick in the back of the head. He had to use two canes to walk for the rest of his life after the riot. He joined the fray with his revolver in hand to help freed men attend a hearing they had set for later in the day. They were seeking a peace bond against a local white man after an altercation. They were threatened by whites and told not to attend the hearing. Blacks had no rights to go to court during Virginia slavery, and Lewis Ruffner realized that the hearing would be an important lesson in town, that freed people could have their civil rights protected by the courts.[40]

The Fergusons after the riot courageously continued to pay for their new home in town. Race tensions two months after the riot led to the savage beating of a black man in Malden. The next month, the governor was asked by county officials to help stop blacks from being stoned and shot at on the streets of Malden. They also asked the governor not to make their request public, since secret society members were widely supported in the community.

The Fergusons stayed in their Malden home, surviving as one of the first black families to own a home there. Home ownership fairly marks the beginning of middle class status for blacks in West Virginia, and for the South through the leadership of Booker T. Washington and his American Dream.

The unusual relationship of the Ferguson family and the Ruffner family creates a rare success story for the Reconstruction Era. Radical Republicans in Congress tried to force the idea of equality into the slave societies of the South, using soldiers and bayonets, but with little success anywhere. Although Reconstruction was not ordered in West Virginia, the Congressional efforts for equality influenced the Ruffners and other sympathetic state leaders to accept equality for freed people. During the turmoil of the Reconstruction Era, the success of young Booker's boyhood heroes in building a black middle class gave him the hope and vision to pursue equality through education and fair opportunity for common people in the Deep South. His heroes were members of his family and their independent church community, who created a legacy of local, state, and national black leaders before and during the modern civil rights era.

An 1872 Photograph of the Fergusons' Second Home in Malden. Purchased in 1869 as shown in The *Outlook Magazine* in 1900 – *Author's Collection*

In America, during and after Reconstruction, the idea of equality continued to be subordinate to the overriding Anglo-Saxon idea of white superiority. Many whites thought that blacks should be treated as needy children. The Ruffners would agree until they met the Ferguson family and their talented son, who came to town with only one name, "Booker." He added the last name "Washington" when he was nine years old, and later the famous "T." for "Taliaferro."

Booker T. Washington's boyhood years soon after the Civil War were the most uncertain times in American history. When the butchery of the Civil War ended, four million people formerly held in slavery were free to leave their places of captivity, but very few had any place to go. The death toll in the war was horrific. Of the 3.5 million men who served as soldiers in the war, some 600,000 were killed. There were perhaps another 50,000 civilians who died on both sides. The tragedy of the South after the war was that one-fifth of all southern men of military age were dead. With death touching every family in the South, a legacy of lost Confederate glory arose and encouraged whites to celebrate a romantic memory of slave times in the South, which was later accepted in the nation as a whole. That legacy would endure into the twenty-first century as the national story of southern culture.

Most all interactions of blacks and whites soon after the Civil War were social experiments for the work, living and survival of freed people. They had to overcome demeaning images in books and popular minstrel shows. Many catchy tunes about living in the Upper South were part of the popular white culture, such as "Carry Me Back to Old Virginia" and "My Old Kentucky Home." These songs were popular songs used in minstrel shows before the Civil War.

Jim Crow was the name of a lead character in minstrel shows. The term "Jim Crow" is today a depreciating term used for laws and social codes that support separation and subjugation of black people. In the shows, Jim Crow was portrayed by Thomas Rice. Touring minstrel shows were popular with white people for over a century, to laugh at people who were held in slavery and then to laugh at people who were to be shunned in segregation. The shows promoted stereotypes of blacks as inferior beings. Starting in the 1840s, traveling minstrel shows had white actors in black face entertaining white people with jokes and skits showing black people to be ignorant, dishonest, and lacking in social graces and common sense. The "infectious music and dance" of people held in slavery was an important part of the shows because white people found the music very entertaining. Historian Charles Sellers wrote that minstrel shows "inculcated racism but also appropriated the vitality of black expression to other white needs" to degrade and suppress black people generally. "Blackface" racist entertainments were popular with glass workers in the 1890s and across the south until after the Second World War.[41]

In Malden, after the war, many freed people stayed on to work in salt factories and coal mines for decent wages that were likely equal to wages for white workers, allowing freed people in the Kanawha Valley to purchase homes and build a middle class community in the first generation after slavery. They were social pioneers and the prophets of change for later generations. With education, their children became professionals and community leaders who spread the message of middle class values across the state and well beyond its borders.

This work will introduce the reader to new information on young Booker and his boyhood heroes and the historic legacy of leadership they initiated. It is noted that much of the new original material was discovered and shared by Gerald Ratliff, a Malden historian, photographer and retired journalist. The legacy of black leaders for the nation from West Virginia is outstanding. It begins with Booker T. Washington and continues in the careers of national leaders who followed him in the modern civil rights movement. Three giants of the movement are from one historic church, First Baptist Church of Charleston. The capstone of the leadership of Booker T. Washington and his heroes is the election of an African American as president of the United States in 2008. This legacy should be celebrated as a monument to Booker T. Washington's heroes who started their own proud black community with faith that the country they loved would become a more "holy nation" where equality, liberty, democracy, and social justice would overcome white supremacy, at least "someday."

The success of young Booker's boyhood heroes in building a black middle class gave him the hope and vision to carry the American Dream to the Confederate South and the nation. This work is about his journey of hope and faith presented with a story of good people in a mountain industrial town who live simple lives as good neighbors and help change the history of the modern world.

Louise McNeill Pease, Poet Laureate of West Virginia - *Image Courtesy of West Virginia State Archives*

Old salt well derrick -- *Image Courtesy of West Virginia State Archives*

Chapter 1

The Wilderness Of Western Virginia

Frontier Values in the Mountains

The ideas of Reconstruction for equality and fair play were a success in Malden. Congress did not impose Reconstruction in West Virginia because it was a loyal state. The state's heritage provided better human relations for freed people because its value structure was centered on a strong work ethic, self-reliance and respect for the individual. Those ideas were supported by a frontier social system that gave little value to birth status. These values were very different from the aristocratic ideas of the Confederate South, especially those dominant in eastern Virginia before and after the Civil War.

Booker's boyhood after the war begin in the rugged mountain and valley topography of West Virginia which had been settled only 70 years before. In the Kanawha Valley, the values of its hardy pioneers continued. In all generations, mountains define, focus, secure, and inspire the people who live and go among them.

Poet Laureate of West Virginia Louise McNeill Pease captured the magic of the mountains in the poem, "Over The Mountain" in her book of poems, *Hill Daughter,* published in 1991. This was one of two books she published while living her last years in Malden.

When I was a child and we lived at home
In our farmhouse under the mountain's comb,
The meadows stretched from our wide front door,
And the fields ran down to the river's shore;
But behind our house, to the west and north,
The mountain reared, from the earth reared forth-
A king of dark, with a rocky crown,
The mountain stood, and its dark fell down
In shadowed length on our wide front door,
Across our fields to the south and shore.[42]

Some think that from folklore mountains have a spirit and orienting force of terrain that can both limit and protect. Others could say the force is the heritage of a rugged, pioneering people, who embraced the struggle to survive and make the mountains and valleys habitable and nurturing. All of those factors combine to make people forever "mountaineers." Governor Bob Wise said in his State of the State Address on February 14, 2001:

> Every West Virginian senses at some time as evident truth: God walks among these West Virginia hills. From the smoky mist rising from every hollow - to the deer raising her head from the mountain stream - to neighbors that gather 'round in times of hardship and grief and in times of joy. West Virginia is a special place.[43]

Mountaineers know their roots and are oriented to place by imposing and distinctive horizons. They know direction by mountain shapes that never change unless by the acts of man. The horizons of flat-land are straight lines in the distance, and they do not orient or secure people to place even those who grow up there. The landmarks in flat-lands are only those which are constructed by man. The beauty and wonder of flat-lands are in the expanse of possibilities and opportunity. To pioneer farmers from the East the open expanse of the Northwest Territory we now call the "Midwest" presented unlimited opportunity for land that was open, rich and ready for their work and their families. The whole of the Northwest Territory, from Ohio to Minnesota, is a farmer's dream and the source of great wealth for America for over two centuries, and today.

Among the hills, mountaineers can focus and bloom and spread like rhododendron. On flat land, many feel a palpable loss of orientation and lack of spirit felt in their home mountains. This sense of place and home have people of the mountains often say, "Once a mountaineer, always a mountaineer."

Dr. Henry Louis Gates, Jr., a leading African American historian, grew up in West Virginia mountains in Piedmont, Mineral County, and spent time living in the Charleston area. He has written that his growing up in mountains and being a mountaineer has been as profound an influence for his personality as has been the influence of his race.[44]

> There is something compellingly peaceful about a mountain range rimming a river, and Charleston the state capital, is on the Kanawha River, in a beautiful river valley, surrounded by gently rolling hills—a most idyllic valley, too, befouled only by the stench of the Union Carbide plant located there. Still those mountains have had a salient effect on all of us who grew up in them. I have often thought that being a "mountaineer" –that is the state's nickname for its citizens --was as

important in shaping the peculiarities of my personality as was being black, more so, in some ways, like stubbornness, and hardheaded resoluteness and individualism.[45]

In the early 1800s, the mountain culture of Malden and western Virginia was egalitarian and merit-based. Mountain terrain limited the development of early towns with formal social institutions, in turn encouraging strong egalitarian attitudes and beliefs. These beliefs evolved into a democratic social order. Most mountain people owned their land and cultivated it with family members. Few used slavery for gain. Only about 15 percent of households had enslaved people in western Virginia, making the institution of slavery much less important than it was in eastern Virginia.[46] But the Malden salt industry in the Kanawha Valley was built on the crushing labor of enslaved Virginians, and it would impact the nature, size and politics of the new state.

When Booker's mother, Jane Ferguson, brought her three young children to Malden after the Civil War, they immediately benefited from frontier values, because they were treated with respect as hard workers. The single most important standard for earning respect and community status was a strong work ethic. Those values continue today. Social status in the mountains was not in three levels for upper, middle and low. Status was based on work ethic and clean living. People could be divided simply, between "respectable" and "not respectable", with each community defining the criteria for these groups.[47] At first, freed people were "not respectable" simply because of their race, but thanks to the leadership of Jane Ferguson, Washington Ferguson, and their friends, that status would change before young Booker's eyes as he grew into a young man.

The Ferguson family would learn immediately on arrival in Malden that a strong work ethic would be their salvation as a "family." Their work in a merit-based mountain community would be rewarded. This was not true for freed people throughout the Confederate South. These values today support the culture and life of the Kanawha Valley and West Virginia. A secure family was a natural human bond which was denied to enslaved people by Virginia law. They shared a family bond as allowed by custom until disrupted painfully when members of the family--children or adults--were shipped away as commodities to plantations in the Deep South. Historian Kenneth M. Stampp at the University of California at Berkeley estimated that 300,000 Virginians were sent south from 1830 to 1860, disrupting those lives and the lives of hundreds of thousands of loved ones left behind in Virginia.[48] Enslaved people in Virginia were more valuable for sale south than for work production in the thirty years before the Civil War. Leasing as well as sales into the slave trade disrupted family life in Virginia. Half of the enslaved people in the Kanawha Valley by 1850 were leased far away from their homes and loved ones in eastern Virginia.

In eastern Virginia and most of the developing Confederate South, aristocratic values were well established. Many community hierarchies were based on the English model for birth status as the key to social prominence. Some aristocratic English families relied on a deeply held belief that they were anointed by God through their birth status to dominate and control others. This anti-democratic idea was espoused by John C. Calhoun of South Carolina. He said that the nation could not be wealthy unless one portion lived on the labor of the other portion. He was an early supporter of state nullification of federal tariff laws in the South in 1832, based on a theory that states had sovereign rights superior to federal law. This theory of sovereign states' rights was repelled for a time by President Andrew Jackson in his strong response to the nullification protest. The theory was used to protect slavery until the Civil War, and it led to a successful argument made before the United States Supreme Court after the Civil War to protect Jim Crow state segregation laws denying federal civil rights. [49]

The mechanical revolution would eventually change the requirement for manual labor in general, but elitism in the social order persisted in the North and South, encouraging a romantic ideal for the aristocratic families in the South that extended for over a century after the war. The theme of a lost glory of the Confederate cause was celebrated. The myth of the ideal southern man was romantic. He was in the "ideal" a swashbuckling fellow who always was above ambition and disdained vanity. He was ever suspicious of accumulated power and never appeared to seek to make money, but in some way he was affluent. He did not give orders but in some way, he was followed. He did not work but in some way he was accomplished.[50]

The ideal southern man was very different from the iconic western frontiersman and yeoman farmers who conquered rough mountain terrain to establish settlements and plant a frontier culture that endures. State Poet Laureate Louise McNeill expressed the magic of the yeoman culture of the hills in her poem, "West Virginia" from *Hill Daughter* published in 1991.

> Loved and treasured, earth and star,
> By my father's fathers far---
> Deep-earth, black-earth, of-the-lime
> For the ancient oceans' time.

Plow-land, fern-land, woodland shade,
Grave-land where my kin are laid,
West Virginia's hills to bless--
Leafy songs of wilderness;

Dear land, near land, here at home--
Where the rocks are honeycomb,
And the rhododendrons...
Where the mountain river runs.[51]

Nature's Division of Virginia: East and West

To understand the division of Virginia into east and west requires appreciation of the very different economies and aspirations of the two regions. In the western mountains, pioneers had day-to-day issues of human survival. Those issues were very different from the patrician concerns for protection of privilege enjoyed by Virginia aristocrats living east of the Allegheny Mountains.

Granville Hall, a journalist and reporter for the statehood convention in Wheeling, wrote poetically about the differences between eastern and western Virginia:

Mountain barriers had been reared by nature between the two sections. On one side of them the waters flowed toward the old world of vested privilege; on the other toward the new, the free, the possibilities of the future and the unknown. Commerce divides with the water-sheds and flows with the streams. The interests and purposes of men follow commercial lines.[52]

In the western wilderness, with survival at stake, the birth status of a person was of little help in the struggle to survive. What mattered was whether or not a neighbor of any status or race could help defend the family from wild animals or dangerous people, and who could help build up the community. Survival on a hostile frontier was the goal of life. Until towns grew with industry and agriculture, English style birth status offered little to struggling pioneers. Established plantations and English culture in eastern Virginia made aristocratic birth status a key to social interactions and political influence.

Some of the aristocratic style of eastern Virginians may have come from Cavaliers who emigrated there as British exiles after Parliament won the British Civil War against King Charles I and his supporters who were called Cavaliers.[53] The King was beheaded for treason in 1649, and Parliament ruled without a monarch until Charles II assumed the throne in 1660. Folklore has the Virginia nickname, the "Old Dominion," coming from that time. The deposed king's son was returned to the British throne as Charles II, but not until after loyal Cavaliers in Virginia offered him the Virginia colony as his kingly "dominion." Charles was said to be ever grateful for the Virginians' offer of a dominion while he waited to return to the British throne. Virginia has Old Dominion University in Norfolk. The mascot of the University of Virginia is a Cavalier with feather-plumbed hat. The sports team mascot of West Virginia University is a mountaineer with musket and coonskin cap.

In the 1700s, there were few native settlements located in the western Virginia territory that would become West Virginia. The mountains and valleys were used as hunting grounds, sometimes between competing tribes. Two thousand years before European exploration, the Mound Builders in the Adena period came to the Ohio Valley and the Kanawha Valley. They constructed huge dome shaped earth works as burial mounds that can be seen today in South Charleston and Moundsville. Native tribes claiming hunting rights in the 1700s included Shawnee people in the Ohio Valley. The Tuscarora people lived along the Potomac River, and the Delaware people were in the Northern Panhandle. The smaller Mingo tribe had settlements across the Ohio River from the area surrounding today's Wheeling. Native Cherokee people from North Carolina hunted in southwestern Virginia from time to time, but they had little presence in western Virginia compared to the Shawnee.[54]

Attacks and counterattacks on villages and settlements were savage with scalps taken on both sides. Each side demonized their enemies. Some native tribes were claimed to be cannibals by tradition against conquered tribes, according to an account by Charles Johnston.[55] This claim and reports of savagery by warriors were regularly made to settlers, inflaming passions for revenge. Both sides were fierce, vengeful and deadly.

The Allegheny Mountains created a high physical barrier to social and economic interaction between established ways of the old families and power brokers in eastern Virginia and the rugged western pioneers who were mostly Scot-Irish and German settlers.[56] These settlers survived on a dangerous western frontier that stretched from the Valley of Virginia west to the Ohio River. The Valley goes north and south from Pennsylvania to the Carolinas and is part of the Great Appalachian Valley. It was used for regular migrations of settlers. In Virginia, it furnished a route south for early German and Scot-Irish settlers from Pennsylvania to settle in the western mountain valleys along the Potomac River and Shenandoah River.

Germans formed the first settlement in today's West Virginia, on the Potomac River at Mecklenburg now named Shepherdstown. German immigrants were quick to assimilate much of the official English-speaking culture, while maintaining their ancestral folkways. Scot-Irish immigrants came from Ulster in northwest Ireland and were joined by immigrants from the border regions of North England. From 1715 to 1775, as many as 250,000 immigrants came from Ulster and North England to the American back country. They came in family groups. Most Scot-Irish settlers were fierce patriots for the new republic. They were poor and not welcomed by the established English proprietors of coastal colonial areas. Their brethren Scots from the old country Highlands immigrated to the Carolina back country and most were loyal to King George in the Revolution.[57]

The culture of Old Virginia from colonial times was affected by its diverse subcultures. Different words are used in different regions relating to the folkways of the regions. Earthworms are angleworms, fishing worms and red worms depending on the region. Griddlecakes and pancakes are hotcakes and flannel cakes. Living rooms can be parlors, sitting rooms, chambers and front rooms.[58]

But the differences between eastern and western Virginia before the Civil War were not matters of subculture or language. They arose from differences in geography, cultural values, heritage, and social and political values. The differences created constant strife between east and west. For his 1835 critique of America, Alexis de Tocqueville traveled widely, and made a trip through western Virginia from Wheeling to Cincinnati. He noted that, overall, western settlers were of a different European stock than the English in eastern Virginia. Early settlers in Virginia were also a different kind of people from those who settled in New England. Robust settlers in New England included Puritans who were fleeing religious and social persecution during the reign of King James I of England. The Puritans were unified by the idea of a new society with no lords and only common people. They were intelligent, religious and educated people. By contrast, Virginia was settled by adventurers who created slavery to build a lucrative economy with tobacco production. Most colonists outside New England were generally of a different kind. By 1770, one-half of the white population living south of New England came to America as bond servants and about half were of "non-English origins."[59]

In New England, settlers came to establish a new social order based on liberty and equality. They "landed on a barren coast" and established their first village at Plymouth, after failing to sail farther south to northern Virginia as first intended. They adopted the Mayflower Compact which was the first social contract or constitution in North America, about one year after the first Africans were brought to Jamestown in 1619. The Mayflower Compact was a document of self-governance supported by the idea of sovereignty in the Puritans as a group who were agreeing to be governed. It was signed on November 21, 1620, over 150 years before Jean-Jacques Rousseau's influential book, *The Social Contract,* which proposed that sovereignty for a government's right to govern must be based on the consent of those who would be governed. For the 1787 Federal Constitution, it was the sovereignty of "We the People." For the 1620 Mayflower Compact, it was the Puritan colonists who by their consent joined in "a civil body politick" for the "better ordering and preservation" of the colony with "just and equal laws" for "the general good of the Colony, unto which we promise all due submission and obedience."[60] The ideas of the Puritans in the Mayflower Compact, for liberty and equality based upon independent sovereignty and dutiful service to the community as a whole, would be influential in the development of new ideas and free spirits in the thirteen British colonies, leading to creation of the United States and its Federal Constitution, 167 years after the Mayflower Compact.

In Connecticut, in 1639, three towns joined in "Fundamental Orders" to establish a federal system of democratic governance which was a precursor to the federal government created by the Federal Constitution a century and a half later. The document was signed in Hartford at a convention of the towns to establish a representative and limited central government. Vincent Wilson, Jr., wrote that the document was also notable for the absence of any reference to Parliament or the Crown. "In the wilderness along the Connecticut River, the three towns had, in fact, come close to creating an independent commonwealth."[61]

All colonies and states in the new nation legalized slavery. But Virginia was the leading slave colony and state, and it was strongly criticized by Alexis de Tocqueville. In the 1830s, after Britain abolished slavery, Virginia was prosperous selling people held in slavery as commodities to the Deep South. The sale of each person disrupted slave families and their "kin networks," which included family friends and more distant relations. Alexis de Tocqueville stated in his 1835 book *Democracy in America* about the beginnings of slavery and its ill effects on society in Virginia and the South:

[Virginia was founded by] seekers of gold, adventurers without resources and without character...No lofty views, no spiritual conception, presided on the foundation of these new settlements. The colony was scarcely established when slavery was introduced; this was the capital fact which was to exercise an immense influence on the character, the laws, and the whole future of the South. Slavery...dishonors labor; it introduces idleness into society, and with idleness, ignorance and pride, luxury and distress. It enervates the powers of the mind and benumbs the activity of man. The influence of slavery, united to the English character, explains the manners and social condition of the Southern States.[62]

German and Scot-Irish Pioneers in Western Virginia

Many settlers in the Valley of Virginia and across the mountains from eastern Virginia, were Scot and German Protestants. Scot Protestants, who came from Ulster in northwest Ireland, were called "Scotch-Irish" in America. They were independent free-spirited Presbyterian followers of John Calvin and John Knox. Many western settlers were German immigrants, who were Baptists, Dunkards, German Baptists, Mennonites, and other free thinkers. Settlers of German descent were often antislavery and few of them held people as slaves.[63]

Historian Carter G. Woodson, who was a dean at today's West Virginia State University and is the father of Negro History Week that later became Black History Month, wrote of the different rugged pioneers who settled in the mountain areas of western Virginia:

Among the Germans were Mennonites, Lutherans, and Moravians, all of whom believed in individual freedom, the divine right of secular power, and personal responsibility. The strongest stocks among these immigrants, however, were the Scotch-Irish, 'a God-fearing, Sabbath-keeping, covenant-adhering, liberty-loving and tyrant-hating race,' which had formed its ideals under the influence of philosophy of John Calvin, John Knox, Andrew Melville and George Buchanan. By these thinkers they had been taught to emphasize equality, freedom of conscience, and political liberty. These stocks differed somewhat from each other, but they were equally attached to practical religion, homely virtues and democratic institutions. Being a kind and beneficent class with a tenacity for the habits and customs of their fathers, they proved to be a valuable contribution to the American stock.[64]

Most British immigrants were religious people seeking a new life with personal freedom away from the English Episcopal Church, which was headed by the British monarch as an arm of the state, and supported by unpopular colonial taxes. Dr. Henry Ruffner, a frontier Presbyterian minister from a German immigrant family, stated this analysis in a Fourth of July Speech in the Kanawha Salines in 1856. It was a published speech extolling the Union and the many different white immigrants who joined in the "American mold" and formed the "national character." Fully adopting the idea of white superiority, he excluded the "African race" from the national mold and character, because they were different "not by the will of man, but of God, who made us all."

> I would not, as some do, attribute our progress to a physical superiority of the Anglo-Saxon race, to which the majority of the British people and the early settlers in this country belonged. But much, very much, is due to the religious character of the early colonists, and to the principles of civil liberty which they brought with them. The great majority were Protestant Christians, accustomed to free thought and action, under a free system of government in Church and State. They gave to colonial society and institutions their first form and movement. From these, the growing colonies never departed, and the revolution only shook off the encumbrance of foreign domination, and gave to the American character and institutions a free development. From the beginning, and more in after times, our American population has been composed of diverse races. Now, the majority of our citizens are of German, Low Dutch, Irish, Welsh, and French descent, with a sprinkling from other nations of Europe. Yet whatever may have been the origin of our mature population all have been cut in the American mold, and conform to the national character. The same general spirit of industry, enterprise and personal independence, distinguishes them from other nations and makes them indistinguishable from one another. It is only the African race, bond and free, who are of so different a type from the rest, that they cannot incorporate with the mass; but must remain ever distinct not by the will of man, but of God, who made us all.[65]

Many Virginians in its coastal regions called "Tidewater Virginia" were uncertain about the migration of fiercely independent groups of Protestants into the Valley of Virginia and west into the Allegheny Mountains. Some viewed these rugged settlers as rabble compared to the genteel planter class of English stock, who were Episcopalians and enjoyed their society in English style. The churches of German immigrant families generally opposed slavery like those of the Lutherans in the family of David Ruffner and the Mennonites in the family of his wife, Anna Brumbach Ruffner. Any church in which German immigrants played a major part opposed slavery.[66]

The opposition to slavery in German churches was somewhat less than the opposition of the Methodist Episcopal Church, but opposition to slavery by German immigrants was strong. During the Civil War, German immigrants in Texas and elsewhere in the South were brutally attacked for their opposition to slavery and supposed disloyalty to the Confederate cause. In Louisa County, Virginia, German store owners were forced out of the county by masked men threatening to burn their property. In Texas, many German immigrant men were hanged and shot and a number were massacred after surrendering to Confederate troops.[67]

Thomas C. Miller and Hu Maxwell wrote of the German opposition in *West Virginia and Its People*:

> The Baptists, Presbyterians, and also practically all denominations in which the German element was large, were not much behind the Methodists in [their] opposition to slavery, though some of them did not so frequently or so loudly lift their voices against it.[68]

By contrast, the Episcopal Church in Virginia "had little to say in opposition to slavery," and it was not able to grow in western Virginia until after the Civil War when "slavery became a thing of the past." Before the Civil War, there were fewer than a dozen parishes in the western mountains. William Meade, the Episcopal Bishop of the Diocese of Virginia during the years of forced migration of thousands of people to the Deep South, early in his career was a reformer who was educated at Princeton College, an antislavery institution. He initially favored the enlightenment of enslaved people with literacy training, but later joined other Virginia leaders in opposing slave literacy after an enslaved, educated man, Nat Turner, led a bloody rebellion in 1831. Slaver religious scholars would point out that, in the New Testament, St. Paul attacks cruelty to slaves, but he does not attack the slavery relationship or the existence of slavery.[69] One commentator stated that a beneficial aspect of this scripture is that it at least showed slaves that their masters on earth had a master in heaven.[70]

Accepting this slaver interpretation of scripture, Bishop William Meade preached to people held in slavery that they should give over their physical lives on earth to total obedience to slavers and accept as their Christian duty, the requirement that they wait to enjoy a true and glorious freedom with God in heaven. The flight of freed people from white led churches after the Civil War can be fully understood after reading these words that Bishop Meade preached as the religious leader of the Virginia Diocese of the Episcopal Church. They are chilling words to read and difficult concepts to grasp.

> If, therefore, you would be God's freeman in heaven, you must strive to be good, and serve him here on earth. Your bodies, you know, are not your own; they are at the disposal of those you belong to but your precious souls are still your own, which nothing can take from you, it if be not your own fault....I now come to lay before you the duties you owe to your masters and mistresses here upon earth. And for this you have one general rule, that you ought always to carry in your minds; and that is to do all service for them as if you did it for God himself....when you are idle and neglectful of your masters' business, when you steal, and waste, and hurt any of their substance, when you are saucy and impudent, when you are telling them lies and deceiving them or when you prove stubborn and sullen, and will not do the work you are set about without stripes and vexation,--you do not consider, I say, that what faults you are guilty of towards your masters and mistresses are faults done against God himself, who hath set your masters and mistresses over you in his own stead, and expect that you would do for them just as you would do for him....your masters and mistresses are God's overseers...and God himself will punish you severely for it in the next world, unless you repent of it....[71]

Some religious leaders counseled slavers that God expected them to use physical punishment to guide and control the behavior of enslaved people. Tennessee's William "Parson" Brownlow stated, "The Scriptures look to the correction of servants, and really enjoin it, as they do in the case of children. We esteem it the duty of Christian masters to feed and clothe well, and in the case of disobedience to whip well." Heavy reliance on physical punishment was a racist response founded in belief in the inferiority of black people.[72]

Despite antislavery heritages of immigrant churches, by the time of John Brown's raid on Harpers Ferry in 1859, most churches had dropped formal protests of slavery, other than Quakers who worked relentlessly to end slavery and provide for the education of enslaved and free blacks. The Episcopal Church in the South was led by a number of Bishops who were strong advocates for slavery, in addition to Bishop William Meade in Virginia. The co-founders of today's University of the South were bishops who supported slavery. Bishop Leonidas Polk became a confederate general and Bishop Stephen Elliott called "slavery a 'sacred charge' and 'a great missionary institution...arranged by God,'" echoing the sentiments of Virginia Bishop Willaim Meade. This leadership of the southern

Episcopal Church caused Union soldiers across the South to commandeer Episcopal churches, as slaver churches, for their offices, quarters and stables. [73]

Most Scot-Irish settlers came to Virginia through central Pennsylvania. Folklore has the term "Hillbilly" coming from the Scot-Irish through the rich and popular music they played in the mountains. Coming from Ulster, it is thought that many of their ancestors supported William of Orange in 1640 in the Battle of Boyne against Irish Catholics, and were known as "Billies." It was common for immigrant Scot-Irish to play banjos or dulcimers and sing songs of "Billie of Orange." Their music was rich with storytelling. The term "Hillbilly" can also mean a friend from the hills. The modern term is not known to have appeared in print until the late 1800s when "Hillbilly" was used in an article in the *New York Journal*. As hillbillies in the Appalachian South, the Scot-Irish were part of a sturdy breed whose music helped create a mountain culture. "Hillbilly Music" is an important genre in country music today. [74]

At least seventeen American presidents are thought to be descendants of Scots from Ulster in northwest Ireland. They include Andrew Jackson, James K. Polk, James Buchanan, Andrew Johnson, Ulysses S. Grant, Chester A. Arthur, Grover Cleveland, Benjamin Harrison, William McKinley, Theodore Roosevelt, Woodrow Wilson, Harry Truman, Richard M. Nixon, Jimmy Carter, George H. W. Bush, William Clinton, and George W. Bush. [75]

Scot-Irish and German settlers were determined, hardy, and fierce in protecting and advancing their separate immigrant settlements. They were an imposing presence on the Virginia frontier before and after the Revolutionary War. Most western settlers immigrated from states north of Virginia through the Valley of Virginia and the Great Valley of the Appalachians, which stretches seven-hundred miles through a long plateau of arable land from the mountains of Albany, New York, to the Carolinas. It was America's first "Midwest," and created a long conduit for ongoing migration of settlers in the eighteenth century. These pioneers had fundamental differences with established Virginians who lived east of the Valley of Virginia. They considered themselves equal to eastern aristocrats. They believed first in individualism and they were, for themselves ever ready to fight against Aristotle's idea in *Politics,* that some men were born to be slaves. [76]

These immigrant pioneers would create a new elite class based on success in agriculture and business, and eventually in manufacturing after the salt industry was started by the Ruffner family. The Ruffners were German stock but readily exploited enslaved people in their salt factories. These settlers built new communities and pioneered new social institutions unlike those in eastern Virginia, where English society was imitated with large agricultural estates worked by slave workers. Generally, those estates were passed on to the oldest male heir of the family. [77]

Professor Charles H. Ambler in *A History of West Virginia* wrote that immigrant settlers would Americanize the expansion west of the nation's frontier with ideas of equality and democracy. He thought that the character of the society that was established upon the Virginia frontier augured well for the future of western expansion.

> The Scot-Irish were bold, enterprising, and fearless, whereas their German and Dutch neighbors were methodical and frugal. In the combination of the stocks with those of purer English origins coming from the East through Virginia, the Americanization process was noticeably accelerated. Tradition as well as environment predisposed the practice of equality; and religion, whether Mennonite or Moravian, Lutheran or Presbyterian, confirmed local settlers in democratic habits of mind. To such leaders had fallen the task of carving out an empire in the West.[78]

Virginia Aristocrats Versus Mountain Pioneers

The differences in eastern and western Virginia were many. Professor Oscar Lambert wrote, "Discord between the two regions did not happen by accident, it was inevitable."[79] The different terrain, economies, social structures, immigrant stocks, and religious affiliations meant conflict and discord on most every subject. William P. Willey, an early professor of law at West Virginia University, analyzed the eastern Virginia aristocrat:

> The eastern Virginian was and is, and always has been a very peculiar type of American citizen. He was an aristocrat by nature. He banked on his blood. His title to nobility arose in proportion to the intimacy of his alliance with the first families of Virginia....Caste was as well defined and pronounced in the population as under an absolute monarchy. The poor white trash had no standing that a member of the first families of Virginia was wont to respect. Many of the notions that obtained under the old feudal system, where the baron built a castle and walled himself in from the vulgar contact of the plebeian and put on great pomp and ceremony, seemed to have been imported to Virginia. The lordly owner of a Virginia plantation surrounded himself with slaves and established himself in a mansion that was inaccessible to the common herd as a feudal castle.[80]

Many in eastern Virginia followed the English nobility's tradition for the inheritance of whole estates by the oldest son, generation by generation. In England, this practice, called primogeniture, kept large estates in the control of one family line with a title of nobility attached to the owner of the estate. Younger male and all female children were expected to benefit the family by profitable marriages and businesses. English-style society was not limited to eastern Virginia. Alexis de Tocqueville observed that many English aristocrats settled throughout the colonies southwest of the Hudson River. He found that New England was different from the states to the south, because intellect and education were highly valued and were new sources of power and social status.[81] That tradition continues there with considerable family status attached to a member of the family attending an elite prep school, academy, college or university. Ivy League schools lead the way for elite status.

German and Scot-Irish settlers fully supported democratic ideas and frontier values for independence, equality, and individualism. They adopted a democratic tradition for inheritance, where children were treated equally and the first-born son was given no more than his siblings. Gender matters little in a share-and-share-alike system of fairness and equality. Children succeed or fail on their own merits. Alexis de Tocqueville explained in *Democracy in America* how important this democratic tradition can be to society itself. It invigorates a society and its economy by changing the interactions of heirs in favor of ambition, merit and innovation. Equal inheritance eliminates aristocracy bestowed by birth:

In virtue of the law of partible inheritance, the death of every proprietor brings about a kind of revolution in the property; not only do his possessions change hands, but their very nature is altered, since they are parceled into shares, which become smaller and smaller at each division. This is the direct, and as it were the physical, effect of the law. It follows, then, that, in countries where equality of inheritance is established by law, property, and especially landed property, must constantly tend to division into smaller and smaller parts...But the law of equal division exercises its influence not merely upon the property itself, but it affects the minds of the heirs, and brings their passions into play. These indirect consequences tend powerfully to the destruction of large fortunes, and especially of large domains.[82]

Alexis de Tocqueville thought that a democratic approach to inheritance by equal shares directly encouraged the entrepreneurship of heirs. The breakup of large estates limited family wealth and showy signs of riches. The talents and hard work of the heirs, instead of the luck of their birth order, would carry them through life. He wrote that equal distribution to heirs was the "last step to equality" in

America. Thomas Jefferson, in his 1785 *Notes on Virginia*, proposed changing Virginia law on inheritance, for parents who leave no will to a democratic model with children sharing equally in the estates. When a different distribution of assets is intended, a last will and testament would be required. The proposed law was adopted in Virginia and throughout the nation.[83] It continues as the law of inheritance in America.

Alexis de Tocqueville also predicted that, with America's growing mechanical revolution, the last step to equality through equal inheritance would create a new American aristocracy of manufacturers and businessmen. He could observe that to happen in the Kanawha Valley, where the families of successful salt industrialists married into other successful families in multiple generations on a regular basis. Such marriages were seen as favorable in helping to advance the business interests of the families.

Western Virginia settlers widely embraced a merit-based value structure, where skill and work of the individual were respected and rewarded regardless of birth status or social class. Professor Charles H. Ambler wrote that the culture of West Virginia has always been democratic equalitarianism:

> The pride and boast of this frontier society was its democratic equality. If one person had a better house and better furnishings than another, his good fortune was due largely to his greater industry and skill....[84]

This high value on merit and respect for individual effort and skill endures in West Virginia mountain communities. It is common today to see economic diversity in mountain communities, a rare quality in the culture of sameness in many suburbs especially those spread across flat-lands. In mountain hollows, a large modern landscaped home may sit between older, smaller homes and mobile homes, some owned by families who may follow a clannish Scot-Irish heritage. In mountain culture, the love of place overcomes economic status. The love of family and place in sheltering mountains orients people to their own communities and encourages them to know, appreciate and value their families and neighbors.[85] The idea of equal individual status for place and clan in a community is foreign to the idea of class separation by races, cultures, or finances. These values support equality and diversity. Individual merit helped hard working freed people after the Civil War to become respected neighbors in Malden and throughout West Virginia. Young Booker would observe his boyhood heroes using middle class values to establish themselves and their community with the respect that comes from equality based on the merit of the individual in society.

This economic diversity is in contrast to many places of today's American suburban culture, where grouped sameness can be a status indicated by zip code. Place can become a temporary status point to be improved upon by strategic moves to "better" and less economically diverse subdivisions. Such "better" subdivisions have larger houses with more distinct landscaping and greater amenities and somewhat less sameness, but they are marked with less economic diversity.

American popular culture embraces sameness as a satisfying, predictable quality for the day-to-day routines of life. Comforting fast foods are produced for all to enjoy with a reliable sameness, assuring every American that the chain restaurant hamburger enjoyed yesterday is the same one to be enjoyed today or tomorrow. Fast foods are now both sustaining and iconic for American culture around the world. The mechanical revolution introduced "mass" everything and with it, sameness. Between mountain horizons each place and each person are special and individual, creating a culture of egalitarian values supported for past generations by old-fashioned home cooking and canning and quilt making--with very little in the way of sameness.

Daniel Boone - *Image Courtesy of the Library of Congress*

American Progress by John Gast - *Image Courtesy of the Library of Congress*

Chapter 2

Settlers Push West
Into Native Hunting Grounds

Virginia Settlers Defy King George's Ban on Western Settlements

After the French and Indian War, in 1763, Virginia settlers were banned from making new settlements west of the crest of the Allegheny Mountains. A Proclamation of King George III banned settlements in the mountains west of a line drawn between what would be today from Preston County to Pocahontas County. The King wanted to protect native hunting lands in the West in order to create a new relationship with native peoples, like the relationship the French enjoyed before their war with the British.

Well before the Revolution, British leaders were becoming concerned with aggressive colonists who were beginning to show independence with their economic success. In the colonies, there were rising expectations of wealth and self-government. White colonists generally had a much higher standard of living than the common English family. Colonists openly challenged British control of their colonial governments and growing economies. As revolutionary agitation grew in prosperous New England, the British wanted to solicit native tribes to be allies along the western wilderness territories of its thirteen coastal colonies.

Scot-Irish and German settlers readily violated the proclamation. These settlers were not known for loyalty to the British King, or his Episcopal Church, or for any idea that native peoples deserved to be undisturbed in their hunting lands that spread across the western mountains. The settlers most ready to defy King George were descendants of the Scots who held the north of Ireland for King William. Scot ancestors had pushed Irish Catholics off their lands to establish a loyal colony in northwest Ireland, and they were prepared to do the same for their settlements in the western mountains of Virginia. Any limitation on new settlements was aggressively opposed, whether presented at law with a royal proclamation or by the presence of native peoples. Settlers readily built settlements with forts in territories controlled or claimed by native tribes. The forts would be essential in the settlers' war in 1774. Settlements in the western mountains of Virginia would lead to the migration of white settlers into the Midwest.[86]

Virginia authorities did not enforce the King's ban on settlements. Most all Virginians strongly objected to it. Expectations for growing wealth were tied directly to the ownership of new lands in the West. These lands would benefit all, including poor pioneers willing to settle their families there and the rich land speculators in eastern Virginia who wanted, where feasible, to encourage large slave estates in river valleys in the West.

Scot-Irish and German settlers had been successful in separate settlements in the Valley of Virginia. They fared well in the western mountains east of the Ohio River. The natural protection of the mountain terrain, good water, and abundant timber were ideal for the simple farming techniques and the pioneer culture of these settlers.[87]

Formal surveys of title were not available, and new settlers used "Tomahawk Rights" to begin farming on the forbidden wilderness lands. These claims of ownership were established by chopping trees on the perimeter of claimed lands, and they were respected by other settlers and frontiersmen. Many claims were later legalized under Virginia law, where no conflicting claims were a problem. Settlers could also claim land rights by planting acres of corn and by establishing formal settlements. Verifiable land titles in western Virginia would be a major problem for settlers and later for mineral developers, particularly in the years of resource development after the Civil War.[88]

The settlement ban was lifted after five years, in 1768, following a treaty with the Iroquois Six Nations that ceded to King George III land rights covering some 4,950 square miles and comprising much of today's West Virginia. Benjamin Franklin and others wanted to create a fourteenth colony out of those lands, to be named Vandalia, with its capital to be built at Point Pleasant.[89]

Settlers willing to go into western Virginia were from many religious and national groups, but predominantly they were Scot-Irish and German settlers who had little or no loyalty to a British monarch. Many colonists shared resentment of the Crown for a variety of reasons. The ban on settlements started agitation against King George in Virginia. Many settlers and other Virginians began to see King George as an oppressor demanding unpopular taxes and absolute control over their colonial government. The King's new taxes were used to cover his high war debt for driving the French out of North America. Taxes put on paper, documents, glass, lead and tea were symbolic of the dominant relationship of the King and Parliament to the colonies, which had no representation in Parliament. Colonists strongly opposed these taxes and any attempt by the British to impose its control over colonial affairs. "Taxation without Representation" became a battle cry for colonists who wanted self-government. The strongest opposition to British control was in commercial New England and in the upper classes throughout the colonies. Protestant settlers specifically objected to paying taxes to support the Episcopal Church, which had been headed by the British monarch since Henry VIII. The idea of independence from Britain began to take hold in the colonies.

Scot-Irish and German pioneers forever imprinted defiant individualism on the society of western Virginia and frontier America. For these settlers, democracy was more of "a social instinct" than a political theory. Their fierce independence and fighting skills would be important in the Revolutionary War some 12 years after the French and Indian War. At the start of the Revolutionary War, frontiersmen were mustered from around Sheperdstown and Winchester to make a "beeline" to aid the Continental Army. Their famous 600-mile "Bee-line March to Cambridge" from Virginia at the start of the Revolutionary War began in Shepherdstown and finished in Cambridge, Massachusetts, 24 days later. The militia wore buckskin suits and coonskin hats and caused a sensation for staid New Englanders. They gave the army "color and momentum." They injected "into it a driving power and enthusiasm that contributed much to its ultimate success."[90]

George Washington Explores the Kanawha Valley

In 1770, in a quiet time on the frontier, well before colonists and the British went to war in the Revolution, George Washington led a travel party to explore the Ohio River and the lands east of the mouth of the Great Kanawha River at today's Point Pleasant. They wanted to determine what lands there might be used to reward militiamen for their service in the French and Indian War and what lands they could purchase and sell for good profit. It was common for wealthy men to buy up the land grants of common militiamen to form major frontier settlements.

In 1770, Mingo Town was an established native town on the west side of the Ohio River near Yellow Creek, some 70 miles down-river from Fort Pitt in the area across the river from today's Wheeling.[91] When George Washington's party went to Mingo Town, it had 20 cabins and 70 Natives who were known to be a peaceful tribe, helpful to whites traveling on the Ohio River. The Mingos had been living there in a permanent trading settlement since the end of the French and Indian War in 1763. The town was a reliable resting place for traders and explorers. The Washington party was welcomed and protected as visitors.

The name "Kanawha" became used for the major river tributary of the Ohio River at today's Point Pleasant. The Great Kanawha River begins in North Carolina, where it is called the "New River." The New River is now a Federal American Heritage River which is protected as one of the nation's most scenic rivers. It is famous round the world for white water rafting and adventure sports.[92] Flowing through North Carolina, Virginia and southern West Virginia, the New River is unusual because it flows north due to mountain terrain. It then flows through the majestic New River Gorge to picturesque Kanawha Falls in Fayette County. Above Kanawha Falls is a wide and peaceful river basin where the New River is joined by the Gauley River to become what is called the "Great Kanawha River." The "Little Kanawha River" is a major tributary of the Ohio River near Parkersburg where the state's oil industry started in the time of the Civil War.

When George Washington traveled down the Ohio River to the Great Kanawha River, he wanted to determine if there were lands there that would be suitable for large slave plantations. The rivers made these lands fully accessible by water, which was the only comfortable transportation of the day. George Washington was well-known as a surveyor and land speculator. Lord Fairfax, who was Virginia's largest land owner, was George Washington's mentor in his teen years as a beginning surveyor. With such a great mentor and his favorable marriage to a very wealthy widow, George Washington became a leading planter, land speculator, and slaver. His enslaved workers produced massive amounts of tobacco reaching a peak of 89,000 pounds in 1763. Historian Charles H. Ambler wrote that in addition to tobacco, George Washington "owned, bred, and sold Negro slaves, and he grew corn, wheat, oats, rye, and barley in large quantities." He had his "own mill and his own still." By 1772, his lands east of the Alleghenies aggregated more than twelve thousand acres. He and other eastern Virginia land speculators were committed to opening the western territory to new settlements. He eventually would own thousands of acres west of the Alleghenies.[93]

On this 1770 journey of exploration, George Washington took his best friend, Dr. James Craik, who was his personal physician and later would be appointed by President Washington as the Physician General of the United States Army. Another respected friend on the journey was a surveyor, William Crawford. They were served by enslaved people. The party traveled through the Valley of Virginia, then overland north and west to Fort Pitt on the Ohio River. They made several camping trips up and down the Ohio. The Mingo settlement was one of the few permanent settlements at the time on the Ohio River. In 1770, there were no permanent white towns on the Ohio River south of Fort Pitt and none eastward for over 50 miles on the north side of the Great Kanawha River.[94]

Today's Marietta, Ohio, would become the first major white settlement in the Northwest Territory, established in 1788, eighteen years after George Washington's exploration journey. The new town was originally known as "Adelphia," meaning "Brotherhood." Marietta was the first planned city of the West,[95] on the west side of the Ohio River some 65 miles north of the wide mouth of the Great Kanawha River at today's Point Pleasant.

George Washington wrote in his journal that Mingo Town was a comfortable place to rest and get provisions. The town was near Yellow Creek.[96] His party camped at Mingo Town several times and had horses brought there. At Mingo Town, they saw 60 warriors from the dominant confederation of native tribes, known as the Six Nations. The warriors were going to Cherokee territory to battle the Cuttabas. Native tribes fought each other for domination of their territories. The battles were bitter. When native tribes united against white settlers, they were a formidable force.

The hosts in Mingo Town greeted the Washington party warmly and with ceremony. They warned their guests of a recent murder of a white man down-river, but it turned out to be an accidental drowning. The Washington party met with Chief Kiashuta down-river. The Chief was trusted because he had helped young George Washington 17 years before in a visit he made in 1753 to the French. Chief Kiashuta advised the Washington party that the lands they would see along the Kanawha Valley were on a narrow river plain generally, with fertile bottom lands at the mouths of creeks flowing into the river. George Washington had hoped to find wide, large valleys where major slave estates could prosper, like in eastern Virginia. Chief Kiashuta's information was discouraging, but accurate.

The Washington party continued their exploration to the mouth of the Great Kanawha River. Some 200,000 acres had been given by land grants to militia veterans of the French and Indian War. Always looking for good agricultural lands, George Washington planned the trip to shop for expansive bottom land along the Great Kanawha River that he and other land speculators could buy from militiamen who had no interest in settling in the west. The party traveled into today's Mason County and Putnam County, but not on east to the Elk River in today's Charleston. The rugged terrain and narrow river bottoms were well described by Chief Kiashuta. George Washington concluded that the river valley would be settled in small tracts and they would likely be subject to flooding.[97]

This exploration journey would be important, not for its financial benefit to the leaders of the party, but for what it would mean for the future of the local area. George Washington and his friend Dr. James Craik would own lands in the Kanawha Valley, but few would be suited to a major slave plantation. George Washington's lands would attract family members to live in the

Kanawha Valley. The lands purchased by Dr. Craik caused his grandson and namesake to come to the area after college.

Reverend James Craik would become an important state leader in Kentucky vigorously opposed to secession. After the Civil War, he would be the Episcopal churchman who would reunify Confederate dioceses to the national church as soon as the war was over. In 1839, in Charleston, Reverend Craik left his law practice to serve as a rector of a new church, St. John's Episcopal Church, which he helped establish with other early trustees, Joel Shrewsbury, Henry Rogers, and Alexander W. Quarrier.[98] The deed to the first church property was dated February 16, 1835 and written to them as trustees, along with Bishop William Meade and Rector John B. Martin as additional grantees.

George Washington finished his party's peaceful journey at Fort Pitt, where he hosted an extravagant dinner for his companions at a cost of over 26 pounds. Although disappointed in the narrow river plains, by the end of the Revolution, George Washington owned over 43,000 acres in the Kanawha Valley. The Kanawha County Land Books show that in 1797, the last year of his Presidency, George Washington owned over 26,500 acres. If his largest holdings were combined in a single parcel on the Great Kanawha River, it would be two miles deep from the river edge and extend 50 miles, a distance equal to the distance from today's downtown Charleston to Point Pleasant.[99]

Nothing on George Washington's quiet journey in the valleys of the Ohio River and the Great Kanawha River foretold the carnage of the frontier warfare that would follow in four years or the tragic fate of his friend William Crawford during the Revolutionary War.

Capture and Torture of William Crawford

William Crawford, the third member of the Washington party, was an important figure in western Virginia history. He would become a commanding officer in Lord Dunmore's army four years after the journey with George Washington. In 1774, he had constructed Fort Henry in today's Wheeling and Fort Gower, a stockade across the Ohio River from today's Parkersburg. These forts were constructed for the Virginians' march to the Battle of Point Pleasant. William Crawford spent three years surveying in the area. He also led raiding parties against native warriors and their settlements.

During the Revolutionary War, in 1782, while leading an army into Sandusky, Ohio, he was captured by native warriors soon after a massacre by whites of a peaceful Moravian village. While he was not responsible for the massacre, he was horribly tortured to death as revenge for the massacre.[100]

William Crawford pleaded with the warrior leader and a white man named Simon Girty to prevent the torture, but he was told that he had to be tortured for the killing of peaceful Moravian natives, since the warriors did not capture the white leader of that raid. One account asserts that the son of William Crawford may also have been tortured and killed with him.[101] Other accounts do not include his son in his father's horror.

The torture was inhuman beyond description. William Crawford was tethered to a pole naked, and he was shot with 70 rounds of hot salt peter that burned under his skin, from neck to feet. Most shots were to his groin. His ears were cut off, and he was stabbed with flaming sticks, one of which hit in his eye. Embers were thrown at him. He prayed out loud and begged to be shot dead by Simon Girty. William Crawford fell to the ground and was scalped alive and, finally--but not mercifully--he burned to death.[102]

William Crawford was a man of great stature and notoriety on the frontier. His torture inflamed settlers for full revenge and the disdain of Simon Girty. For settlers, it was used as proof that native peoples were "uncivilized" and deserved to be treated with cruelty.

English law provided a horrible torture for treason that included a sentence where the accused traitor was hanged by the neck not to die but to be disemboweled and, while alive, to see his bowels burned in front of him. He would then be beheaded and quartered and his remains delivered to the monarch for disposal along with ownership of the traitor's family estate. While death for treason in some cases may have been more immediate than what William Crawford endured, its intention was no less cruel.

It should be noted that, in context, hanging in the nineteenth and twentieth centuries was considered a kinder form of punishment by causing immediate, painless death without torture. But it was not always immediate or painless. It is said that Mary Surratt and the conspirators who were hanged with her after the assassination of Abraham Lincoln, took five full minutes to die while dangling in air.[103] No culture can fairly claim a superior "civilization" over such tortures.

While on the terrible topic of torture and death for treason, it should be remembered that the American Revolution was high treason against the British Crown, and its leaders in Virginia and other colonies were put in jeopardy of torture and death as traitors under English law. They could be hanged by the neck and disemboweled while alive and then beheaded. After death they could be quartered with their remains denied to their family leaving only the horror of their torture and death as the last memory of their loved one. Their family estates could be forfeited to the Crown and their family reputations ruined.

These tortures for treason were disfavored in the 1700s and eliminated in English law in the 1800s, but they were available during the American Revolution. Mercy for a traitor would have been to be simply beheaded or hanged.[104]

The conscious acceptance of this extreme and horrible fate by George Washington, Thomas Jefferson, John Adams, Samuel Adams, Benjamin Franklin, Alexander Hamilton, Patrick Henry, Richard Lee III, Richard Henry Lee, and others should greatly credit their extreme sacrifice in order to establish for future generations a new republic based on the ideas of equality and liberty notwithstanding their use or acceptance of slavery in their time. Some of these men were not slavers and George Washington freed the enslaved people in his personal estate in his will.[105] Hindsight judgments of any nature, which can be made now, some two and a half centuries later, about their intentions, duties, and service, should account for the sacrifices made in their day.

Massacre of Mingo Village Starts All-Out War

In April 1774, a terrible massacre by whites of a native village of children, women and men at Yellow Creek not far from Mingo Town started an all-out frontier war. The uneasy truce before the war between the Shawnee and Virginia settlers was over.[106] There were attacks on both sides against native villages and white settlements. Native families were massacred, and settler families were massacred. The once peaceful and friendly Mingos joined other tribes on the attack for revenge against any and all settler families throughout western Virginia.

The war became known as "Lord Dunmore's War," but it should have been named the "Virginia Settlers' War" or the "Settler and Indian War." Lord Dunmore was the last royal governor of Virginia. In 1774, he conceded to settler demands to supply an armed force sufficient to drive Shawnee and other tribes out of the Ohio River Valley---forever. The war would put in place a chain of events that would affect the military strategies of the American Revolution, the formation of new western boundaries for the United States, and the migration of pioneers into the Midwest.

The call for militia was answered widely by yeomen farmers and their area leaders throughout the Valley of Virginia and western mountains.[107] Historian Edmund S. Morgan wrote:

> The yeoman farmer, standing four square on his own plot of land, gun in hand, and virtue in his heart, was thus the ideal citizen of a Republic.[108]

Yeomen farmers were fierce fighting men. The plan for the war was to destroy native villages west of the Ohio River. The settlers wanted to force native peoples to live farther west with no access to Virginia's western mountains and the Ohio Valley. The military operation was intended to secure settlements throughout western Virginia, including in today's Kentucky. It would be a beginning of "Manifest Destiny" as settlements would spread relentlessly west across the continent, taking native lands and foreign territory, and ultimately pushing native peoples and their cultures to near extinction.[109]

Settler Militia is Ready for Long Campaign

The armed force was separated by Lord Dunmore into two armies, one that the royal governor himself would lead north to Fort Pitt and then south down the Ohio Valley. The other army would be led through the Kanawha Valley by General Andrew Lewis, a good friend of George Washington. His father, John Lewis, was a Scot from Ulster. General Lewis lived near today's Salem, Virginia

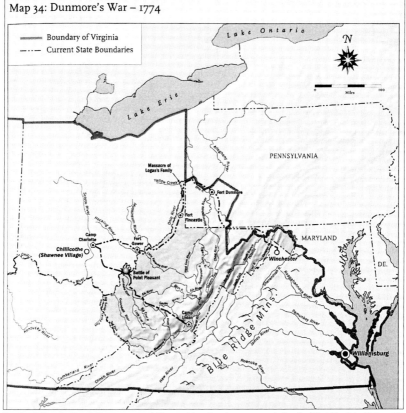

Routes taken by Lord Dunmore and General Lewis – *Image permission by West Virginia University Press, Source: Frank S. Riddle. A Historical Atlas of West Virginia, 2008."*

in the Shenandoah Valley. General Lewis would serve four years in the Revolutionary War, surrendering his commission in 1780 and dying soon thereafter.[110]

The royal governor's army included about 1,300 men who were either settler militia or regular British army troops. The Lewis division in the south had a settler militia of about 1,000 men with no British troops. The plan of the march was for the royal governor's northern army to go south from Fort Pitt along the Ohio River and join forces with the southern settler militia army. At this time, all of the territory across the Ohio was considered, at least by Virginians, to be Virginia territory. Virginia would not cede its territorial rights west of the Ohio River until 1781.

On the march, Lord Dunmore separated his northern army into two divisions, one he commanded and the other was commanded by William Crawford, who was assigned 500 men who were supplied with 200 cattle and 50 packhorses. His division constructed Fort Gower on the west side of the Ohio River and they were joined by Lord Dunmore's division traveling with 100 canoes. It had been agreed to have Lord Dunmore's army from the North proceed south along the Ohio River and meet General Lewis' army at Point Pleasant where General Lewis thought they were to build a fort before crossing the Ohio.[111] General Lewis mustered the southern settler militia at Camp Union, near today's Lewisburg.[112] Their supplies reveal the plan for a very long siege in the Ohio territory. Historians Thomas Miller and Hu Maxwell describe the vast supplies for the campaign:

> The cattle were driven, and the flour was carried on packhorses west of Staunton. The quantity of flour accumulated was 160,000 pounds, or 800 barrels. It was gathered from an extensive region, for at that time there were no large stores and mills as at present. The expedition had 800 packhorses. There being only paths across the Allegheny mountains and westward, it was impossible to use wagons. The load for a horse was about 200 pounds, or one barrel of flour. The horses were barely sufficient to carry the supply of flour, had there been nothing else, but the flour was only a portion of the stores. There were salt, tools, tents, blankets, and many other things that the army could not go without....Loads were carried from Staunton to Warm Springs as one relay; Warm Springs to Lewisburg, or Camp Union, was another; the next carried the supplies to the mouth of the Elk river, the site of Charleston; and from that place to the mouth of the Kanawha much of the stores was transported by water in canoes.[113]

In early September 1774, General Lewis' militia army began their march from Camp Union to the mouth of the Great Kanawha River on the Ohio River at today's Point Pleasant. Like the royal governor did with his northern army, General Lewis divided his militia army into two divisions with their own commanders. The plan of the march was for the divisions to follow the same trail, but leave Camp Union at different times. Colonel Charles Cameron Lewis, the brother of General Lewis, commanded the first division with 600 men who were supplied with 108 cattle, 500 packhorses and 54,000 pounds of flour. Colonel Lewis led the way leaving camp on September 6. The second division left six days later on September 12, under the command of Colonel William Fleming. He took his 450 men on the trail with 18,000 pounds of flour and the requisite number of packhorses and cattle. General Lewis accompanied the Fleming division.[114]

General Lewis' militia divisions had to cross two mountains to go into the Great Kanawha River Valley at picturesque Kanawha Falls. The river is considered to be "formed" at that spot by the junction of the Gauley River and New River. The southern militia followed an old, narrow buffalo and native trail that passed over the mountains and through the river valley. The trail was narrow and rough and the packhorses and cattle needed more room and a better road. The settler militia cleared and constructed a rough road as they marched. The road was made to move men, cattle, horses and vast supplies. Their road has been used with upgrades for centuries as a midland route from eastern Virginia to Lexington, Kentucky. Today, it is U.S. Route 60, known in history as the "Buffalo Trail," the "Lewis Trail," and, more formally as a toll road, the "James River and Kanawha Turnpike,"[115] It is today designated as the Midland Trail Scenic Highway, the first designated scenic highway in the state.

The Lewis Trail is today followed generally by a two-lane highway between White Sulphur Springs and the Huntington area. It passes through the Kanawha Valley to Malden and Charleston after passing through scenic Hawks Nest State Park in Ansted, on a cliff high above the New River. It is near the New River Gorge Bridge, not far from Quinnamont where the southern West Virginia coal industry began in September, 1873, with the first shipment of coal on the new C & O Railway by Joseph Lawton Beury. The rich history of the area is interpreted at a federal visitors center, located near Fayetteville at the north end of the New River Gorge Bridge. The Bridge is a wonder of the world, as one of the longest single span bridges anywhere. In the surrounding bridge area, there are many adventure sports, such as whitewater rafting, zip lining, kayaking, bass fishing, battle games, mountain biking, rock climbing and others. The bridge can be toured by walking below the road surface along the steel beam supports with the river in full view 876 feet below. Free base jumping into the Gorge is organized one day per year for Bridge Day, a traditional Fayetteville community festival in late October when fall foliage is at its peak color. The rapids on the New River and Gauley River are known around the world. They can provide calm or boisterous river rides. In autumn, rafting on the lower Gauley River can be 11 miles of Class V rapids with a 12-foot waterfall. Less vigorous sports like trail and mountain hiking round out adventures accessible from the Midland Trail Scenic Highway, U. S. Route 60. The bridge is part of a four-lane freeway system for U. S. 19 and Interstate 79, going north from Beckley to Summersville and on north to Morgantown. [116]

Militia Marches to Point Pleasant
Passing by Salt and Gas Springs

On the march to the Ohio River, settlers passed a natural gas spring and a salt spring. The two phenomena were natural curiosities a few miles apart, east of today's Charleston. As natural wonders, they were popular to early visitors in the Kanawha Valley and became well-known throughout Virginia.[117] The early discoveries of these springs are memorialized with a monument at today's DuPont Middle School, at the location of the natural gas "Burning Spring."

Militiamen first saw Burning Spring where natural gas came out of the ground and would ignite into a large column of fire that could burn for days. Burning Spring is recognized today as the site of one of the first discoveries of natural gas for the western world. By 1780, Governor Thomas Jefferson issued a patent for Burning Spring with 250 acres. Andrew Lewis and his friend George Washington who never saw it, took title to the spring and acreage. George Washington refers to the spring in his will. They bought the property "on account of a bituminous spring which it contained to burn as freely as spirits and is as difficult to extinguish." Andrew Lewis shared George Washington's interest in natural curiosities as well as military affairs. Andrew Lewis died in 1780 and under Virginia law, at his death, George Washington owned the spring outright as the survivor of them. The heirs of Andrew Lewis objected, and their objections were later honored by Dr. Lawrence Washington, a great nephew of George Washington and the son of Martha Dickinson Shrewsbury who lived nearby. She was a daughter of salt industrialist John Shrewsbury and niece of Joel Shrewsbury.[118]

Second, about 5 miles west, the settler militia passed by the "Salt Lick" which was made by a natural spring of salt water near the Great Kanawha River at the mouth of Campbells Creek. John Dickinson was on the march of militia as a captain from Bath County. He saw the salt spring and acquired a patent for 502 acres including the salt spring. In 1794, he would sell the tract and salt spring to Joseph Ruffner. He bought the patent without seeing the spring or its surrounding property. This event would be the beginning of the salt industry in the Kanawha Valley.[119]

On September 30, 1774, the settlers' militia camped near the Elk River wilderness in today's downtown Charleston. From there, the militia traveled along the Great Kanawha River to its mouth on the Ohio River at today's Point Pleasant.

On October 9, 1774, the settler militia camped on the Ohio River at a peaceful spot along the wide waters of the Ohio River where it was joined by the Great Kanawha River. The plan was for the militia to build a fort and cross the river to begin the march to native settlements when they were joined by Lord Dunmore's army.

The next morning, against orders of the day, several militiamen scouted for game away from camp and discovered a native war party. It turned out to be the native army ready to surprise and destroy General Lewis' militia before it could be joined by the northern army. One of the men made it back to camp and warned the others of the coming surprise attack. The settlers soon found themselves under attack by a large force of warriors from several tribes led by a very able Shawnee field commander, Chief Cornstalk. He was joined by Chiefs Logan, Red Hawk, Blue Jacket, and Elinipsico.[120] Colonel J. L. Peyton wrote in his history of Augusta County of the fateful battle on October 10, 1774.

> It was, throughout, a terrible scene—the ring of rifles and the roar of muskets, the clubbed guns, the flashing knives—the fight hand to hand—the scream for mercy, smothered in the death-groan—the crushing though the brush—the advance—the retreat—the pursuit, every man for himself, with his enemy in view—the scattering on every side—the sounds of battle, dying away into a pistol-shot here and there through the wood, and a shriek….No language can adequately describe it.[121]

They held their ground all day against the attacking warrior army. The settlers may have had the larger army. The weather was clear and pleasant, and the rivers were low. The battle was intense with no food or rest for the militiamen or the warriors, all day. The battle ended at dark with retreat of the warriors across the Ohio River on the order of Chief Cornstalk.

The settler militia lost 82 men. Most notably they lost Colonel Charles Cameron Lewis. He wore into the battle, a red British military uniform. His red coat was inspiring to his men, but among the militiamen, many of whom were dressed in dull garb to fight frontier style, the red coat made Colonel Lewis an obvious target. Some militia used dyed buckskins in a variety of colors, even red, but a bright red British officers' coat would make an easy target for native warriors. Lewis County is named for Colonel Charles Camron Lewis. He was a known frontier hero and his descendants in Malden became major salt industrialists and, later in Charleston, they became prominent bankers with the Dickinson family. After the warriors withdrew, the militia men collected 17 scalps and hung them on a pole near the river bank.[122]

Shawnee Chief Cornstalk knew after failing to overwhelm the Lewis army that he could not stop the onslaught of the Virginian armies soon to join into a mighty fighting force. The combined armies could not be repelled by his outmanned warrior army. He hoped he could win in a surprise attack and rout the southern militia army before it could be joined by Lord Dunmore's army. Chief Cornstalk believed his warrior army would be crushed on the west side of the Ohio River by a long campaign against native settlements. His enemy had the manpower and supplies to destroy all native villages in the Ohio Valley and westward. This left Chief Cornstalk with no good choice in the matter. It was devastation or peace.[123] He bargained for peace with Lord Dunmore.

Chief Cornstalk would become a friend to the settlers, creating a three-year peace in the West in the important first years of the Revolutionary War. That peace ended when Chief Cornstalk was murdered on November 10, 1777. He was under guard at Fort Randolph near Point Pleasant when he was murdered. Later, when the settlement at Point Pleasant did not grow, local people thought that his cruel murder put a curse on the area. His death was a great tragedy, and if curses were in fact so made, his murder would have created an unsurmountable curse at Point Pleasant.

General Andrew Lewis told his son that Chief Cornstalk was "the most dignified looking man, particularly in council, he ever saw." Colonel Benjamin Wilson wrote about the commanding presence of Chief Cornstalk at Camp Charlotte,

> [H]is looks, while addressing Lord Dunmore were truly grand and majestic, yet graceful and attractive. I have heard the first orators in Virginia—Patrick Henry and Richard Henry Lee—but never have I heard one whose powers of delivery surpassed those of Cornstalk on this occasion.[124]

It was a senseless killing of a great leader and peacemaker. His murder was an outrage to native peoples and to most Virginians. Theodore Roosevelt wrote that Shawnee Chief Cornstalk died a "grand death by an act of cowardly treachery on the part of American foes; it is one of the darkest stains on the checkered page of frontier history." The murder ignited native attacks throughout western Virginia.[125] The three-year peace on the frontier was over.

Settlers' Militia Secures Western Border of America

The victorious and emboldened settlers in General Andrew Lewis' militia left Point Pleasant without joining the delayed the northern army and without building a fort as planned. They crossed the Ohio River to begin their long campaign to drive native villages out of the Ohio Valley and beyond.[126] General Lewis had the supplies needed to continue the mission into winter, but Lord Dunmore sent word to General Lewis that a treaty had been made with Chief Cornstalk on behalf of all the warrior tribes. The royal governor advised General Lewis that the settlers' war was over and all advances against native villages were to stop. General Lewis's victorious militia army continued to march, and Lord Dunmore himself traveled to meet General Lewis and command him to stop his militia's advance toward the native villages.

Lord Dunmore would become unpopular with Virginia settlers because he abruptly ended the war after a one-day battle. Many thought he did it in order to help the English Crown against the settlers' interests. It was believed by many settlers that he intended from the start to solicit warrior allies for the King for his troubles brewing with New England colonists. The Boston Tea Party took place on December 16, 1773, eleven months before the Battle of Point Pleasant.[127] The governor's true intentions at the time are not known. There is no doubt that he saved a terrible attack on native settlements. The withdrawal of the well-prepared settler militia left native villages in the territory north of the Ohio River for almost 20 more years until 1794, when General Anthony Wayne would push natives out of the territory with his complete victory at Fallen Timbers on August 20, 1794 near today's Toledo, Ohio.

Lord Dunmore became the enemy of western settlers during the Revolutionary War. The war started on April 19, 1775, six months after the Battle of Point Pleasant, in Massachusetts near the bridge at Concord going to Lexington. It is unknown which side fired the first shot. In a poem, "Concord Hymn" by Ralph Waldo Emerson, it was immortalized as being a shot made by the local farmer militia.

> By the rude bridge that arched the flood,
> Their flag to April's breeze unfurled,
> Here once the embattled farmers stood;
> And fired the shot heard round the world.[128]

After that shot, Lord Dunmore, as royal governor, supported his British King at all costs. He issued a proclamation to set free any enslaved men who were held in slavery by rebellious slavers and agreed to join the King's army. Andrew Lewis led a colonial army against Lord Dunmore forcing him out of the colony and onto a British ship. The Governor's call for slave recruits was answered by the thousands. For the Continental Army, about 5,000 people held in slavery joined and were emancipated for their service--if permitted by their slavers.

Lord Dunmore proclaimed that their rebellious slavers were traitors to the King. His emancipation proclamation was issued on November 7, 1775.[129]

I do require every person capable of bearing Arms, to resort to His Majesty's STANDARD, or be looked upon as Traitors to His Majesty's Crown and Government, and thereby become liable to the Penalty the Law inflicts upon such Offences; such as forfeiture of Life, confiscation of Lands....And I do hereby further declare all indentured Servants, Negroes or others, (appertaining to Rebels,) free that are able and willing to bear Arms, they joining His Majesty's Troops as soon as may be, for the more speedily reducing this Colony to a proper Sense of their Duty, to His Majesty's Crown and Dignity.[130]

The Proclamation was selective like Abraham Lincoln's Emancipation Proclamation would be a century later, to free only people enslaved by rebellious slavers. The bondage for loyal slavers was left intact. Throughout the colonies emancipated slaves joined the British army numbering in the thousands. After the War, many freed people were evacuated by the British army to Canada and London.[131]

Suspicious settlers thought the early end to their war with a one-day battle at Point Pleasant was a planned scheme to create a western front for the British King against the colonies. Virginia settlers were outraged to discover that Lord Dunmore met with a warrior chief the day before the battle. Some settlers thought that the royal governor knew in advance of the planned surprise warrior attack on General Andrew Lewis' militia. It is interesting that General Lewis received no orders or communications from Lord Dunmore on his march, until the order to stop advancing toward native settlements.[132] Some Virginians claimed that Lord Dunmore hoped General Lewis' militia would be defeated. Aid to the enemy would be a treasonous act by the governor, even during the tensions of the early Revolutionary period which were spreading throughout the colonies. Without doubt, the settlers' one-day decisive victory at Point Pleasant ended any chance of a second English front for at least the first three critical years of the Revolutionary War, before the tragic murder of Shawnee Chief Cornstalk.

Perhaps peaceful purposes were intended by Lord Dunmore. Massacres on both sides started the settlers' war after whites massacred families on Yellow Creek near Mingo Town. Mingo Chief Logan's entire family was killed on the west side of the Ohio River.[133] The slaughter of his family turned Chief Logan and his tribe from friends of the settlers into vengeful enemies. After the Battle of Point Pleasant, Lord Dunmore invited Chief Logan to a peace conference with Chief Cornstalk and others.

Chief Logan replied in a letter to explain the Mingo attacks on former friends. He wrote with such eloquence in English that some questioned whether he alone wrote it. Historian John P. Hale dismissed such questions by writing that it had also been doubted that Thomas Jefferson wrote the Declaration of Independence, that Shakespeare wrote Hamlet, and that William Tell was more than mere myth.[134] Chief Logan writes a prophetic plea for native peoples as Americans began their push westward to the Pacific Ocean.

I appeal to any white man to say if he ever entered Logan's cabin hungry and he gave him not meat; if ever he came cold and naked, and he clothed him not. During the course of the last long and bloody war [the French and Indian War], Logan remained idle in his cabin, an advocate of peace. Such was my love for the whites that my countrymen pointed as they passed and said: 'Logan is the friend of the white man.' I had ever thought to live with you, but for the injuries of one man. Colonel Cresap, the last Spring in cold blood and unprovoked, murdered all the relations of Logan, not even sparing my women and children. There runs not a drop of my blood in the veins of any living creature. This called on me for revenge. I have sought it. I have killed many; I have glutted my vengeance. For my country, I rejoice at the beams of peace; but do not harbor a thought that mine is the joy of fear. Logan never felt fear. He will not turn on his heel to save his life. Who is there to mourn for Logan. Not one.[135]

The settlers' decisive victory changed the history of the continent. Professor Phil Conley summarized the important consequences of the battle at Point Pleasant. The battle broke the spirit of the native tribes and prevented an expanded all-out settler war. It created a peace on the western frontier for the first three important years of the Revolution, eliminating a western front for the British supported by native allies in the Ohio River Valley. It assured the ready settlement of western Virginia, which then included all of Kentucky. The original English land grants provided that the Midwest belonged to Virginia all the way west to the Pacific Ocean. With new and growing settlements, Kentucky would become a separate commonwealth in 1792 with the consent of Virginia, as was required by the then new Federal Constitution for property taken by a new state from an existing state. The settlers' war was also a training ground for many militiamen in the Revolutionary War and for many national and state leaders who, after the Battle of Point Pleasant and the Revolution, would seek their fortunes in the Midwest.[136]

The most important impact of the Battle of Point Pleasant was in the negotiations for the Treaty of Paris to end the Revolutionary War. It prevented Britain from insisting that the new nation's western boundaries be set at the banks of the Ohio River. The treaty was signed on September 3, 1783. Before the war, in 1774, Parliament passed the Quebec Act to make the Ohio River the western boundary of the troublesome American colonies. All lands west of the Ohio were to be the territory of Canada, Britain's new obedient province after the French and Indian War. By the end of the eight-year Revolutionary War in 1783, the expanded settlements of German and Scot-Irish pioneers in the mountains and valleys of western Virginia, effectively made the Ohio Territory and all parts of the Midwest, *de facto*, the sole territory of the new United States. It was not the territory of Canada, which was the King's only province in North America that remained loyal.[137]

The 1783 Treaty of Paris made the Mississippi River the western border of the United States, a border that would be expanded greatly with the Louisiana Purchase in 1803. That purchase from France in 1803 opened the entire continent to settlement in the age of wagons and boats--before the times of steamboats and canals, and then railroads--all leading to continental migration and inevitable conflicts with native peoples and Mexico.[138]

Historian H. G. Wells wrote that railroads and the printing press made America a nation. He thought that railroads linked the nation's economy and diverse populations, and the printing press linked all Americans to the idea of democracy. Railroads opened flat-lands and valleys but would bypass and isolate mountain regions because track mileage there was costly. Constructed tracks in the southern Appalachian region were half the mileage of tracks in southern valleys and plains.[139]

The spirit of revolution was everywhere, and western Virginia settlers were ready for it. Their true loyalties were expressed at Fort Gower, on November 5, 1774, when Virginia militiamen issued a landmark declaration of their loyalty, first to America and then to the King.[140] They were preparing to return to their homesteads three weeks after the triumph at Point Pleasant. The Fort Gower Resolves declared first loyalty to American liberty, but more significantly, they announced a growing brotherhood of colonists willing to speak with one voice in opposition to British controls and taxes. That voice would be for protest and then revolution. The defiant individualism of the settler militiamen made inevitable such resolutions of protests against the sovereignty of the British King.

The victorious militiamen after the Battle of Point Pleasant resolved:

[A]s attachment to the real interests and just rights of America outweigh every other consideration, we resolve that we will exert every power within us for the defense of American liberty, when regularly called forth by the unanimous voice of our countrymen.[141]

Their declaration followed the Fairfax County Resolves issued on July 18, 1774, by George Mason and George Washington to set out the clear expectations of Virginians for liberty with unalienable rights against the British Crown.[142] These Virginia ideas leading to high treason against the British Crown would give purpose to the Revolution to create a unified republic.

Royal Governor's Palace, Williamsburg, Virginia.
Image Courtesy of the Library of Congress

Monument at Point Pleasant, Tu-Endie-Wei State Park, West Virginia
Image taken by Brian M. Powell, Licensed under CC BY-SA 3.0

Chapter 3

Virginia Leads In Revolution For A Unified Slave Nation

Militiamen Lead Continental Army and Expansion West

General Andrew Lewis' militia was a talented group of about 1,000 Virginians who would become national and state leaders for the Revolutionary War and for the nation's expansion into the Midwest. From those men, there would be leaders of states that did not exist at the time of the battle.

Historian Virgil Lewis in *History of the Battle of Point Pleasant*, wrote that the settlers' militia had many Virginians who distinguished themselves in the Revolutionary War. Six militiamen became generals. "Indeed, it is a matter of history that these Point Pleasant men were on nearly every battlefield of the Revolution." He detailed the battles:

> They won the Battle of Point Pleasant, which changed the course of history on this continent; and when the War for Independence came, they met the heroes of Lexington, Concord, and Bunker Hill, and together with them were at Monmouth, Brandywine, King's Mountain, and Yorktown. Seven officers in the Battle of Point Pleasant rose to the rank of general in the Revolutionary Army; six captains in the battle commanded regiments on continental establishment in the war for independence; four officers in the battle led the attack on Gwynn's Island, in Chesapeake Bay, in July 1776...one captain in that battle was the most prominent American officer in the battle of Brandywine where he was severely wounded; another officer in that battle led the advance at the storming of Stony Point, one of the most daring achievements of the Revolution; still another officer in that battle, won lasting fame as the "Hero of King's Mountain." Hundreds of men in that battle were afterward on revolutionary fields and many of them witnessed the surrender of Cornwallis to the united armies of the United States and France, at the close of that struggle at Yorktown.[143]

Virginia militiamen would go on to be leaders of national, state and local governments with expansion of settlements into the Midwest. Nine of the

1,000 men would serve in Congress and four would be state governors. About one hundred would be state legislators. Virgil Lewis wrote about the militiamen who became leaders:

> Six of them afterwards occupied seats in the American House of Representatives; three of them were members of the United States Senate; four of them became governors of states; one of them a lieutenant governor; one of them a Territorial Governor; one of them military and civil commandant of Upper Louisiana; one of them a surveyor-general of one of the thirteen original states; one the father of a governor of Virginia; one, the father of a supreme judge of Kentucky; one of them the largest manufacturer and wealthiest man in eastern Ohio at the time of his business career; one of them president of the Bank of St. Louis; one of them a framer of a constitution for Ohio; one of them a receiver of public monies in a western State; and a hundred of them state legislators and framers of state constitutions....[144]

Virgil Lewis also found the names of Virginians in the Battle of Point Pleasant to be memorialized in the names of counties and towns in nine states.

> Their names are all around us. Of the men who made national history at Point Pleasant, the name of one is preserved in that of a county in Pennsylvania; the names of three in those of counties in Ohio; of four of them in county names in Indiana; of four of them in the names of counties in Illinois; of four of them in county names in West Virginia; of five of them in the names of counties in Tennessee; and ten of them in the names of counties in Kentucky. Towns named in memory of men who were in the battle of Point Pleasant are found in many states, prominent among them being Christiansburg, Virginia; Lewisburg, and Clendenin, West Virginia; Flemingsburg and Harrodsburg, Kentucky; Clarksville and Sevierville, Tennessee; and Shelbyville, Indiana.[145]

The settlers' war, Virgil Lewis contended, was a struggle between "civilization" and "barbarism." He contended that General Andrew Lewis' 1,000-man militia had advanced civilization by driving barbarism from the "forests of western Virginia." This view was shared by many people in the Kanawha Valley in the nineteenth century, many of whom were the grandchildren of these early settlers.[146]

"Civilization" in general has been an idea used for centuries by dominant cultures to justify the subjugation of peoples with different cultures.[147] In America, like in Europe, the pursuit of "civilization" has usually included the advance of Christianity especially by Spanish conquerors. Americans used the advance of "civilization" to justify the nation's western expansion to replace the cultures of native peoples. It was also used as proof that slaves were better off in slavery, because in Africa they were "uncivilized" and, absent white supervision, they would by their dangerous nature regress to the barbarism of their cultures in Africa.

A long-lasting aftermath of the settlers' conflicts with native warriors was a virulent racism against all native peoples that continued well into the twentieth century. Chilling discussions of race and cultural inferiority appear in a number of books, such as the *Chronicles of Border Warfare* by Alexander Scott Withers. Strong resentments of native peoples by descendants of settlers are expressed a century later in a state history written in 1904 for the West Virginia State Superintendent of Free Schools. It states that for the first 67 years of settlement "there was little else than savage warfare in West Virginia until General Wayne, in 1794, broke the savage power at the Battle of Fallen Timbers on the Maumee River." His victory signaled the end of native control of the continent. It also ended British interference from Canada in America's western expansion in the Midwest two decades before the War of 1812.[148]

No history by West Virginians of the Battle of Point Pleasant is complete without acknowledging that Congress recognized the settlers' war in the Ohio Valley to be part of the Revolutionary War. On May 30, 1908, when Theodore Roosevelt was president, Congress declared the Battle of Point Pleasant to be the first battle of the Revolutionary War, at least as a political fact, if not a historic one. That battle's first shot was not heard around the world, but its impact dramatically changed what shots would be needed six months later and for the first three years of Revolution. Regardless of the Battle's "firstness," the settlers' war directly helped win the Revolutionary War and start the western expansion of the nation with a legacy for pioneer settlements by rugged individuals whose march would be stopped only by the eastern shore of the Pacific Ocean.[149]

Virginians Lead the Nation to a New Federal Government

Four years after the end of the Revolutionary War, Virginians led the movement to create a strong central government. In Philadelphia, the summer of 1787, from May to September, the Constitutional Convention met for the purpose of revising the existing weak national government under the Articles of Confederation. But in secret they debated and drew up an entirely new federal system of government with a national government and state governments, with all to be sovereign in separate spheres. Twenty-five of the fifty-five delegates, or almost half were slavers.[150]

On September 17, 1787, after many compromises, thirty-nine of the fifty-five delegates, or 71 percent, signed the Constitution.[151] The leaders of the Convention were men of the Enlightenment and they believed in original sin and slavery. They worked hard for a government based on law and moderation, and fully flexible for change in new generations. The signed document was then sent to the states for ratification by special conventions, not by the state legislatures which had voted to send the state's delegates to Philadelphia. The special convention process cleverly bypassed local power elites in favor of greater citizen participation. Many state leaders were surprised at the special ratification process which relied upon the very new idea of government authority, or "sovereignty" residing in the "people" instead of their elected representatives. Each of the states were required to conduct conventions to vote for or against establishment of the new federal system of government. The Federal Constitution was to be approved by nine states voting to ratify, but all knew a unified government required unanimous approval of the states.

During the ratification process, there was no language to guarantee rights to individuals to protect them from a strong central government. Federalists, including James Madison, Alexander Hamilton and John Jay, each of whom were slavers, promised that civil liberties would be added by the new government as a first order of business. The new Congress wrote and proposed for ratification the first ten amendments to the Federal Constitution, known as the Bill of Rights soon after it was organized. True to his word, and the Federalist Papers, James Madison, as a member of the House of Representatives wrote amendments guaranteeing individual liberties, which were passed by the House on September 24, 1789 and by the Senate the next day. The first ten amendments to the Federal Constitution, called the Bill of Rights, were ratified by the state legislatures two years later on December 15, 1791.[152]

The amendment process for the Bill of Rights used by Congress has been followed for every amendment in the history of the Federal Constitution. That amendment process has Congress approving specific language for each amendment, which in turn must be approved in the same language by three-fourths, or currently 38 of the 50 state legislatures. Article V of the Federal Constitution allows for another amendment process which is wide open and dangerous. It allows a Constitutional Convention to be called by the votes of two thirds of the state legislatures, bypassing Congress and leaving the full nature, scope, and language of all amendments to be decided at another secret convention. With the precedent of the secret Philadelphia Convention creating--to the complete surprise of the nation and world--an entirely new government well beyond its authorized purpose, such an amendment process by a runaway convention could pose the greatest threat of destabilization of the republic since the Civil War. The only check on preserving individual rights and the constitutional system known today would be after a contentious and uncertain ratification process where each state legislature would have to debate and vote to ratify or reject the amendments or perhaps a full rewrite of the Constitution. Both amendment processes require ratification by three-fourths, or now 38, of the state legislatures to ratify the amendment--or a rewrite of the Constitution which could provide for a different ratification process like was done in the Philadelphia convention. The National Archives has engraved on a wall near the original Bill of Rights an important reminder about our heritage and how fragile it is: "Eternal vigilance is the price of liberty."[153]

In Philadelphia, George Washington of Virginia was elected unanimously to preside over the convention. His support gave legitimacy to the secret convention and its new concept of a unified federal union. He was the nation's first citizen and national hero. There was no question that this beloved Virginian was "first in war, first in peace and first in the hearts of his countrymen."[154] He is one of very few conquering generals in world history who declined to become the ruler over territories he conquered. George Washington did not want to be a king. He had no children to whom he could pass a crown. He was a republican patriot in every sense of the term, because he was committed to the ideas of liberty and equality, but like other Virginians, he was a slaver. His service to the nation was high treason against the British Crown, and it was a great sacrifice to him and his family. His service is glorious because he dedicated his life to building a new national republic, not for personal gain or glory. Like other founders of the new republic, he built his family's fortune at the expense of the families of the people he held in slavery. The founders of the nation are our national family, and we can respect them, like we do our family members despite differences that arise. We should acknowledge, consider and discuss their sacrifice, inconsistencies, and imperfections as readily as we may do for beloved family members. Slavery cannot be defended but it can and should be studied, discussed and better understood.

George Washington had been hesitant to attend the convention in Philadelphia, but he was persuaded by James Madison and others to attend. He had retired from public service to manage his large slave estates. He did not desire the role of presiding officer, but he accepted it as his duty as the leader of the nation. During the four months of debate on the Constitution, he did not speak on issues, but it is written that he used gestures to indicate his opinions on matters under consideration. At the end, he strongly supported the Constitution, and signed the document at the top as the leader of the convention.[155] He may have been the first man to sign the document.

Virginian James Madison was a key leader in organizing the Philadelphia convention. He convinced George Washington to attend. He is properly known as the "Father of the Constitution" for his negotiated compromises during the convention and for his later brilliant support for ratification as one of the authors of the *Federalist Papers*. American government today using three branches with a system of checks and balances can be traced largely to his work for the Federal Constitution.

James Madison, with strong support of George Washington, worked to convince delegates from all states that a new central government with a strong executive and a new federal executive and judicial system was needed. The new government would replace the weak confederation of independent, sovereign states set out in the Articles of Confederation. The Confederation was created by the Continental Congress and ratified by the 13 states. It became effective on March 1, 1781, six months before Yorktown. The Confederation was an ineffective government. It had no national executive and no judiciary.[156] It left sovereignty to each state, with what would be called "states' rights," to do in their borders anything its government desired, without regard for a national good or any responsibility to help solve national problems. Each state had one vote in Congress regardless of population. The new Madison government would give large population states numerous seats in the House of Representatives.

The Articles of Confederation confirmed that each state had the powers of sovereign nationhood in their borders. They set tariffs against other states, printed their own currency, limited travel between states, and refused to allow for collection of out-of-state debts. There was no national tax, economy, or army, and each state had to pay its own debt for the eight-year Revolutionary War.[157]

The commerce and finances of the new nation were the concern and province of Alexander Hamilton. He was an organizer of the Philadelphia convention and an early leader for a strong central government. He wanted a unified country and thought that a national economy would unite the states in all matters. He favored national debt to replace state debt from the Revolution. He was so intent on centralization of the national debt that he agreed with Virginians for the capital of the new nation to be built on the Potomac on land surrounded by the nation's two leading slave states, Virginia and

Maryland. That location for the District of Columbia put the national capital near Mount Vernon, the home plantation of George Washington.[158] The capital city would be given his name.

Alexander Hamilton also thought that unification would come with a national currency and a central bank. A national currency was needed to replace unreliable and separate state currencies to encourage trade between states and foreign businesses. A central bank was to support and stabilize local banks and the financial system as a whole. He envisioned America to have a major economy in the world based on manufacturing and world trade. Thomas Jefferson had a different vision, for an agrarian economy of large and small farms. Hamilton's world view was correct. He supported Wall Street commodity markets.[159] Some contend that the ideas of Alexander Hamilton for banking and financial systems are used in the world's economy today.

The debt of individual states was an important issue of the day. It was a crushing burden for some states. Many militiamen had not been paid fully for their service in the Revolution. New taxes were needed and this added to financial and political problems of individual states. By1786, in Massachusetts, the tax and payment problem for former soldiers in the western part of the state was so great that Captain Daniel Shay organized a militia of over a thousand men to march on Boston. They were turned back by Massachusetts militia but it was obvious that a new form of national government with the power to tax and to raise a national army was needed for internal stability as well as external security. Shay's Rebellion was one of the most important events in American history, as a lead-up to the Philadelphia Convention the next year, in 1787.[160]

Sovereignty in "We The People" is Established

There was strong opposition in many states to a new central government. When the proposed constitution was revealed to the public, opposition focused on the opening words, "We the People" and to a lesser extent to the words, "of the *United* States of America." The term "united" appears in the heading of the Declaration of Independence, but it is in very small letters so the phrase, "States of America" was emphasized. The Federal Constitution's headline letters make "united" the same size as "States of America," indicating an important shift to an effective central government and a new identity as a nation.

The three opening words, "We the People," created a sensation for the advocates of sovereign states' rights. These words announced clearly that the new federal government derived its sovereignty from the people "of the United States" as a whole, not from the individual states or their elected legislatures. That sentiment for a new national sovereignty is the foundation of the Federal Constitution. The opening words surprised many and delighted many.

> We the People of the United States, in Order to form a more perfect Union, establish Justice, insure domestic Tranquility, provide for the common defense, promote the general Welfare and secure the Blessings of Liberty to ourselves and our Posterity, do ordain and establish this Constitution for the United States of America.[161]

Opponents of the new national constitution were surprised by the proposed federal government which was to be superior to their state governments in all commercial and national security matters. Proponents contended that a federal system with a central government was needed to assure that truly national interests for the economy and national security would be secured. Opponents thought that states' rights should be above federal rights in most all spheres, especially commercial. The ratification process underscored that the proposed federal government would be founded on a national sovereignty of "We the People," not on a combined sovereignty granted from time to time by separate states or their governments. Philosophically, these different ideas of sovereignty and government powers would be an issue finally decided by a bloody civil war over slavery. The advocates of states' rights who were opposed to an effective national government made ratification in the state conventions controversial, difficult and uncertain, especially in major states like Virginia and New York.

The idea that sovereignty rests on the agreement of the governed, or "We the People," came after Jean-Jacques Rousseau published *The Social Contract* in French in 1762. It was translated into English and published in 1782, five years before the convention in Philadelphia. The book captured the imagination of many American leaders, including some of the Founding Fathers. Jean-Jacques Rousseau presented the idea that the sovereignty of government rests solely on the consent of the people to be governed. The new Federal Constitution was seen as a written contract to be adopted by the people for their nation. This idea was radical at the time. It denied the sovereignty of monarchs and state governments. It affirmed the 1620 Puritan ideas used for the Mayflower Compact where they agreed jointly to bind themselves to a body politic with the duty to make it benefit the community as a whole through just and equal laws.

Historian H. G. Wells gave credit to Jean-Jacques Rousseau for today's democratic sentiment. Rousseau's idea of sovereignty was revolutionary because it meant that the people had to give consent to be governed by their rulers. This idea of sovereignty would be used to the extreme in the bloody French Revolution a few years later. Some think that the idea of national sovereignty would have been much less popular in America, if the French Revolution had preceded the Philadelphia convention.[162]

The key fight in the Constitutional Convention was over slavery but the document was written carefully to minimize the issue that divided many Americans. The words "slave" and "slavery" do not appear in the ratified document.

Slavery is Approved in Constitution by Implication

The Federal Constitution was the product of four months of closed-door meetings with compromise after compromise. It did not outlaw slavery. Slavery had been institutionalized by eastern Virginia aristocrats for its dominant tobacco industry some five generations before. The high ideals of the Revolutionary War caused northerners to begin to abolish slavery in their states, but most southern states were dependent on slavery for their agricultural economies. The southern states had become slave societies. The Revolutionary War and poor soil conditions, followed by keen competition from Kentucky and North Carolina, combined to force Virginians away from their dependence on tobacco and toward other cash crops, including corn, wheat, dairy and some vegetables and fruits. For production of those goods, Virginia was overpopulated with people held in slavery.[163] Many predicted that slavery would end in Virginia after the once high profit tobacco industry no longer dominated its economy. Virginia slavery was saved in the nineteenth century only by the new cotton industry's need for almost one million slave workers, which in turn made people enslaved in Virginia valuable, creating a livestock commodity export industry in eastern Virginia.

James Madison from eastern Virginia authored many key compromises in Philadelphia, and he is properly called the "Father of the Constitution." He is the architect of the federal system of government. He was visionary in designing the federal system with three branches of government for the separate functions of governance, including the power of the federal judiciary to overrule any state laws that violated the Federal Constitution. He brilliantly defended the new government and constitution in the *Federalist Papers*, and later in the Virginia convention for ratification.[164] He was a genius and a slaver.

First and foremost, in the Philadelphia convention, Madison was a political realist. He understood clearly that the economic interests in the new nation would determine the success or failure of the new constitution during the ratification process.[165] New England businessmen and southern slavers had to be accommodated for their different interests in order to win ratification state by state. He understood there would be conflicts, creating factions based on those economic interests. He navigated the various economic interests of the convention delegates and their represented states, by making tradeoffs and compromises he thought were needed to secure his goal of a constitution for a unified nation with a federal government ratified by all or most all of the states. He wrote in *The Federalist:*

> The most common and durable source of factions has been the various and unequal distribution of property. Those who hold and those who are without property have ever formed distinct interests in society. Those who are creditors, and those who are debtors, fall under a like discrimination. A landed interest, a manufacturing interest, a mercantile interest, a money interest, with many lesser interests, grow up of necessity in civilized nations and divide them into different classes, actuated by different sentiments and views.

Slavery was central to the compromises needed to finalize the new constitution and those compromises rested on the economic diversity of the nation. Southerners did not want Congress to control slavery or commerce. They wanted slavery protected and for all votes on commerce bills to be approved by votes of two-thirds of the members of both houses. New England delegates wanted commerce bills to become law by majority votes to protect their business interests, and many northerners wanted slavery abolished.[166]

The "elephant" in the convention hall was slavery. No one wanted to admit that the issue would absolutely, completely control the success or failure of their proceedings in Philadelphia and in the ratification process. Delegates believed that the fate of the new nation as a unified republic was at stake. The slavery issue was so tender that it had to be legalized by implication without use of words directly referring to "slavery" and "slaves." Instead, circumlocutions were used for people who were slaves, like the term, a "person held to service or labor."[167] Professor Ira Berlin explained the importance of slavery at the time and how it led to a revolutionary civil war to remake and unify the nation.

The coincidence of slavery's destruction with the revolutions that made the American Republic in 1776 and then remade it in 1861 reveals the extent to which slavery was woven into the fabric of American life. For most of its history, the American colonies and then the United States was a society of slaves and slaveholders. From the first, slavery shaped the American economy, its politics, its culture, and its most deeply held beliefs. The American economy was founded upon the production of slave-grown crops, the great staples of tobacco, rice, sugar, and finally cotton that were sold on the international market and made some men extraordinarily wealthy. That great wealth allowed slaveholding planters a large place in the establishment of the new federal government in 1787, as planters were quick to translate their economic power into political power.[168]

Three provisions to protect slavery were demanded by southern delegates in the compromises to create a new republic. Their concern was heightened because, at the same time the delegates were meeting behind closed doors in the summer of 1787 in Philadelphia, the Congress on July 13, 1787, publicly adopted the Northwest Ordinance with a ban on slavery in the new territory. That Congress was organized during the Revolutionary War under the Articles of Confederation with each state having one vote. Not all states were represented for the vote in Congress but the southern states which were represented did not oppose the ban, indicating there may have been more general support for abolition, or even gradual emancipation, than the leaders of the Philadelphia convention may have perceived. Their perceptions may have been heightened because they were themselves slavers. At this time, slavery was centered in Chesapeake Bay states when they were experiencing economic stagnation because the tobacco and slavery industry was in decline creating an overpopulation of slaves. It would be a decade before a new cotton economy in America would change the nature of slavery and the political posture of the issue of slavery for the next seventy years, until the Civil War. The Northwest Ordinance was a landmark policy document. First, it banned slavery in the new territory north and west of the Ohio River, helping to confine slavery to the southern and southwestern states, and, second, it adopted the policy that all new states would be added to the Union as equal partners to other states.[169] Article Six of the Northwest Ordinance reads:

There shall be neither slavery nor involuntary servitude in the said territory, otherwise than in punishment of crimes whereof the party shall have been duly convicted....[171]

Language in the article in the Ordinance banning slavery, Article Six, was later adapted for the Thirteenth Amendment to the Constitution ratified after the Civil War on December 6, 1865. It also is similar to the language in West Virginia's statute abolishing slavery passed by the Legislature on February 3, 1865 with substantial majorities in both houses.[170] The Ordinance also has a proviso clause for return of escaped slaves similar to the one adopted for the Federal Constitution two months later at the end of the Philadelphia convention. The fugitive slave proviso may have been the reason for the lack of opposition to the ban on slavery.

In Philadelphia, the compromises over slavery were three. First, a provision for calculation of representation in the House of Representatives and the Electoral College was used to increase the voting power of slavers by counting people in their districts who were classified as not free and could not vote, at the rate of an extra three-fifths of a person for each enslaved male.[172] It is remembered that the right to vote for women came in 1920, over a half century after the Civil War, upon ratification of the Nineteenth Amendment to the Constitution.

Second, a provision banned Congress from outlawing the importation of kidnapped people from Africa during the first 20 years after ratification.[173] When the twenty-year time was up, Congress voted to outlaw the international slave trade effective in 1808. This greatly helped eastern Virginian slavers because a ban on new slaves kidnapped from Africa limited competition for sales of Virginians who were born slaves. Livestock commodity sales of Virginians would increase as the cotton, sugar cane and tobacco industries grew in the Deep South and West.

Third, with little debate from delegates who were exhausted after four months of work, delegates at the end of the convention adopted a clause to require slaves, who were called persons bonded to service to another, to be returned to that person when they escaped. This simple clause to require return of escaped slaves to their slavers was likely taken from the Northwest Ordinance passed by Congress in July two months before. In the Northwest Ordinance it is in a proviso added to the clause banning slavery in the territory. The demands for return of fugitive slaves would cause turmoil before the Civil War. Interestingly, the Fugitive Slave Act would be used to expand the power and reach of the federal government, against people in the North who wanted to keep and protect fugitive slaves. Southerners wanted fugitive slave laws enforced by federal authorities, but in other matters of states' rights and sovereignty, they widely opposed any action by federal authorities against states or local govenments.[174]

Supreme Court Justice Thurgood Marshall wrote that the Constitution we celebrate today is one that has replaced the one proposed by the Founding Fathers. It is not the one voted in Philadelphia. He called that document "defective from the start." He stated that when Americans cite to the "Constitution" they should invoke a concept that is vastly different from what the Founding Fathers began to construct two centuries ago.

> [T]he government they devised was defective from the start, requiring several amendments, a civil war, and momentous social transformation to attain the system of constitutional government, and its respect for the individual freedoms and human rights, that we hold as fundamental today.[175]

The Constitution voted in Philadelphia reflected a very different time in America, when life--political and social--was controlled by the idea of white superiority. With the very close votes for ratification in the state conventions, it is obvious that language abolishing or guaranteeing slavery would have defeated ratification in enough states to divide the nation in 1787. If America were to be unified, at that time, it had to be unified as a slave nation. Slavery was widespread and fully supported by the dominant idea of white superiority. New Yorkers Alexander Hamilton and John Jay held people in slavery. The acceptance of slavery in the Constitution is one of the most important compromises in world history. It would soon divide the new nation into North and South, enslaved and free. It set a path to civil war.

Slavery was the foundation of the nation's economy. European governments were confident that the nation after the Revolution would not survive with 13 independent states claiming independent sovereignty.[176] The War of 1812 would end that possibility when patriotism unified the nation behind the new federal government and against an old enemy, Great Britain.

Debates in state ratification conventions over the new Federal Constitution reveal that Virginia leaders in Philadelphia wanted to assure that courts could not automatically abolish slavery in light of the inspirational language of the Preamble of the Federal Constitution hailing "the Blessings of Liberty to ourselves and our Posterity" and language in the Declaration of Independence proclaiming the founding ideas of liberty and equality. The slavery references, using words other than slavery, gave protection to the slave-based economy of Virginia and other southern states.

Slavery had been an important issue in 1776 during consideration of Thomas Jefferson's draft of the Declaration of Independence. It was written eleven years before the Constitution. Thomas Jefferson was appointed to a committee to draft the document. Benjamin Franklin declined to write the document, and John Adams encouraged Thomas Jefferson to write it, because he was a good writer and, unlike himself, Thomas Jefferson was a popular man in the convention. The document was his own to write. [177]

Thomas Jefferson's draft was accepted in full except for language he used to condemn the British Crown for forcing slavery into the colonies. He used language which was in step with the oratory of the document's high principles for liberty and equality for all men. It was readily voted out of the Declaration of Independence:

> [The British king] has waged cruel war against human nature itself, violating its most sacred rights of life and liberty in the person of a distant people [Black Africans] who never offended him, captivating and carrying them into slavery in another hemisphere, or to incur miserable death in their transportation [across the Atlantic].[178]

The language was removed at the insistence of southern delegates.[179] The claim against the King is correct. When colonies tried to ban slavery, the British government overruled them. In 1711, British authorities overruled the Pennsylvania colony legislature's ban on slavery. In 1713, the Treaty of Utrecht gave Britain the slave trade. In that year, the Crown Colony of Georgia was established and slavery was not allowed in the colony until 1749 when the British Parliament approved a repeal of that prohibition on slavery in the colony. In 1760, the South Carolina colonial legislature ended slavery, but the British government overruled the colony's legislation, leaving slavery in effect. Also, the rejected draft paragraph shows that Thomas Jefferson was caught up in revelry for true, consistent principles of liberty and equality for all. He saw the Revolutionary War as fully justified by those noble ideas. Some commentators think that the day-to-day experience with slavery made the men of revolutionary times very protective of the ideas of liberty and equality. It is thought that Virginia slavers may have become rebels, because they feared for themselves the same domination by British lords that they used against the people they held in slavery.[180]

Virginia's Ratification Needed for a Unified Nation

Virginia's approval of the new Federal Constitution was vital to the creation of a unified republic and the acceptance of a national government. Four days before the vote in the Virginia convention, New Hampshire's state convention ratified the Federal Constitution, making it the ninth state to ratify and thereby, technically at least, enacting the new Federal Constitution by its own terms under the specified ratification process. But acceptance of the new federal system of government needed unanimous approval of the states, especially in Virginia, and later in New York.

From the beginning of the first settlements in America, Virginia was the most important and influential colony. It was largest by area and population. It had one sixth of the population of the nation at the time of the Philadelphia convention in 1787. Virginia greatly increased its slave population in the years in the era of the Revolutionary War. In 1743, Virginia had 42,000 enslaved Virginians and increased that number by 1782 to 259,000. It is thought that as many as 400,000 people were kidnapped from Africa in this time and taken to the mainland colonies, with half of that number, or 200,000 people, being imported to Virginia, explaining the great increase in the number of enslaved Virginians in the Revolutionary era.[181]

Virginia's influence in the new nation was remarkable. Virginia provided the military leadership and top general who won the Revolutionary War, and it would provide four of the nation's first five presidents each of whom were major slavers. Through 1850, it provided seven of the first twelve presidents. Many important Founding Fathers were from Virginia and they protected their state's economic interests in slavery. John Marshall, the nation's most important Chief Justice of the United States Supreme Court, was a Virginia

slaver. Virginia Presidents attended to the needs of Virginians and their economy. George Washington located a major federal armory at Harpers Ferry in Virginia, and Virginians helped secure one of the first major federal public works projects in the National Road to Wheeling, which would become Virginia's second largest city after Richmond.[182]

In the debate at the Virginia ratification convention in 1788, James Madison admitted that the purpose of the language banning international slave trade until after twenty years

Illustration of Independence Hall, Philadelphia Pennsylvania by Benson J. Losing and F. Schuyler Mathews, c. 1892.
Image Courtesy of the Library of Congress

was to assure slavers that slavery could not be abolished in those first twenty years of the new government. That provision was used to get support for ratification from delegates to state conventions in southern states, including Virginia. The concern was well founded after Congress during the Philadelphia convention outlawed slavery north of the Ohio River by the Northwest Ordinance which it adopted in July 1787.[183]

James Madison struggled with the obvious inconsistency between the ideas of the Revolution and the denial of liberty and equality to people who were held in slavery throughout the nation. He said that he believed that slavery was "dishonorable to the National Character." Due to financial problems later in life, like his friend Thomas Jefferson, James Madison did not free the people he held in slavery. One of James Madison's friends urged him to free them as an important legacy for his national service. James Madison wrote to the friend that, with such great generosity as the friend proposed, that he hoped freed people could manage to change the color of their skin. James Madison thought that the distinct skin color of slaves limited their ability to ever participate in American society. He also thought that, since he was a kind slaver, the people he held in slavery were better off enslaved with him than elsewhere as free people. That can be seen as a statement against the harsh treatment of freed people who were often ostracized and pushed out of the South.

In 1829, at a Virginia state convention to revise representation for Virginia's House of Delegates, James Madison stated that the three-fifths extra representation clause revealed the character of people by showing that slaves should be considered, as much as possible, as human beings and not as "mere property."[184] It is true that persons not free were identified by implication in the constitution document as human beings, but a better explanation is that slavery gave Virginia and other slave society states significantly greater representation in national affairs to prevent any interference with slavery and other southern interests in Congress and by the election of presidents who might be antislavery. Most of the presidents before 1860 were slavers. Approval of slavery in the Constitution by implication was also intended to limit courts from finding slavery itself was a violation of basic guarantees of human rights to liberty and equality.

Constitution Wins Close Vote in Virginia Convention

Opposition to the Federal Constitution in Virginia was strong. Many important leaders objected to the new national government because it limited the sovereignty of Virginia and had no bill of rights to guarantee basic freedoms and liberties against what would be a powerful national government. It gave Congress control over slavery. Many states had constitutions with a Bill of Rights to guarantee fundamental human rights of liberty and equality.

Virginia's leaders were divided over the new constitution. George Washington and James Madison were formidable supporters of its new federal government system. Patrick Henry of "Give Me Liberty or Give Me Death" fame aggressively opposed the Federal Constitution. He opposed a centralized government in any form. He also was not swayed by Federalist promises that a Bill of Rights would be added to the Constitution after the new Congress was organized. When the Federal Constitution was up for ratification, the Bill of Rights was merely a promise in the *Federalist Papers*. Its essays were written by Alexander Hamilton, James Madison, and John Jay to support the new constitution in the state ratification conventions. Alexander Hamilton wrote 51 of the 85 Federalist Papers.[185]

Many people asked what protections would citizens have against a strong central government. The new system had a president instead of a king, but would a president be any different from the British King they overthrew in the Revolution? There was no limit on the number of terms a president could serve. They asked about sovereign states' rights. Many state leaders nationwide asked these questions. In Virginia, a close convention vote was predicted. The day was won for the new Federal Constitution on the clear and repeated promise that a Bill of Rights would be approved by the new Congress and ratified by the states. In states with high debt like Massachusetts and South Carolina, the promise that the new Congress would assume sole liability for each state's debt from the Revolutionary War was very popular. Virginians did not generally favor the assumption of state debts from the War by the national government.[186]

In June 1788, the next summer after the Philadelphia convention completed its secret work, Virginians met in convention to consider ratification. It had 170 delegates with 168 voting. The portion of western Virginia mountain territory that would become a new state in 1863 had few delegates. [187]With Patrick Henry leading the opposition to ratification, the vote was too close to predict. George Washington planned not to attend the Virginia convention for ratification. When the Virginia vote was in doubt, he and other supporters of the Federal Constitution became alarmed. To avert disaster, the General sent messages to the western delegates asking them to come to the aid of the nation as they had done for him as their leader in the Revolutionary War. The Society of Cincinnati, formed at the end of the war by commissioned officers to preserve the ideals of their service, was used to communicate to former Revolutionary War soldiers.

The western delegates answered his call and voted overwhelmingly for the new constitution. With their votes and the votes of delegates from the upper Valley of Virginia and Potomac River area, Virginia ratified the Federal Constitution. The final convention vote for Virginia's ratification was 89 to 79, a slim 10 vote majority. The votes of six more men against ratification would have put the nation in disarray and would have assured conclusive defeat a few weeks later in the New York convention. In that state, Alexander Hamilton was able to lead the convention to ratify the Federal Constitution by a majority of only three votes, with 30 for and 27 against ratification. While six delegates from western Virginia voted against the Federal Constitution, eighteen voted for it.

Only with the votes of western Virginia delegates was the Commonwealth's ratification won. Its ratification would unify and stabilize the new nation with a strong central government for seventy years. Without Virginia's ratification, the new nation would have had a federal government considered illegitimate in several states including Virginia, the most influential of the thirteen states. A new national constitutional convention would have been needed. If a failed ratification had defeated the constitution movement, the nation might have formed two or more separate nations, divided not by language, cultures, religions, history, community values or customs. The nation would have been divided by slavery. The key western votes following the leadership of George Washington and James Madison and close votes for ratification in other states, gave America its new federal government and a constitution for "We the People," which included white men but not men held in slavery or women of any race or status.[188]

The separate sides of the debates over ratification set the political philosophies of the nation's first two political parties which would emerge after President Washington's two terms as president. The "Federalists" were led by John Adams and Alexander Hamilton, and "Republicans" included James Madison and James Monroe who followed the leadership of Thomas Jefferson. Thomas Jefferson became a bitter enemy of many Federalist leaders and was disdained by Martha Washington who shared her husband's cynicism about him. She called Thomas Jefferson "one of the most despicable of mankind" and "the greatest misfortune our country has ever experienced."[189]

The close ratification vote in Virginia reveals that the Federal Constitution would have failed by a large margin if references favorable to slavery had not been added to give implied approval of slavery, at least in the early years of the republic. It is speculation that a gradual emancipation clause might have been accepted if antislavery voices had been stronger in the secret convention. James Madison's political judgment of the immediate effect was as strong as his skills at compromise and personal leadership. He and the other Federalists kept the nation unified with a Federal Constitution built upon many compromises. As the Federalists put off a political solution to the issue of slavery for future generations, they created a divided nation, institutionalizing two opposing societies to be divided later between two regions, North and South. They also constructed a direct path to war between those regions.

The votes of a few men carried the first proposed Federal Constitution through the ratification process. Their personal success presents an important lesson in leadership that individual vision, foresight, and risk-taking can make a lasting difference in the history of the world. For that, such leadership, one person at a time, may be credited as exemplary, but in the realm of human affairs and government, the outcome of such leadership must be judged on it's merits for social justice and fairness.

Such a lesson in leadership brings into focus questions for the ages on America's constitutional slavery. If the first draft of the proposed Federal Constitution had been rejected in Virginia or in New York or by a number of other states for or against slavery, the question arises, would its rejection have created a fair opportunity for open debate over emancipation of people held in slavery sometime in future generations? Would there have been a good chance for a better union of states with a government founded initially on the ideas of liberty and equality for all people, including people who were enslaved? Would a second convention with open public debate--not in secret--have produced different compromises in favor of emancipation especially if it brought to the stage new leaders who were opposed to slavery or at least less supportive of slavery?

Slavery in 1787 was not such a dividing issue, because the idea of white superiority was held almost universally by the dominant white majority. More questions arise in flat hindsight. With new leadership on compromises made after open debate, could the next draft have scheduled gradual emancipation of enslaved people, or in another way directly challenged the idea of white superiority. If gradual emancipation had been scheduled and proposed to the 13 states, would nine states have ratified the document and then used force to keep dissenting states in the union of the "United States?" Or if there were a war over the ratification process and majority state demands for unity at that time, would that war have killed hundreds of thousands fewer soldiers or resulted in a more just post-war inclusion of enslaved people into the full life of the nation, whether one free nation and one slave nation. Would the division of the nation at the outset have forced better compromises and gradual emancipation of people held in slavery?

It is very likely that a failed ratification process over the issue of slavery would have encouraged silent antislavery leaders to step forward on the issue of slavery. Benjamin Franklin, John Adams, or even George Washington might have felt called upon to use their influence to mediate on the issue, perhaps for some form of gradual scheduled emancipation. Some Founding Fathers had antislavery sentiments. Benjamin Franklin was a leader for abolition in Pennsylvania and signed an early abolition petition filed with Congress. John Adams opposed slavery with encouragement of his wife, Abigail Adams, but he was not a popular leader in the Convention. George Washington, a major slaver, wrote in a letter "An evil exists which requires a remedy." He was the key person in the Convention. He emancipated his personal slaves at his death, but not earlier. In Philadelphia, it appears that none of these men, nor any other delegates took a leadership role on the issue of emancipation. Of course, early division of the "United States" may have brought on direct interference from European powers. Would that interference have been to end slavery or, perhaps, to preserve it for cheap labor for cotton manufacturing?[190] For the first national republic in two thousand years, the issue of unity was delicate and was protected over the concerns for the humanity of people held in slavery. Over 40 percent of those people lived in Virginia.

A rush to question the outcome of the first constitution is tempered by the defense by a commentator, Calvin Colton. He wrote that the compromise to keep slavery to preserve early unity of the nation was essential to making the republic's revolution a success.

> But for the compromise, the struggle and cost of the American Revolution would in all probability have been wasted. It was indispensably necessary to save and secure the freedom and independence we had acquired…. The arrangement, as finally adjusted and ratified, was regarded by our fathers as one of great solemnity and of unspeakable importance. It was viewed with a kind of religious awe, and with conscientious respect…. –a feeling that has been cherished from that time to this, and ever ought to be cherished.[191]

His argument is difficult to challenge in light of the monarchy-dominated world surrounding the new republic. But ignoring the humanity of ten percent of the population of a republic merely postponed the division of the republic with a civil war seventy years later. As a fundamental issue of social justice in a republic, such a civil war was likely "inevitable." In flat hindsight, the American Civil War is called by many as "inevitable," but lessons in leadership show that a few men of different experiences and leadership goals may have created a government and society with people emancipated from slavery, perhaps gradually, in a unified nation with no path to a bloody civil war that would kill 600,000 American soldiers. Today, the same percentage of deaths to the national population would mean the deaths of some seven million souls.

The American Civil War was a second war of rebellion and, for southerners, it was to undo the success of the first war of rebellion by destroying the federal government that the Founding Fathers created. The Civil War was fought by southerners to withdraw Confederate states with slave societies that did not exist during the era after the Federal Constitution was established. It took the migration of almost one million people held in slavery, many from Virginia, to create those rebellious states. These people forced out of their homes to move to the new South were excluded from the social contract of "We the People," because of the dominant idea of white superiority. A constitution based on the ideas of liberty and equality for all people, even if only to be gradually included, was not impossible in all events. Slavery is thus the original sin of the nation and the sole cause of the Civil War, pure and simple.

Because of the speculation involved, it must be acknowledged that professional historians properly shun "what if's" presented in hindsight. But the lessons to be learned about leadership are different and must be taught in light of the "what if's" of historic events and leaders, and how justice and the protection of humanity and peace can be lost or won by hard work, focus, vision, courage, self-sacrifice, compromise, preoccupation, exhaustion, and, most important of all, the hope for social justice, or the loss of that hope. There were thousands of leaders in America, after adoption of constitutional slavery and before the Civil War, who may have been able to lead the nation away from its path to war. They did not, but their failures did not make the deaths of 600,000 soldiers in a civil war seventy years after the Philadelphia convention "inevitable." The lessons of the leadership from that era show instead that visionary, courageous leadership in Virginia, like its strong leadership for the founding of a unified republic, could have stopped its secession and thereby saved most of those lives. But the second generation of Virginia leaders failed to measure up to the first eastern Virginia leaders. They were enjoying the prosperity of a new slave livestock industry for commodity sales to new slave societies. The economic dependence of eastern Virginians on slavery brought about the war, which was needed to assure and protect for all people --including those held in slavery-- as President Abraham Lincoln reminded at Gettysburg, that "government by the people, of the people, and for the people, shall not perish from the earth."[192]

Abraham Lincoln Delivering Gettysburg Address - *Image Courtesy of West Virginia State Archives*

Opening words for the Declaration of Independence, 1776, and the U. S. Constitution, 1787.

Chapter 4

Joseph Ruffner Moves His Family To Western Frontier Of Virginia Along The Great Kanawha River

Clendenin Settlement on "Great Kennawa" River

The settlement of Charleston on the Great Kanawha River at the mouth of the Elk River was established by four Clendenin brothers in 1788. Robert Clendenin, Alexander Clendenin, William Clendenin and George Clendenin, the family leader, wanted to attract settlers to the town they named "Charlestown," in honor of their father Charles Clendenin. They were Scot-Irish settlers on the western Virginia frontier. Daniel Boone was living near their frontier town. They called the river the "Great Kennawa River," to distinguish it from the smaller Little Kanawha River which flowed into the Ohio River at today's Parkersburg. The river starts as the "New River" in North Carolina and continues with that name into Virginia and West Virginia until it is joined by the Gauley River, and takes the new name "Great Kanawha River."[193]

Historian John P. Hale, in 1891, suggested that the Legislatures of the states where the Great Kanawha River flowed agree to rename the full length of the river from North Carolina to the Ohio River, the "Great Kanawha River." That name would be true to the common tradition for naming rivers with the name used at its mouth. He contended that the Great Kanawha River was not formed as a river at Kanawha Falls but was simply joined by the Gauley River at that place.

He wrote that the name "Kanawha" was "likely derived by evolution from the name of a tribe of Indians who dwelt along the Potomac River westward to the New River." These native peoples were a branch of the Nanticoke tribe and were variously called, Conoys, Canaways and Kanawhas. The word "Kanawha" is the native word for "wood," but he contended that natives did not mean to call the Great Kanawha River the "River of Woods." He thought the term comes from the name of an early western explorer Colonel Abraham Wood who discovered a new river "at the other end" in the hills of North Carolina. Dr. Hale insisted that the name should be either "Kanawha" or "Woods River," and never referred to as "Kanawha, the River of Woods."[194]

John P. Hale wrote of these rivers with personal, unique authority. In 1775, his great grandmother, Mary Draper Ingles, was captured at home in today's

Hale House, Circa 1838 – *Author's Collection*

Blacksburg and taken by native warriors along the New River and the Great Kanawha River across the Ohio River to their village in today's southeastern Ohio. He wrote that Mary Draper and her husband William Ingles, a Scot immigrant, were "in 1750, the first white couple wedded west of the Alleghenies in America."[195] It was common for warriors to kidnap well-to-do women and children who could be returned to their families for ransom. She showed her captors how to make salt at a spring later called "Salt Lick" or "Buffalo Lick" at the mouth of Campbells Creek near today's Malden. She is the first white known to have made salt in Malden. She escaped from the native village and walked from Ohio following the rivers back to her home. Her tortuous journeys are legendary and the story of a popular book, *Follow the River* by James Alexander Thom.

The current spelling, "Kanawha," would be used for the new county that George Clendenin in 1788 lobbied the Virginia General Assembly to create out of the large western counties of Greenbrier and Montgomery. The County of Kanawha became official on October 1, 1789. That was an important year. It was the year the Federal Constitution took effect, and its first Congress assembled and George Washington was inaugurated as President in the nation's capital in New York City.[196]

George Clendenin was the leader of his clan. He is an American frontier hero. He fought in the American Revolution and served as a western delegate to the Virginia convention which approved ratification of the new Federal Constitution. He was elected to represent Greenbrier County in the Virginia convention. Kanawha County would not be established by the General Assembly until the next year.

The Clendenin settlement had a fort and only seven houses nearby. It was incorporated as a town in 1794, with the name "Charleston," and town trust-ees were pioneer settlers: Andrew Donnally, Sr., George Alderson, William Clendenin, John Young, Reuben Slaughter, John Morris, Sr., Leonard Morris, William Morris, and Abraham Baker. By 1800, Charleston had 65 residents, 12 houses and a jail and courthouse. The next year a post office was established in town with the name "Kanawha Court House." In 1810, Kanawha County had 3,866 residents and 352 people held in slavery. Most of the population was up-river from Charleston in the salt works that surround today's Malden.

The property of the Clendenin settlement was purchased from the prom-inent Bullit family in eastern Virginia, when the Kanawha Valley was a com-plete wilderness. Thirty-six town lots were surveyed, but settlers did not come to the new town. A year after Charleston was incorporated, the Clendenins gave up on their town plan and sold the fort and town to Joseph Ruffner. This would begin a great frontier industrial era for the Kanawha Valley, which be-came known throughout Virginia as the "Kanawha Salines." The salt industry would begin with Joseph Ruffner's sons drilling a deep salt well in 1808, pro-ducing a strong salt brine near the salt spring at the "Salt Lick" used by Mary Draper Ingles. [197]

For security from native attacks, the Clendenins constructed a fort, they named Fort Lee for Henry Lee, III, who was governor of Virginia from 1791 to 1794. He is known as "Light-Horse Harry" Lee, a cavalry hero of the Revolu-tionary War. He was a popular statesman who, with Patrick Henry, opposed the Federal Constitution in the years before his election as governor. Henry Lee is remembered for his eulogy for George Washington proclaiming the great Vir-ginian was "First in war, first in peace, first in the hearts of his countrymen."[198]

Governor Lee was in a prominent old Virginia family. His cousin was Patriot Richard Henry Lee, who in June 1776 in the Second Continental Con-gress moved a resolution for independence of the thirteen colonies from the British Crown. The resolution was high treason because it was to forever end any possibility of return to British control. The resolution proclaimed that the colonies "are, and of Right ought to be, Free and Independent States, that they are Absolved from all Allegiance to the British Crown, and that all political connection between them and the State of Great Britain is, and ought to be, totally dissolved." Richard Henry Lee's resolution was adopted with Virginian leadership on July 2, 1776. The Declaration of Independence, written by a Virginian, was adopted on July 4, 1776.[199]

Henry Lee, III, is also known in history as the father of Confederate Gen-eral Robert E. Lee. Later in the governor's life, he fell into debt and was in debtor's prison for several years while the future Confederate general was very young. It was Robert E. Lee's marriage into the wealthy Custis family that gave him an early fortune. General Lee's wife, Mary Anna Randolph Custis, was the great-granddaughter of George Washington's wife Martha Dandridge Custis Washington. The Lee family home across the Potomac River from the Lincoln Memorial was known as the "Custis-Lee Mansion" until recently when the federal government changed its name to "Arlington House: The Robert E. Lee Memorial." The mansion museum is surrounded by Arlington National Cemetery. The memorial for the burial site of John F. Kennedy with the Eternal Flame is nearby in the national cemetery.[200]

The Clendenins moved to Kentucky after the sale of Charleston. Like other entrepreneurial pioneers of their day, when one idea was not a success, they just moved west to a new place with a better idea. This confidence and sense of improvement by moving west would be an important sentiment for Americans in the nineteenth century. By contrast, many Europeans were forced to travel to America for a better life in order to leave behind lives of desperation at home.

Joseph Ruffner Envisions an Iron Industry
for Growing Markets on the Western Frontier

In 1794, the threat of western warfare with natives ended with General Anthony Wayne's defeat of native tribes at Fallen Timbers, near today's Toledo, Ohio. That battle pushed native settlements out of much of the Midwest which effectively ended much of the British interference with American expansion into the Midwest, at least until the War of 1812. It helped secure the northern border with Canada and left the Ohio Valley and Kanawha Valley relatively free from native attack.[201]

General Wayne's victory was what General Andrew Lewis planned but was stopped by Royal Governor Dunmore. Fallen Timbers was eleven years after the Treaty of Paris was negotiated to end the Revolutionary War in 1783. It was six years after the new Federal Constitution was narrowly adopted in 1788. The states of Vermont and Kentucky had joined the Union by 1792. Ohio was then a territory, set to become a state in 1803.[202] Joseph Ruffner and all Virginians could have seen the opening for new settlements, but few men saw the unique opportunity for industrial production that could be shipped from the Kanawha Valley to the West with only limited competition from east coast producers. With mountain barriers, and before the era of canals and railroads, any product made in the East could not easily compete in western markets with goods made in the West. The small New England weaving mills on the Blackstone River in New England were starting to generate interest in factories for mass-produced products. Eastern Virginia had iron and coal industries but no access to markets in the expanding West.

Joseph Ruffner was a good businessman and the Ruffner estates in Luray grew to be very productive. But when two barns were burned by arson, he began looking west to move his family and build a new fortune, with iron furnaces or other operations to supply new settlements and markets across the Midwest. The iron industry was popular in eastern Virginia but without river transportation it could only serve coastal and bay areas in the East.

He began to dream of a major industry to serve new markets from the Great Kanawha River which he envisioned opening soon in the Midwest. In 1794, the western boundary of the new nation was the Mississippi River. He could envision new markets, first, in the Ohio Valley and later throughout the Northwest Territory and south as far as New Orleans, which then belonged to Spain. A decade later the Louisiana Purchase would move that western boundary to the Rocky Mountains and unleash great expectations for a continental boundary formed by the Pacific Ocean.

The Louisiana Purchase has been called the greatest land transaction of all time. It was made in Europe in 1803 to convey lands belonging to native tribes and nations west of the Mississippi River. It greatly increased the size of the United States at the expense of native peoples, and presented new opportunities for vast expansion of white settlements. It also allowed for expansion of slavery south of the Ohio River and along the Mississippi River. "By 1850, southerners, like other Americans, possessed a swaggering sense of expansionism."[203] The expansion to new territory would put slavery in the center of a growing storm of discord and violence.

The nation's expansion across the continent was unlikely in 1794, when Joseph Ruffner was deciding how his family could benefit by moving to the wilderness of western Virginia. He wanted to help each of his sons begin successful careers. Their individual prospects would be limited in the agricultural economy of the Valley of Virginia. He rejected the English custom for inheritance of family estates by the first-born son. He did not want to create a landed aristocracy for his oldest son, David Ruffner. The area attracted immigrants from northern states and was becoming more and more populated. He had a visionary mind and a pioneer spirit. A move to the West would put at risk the fate of his family and his fortune in a wilderness territory.[204] But he was restless to make a new life and had the vision and grit to do it for his family's future. At 54 years of age, he was ready to take the risk. He left the family estate in Luray and moved his family to the Kanawha Valley.

Virginia Iron and Coal Industries Have Only East Coast Markets

Prosperous industries in eastern Virginia were well known to Joseph Ruffner. Major iron and coal industries were being developed. But these industries shared a common problem. Their markets were limited to the East. The Kanawha Valley did not have that limitation. Native peoples had been pushed out of the area, and river transportation meant western markets on the Ohio and Mississippi Rivers could be supplied by any industry along the Great Kanawha River. At first, Joseph Ruffner envisioned an iron industry for his family.

Eastern Virginia and Maryland had iron factories that worked about 70 slave workers and that number grew to 90 by the Civil War.[205] Virginia iron producers used charcoal processed from wood to fuel their iron furnaces. Wood was plentiful for fuel in Virginia. About 19 cords of wood would make 750 bushels of charcoal needed each day to produce 5 tons of iron, out of 12 tons of iron ore. Iron furnaces generally operated round-the-clock. By 1806, British iron producers had stopped using charcoal from wood in favor of coke made from coal. Coal-based fuel burned hotter than charcoal in new "hot blast" furnaces. With coke as a fuel source, iron furnaces could handle as much as 90,000 tons of iron ore every year. Due to limited coal reserves, Virginia's iron industry continued to use charcoal until the 1870s, when it was replaced with coke shipped by railroads.[206]

In the coal industry near Richmond there were, at minimum, 40 coal companies operating from the American Revolution to the Civil War, in what was called the "Richmond Coal Basin." The first commercial coal in the United States was produced there. A major coal operation could use as many as 1,600 to 1,900 slave miners.[207] Coal operators used enslaved people for their operations in the early 1800s to produce surface coal with primitive trenching techniques. Surface mining was replaced with underground deep shaft mining and the invention of underground room and pillar mining. Virginia began its coal industry before the Revolutionary War.

Virginia supplied coal to Philadelphia, New York and Boston as early as 1789. Before the War of 1812, eastern Virginia's early iron and coal products were marketable only to cities and towns along the Atlantic Coast. Some iron furnaces were in western Virginia in Monongalia, Hancock and Jefferson counties before the end of the 1700s. Some of these western furnaces had river access to the Ohio River. The best-known western furnace was one built along the Ohio River in 1790 by Peter Tarr in Hancock County. The first furnace to operate was Bloomery, constructed 30 years before near present day Harpers Ferry in Jefferson County. There were an estimated 35 furnaces before the Civil War. Few furnaces survived the war. But it would be salt, not iron, that would fulfill Joseph Ruffner's dream for a Ruffner industry on the western frontier.[208]

Salt Factories at the Beginning of the Industrial Revolution

While Joseph Ruffner was looking west for a new industry and frontier borders were expanding, a mechanical revolution was beginning in New England for manufactured thread spun in mills with water power. The mechanical revolution at the start of the nineteenth century developed a political and social movement which historians call the "Industrial Revolution." It began with a spinning mill established by Samuel Slater in Rhode Island. Other small water-powered spinning mills were established in Massachusetts and Rhode Island, first along the Blackstone River.

These "first factories" were very modest and employed few workers. They were small water-powered spinning operations which produced thread that in turn was farmed out to home workers to weave into cloth. They started with Samuel Slater's first successful spinning machine in 1790. In 1793, he helped build the first cotton textile mill to spin thread. The Blackstone River Valley is called by some, among others, the "Birthplace of the American Industrial Revolution."[209]

In the nineteenth century, cotton became the preferred cloth for clothing replacing wool, flax, and other heavy, scratchy fabrics. Mechanical innovations and new production systems changed how cloth was made, dramatically reducing the weaving work women needed to perform at home to make clothing. All home spinning and weaving would eventually be replaced by textiles made in large mill factories such as the first factory operations started in the 1820s in Lowell, Massachusetts.[210]

It is well considered that the American Industrial Revolution was fully launched with the mill established by Francis Cabot Lowell on the Charles River in Waltham, Massachusetts in 1815. His mill was the first to produce cotton cloth making it the "first mill to spin, card, and weave cotton under one roof." His concept for mass production of finished cloth in major factory systems was revolutionary, and that concept was carried on after his death in 1817 by investors who built America's first major factory systems with free labor in a town they called Lowell. Most laborers there were young farm girls. The factory systems in Lowell started the demographic, social and political changes associated with the "Industrial Revolution," following a mechanical revolution. Francis Cabot Lowell's Waltham factory began its water-powered loom on February 2, 1815, making it the "first time in the United States when cotton was manufactured into cloth by machinery."[211]

The term "Industrial Revolution" was first used by Frederick Engels and then John Stuart Mill in the mid-1840s.[212] It signals the changes in economics and society, caused by mechanical innovations in the manufacture of items in factories instead of by home cottage industries usually associated with subsistence agriculture. Factories are places where the work is organized by bringing workers to equipment to mass produce items or natural resources more cheaply than could then be produced by individual artisans and laborers in home cottage industries. By providing home workers with affordable goods like thread and later woven cloth, home workers had more time to craft products they could make and sell on their own. Farmers could put more time in farming to grow cash crops for sale rather than their own consumption. As workers left the land for factories and sweat shops, they became buyers for agricultural and manufactured goods. As factory work and manufactured goods expanded, mass production techniques were used for more and more goods with more workers leaving farms to fill factories in urban areas, creating expanded markets for sales of even more manufactured goods and goods specially crafted at home until the home goods were replaced with more factory-made goods. Markets and innovations expanded the production and demand for manufactured goods, and spread factories and the Industrial Revolution across the nation.

The Industrial Revolution reorganized the work and more importantly, the day-to-day lives of workers and small businessmen. Eventually, it changed where people lived and how and why they worked. It encouraged migration to urban areas and reorganized society. The American economy at the beginning of the nineteenth century was very different from the one at the end of the nineteenth century when the nation's industrial economy soared to first in the world. The Industrial Revolution transformed the demographics, economy, social life, politics, and culture of America in the nineteenth century. It did so on the labor of people in slavery especially in the cotton and slavery industry where over a million people held in slavery produced cotton for textile factories in New England, Britain, and across the world.

The important part of the Industrial Revolution was the creation of markets for mass produced goods. The expansion of markets for industrial-made goods made the Industrial Revolution a revolution of society and work. Work in textile mills and small workshops had a ripple effect. It took workers off farms in the North and made them into customers for farm and ready-made goods, such as furniture, clothing, shoes, and other household goods that could be made first in small workshops and then in factories. These small workshops, known in New York as "sweat shops," could make clothing, furniture, leather goods and hats.[213]

The mechanical revolution started America's slow march away from brute agricultural labor in favor of the efficiencies of mechanical innovation and manufacturing. America became an industrial giant in the world economy, just as Alexander Hamilton envisioned a century before. He was certain the nation would be unified if it had a national currency, banking system, and integrated economy. For him these unifying elements were the best reason for a strong central government, currency and banking system.

Lowell, Massachusetts, with its investors in the Boston Manufacturing Company, has many titles related to its early factory systems including the "Cradle of the American Industrial Revolution," the "Birth Place of American Industry," and the "Place the Industrial Revolution Began." It was the first large scale town built for factory production in America starting with its first major factory in 1822. Machinery and new labor systems for housed workers were used in Lowell for the booming textile industry, because of the demographic, social and political changes started in the 1830s by Lowell's extensive cloth weaving factory systems.

Lowell's success well after the Kanawha Valley factory furnace systems were developed, constructed and producing millions of pounds of salt for shipments in specially made barrels on specially made flatboats to western markets hundreds of miles away.[214] The salt industrialists' use of slave labor greatly limited the demographic, social and political changes patterned in the Industrial Revolution in New England. The salt industrialists had the mechanical innovation and heavy factory systems, but no new markets were created by the slave work force and no society-wide changes occurred. The Virginia slave society remained.

The Ruffners and other Kanawha salt producers, who were called "salt makers," were among the earliest major industrialists in America. They were the first true industrialists on the western frontier. The term "industrialist" was not used in the salt and slavery industry likely because the concepts of factories and industries were not developed so early in the mechanical revolution, before it evolved into the Industrial Revolution. The largest factory in New England in 1820 employed about 350 workers, when five years earlier there were over fifty furnaces blazing day and night producing millions of pounds of salt in salt factories called "salt works," again a term used before the concepts of industry and factories were widely known.[215] In 1820, there were 1,073 slaves in Kanawha County involved directly or indirectly in the salt and slavery industry. But the mechanical revolution in the Kanawha Salines did not carry with it the social, economic and cultural changes that occurred in New England with cotton cloth manufacturing. Slave labor minimized the impact of the industry because it did not directly create new markets for goods to be manufactured and sold. Without creating new markets, the salt industry had a minimal impact on Virginia's slave society in the beginning of the American Industrial Revolution. While the Kanawha salt makers helped open up settlement and the beginning development of the Midwest with their salt production, they did not create an "Industrial Revolution" there or in slave-rich eastern Virginia.

The eighteenth-century coal and iron industries in the Richmond area were not the beginning of the Industrial Revolution because they also did not directly change the lives of families, or encourage urbanization or new markets or affect home and cottage industries. Nor did they lead to new product manufacturing like the factory systems did in New England transforming its economy from small scale farming into huge industries for mass production. The same can be said of the salt and slavery industry in the Kanawha Salines. Most all workers were forced into the industry and half of its workforce were people leased from central and southwest Virginia. They did not bring their families with them and the product produced was a natural resource and did not replace a home or cottage made good that in turn created new markets for new goods. Its effect was indirect and widely spread, well beyond its wilderness area. Kanawha salt had a major influence on development of the Midwest by providing a means for meats to be stored, shipped and consumed, and it led to new livestock production and a meat packing industry in Ohio and the Midwest. It encouraged new settlers to locate there. But the impact was much less important in the changing demographics and economy of its region, than the impact of the New England cotton cloth industry on its small-scale farming and cottage economy. It was not a localized impact, and it did not touch every person who lived there, changing how and where they lived.

The socialization of cotton factory workers was a matter of free choice, which made that workforce a new market for mass produced goods. The socialization of enslaved salt workers had little impact because they were forced to produce salt based on the cruelty of slavery in Virginia, not new market influences. The salt factories brought new people to a wilderness area but did not uniquely change existing economic and social systems there, like the mechanical revolution did in New England and elsewhere, directly starting the American Industrial Revolution. But with the remarkable success of water-powered textile spinning mills in New England, the Ruffner patriarch, Joseph Ruffner, could easily envision that a product could be mass produced for near monopoly sales in growing western markets. He knew that a major industry, such as one for iron—or salt as he later discovered—could prosper with good river transportation systems and abundant product resources. He understood the power of new markets and mass production. He was one of the western frontier's earliest capitalists. His sons would make an industry boom before the Industrial Revolution could be conceptualized or named some three decades later.

Joseph Ruffner Buys Kanawha Salt Spring
and Explores Western Virginia Frontier

The Ruffners were pioneers and innovators by instinct. In 1794, as Joseph Ruffner began to explore for his family's future on the western Virginia frontier, he met John Dickinson, at his home at Cow Pasture, some 20 miles from Clifton Forge. John Dickinson told him about the Kanawha Valley and his property there which was granted as a patent covering 502 acres that surrounded a natural salt spring along the Great Kanawha River. The salt spring property was at the mouth of Campbells Creek, named for James Campbell, an early settler who did not remain in the Valley. It was not far from a settlement and fort owned by the Clendenin brothers. John Dickinson had been a colonel of militia during the Revolutionary War. Colonel Dickinson saw the salt spring when he was on the march of General Andrew Lewis's militia to the Battle of Point Pleasant. He was wounded there as a captain of militia.[216] The natural salt water spring was known as the "Salt Lick" or "Buffalo Lick." Buffalo were attracted to the salt spring and were regularly hunted there by natives. Nineteen years before the march to Point Pleasant, in 1755, Mary Draper Ingles was captured by warriors, and forced to make salt for her captors at the "Salt Lick".[217]

Joseph Ruffner envisioned the mass production of salt for sales in western markets to be a good industry for his family. Salt was an essential ingredient for packing, storage and transportation of meats. In the spring of 1795, he began his personal travels into western Virginia to see the salt spring property that he purchased before he saw it or any of the property surrounding it. True to his nature, he explored alone on horseback for hundreds of miles over the Allegheny Mountains from Luray and the Valley of Virginia to the Kanawha Valley. His route apparently was along the Greenbrier River to the New River and onto Kanawha Falls where the Gauley River joins the New River and the Great Kanawha River begins.[218]

A well-known Charleston storyteller, Paddy Huddlestone, is credited in local histories to have witnessed Joseph Ruffner on his journey crossing the Gauley River in high current. The story was told by Paddy Huddlestone to John L. Cole, a relative of Daniel Boone's wife and the grandfather of Malden's last salt family heirs, Martha Darneal Cole and Llewellyn Shrewsbury Cole. They enjoyed displaying a powder horn used by Daniel Boone. Paddy Huddlestone reported, many years later, that he saw Joseph Ruffner build a log raft with nails he carried in a satchel. He then boarded the raft and floated it on the current while holding the tail of his horse as he pushed the horse into the current. The horse pulled him across the river on the raft where he dismantled the raft, retrieved each of the nails for his satchel and proceeded on horseback. The story has some

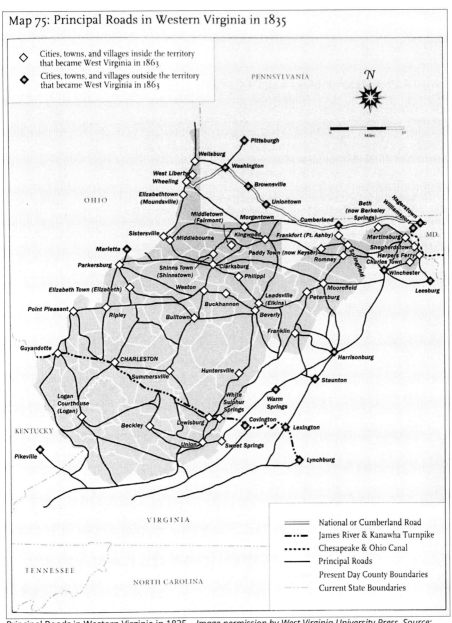

Principal Roads in Western Virginia in 1835 – *Image permission by West Virginia University Press, Source: Frank S. Riddle. A Historical Atlas of West Virginia, 2008."*

validity, at least as folk lore, because it so well demonstrates the fearless pioneer spirit, ingenuity, and grit of the Ruffner family. [219]

Ruffner Family Moves to the Kanawha Valley

In September 1795, Joseph Ruffner moved his family to the Kanawha Valley. It was a month-long journey. He had been married to Anna Heistand Ruffner for 30 years, since 1764. They had six sons and two daughters. The children ranged in ages from 14 to 31.

The sons went with them to the Kanawha Valley. Their oldest son, David Ruffner, was the only son who was then married. He had three children and joined his parents a year later. Their daughter, Esther Ruffner, died at age eighteen. Their daughter, Eve Ruffner, was married to Nehemiah Wood, Jr. They stayed in the Valley of Virginia and later moved to Ohio. The Ruffners remained a prosperous family in Luray. Failure in the west would likely bring Joseph Ruffner and his family back to the Valley of Virginia.[220]

The Kanawha Valley had few settlements along the Great Kanawha River between the Clendenins' town at the mouth of the Elk River and today's Point Pleasant on the Ohio River.[221] St. Albans had a settlement and fort on the south side of the Great Kanawha River, but there were no settlements on the north bank of the river. It had been a popular hunting ground for native peoples, mostly traveling from Shawnee villages in today's southeastern Ohio.

The area was full of game. It was believed that Anna Heistand Ruffner encountered the last panther or mountain lion roaming in the area. It was a big cat. The place is at today's Greenbrier Street then known as Ruffner Hollow, just north of the large Ruffner farm which was located at today's State Capitol grounds.[222] The student mascot at Charleston High School was the Mountain Lion. Its successor high school, Capital High School, located near Ruffner Hollow on Greenbrier Street, adopted the Cougar as its mascot. Virginia settlers could have called either big cat a "panther."

The area was not completely secure from warrior attacks since a settler had been killed in1794, about a year before the Ruffners arrived. There had been a full-scale attack on the Clendenin's Fort Lee in 1789, some five years before the Battle of Fallen Timbers. The Fort Lee attack gave rise to the legend of Mad Anne Bailey, a frontier scout, who was heralded as a heroine for saving the fort by riding to a fort near today's Lewisburg and back with gunpowder to win the siege. The accuracy of the account of a 224-mile round trip by horse can be questioned, but, as the rare legend of a courageous woman pioneer, it is celebrated by West Virginians.[223]

When Joseph Ruffner came to the "Salt Lick," he found good bottom-land west of the salt spring property toward the Elk River where the Clendenins had their town. The town had been incorporated the year before he arrived, and Kanawha County was six years old. Settlers were slow to move into the

Kanawha Valley until peace became certain. Peace would not come to western Virginia until after the 1794 Battle of Fallen Timbers. The Clendenins had established their small pioneer town early in the settlement of western Virginia, and were looking for a buyer so they could move on west to Kentucky.

Ruffners Purchase a Village and Fort at Charleston

Soon after arrival in the Kanawha Valley, Joseph Ruffner purchased from George Clendenin and his wife, Jemima Clendenin, the family's Fort Lee, and the town with seven houses. Twenty years later there would be over 50 salt furnaces operating day and night on both sides of the river east of Fort Lee.

The purchase included at least 1,000 acres on the north side of the river in several major tracts, including today's downtown Charleston and much of the narrow valley plain stretching six miles toward the "Salt Lick" at Campbells Creek. After the move of his family to the Kanawha Valley, he continued to purchase lands including over 6,000 acres west of town.

Joseph Ruffner was a remarkable man. He made "a success of everything." Historian W. S. Laidley wrote that Joseph Ruffner owned "all the salt property then known and, with the beginning of a new county, and a new town, and a new business, in a new world, he invested heavily and wisely."[224]

Joseph Ruffner was civic minded, a legacy he passed on to his children and grandchildren. He was respected for his interest in "every proposition that had, for its purpose, the aiding and upbringing of the town or the county. He was an active energetic, full of a go-ahead spirit and determination."[225] His flat-land farm is now Charleston's downtown area. The State Capitol stands today at the center of farm lands where he and his wife built a two story log cabin.

Cabin built by Joseph and Anna Heistand Ruffner – "Rosedale" – *Image Courtesy of the Library of Congress*

Chapter 5

Ruffner Dream Of A Major Industry Becomes A Rich Reality

Rough Start to a Major New Industry

In 1797, Joseph Ruffner leased the salt spring at Campbells Creek to the Kanawha Valley's first salt maker, Elisha Brooks. The first commercial salt production was not industrial. It started simply with twenty-four iron kettles, heated by wood to boil off water in the weak brine that came out of the natural spring at the "Salt Lick." He could make about three bushels or 150 pounds of salt per day. That was a meager start to an industry needed to preserve meats for thousands of people in growing western markets.[226]

Joseph Ruffner was happy to spend his personal time working his productive farm property, as he had done in Luray. He never made salt himself, but he dreamed his sons would mass produce salt. He left that work in his will to his oldest sons as a dutiful legacy. On March 23, 1803, at age 62, Joseph Ruffner died leaving a large estate which included three people he held in slavery. He divided his property among his children to encourage their entrepreneurship. His estate plan was democratic according to what Alexis de Tocqueville called equal inheritance and America's "last step to equality."[227]

Joseph Ruffner's dream of an industry to mass produce salt was passed by his will to his oldest sons, David Ruffner and Joseph Ruffner, II. The will was dated February 21, 1803 a few weeks before he died. The two oldest sons were to produce salt at the salt spring property in one year and share proceeds with each of their brothers other than Samuel, who was a disabled brother to be provided for by contributions of his brothers.[228] If the two sons failed to produce salt in the year after Joseph's death, ownership of the property would go to their youngest brother, Abraham Ruffner, unless the property were sold and, in that event, Abraham was to be paid the sum of "£750 Virginia Money."

The deed to the salt spring property cost 600 pounds sterling, which was estimated a century later by Joseph Ruffner's great-grandson, W. H. Ruffner, to equal about $2,000.00. Importantly, Joseph Ruffner agreed to an additional bond to pay 10,000 pounds sterling, if the property should produce high levels of salt. The bond amount would be about $33,000.00 if it became due, according to the great-grandson's calculations. The Ruffner brothers were slow to start drilling and they hoped to eliminate the bond payment, by drilling the first well on land just east of the Dickinson tract. Litigation ensued over the bond payment and the Ruffner brothers' ownership of the salt spring property under the terms of Joseph Ruffner's will. Abraham Ruffner, the youngest brother, grew tired of waiting for payment from his brothers, and, in 1806, three years after his father's death, he sold his interest in the salt spring property to Andrew Donnally, Jr.[229]

By 1810, the Ruffner brothers had to pay installment payments on the bond to Colonel John Dickinson's heirs in the form of "good, merchantable salt." Litigation over ownership rights between the Ruffner brothers and Andrew Donnally, Jr., would not be settled until 1822 when a deed for the salt property was made to the brothers by Andrew Donnally, Jr..

The bond payments went to the families of Samuel Shrewsbury and John Shrewsbury. Their father-in-law, John Dickinson, had conveyed his property in the Valley to them in 1796, and they had been living there since 1798. Their families were well established when the Ruffners began digging their first well on the Anderson tract. They were ready to make salt if the Ruffners succeeded as drillers. The payments may have launched their early salt businesses.

The litigation over ownership of the salt spring property led to a family fight at the Kanawha Courthouse. David Ruffner was jailed and fined for striking Andrew Donnally, Jr., with a Dutch anvil, and for assaulting his servant. The father of Andrew Donnally, Jr. was Colonel Andrew Donnally, Sr., an incorporator of the Town of Charleston, a major salt industrialist and member of the Kanawha Salt Company in 1817.[230] Joseph Ruffner, Jr. was fined for aiding and abetting and for concealing the act. They had to post a $500.00 bond to assure good conduct for a year. As leading citizens on the frontier, the Ruffner brothers had little trouble over the assault and eventually worked out their conflicts with the 1822 settlement.

Ruffner Brothers Drill First Deep Well in America

In 1808, after more than one and a half years of drilling through bedrock, David Ruffner and Joseph Ruffner, II, drilled the first deep well in America, and perhaps in the western world, to start a major extractive industry in the Kanawha Valley. This was fourteen years before the first major Lowell factory was operating in Massachusetts in 1822. During and after the War of 1812, the Kanawha salt industrialists had major salt factories and related operations producing and shipping millions of pounds of salt to western markets on the American frontier.

All elements necessary for a salt extraction and production industry were available in the Kanawha Valley, except for a strong salt brine. First and foremost, the industry's major markets would be secure from eastern competition. There was ready access to river transportation, boat building and barrel making, and reliable fuel sources from abundant woods. Slavery could be relied upon for a steady workforce. Less tangible elements were the Ruffner gifts for innovation and self-determination. The brine was piped, first in wooden pipes and then in metal pipes, into furnaces to evaporate water in the brine, using wood and later, coal as fuel for new factory processes which were invented on site time after time. The mechanical innovation of the Ruffner brothers would carry the day for drilling, especially from Tobias Ruffner, who was a blacksmith with a genius for the engineering of drilling equipment and processes.

Industrial salt operations required collection of strong brine from deep wells near a factory. Those wells were a major innovation at the very beginning of the mechanical revolution. While the Ruffners were the first to drill deep wells in America, they were not the first to drill deep wells on the globe. In China, salt was produced from deep wells hundreds of years before, as early as 300 A.D. Those salt industrialists were so advanced that they drilled two wells side by side, one well to produce brine and one well for natural gas to fuel their salt furnaces to boil off the water in the brine.[231] This advanced Chinese technology was unknown to the Malden salt industrialists.

By 1815, in a narrow six-mile river plain there were over 50 salt wells and furnace factories operating. The industry adopted a very early use of coal for mass production. Coke from coal was being used in Britain for iron production but wood was the fuel of choice in Virginia. The salt and slavery industry required extensive timber operations for barrels and flatboats to be used for shipping on rivers to western markets. Factory-produced Kanawha salt required shipments in thousands of barrels, on hundreds of boats, for hundreds of miles to frontier markets in the West. Boats could leave the Kanawha Valley and go down river onto the Ohio River to new towns that would become the cities of Cincinnati and Louisville, and onto the Mississippi River west and south, sending salt through the Northwest Territory to Missouri, Tennessee, the undeveloped Deep South, and New Orleans.

For the Ruffners, the key element missing was an industrial strength brine. The salt spring water at the "Salt Lick" was too weak for mass production. David Ruffner and his brothers assumed, apparently on faith, that a stronger brine could be discovered by digging underground and below bedrock. There was no geology or other science to challenge that assumption or to support it. When the Ruffners began digging and drilling, no one knew the demanding work required. Deep well drilling through bedrock was unknown. Searching for a stronger brine below bedrock required an article of faith and relentless hard work.[232] With a salt spring at the land surface, Joseph Ruffner, and his sons, assumed that the brine below ground would be stronger. They would never guess before they started drilling that a stronger brine would require 18 months of drilling through over 50 feet of bedrock.

Other innovations of the Ruffners in the first two decades of their industry included the early use of steam engines at a time when some states had few factory steam engines in their borders. The Ruffners perfected drilling tools, bits, casings, tubing, and implements commonly used today for the oil and natural gas industries. Auger tools were invented by Tobias Ruffner. The tubing that salt industrialists developed was made at first from wood and then, by blacksmiths who were the mechanical engineers of the day, from tin followed by copper and iron.[233]

A pioneer drilling device used in the oil and gas industry today was not invented by the Ruffners. It was made by William "Billy" Morris, whose family was one of the earliest to settle in the Kanawha Valley. He invented a long double link metal device, with jaws that fit closely, to slide loosely up and down while a sinker and chisel-bit cut a hole in the rock and soil below it. He decided not to take a patent on the device he called "jars," intending it to be a benefit to mankind. John P. Hale wrote that for this invention, made around 1840, Billy Morris should be ranked with the inventors of "the sewing machine, reaping machine, planing machine, printing cylinders, cotton gin, etc."[264] Tobias Ruffner and his brothers deserve equal credit in the history of engineering for both their drilling techniques and inventions for salt factory production.

The invention of percussion drilling should be celebrated. Mechanical inventions and processes are not inevitable other than in flat hindsight. It must be remembered that the wheel was not employed for hauling in the western hemisphere before the conquests of Europeans.[234] Also, it took over thirty years for the salt industrialists in Malden to realize that the natural gas spoiling their salt wells could be used cheaply to fuel their salt furnaces.

The Ruffner brothers reached a strong brine after a number of failed attempts and months of nonstop digging and drilling with make-shift equipment and tools supplied by Tobias Ruffner. The work was continuous by enslaved and free workers, and at least one Ruffner teenager, Henry Ruffner. The final well drilling started in the summer of 1807 after the drilling had gone on "eight or ten months with eight or ten hands." The drillers "reached the point for beginning the hole in the rock and were encouraged by finding that the water which oozed into the gum from below was much saltier than the water which was found at the Salt Spring." At seventeen feet, the bedrock became softer and the auger tools descended rapidly.[235] With stronger brine than before below deeper bedrock, the Ruffners began building their first furnace. They continued drilling and drilling into bedrock until February 11, 1808, when David Ruffner and Joseph Ruffner, II, piped their first draw of brine from the well into their furnace. That day began production in an industry to serve salt consumers throughout the frontier West. It was two years after the Lewis and Clark Expedition returned from the Pacific Ocean, reporting on a new world in the West. Thomas Jefferson was president, and it was at the beginning of the American Industrial Revolution. [236]

A popular British historian, Alistair Cooke, wrote that salt was an essential ingredient in America's expansion to the West because it was needed by pioneers for the preservation of their meats. He wrote that Daniel Boone considered three things essential in life, "A good gun, a good horse, and a good wife." Another essential was "salt" to preserve meats. This followed upon the lead of Historian Frederick Jackson Turner who stated by broad generalization that the availability of salt on the western frontier had a direct impact on expansion west, first limiting expansion before salt became readily available and then encouraging it after salt became abundant. Pioneer settlers were encouraged by the Lewis and Clark Expedition to move West along the Ohio River to the Mississippi River and Missouri River. They needed salt to make their meats portable, traveling through the Midwest in uncertain and dangerous terrain. This vast new American territory would be supplied for decades by salt produced from the strong Kanawha brine.[237]

History of True Pioneers Does Not Repeat Itself

John P. Hale, historian and prominent salt industrialist, opened his seminal work, *Trans-Allegheny Pioneers,* with the all-telling sentence, "Pioneer history does *not* repeat itself."[238] In that book, he commemorated the Ruffner achievement in drilling their first deep well on the western Virginia frontier.

[I]t is difficult to appreciate the difficulties, doubts, delays and general troubles that beset them then. Without preliminary study, previous experience or training, without precedents in what they undertook, in a newly settled country, without steam power, machine shops, skilled mechanics, suitable tools or materials, failure, rather than success, might reasonably have been predicted.[239]

It turns out that necessity was the mother of the Ruffners' invention of modern drilling. David Ruffner had to succeed in his drilling. His son, Henry Ruffner, wrote a friend several decades later that his father sank "hollow sycamore trees into the mud, until we were all sick of it, but my father was deeply in debt and it was sink or nothing."[240] It took tenacious, step-by-step, deep well drilling with tools and processes the Ruffners had to invent as they went along. After a year and a half of digging and drilling that started in 1806, the Ruffner salt well went from folly to a special mark in the history of the world on February 11, 1808.

These sons of a Virginia farmer, who could only dream of being industrialists, are recognized today for their "momentous impact on the modern world," through their drilling inventions that opened the nation's oil and natural gas industries.[241] David Ruffner, Joseph Ruffner, II and Tobias Ruffner are heroes for the drilling industry. The techniques and equipment the Malden industrialists created are used today by the drilling industry worldwide. For modern drillers, Malden is the "alpha," or the beginning of their industry.

Drilling Success Starts Golden Salt Rush

The Ruffner deep well drilling set off a salt boom in the Kanawha Valley. The first wave of land speculators led a wild rush for hundreds of thousands of acres in the area of the Kanawha Valley. By 1810, major investments were being made in salt properties and production factories. Kanawha County land tax records show that in 1814, speculators owned unimaginable tracts. George K. Taylor owned 585,000 acres valued on the tax books in 1814 at $99,440.00, and Robert Morris owned 542,715 acres valued at $92,261.60, and Thomas Rutter & Co. owned 174,672 acres valued at $29,694.24.[242]

Deep brine wells made a compact river valley area an island of intense new industrialization on the American frontier from 1810 to 1815. As a factory-based industry, it was remarkable for its size and location in a wilderness well away from eastern markets, salt competitors and early textile factories. It is said that cotton made the "cradle of industrialization."[243] If so, the early salt factories in the Kanawha Valley were the "cradle of frontier industrialization."

In 1810, two years after the Ruffner well first began producing industrial strength brine, there were sixteen salt furnaces producing in the Kanawha Valley to burn off water in the brine. By 1815, salt furnaces were producing six hundred thousand bushels, or 30 million pounds of salt per year. The area became known nationwide as the "Kanawha Salines." That year there were over 50 furnaces boiling off water from brine.[244]

Wheeling, Wellsburg, and other Virginia towns on the Ohio River were starting small industries, but none on the scale of the salt factories in the Kanawha Salines. Wheeling was growing as the second largest city in Virginia because of its location on the Ohio River at the end of the new federal highway known as the "National Road." That key east-west road was one of the federal government's first large public works projects. It was officially completed in August 1818, to Wheeling from Cumberland, Maryland. Wheeling accommodated thousands of pioneers on the road traveling West, with its small factories and cottage workers making goods for travelers. The new Ohio River industries would not become major industries until a number of years after the salt and slavery industry was booming.[245]

The Ruffner family was joined by Shrewsburys, Dickinsons, Lewises, Donnallys, and many others who would become "Salt Kings," businessmen who made over $50,000.00 per year. They were a *nouveau riche* industrial elite who mass produced and shipped salt to markets in the growing Midwest, just as Joseph Ruffner had dreamed when he risked family and fortune to move to western Virginia. It is said that he invested wisely in property, but without question his greatest investment was in his family who would create the first major industry in the West and bring a new population center to the wilderness he purchased for them in the Kanawha Valley.

Human relations in Malden before and after the Civil War are fairly unique because of the centering vision and determination of the pioneer Ruffner family and their community's pioneer values. Dominant values included respect for the individual and a strong work ethic, and fundamental principles of liberty and equality, despite use of Virginia slavery to work their new industry. Their success and inconsistencies on principle mirror the nation that was America at the time. Their legacy of pragmatic values started when Thomas Jefferson was president. It ends with Booker T. Washington taking a gospel to the nation for middle class values that he observed his boyhood heroes use to build an early black middle class in Malden. He would enshrine these values as his plan to expand the American Dream to all Americans.

Western Virginia Coal Industry Begins as Fuel for Salt Furnaces

In the Kanawha Valley, the Ruffners established a succession of new industries that would produce coal, oil, natural gas and chemicals. The population center that grew up around their town in the western Virginia wilderness would expand the borders of the new state of West Virginia, to include southern counties that would later define West Virginia as a "Coal State" for its first

150 years.[246] Absent such an important population center, it is likely that the Great Kanawha River and Gauley River would have been the natural southern borders of a small state with Wheeling as its capital and the center of its commercial and political life.

The production of coal, oil, and natural gas after the Civil War, and chemicals in the twentieth century, were all spurred by the success of what started as a Ruffner folly in 1808. Crude but effective tools and techniques were used for the first deep well, to reach an ancient underground salt sea which extends from Malden to Michigan. Malden salt industrialist Charles Reynolds was able to drill as deep as 1,700 feet in an effort to get the strongest brine possible, to save fuel costs in burning off water in the brine.[247]

In early years of production, wood was the only fuel for the salt furnaces. As timber was stripped from nearby hills, in 1817, David Ruffner and his brother, Tobias Ruffner, began an important innovation by using out-crops of coal to fuel their salt furnaces. Other salt industrialists were reviewing their use of wood and the possibilities of using coal at the time. David Ruffner was the first industrialist to successfully use coal in western Virginia. This was one of the earliest uses of coal for major factory production, and it began the commercial coal industry in today's West Virginia. James Monroe became president when David Ruffner first used coal. Eventually, between today's Charleston and Belle, many short-spur railroad tracks were laid for carts to carry coal from hollows to the river. There were few major factories in America at the time, and wood or water power were used for fuel energy. Coke from coal was used as a fuel for iron furnaces, but for little else. Coal was used by blacksmiths, but not in large quantities.[248]

Fuel coal was not an immediate success in the salt furnaces. Coal slag clogged furnace grates slowing production. In 1828, David Ruffner's son, Henry Ruffner, while teaching Greek and Latin at Washington College, invented a steam process to remove the coal slag, making coal the fuel used for the whole industry.[249]

By the 1850s, coal was being exported to commercial markets outside the Kanawha Valley, beginning a major export coal industry in western Virginia that would become a giant producer for America's industrialized economy into the twenty-first century.[250]

State Inspectors and Tariffs Protect Kanawha Salt Brand

To protect their brand of "Kanawha Salt," salt industrialists had the Virginia General Assembly to enact regulatory laws to control marketing of Kanawha Salt and its brand name in order to guarantee product quality and limit competition from producers outside the area. The Kanawha salt industrialists wanted uniform standards for purity, quality and quantity to preserve the reputation of "Kanawha Salt."[251]

On May 1,1814, the General Assembly required "a person of good repute and who is a skillful judge of the quality of salt" to be elected by the county court as a salt inspector. In 1833, legislation required two salt inspectors to be elected. These regulations were similar to the British monarchy's restrictions for marketing of special products. State inspectors checked labeling, salt quality and the weights of loaded barrels. Salt produced outside of the Kanawha Salines area could not use names to imply that it was produced there. Regulations to protect the brand name helped shore up profits.[252]

Jesse Boone, son of Daniel Boone, was a salt inspector who, it has been written, served as an early salt inspector in the Kanawha Salines.[253] That claim has been disputed since the Boones left the area a number of years before.

Salt industrialists liked protections at law that limited competition. They strongly supported national tariffs on importation of salt to limit competition from foreign salt, primarily from Great Britain. They supported the Whig Party and it's high tariff policies to protect the interests of American manufacturers including those in New England and the Kanawha Valley. William Dickinson, Jr., apparently named his sons for prominent Whigs: Henry Clay Dickinson and John Quincy Dickinson. Senator Henry Clay would help found the American Colonization Society (ACS), an organization for southerners who supported slavery and wanted an alternative to unrestricted emancipation and equality of citizenship. Kanawha County had a local chapter of the society. Henry Clay stayed overnight at Holly Grove, Daniel Ruffner's stage coach inn in Charleston. John Quincy Adams, after his one term as president, was a long serving antislavery congressman.[254]

Rachel Grant Tompkins, who was a leading woman salt industrialist after the Civil War, said simply that the industry was profitable with salt tariffs and unprofitable without them.[255] Tariffs to protect early American industries were important national political issues before the Civil War.

Oil and Natural Gas Pollute Salt Wells and Start New Industries

The ancient salt sea below Malden was layered with natural gas and oil that would flow into wells along with salt brine. Oil flowed into many wells in varying quantities. For deeper wells, oil could come up in very large quantities. Some wells were estimated to discharge as much as 25 to 50 barrels of oil a day. Oil had no value at the time. It was a major nuisance for the salt industrialists. Salt workers discharged oil directly into the Great Kanawha River, which was given the nickname "Old Greasy," because of the eerily iridescent color of the oil on the water surface.[256]

Oil and natural gas industries before and after the Civil War greatly benefited from the Ruffners' industrial innovations and processes. Ruffner drillers were widely known and respected. In 1859, Ruffner drillers were called to Titusville, Pennsylvania, to drill the first oil wells where Edwin Drake is credited with starting the American oil industry. His first well began producing oil on August 27, 1859, two months before John Brown's raid at Harper's Ferry. The history of oil has dominated international politics ever since Edwin Drake set off the oil rush in Titusville just before the Civil War. It is noted that as early as 1815, oil in western Virginia near the Little Kanawha River in Wirt County was being produced on Hughes Creek. By 1857, before the Drake wells were drilled in Titusville, substantial quantities of natural lubricating oil were discovered along Oil Spring Run. A railroad station was built in the area which was named "Petroleum." Major oil production at "Burning Springs" in Wirt County began in 1866 with two deep wells drilled by William McConaughy and John Jones at an average of 850 feet. The first well began producing oil on March 15, 1866, at the rate of 400 barrels per day and the second well began producing on April 2, 1866. It caught fire burning an estimated $16,000.00 of oil before the fire was extinguished.[257]

To salt industrialists, natural gas was a dangerous nuisance. It is impossible to estimate the volume of gas that regularly vented in the salt wells. John P. Hale wrote cleverly that any such estimates should be taken with a *"grano salis."* The first salt well which is known to hit natural gas was by James Wilson by accident in 1815 in downtown Charleston not far from the location of Fort Lee.[258] He was drilling for salt.

The first industrial application of natural gas in America was in 1841, at "Burning Spring" for the salt works of William Tompkins, some 33 years after the first successful Ruffner well in 1808. Chinese salt industrialists drilled for natural gas to fuel their salt furnaces but their technology was unknown to the Kanawha salt industrialists. William Tompkins used natural gas to light his operations for night work. Credit for the western world's discovery of natural gas at Burning Spring is given to John Van Bibber. In 1773, he saw the natural gas spring a year before General Andrew Lewis marched his militia by the natural phenomenon in 1774. Following William Tompkins, in 1843, the Dickinson & Shrewsbury partnership drilled down 1,000 feet near Burning Spring and "tapped nature's great gas reservoir of this region." Other salt industrialists drilled for natural gas. The Tompkins salt works were located at today's DuPont Middle School, where a monument is located commemorating the discoveries of natural gas and underground salt water.[259]

Industry Expands on Salt Monopoly in War of 1812

The War of 1812 created a monopoly bonanza for the salt industrialists. It spurred immediate expansion of the industry. The war forced American entrepreneurs across the nation to make rapid adjustments in their businesses for a wartime economy. Trade with Britain was stopped until the end of the war in March 1815. For the three years of the war, American investors had to turn to local businesses for new profits. The first factory buildings were modest, built for textile production in New England. The number of new textile mills in New England increased significantly between 1807 and the end of the war in 1815.[260]

Fortunately for new Malden salt industrialists, the War of 1812 produced a high demand for salt and limited competition from British salt in western markets. By 1814, eight years before the Lowell factories in Massachusetts were in operation, over 600,000 bushels were already being shipped from factories in the Kanawha Valley. In this time, each bushel of salt required the evaporation of about 70 to 100 gallons of water. Before and after the War of 1812, British ships carried cheap salt to New Orleans as ballast. The war gave Malden salt industrialists a monopoly for three years in all Western markets along the Ohio River and Mississippi River. At the time, no alternate interior water routes to the West were available for salt produced in the East. [261]

Salt production was essential for the success of new meat packing industries along the Ohio River. The first primary market for salt was in Cincinnati which was becoming a major city in the West, due in large part to its booming pork packing industry. The mass production of salt in the Kanawha Salines could hardly meet demand until after the War of 1812. In these years, salt industrialists enjoyed the riches of monopoly and they began overproducing salt.

This level of salt production required constant fueling of furnaces and the mass production of flatboats and barrels to ship the salt by water to western markets. The industry required ancillary development of adjacent lumber and coal resources and an explosion of cooperage, boatbuilding, shipping and blacksmithing. To support the industry, thousands of dollars of agricultural produce was needed each year, along with 1.7 million bushels of coal, 142 tons of iron, 130 thousand salt barrels worth $32,000, and payments of about $8,000 to blacksmiths and to mechanics. In 1818, the salt factories were surrounded with shanties for 800 to 1,000 workers, slave and free, and little else. By the

1830s, new businesses were established and towns in Malden and Charleston began to develop in the Kanawha Valley.[262]

These new industrial operations were producing and shipping mass quantities of salt before the time of steam engines, steamboats and railroads. In 1825, the Erie Canal in New York was completed at a cost of $6 million which was about $5 per New Yorker. It was 363 miles long, forty feet wide and four feet deep. With smaller canals in Ohio, and later in Pennsylvania, the competition from those states for western salt sales became overwhelming. By the 1850s, the out-of-area competition doubled its salt sales and greatly reduced the sale and marginal profits of the Kanawha salt industrialists. A number of salt producers in the Kanawha Valley were forced out of the industry in the decade leading up to the Civil War.[263]

Peak production years for the salt and slavery industry were from 1846 to 1852. The highest year was 1846 with 45 salt furnaces producing about 161 million pounds of salt, which was shipped as more than 3.2 million bushels of salt. Hundreds of flatboats constructed on the Great Kanawha River floated cargo down-river as far south as New Orleans. Flatboats had no means for return trips up-river. At their destination, flatboats would be dismantled and sold for wood. The boaters would then return to Malden overland or later on steamboats when they began navigating the Ohio River. After 1820, the industry used steamboats that could power up and down rivers in times of favorable water levels. Several major salt industrialists had steamboats, but most salt was shipped by flatboats down-river because they could move in shallow river waters common on the Great Kanawha River for three to four months a year, before the age of river lock and dam systems. Andrew Donnally, Sr., floated the first steamship, which he named the *Andrew Donnally,* up the Kanawha in 1820. He was a rugged salt industrialist who had extensive investments in early steamboats. He was reported to say, when any of his boats sank, that if no boatman had drowned, it was not a "fair sink." He owned much of the Greenbrier Valley and sold his holdings there to move to west in the early years of the Clendenin settlement. He was an incorporator trustee for Charleston in 1794. He was known as a frontier hero for defense of his fort in today's Greenbrier County, which was attacked in 1778 by warriors after the three-year frontier peace ended in 1777.[264]

The early salt monopoly created a moneyed aristocracy in the Kanawha Salines. Henry Ruffner wrote that there was "unbounded wealth" in the Kanawha Salines. A number of salt industrialists became Salt Kings, including the Malden families prominent in the industry: the Ruffners, Shrewsburys, Dickinsons and Lewises. The salt boom started Charleston to grow replacing rough log homes with frame homes on Front Street along the Great Kanawha River, away from noisy and foul-smelling salt factories up-river around Malden. The first three frame homes in Charleston were built in 1812 to 1815. The Ruffners and other early settlers lived in log houses, and by the 1830s, fine homes made of brick and framed wood started to appear in Charleston and in Malden, which was then called Saltborough. The Craik-Patton House, now a period home museum, is an example of how the Salt Kings began to live in the 1830s.[265]

Many "Salt Kings" were members of the masonic lodge organized in Malden in 1827. The list of members of Salina Lodge No. 27 of the Ancient Free and Accepted Masons, (A. F. & A. M.) presents a "Who's Who" of salt industrialists and community leaders: Samuel Shrewsbury, Sr., Jacob Darneal Shrewsbury, L. B. Shrewsbury, Littlebury Shrewsbury, Henry Clay Dickinson, John Quincy Dickinson, John Dickinson Lewis, Charles Ruffner, Richard E. Putney, Moses M. Fuqua, Joseph Lovell, James Hewett, John Parks, J. W. Reynolds, James MacFarland, John H. McConihay, John F. Hubbard, James Norton, C. N. Coleman, William S. Summers, Samuel L. Cabell, Alexander W. Quarrier, Spicer H. Patrick, and John L. Cole.[266] The Lodge met in the Episcopal Church in Malden which was started by Joel Shrewsbury as a mission church of St. John's Episcopal Church in Charleston while James Craik was rector. Salina Lodge No. 27 later purchased a building beside the Kanawha Salines Presbyterian Church and now has its lodge hall on the main street in front of the old Presbyterian church.

The homes of Salt Kings were modest compared to the palatial mansions on cotton plantations where King Cotton reigned from 1830 to the Civil War and beyond. David and Anna Ruffner likely built their home in the 1830s near his Malden salt factory, with separate dwelling spaces, one for them and one for their son Lewis and his family. It was a sizeable but modest home in a U shape with two story gabled wings and attic rooms joined by a large front porch and connecting rooms behind the porch.[267]

The Ruffner family prospered. In 1815, Daniel Ruffner built "Holly Grove" in Charleston as a stately brick home and stage coach inn for travelers on the nations midland route, the James River and Kanawha Turnpike, going from eastern Virginia toward Lexington, Kentucky. The home and inn were on prime farm land inherited from his father, Joseph Ruffner. His father and mother lived there in a two-story log house called "Rosedale."

The site was selected by the Ruffners for its flat bottom land near a small fort structure built a mile east of the Clendenin's Fort Lee. The log house, "Rosedale," has been moved from downtown Charleston and reassembled on the site of the Craik-Patton House which also was relocated from Charleston to its site on the river near Daniel Boone Park. The Park is near the location of a cave on the north side of the river, used by Daniel Boone when he was there to make salt at the salt spring or to track game in the area. The cave was taken when the river road was expanded. He had a cabin on the south side of the river. In 1791, he represented Kanawha County in the Virginia Assembly.[268]

Holly Grove was red brick constructed in a plain Federalist style consistent with the Ruffner style of living. The home stands today next to the Governor's Mansion on the grounds of the State Capitol. The home was embellished in 1902 with a graceful rounded front portico by James Nash. A stone in the shape of an "L" stands on the sidewalk in front of Holly Grove. It is a horse-mounting platform. When it was removed after sidewalk repairs a number of years ago, it was readily reinstalled once its antique use some 150 years before was discovered. Holly Grove was on the James River and Kanawha Turnpike carriage road, which is now U.S. Route 60. It follows the road made by the militia with General Andrew Lewis for the march to Point Pleasant. Many notable persons traveling the James River and Kanawha Turnpike stayed at Holly Grove including Andrew Jackson while president, Henry Clay, and Sam Houston, who was a family friend.[269]

Holly Grove Mansion - *Image in Public Domain*

Chapter 6

Attorneys As "Shock Troops Of Capitalism" Rewrite Legal Doctrines At The Beginning Of The American Industrial Revolution

Salt Industrialists Create the First Business Trusts

After the War of 1812, salt profits dropped with new competition in western markets and because of local overproduction. In 1817, to increase salt profits, a brilliant young attorney, Joseph Lovell, joined by David Ruffner and other major salt producers, created a contract association of industrialists named the "Kanawha Salt Company" to limit salt sales and production.[270] This contract association and its successors are some of the most enduring innovations of the early industry. The company was a business association that would grow into a weak cartel, but it had only limited success in Malden. This business formation was later used in the Gilded Age to create giant monopoly businesses.

Joseph Lovell named and founded the association as the "Kanawha Salt Company." It required participating industrialists to agree on fixing prices, setting limits on the amounts of salt they would produce, and dividing up salt markets for participating salt producers.[271] The leading salt partnership, Dickinson & Shrewsbury, and its principal partners, did not join any of the business associations designed to restrain trade. They benefitted from restraints on the salt trade, but remained independent of the first company and its successors.

Professor John E. Stealey, III, of Shepherd University is the dean of historians in West Virginia. In 2000, he published a book on the Kanawha salt industrialists' restraints on trade. In *Kanawha Prelude to Nineteenth-Century Monopoly in the United States: The Virginia Salt Combinations*, he concluded that the Kanawha salt producers' business formations to restrain trade were the predecessors of trusts and monopolies in the Gilded Age. In America today, such restraints on trade are illegal, but they can be used in international trade to control prices and profits in worldwide industries such as the oil industry.

Professor Stealey is the only professional historian who has extensively researched and published on the antebellum Kanawha salt and slavery industry. His seminal work on the industry is *The Antebellum Kanawha Salt Business and Western Markets*, published in 1993, and now in its second printing. He comprehensively reviewed and analyzed the industry from its pioneer beginnings, detailing activities, innovations, and developments of the Ruffners and other industrialists. He reviewed their business combinations, the use of Virginia slavery, and the economics of the industry in supplying western markets. The industry was explored through its great success and its decline in the 1850s and 1860s resulting from increased competition from new salt producers with access to the Ohio Valley, using canals in Ohio, New York and Pennsylvania. Railroads would move Americans west and the meat packing industry west to Chicago which would be served by salt producers in Michigan and the Great Lakes.[272]

The salt business combinations took a number of forms in Malden, beginning with the Kanawha Salt Company as an association in 1817, and with business trust formations which followed in the 1820s and 1830s representing the "earliest known trust formation in American industrial and legal history." [273] These business combinations set prices, limited production and assigned markets for salt sales. The Ruffners were leaders in the "Kanawha Salt Company," and the succession of monopolistic associations that followed. They were also leaders in the establishment of private corporate joint-stock companies and sales agencies for Kanawha salt.

The master mind of business trusts was Joseph Lovell. He married American royalty when he married a niece of George Washington, Betty Washington Lewis. He was the son of an English lord and the stepson of one of Richmond's richest merchants, James Bream. As a young attorney, he scouted business opportunities for his stepfather including opportunities from his own clients. His prospecting was so successful that, in 1818, the Bream family moved to Charleston. Descendants of Joseph Lovell today have important letters that he wrote to his stepfather about his business dealings, loans from his family, prospects for investments and the creation of the Kanawha Salt Company. In one letter to James Bream in Richmond dated January 6, 1817, Joseph Lovell suggested to his stepfather that he could purchase property from Daniel Ruffner for $25,000.00, and he also named prominent salt industrialists as possible directors of an association he proposed to name the "Kanawha Salt Company," including William Steele, Colonel Andrew Donnally, Sr., John Reynolds, "Joel Shrewsbury, and myself." Although an early participant, Joel Shrewsbury would keep his salt partnership, Dickinson and Shrewsbury, away from membership in the salt combinations and trusts while enjoying their benefits in increasing salt prices for all producers including the partnership.[274]

Joel Shrewsbury was a business leader who made the partnership the leading salt producer in the Kanawha Valley. He set up early operations of the partnership for multiple salt factories and major agricultural operations. His partner, William Dickinson, Sr., remained in Bedford County in the early years, where the partnership began with a family store.

On November 10, 1817, some ten months after Joseph Lovell's letter, the Kanawha Salt Company was formally organized when the salt industrialists as "subscribers" signed its Articles of Agreement. The men named as subscribers in the declaration of the articles included Joel Shrewsbury's brothers, Samuel Shrewsbury, Sr., and, John Shrewsbury, and John D. Shrewsbury, and three Ruffners, David Ruffner, Tobias Ruffner and Daniel Ruffner, along with Isaac Noyes, Bradford Noyes, Andrew Donnally, Sr., John Reynolds, Aron Stockton, Charles Morris, Leonard Morris, Alexander Grant, W. Steele and Company, John J. Cabell, Stephen Radcliff and Joseph Lovell. Alexander Grant's name was scored out of the document, including his signature written on the Articles.[275]

Joel Shrewsbury's name is in the document and he is assigned production limits but his signature does not appear on the page with the other subscribers' signatures.[276] He regularly used his work for the partnership as a shield from the requirements of membership in the salt combinations to follow. The Articles listed him as a subscriber. He is the only listed subscriber who did not sign the document.

The Articles of Agreement set out production limits for the named subscribers, including the one assigned to Joel Shrewsbury for 30,000 bushels in the year 1818. The production limits reveal the relative size of the separate operations for the listed salt industrialists. Some subscribers are listed together for a single limit. They are usually family members. The highest single limit was for William Steele & Company at 53,000 bushels. When added to William Steele's personal limit of 20,000, the total was 73,000 bushels. David Ruffner and Andrew Donnally, Sr., had the second highest single limits at 40,000 bushels each. The limits for the three Ruffner subscribers totaled 69,000 bushels, which was the highest for a family of industrialists. R. E. Putney, a son-in-law of David Ruffner, signed as a subscriber but he was not listed in the declarations of the Articles, and he did not have a production limit listed in his name. He likely signed to join in with David Ruffner who may have been his partner in a salt factory. They would be lead partners later in the subdivision of Malden in the 1830s for the town of "Saltborough." The Shrewsburys, including Samuel, John, and John D. Shrewsbury, had a combined limit of 32,000 bushels which if added to the limit for Joel Shrewsbury made the family total 62,000 bushels. The Articles were in effect for only the first of its five planned years because of the Panic of 1819, the nation's first widespread financial crisis and economic collapse.[277]

Attorneys Secure Industrial Investments with New Legal Doctrines

Joseph Lovell's idea of a monopoly business trust came at a time when modern American contract and corporate law doctrines were in their early development. Commodity and stock markets were being developed. Shareholding in corporations among many investors as a way to capitalize new major investments was beginning. The investors in the Lowell factory systems were early to use this means of raising investment capital. Contract law began to change. Capitalists wanted to protect their investments with contracts that could be enforced with speed and predictability, especially as they invested with entrepreneurs in new businesses at the start of the mechanical revolution. The mechanical revolution reduced the manpower needed to mass produce goods using factory systems, but it greatly increased the capital investments for equipment and facilities needed to replace manpower.

In the early1800s, American contract law was evolving to meet the requirements of entrepreneurs and investors in the mechanical revolution. In the 1700s, most corporations were chartered by legislative bodies for costly public benefits which today are performed by governments, such as to construct bridges, highways and canals.[278] The corporate bodies created by legislatures were not suited for fast moving capital investors. They wanted to strike lucrative bargains and protect those bargains with contracts that could be enforced by or against new private corporate formations.

In Malden, salt factories were capital intensive. Historian and salt industrialist, John P. Hale wrote in 1891 that a good salt well cost $1,200.00 to $1,500.00 and required 60 to 90 days to drill and ream a boring hole. Then a salt furnace would be built at a cost between $40,000.00 and $100,000.00 in nineteenth-century currency. He wrote that even an inefficient furnace would produce 100 bushels of salt using 125 bushels of coal.[279]

Lawyers became what Historian Charles Sellers called "shock troops of capitalism" to protect capital investment by revising contract law to make contract enforcement more predictable and by creating new private corporate formations to operate new and expanding industries. Malden attorneys were at the forefront of developing business trusts and other corporate formations for private joint-stock companies and sales agencies.[280]

As factory systems emerged, capital investments became necessary and very substantial. New industrialists had to recruit skeptical investors who demanded proof that their investments would be valuable, and their bargains would be fully realized. Investors wanted certainty in the enforcement of their contracts. In the 1700s, a simple private agreement was not automatically enforceable merely because the parties agreed to its terms. Investors feared their investments were in jeopardy under old contract law doctrine. At the time of the Revolutionary War, contracts were enforced in court with jury trials where jurors would decide, first, if the contract was fair to both parties and, second, if there was some public benefit to support the agreement.[281] Jury verdicts were unpredictable on these issues.

Entrepreneurs and investors wanted the language as set out in their contracts to control enforcement, with interpretation of the language to be made by judges, not juries. In the early years of the mechanical revolution, investors were looking for safe profits, especially in new commodity markets during and after the War of 1812. Contract law began to change to give more certainty and predictability to private agreements and to new corporate organizations.[282]

The emerging doctrine for contract law made contracts enforceable so long as they represented a mutual agreement of the parties, which today requires what is called "a meeting of the minds." The determination of whether or not there had been a meeting of the minds was to be made by a judge, based on the plain language of the contract. Other considerations became irrelevant, such as traditional concerns over fairness to the parties and possible public benefits. The new inquiry in court was limited to the words used in the contract and rarely involved the circumstances of the making of the contract or any surprise benefits or losses, unless the parties could show misrepresentation, fraud or unfair advantage in making the contract. Judges reviewed the contract language and little else. The new doctrine for a "meeting of the minds" made enforcement swift and certain, giving investors and entrepreneurs the comfort they required for major investments. The parties were assured success in court, so long as their lawyers properly spelled out their expectations in the language of the contract.

The emerging contract law meant that new legal business formations such as joint-stock companies, private corporations, and sales agencies were secure for new capital-intensive industries like textile mills and salt factories. Salt industrialists began using private corporate formations which before had been granted by acts of government. This put predictability in capitalism and economic development as a whole, enhancing rapid growth of industries by helping secure more and more entrepreneurs and their investors. By the end of the nineteenth century, with this new doctrine for contracts, American capitalists developed the nation into the most powerful industrial nation in the world.

Malden industrialists, led by David Ruffner, were leaders in forming private corporate joint-stock companies. Professor Stealey wrote, they "refined the organization and operations of contemporary joint-stock companies and sales agencies." Joint-stock companies were used for the salt combinations, and for David Ruffner's organization of Mercer Academy. It was approved as a joint-stock company by the Virginia General Assembly in 1818. He also used a joint-stock company for his Saltborough subdivision development for the planned town that is today Malden. Lewis Ruffner operated a sales agency in Louisville for Kanawha salt interests for 12 years. [283]

Just like the Ruffners who drilled a deep well and then had to create a salt production industry, lawyers in the salt and slavery industry formed a new business trust and then had to develop across-the-board safe, reliable corporate and other business legal formations, such as partnerships, private corporations, joint-stock companies and sales agencies to encourage investments in their capital-intensive industry. Salt industrialists relied on small groups of major investors to fund their operations often by using joint stock companies and thereby creating an industrial aristocracy in Malden. In Boston, corporations were formed by wealthy investors to raise capital for new textile mills, who in turn sold shares more widely, establishing the modern use of corporate shares to finance major new ventures. Corporate shareholding was an outgrowth of joint stock companies used in the time when corporations needed to be chartered by legislative bodies. It allowed middle class investors to participate in the speculation and the profits and losses of major new operations.

Lawyers would be important later in the nineteenth century to secure land titles for new coal, oil, and gas industries. Professor Stealey found that some of "the most creative intellectual accomplishments in Appalachia and West Virginia have been achieved by attorneys regarding land titles and natural resources." These topics, he contends, "beg for historical discovery." [284]

Joseph Lovell's business trust model would later be used for market domination and monopoly after the Civil War by Booker T. Washington's patrons in industry, John D. Rockefeller, Andrew Carnegie, and others who used restraints of trade to build empires of wealth in America's Gilded Age.[285]

Business Trusts Have Limited Success in Malden

The Kanawha Salt Company was planned for an initial period of five years, through 1822, but lasted only one year because of the Panic of 1819. The business panic began with failing western banks.[286] Many local banks were not reliable in this time. In later years, the salt industrialists used successor trusts but none were complete monopolies, because some of Malden's leading industrialists declined to give up control of their production, like the Dickinson & Shrewsbury partnership. That partnership was what Professor Stealey called a "militantly independent partnership." It enjoyed the benefits of the business trusts but operated outside of their restrictions and limitations.

Without full participation by all of the major industrialists, the Malden business trusts had limited success in shoring up profits. Increased production led to overproduction, which in turn drove salt prices down and profits lower. Profits of the salt industrialists suffered with each new innovation or efficiency that increased production.

The most successful business combination was Hewitt, Ruffner & Company. For four years, from 1836 to 1840, it was led by James Hewitt and Lewis Ruffner, who was managing his father's businesses. Hewitt, Ruffner & Company was successful because it was able to manage and limit all salt production in Malden with voluntary cooperation of Dickinson & Shrewsbury and other non-members.[287]

Business trusts were used for predatory business practices after the Civil War and into the Gilded Age, until they were outlawed in 1890 by the Sherman Anti-Trust Act. Because American law does not control international affairs, the Organization of Petroleum Exporting Countries, known as OPEC, operates openly as an international oil cartel, acting to affect prices and limit production to stabilize and increase profits for member nations.[288]

RUFFNER FAMILY TREE

Revised December 2019

IN VALLEY OF VIRGINIA--LURAY

*Peter Ruffner---*Mary Steinman
|1713-1778| |1714-1798|

CHILDREN IN LURAY
*Joseph Ruffner   Reuben R. Ruffner
Benjamin Ruffner   Tobias Ruffner
Catherine Ruffner   Elizabeth Ruffner
Peter Ruffner (Jr.)   Emanuel Ruffner

IN KANAWHA VALLEY--CHARLESTON

*Joseph Ruffner---*Anna Heistand
b.|09/25/1740| b.|10/15/1742|
d.|03/23/1803| d.|08/29/1820|

CHILDREN IN LURAY
Esther Ruffner   ***Samuel Ruffner**
*David Ruffner   Eve Ruffner
*Joseph Ruffner II   ***Daniel Ruffner**
*Tobias Ruffner   ***Abraham Ruffner**

*David Ruffner----*Anna Brumbach
b.|06/18/1767| b.|11/11/1766|
d.|02/01/1843| d.|11/22/1852|

CHILDREN IN MALDEN
*Henry Ruffner
*Ann Eve Ruffner
*Susan B. Ruffner
*Lewis Ruffner

*Dr. Henry Ruffner----*Sarah Lyle
b.|01/16/1790| b.|1787|
d.|12/17/1861| d.|1849|

CHILDREN IN LEXINGTON
*William Henry "W. H." Ruffner
*David Lewis Ruffner
Julia Elizabeth Stuart Ruffner
Anna Brumbach Ruffner

*Dr. Henry Ruffner ----*Laura J. Kirby
2nd Marriage   b.|1828|

*Lewis Ruffner-----*Elizabeth Shrewsbury
b.|10/01/1797| b.|10/01/1804|
d.|11/19/1883| d.|01/05/1843|

CHILDREN IN MALDEN
Madeline Eloise Ruffner   Lewis Ruffner, Jr.
David Henry Ruffner   Julia L. Ruffner
Sarah Ann Ruffner   Henrietta Ruffner
Joel Shrewsbury Ruffner

*Lewis Ruffner ----*Viola Knapp
2nd Marriage   b.|1812| d.|1903|

CHILDREN IN MALDEN
*Ernest Howard Ruffner
b.|06/24/1845| d.|05/24/1937|

*Stella Blanche Ruffner

*Detailed Information is Provided in the Text.

Chapter 7

Ruffners Bring Civic Improvements, Education, And Religion To The Western Frontier

New Town is Established Named "Saltborough"

David Ruffner was civic minded and a shrewd businessman. He wanted a town for workers and owners of salt factories closer than the village of Charleston where the county courthouse was located some six miles west of his home and factory. He wanted it on his land. He had moved to the "Salt Lick" area in 1805, and wanted to create a town and sell lots. He organized a joint stock company to create a planned town that became today's Malden.[289] With the help of his son-in-law, Dr. Richard Putney, David Ruffner planned and laid out the town, which they named "Saltborough" with a business area, home lots and generous alleys in the rear of the lots. Dr. Putney was married to Ann Eve Ruffner, the elder daughter of David Ruffner.

Home of Dr. Richard E. Putney and Ann Ruffner Putney, C. 1836
Photo by Jon Linville, Voyager Gold Media

The river front was set aside as a park for the recreational use of the owners of lots in the town. A steamboat landing would be put on the east side of the river front. A ferry was operated there into the early twentieth century. Before piped water supply, the ferryman would provide river water in barrels to residents who would keep the water in a trough until taken indoors where it was properly boiled for any use whether cooking, washing, bathing or cleaning.

The town grew with hotels, small businesses and houses between the salt factories. In 1818, the area had slum shanties for eight hundred to a thousand salt workers. Henry Ruffner called it "the wickedest and most hopeless part of Kanawha." By 1830, the Ruffner family's town had its first hotel, and twenty dwellings, three stores, two churches, a post office, a cooper shop, a barber shop and a tailor shop. A second hotel was added in 1834. By 1850, the town had added churches, and several stores. Methodists met in a small brick church on a main commercial street, and Presbyterians met in a sizeable brick church built by David Ruffner, which had been formed in 1819 by Henry Ruffner. The Ruffner slave quarters were located near their salt well and factory at the mouth of Campbells Creek in an area called "Tinkersville." It is today a coal depot for shipments by Charles Jones' family barge company. He maintains a river museum collection on the site.

"Saltborough" has had several names. Following the salt boom of the early 1800s, the salt producing area of the Kanawha Valley as a whole was known across the nation as the "Kanawha Salines." After the name Saltborough began to fade in the 1840s, the Ruffner town was informally called "Terra Salis." In the 1850s, the name "Malden" became popular. By 1855, the name Malden appears in the county assessor's land books. The name is commonly used in deeds written in the late 1850s. The area became a local tax district with the name of Malden after the Civil War. The town was incorporated in the name of Malden for a brief time until the town marshal, Allen Belcher, was killed in a shootout on November 15, 1881, at today's intersection of Commerce Drive and Salines Drive. The town was incorporated a second time, but again its charter was not continued.[290]

Today, Malden is a village in Kanawha County without incorporation. The origin of the name Malden is unknown. There was a newspaper article in the *Charleston Gazette* on June 17, 1915, about a reunion planned for Malden, and it states simply that a salt maker named Hewitt came from Malden, Massachusetts, and "brought the name with him." James Hewitt was a major salt industrialist in Malden in the 1830s and 1840s and he may have been the source for the name "Malden." From 1836 to 1840, his company's version of the salt trust, Hewitt, Ruffner & Company, became the only fully successful salt business trust because all producers cooperated in fixing prices and con-

Saltborough East of Ruffner Farm and Saltworks. – *Photo by Jon Linville, Voyager Gold Media*

trolling production and markets.[291]

As an industrial town by any name, Malden was a dismal place to live and work. There were smoking boilers with fire and smoke fouling the air day and night. An interesting story is told that in the spring of 1835, a young balloonist by happenstance flew over the Kanawha Valley at night. Richard Clayton was in a hot air balloon that escaped its moorings in Cincinnati due to high winds that carried him east into darkness. After many hours, he discovered where he was flying when he found himself in smoke and could see fires spread out along a river valley. He knew he was above the salt factories along the Great Kanawha River. The story tells that he landed safely two hours later in today's Summers County.[292] The valley was well known nationwide at the time but very few ever saw it from the sky.

In addition to fire and smoke, there were loud industrial noises and the sight of rough working men, "the roughest that can be seen, half naked" working in "the mournful screeching of the machinery, day and night," as Anne Newport Royall wrote in her 1826 travel book, *Sketches of History, Life and Manners, in the United States*. She was from Sweet Springs in Monroe County. As an early woman writer, journalist, and newspaper editor, Anne Royall is considered to be one of America's first professional women journalists. There is a story that she once forced President John Quincy Adams to give her an interview, after his swim in the Potomac River, by sitting on his clothes.[293]

David Ruffner is The "Father Of Presbyterianism"

David Ruffner brought social order to the industrial Kanawha Valley. He was a justice of the peace and a longtime member of the county court. He was elected to the Virginia General Assembly five times in 1799, 1801, 1802, 1804 and 1811. He was elected in 1811, after he had been jailed and fined for striking Andrew Donnally, Jr., at the courthouse with a Dutch anvil over ownership of the salt spring property on Campbells Creek. David Ruffner was a member of the county court for 53 years.[294]

While his public service career was important, it was his leadership for religion and new churches that would be his longest lasting civic contributions. He introduced religion on the western Virginia frontier. He was called the "Father of Presbyterianism in the Kanawha Valley." In 1819, it was written that the state of society in the Kanawha Salines was "deplorably immoral and irreligious." Early church services were conducted by his older son, Reverend Henry Ruffner, soon after he became an ordained Presbyterian minister. Young Reverend Henry Ruffner converted his Lutheran father, David Ruffner, to the Presbyterian Church.[295]

On March 14, 1819, Reverend Henry Ruffner formally conducted the first Presbyterian church service in the Kanawha Valley at Mercer Academy, helping his father and others organize Presbyterian churches in Charleston and in Malden. The Charleston church divided in 1872 over Union and southern sympathies. The "southern" First Presbyterian Church built a domed sanctuary in 1915 designed by architects Weber, Werner, and Adkins copying the design of Stanford White's New York Madison Square Presbyterian Church. The "northern" Kanawha Presbyterian Church built the first major church structure in the Valley in 1885, adding six dazzling Tiffany windows at the turn of the century. The Kanawha Salines Presbyterian Church today is the quaint house of worship built by David Ruffner in 1840, brick by brick. These churches have been active houses of worship for over 200 years.[296]

The Malden church was constructed by David Ruffner during his retirement. It was completed in 1840, three years before he died and about ten years after he and his son-in-law, Dr. Richard Putney, subdivided lots for "Saltborough."[297] David Ruffner had constructed not far from his home, an early meeting house, or community building. It was built on his farm not far from the mouth of Georges Creek on the river. It was called the Ruffner Meeting House, and served as a Presbyterian church. It was "sufficient to accommodate perhaps 200 people." Before 1840, it was the town's "center of

Kanawha Salines Presbyterian Church, 1840 – *Image Courtesy of West Virginia State Archives*

View of Slave Balcony, Interior of Kanawha Salines Presbyterian Church – *Image Courtesy of the Library of Congress*

moral, religious and educational operations." He made it available to churches and other groups. David Ruffner took great pride in the Kanawha Salines Presbyterian Church. He supervised placement of every brick. He had a course of brick taken down which had been put up when he was away.[298]

David Ruffner understood the humanity of the people he and others held in slavery, but he kept them in slavery as a leading salt industrialist and Salt

King. Slavery gave him and other southern salt industrialists a major competitive advantage over northern salt industrialists who had to pay wages and perhaps board for their workers. His German heritage, his service to the community and his business practices were inconsistent.

David Ruffner included areas in his churches for people to worship who were held in slavery. The Kanawha Salines Presbyterian Church has a balcony built for them, which young Booker may have been required to use after the war when he accompanied Viola Ruffner to her church. He may have attended while employed by Viola Ruffner, at least for special occasions. It is reported that he learned his catechism in the kitchen of the minister of the Presbyterian church. But he is known as an active member of his family's church, the African Zion Baptist Church.

That church was begun by devout Christians who were enslaved by the Ruffners and, perhaps other slavers. They would form their own faith community in 1852 under the leadership of Pastor Lewis Rice at Black Hawk Hollow, which is today's East Point Drive, east of Charleston and several miles from the Ruffner slave quarters at Tinkersville. There may have been a white pastor try to start services for blacks at Black Hawk Hollow some years before, but members of the African Zion Baptist Church have always dated their church from 1852, with no direct white leadership at any time. Pastor Rice's secret services before the war, could be punished with 39 lashes. With the encouragement of David Ruffner's son, Lewis Ruffner, during slavery in 1863, those Christian believers organized their own church, as the state's first black Baptist Church. Church services of the "Mother Church" started in the cabin bedroom of Pastor Rice in the Ruffner slave quarters. Many people freed themselves after the Emancipation Proclamation was issued, leaving the area during the war, but a number of the Ruffner slave workers stayed on. At the end of the Civil War in1865, Lewis Ruffner agreed to the construction of a church in his former slave quarters which would be used more as an early school than for church meetings. After the war, the African Zion Baptist Church would become the center of a community of freed believers and black leaders who would launch the career of Booker T. Washington and his American Dream for all. [299]

Ruffners Support Free Public Education

Throughout the nineteenth century, the Ruffners were the leading Virginia educators who supported state funding of public schools. Dr. Henry Ruffner before the Civil War and his son, Dr. William H. Ruffner after the war, were pioneer advocates in the South for universal free public education. They were both nationally known as educators and for their free thinking and success. The Ruffners opposed plans for public education without government funding for poor children.[300]

In 1817, former President Thomas Jefferson proposed a plan to establish public schools statewide and to establish a state-supported university in his hometown of Charlottesville. At the time, the College of William & Mary in Williamsburg was Virginia's leading established college. Washington College in the Valley of Virginia at Lexington had been established with a bequest from George Washington but it was not the equal of William and Mary. Thomas Jefferson opposed government funds for public schools but he wanted government funding for an elite university in his hometown of Charlottesville. He proposed a system of public education that would have districts about six-mile square throughout the state with one school house each. Students could attend without tuition for only three years, and they would owe tuition for longer times of study. There was no provision for poor students to have tuition waived. High schools would be available to good students. He wanted government taxes only to be used to support a new university. The idea of public schools for the masses was contrary to the value structure of most eastern aristocrats. Clearly, those aristocrats opposed paying a tax themselves to support public schools. Thomas Jefferson did not oppose public education; he just did not want the government to pay for it.[301]

Charles Fenton Mercer, a member of the General Assembly's House of Delegates, led opposition to the Jefferson plan. He favored a plan for public schools that would be free with support from state tax revenues. His plan was popular in western Virginia and supported strongly by the Ruffner family. He wanted public schools open to all children. The Jefferson plan would rely on parents and others to support public schools with tuition and contributions.

Delegate Mercer fought to have state government at least cover the tuition of poor students. He was able to maneuver a complete standoff with Thomas Jefferson's friends in the State Senate. While eastern Virginian leaders opposed universal education and any plan for a tax to fund it, they readily supported the Jefferson plan to establish an elite state university available to educate the children of aristocratic families.

As Thomas Jefferson saw his hometown university plan going down to defeat, his friends in the Senate accepted a compromise to create the University of Virginia as a state-funded institution and to provide public school funding for children whose families could not afford to pay tuition. Compromise legislation was enacted on January 25, 1819. Professor Charles H. Ambler summarized what happened: "Jefferson's friends accepted a system of public education in which they did not believe in order to get a university."[302]

True to its founding purpose, the University of Virginia served the aristocratic families of eastern Virginia and other states with slave societies. The university in Charlottesville was in the eastern part of the state. It was called the "seminary of the privileged class." It was generally avoided by families in western Virginia. In 1859, of the 370 students at the University of Virginia, only 17 were from west of the Blue Ridge Mountains. Western Virginia students attended Washington College, Bethany College and schools in Ohio and Pennsylvania. At Marietta College in Ohio across from Parkersburg, there were 15 western Virginia students enrolled, just two less than the number at the University of Virginia. In today's Huntington, Marshall University was started as an academy in 1837. It was named for Chief Justice John Marshall and became a college in 1858.[303]

It is remarkable that the University of Virginia had only 10 percent of its students from west of the Blue Ridge Mountains, but it received a majority of all state education funds. Ironically, most of those state education funds were generated in western Virginia by land sales for delinquent taxes.[304]

For Washington College, President Henry Ruffner actively recruited western Virginian students and elevated the quality of education at the college. The college was started as Augusta Academy in 1749 by pioneer Scot-Irish Presbyterians with no official church status. It was renamed Liberty Hall in 1776 by enlivened patriots. In 1796, George Washington, while serving as the nation's first president, contributed $20,000 of James River Canal stock to the failing school. Liberty Hall was able to upgrade its curriculum to college level, and the college was renamed for its great benefactor.[305]

In 1840, Bethany College was established north of Wheeling by Alexander Campbell near his home place and farm. He was the national leader for a new Protestant denomination he had organized as the "Disciples of Christ." It continues today as a major Protestant denomination known as the Christian Church. Alexander Campbell did not actively oppose slavery. His views on slavery were complex. Bethany College was popular with southern aristocratic families, although it was technically in the North, being north of the Mason-Dixon Line, the traditional dividing line between North and South. The Line was surveyed as the southern border of Pennsylvania from 1765 to 1767 by Charles Mason and Jeremiah Dixon, expert surveyors from Britain. As a representative at the 1829 Virginia Constitutional Convention, Alexander Campbell championed the cause of free schools and public education, and he argued for an end to slavery.[306]

Archibald W. Campbell was Alexander Campbell's talented nephew. He was a newspaper man known for his fierce advocacy for a new state during the Civil War. He was the courageous abolitionist editor of the *Wheeling Daily Intelligencer* which he began publishing in 1856. He is appropriately called by many in the Wheeling area the "Father of West Virginia." Others say that distinction belongs to the political leader, Francis Harrison Pierpont from Marion County, who served as the governor of the restored Virginia government loyal to the Union. Governor Pierpont mustered over 12,000 enlisted men in the first six weeks of his term. Thirty thousand Union troops would come from northwestern Virginia. There are limited records for the number of Confederate soldiers from that area. Historian Phil Conley thought for Confederate soldiers in that area "there were certainly not less than ten thousand."[307] In Virginia, many soldiers likely made the decision on which army to join, more from the viewpoint of at whom would they be shooting, than what political, social or other loyalty they had for a specific idea, cause, or side.

It is noted that the University of Virginia, today a leading academic institution, accepted its first black student in 1950 after federal litigation, where the court rejected the university's claim that the exclusion of black students was based on the state's constitution, laws and customs. In Virginia, both the University of Virginia and many of the state's higher education institutions did not allow women and men to be students together for over a century after the Civil War. In 1969, women were admitted to all colleges of the University of Virginia. At West Virginia University, women were excluded for its first two decades until the fall semester in 1889 when ten women were enrolled for the first time. Agnes Westbrook Morrison enrolled in the University's College of Law, and, in 1895, she became one of the first women in America to graduate from an established law school.[308] West Virginia University is today a top-level research institution which saw its Center for Alternative Fuels, Engines and Emissions discover and expose an international criminal fraud by German car giant Volkswagen for installing devices to cheat on pollution emission standards. Volkswagen recalled 8.5 million cars in Europe and offered to pay $15 billion in settlement.[309]

Ruffners Help Establish Mercer Academy in Charleston

David Ruffner helped organize Mercer Academy in downtown Charleston. He gave land for its use and organized it as a joint-stock company with a board of trustees. Though not a college, the academy was equal to many colleges of the day. Mercer Academy was named for Charles Fenton Mercer for his legislative fight to secure state funding for free public schools. The Ruffner educators were champions for free public school education in Virginia. They believed that democracy to succeed needed voters with some level of education. Mercer Academy was the first and only major school in the Charleston area before the Civil War. Mercer Academy was unusual for its day in educating southern men and women together. It was incorporated on November 29, 1818. The Mercer program for free public schools was favored in western Virginia but widely opposed by aristocrats in eastern Virginia.[310]

Professor Charles H. Ambler wrote that Mercer Academy was known as a pioneer "log college" of the "first quality." It was an upper level school. Henry Ruffner, David Ruffner's older son, organized and opened the school in 1818 in a two-story brick building at today's Hale and Quarrier Streets. He was the area's first ordained Presbyterian minister.[311]

Universal public education was a *cause célèbre* of the Ruffner educators. Dr. Henry Ruffner was an early supporter of local property taxes to pay for free schools. After decades of work, in 1846, the Virginia General Assembly allowed 16 of its 132 counties to establish free public schools with property taxes to be voted on by referendum. Only three counties, Kanawha, Jefferson and Ohio, approved the taxes to fund their public schools. These counties would become part of West Virginia, and they would have the only free public schools in the state when it was formed. The schools were for white children. The first public school for black children would start in Parkersburg during the Civil War. The second one would be in Malden started by the community of enslaved believers who formed the African Zion Baptist Church at the Ruffner slave quarters.[312]

The Ruffners' main business competitors, the Dickinson & Shrewsbury partnership, aggressively opposed property taxes on their businesses and convinced the General Assembly to eliminate a school tax following the partners' confrontation with the Kanawha County Sheriff over his attempts to collect property taxes owed by the partnership. Historian Charles Ambler wrote that, as a delegate in the new West Virginia Legislature, "Louis[sic] Ruffner" resisted property taxes for school support. He wrote that Delegate Ruffner sought to delay for two years a tax for public school support in order to allow voters to approve or disapprove the tax. When that proposal failed, he had the maximum levy rate reduced by one-third from 15 percent to 10 percent.[313]

After Henry Ruffner left the Kanawha Salines to teach at Washington College, the Ruffners' Mercer Academy was under the active leadership of Herbert P. Gaines, publisher of the *Kanawha Spectator,* a Charleston newspaper. His academy had the curricula of a college. He used a method of instruction which was intended to be precisely what was used at the College of William & Mary.[314] Principal Gaines offered classes in literature, English grammar, arithmetic, bookkeeping, Euclid's elements, surveying, navigation, logic, rhetoric, history, algebra, moral philosophy and economy. Greek and Latin and other languages were taught and the quality of instruction made it equal to many of the best colleges of the time.

Mercer Academy was supported by private tuition from students. It was never supported by members of the Ruffners' Presbyterian church nor was it dependent on the Ruffner family for financial support. In 1826, academy tuition was $8.00 to $10.00 per session depending on the course of instruction. Weekly boarding charges were $2.75 in private homes and $3.00 in "public houses." The school trustees controlled its property, including the real estate furnished by David Ruffner, whose second son, Lewis Ruffner, was a trustee of the academy and taught some classes there before the Civil War.

The academy building was the only place in town where as many as 50 people could be seated. David Ruffner's meeting house in Malden could accommodate 200 persons. For celebration of the Fourth of July 1826, George W. Summers of Charleston, who was western Virginia's leading Whig politician, gave a celebrated oration in the upper hall of the academy.

In the 1850s, David Lewis Ruffner, the younger son of Dr. Henry Ruffner, was a teacher and a principal at Mercer Academy. He was also captain of the second organization of the Kanawha Riflemen in 1858. It was organized for the sons of Charleston's aristocratic families. The elite corps' first organization was in 1856 by Captain George S. Patton, grandfather of the famous general in the Second World War with the same name. As the Civil War was starting, the Kanawha Riflemen became a Confederate regiment under the command of George S. Patton. In 1861, he was promoted by the Confederacy to Lieutenant Colonel. David Lewis Ruffner was the namesake of the area's leading Unionist, Lewis Ruffner, who was his uncle and a trustee at the academy. It was a time of deeply divided political and family loyalties. [315]

Ruffners are State Leaders for Higher Education

Dr. Henry Ruffner was widely respected as president of Washington College. He elevated the quality of the college. In 1838, he was granted a prestigious honorary doctorate of divinity degree from Princeton College. He was a known author, theologian, and free thinker. While serving as a college president, he had a church near Lexington where he preached each Sunday. While he greatly improved the level of education at his college, his legacy as an educator comes from his work for tax supported public schools. Further, he supported the establishment of normal schools throughout Virginia to train teachers to high professional standards, suggesting that teaching should be developed into a profession.

In 1841, a state education convention was convened in Clarksburg to propose changes to the state's public education system. As president of a leading college in Virginia, Dr. Henry Ruffner proposed what was named the "Ruffner Plan," to create a new state system for free public education including high schools. It would be a state system of public schools, that his son, W. H. Ruffner, would adapt as Virginia's first State Superintendent of Public Instruction during Reconstruction. His son's success would make him a leading national educator.[316]

Mercer Academy Closes With Damage in the Civil War

Mercer Academy was active until 1862 when the Union army used it to store supplies. Professor Ambler wrote in his extensive work, *History of Education in West Virginia from Early Colonial Times to 1949*, that the academy was burned on September 12, 1862 in a fight for control of Charleston between Confederate General W. W. Loring and Union Colonel Joseph A. J. Lightburn of Lewis County. Mercer Academy was never restored as an academy. The fire almost destroyed the building, but when Union troops took back the town, they filled in the walls and added a roof. It was used by the troops until July 1865, when it was deserted and then used temporarily for what would become a very important black Baptist church. Reverend F. C. James left the pulpit of the African Zion Baptist Church in Malden, and later started the legendary First Baptist Church of Charleston in the old academy building. By 1873, he had a church erected on Washington Street near Dickinson Street. This church would become one of America's most important black churches of the twentieth century.[317]

Mercer Academy was a casualty of the war in 1862 because Union soldiers burned its building as they fled town. A warning to leave town was delivered personally to the Ruffners by Union Colonel Lightburn.[318] At the time, Lewis Ruffner was a Major General of Union Militia, commissioned four months before on May 7, 1862 by the restored Virginia government. Colonel Lightburn was a boyhood friend of Thomas "Stonewall" Jackson. While most Ruffners were Confederates, the Malden patriarch of the family, Lewis Ruffner, was a famous Unionist. His commission made him a target for killing or arrest, and it subjected his business and farm properties to foraging and destruction. But, with great providence, he was not injured or captured, and his property was not ravaged. Lewis Ruffner's standing in the community may have limited his personal jeopardy. He may have left the area, perhaps with Union troops. He had property in Kentucky. There are no known records or accounts of him during the time when confederates took over Kanawha County. A Confederate army takeover of the town occurred only once during the war in 1862.

In the twentieth century, Mercer Academy was memorialized as Mercer School, which was established as the segregated elementary school for Charleston's fashionable East End residential neighborhood. Mercer School was integrated by black students and Minnie Wayne Cooper and other African American teachers soon after the Supreme Court struck down public school segregation in 1954 in *Brown v. Board of Education.* State government and many local school boards supported early integration of schools. Mrs. Cooper was a well-respected elementary teacher who became accepted as a preferred teacher by Charleston's elite families. Mrs. Cooper proudly told a story of her first year at Mercer School, when a prominent white mother strongly objected to having a black teacher for her second-grade student. By Halloween, the mother sent a maid to deliver cookies and a message to Mrs. Cooper that she was the best elementary teacher any of her children had ever had.[319]

Mrs. Cooper and her husband, Robert Cooper, lived in her parents' modest home between the Kanawha Salines Presbyterian Church and the river in Malden, not far from the town's commercial boat landing which was still in use when she was a child. She could remember visits by "Uncle" Booker. He would give her dolls and toys on most of his visits. She was eleven when he died in 1915.

Mrs. Cooper was a granddaughter of Caroline Wayne who was an original member of the community of enslaved Christian believers who started worshiping in 1852, in secret at Black Hawk Hollow. That community of believers would establish the first black Baptist church in the state, the African Zion Baptist Church in Malden.

Minnie Wayne Cooper became a leader in her grandmother's church, where Booker T. Washington was a member his entire life. As a teenager, he was secretary of the church. Minnie Wayne Cooper, Reverend Paul Gilmer, Sr., and Anna Evans Gilmer worked together to preserve the church at the end of the twentieth century when it no longer had an active congregation.

African Zion Baptist Church – *Images Courtesy of West Virginia State Archives*

African Zion Baptist Church – *Images Courtesy of West Virginia State Archives*

African Zion Baptist Church – *Images Courtesy of West Virginia State Archives*

Chapter 8

The Salt Aristocracy Of Malden

Success of "Salt Kings" Creates an Aristocracy

The families of salt industrialists created an aristocracy of manufacturers and businessmen like those seen for industrial entrepreneurs by Alexis de Tocqueville. These families advanced their businesses with innovation, hard work, savvy business acumen, marriages, and slavery. In Malden, they made advantageous marriages in several generations. The four leading Salt Kings lived in Malden. They were General Lewis Ruffner, William Dickinson, Sr., Joel Shrewsbury and John Dickinson Lewis. Other successful salt industrialist families included Donnally, Smith, Noyes, Tompkins, Reynolds, Hale, Laidley, Summers, Stockton, Cabell, Quarrier, Morris, Lovell, Grant, MacFarland and a number of others. These names of prominent salt industrialist families in the nineteenth century, most all of whom held people in slavery, are used for street names in today's downtown Charleston.

Dickinson-Lewis Family

The Dickinson family in Bedford County, Virginia, started with Joseph Dickinson who was a successful tobacco planter. Joseph Dickinson married Elizabeth Woolridge and they had five children. He had a store which he operated in partnership with his son, William Dickinson, Sr., and two of his sons-in-law. When he closed out his partnership, a new partnership was started by his sons, William Dickinson, Sr., and Pleasant Dickinson with their brother-in-law, Joel Shrewsbury, who had married their sister, Sally Dickinson. This second partnership was formed to operate a family store in Bedford County.

In the second partnership, William Dickinson, Sr., was the dominant partner and his brother, Pleasant Dickinson, was an associate partner. Joel Shrewsbury's early success brought his partners to Kanawha County. William Dickinson, Sr., strongly objected to Pleasant Dickinson's marriage in Bedford to "the widow Brown," and forced him out of the partnership. Pleasant Dickinson may have stayed or returned to the Kanawha Valley. A person named Pleasant Dickinson is listed in Lewis Ruffner's cash account book showing payments in 1839 by Pleasant Dickinson. Other than those few listings, the book contains almost no other persons named Dickinson.[320]

Joel Shrewsbury was the leader of the partnership in Kanawha County. By 1850, the partnership had the most successful salt operation in the Kanawha Valley. It had multiple salt factories and 232 persons who were enslaved and working for Dickinson & Shrewsbury.[321] It is likely that the partners leased slaves, and held people in slavery as residents. The partners held people in slavery individually as well. The partnership had diverse business interests. It was nimble and innovative. It had multiple salt factories but it also supplied food and services to workers in other salt operations. Slave work was organized to alternate between salt production and farming as needed. In 1843, at its factory at Burning Spring, the partnership was the second operation known in the western world to use natural gas for an industrial fuel.

By 1820, William Dickinson, Sr., was living in the Kanawha Valley. He was known as a strict businessman. His son, William Dickinson, Jr., worked in the family businesses in Bedford County for a number of years before coming to the Kanawha Valley. He was known as Colonel Dickinson and was well liked in the Kanawha Valley.[322]

William Dickinson, Sr. and Joel Shrewsbury are famous in local history for suing each other in 1856 as elderly men during the acrimonious dissolution of their 45-year partnership. Joel Shrewsbury died at age 80 in 1859. William Dickinson, Sr. died four years later in 1863 in his early nineties. A key issue in court was what part Pleasant Dickinson played in the partnership. In 1866, several years after the deaths of the partners, the court divided the partnership with seven-twelfths awarded to the heirs of William Dickinson, Sr., and five-twelfths to the heirs of Joel Shrewsbury.[323]

John Dickinson Lewis was the grandson of Colonel Charles Cameron Lewis who was killed at the Battle of Point Pleasant. He came from Bedford County to the Kanawha Valley to work as a clerk for the Dickinson & Shrewsbury partnership. His great success with another salt company, Armstrong, Grant & Company made him a major salt industrialist, land speculator, and leader in business consolidations. John Dickinson Lewis was a leading member of Malden's St. Luke's Episcopal Church. He purchased from Tobias Ruffner land for his home and salt operations west of David Ruffner's farm, factory and slave quarters at Tinkersville near the mouth of Campbells Creek.[324]

Colonel Lewis' namesake was Charles Cameron Lewis, a son of John Dickinson Lewis and Ann Dickinson Lewis. After the war, he became a stockholder and officer in Kanawha Valley Bank. The Dickinsons and Lewises intermarried. Charles Cameron Lewis' sisters married the two sons of their uncle William Dickinson, Jr.. They were in the Confederate army, Henry Clay Dickinson and John Quincy Dickinson. The sisters were Sallie Jane Lewis and Mary Dickinson Lewis.[325] Their mother, Ann Dickinson Lewis, was the sister of William Dickinson, Jr., the only son of William Dickinson, Sr.

In 1867, the Dickinson and Lewis families started the Kanawha Valley Bank in Charleston. It has been known primarily as the Dickinson family bank. It was started the year after the court decision on the Dickinson family's partnership shares and two years after the Civil War.[326] William Dickinson, Jr., started the bank with an investment of $10,000.00 and his sons each invested $5,000.00, giving them two-thirds control of the bank. Two other investors who were not members of the Dickinson family invested $5,000.00 each. The first meeting of investors was in the Frankenberger Building in Charleston on April 8, 1867. In its second year of business, the bank produced a net profit of over $13,601.36 for a 30 percent return on investment. In this time, the Dickinson and Lewis families began to expand their business operations beyond salt production.[327]

The Dickinson-Lewis family continued in the salt business until 1945, but it was banking and other business enterprises that produced the family's business success in the twentieth century. William Dickinson Jr., lived until 1881 when his son, John Quincy Dickinson took over the family businesses and built the family financial base by capitalizing on the growing coal, gas and timber industries in southern West Virginia. It is written that John Quincy Dickinson invested in sugar plantations in Cuba, and in lands in Chile, Mexico, Florida, and West Virginia.[328]

John Quincy Dickinson became the lead banker for the Dickinson and Lewis families following the death of his father, William Dickinson, Jr. His older brother, Henry Clay Dickinson, was a favorite of their grandfather, William Dickinson, Sr., but he died early at age 41 when he was serving as the second president of Kanawha Valley Bank and the first Democrat mayor of Charleston, elected at age 40. The early death of Henry Clay Dickinson opened the door for his talented younger brother to take charge and begin building the family fortunes. The investments in coal, natural gas, oil and timber industries were made as those industries were ready to boom once railroads in 1873, opened southern counties in West Virginia, to full resource development. In his role as banker, it was said by Mary Lee Settle, a renowned author and member of the William and Rachel Tompkins family, that John Quincy Dickinson would sit "in judgment over the wilder men of the valley" as the "priest of their money or lack of it." She wrote that he told a Tompkins heir who needed a loan after losing money out of state in a business panic, that the Dickinson family kept its money in the ground, and he suggested that the Tompkins family do the same.[329]

In the 1890s, in two business panics, John Quincy Dickinson famously deposited to the family bank, Kanawha Valley Bank, sums totaling $100,000.00

from his personal funds to prevent runs on the family bank. He knew his personal guarantee and the bank's faithful payment every year of a six percent dividend despite times of bank panic would keep the family bank in business. Kanawha Valley Bank prospered for over a century expanding in the 1980s to become One Valley Bank, the state's largest bank at the end of the twentieth century. The bank was purchased by Branch Banking and Trust from North Carolina and lost its identity with Malden.[330]

John Quincy Dickinson Home at Quincy 1980s photo – *Image Courtesy of West Virginia State Archives*

Three young Dickinson women married three Shrewsbury brothers. Joel, Samuel and John. Two were sisters in Bath County. The third was in Bedford County. The Dickinsons and Shrewsburys were old Virginia families and marriages of close cousins were not uncommon.

The Dickinson family of Bedford County were not close relations to the Dickinsons in Bath County. It was John Dickinson of Bath County who sold the Salt Lick spring to Joseph Ruffner. The Dickinsons in Bedford County were initially farmers and then businessmen. The three Shrewsbury men were pioneer salt industrialists. They were married in the time of the new Federal Constitution.

There were other marriages in multiple generations between the Shrewsburys and Dickinsons at least until the breakup of the Dickinson & Shrewsbury partnership in the late 1850s. It is said in the Shrewsbury family that all Shrewsburys, male or female, who had the middle initial "D" had that initial for either the name Dickinson or Darneal.[331] Their genealogy bears out this family tradition.

Shrewsbury Family

The patriarch of the Shrewsbury family in Malden was Joel Shrewsbury. He was a leading industrialist who also served the community. He became very wealthy as a pioneer salt industrialist. At his death in 1859, he had 72 properties, thousands of acres of valuable coal lands, salt furnaces, and 101 people held in slavery that he named in his will and divided as property among his descendants. He specified in his last will and testament that the people held in slavery were in no event to be sold, and they could choose with which of his children they preferred to live, or they could choose to reside on and cultivate small plots on his lands. His executor was "to exercise a general supervision over said servants, and see that they do not come to want." A commentator, D. C. Gallaher, who wrote a detailed family history of prominent families in the Kanawha Valley, commended Joel Shrewsbury and his will, noting, "the striking tenderness of the testator towards his descendants, and his slaves as well, and is itself a commentary upon the ignorance and unjust prejudices of the maligners of slave owners."[332]

Joel Shrewsbury started the partnership with two brothers-in-law, William Dickinson, Sr. and Pleasant Dickinson. He started partnership operations in the Kanawha Valley during the War of 1812. The Dickinsons & Shrewsbury partnership, as it was first named, became the Ruffners' primary competition. After Pleasant Dickinson was pushed out of the partnership, it was known as Dickinson & Shrewsbury.

The partnership became established in the Kanawha Valley after Joel Shrewsbury settled there during the salt boom years before and during the War of 1812. He came initially to visit his older brothers, Samuel Shrewsbury, Sr., and John Shrewsbury who moved to the Kanawha Valley from Bath County, Virginia, in the mountains west of the Valley of Virginia. They started at a stone house that is preserved today as a frontier home museum by the Town of Belle. It was constructed by Samuel Shrewsbury, Sr., and Mary "Polly" Dickinson Shrewsbury, whose father, John Dickinson, gave her husband and her sister's husband all his property in the Kanawha Valley in 1796. The brothers moved there in 1798 a full decade before the Ruffners' drilling was a success. They were ready to produce salt apparently in anticipation of the success of some salt makers. By 1810, they were producing salt. For most of the eighteenth century, women could not own land if they were married.

Joel Shrewsbury was civic minded. He helped organize two of the early Episcopal churches in western Virginia, at Charleston and Malden. The first Episcopal parish in the area was St. Mark's Episcopal Church which continues today in St. Albans, on the south side of the Great Kanawha River. While St. Albans is in Kanawha County it is not considered to be part of the "Kanawha Salines" which was primarily on the north side of the Great Kanawha River between the Elk River in Charleston and the Malden-Belle-Quincy area.

In Malden, Joel Shrewsbury constructed St. Luke's Episcopal Church as a mission church of St. John's Episcopal Church in Charleston. The mission building was poorly constructed and collapsed before the Civil War. The mission church property shared a boundary line with the lot and house sold after the war to young Booker's family by a grandson of Joel Shrewsbury.[333]

Joel Shrewsbury was a founding trustee of St. John's Episcopal Church in Charleston along with attorney James Craik who became a priest there. Later in Louisville, Kentucky, in the 1850s, Reverend James Craik was a leading Unionist and churchman for the national Episcopal Church.[334] His wife, Juliet Shrewsbury, was the daughter of Samuel Shrewsbury, Sr., and the niece of Joel and John Shrewsbury.

During the Civil War, St. John's Episcopal Church, like its peer Episcopal churches in the South, was known as a "Confederate Church." Prominent leaders of the Episcopal Church in the South strongly supported the full bloom of slavery. Many Episcopalians and Presbyterians in Charleston came from eastern Virginia to the booming salt and slavery industry. The St. John's Episcopal Church located in Richmond was the home of the Virginia diocese and its bishop, William Meade. It was there that Patrick Henry proclaimed, "Give me liberty or give me death."[335] The salt aristocrats intermarried in multiple generations, and, by the 1830s when the Charleston church was established, they had an industrial aristocracy of wealth in western Virginia based on business success instead of birth status.

The Charleston St. John's Episcopal Church congregation included many of the Valley's leading salt industrialists and slaver families. Its church building was commandeered by Union soldiers. It was customary for Union troops to take over Episcopal churches in the South and leave them damaged as spoils of war against Episcopal slavers who most always supported the Confederacy.[336] They left the building in shambles.

Union soldiers at St. John's Church ordered A. T. Laidley, a leader of the congregation, to include in the standard Sunday School service a prayer for President Abraham Lincoln. The prayer was declined because it was not allowed as part of the prescribed, formal services of the church. After he was threatened with burning of the church and his own imprisonment, he fled town for the duration of the war.

Church services were not held again until after the war.[337]

Joel Shrewsbury's older brothers, Samuel Shrewsbury, Sr., and John Shrewsbury, were early salt industrialists in the Kanawha Valley. They married sisters and their father-in-law conveyed his property to them for his daughters' benefit. By 1810, they were making salt just two years after the Ruffner well was productive. Samuel Shrewsbury married Mary "Polly" Dickinson and their tenth child, Juliet Shrewsbury, married James Craik. John married Martha Usher Dickinson and their son, Samuel Shrewsbury, Jr., married Laura Angela Parks, a great-niece of George Washington.[338]

The two Shrewsbury brothers were the sons-in-law of John Dickinson, the man who sold the "Salt Lick" to Joseph Ruffner. He was wounded both in the Battle of Point Pleasant and at the Cowpens in the Revolutionary War, where he met his future son-in-law, Samuel Shrewsbury, Sr. For the purchase of the salt spring property by Joseph Ruffner, he required a special bond for an increased payment in the event the salt spring produced high levels of salt. John Dickinson conveyed his properties in the Kanawha Valley to the two Shrewsbury brothers on October 8, 1796. They moved to the property with his daughters two years later. They invited their younger brother, Joel Shrewsbury, to visit to show him the Kanawha Valley and the likelihood of a new pioneer life there. That visit may have encouraged Joel Shrewsbury to begin operations for his partnership there, once salt production started in earnest in 1810. At the time, the partnership was operating a store in Bedford County. When Joel Shrewsbury joined in the salt and slavery industry, it was primarily through his partnership, Dickinsons and Shrewsbury.[339] The two Shrewsbury brothers would have benefitted from the family's litigation against the Ruffners to enforce payment of the bond for Joseph Ruffner purchase of the "Salt Lick" spring property.

A prominent son of Joel Shrewsbury was William Dickinson Shrewsbury. He was a salt industrialist whose wife was Martha Darneal of a well-to-do family in Kentucky. They had 16 children and lived in the Welch-Oakes-Jarrett House that stands today on the river front near Malden's former steamboat landing. William Dickinson Shrewsbury was the justice of the peace who was to hold a hearing for a peace bond petition in 1869, on the day a race riot broke out in Malden between the two court parties, one white and one black, and their friends, near the newly purchased home of young Booker's family. In contrast to the great success of the Dickinsons after the war, William Dickinson Shrewsbury had financial difficulty in the 1850s. It is noted that generally, the younger generations of Shrewsburys who followed the three Shrewsbury brothers did not succeed in business. A decade before the riot, the people William Dickinson Shrewsbury held in slavery had to be sold for his debts. His

The Old Stone House, Samuel, Jr. and Polly Shrewsbury Home – *Author's Collection*

father, Joel Shrewsbury, purchased the slaves and gave them in trust as a life estate to his wife, Martha Darneal Shrewsbury, for the term of her life.[340]

A son of William Dickinson Shrewsbury and Martha Darneal Shrewsbury, was Robert Peal Shrewsbury, who was the grandfather of the Malden "Cole Sisters," Llewellyn Shrewsbury Cole and Martha Darneal Cole. They were well-respected school teachers and the last residents in Malden of the old salt families. They enjoyed repeating the old-time cautionary phrase used in Malden to "never have anything to do with high water or ignorant people." Their grandfather, Robert Peal Shrewsbury, told his family that after he took off his hat to Booker T. Washington at a speaking event at the Malden ballfield, he was promptly criticized for doing so, and replied "Since he took off his hat to me, I was not going to let him be more polite than I." His brother, Jacob Darneal Shrewsbury, sold to Booker's family their new home 7 weeks before the Malden race riot. He was 26 years old and a nephew of Elizabeth Ann Dickinson Shrewsbury Ruffner, who was the first wife of Lewis Ruffner.[341] Lewis Ruffner was permanently disabled from injuries he received in the race riot.

Craik-Shrewsbury Family

The Craik family was close to George Washington's family in three generations. The Washingtons were royalty in America. George Washington's best friend was Dr. James Craik, a Scot immigrant physician and plantation owner, who was educated in Edinburgh, Scotland. He settled near Mount Vernon and married a relative of George Washington's mother. Dr. Craik traveled with George Washington and William Crawford to Mingo Town in 1770. He would be the attending physician at the deaths of the former president and his first lady, Martha Washington.[342]

Dr. Craik's son, George Washington Craik, was helped with his education by the Washington family. He served as the personal secretary to the president. His son, Reverend James Craik, became an important leader in Kentucky for the Union and the national Episcopal Church after the Civil War.

The grandson came to Charleston because his family's lands there were purchased after the 1770 trip by George Washington and Dr. Craik into the Ohio Valley and Kanawha Valley. Reverend Craik was first an attorney and then a trustee, deacon and rector who organized the Charleston parish into St. John's Episcopal Church, and it became known as a church for salt industrialists and slavers.

In 1844, Reverend Craik and his wife, Juliet Shrewsbury Craik, were called to Louisville for him to serve as rector of Christ Church. She was the granddaughter of Colonel John Dickinson who conveyed the salt spring to Joseph Ruffner.[343] The Craiks' church in downtown Louisville stands today as the city's oldest house of worship. It has a large stained-glass window of Juliet Shrewsbury Craik in the sanctuary.

Reverend Craik was a well-known and influential minister in Kentucky's Episcopal Church. He had a national reputation as a conservative Episcopal churchman. He is credited for using his personal influence with legislators and other leaders to help keep Kentucky in the Union as a border slave state. After the war, he was a leader in the national church hierarchy and, as the President of the House of Deputies, despite opposition, he was able to masterfully reunite all of the southern Episcopal Dioceses to the national church soon after the Civil War. Some Protestant denominations which split before or during the war did not reunite for generations. Reverend Craik saved his church as a united national church. In 1873, his very conservative leadership pushed Kentucky's Assistant Bishop George David Cummings out of the church, who then established a new denomination known as the Reformed Episcopal Church. Reverend Craik opposed Bishop Cummings for what then was seen by conservatives as a heresy: the conducting of a joint communion service with Presbyterians. At his death in 1883, Reverend Craik was revered as one of the leading churchmen of Kentucky and the national Episcopal Church.[344]

In Charleston today, the home of James and Juliet Craik is the city's premier period home museum.[345] It is named the "Craik-Patton House" for the Craiks and for the prominent Patton family who lived there during the Civil War. George S. Patton was a Confederate military leader of the Kanawha Riflemen. He died on September 25, 1864, from wounds in the Battle of Winchester, Virginia. His grandson of the same name was the Second World War general who led victorious troops in the Battle of the Bulge in 1944 and 1945.

Craik-Patton House – *Authors Collection*

Ruffner Family

Peter Ruffner started the Ruffner family in America in 1732 when he arrived at age nineteen in Lancaster County, Pennsylvania. Many German immigrants settled in that Quaker colony. The Ruffners were a German-speaking family. He came from an area near Germany's border with Switzerland. He had the physical attributes of George Washington. It was reported that he was six feet, three inches tall, attractive, intelligent and powerful. Seven years after he arrived, perhaps at the end of a time of indentured servitude for payment of his passage, Peter Ruffner made a favorable marriage with Mary Steinman, the daughter of a wealthy German land-owner who gave them a large estate in the Valley of Virginia, near today's Luray, Virginia.

Ruffner descendants still live in that area, as well as in the Kanawha Valley and across America.[346]

The Ruffner family prospered in Luray with children and growing estates. Peter and Mary Ruffner had eight children: Joseph, Benjamin, Catherine, Peter Jr., Reuben, Tobias, Elizabeth and Emanuel. Peter Ruffner died in 1778 and his wife, Mary Ruffner, died twenty years later. They were a major land holding family.[347] German and Scot-Irish settlers maintained separate settlements at this time in the Valley of Virginia, likely due to early language and cultural differences. The Ruffners owned farm-lands extending ten miles along a creek. They expanded their first location by purchasing lands from the estate of Lord Fairfax, who owned most of the northern Virginia colony at the time of the Revolutionary War. Lord Fairfax died as a loyal subject of King George on December 9, 1781, only two months after the British lost the battle at Yorktown.

In the early 1790s, the Ruffners discovered the "Ruffner Cave" which is today known as the Luray Caverns. This began as a tourist attraction in 1878 and was part of Virginia's tourist industry, which then was centered on many sulphur and hot springs in the state. The state's tourism industry continues to be prominent in its economy. By 2017, tourism brought to the state $25 billion in business activity and government revenues of over $1.7 billion. Much of Virginia's tourism is based on its history, and some interpretation of its slave past is presented in a number of venues. The state tourism industry has been booming for many years. Thirty years ago, in 1987, tourism brought to Virginia revenues totaling $3.6 billion or then 19 percent of the state's business revenues. It created 157,882 jobs and generated tax revenues of $365 million. Its tourism business in 1987 was second in the South only to Florida. Today it rivals tourism anywhere.[348]

Before the Civil War, in the Allegheny Mountains of western Virginia, there were numerous water springs considered good for health, and they attracted a large tourist trade to resort hotels located at the springs. There were naturally heated springs, in Berkeley Springs, and in Bath County at Warm Springs and Hot Springs where the charming Homestead Resort and Spa is located. Monroe County was popular with resorts at Red Sulphur Springs, Salt Sulphur Springs and Sweet Springs. The latter two springs have resort buildings still standing. The Old Sweet Hotel established in the late 1700s is said to have been designed by Thomas Jefferson. W. H. Ruffner frequented these resorts to improve his health in the 1850s.[349]

The "Queen of the Watering Places," leading all resorts, was the Old White Hotel at White Sulphur Springs. Today, the Greenbrier Hotel Resort reigns there amid 11,000 acres on mountain estate grounds with unmatched interiors by legendary New York designer Dorothy Draper. In eighteen months, in 1946 and 1947, she purchased over 34,000 pieces of furniture, 45,000 yards of fabric, 40,000 gallons of paint and 15,000 rolls of wallpaper for her complete redecoration of the hotel building. As the state's largest hotel and resort, it entertains thousands of guests and visitors every month, who, in grand style or sporty attire, can "take the waters" of Old Virginia.[350]

The oldest son of Peter and Mary Ruffner was Joseph Ruffner. He was a good businessman and his estates grew to be very productive. Joseph Ruffner married Anna Heistand, and they had eight children including: Esther, David, Joseph II, Tobias, Samuel, Eve, Daniel, and Abraham.[351] In 1794, Joseph Ruffner envisioned a great bounty in western Virginia which had just become safe for new settlements after General Anthony Wayne defeated native tribes at the Battle of Fallen Timbers. This battle left Virginia settlements in the Ohio Valley and Kanawha Valley in peace for the first time. It led to a rush of surveyors and land speculators, and it began the push for migration of white settlers to the Midwest.[352]

As a third-generation German immigrant family, the children of Joseph and Anna Ruffner spoke German at home, and members of the family were Lutherans and Mennonites. Their eldest daughter, Esther, died when she was eighteen years old. Their eldest son, David, would build on his father's industrial dreams by creating the two largest industries in the Kanawha Valley, salt and coal. He would make major civic developments in the valley including a school, churches, and layout of the industrial town of Malden.[353] David Ruffner married Lydia Anna Brumbach, and they had four children. His two sons would be state leaders in their own right for education, religion, free thinking, engineering, and statesmanship. His grandsons would be important leaders for river development and education.

Joseph Ruffner, II, helped his brother David to drill their first salt well. They found a strong brine on the river's edge of the Great Kanawha River. In November 1807, they set up a furnace ready to produce salt from brine from their first well on February 11, 1808. That day their industry started in the Kanawha Valley. Three years later, in 1811, he moved to Cincinnati, Ohio, where he was a large landowner and served as a judge, and became involved with the Ohio canal system. The grandson of his brother, David Ruffner, named Ernest Howard Ruffner, would become an important federal engineer on the Ohio River when he lived in Cincinnati. [354]

Another talented son was Tobias Ruffner. He was a very successful blacksmith who could cleverly forge most any tool or implement.[355] He would be known today as a brilliant mechanical engineer. He is not given enough credit for the mechanical innovations he made day-to-day to turn Ruffner drilling from folly into a booming frontier industry.

Samuel Ruffner was burned as an infant and disabled. His brothers agreed to take care of him after the death of their father. Samuel married and had four children.[356]

The youngest daughter was Eve who married Nehemiah Wood, Jr. In 1805, before the first Ruffner well was drilled, they moved to Gallia County, Ohio. They owned major tracts of land. Their home and farm land on a 900-acre tract have been used by the Bob Evans family.[357]

Daniel Ruffner lived with his parents in Charleston on their farm at today's State Capitol. In 1815, he built a home and inn he named "Holly Grove." It is today preserved as a state office building next to the Governor's Mansion. He had seven children with his first wife, Elizabeth Painter, and seven with his second wife, Elizabeth Honeyman Singleton. In 1809, he was a justice of the peace. He farmed the home place and a large tract north of town. He had a salt furnace on the home property. In 1853, he purchased a farm called Mount Vernon in Kentucky and later retired there.[358]

Abraham Ruffner was the youngest child of Joseph and Anna Heistand Ruffner. He sold his interest in the Salt Lick spring to Andrew Donnally Jr., in 1806, and contentious litigation ensued between Andrew Donnally and Abraham's brothers over ownership of the salt property. The litigation ended in 1822 with a deed of the salt spring by Andrew Donnally, Jr., to David and Joseph Ruffner. Abraham Ruffner moved his family in 1818 to Cincinnati, Hamilton County, Ohio, to join the family of his brother, Joseph Ruffner, II.[359]

The talents of the Ruffner family seem unlimited. Their success was broad and guided by David Ruffner. The Ruffners had "an uncommon ingenuity and rare gifts for improvisation."[360] They invented modern drilling techniques and established the first heavy industry for mass production of natural resources on the American frontier. They pioneered new factory systems a few years after they invented deep well percussion drilling for the western world. In 1817, they started the coal industry in western Virginia to fuel their factory furnaces. Their factory and distribution systems came at the beginning of the mechanical revolution before the Industrial Revolution was developed.

The Ruffners were accomplished pioneers in engineering, industry, business, education, religion, town planning, public service and state making. They developed a commercial, social and political center for their industry in the Kanawha Valley that, in turn, would make Charleston the state capital and the center of the coal industry and a modern chemical industry.

The Ruffners have been relegated in history to being a wealthy family who hired young Booker T. Washington to work in their home, and from whom he learned the value of work.[361] This author is unable to name any other family in American history, with five members, who have been outstanding pioneers and leaders in so many fields. Young Booker observed the family closely, and appreciated the wonderment of their heritage as pioneers and courageous free thinkers. He could think that if the Ruffners could conquer the frontier of western Virginia, he could do the same in the Deep South frontier of racist human relations after Reconstruction.

The pioneer Ruffner family influenced Booker T. Washington at the age when boys use hero worship to develop their value systems and vision for life. He and his family worked for Lewis and Viola Ruffner. His stepfather, Washington Ferguson, worked in the Ruffner salt factory and coal mines, while he was a leased slave before the war. In 1864, he emancipated himself from slavery in Confederate Virginia, and came to Malden to work for the Ruffners, and there he finally became a free person a year later in 1865. After Jane Ferguson brought her young children to Malden from Virginia near Roanoke, in 1865, she worked for the Ruffners as a chambermaid, and then as their cook.[362] She had her younger son, Booker, who was only nine on arrival, to live with the Ruffners early on as a house and garden worker, knowing he would greatly benefit from what he would learn there, well beyond the benefit to the family of his wages later needed to pay their home mortgage.

She was ambitious for her children, and she was likely the parent who pushed for the family to purchase a home in Malden from Lewis Ruffner's nephew. The clear purpose was to integrate the town and show all that they and their friends deserved to be equal as well as free. It took the family a mile away from their friends in the former Ruffner slave quarters, and their work and school and church in order to live among white families unsure about their neighbors' intentions and their own community status. Young Booker lived in the Ruffner home for a number of years before going to Hampton Institute in 1872, at age 16, which was some seven years after he arrived in Malden. The exact number of years he lived with the Ruffners is unknown, but it was likely that most of his formative years were spent with them and his mother, their cook, before he went away to school at Hampton.

David Ruffner:
Inventor and One of America's First Industrialists

David Ruffner was a gifted and hardworking young man. His early schooling was in both English and German. He learned spoken English from a store-keeper in Luray. He spoke with a slight German accent. He married Lydia Anna Brumbach. A grandson remembered the marriage was "a happy marriage. The sweet face, deep blue eyes, and gentle temper of the wife softened the sterner, and developed the more amiable qualities of the husband." She would be called "Mother Ruffner" in her later years. They had four children who were Henry, Ann, Susan, and Lewis. After his father Joseph Ruffner moved his family to Charleston in 1795, David Ruffner followed with his young family to Charleston, leaving Luray on October 20, 1796 and joining his parents two weeks later on November 3, 1796.[363] The last child, Lewis, was born at Fort Lee in 1797.

By 1810, early in the American Industrial Revolution, David Ruffner had salt industrialists using factory systems more extensive that the small textile spinning operations in New England, and more than a decade before major factory operations started in 1822 in Lowell, Massachusetts.

The "first-born child" of the small textile mills that started the American Industrial Revolution were the factory systems started by David Ruffner for the Kanawha salt and slavery industry. The leading industry on the American frontier was in the Kanawha Valley, and it was there because of David Ruffner and his brothers, Tobias and Joseph Ruffner, Jr.[364]

David Ruffner's business success and community service are legendary. The sons of David Ruffner and Anna Brumbach Ruffner would become important state leaders in Virginia. Their older daughter, Ann Eve Ruffner, married a physician and successful salt industrialist, Dr. Richard Putney. He helped David Ruffner lay out lots to create a town they called "Saltborough" in 1830. Dr. Putney sold the river front land for salt factories to the Dickinson & Shrewsbury partnership that is today's pastoral Dickinson family farm they call "Kanawha Salines." The Federal style brick Putney home is preserved as a private residence with white painted brick on the main street in Malden.

The second daughter of David and Anna Ruffner was Susan B. Ruffner, and she married a salt industrialist, Moses Morton Fuqua. In 1840, their family moved to Missouri.[365]

David and Anna Ruffner had two sons, Henry and Lewis, who would rival the impact that his parents had on Malden and the Kanawha Valley. In their older years, David and Anna Ruffner enjoyed visits from a gifted grandson, William Henry Ruffner, who was a son of Henry Ruffner. William Henry or

W. H. Ruffner, was a bright, intelligent young man who had the Ruffner grit, work ethic, and gift for success. He was a Renaissance man like his father, who had served as president of Washington College. Henry Ruffner and his son, W. H. Ruffner, would be leaders for public and higher education and both would have national reputations for outstanding work in a number of areas, including education, religion, writing, and free thinking. Dr. W. H. Ruffner as Virginia's first Superintendent of Public Instruction during Reconstruction would be called the "Horace Mann of the South."

David and Anna Ruffner also helped a young man from Pennsylvania named William Swan Plumer who became an important Presbyterian minister, religious scholar and writer. He came to Malden in 1819 when he was 17 years old. David Ruffner "took him off a store boat and set him to teaching a school, which he raised for him." The Ruffners helped the bright young man to attend the schools associated with the Ruffner family. He went first to Reverend John McElhenny's academy in Lewisburg, from 1820 to 1822. Next, he attended Professor Henry Ruffner's Washington College from 1822 to 1825, and later he attended the Princeton Theological Seminary in New Jersey. William Swan Plumer would become one of the leading churchmen of the nineteenth-century Presbyterian Church. He was a minister of a number of important churches. He was a nationally recognized author who published many books. He started, in Richmond, the paper, *The Watchman of the South,* and he is one of the best-known students of Princeton Theological Seminary. He received four honorary degrees and is recognized as one of the leading intellectuals of the Presbyterian Church in the nineteenth century. [366]

When David Ruffner died in 1843, he was memorialized as a great civic leader, industrialist, engineer, and town planner. He established social and religious order on the frontier during America's early industrial years through the Age of Jackson.[367] His sons would do even more for social justice in the nineteenth century, by helping save the Union, organize a new state, and establish free public education for white and freed children after the Civil War. Most notably, his younger son and his wife, Lewis and Viola Ruffner, became champions for the civil rights of their freed neighbors who were a community of Christian leaders ready to encourage and empower the brilliant career of Booker T. Washington.

Henry Ruffner:
Antebellum Virginia's Leading Educator

Dr. Henry Ruffner, the older son of David and Anna Brumbach Ruffner, was an educator, minister, writer and free thinker. He was a leading educator in Virginia before the Civil War. He was president of Washington College, to-day's Washington and Lee University. In 1838, Princeton College recognized him with an honorary doctorate degree.[368] While teaching Latin and Greek at Washington College, he invented a steam process to strip coal slag from his father's salt furnaces, leading to the use of coal by all salt industrialists.

Henry Ruffner (L), Leading Virginia educator and free thinker – Image *Ruffner Family Association Collection* William H. Ruffner (R), the first superintendent of Virginia's public school system. - *Image is a Public Domain photographic print by M. Miley & Son of Lexington, 19th Century.*

On March 14,1819, soon after young Henry Ruffner was ordained, he conducted the first Presbyterian services in the Kanawha Valley. He helped his father establish early Presbyterian churches that remain in service today, as First Presbyterian Church of Charleston, Kanawha Presbyterian Church, and the historic Kanawha Salines Presbyterian Church in Malden.[369]

Dr. Henry Ruffner was known nationally for the 1847 Ruffner Pamphlet proposing the abolition of slavery in "West Virginia." The pamphlet was a scholarly economic analysis of how slavery in Virginia was preventing population growth and economic development, which, at the time was being enjoyed by northern free states. He opposed sales of people held in slavery as livestock commodities for profit. The pamphlet did not propose to end eastern Virginia's slavery or its lucrative slave livestock industry. Abolition would be limited to the area he termed "West Virginia." It should be noted that his proposal for abolition would have eliminated slave labor in the Kanawha salt and slavery industry. Two years before he published the pamphlet, in 1845, he had his son sell his Malden salt factory in the peak production years of the industry. This salt operation Dr. Ruffner inherited from his father. He argued that the northern free states had moved well beyond agricultural economies to manufacturing and modern business economies, while the population growth and economic development in southern slave states were stagnant by comparison. He used inappropriate terms for male and female slaves. He contended that Virginia's economy had more industrialization than other southern states, but its population and economic growth lagged behind the northern free states. In the pamphlet, he argued that slavers in Virginia were investing too much of their capital in people who were to be sold by the thousands in the slave trade.[370] He warned that when the cotton industry was over populated with slaves, the economies in western and eastern Virginia would fail. Unless slavery were abolished in "West Virginia."

The pamphlet caused a sensation across the nation. Northerners hailed it as a new day in the South, and southerners called for Dr. Henry Ruffner's exile from Washington College and the South. Southerners attacked him for heresy against the culture of the South. He would leave Washington College in 1848, about a year after publication of the pamphlet. In 1849, he was granted an honorary Doctor of Laws Degree from Washington College. Following the death that year of his wife, Sarah "Sally" Montgomery Lyle, he moved to Louisville to be near the family of his brother, Lewis Ruffner. Soon thereafter he married Laura J. Kirby from Cincinnati. He was 59 years old. In the early1850s, Dr. Ruffner and his bride and oldest daughter moved to Malden to farm and raise sheep. He set up a private academy he called "Mt. Ovis Academy." When he sold his salt property to Jacob Darneal, he purchased mountain lands lying around at the headwaters of Blue Creek, Campbells Creek, Mill Creek and Indian Creek, an elevated area about seven miles from the river at Malden.

As a scholar and writer, Dr. Henry Ruffner wrote extensively on history and Calvinist theology. He wrote fiction for magazines and a novel, and he published sermons and public addresses in pamphlet form. In the first year of the Civil War, while living in Malden and ministering at the Kanawha Salines Presbyterian Church, he became depressed and debilitated. His pamphlet had been a major political issue in the state election for governor in 1859 when a signer of his pamphlet, John Letcher, was attacked for his apparent flip-flop on the issue of abolition in the western counties. He won his election.

Dr. Ruffner weathered the first storm over the pamphlet a decade before but the election debate disturbed him, and the war that followed he saw as a tragedy. He closed Mt. Ovis Academy in 1861. The academy was well patronized with the sons of notable families. He continued to serve as a minister at the Kanawha Salines Presbyterian Church after he closed Mt. Ovis Academy. The academy was well patronized with the sons of notable families, but his health began to fail after Fort Sumter was attacked. With most all of the young men in the Ruffner family joining the Confederate army, the old Union man lost his spirit for life and died in Malden on December 17, 1861.[371]

Dr. Henry Ruffner was born near today's Luray, in the Valley of Virginia on January 16, 1790. He was named for his mother's father, a German immigrant Mennonite minister, Reverend Henry Brumbach, who died in 1799. Henry Ruffner was a brilliant man who excelled in most every activity he tried. He helped dig his father's first deep well in 1808 when he was 18 years old, digging as he wrote, until he was "sick of it."[372]

He attended the Lewisburg Academy and boarded with Reverend John McElhenny, who was the legendary Presbyterian minister at the Old Stone Church that remains in use in downtown Lewisburg today. Reverend McElhenny was minister of that church for 62 years. He was principal of the Lewisburg Academy which he started in his home in 1808 through 1827. Reverend McElhenny served as chair of its board of trustees until 1860. He had attended Liberty Hall Academy before its name was changed eventually to Washington College. Henry Ruffner's father, David Ruffner, was an early member of his board of trustees. In 1874, the academy was given to a local women's school and later became Greenbrier College.[373]

Young Henry was a star pupil and the Lewisburg Academy's most acclaimed graduate. The Lewisburg Academy was important because it schooled Presbyterian ministers for pulpits throughout the West. Presbyterian ministers were educated professionals in the pioneer West, and some have said these ministers did more for education than they did for religion. That was true for Reverend Dr. Henry Ruffner because of his work as an educator, scholar, writer and free thinker.[374]

Lewis Ruffner:
Salt and Coal Industrialist and State Maker

Lewis Ruffner was the younger son of David Ruffner and Anna Brumbach Ruffner. He was a business leader and legislator who helped establish the new State of West Virginia. His second wife, Viola Ruffner, was a "Yankee" lady with northern ideas. She and her husband would be important mentors to young Booker who lived with them in his formative years. Lewis Ruffner followed in the footsteps of his father, David Ruffner. He was a businessman and slaver, and at times taught school.

Lewis Ruffner, Salt Manufacturer, Slaver and Leader for the Union – *Ruffner Family Association Collection*

In 1821, at age twenty-four, Lewis Ruffner was elected to a one-year term in the Virginia General Assembly in Richmond. In 1823, at age 26, his father retired and turned over his extensive salt businesses to him. Lewis Ruffner was elected to the legislature for terms in 1825 and 1826 and then he retired from politics until the Civil War. He was a strong Union supporter and was elected as a delegate from Kanawha County to the Wheeling Conventions which first created a restored Virginian government loyal to the Union, and then established a new state. He served in the new state legislature during the war, in 1863 and 1864. The new state took the name "West Virginia," which his brother, Dr. Henry Ruffner popularized in his 1847 pamphlet, proposing the abolition of slavery in the western area of Virginia extending from the Blue Ridge Mountains to the Ohio Valley.[375]

Delegate Ruffner hoped the state would be called "Kanawha," and that the new state government would compensate him for emancipation when the time came for freedom for all people held in slavery--if the Union won the war. He served as a Kanawha County Delegate in the first two years of the new state's legislature in 1863 and 1864. In the first year, his friend and fellow slaver from Kanawha County, Spicer Patrick was elected Speaker, the state's first speaker of the House of Delegates. Delegate Ruffner served as the Chair of the important Taxation and Finance Committee. Spicer Patrick had been a Kanawha County Delegate to the Richmond secession convention, where he and the other three local delegates voted no on secession.[376] Delegate Ruffner appears to be Majority Leader in marshaling motions on the floor of the House to move along the leadership's legislative agenda. In 1863, the legislature convened on Statehood Day, June 20, 1863, and met each month for the rest of the year organizing the new state.

Lewis Ruffner's family members were Confederates. They were soldiers and sympathizers. Lewis Ruffner courageously became the leader for the Union in the Kanawha Valley. He was the only openly Union man in his family. He defied both his family and the families of other prominent salt industrialists who refused to support the Union.

Lewis Ruffner was born on October 1, 1797, as the Ruffners' fourth child. Some historians have written that Lewis Ruffner was the first settler child born in Charleston. Other information indicates that a Clendenin child was born at Fort Lee before it was purchased by the Ruffners. Lewis Ruffner attended school in Charleston, and later, he followed his brother, Henry, who was seven years older, at the Lewisburg Academy, studying with Reverend John McElhenny. He spent a year at an academy in Cincinnati. In 1816, he again followed his brother, attending Washington College in Lexington.[377]

On November 2, 1826, Lewis Ruffner married Elizabeth Ann Dickinson Shrewsbury, the daughter of leading salt industrialist, Joel Shrewsbury, and his wife, Sally Dickinson Shrewsbury. In 1827, Lewis Ruffner was an innovator in his father's salt businesses. With Frederick Brooks, he helped introduce steam engines to the industry. In 1828, he was selected by the Virginia governor to serve as a justice of the peace and as a member of the county court. He continued control over his father's extensive salt businesses for twenty years.

W. H. Ruffner wrote in 1901 that David Ruffner built the Ruffner home place in 1805 on the George Alderson tract near the salt spring. He wrote that it was later occupied by Lewis Ruffner and that his descendants still lived there in 1901. Descendants of Lewis and Viola Ruffner lived on the property until the 1950s. When they subdivided and sold lots in the 1940's, they added to their deeds a covenant that the purchasers would not sell to persons of African descent. The year 1805 is too early for construction of David Ruffner's house. That estimate is too early for a frame house in Malden. John P. Hale reports that the first three frame houses in Charleston were built in the years 1812-1815. The year 1805 was three years before the first salt well was drilled and at a time when David Ruffner may have been in some financial distress, according to Henry Ruffner's letter to a friend many years later. The year 1805 was after David Ruffner's inheritance from his father and well before the bounty of the salt and slavery industry made "Salt Kings." Log homes were common in 1805 and the home which lasted well into the twentieth century had a painted plank exterior and double sash windows. The home was built in two main sections or wings to accommodate two families, likely after Lewis Ruffner and his first wife, Elizabeth Dickinson Shrewsbury Ruffner had children in the 1830s. David Ruffner died in 1843. It is more likely that the Ruffner home place was built when Lewis Ruffner was managing his father's businesses in the 1830s. It no longer stands in Malden.[378] The street to the home place is named

General Drive.

In 1829, Lewis Ruffner paid dues to the American Colonization Society, which had been established by Henry Clay as an alternative to emancipation with freedom and equality. Southerners who objected to slavery often supported the idea of deporting to Africa people as they were freed. When abolitionists in the North began attacking the slave industry in the 1830s, the backlash of public opinion in the South was so strong that no southerner who opposed slavery could do anything publicly other than support a back-to-Africa movement for people who may be freed. Virginia had a statute making antislavery publications illegal. After the 1831 Nat Turner Rebellion, open opposition to slavery was deemed a treasonous attack on genteel southern society. It was also a dangerous opinion to express openly in the South.[379] The cutoff of fair political debate in the South on the issue of slavery before the Civil War was a major factor directing the republic to a final political--and necessarily violent--"solution" to that issue.

In 1839, Lewis Ruffner was made a commissioner of a local bank established by the Virginia General Assembly. He and his father-in-law, Joel Shrewsbury, were interlocking directors for the bank and the business salt trust known as "Hewitt, Ruffner & Company." From 1836 to 1840, the salt company was the most successful of all prior business trusts in shoring up salt profits with prices above competitive levels. Lewis Ruffner and Joel Shrewsbury used their dual positions as bankers and bank customers to secure credit on favorable terms for their businesses. The Dickinson & Shrewsbury salt partnership worked voluntarily with Hewitt, Ruffner & Company to keep up the prices of salt. That salt company was in a line of successor companies to the Kanawha Salt Company formed by Joseph Lovell in 1817 with David Ruffner and other leading salt industrialists.[380]

Chapter 9

Lewis Ruffner Rebuilds His Life After The Deaths Of His Beloved Wife And Father

Fateful Days in 1843 Change Lewis Ruffner's Life

Lewis Ruffner operated his father's extensive businesses for 20 years. He lived in his parents' home with his wife and their seven children, ages two to 16 years. All was well until early 1843, when, in less than a month, Lewis Ruffner lost his married life and his businesses. His wife, Elizabeth Ann Dickinson Shrewsbury Ruffner, died on January 5, 1843, and his father, David Ruffner, died three and a half weeks later on February 1, 1843.[381] The date of her death has also been reported as January 23, 1843. The marker for her grave, which is located at Spring Hill Cemetery in Charleston among Shrewsbury graves uses the date of January 5, 1843.

Suddenly, Lewis Ruffner had small children to care for and no businesses to manage. In a will made a number of months before his death, David Ruffner divided his estate among his widow, Anna Brumbach Ruffner, his two sons and two sons-in-law. At law, his daughters could not own property in their names while married. Their husbands took over their property as their trustees. Anna Brumbach Ruffner was given the family home for her lifetime and the people who were held in slavery.

With equal division among his children, David Ruffner rejected the English nobility rule for giving entire estates to the oldest son. The tradition of democratic equal property inheritance, as identified by Alexis de Tocqueville, was used by David Ruffner, as his father had done before him. They and other salt industrialists had democratic sentiments and tried to benefit their heirs equally with no pretense for creating a large estate and a landed aristocracy in the Kanawha Valley. They hoped each heir would be productive with their shares of their estates.

In his will, David Ruffner expressed appreciation for Lewis Ruffner's special work for him and the family by giving Lewis a greater share of the estate because he had lived with him and his wife in their older years, and he had managed well the family's businesses. David Ruffner's widow, Anna Brumbach Ruffner, lived nine more years at the family home in Malden until 1852, when she died at age 86.[382]

As he reordered his life, Lewis Ruffner had his inherited share of his father's businesses to manage, and he needed a governess for his young children.[383] He employed Viola Knapp, an attractive and educated 31-year-old woman from Vermont. She would change his life.

Marriage of Lewis Ruffner and Viola Knapp, a "Yankee" Lady

Lewis Ruffner and Viola Knapp were married in Cincinnati on December 3, 1843, the same year that Lewis' first wife died in January. Born in 1812, Viola Knapp was 15 years younger than Lewis Ruffner, who was 46 years old. Their age difference was much less than the 38-year difference in the ages of his brother with his second bride.[384]

For her wedding, Viola Knapp was chaperoned by Lewis Ruffner's young nephew, W. H. Ruffner. He was the son of Dr. Henry Ruffner, and he became her good friend. She found few friends in Malden. She was never accepted by the Shrewsbury family, including her older step children in part because of her strict "Yankee" ways and, perhaps, because her marriage came so soon after their loved one's death early the same year. Southern mourning periods for men were not long. They were longer for women, at least six months. The months were observed by wearing only black clothing at limited public activities. But a new marriage with a "Yankee" nanny, while living in the marital home, even with a mother-in-law there, might have rubbed against the town's southern and clannish sensibilities.[385]

Viola and Lewis Ruffner are today known in history for their employment and help to young Booker T. Washington. They also helped Christians they held in slavery to formally establish their own church in the Ruffner slave quarters, and later they helped the church to move to town in Malden. Lewis Ruffner was severely injured and permanently disabled from a head injury received in a race riot in Malden when he joined a melee to protect the rights of blacks to go to a hearing for a peace bond. The Ruffners should be celebrated for overcoming the established family idea of white superiority and becoming champions for the rights of freed people to be equal neighbors in Malden.[386]

Lewis Ruffner's Talented Nephew, William H. Ruffner

Dr. Henry Ruffner's son, William Henry Ruffner, or W. H. Ruffner, became Virginia's first state superintendent of public instruction. During Reconstruction in Virginia, in his first year, he had about 130,000 students in almost 2,900 public schools. He was the leading educator in the South. His success was recognized nationwide and copied by other southern states. He helped establish Virginia Tech in 1872 as Virginia Polytechnic Institute and was president of today's Longwood University which he helped start in 1884 as one of Virginia's earliest normal schools to train white women to be teachers. Virginia Tech's highest service honor is the William H. Ruffner Medal.[387]

Dr. W. H. Ruffner became a nationally known author and educator in the North and South. In 1874, while he was state superintendent, Washington & Lee College awarded him an honorary Doctor of Laws degree, the same degree awarded to his father in 1849. The college was renamed in 1870 immediately following the death of its president, the former Confederate General, Robert E. Lee. He had been appointed in the months after Appomattox. President Lee revitalized the college after difficult war years. He supported W. H. Ruffner to be selected by the Virginia General Assembly as the first state superintendent of public schools. [388]

In Malden, W. H. Ruffner visited his grandparents, David Ruffner and Anna Brumbach Ruffner on a regular basis, as a child and young adult. He also visited his father after he returned to Malden in the early 1850s to establish a school called "Mt. Ovis Academy," on lands he owned not far from Malden. William H. Ruffner was born in 1824 while his parents were living near Lexington, Virginia, and his father, Dr. Henry Ruffner, was a professor at Washington College. W. H. Ruffner followed directly in the footsteps of his father by studying at the college and becoming an ordained Presbyterian minister. He married Harriet Ann Gray who was in a wealthy aristocratic family in the Valley of Virginia. He was a life-long, loyal Virginian. Like Dr. Henry Ruffner, he was first a minister and then an educator and free thinker. He opposed slavery before his father's famous 1847 Ruffner Pamphlet. He favored colonization of freed people in Africa, as did many southerners who questioned slavery. As a southern Presbyterian, like his father, W. H. Ruffner opposed slavery generally, but he saw in slavery no evil against God's will. The Ruffners were paternalistic and pragmatic about slavery in their public philosophy and writings. They owned and used slaves to build new industries of salt and coal, creating great wealth for their family but no wealth and little benefit for the families of the people they held in slavery.[389]

He was a gifted young man who handled the business interests of his father in Malden when he was nineteen years old. He rebuilt his father's salt factory after a fire and then sold it in 1845, to the delight of his father, for $25,000.00 to salt industrialist, Jacob Darneal, who was the father of Martha Darneal Shrewsbury and the grandfather of Jacob Darneal Shrewsbury, the young man who sold Booker's family their home in 1869. W. H. Ruffner traveled to collect salt debts for his father in western salt markets, bringing home collections totaling more than $12,000.00. He carried the collections in cash because the banking system in the West was questionable. Western banks and their bank notes were unreliable. He was reliable and self-confident.[390]

In 1849, at age 25, W. H. Ruffner was a chaplain at the University of Virginia. The university faculty wanted a lecture series to improve the reputation of the school. He set up a major seminar of nationally known theologians including his father. When it was publicized that Dr. Henry Ruffner would be one of the lecturers, the state-funded university was attacked for inviting a so-called abolitionist to speak. It was suggested that state funding be withheld from the university until Dr. Ruffner was removed from the program. The initial fire-storm subsided, and the lecture program was a great success. Dr. Ruffner's paper argued forcefully that the presence of miracles on earth was evidence of the existence of God. Chaplain Ruffner was lauded by his peers for greatly improving the academic standing of the university while making a substantial profit from popular nationwide sales of symposium papers.[391]

In 1851, W. H. Ruffner was called to be the minister of the Seventh Presbyterian Church in Philadelphia. He wrote an anonymous paper there criticizing the National Presbyterian Church for failing in its duty to help the poor. It caused a sensation and much debate. He left Philadelphia when his health began to fail. He would go to many springs in Virginia for his health, including White Sulphur Springs, considered the "Queen" of spring resorts.[392]

The Civil War divided the Ruffner family like many families in the border states. W. H. Ruffner was a Confederate. His uncle, Lewis Ruffner, was the Kanawha Valley's leading Unionist. His father, Dr. Henry Ruffner, had been a strong Unionist before the war but became silent in the first year of the war, perhaps because his sons were Confederates. As an 1867 graduate of West Point, Ernest Howard Ruffner, the son of Viola and Lewis Ruffner, would have been one of a very few Ruffners who would be Union supporters during the war. It was a time of family discord across Virginia. The Ruffners' peaceful Mennonite heritage was in the distant past. W. H. Ruffner tried to join the Confederate army, but he was turned away due to poor health and as an ordained minister. His younger brother, David Lewis Ruffner taught at Mercer Academy in Charleston before the Civil War and helped George S. Patton organize the elite Kanawha Riflemen.[393] As the war began, his uncle and aunt, Lewis Ruffner and his "Yankee" wife, Viola Ruffner, and their son at West Point, stood alone publicly among Ruffners as known Union supporters.

Lewis Ruffner in Louisville as Sales Agent for Kanawha Salt

In 1845, less than two years after his second marriage, Lewis Ruffner moved his family to Louisville, Kentucky. He served for twelve years as a sales agent for Malden salt producers. Louisville was a growing western city. It was a dynamic economic and social center on the Ohio River. It was accessible by boat from the Kanawha Valley, and attracted its elite families. By this time, Lewis Ruffner had lost control of his father's separated businesses. Louisville may have given Viola Ruffner some personal relief to be away from family members and neighbors who did not accept her in their aristocratic southern society. She was known to suffer for years under disapproving eyes. In 1844, Lewis Ruffner advertised to sell his inherited salt interests in a Charleston newspaper, *The Kanawha Republican*. A year later Ernest Howard Ruffner was born, the first child of Viola Ruffner and Lewis Ruffner. They named their second child, to grow to maturity, Stella Blanche Ruffner who married Robert H. Wiley, and they would have a family and live on the Ruffner farm for the rest of their lives into the mid-twentieth century. Their granddaughters would be on the Ruffner property until well after the Second World War. [394]

Viola and Lewis Ruffner Return to Malden with New Ideas

Lewis and Viola Ruffner returned to the Ruffner home place in 1857, five years after his mother passed away on November 22, 1852. Lewis Ruffner left Louisville with an evolving view of slavery. He would have been greatly in-fluenced by his gifted "Yankee" wife from Vermont and to some extent by his membership in an emancipation society. On February 22, 1849, *The Louisville Examiner* reported that Lewis Ruffner joined an emancipation society led by Bland Ballard, a well-known attorney who opposed slavery and was a strong supporter of the Union. He was a namesake of his grandfather who was a pioneer in Kentucky. During the war, he was named a federal district judge by Abraham Lincoln, when his predecessor resigned to join the Confederacy.[395]

While Lewis Ruffner was in Louisville, his brother, Dr. Henry Ruffner, moved there for a time and wrote newspaper articles favoring emancipation, some of which were written under assumed names. The influence of Lewis Ruffner's older brother may have been important, although Dr. Henry Ruffner had convinced himself that blacks were inferior beings.[396]

First Page of Kanawha Salt Company Agreement, c.1817 - *Image Courtesy of West Virginia State Archives*

Chapter 10

The Horror Of Slavery

People Adapt to Slavery by Building Families and Kin Networks

The most important story of slavery is about how people held in slavery were able to form and keep relationships with marriages, adoptions and extensive kin networks. Their success is remarkable and admirable. Against many odds, they made family bonds and connected widely to people who were beloved by their immediate families but not always related to them. Those connections extended well past the plantation or farm where they were held in slavery.

The slave family was the center of all life for education, governance, vocational training and socialization, Slave families guided the courting practices, marriage rituals, child-rearing practices, and the division of domestic labor. Slave families grew and were stable in the years following the Revolutionary War. They were the stabilizing social centers of slave economies and the resistance of enslaved persons to abusive slaver control. People held in slavery worked for their families for their diet, clothes, and household goods, all at subsistence level or below.

In the Upper South, slave families often could cultivate small plots for their own goods and craft goods in what spare time they had. They could raise livestock such as pigs and fowl, and make goods for sale to slavers and at market. They could do "overwork" or extra work for goods or payments. Slave economies involved older and young workers. In the Deep South some of these small economies of slaves who were forced to migrate south were reestablished and some were not. The move to the Deep South disrupted slave economies until they were reestablished in some form. Slavery in different regions took on different forms. Any time slavers allowed slave families to have their own goods for market or sale to the slaver, such privileges were taken as entitlements, and there was no turning back without extreme resistance from slave families.[397] Resistance could range from sullen attitudes, work slowdowns, cheating on cotton weights with wet cotton or rocks, or at the extremes with refused whippings, arson and poison. Both slavers and overseers could be the objects of disfavor.[398]

Historian Eugene D. Genovese, in his 1974 book, *Roll Jordan Roll: The World the Slaves Made,* writes extensively about the lives of slaves throughout the South. He uses slave narratives, some plantation records and other sources to describe life for slaves in the quarters and as workers. He found the relationships of slavers and slaves were compatible on the whole with the slavery system designed to force work by slaves for the sole benefit of slavers. Historian Genovese thought that what he called "protection and reciprocity" were keys to the relationship of slaver and slave. He found the system was regular and predictable, and in turn that slaves received "protection and succor" from the slavers, from starvation and loss while living at or below subsistence level. Many people who were considered by slavers as compliant, or "good Negroes," may have given in to the regime of a plantation, but they could explode with anger or plot resistance when perceived rights and duties were violated by slavers. They "did not surrender their will or their honor." They cooperated and "stayed in place so long as their expectations did not suffer a severe jolt and so long as they did not feel betrayed."[399]

Historian Eugene D. Genovese wrote that slavers regularly complained that slaves were not grateful for the subsistent level life that was given to them to live. Some slavers expressed a sense of duty to their slaves. Many slavers claimed a duty to care for older and infirm slaves. One southern writer said that "pauperism is prevented by slavery." A slaver in South Carolina said self-righteously, "It is the slaves who own me. Morning, noon, and night, I'm obliged to look after them, to doctor them, and attend to them in every way.[400]

The conditions of slaves have been regularly compared to other subsistence level workers around the world, and many commentators of the day wrote that slaves were treated as well as others in housing, diet, clothing and medical care, each missing the point that the deprivations of one people should not be used to prove or disprove the deprivations of other peoples. Six authors are cited by Historian Genovese for finding that slaves lived in better housing than poor subsistence level workers in New England, Chile, England, Scotland, and Europe generally. The absence of common slave kitchens is considered proof that slaves had single cabins which would support slave family structures. The families could feed and care for their individual needs. Only Polish poet Julian Ursyn Niemcewicz is cited for his 1798 opinion that the conditions of the slave quarters at George Washington's Mount Vernon were "far more miserable than the poorest of the cottages of our peasants." He is noted to not be fully creditable. Journalist Frederick Law Olmsted wrote that the housing of southern yeoman farmers in the South living in hovels was worse than the single-family housing provided to slaves, and the white farmers who were living in homes were only a notch better off than slaves in the quarters.[401]

There has been research on the demographics of slave families in Virginia. A large plantation called Mt. Airy had detailed records of 668 people enslaved and sales of 121 people –or eighteen percent—away from plantation properties. Its records were studied by Professor Richard S. Dunn at the University of Minnesota. He found the plantation's slaves increased in fifty years from 200 to 700. Of slaves sold, 55 percent were between ten and 30 years old, and 20 percent were over 30 years old. For slaves sold, one-tenth were under ten years old, likely many were sold with their mothers. Frequently girls were separated from their mothers at age nine, before puberty.

Professor Dunn found the life spans of slaves on the Mt. Airy plantation were good except for infants and children who had very, very high mortality rates. Children under ten years old were 48 percent of total deaths. The plantation's high rate of infant and small child mortality is consistent with reports from other plantations where 25 percent of babies died and almost an equal percentage of small children died by age 10, for the shocking total of one-half of children under the age of ten years. The deaths of slaves over 30 years old were 43 percent and only nine percent were from 10 to 30 years old. Eighty percent of women reached menopause. Ninety percent of the women enslaved at Mt. Airy had children, and Professor Dunn found no evidence of forced practices for childbearing.[402]

In 1790, Virginia had 42 percent of all slaves in the nation and its tobacco economy was in decline. There was overpopulation of Virginians held in slavery, and the values of those Virginians were low in 1800. When the cotton industry needed hundreds of thousands of slaves in the Deep South, and its demand for slaves drove sale prices up for multiple decades it created a slave selling commodity industry in the upper south, more in Virginia than any other state. As the cotton and slavery industry grew and became lucrative, a mass migration of slaves was started, and it changed the nature and places of slavery in the nation. Many of the enslaved people who were moved to the Deep South were moved at first as transfers of whole plantations by slavers and their families from Virginia and other Upper South states. As cotton, sugar cane, rice, and tobacco plantations developed across the Deep South, more and more workers were needed and slave traders began handling sales and purchases for wealthy plantation owners, who were able to use less of their personal time for their lucrative businesses.

Virginia's slave livestock commodity industry in Virginia boomed as the value of people to be sold almost doubled, making all people held in slavery more valuable as commodities than for their value as workers. Virginia slave families were encouraged to have and enjoy children. For such commodity sales, control over reproduction was not necessary to create a natural increase in the slave population sufficient to supply thousands of young slaves to plantations in the Deep South. As the migration was forced on hundreds of thousands of people by slave sales and plantation transfers to the Deep South, the slave family structure and kin networks were destabilized. All were threatened and their close-knit members were traumatized by losing a loved one or by the constant threat of losing a loved one. But again, the people held in slavery adapted and continued to be grounded in these family structures and values.

Slave Pen in Alexandria, Virginia – Images Courtesy of the *Library of Congress*

In 1976, Historian Herbert G. Gutman at the City University of New York published an important book on slave families, *The Black Family in Slavery and Freedom, 1750-1925*. It applied statistical analysis to show successful adaptations to the limitations of slavery. In a book review, Lewis Suggs wrote that Professor Gutman's book broke sharply with tradition and signaled a new era in Black Studies. The book used a scientific approach with a stream of statistics and charts and tables. Professor Gutman showed, first, that the black family adapted and survived slavery and, second, that the popular idea of a matriarchal family structure in slavery was not true. It was pure myth. Professor Gutman was also credited with showing how adapted families were agents to transmit values through different generations, establishing definite familial and cultural connections between the eighteenth-century slave family and twentieth-century African American families in the urban South and North.

After emancipation, many people stayed in the areas of their birth and stayed in the countryside generally. They were place-oriented. They did not move far. Only three percent had moved out of the South by 1870. Between the Civil War and the beginning of the twentieth century, the regional distribution of the black population between North and South had changed very little.[403]

Professor Gutman wrote about the importance of established family commitments in slavery as they were continued after emancipation.

> The slaves had created and sustained very important familial and kin sensibilities and ties. The choices so many made immediately upon their emancipation and before they had substantive rights in the law did not result from new ideas learned in freedom and were not the reflection of beliefs learned from owners. Such behavior had its origins in the ways in which Africans and their Afro-American descendants had adapted to enslavement.[404]

Professor Gutman studied adapted black family unions and kin networks in the Upper South and Lower South. Slaves made families with blood relatives and other favorite persons who were included in expanded kin networks. He wrote that most historians study and record what slavers and their society did to people they held in slavery rather than what reactions and adaptations those people used to endure and survive under such treatment in a society that denied their humanity. This approach to the study presents a valuable, essential viewpoint.

Professor Gutman researched extensively through a variety of statistical data and made findings about the adaptations of people held in slavery for long standing family structures which they continued after slavery. While documentation of slave life is very limited before the Civil War, Herbert G. Gutman obtained valuable data on slave marriages and kin networks from post-slavery marriage registration questionnaires in Mississippi and from a variety of information on slavery in Virginia and North Carolina. He also studied child and adult naming customs of slaves, which he found to show the strong presence of fathers in slave family structures.[405]

For persons held in slavery, marriages were solemn commitments. Marriage ceremonies were used for some but not for all unions. In the District of Columbia, only half of the people held in slavery used marriage ceremonies.

Conventional Christian ceremonies with ministers, black and white, were used along with more traditional ceremonies like jumping the broom, which had a spiritual significance. Some slaves used a blanket ceremony where two blankets would be placed side by side symbolizing a family union.[406]

Naming customs were found by Professor Gutman to reinforce kin networks and revealed fathers to be very much involved in the lives of their children. The names "Uncle" and "Aunt" were used to greet, address and refer to adults who were respected, whether or not they were blood relatives. These names expanded kin networks to friends of the family. Slaves chose names of fathers and other blood relatives for male children, but, interestingly, few female names were taken from slave mothers. The common use of father names "strongly disputes frequent assertions that assign a negligible role to slave fathers." Fathers were often separated from their children by the limitations of slavery but many fathers took pride in and cared for their children, while adapting to the forced limitations of slavery. Most slavers did not seem to be involved in child naming, but some did. Most slaves did not take the names of recent slavers but they would sometimes use a prior slaver's family name as a way of connecting to or commemorating a prior kin network.[407]

In Virginia and North Carolina, Professor Gutman found many long-lasting, committed relationships in the counties with information available. It is noted that slaves were held on small farms across Virginia, and it has been thought that the closeness to the slaver family may have encouraged longer-lasting relationships and more control by slaves of their day-to-day lives.

Professor Wilma A. Dunaway at Virginia Polytechnic Institute and State University found from her review of post-war manuscripts by former slaves in the southern Appalachian region, that slaves on small farms were more often physically punished and abused than those on large plantations. She wrote that such a finding on small operations had been confirmed in slave studies around the world. In the southern Appalachian region manuscripts, ex-slaves reported that their slavers were obsessive about punishment. The people held in slavery were punished nearly five times more frequently than people in slavery elsewhere in the nation. Booker and his family lived on a small slaver farm in Hales Ford, and he saw his uncle strapped to a tree and whipped.[408]

Professor Gutman found in counties with large plantations many slave relationships were long-lasting, and that long-lasting relationships were not limited to slaves with elite skills, but were present with field hands and farm laborers. In the Lower South, where Virginia slaves were sent when "sold south," he found many slaves who had been in committed relationships that were forced into separation by their migration south.

For Mississippi, Professor Gutman studied marriage questionnaire responses from freed people in over 4,600 slave marriages registered there after the Civil War. He found that slaves reported family racial mixing with whites to have occurred with ancestors who would have been living in the 1700s and early 1800s in the Upper South, including Virginia. But racial mixing in the Deep South after migration was much less.[409]

Slave families were often generous to other slaves and readily adopted orphaned children. Booker's parents adopted a young boy after they moved to Malden. The people held in slavery were generous and cared for children--their own and others. They would give slower workers some of their own goods so it would not be obvious that they were less productive and could be punished. This was called "evening up" to keep slower workers from "coming up short." They helped other slaves, including runaway slaves. They would slip food to underfed slaves on nearby plantations.[410]

The slave family was the center of resistance to whites, and great care was taken in all interactions with whites. Persons held in slavery had personal codes of honor. They showed respect to other slaves, and they did not report on other slaves. Slave children were taught not to listen to adult slaves, so they could not be interrogated or accidentally tell slavers what was said or being thought by slaves in the quarters. Also, children were trained to spy on the slaver family to know what they were planning or what problems might be presented to the slaves. Children could also be used to give misleading information to whites. Violence by slaves against slaves would sometimes occur, especially if a slave was discovered to be a "traitor" to the slave community. [411]

Slaves would respond to slavers very differently from how they interacted with each other. Open rebellion was certain to be defeated, so indirect resistance was used such as work slow-downs, destruction of tools and property, and, at time, arsons. Kin networks discouraged running away and other forms of resistance to the demands of slavery. Running away was not a good alternative for most slaves, since abject loneliness accompanied escaped slaves who left nurturing families and kin networks. Eighty percent of runaway slaves were between the ages of 16 and 35. Older slaves rarely sought to escape.[412]

The lack of open resistance and defiance was taken by slavers, and by history writers until recently, to show acceptance of a supposed mutual benefit in the slave relationship. There was no mutuality in that relationship, and the lack of resistance shows how effective cruelty was in the slave system and how slaves were able to adapt to protect their families, which was their number one and perhaps only priority while they were held in slavery. Some whites thought the failure of slave husbands and fathers to directly resist the restraints of slavery in regard to women and children in their families and kin networks showed a weakness of character and courage. But such an unfair, harsh assessment ignores the impossible choices that slaves-- men and women--had in trying to protect against separation and loss of loved ones or against the will and whim of evil slavers, especially when whites considered any such questioning of their authority as "impudence" --the most serious offense in slavery.

Observations of Slavery in 1856 in the Coastal States

Frederick Law Olmsted, who became the premier landscape architect in America, designing Central Park in Manhattan and the grounds of the Biltmore Estate in Asheville North Carolina, traveled in 1856 through the Coastal States of the South as a journalist and social critic. He wrote that some people thought the steady reduction in slave populations in old slave states of the Upper South like in Virginia could grow so great with a progressive slave trade for cotton production, that it "would gradually draw off all of the slaves from Virginia and that state would thus be redeemed to freedom."[413]

He viewed people in slavery and wrote that they were clothed and fed as well as most any working people, so he was told. He was told that slave men were generally furnished three shirts, one blanket, and one felt hat. They were given coat and trousers for winter and a jacket for summer possibly. They received two pairs of strong shoes or perhaps a pair of boots and lighter shoes for harvest. Women had "two dresses of striped cotton, three shifts, two pairs of shoes, etc." Other commentators have noted that clothing was less generous than his description. He noted that children wore long shirts, and he considered medical care for people held in slavery to be good.[414] It is difficult to know if his description of the clothing allowances and medical care were fair assessments sufficient to support broad generalizations of treatment across the south, especially for field hands and rural workers.

The costs of maintaining slaves was estimated to be much less than the costs to board free labor. For a "first rate, hard-working" slave, the board would be about $30.00 per year. His clothing would be about $10.00 per year and his food $20.00 per year or five-and one-half cents a day. Traveler Olmsted noted that a Maryland slaver estimated his costs to maintain a working slave totaled about $45.00 per year.[415] In contrast, he estimated the lowest paid free agricultural laborer had board costs of at least 21 cents per day or $1.50 a week or $78.00 per year. In the end, he was confident that freed workers in the North were "ordinarily better fed and clothed" than slave workers in the South.

Traditionally, the written history of Virginia slavery has presented the idea that day-to-day slave life was not all that bad. Slaves were given food and clothes and a dry place to sleep. They also were able to observe and learn in a "civilized society" as history writers stressed over and over for the first century after the Civil War. It is true that Virginians held in slavery were considered to have better treatment than the people forced to work on cotton plantations, many of whom had been sold from Virginia.[416] But it cannot be fairly said the lives of people held in slavery were in effect "not all that bad." People held in slavery lived with terror in horror.

On his travels, enslaved people were observed to be fast asleep on the floors of the hallways in his hotel wearing their usual clothes. He was advised by a "gentleman, that negroes never wanted to go to bed; they always preferred to sleep upon the floor." He was disturbed to be told of cruel treatment of people in the area. One person was whipped to death and several others were maimed for life, but he was assured that the "whole community were indignant when such things occurred, and any man guilty of them would be without associates, except of similar character."[417] Such fictions were needed for slavers' guilt to help them rise above the shame they lived with everyday.

The demographic shifts in slave populations were notable. They changed the nation's economic, demographic and political landscape. In 1800, 75 percent of all enslaved Americans lived on the Atlantic Coast between the Delaware River and the Savannah River, but by 1860 after sales and forced transfers to the Deep South of hundreds of thousands of people, that number fell by almost a half to 40 percent.[418] As export sales grew more and more profitable, Virginia investors could finance new industries and they became less dependent on plantation crop production. But they also became more and more dependent on the state's slave commodity industry.

The prices for people sold as observed by Frederick Law Olmsted in 1856, help explain the dramatic shifts in slave populations from the Upper South to the Deep South. Men 18 to 25 years old were sold for $950 to $1,300 depending on their overall condition. It is noted that homes and farms could be purchased for these sale amounts. Boys who were five feet tall were priced $850 to $950 and small boys only four feet tall were sold for $375 to $450. Young women were $700 to $1,000, and girls who were five feet tall were sold for $750 to $850. If they were only four feet tall, girls were sold for $350 to $452.[419] Especially beautiful young women or girl slaves could be sold for much, much higher prices to slave traders who would sell them to be prostitutes and slaver mistresses. As a system of cruelty, slavery could not be limited by Christian values.

Thousands of Virginians Separated from Their Slave Families and Friends

Forced separations of family members and members of kin networks affected millions of people across the Upper South. The separations were used to signal and protect the absolute authority of slavers while assuring the "perfect" submission of slaves. The fear of a loved one being sold away to the slave trade paralyzed most people held in slavery, preventing any form of open resistance or mere questioning of slaver demands and expectations. Forced separations were the ultimate tool to mandate obedience in family groups.

Professor Ira Berlin wrote broadly that, as "coffles of slaves trudged from the seaboard South by the thousands, slave spouses came to understand the fragility of the marriage bond, and slave parents came to realize that their teenaged children could disappear never to be seen again." He estimated that sales to the Deep South shattered approximately one slave marriage in three and separated one-fifth of all children under fourteen from one or both of their parents.[420]

Professor Gutman studied carefully in detail the forced separations of slave spouses and children. Separations could be brought on for a number of reasons. Thousands of slaves were sold away in the slave trade from their loved ones for slaver debts or profits. Others were forced to move in transfers of plantation operations with groups of slaves. These forced group transfers were more common in the early nineteenth century when slavers in the Upper South were developing new cotton plantations. The sales of slaves into the slave trade are the story lines of *Uncle Tom's Cabin* and the song, "My Old Kentucky Home." In each, a beloved slave is sold-down-river to sugar-cane fields from Kentucky because his slaver had debts to pay.[421] People held in slavery had market value. They could be mortgaged for their own purchase price or for purchases of other property like land or business goods. When debt was a problem, slaves were the assets that could be relied on to cover the debt.

Professor Gutman did not have data to study the forced separations of children from their parents and family groups. He found no evidence of forced childbearing. But the anguish and despair over separation from children was obvious without numerical proof. These separations were damaging to the children and their families.

These were adults, not children, being separated by sale.... If the number of children sold from individual families also was known, the percentage of slave families, not slave marriages, broken by the sale of any members would greatly increase.[422]

In his study of forced slave separations, Professor Gutman found half of the slaves who were at least 40 years old during the Civil War had been separated voluntarily or involuntarily. For slaves over 20 years old, nearly one in nine were separated from a spouse by force. The number of forced separations rose for persons over 30 years of age, to one in four for men and one in five for women. He found that for young slaves during the Civil War, about one in ten had experienced juvenile separations showing, that just before the war, slavery continued to retain what he called "its grimmest quality," which was the breakup of families and the damage inflicted on husbands and wives, parents and children.[423] With one in ten slave marriages ended by forced separations, Professor Gutman wrote,

What percentages of slave marriages...had to be ended by force or sale to make slaves understand owners' power? Ten percent would have been more than adequate. [424]

Professor Gutman explained that while his limited data showed a majority of slaves were not forced to separate from a *spouse*, the cruelty of forced separation was nevertheless overwhelming to those spouses who were subjected to it. Worse, he did not have available data on the *hundreds of thousands of children* who were separated early from their parents and kin networks. Their forced separations could come at a full range of young ages.

Hundreds of Thousands of Virginians
are sent to the Deep South

Virginia exported more people than any other state. Virginia had a very high population of slaves, and the natural increase in that population meant that young slaves, more men than women, could be sold south as commodities for profit. Two-thirds of the persons sold were male. Sales of slaves outside of plantation groups usually involved men sold alone without spouses or family. Most people who were sold south were from Virginia and other Chesapeake Bay states.[425]

From 1800 to 1860, perhaps one million people held in slavery in the Upper South were taken out of their homes and moved to Deep South plantations to work in booming cotton, sugar-cane and tobacco plantations. The nature of the migration has been debated by historians, whether it was by sales into the slave trade or by transfers of plantation groups. All agree that both forms of migration were used. The number in the slave trade versus the number in plantation transfers affect how much trauma was inflicted by the migration. Sales into the slave trade meant contacts with loved ones were terminated—forever.

Early in the nineteenth century, thousands of slaves were transferred to the Deep South in groups by planters seeking more profitable businesses in the West, for themselves or family members. But after plantations were well established, and more and more slaves were needed to work expanding operations after 1820, individual slaves and small groups of slaves were regularly purchased from slave traders in the slave trade that was disdained by most slavers but it was used for investments and to pay debts on a regular basis. These sales in Virginia made its slave livestock industry boom in the last 30 years before the Civil War.

Professor Ira Berlin of the University of Maryland found that a minority of planters moved with their slaves to the Deep South. He found they were a small part of the migration south, because most slavers relied on "smugglers, kidnappers and traders to build their labor force."[426] He explained the forced migration of slaves as involving two types of transfers, one by plantation groups and one by separate commodity sales to slave traders.

Hundreds of thousands of slaves marched west with their owners, their owners' kin or their agents as the shock troops of the massive expansion of cotton and sugar production in the states of the lower South. Seeing opportunities westward, some prominent planters transferred their entire retinue of slaves to new plantation sites. Others, perhaps a bit more cautious, moved with a few chosen hands—generally young men—to begin the creation of new empires of cotton and cane. Once settled, additional slaves followed. Through the first two decades of the nineteenth century, planters in transit carried most of their slaves with them to the interior. Having brought their own slaves South, some slave masters—wanting to augment their labor force—journeyed back to the seaboard to purchase others. A few shuttled back and forth, buying a few slaves at every turn. But over time the westward-moving slaveowner surrendered control of slave transit to a new group of merchants whose sole business became the trade in human beings. Although the balance between the two trades was forever changing, it fell heavily in favor of the slave traders. The number of black-belt and delta planters who returned to the seaboard to purchase slaves declined, leaving slave traders in command. During the course of the nineteenth century, traders carried roughly two-thirds of the slaves from the seaboard to the interior.[427]

The trade for individual slave sales boomed in the 1850s. In 1852, there were 28 slave traders listed in a Richmond directory and others in related fields. By 1860 the numbers increased to 18 traders, 18 slave sales agents, and 33 auctioneers. The domestic slave trade grew so rapidly across the South in the 1850s that there was a "Negro fever" for slave investments. In 1859 to 1860, as much as $150 million was paid to purchase people, or about four percent of the overall value of the four million people held in slavery at the start of the Civil War.[428]

In most all slave exporting states, there were no restrictions on selling slaves separate from family members, even babies, toddlers, and small children. Slave traders purchased and sold single small children on a regular basis. They advertised for children with ages of six, seven, eight, and nine years old. Small children at these ages were expected to work at some labor to help pay for their living costs. It has been written that the separations of children from their slave families were generally at times that were age-appropriate for any children to leave home. These advertised child ages are not appropriate ages for children to leave home even for children in the nineteenth century. Most children who worked in these age groups in the Victorian Era were working with family members, often on a piece work basis to increase the family income, not to live independently. Also, most children and adults who were forced away from their homes, lost all possible contact with their families. Once a person went into the slave trade there was little hope to reconnect to family and kin networks. [429]

Transfers of slave operations to the West were important in the early years of growth of the cotton, sugar cane, and tobacco industries. But after plantations were developed, many of the people forced into the migration were sold through slave traders as single person sales or small group sales. These sales by slave traders were dominant in the thirty years before the Civil War after the time that transfers of whole plantation groups were common. In later years, there was a "Negro fever" for investments in people bought and sold in the slave trade, after people became valuable as commodities. This was especially true in Virginia which became the leading slave exporting state.[430]

In Virginia, every sale of an individual into the slave trade created hardship for the family left behind. Likewise, the removal of a plantation group of slaves meant forced separations for many slaves in and out of the group, because many family members were living on multiple farms and plantations in their areas in eastern Virginia. With so many slave operations, it was common in eastern Virginia for people who were held in slavery to have spouses on different plantations and farms.[431] Booker T. Washington's mother, Jane Ferguson, married Washington Ferguson who lived on a nearby farm. He was far away from home when leased to the Kanawha Valley salt factories. Transfers of a plantation group would affect many relationships of the separated people. When kin networks are considered, it can be appreciated how far the pain and loss could extend beyond the separated person's immediate family.

From 1826 to 1834, Virginians were about 38 percent of all people sold in the slave markets of New Orleans and Natchez. When the percentages of sales for the other two Chesapeake states were added to Virginia's percentage, the number grew to 71 percent. Slave selling in Virginia was spread throughout the eastern part of the state with many counties sending enslaved people to Louisiana slave markets for sale in the years from 1829 to 1831. It is estimated that over the decade of the 1820s, Virginia exported 76,000 slaves to the Deep South. Maryland and the District of Columbia exported 35,000 slaves.[432] Estimates for the number of people forced to migrate in the six decades before the Civil War range between 700,000 and one million.[433]

It has been contended that most of the transfers were with slavers moving their operations west to more fertile lands, limiting the sales of individuals into the slave trade to as little as 16 percent. That claim has not been supported with statistical evidence. In 1974, Economist Robert William Fogel and Professor Stanley L. Engerman stirred controversy on the issue of plantation transfers versus individual slave trade sales in their book, *Time on the Cross: The Economics of American Negro Slaves*. They calculated that 835,000 slaves were moved to the Deep South and only 16 percent, or about 2,500 slaves per year, were sold in the slave trade from the entire Upper South. They asserted, but did not substantiate with statistics or other information, that the other 84 percent were sent south in plantation transfers-some 701,000 slaves. Writers in the nineteenth century during the mass migration discussed freely the high numbers of sales in the slave trade and few refer to plantation transfers. No historian before or since has agreed with their estimates. It is an important point because it improperly minimizes the effect of the separations on slave families and kin networks by what was called the "Second Middle Passage."[434]

The numbers of people sent to the Deep South and West have been discussed and disputed.[435] While both types of migration were used, it is difficult to know exact numbers for each type. It is a crucial finding because plantation transfers would be less disruptive, painful and controlling of slaves left behind than individual, perhaps sudden sales into the slave trade where the people sold would be lost to their loved ones forever. They would have no record or information on the loved one's condition or whereabouts. Plantation transfers would be much easier for the slaves left behind. They would know generally where their loved ones were sent and with whom. The person forced to migrate would be with people they knew, and they would be comforted to know that the people left behind might know where they were settled. It is important for enslaved Virginians because about 85 percent of the people sent south were from the East Coast States of Virginia, Maryland and the Carolinas. If slave groups and families were kept together and not sold individually in the slave trade, the horror of forced separations decried by many historians, including Professor Herbert G. Gutman, would be less. Professor Gutman found there was no evidence to support the Fogel-Engerman precise claims for 84 percent plantation transfers and 16 percent sales into the slave trade. Professor Gutman wrote a book, *Slavery and the Numbers Game: A Critique of Time on the Cross* to directly challenge in detail the findings of Fogel and Engerman. [436]

Sale to a slave trader was a death-like experience for the people left behind. It meant that a loved one could be stolen away at any time and marched in a coffle to be auctioned, perhaps multiple times, to unknown slavers in unknown places, to do unknown, heavy gang labor in unhealthy and life-threatening jobs and perhaps with forced immoral duties and death punishments. That is the outline of the fictional story of *Uncle Tom's Cabin* that could become real life for every enslaved person any day of their lives in slavery. Most white southerners did not like the book and one writer called the cruelty displayed in the book, essentially a "falsehood."[437]

While it is hoped the horror of separated and sold persons in the slave trade was in fact much less than what others have found, it appears an estimate of 2,500 sales for all slaves sold from the Upper South in one year is much too low. The successful slave trade firm of Franklin & Armfield alone sold at its peak "as many as a hundred slaves" every two weeks, which could be as many as 2,600 people in a year. The migration from Virginia was estimated by Professor Kenneth M. Stampp to have been 300,000 in the three decades between 1830 and 1860, with the majority of people, he thought, to have been sold in the slave trade and not by plantation transfers.[438] With so many people being sent from Virginia in those years, it seems impossible 84 percent could have been by plantation transfers.

The analysis by Economist Fogel and Professor Engerman fails to account for the slave trade sales by individual slave traders and firms and the many sales in market cities other than New Orleans, including Natchez, Richmond, Norfolk, Alexandria, Baltimore, and Charleston, South Carolina, where sales could have been by or to ultimate plantation users who may have traveled to exporting states to get good bargains on price or better commodity choice selections. Slaves as commodities were major investments.

In all, the numbers indicate the slave trade was much greater than 16 percent of all persons relocated to the Deep South. An estimate by Historian Ira Berlin that 67 percent of the sales were in the slave trade from 1820 to 1860 seems more appropriate for a society where slave coffles could march up to two hundred slaves, likely for both types of migrations. Professor Wilma A. Dunaway estimated from ex-slave narratives that about one-third of slaves were sold in the slave trade, which would be double the estimates of Economist Fogel and Professor Engerman. Her estimate would total about 270,000 to 330,000 people from the Upper South. Annual exports of Virginians from 1830 to 1860 have been estimated to total between 6,000 and 9,000. These three decades are in the time when Historian Berlin estimates that plantations had made slavers very rich, and they began to let slave traders take over their slave procurement practices.

These numbers on plantation transfers and sales in the slave trade do not include the extensive sales of slaves intra-state in Virginia, Kentucky, and the Carolinas, or the major Virginia business of leasing slaves to work away from their slavers and families. Historian Bancroft estimated that Richmond had 5,000 slaves leased for work in its area, and the state as a whole had 15,000 slaves leased. In the Kanawha Valley in 1850, there were 1,500 or about half of all persons held in slavery there. They were most all leased far away from their homes and families in eastern Virginia. For leased persons in all of the southern slave states, there were likely 60,000 people working under lease at any one time before the Civil War. Finally, it is fair to add that these numbers do not include the estimated 600 convict slaves that Virginia exported to the South from 1800 to 1850.[439]

Economist Fogel and Professor Engerman cite little support for their 16 percent estimate. Most notably, their analysis fails to cite any supporting evidence for their extreme calculations, through slave narratives, or news accounts, novels, popular songs, stories, tax records, demographic information, or other materials to support their contention that plantation transfers of over 700,000 people in fact occurred without the slave trade being involved in those plantation transfers. There is considerable evidence to the contrary.

In 1832, Thomas Dew, a professor at the College of William & Mary, took pride in the sale of thousands of slaves from Virginia. He extolled slave sales into the slave trade as a "source of wealth," and without slavery, Virginia would be a "desert." He contended that most of the slaves who were sent out of Virginia were sold as commodities in the domestic slave trade. He did not refer to plantation transfers.[440] Professor Dew wrote:

> Virginia is, in fact, a negro raising State for other states, she produces enough for her own supply and six thousand for sale…. Virginians can raise [them] cheaper than they can buy; in fact, it is one of their greatest sources of profit. In many of the other slaveholding States, this is not the case, and consequently, the same care is not taken to encourage matrimony and the rearing of children.[441]

Many white Virginians in slave times did not like the idea that the state was rearing slaves for market as livestock.[442] They considered owning slaves, who were very costly to purchase and maintain, to be clear indicia of a higher and more sophisticated class. Slaves were worth individually more than many homes and farms of poor whites. If the cost of a slave were on average $700, the purchasing power of that sum today would be in the range of about $20,000.00.[443]

Professor Thomas Dew estimated that the number of slaves sold out of state to the slave trade was 6,000, but Historian Frederic Bancroft found the number was almost double the Dew estimate in the 1830s. Professor Bancroft thought the ten-year annual exports of Virginia slaves in the 1830s averaged 11,800 for a total of 117,938 slaves. Slave sales were less in the 1840s and 1850s, despite "Negro fever," when slavery was considered a good, safe investment. For example, in 1860, one estate after the death of the slaver was able to sell 566 people for $580,150 or an average of $1,025 per person. In all, Historian Bancroft calculated that in the thirty years before the Civil War, Virginia slavers alone sold 281,142 slaves with average annual sales of 9,371 slaves for the antebellum period.[444]

Thomas Jefferson Randolph, a contemporary of Thomas Dew, decried the rearing of slaves in Virginia for the purpose of sale as commodities. He did not refer to plantation transfers as significant in his time in the 1830s. He said the slave trade was dishonorable to the patriots of Virginia.

> It is a practice, and an increasing practice in parts of Virginia, to rear slaves for market. How can an honorable mind, a patriot, and a lover of his country, bear to see this ancient dominion, rendered illustrious by the noble devotion and patriotism of her sons in the cause of liberty, converted into one grand menagerie where men are to be reared for

market like oxen for the shambles.[445]

Slaves sold into the slave trade forever lost all contact with loved ones, and their loved ones left in the Upper South would never again know anything about the sold persons—where, what and how they were doing and if they survived the long and dangerous trails of tears away from the Upper South.

Historian Winfield H. Collins asserted with little support in his 1904 book, *The Domestic Slave Trade of the Southern States*, that about three-fifths or sixty percent of the slaves sent to the Deep South were moved in plantation transfers and not through the slave trade. His opinion relies solely on an 1836 news article in the *Virginia Times* that three-fifths or 60 percent of Virginia slaves migrated in plantation transfers. That is inconsistent with the opinions of Professor Thomas Dew and Thomas Jefferson Randolph which were made earlier in the same decade as the news article.[446]It is also contrary to the careful analysis of Dr. Henry Ruffner.

Dr. Henry Ruffner wrote about the issue in the Ruffner Pamphlet he published in 1847. The pamphlet was titled, "Address to the People of West Virginia; Shewing that Slavery is Injurious to the Public Welfare, and That It may be Gradually Abolished, Without Detriment to the Rights and Interests of Slaveholders by a Slaveholder of West Virginia."

Dr. Ruffner, like Professor Thomas Dew and Thomas Jefferson Randolph a decade before, makes no reference whatsoever to plantation transfers. He wrote, "The high price of Negroes in the South caused many to be sold out" of the Shenandoah Valley. He complained that slavery had become a commodity industry and oversupply would destroy western Virginia unless slavery there would be abolished. In the pamphlet, he publicized the term, "West Virginia." Dr. Ruffner envisioned the end of slave sales when the Deep South cotton and slavery industry became saturated with slaves in a declining industry, with lower and lower cotton prices and profits. From the 1850 Census, it was estimated that the Deep South had 1.8 million people in the cotton and slavery industry with 420,000 people held in slavery on plantations of 50 workers or more. Dr. Ruffner saw the end of slave trade sales and total stagnation of the Virginia economy with overpopulation of persons held in slavery. He referred to them as being treated like "woolly-headed" livestock animals. [447]

> The price of cotton has regulated the price of Negroes in Virginia; and so it must continue to do; because slave labor is unprofitable here, and nothing keeps up the price of slaves but their values as marketable commodities in the South. Eastern Negroes and Western cattle are alike in this, that, if the market abroad go down or be closed, --both

sorts of animals, the horned and the woolly-headed, become a worthless drug at home. The fact is, that our Eastern brethren must send off, on any terms, the increase of their slaves, because their impoverished country cannot sustain even its present stock of Negroes. We join not the English and American abolition cry about "slave-breeding," in East Virginia, as if it were a chosen occupation, and therefore a reproachful one. It is no such thing, but a case of dire necessity, and many a heartache does it cost the good people there.[448]

In 1856, Frederick Law Olmsted wrote in his travels about the importance of the slave trade to Virginia slavers. He said, with high prices in the slave trade, people held in slavery became "less productive, but more valuable." It made slavers treat enslaved Virginians better for better sale prices. This aspect of the livestock commodity industry made the costs of care higher. It also changed the type of punishment used against slaves, because scars on the backs of slaves reduced their value for sale. Traveler Olmsted found in general that Virginians held in slavery as "transferrable property" were "better fed, clothed, and sheltered, and the pliant strap and scientific paddle have been substituted as instruments of discipline, for the scoring lash and bruising cudgel." He judged Virginia as a slave society and wrote that he would not "recommend any one in the free States to choose in Virginia a residence for a family."[449]

The long view of history shows that many Virginia slavers during the 40 years before the Civil War sold thousands of people each year into the slave trade, creating an industry for commodity sales for use by others, whether or not childbearing was unfairly encouraged. With the Deep South growing rapidly, the value of slaves in Virginia greatly increased. Also, the end of the international slave trade in 1807 helped increase the values of Virginia slaves. By 1830, slavery was big business in eastern Virginia. Enslaved Virginians became investments, and their value increased, creating a ready market for what were called a special brand of "Virginia Negroes." The prices paid for slaves fluctuated over time. In the 1830s, prices were as high as $1,250 per person and fell to below $700 in the 1840s, then rose again in the 1850s to as much as $1,450.[450] For thousands of slaves each year in Virginia, their sale values grow significantly, especially young slaves from ages ten to 30 years. That made sales to the Deep South attractive to Virginia slavers, and it set their path to a civil war to protect their markets to sell slaves there.

Economist Robert William Fogel in his 1989 follow up book, *Without Consent, Without Contract*, returned only briefly, to the issue of forced family separations in the slave trade. He conceded fully on the issue of plantation transfers by his silence. He cites to the works of three historians who do not support his earlier very low estimates of sales into the slave trade.

First, Professor Herbert Gutman is acknowledged for his research and analysis in his 1976 book, *The Black Family in Slavery and Freedom 1750-1925*. It showed vast destruction of slave families by forced separations of spouses and children whose numbers were unknown. Professor Gutman wrote an article in the *Journal of Negro History* in January 1975 which was published that year as a book, and reprinted in 2003, *Slavery and the Numbers Game: A Critique of Time on the Cross*. He rushed to publish his objections to the Fogel-Engerman estimates on plantation transfers because they were so contrary to his long-studied and statistically-supported research. Professor Gutman wrote there was not "a shred of evidence (or even argument)" … to explain about how Economist Fogel arrived at the statistic of 84 percent. That assessment is correct.[451] Economist Fogel was lauded for his first book for its statistical approach to slave issues, but on the key issue of sales into the slave trade, he failed to use the statistical analysis he proposed for such issues.

Second, Historian John W. Blassingame is cited by Economist Fogel for his the 1972 book, *The Slave Community: Plantation Life in the Antebellum South*, where it was found that forced migration through the slave trade was so extensive that a full one-third of slave unions were "dissolved by masters" using the slave trade, for business profits valued over marriage bonds.[452]

Third, Historian Eugene D. Genovese was cited for his 1974 book, *Roll Jordan Roll*, where his emphasis was on each slave's ever-present terror that a loved one would be sold into the slave trade. The terror paralyzed people into "perfect" submission. It was the very essence of the Horror of Slavery. The threat of a sale to a slave trader was almost as controlling and punishing as the reality of the sale itself. He thought the numbers of persons actually sold in the slave trade were fewer than what others calculated but the data "do not permit precise measurement." He wrote that the looming uncertainty created by the "potential for forced separation—whatever the ultimate measure of its realization--struck fear into the quarters, especially in the slave exporting Upper South."[453] Like the torture of a whip, the threat of sale could be as penetrating as the lash.

Demographic Changes in Virginia's Slave Population

Regular exports of Virginians lowered the natural increase in their population dramatically. There were so many young Virginians held in slavery who were forced to migrate south that Virginia's demographic increase in the state's large slave population was very small. In the 1790s, the growth rate for the slave population in Virginia was 20 percent, and by 1850, it was only four percent, so low that it barely continued to sustain the established slave population. North Carolina and South Carolina, which earlier had been importing people for work production, joined in the lucrative slave migrations and experienced similar slave population decreases.[454]

Exports created a migration out of Virginia so great that the state lost one-half the usual increase in its slave population from 1820-1850. For that thirty-year period, the increase was 64,000 people, whereas the increase in the 30 years before 1820, was over double that number at 156,000 people. The numbers are surprising when compared to white population increases in the same two periods. The white increase was larger in the thirty years from 1820 to 1850 than before. In that thirty-year period, the white increase was 290,000 compared to 161,000 in the prior 30 years.[455]

These numbers show major population changes in Virginia and in the Deep South. If sales of people continued at a rapid pace, it was speculated that the slave trade might take away enough Virginians to allow the state to abolish slavery.[456] With one-third of the state's population held in slavery--one-half million people still residing in eastern Virginia in 1860--such a fortuitous and peaceful end of slavery there seems to have been at best many, many decades away. The pool of young slaves used for Virginia's livestock commodity industry was far from being depleted at the time of the Civil War. In fact, protection of its lucrative livestock industry was a substantial cause of Virginia's joining the Confederacy.

Slaves Submit to Protect Loved Ones from Forced Separation

Out of the turmoil and fear of their sale and move South, many enslaved men and women were forced away from their homes and families. They had to adapt to new lives in the Deep South, most by starting over with new spouses and new kin networks. The forced migration of slaves caused terrible dislocations, upset, grief and losses. When people were sold as commodities to the slave trade, they were cut off from "nearly every human attachment." The high numbers of persons sold, especially young people, would have been devastating to them and to their families left behind.[457]

The essential quality of marriage known today is the security of permanent commitment. That quality of security was denied to spouses and families in slavery. It was replaced by fear and dread of immediate loss of loved ones. For people held in slavery, there were no protections for their chosen lifetime commitments. Slaves were financial investments that could be bought or sold for profits or debts. Family commitments of parents could not extend to children, grandchildren, nieces and nephews when they became valuable for sale. While personal feelings and commitments of slaves were genuine and necessary adaptations, they could never create a secure foundation of familial relationships. For slavers the term "slave marriage" was an oxymoron if the term included a reasonable expectation for secure relationships.[458] It did not.

The threat of sale of a loved one south was the ultimate tool of slaver control over all slave families and kin networks at home. Their members lived with the ever-present torture of the possibility of sale of a loved one to the slave trade. Parents and spouses could not protect others or themselves from most any form of abuse when that threat was hanging over their heads. It was always hanging over their heads. As one slaver advised his overseers "nothing but the lash or fear of being sold kept self-willed," stubborn, or resistant slaves "straight."[459]

There also was the clear benefit to slavers in being able to easily sell to the slave trade any spirited slaves who might cause trouble. Professor Wilma A. Dunaway estimated that in the southern Appalachian region about ten percent of slave sales were for the purpose of removing a slave who resisted authority or posed a threat to the slaver community.[460]

One of the great terrors of any parent's life is the separation or loss of children at any time. Slaves would say that the person lost by sale to the slave trade was "stolen." John Greenleaf Whittier exposes the pain and trauma of a Virginian mother losing her child to the mass migration to cotton, sugar cane, and rice plantations, "where the slave-whip ceaseless swings" in his poem, "The Farewell of a Virginia Slave Mother to her daughters, sold into Southern Bondage."

> GONE, gone--sold and gone,
> To the rice-swamp dank and lone,
> Where the slave-whip ceaseless swings,
>
> ...
>
> Where sickly sunbeams glare
> Through the hot and misty air--
> Gone, gone--sold and gone,
> To the rice-swamp dank and lone,
> From Virginia's hills and water;
> Woe is me, my stolen daughters.[461]

The denial of stable, enduring family structures is a fundamental Horror of Slavery. Informal, hoped for, prayed for, families could not withstand the forces of white domination that could with no notice separate them from their loved ones. Committed unions and networks of adults in slavery cannot fairly be said to make slavery benign or mutually beneficial. They made slave life bearable by a people who refused to be denied their personal humanity and the nurture and benefit of their own familial relationships.

Manhood Challenges in Protecting Families from Separations

Slave marriages provided comfort and support, but could not change the distress over never knowing if loved ones would be sold or leased away. Young slaves had a high risk of being sold south after their values for sale soared from 1820 to 1850. There were no reasonable expectations that children could remain with parents at any ages. Forced separation of slave spouses, married in every sense but in the law, was a constant threat but happened less frequently than the family's separation from children. Southerners accepted the separation of slave families as an "inevitable feature of slavery."[462]

Professor Edward E. Baptist at Cornell University found the psychological damage to husbands and fathers would be deeply disturbing with the various challenges to manhood presented in slavery. In his 2014 book, *The Half Has Never Been Told: Slavery and the Making of American Capitalism*, he analyzed with great care the extreme difficulties that men held in slavery would have had in their adaptation to slaver challenges to their manhood. They were committed and caring fathers and members of families and kin networks that needed to be protected from forced separations by sales into the slave trade. He reviewed the special duty that many men feel instinctively to protect loved ones while being careful to never do anything that might cause harm to them or others. With forced separations possible at any time, in slavery that meant doing nothing to have a slaver select a family member for sale south in the slave trade. Nothing. The psychological damage of this dual role of protector and restrained bystander would be overwhelming. Professor Baptist wrote:

Despite the separations inflicted by forced migration, the slave frontier was actually teeming with fathers. Indeed, it was full of all kinds of relationships-new, rebuilt, flexible.... For father, brother, friends and lovers, the new relationships of flesh, of blood, and of pretend-blood were foundations on which they could stand and feel like men. But relationships were also gate ways to more vulnerability. Many enslaved men were more willing to retreat in order to protect their roles as husband and father than they would have been to protect their own bodies alone. One couldn't live out these ties unless one was still alive. Yet achieving survival by sometime retreating from self-assertion and self-defense required a psychologically difficult sort of thinking about oneself.... [Fathers created families of all sorts, and they would care for the children], feed them and teach them. Because these choices placed them in relationships as husbands or lovers, fathers or brothers, these men often made ordinary virtues central to their own identities, despite all the cultural noise that told them that as men they had failed. And perhaps a man who lived in that way also undermined the white ideal of the man as a vengeful hero.[463]

Some writers have tried to use the lack of open rebellion and resistance by people enslaved on Deep South plantations, especially men, as some evidence of their acceptance of the paternalistic slave cruelty system in return for a subsistence level of support. It also has been claimed that the paternalism of slavers and their encouragement to work with incentives rather than whip punishment shows that slaves accepted that system. That assumption is like the assumption that a deprivation can be used to prove inferiority. It is reminiscent of Historian James Curtis Ballagh's reference in his 1902 *A History of Slavery in Virginia* to what he saw as the ever-happy music played in the slave quarters. The people sang for a voice. They did not sing to express happiness with enslavement. Slaves had to endure to survive. Frederick Douglass commented on the compromises needed for survival as a slave. He said that "endurance" was the "only alternative" because, "I found myself here, there was no getting away, and naught remained for me but to make the best of it."[464]

Adaptations to create family relationships were matters of survival, not proof of a mutually beneficial slavery relationship. They are not proof of acceptance or happy submission. Family adaptations made the crushing burden of slavery one that could be carried for the sake of others who needed help for their survival. They were proof of commitments to loving relationships.

The adaptations of slaves to the many deprivations of slavery, in order to protect and help their relatives and kin networks were sincere, peaceful, honorable, generous and admirable. They were living proof of their high and evolved level of humanity.

Investments in Slaves Protected by Virginia Law, but Not Slave Families

The evil of slavery is best revealed in its use of families and loved ones to enforce obedience and submission. Family groupings were often encouraged on plantations to establish predictable relationships, encourage childbearing, and prevent discord. Family structures helped slavers with many management concerns. Slave marriages were not recognized at law. They were denied protection of law in order to allow for any time when loved ones would be stolen and sold away or leased away. Virginia families could not be made permanent with so many slave sales and forced plantation transfers occurring on a regular basis. By custom, many slavers would keep slave children and older people in family groups where marriages were recognized by slave peers. They would provide for older slaves who could not work, or at least they empowered members of their families to provide for them day-to-day. Slavers generally would not interfere in matters of personal relationships unless discord affected the greater "plantation family."

Family structures encouraged stable conditions for childbearing, as noted by Professor Thomas Dew. Slave growing and selling was a profitable part of the slavery business. Slavers knew that their livestock assets were improved by fertile females. Andrew Burstein in his 2010 book, *Madison and Jefferson,* wrote that Thomas Jefferson acknowledged that a fertile slave mother had greater value than the value of any field hand. At Monticello, slave girls had children at earlier ages than the average for other Virginia plantations and earlier than free women having children in the North. Economist Robert William Fogel and Stanley L. Engerman estimated, in cold cash terms, that the antebellum return on slave investments was as high as ten percent, and it compared favorably to returns on investments in the textile industry at ten and one tenth percent and for southern railroads at eight-and one-half percent.[465]

Slavers could choose to be cruel or helpful depending on how they viewed their investment in human property. They could be "hard, calculating businessmen…with as much shrewdness as could be expected of a northern capitalist." Slavers could cash in on their investments selling children, women and men, through slave dealers or at public auctions in cities with slave markets. The largest east coast city with slave markets was Charleston, South Carolina. Richmond was the center for Virginia's sales of slaves in state and out of state. Other cities had slave markets in Virginia.[466] No established slave market has been discovered in the Kanawha

Valley where there were few slaves living in the area and leasing was used for work production.

Growing Children as Livestock--"Eating Like Pigs"

Children in slavery had the status of livestock like their parents. They could be treated well as personal pets or they could be separated at any time for any reason from their mother, family, or kin network. One commentator was shocked traveling in the South when he saw an infant sold separately from the infant's mother. Only Louisiana had a law to prevent sales of young children away from their mothers. Historian Eugene D. Genovese in *Roll Jordan Roll* wrote generally in very positive terms about the lives of many slave children--playing games and not working until older ages. Early in life they would play with slaver children. He wrote that small children held in slavery enjoyed substantial childhoods before they began their work lives, which he estimates to be older that other historians. Professor Genovese wrote that these children played marbles, hide and seek, horseshoes, stick ball and hide the switch. Girls jumped rope and played ring games. They romped in the woods and enjoyed the out-of-doors. But he notes that the children also played at being whipped using switches and being auctioned off, acknowledging the reality for the important adults in their lives, and for their own futures.[467]

Small children had little value until ready for work at about the age of seven to nine years. Professor Wilma A. Dunaway found that child labor started early in the southern Appalachian region. By age seven, forty percent of boys and about fifty percent of girls were in the workplace. Children eight to ten years old would be put in the fields to work, at first carrying water, then helping to plant seeds. By age 12, they would be weeding and hoeing, pulling weeds, and clearing new ground, thinning corn, and harvesting. Historian Genovese found the requirements for regular work came later than these ages.[468]

Small slave children on a plantation were considered financial investments with the costs of their care, feeding, clothing and supervision being liabilities until they were ready for gainful labor. Their mothers were kept at work after delivery, and older slave women cared for the children. Often times small children were raised by older children. Some slave children wore rags and usually had no shoes. Booker T. Washington wrote that once he received wooden slat shoes with leather straps. Shoes were costly, and oftentimes they were poorly made and did not fit. Many slaves preferred to go barefoot, but slaves always wore shoes and their best clean clothes to church as a matter of respect. Many slavers liked to dispense clothing to slaves with great ceremony to show clothing as gifts of their generosity. Christmas was a time for gifts of clothes and other items for adults and children held in slavery. In Virginia, a slave reported that he had only one shirt and he had to wash it at night and hope it dried by morning. Headkerchiefs were popular to show pride in African origins. In the twentieth century, traditional headkerchiefs fell out of favor, and now, unfortunately, they are not commonly seen.[469]

A deeply disturbing abuse of children and families held in slavery was reported by Historian Genovese. In *Roll Jordan Roll*, he wrote that slave narratives show that some slave children were fed regularly from a trough. "Many ex-slaves describe such scenes" and add that the "quantity of food was inflexible," so that the children scrambled to "slop up" as much as they could as fast as they could. Time and time again, he wrote ex-slaves referred to eating like pigs. Booker T. Washington wrote in *Up from Slavery* that slave children were treated like livestock. They did not have meals. Without referring to eating at troughs, which his mother as a cook would never allow, he wrote "Meals were gotten by the children very much as dumb animals get theirs." No white child ate like a pig. Feedings without meals were to demonstrate to hungry slave children every day that they were livestock animals, not human beings.[470] Is there a cruelty greater than this?

Court-Approved Maiming and Mutilations of People with Free Spirits

Slavery was an economic system supported by cruelty that is hard to imagine today. The ideological basis of slavery was accepted by southerners and by many northerners. Historians and romantics for the Old South like to smooth the rough places in the cruelty system with anecdotes of generosity, claims about generous incentives to work, allowances of land and time off for personal activities and slave-earned personal income, permission to make and visit family and friends off the plantations, affection for mammy caregivers, claims of one big family on plantations, and happy music in the slave quarters.

A North Carolina judge, Thomas Ruffin, wrote an often-quoted simple statement about the true relationship of slaver to slave and the sole purpose of the relationship was to benefit the slaver. It succinctly explains the need for cruelty and how cruelty was part of every moment in the life of every slave, whether they were being whipped or separated from loved ones or under the threat of being whipped or separated from loved ones, or worse. Judge Ruffin wrote, "The power of the master must be absolute to render the submission of the slave perfect." He wrote further.

The end is the profit of the master, his security and the public safety; the subject, one doomed in his own person and prosperity, to live without knowledge and without the capacity to make anything his own, and to toil that another may reap the fruits....that he is thus to labor upon a principle of natural duty, or for the sake of his own personal happiness, such service can only be expected from one who has no will of his own; who surrenders his will in implicit obedience to that of another. Such obedience is the consequence only of uncontrolled authority over the body. There is nothing else which can operate to produce the effect. The power of the master must be absolute to render the submission of the slave perfect.[471]

The system of cruelty should be explored to understand the nature of slavery and the slave societies which the Confederate rebellion sought to protect as social, economic, and political institutions. Part of the system of cruelty was an almost universal refusal to document the instances of individual cruelty outside of judicial process. There are some exceptions.

Advertisements for runaway slaves in the Kanawha Valley indicate that a number of people who escaped may have been tortured with punishments there or perhaps elsewhere. Julius DeGruyter wrote in *The Kanawha Spectator* that advertisement notices in local papers offering rewards for runaway slaves were similar. They are shocking today. Nearly all of the reward notices had the same cartoon of a slave running with a bundle on a stick and general descriptions of the slave such as height, weight, skin tone, approximate age and name to which the runaway answered. These advertisements reveal the difficult relationship of slavers and slaves, both in the cruelty revealed and in the interactions slaves had with whites, where a slave would be described, "Has a down look when spoken to," and "stutters very much when spoken to," and "easily confused when spoken to," and other expressions of dread, anxiety and submission. A woman who escaped slavery to Canada said, "I feel lighter, --the dread is gone.... It is a great heaviness on a person's mind to be a slave."[472]

Shocking descriptions of past torture and punishment appeared in the advertisements for return of runaways with telling identifying information, such as:

'He walks with a limp, where his tendon has been cut;' or 'Has a brand burned on his shoulder'; or 'His right ear has been cut off'; or 'Two fingers have been cut off left hand'; or 'Has an iron collar around his neck.' [Many of these notices concluded with:] 'Has a down look when spoken to.'[473]

The apparent cruel treatment and scars displayed in these fugitive slave advertisements were legal in Virginia as "corrections" for slave behaviors which were to be discouraged and prevented. Physical punishments could make a runaway unique and identifiable. Such punishments could include slitting the nose and amputating ears or some fingers and toes, dismemberment, hobbling, branding, and emasculating. The latter was eventually limited to assaults and threats of assaults on women. It is very important to note that there was no offense in the Virginia slave code or any other law for the rape of a black woman or girl—by a black or a white man. Slave women and girls were given no respect in the formal law.

Felons would have ears "cropped." By the mid-nineteenth century, branding and mutilations declined but were not abolished everywhere. But most "corrections" were done with due regard for the slave's continuing ability to work. Whip scars on the backs of slaves reduced their value and new types of whips, straps and paddles were used in slave exporting states like Virginia to inflict pain without leaving devaluing scars.

One of Virginia's most prominent slavers, Robert "King" Carter in 1707 petitioned a court to "chop off" the toes of two female slaves, named Bambarra Harry and Dinah. The order of the court gave him "full power to dismember." He owned iron foundries, flour mills, textile weaving centers, and blacksmith shops. Mutilations were not uncommon in Virginia and the other Chesapeake Bay states. They presented a "theater of terror—with its army of black amputees hobbling across the Chesapeake landscape."[474]

Prior court approval was generally appropriate for severe "corrections" that would maim, but slavers were given wide discretion for most punishments, no matter how vicious or cruel as long as the slave did not die. In Virginia, it was long accepted that the intentional killing of a slave was murder. In 1851, the Virginia Supreme Court upheld the murder conviction of a slaver for the death of a slave subjected to "cruel and excessive whipping and torture." Also, it was recognized in Virginia that slaves had a right of self-defense, when they saw their lives were in danger. Public opinion supported a slave's right of self-defense.

Historian Eugene D. Genovese wrote that while "Public opinion might remain silent in the face of harsh treatment by masters, it did not readily suffer known sadists and killers." But it appears that public opinion did suffer sadism and murder as part of the slavery system so long as the enslaved victim did not die. The protections of slaves in the South were better than in the Caribbean Islands and in the Spanish and Portuguese colonies where high populations of slaves kept slavers in fear of insurrection and insubordination, and "strangled pleas for humanity," as cruelty there was unbounded. Social controls in addition to law helped prevent some brutality in Virginia.[475]

Slave behavior in Virginia was controlled by a special slave code separate from the common law applied to whites. It was developed by custom in the 1600s and codified in 1705. Virginia used a separate court system to adjudicate slaves for charged wrongs against whites and other slaves. Some of these courts were considered perfunctory especially for less serious offenses. But for murder and other capital offenses, the charges were tried by a formal process. These courts were not perfunctory. Surprisingly, as many as one in five enslaved Virginians charged were not convicted over the period from 1706 to 1865. Historian Philip J. Schwarz found in state records for those 159 years, there were 4,324 cases filed and there were convictions in 3,432 of those cases, with 899 cases where enslaved Virginians were not convicted, representing a 21 percent acquittal or dismissal rate. Historian Schwarz also found that over ninety percent of the murders by Virginians held in slavery were of whites. Oftentimes, in the South, a slave who was convicted of murdering another slave was given a lighter punishment than death, such as branding, whipping, transportation, or a shorter prison term, revealing a greater concern for protecting the financial interests of slavers who would lose a slave to hanging than the life of the murdered slave.[476]

Such apparent due process of law for people held in slavery gave Virginia slavers some comfort to believe that their ownership of slaves was legitimate, subject to rules, and fair to all. Planters liked thinking of themselves as managing a business and a big family. Planters were shrewd and calculating businessmen who adopted the role of patriarch for their "plantation families." Planters would judge and punish slaves for minor slave code offenses and disobedience, and simple impudence, but not major crimes for capital offenses. Capital offenses included insurrection, murder, arson, manslaughter, poisoning, robbery, burglary, theft of high value items, and other serious offenses. In the white code, a white could be put to death for helping slaves escape. Killing runaways was considered justifiable homicide.[477] Roaming night patrols could whip people held in slavery, if caught away from home past curfew, usually at 9:00 p.m., or when they failed to produce a written pass to be away from their homes at any time.

If a slaver lost a slave to a legal hanging, the slaver was compensated by the state for the loss of property. This was to encourage slavers to reveal capital offenses that posed a danger to the slaver community at large. For capital offenses, juries were not used. Local notable citizens, who were appointed as justices of the peace to sit as an "oyer and terminer" court. They would be convened for a speedy public trial, so other slaves would be deterred from similar offenses. Georgia used juries for capital offenses until 1846, when it adopted a special court with judgments which could only be appealed to the governor for pardons.[478]

Some commentators have written that Virginia's use of a speedy and regular process of law for serious slave offenses had the beneficial effect of encouraging a general respect for law in the populace, and, perhaps thereby limiting the "lynch law" of the post-Reconstruction era, and the early adoption of Jim Crow segregation and disenfranchisement laws, which were passed in Virginia later than in other Confederate states. It is true that Virginia took a more moderate path during and after Reconstruction, and that respect for law can change the moral climate of a community. But it must be noted that blacks in the Jim Crow era did not serve in the Virginia General Assembly after 1891, whereas other states had black legislators serving later, in North Carolina until 1894 and in South Carolina until 1904.[479]

Many punishments to control slave behavior could be employed without legal process. Pain, scarring, and humiliation could be used at the whim of slavers. A slave could be forced to work wearing a heavy iron collar on the neck and shackles on the ankles. There were iron head helmets to encase the heads of problem slaves. Various privileges could be limited such as reduced work time, family visits off the property, time to work in garden plots and other income activities of their own, and provisions for food, liquor, clothing, and shelter. Some punishments were tailored to the offense to humiliate. A prominent Virginia planter, William Byrd, forced a slave who had a problem holding his bladder in the night to drink a pint of urine.[480]

Physical punishment usually involved whippings, which by Virginia law could be up to 39 lashes with no court approval needed. Enslaved Virginians would get 30 lashes "should they lift a hand to *any* Christian"--other than a black Christian. Most white southerners accepted whippings as necessary and fully acceptable "if not done cruelly." How a whipping could be done without cruelty is unthinkable today. Professor Kenneth M. Stampp found an "element of savagery" in the treatment of slaves, which it seems southerners might say is a matter of degree and respectable "if not too savage." Slavers also used stocks, jails, and "hot boxes," which were metal and used to confine people in the hot sun. Slavers could hang people by the thumbs as punishment. But the absolute, most controlling and cruel punishment was sale of an offending slave away to hard labor and complete loss of loved ones. Accordingly, most resistance to white control was indirect and hidden from the oppressors.[481]

Whips would cut and scar the flesh on bare backs of men and women. A slaver in Georgia used a special technique for greater cruelty in his whippings. He would whip people by hanging them by their wrists and having them keep one foot on a sharp spike that would stab the foot with body movements during the whipping. Any correction technique that did not produce death was generally considered moderate to achieve complete obedience. Whipping was valued by slavers as a good alternative to other punishments because it was a frightful lesson to the person being whipped and to other people in the area, while the offending slave could be put to work in several days without losing significant work production, as compared to chains, shackles, iron head covers and jail time, "hot boxes" or other incarceration techniques. There are, understandably, few records of whippings or other punishments on plantations. On Highland, a plantation in Louisiana with 200 slaves, there were 160 whippings recorded involving about one hundred of the plantation slaves.[482]

When a slaver's "correction" by whipping caused death under Virginia law, it could be deemed an accidental death. At first in slavery, it was presumed to be accidental, but later it was a case to be considered for charges against the one performing the correction. Georgia enacted a law in 1816 to prevent "unnecessary and excessive whipping" and another statute in 1851 to outlaw "beating, cutting, or wounding, or by cruelly and unnecessarily biting or tearing by dogs." Throughout the South, there are very few cases reported against whites for cruelty. During colonial days, South Carolina and Georgia had statutes to restrain slavers from violence to slaves that injured but did not kill them. Virginia, North Carolina, Maryland and Delaware had no such statutes for nonfatal abuse. The punishments set out in code for whites who would be cruel to slaves could be fines or requirements that the slave be sold and the sale proceeds paid over to the abusing slaver. In 1860, Maryland enacted a restraining statute to require sale of the abused person, but only if the abuse conviction was the *third abuse conviction* against the slaver. Louisiana had *a statute with a fine of one hundred dollars for slavers who "cut out the tongue, put out the eye, castrated or did 'cruelly scald, burn, or deprive any slave of any limb or member.'"* Such statutes and fines were to protect and not punish cruel slavers and the system of cruelty needed for slavery to continue as an institution and an industry. [483]

No black, slave or free, was allowed to testify in any court against any white. South Carolina had a unique evidentiary system to accommodate the lack of slave testimony. The slaver was presumed to be guilty, and he or she could overcome that presumption by simply giving an oath of innocence. To overcome the oath, two white witnesses were required to testify to present "clear proof" of guilt. Blacks could not testify against a white but they could be compelled to testify against another black, so slavers could have evidence to support judicial petitions for "corrections." As noted before, slaves could lose ears, fingers, and toes to mark them for easy identification, and they could be branded with an "R" as a runaway, like common livestock. Runaways could also be killed by designated persons if they did not readily obey orders to return to their slavers.[484]

At law, the slaver and the overseer were responsible for legal "corrections." Only slavers could lawfully abuse, maim, or scar the people they held in slavery. Permission of the slaver was needed for anyone else to intentionally injure a person held in slavery. Cruelty by anyone other than the slaver was a violation of the letter of the law, but traditional social codes in many places might have protected such perpetrators, if people generally approved of the abuse as being needed to "render the submission of the slave perfect." The abuse at law would be to the slaver's property more than to the enslaved human being.

As profitable slave livestock, people could be cared for by slavers and their overseers, properly or improperly. They could be fed well or not fed well, punished harshly or not. Most Virginians held in slavery were provided essentials for living at subsistence level, but nothing at law required any decent care. Peer pressure and social approval were subtle factors in the custom of a slaver's area. But overseers were often rough men hired to manage and encourage people into behaviors that were clearly lucrative to their slavers, like hard work and producing children.

The most effective restraints on abuse by slavers and their overseers, whether physical, spiritual or emotional, were self-imposed and likely encouraged by social standards in their areas. Restraints might also come from family or religious values. Some paternalistic slavers liked to treat their slaves like pets. The protections needed for what were major investments in human property also had to be duly accounted for. It is noted that a healthy young slave could approach today's value of a reasonably priced automobile. In most every case, there would be an overriding concern for financial investments.

In Malden, it is likely that skilled and well-liked slaves had more free movement and social interaction than elsewhere in the South for a number of reasons. Virginia slavery generally allowed for considerable free movement of people held in slavery. In 1850, with 3,100 slaves living in a compact ten-mile long river plain among 12,000 white people, they there were less likely as a group or individually to be openly abused or neglected.[485] Any shocking violence by slavers could be a powder keg. There were regular interactions between many different groups of enslaved people, unlike in agrarian areas. Their industrial work was spaced for idle periods which made interactions more predictable. Discord was discouraged in any slave society, but slavers in the salt and slavery industry had to be reserved in their controls and demands because slaves had freedom to move, plan, and interact, and the considerable power to sabotage expensive factory operations,

In the Kanawha Valley, there were many competing employers, and good workers would have been more valuable to them as individuals, whether owned or leased. With the ever-present fear of a slave uprising, slavers throughout the South were thought to be wise to limit abuse to very special, egregious misbehavior. But slavers in isolated agricultural areas had no need to limit out-of-sight abuse. People held on small farms were much more likely to be abused and punished that on larger operations.[486]

It is noted that Lewis Ruffner advertised in 1844 for the return of at least one person he held in slavery after his father died the year before. The runaway man was named "Gatewood." Salt industrialists would likely pursue fugitive slaves into Ohio. It is perhaps a coincidence with the slave name Gatewood, that the artist Robert Henri's mother was Theresa Gatewood whose parents were Robert Burke Gatewood and Julia Ann Jones Gatewood. Her family owned a hotel in Malden when she married a river boat gambler and real estate developer, John Jackson Cozad. He founded towns using the name Cozad in Ohio and Nebraska. He had an altercation in his town in Nebraska, and shot a man to death. When cleared of criminal charges, he moved the family to Denver and changed his name and his children's names. His son, Robert Henry Cozad, changed his name to Robert Henri. He would become one of America's most acclaimed painters. He was important in the American art movement

known as "The Eight." His works are highly valued all over the world. There is one of his fine portraits, *Kathleen,*"on display as part of the collection of the Huntington Museum of Art in Huntington, West Virginia.[487]

KATHLEEN by Robert Henri – *Painting-Image Courtesy of The Huntington Museum of Art*

People in Chains Walk Trails of Tears

The people who were forced to migrate in slavery to the Deep South, away from their families and kin networks, traveled south walking in chains over hundreds of miles, over trails of tears.[489] For slaves going from central Virginia west toward the Ohio River, their land route was through the Kanawha Valley along the James River and Kanawha Turnpike and then on or beside the Great Kanawha River to the Ohio River and south on the Mississippi River.

The longest of the trails of tears went southwest through the Appalachian Mountain range. There were also trails to Richmond and Charleston, South Carolina, for shipments by boats to ports in the Deep South that could include New Orleans and Natchez. There were regular slave auctions in Richmond and Charleston, South Carolina, where children, women and men were stripped, examined intimately, auctioned and sold as livestock. One traveler in the South was sickened to see an infant at auction sold away from the infant's mother. The traveler was assured that the separation would be temporary since the mother would be sold later.[490] Whether they were unified or not, there was no law in Virginia to prevent sales of children at any age away from their families. "All sales," as an auctioneer could proclaim, "are final."

The mass migration has been called the "Second Middle Passage" of forced relocation, as devastating to humankind perhaps as the First Middle Passage of people from Africa to America.[491] Professor Ira Berlin wrote that the forced migration of slaves ended the paternalistic role of slavers with what people held in slavery could see was a Second Middle Passage in a slave trade as anonymous, dangerous, and mean as the first kidnappings from Africa.

> The Second Middle Passage shredded the planters' paternalist pretenses in the eyes of black people and prodded slaves and free people of color to create a host of oppositional ideologies and institutions that better accounted for the realities of the endless deportations, expulsions, and flights that continually remade their world.[492]

The Horror of Slavery in the forced migration caused fewer deaths than the First Middle Passage, but many people died going to the Deep South. Others committed suicide in the long and difficult journeys. Groups of slaves in "coffles" were expected to walk 20 to 25 miles per day in all kinds of weather and terrain. The travel from Virginia and the other Chesapeake States to New Orleans was hundreds of miles. The distance from Richmond to New Orleans is about one thousand miles. It would take many weeks of walking to complete a trip to most any overland destination. People might be sold only to be sold again to other slave traders on the trip south. Some people were moved by ships or steamboats after extensive walking to a port where more walking in the coffle might be required. Kentucky slaves were "sold down river." It was grueling travel that made the migration south along trails of tears a true Second Middle Passage. The forced migration of almost one million people caused much human suffering in Virginia and the rest of the Upper South for hundreds of thousands of established slave families and kin networks, who were forever separated from stolen loved ones.[493]

Enslaved Virginians would walk long distances chained in "coffles." Slave coffles were cleverly designed to be completely effective to their purpose. People were chained in two lines side-by-side so that the only possible movement of the coffle was forward with all people going at the same time and in line. When a person moved, the chains made noise. Coffle movements required constant co-ordinated effort. If a person stumbled, the whole coffle could fall. Chains could be around their necks, hands and ankles. Spirited people could be forced to wear metal helmets completely encasing their heads. When chained, it was easy for the people to be taken away from their loved ones who would try to say good-bye. Natural body necessities for women and men would be performed while in the coffle. Women and children could be in a two-by-two row coffle or they might follow behind coffles of men. Women and girls had no protection from assaults on their weeks of walking on trails of tears to the Deep South. People chained in the coffles could not help. Resistance to the slave traders was constant and murder and mayhem could break out at any time. Open insurrections were rare and rarely successful, but they did occur. [494]

This mass migration over trails of tears was clearly different from the original travel on slave ships from Africa. A major difference in this forced passage for people away from families and homes in the Upper South was that the people in coffles were in fresh air, and they were fed, because they were too valuable to slave traders to have them die on the trails of tears. But once they were in the Deep South, the average life span for the people moved there was affected. It was said in the sugar industry, that few slaves "lasted 7 years." Professor Edward Ball at Yale University calculated that the average sale price of men and boys was $700.00 and a single coffle with 200 people chained together in double file, was worth $140,000.00, which he stated today could be as much as $3.5 million in one very long coffle. Much smaller coffles also would make sizeable profits.[495]

A heavy traffic of slave coffles over the James River and Kanawha Turnpike to the Ohio River was one of the trails of tears walked by people who were sold and, as their families would say, "stolen" away from central Virginia. The trail was the same trail that was first constructed into a road by General Andrew

Lewis' militia in 1774. It was a major route mid-way in America from Richmond to Kentucky, through the Kanawha Valley. In 1829, the Kanawha Turnpike was said to have carried 30,000 hogs east and thousands of chained people west. One account from Guyandotte, today's Huntington, reported that some 100 slaves were seen traveling on the Kanawha Turnpike with a long wagon train on its way to Missouri.

West Virginia Poet Laureate Louise McNeill Pease, wrote of these coffles of people in "The Autumn Drives," another poem from *Hill Daughter*, published when she lived along the trail of tears in Malden. [496]

> The bison first surveyed this track,
> But now a wider road
> Curls up and down the mountain's back
> And bears a darker load
>
> For on it through these autumn days
> The nameless creatures plod,
> While close behind the drivers raise
> The whiplash and the prod.
>
> The driven coffle of the slaves
> On splayed and blistered feet
> Goes south to market to be sold
> To make the sugar sweet.
>   ....
> The hog---all sixty thousand hogs--
> In herds of dusty black
> Hoof slowly on their pointed legs
> And waddle down the track.
>   ....
> Above the road, the vultures float,
> for weakling things must fall
> And die and slicken with the bloat
> And wait the buzzard's call.
>   ....
> But on and on down these ravines
> And up this wooded shore,
> The slave men trek to New Orleans
> The sheep to Baltimore. [497]

Advertised Brand for Sales of "Virginia Negroes"

Virginians were advertised as a better brand of slaves. They were sold in the South as "Virginia Negroes" to signal a special, superior product that could be expected to be "compliant, gentle, and not broken by overwork." Historian Eugene D. Genovese in *Roll Jordan Roll,* cited writers who found Virginia slaves to be "good-tempered and kind to each other." Also, "Quickness of temper had always proceeded along with extraordinary courtesy." They were seen to be very "mindful of the courtesies due each other. Good day and good health are the daily wishes…."[498]

Virginia sent more people south than any other state, and Richmond was the largest slave market in the Upper South. Despite uncertain data, Historian Frederick Bancroft calculated that in the thirty years before the Civil War, from 1830 to 1860, there were 281,142 people moved to the Deep South from Virginia alone, at the average rate of 9,371 persons per year.[499] Slave selling in Virginia was big business, too big to lose in a war.

In 1857, Richmond had revenue of $4 million, which today could have the buying power of about $117 million. If the persons shipped out of Virginia totaled 281,142 as Historian Bancroft calculated, at the average sale price in Virginia as the place of warehouse origination, assuming an approximate sum of $700.00 each, the gross revenue for sales of Virginians in that 30-year period would be about $196 million and the buying power of that sum today would be about $5.75 billion. The value of the sales in the Deep South could be double the sale price in Virginia. These are rough calculations, and they beg for detailed research into the value of the eastern Virginia slave livestock industry. In the Civil War, almost one-half million Virginians were held in slavery among one million whites in eastern Virginia. These numbers give some sense of the overwhelming investments in people held in slavery in eastern Virginia at the time of the Civil War. [500]

Slave coffles are symbolic of the long terrible march to Freedom. Sad memories of the traffic of chained people walking over trails of tears can be remembered in verses to the song, "Lift Every Voice and Sing" written as a poem in 1900 by James Weldon Johnson in Jacksonville, Florida, for a celebration of Abraham Lincoln's birthday. The music was written by his brother, J. Rosamond Johnson. The song is used widely as an anthem for African Americans and for all people who hope and pray for the end of racism and its scars on the history of America. In 1919, "Lift Every Voice and Sing" was adopted as the official song of the National Association for the Advancement of Colored People, the NAACP.[501]

James Weldon Johnson would become the first African American to serve as the Executive Secretary of the NAACP. Under his leadership, the NAACP expanded across the country and became the leading force to end racism by concerted litigation to force social change. He was ably supported by Walter White and the NAACP organization's monthly publication, *The Crisis: A Record of the Darker Races,* which was edited and written by the genius commentator, author and free thinker, W. E. B. Du Bois, to give voice to the experience, nobility and struggles of blacks in the twentieth century. It had a circulation of 100,000 subscribers, white and black, and it was popular with poor working blacks in the South. It was often militant and always challenged the accommodationist philosophy of Booker T. Washington, which was accepted by many middle class blacks and their clergy who were centered in prominent black churches throughout the South.[502]

"Lift Every Voice and Sing" tells the story of slavery and is inspirational for all generations.

> Stony the road we trod,
> Bitter the chastening rod,
> Felt in the days when hope unborn had died;
> Yet with a steady beat,
> Have not our weary feet
> Come to the place for which our
>   fathers sighed?
> We have come over a way that with tears has
>   been watered.
> We have come, treading our path through
>   the blood of the slaughtered,
> Out from the gloomy past, till now
>   we stand at last
> Where the white gleam of our bright
>   star is cast.[503]

People in Slavery Sing More for a "Voice" Than for Joy

In his 1902 book, *A History of Slavery in Virginia,* Historian James C. Ballagh's account of Virginia slavery assumed the popular Virginia myth of benign slavery and happy slaves living in a mutually beneficial society. He stressed that the slave quarters were places of music, laughter and joy, without mentioning that many slaves had to work from dawn to dark in most months, and then they had chores in their cabins until about ten at night, usually six days per week. Rain days could be joyous times away from scheduled outside work. Many slaves had reduced workdays on Saturdays when they could work on their own economies and self-help. Saturday nights were the times of celebration and parties that would draw slaves from other plantations and farms, for important social breaks in the relentless work required by the threat of whipping. [504] Historian Ballagh wrote of the happy life in the quarters.

> The life in the quarters was one of its own. There was much hospitality and sociability, much dancing, laughing, singing and banjo-playing when the day's work was done. This was the home of the plantation melody and clog dance. There was little that was morose or gloomy about the slave, either at work or rest. If his condition was deplorable it was rare that he recognized it to the extent of allowing it to affect his spirits. [505]

Singing of slaves did not mean they were happy. Music let people in slavery have their own voice and breath. It is unfair to cite adaptations by slaves to terrible conditions as proof of their happiness. There were messages in many songs and hymns, messages about grief and suffering and loss of relatives who were "stolen" away for sale south in the mass migration of people from the border states to the Deep South. [506]

Professor Ira Berlin explained that these messages and reminders were part of the music of forced separations of families and loved ones in the Deep South.

> The music of the quarter was transformed by the great migration, giving rise to a sound whose deep religiosity gained it the name "spiritual" …. They still contained much of the same rhythmic structure, antiphony, atonal forms, and various guttural interjections and were accompanied by hand clapping and foot stomping. They were almost always performed in a circular formation with the singer moving in a counter clockwise direction. The pain of separation—motherless children, for example—and the hope for a better life to which men and women might "steal away" were among the spiritual's most persistent images. Movement abounded in references to roads and rivers, chariots and ships, and eventually trains. Slaves sang of running, traveling, and "travelin' on…." Spirituals…also emphasized place: sometimes the nostalgia for a place lost, the desire to be "returned" and "carried home"; sometimes that other place, of final rewards…black life amid

the second great migration was a process of continuous recreation.[507]

Professor Berlin thought that none of the new forms of black music could match the blues for expression of the black experience dominated by the idea of white superiority.

It was a musical response to white supremacy. Like black churches, schools, and towns, the blues also represented an inward turn—a separate world in which whites could not enter. The blues drew upon long-established African American rhythmic and tonal patterns. At times, it echoed the field shouts and spirituals. And like them, the blues exhibited extraordinary flexibility and range, calling for --indeed demanding--creativity.[508]

In 1856, Frederick Law Olmsted was impressed with the singing of slaves while they worked, which he observed in his travels through the Coastal States as a journalist. He disagreed with a man he met who told him that slaves had inferior music qualities and did "not understand harmony." The man said their songs were "mere sounds, without sense or meaning." Traveler Olmsted wrote of the sweet sounds he heard.

The love of music which characterizes the negro, the readiness with which he acquires skill in the art, his power of memorizing and improvising music is most marked and constant. I think, also that sweet musical voices are more common with the negro than with the white race—certainly than the white race in America….[They would anytime] fall into singing, each taking a different part, and carrying it on with great spirit and independence, and in perfect harmony, as I never heard singers, who had not been considerably educated, at the North.[509]

African American music of celebration, love, struggle, spirit, loss, pain, and life, during and after slavery, has been a unique and distinctive creative expression. It is a "blessing and an ornament to the earth." An apologist for slavery wrote that blacks "give us music of a natural order, full of genuine feeling, opening its way directly to the general heart." African American music is one of the greatest contributions to culture in the world, by any people. It has created or transformed many music genres enjoyed around the world today--blues, spirituals, gospel, jazz, ragtime, rap, rhythm and blues, rock and roll, country, soul, hip-hop and others.[510] It is the voice of a great people with a high culture.

Official State Songs about People "Stolen" Away from Their Homes

There are antebellum songs that have been standards for whites in the South to commemorate the longing of people held in slavery to return home after they had been "sold south" from Virginia or "sold down-river" from Kentucky in the great forced migration before the Civil War. The states adopted their favorite antebellum songs as official state songs. "Carry Me Back to Old Virginia" was the state song of Virginia for 132 years. The official state song of Kentucky continues to be "My Old Kentucky Home," written by Stephen Foster from the story of the antislavery book, *Uncle Tom's Cabin*. It has been modified to no longer refer to "darkies."

In 1997, the Virginia General Assembly withdrew its official status from "Carry Me Back to Old Virginia." The verses refer to the longing of a "darkey" who was sold south. He longed to return to his "Massa and missis" in heaven, if not in the beloved "Old Virginia."[511] There is no resentment expressed for being "sold south."

> Carry me back to old Virginia,
> There's where the cotton and the corn and taters grow,
> There's where the birds warble sweet in the spring-time,
> There's where the old darkey's heart am long'd to go,
>
> ....
>
> There's where I labored so hard for old massa,
> Day after day in the field of yellow corn,
> No place on earth do I love more sincerely
> Than old Virginia, the state where I was born.
>
> ....
>
> Carry me back to old Virginia,
> There let me live 'till I wither and decay,
> Long by the old Dismal Swamp have I wandered,
> There's where this old darkey's life will pass away.
> Massa and missis have long gone before me,
> Soon we will meet on that bright and golden shore,
> There we'll be happy and free from all sorrow,
> There's where we'll meet and we'll never part no more.[512]

Songs like "Carry Me Back to Old Virginia" encouraged whites to believe that the people held in slavery had happy lives with them. The great distance to the Deep South for people sold into the slave trade ended all hopes of return to their families and loved ones back in "Old Virginny."

The state song of Kentucky is today "My Old Kentucky Home." It romances the longing of a slave to return to his loved ones after he had been sold from his cabin home in Kentucky to work on a sugar cane plantation in the Deep South. The state song is played reverently to a standing crowd at Churchill Downs by The University of Louisville Marching Band to start the ceremonies for the running of the Kentucky Derby the first week of May each year. The Kentucky General Assembly changed the lyrics for the official state song by removing the words "darky" and "darkies," and replacing them with "people." With these words changed, the reference to slavery is less obvious, and blacks are more respected as people. But the impact of the song as a memorial to people sold down river during the Horror is removed.[513]

Stephen F. Foster originally intended the song to be antislavery by directly referring to the plight of Uncle Tom, the sympathetic fictional slave in *Uncle Tom's Cabin*. The song presents the story of Uncle Tom as the lead character in the book. He is beaten to death on the orders of his evil new slaver, Simon Legree. Kentuckians who were sold to the Deep South were said to be "sold down-river," because the Ohio River and Mississippi River carried them to southern slave markets and large plantations. To popularize the song in the South where the book was unpopular, Stephen F. Foster altered the song sheet to delete references to Uncle Tom.[514]

"My Old Kentucky Home" became a hit throughout the South as it endures today. Uncle Tom was sold to hard labor in the Deep South. Uncle Tom, like the unnamed character in the song, had to leave his happy cabin where the young folk would roll on the floor, in order to go to hard labor in sugar cane fields because hard times fell on his slaver, forcing the slaver to sell his prized slaves to cover his debts.

In hot, humid weather, the labor of slaves in sugar cane fields was hard. Some have estimated that life expectancy in the sugar cane fields was only seven years. Thousands of Kentuckians were sent to southern fields "where the sugar canes grow." The debts of Uncle Tom's slaver are the "Hard Times" that came "knocking at the door." This meant the slave had to leave his cabin home, bow his head and bend his back in the sugar cane fields. The song says the slaves had a few more days till they would totter on the road, and "Then my old Kentucky Home, good-night!" When Uncle Tom refuses to tell Simon

Legree where two escaped slaves could be captured, he is beaten to death for his loyalty to his friends. [515]

The "good-night" for Uncle Tom was death as a sacrificing Christ figure. For others it was the end of all contacts with families and kin networks in their Kentucky home. These are some of the verses of the state song, with original references to African Americans as "darkies" included:

> The sun shines bright in the old Kentucky home,
> 'Tis summer, the darkies are gay,
> The corn top's ripe and the meadow's in the bloom,
> While the birds make music all the day.
> The young folks roll on the little cabin floor,
> All merry, all happy, and bright:
> By 'n by hard times comes a knocking at the door,
> Then my old Kentucky Home, good night.
>
> ....
>
> Weep no more, my lady, Oh! weep no more to-day!
> We will sing one song for the old Kentucky home,
> For the old Kentucky home far away.
>
> ....
>
> The head must bow and the back will have to bend,
> Wherever the darkey may go:
> A few more days and the trouble all will end
> In the field where the sugar-canes grow.
> A few more days for to tote the weary load,
> No matter, 'twill never be light,
> A few more days till we totter on the road,
> Then my old Kentucky Home, good-night![516]

A popular West Virginia state song, "West Virginia Hills," refers to a romantic longing of people to be in the "Mountain State," by people from its mountains--not by people who were enslaved there. It is one of four official state songs of West Virginia. Two other songs are less known, "This is My West Virginia" and "West Virginia, My Home Sweet Home." In 1885, Ellen King wrote the ever-popular state song, "The West Virginia Hills."

> Oh, the West Virginia hills!
> How majestic and how grand,
> With their summits bathed in glory,

> Like our Prince Immanuel's Land!
> Is it any wonder then,
> That my heart with rapture thrills,
> As I stand once more with loved ones
> On those West Virginia hills?[517]

The most popular recent state song for West Virginians who long to return to their "mountain mamma" in the Mountain State has become, "Take Me Home, Country Roads." It is also referred to as "Almost Heaven, West Virginia." The song was a 1971 international hit sung by John Denver and written with Taffy Danoff and William T. Danoff. The song refers to ageless mountains that define, protect, and nurture mountain people.

> Almost heaven, West Virginia,
> Blue Ridge Mountains, Shenandoah River,
> Life is old there, older than the trees,
> Younger than the mountains, blowing like a breeze
>
> Country roads, take me home
> To the place I belong,
> West Virginia,
> Mountain mamma, take me home
> Country roads[518]

It should be noted that the Blue Ridge Mountains and Shenandoah River are central features of Virginia. They become part of West Virginia in the Eastern Panhandle near Harpers Ferry. It is said that first inspiration for the song came to the authors while passing through Maryland country side, but the song was adapted to put "mountain mamma" in the state of West Virginia.

John Denver performed the song on September 6, 1980 at the first football game played at today's West Virginia University's Mountaineer Field.[519] The song is a rallying cry for West Virginians. It is used at many events. Most notably, Mountaineer football fans use the song as part of the revelry of their games, swaying and singing, "Almost heaven, West Virginia...."

Advertisment for Auction and Sale of Negros, Atlanta Georgia - *Images Courtesy of the Library of Congress*

Chapter 11

Cotton Booms And Virginia Prospers With Slave Selling Livestock Industry

Economic Impact of the Cotton and Slavery Industry

Slavery was not incidental or a mere social tradition. It was not a holdover of colonial culture in the South. It was one of the primary factors that produced national growth and prosperity before and after the Civil War. After the war, when restoration of the cotton industry was considered vital to the nation's post-war economy in the South and the North, cotton plantations were readily restored to their rebel owners for creation of a sharecropping system to keep freed people, and poor whites, in place picking cotton needed for textile factories in New England and Britain. Cotton was the most sought after product in the world and it is everywhere today, an intimate part of our lives. The cotton industry formed the economic and social structure of the South for generations, at least until the Great Depression when mechanical cotton pickers replaced human "hands" in the cotton fields.[520] The nation's industrialization and dominant position in the world economy in the early twentieth century started with the cotton and slavery industry.

The history of America has been a history of slavery in many contexts. The nation's original sin began with the idea of white superiority which supported the use of slavery for a major economic benefit to tobacco producers in Jamestown. The idea continued full force before the American Revolution until its economic benefit waned with falling tobacco production in Virginia and other Chesapeake Bay states where most slaves lived in 1790. At this time, when the Federal Constitution was ratified in 1788, slavery was a peculiar social institution, and it might have withered away as predicted by Thomas Jefferson and others, but Eli Whitney's cotton gin made cotton marketable and created a great demand for slave workers in the Deep South to pick cotton for export to New England and Britain in the world economy.

The cotton and slavery industry is now being viewed as the driving force for the American Industrial Revolution. It created the forced migration to the Deep South of as many as a million people held in slavery in the Upper South. After the War of 1812 slavery drove industrialization with new factory systems to make cotton cloth in New England. It made the national economy one of the fastest growing national economies in the world.

Historian Sven Beckert has written that slavery "stood at the center of the most dynamic and far reaching production complex in human history." Another historian, Edward Baptist, has asserted that slave labor used in the cotton industry was driven by "whip torture," and that brutal work conditions made the cotton and slavery industry the clear leader of the American economy. These conclusions about work conditions and the nature of the cotton industry and its impact on the national and world economies have been the subject of a keen academic debate,[521] like the debate over the forced mass migration of slaves either by plantation transfers or by sales into the slave trade.

The tobacco and slavery industry in the Chesapeake Bay colonies began the nation's use of thousands of agricultural workers in an export industry. Slavery was instituted for tobacco production which became the engine of the colonial economy of Virginia, Maryland and Delaware. In 1628, at the beginning of the tobacco industry, new planters produced one half million pounds of tobacco. By 1639 that number grew to 1.5 million pounds and it was 53 million pounds in 1753, just before the Revolutionary War. Tobacco production required a large work force. By 1775, the Chesapeake Bay colonies had taken 160,000 people from Africa into slavery. Another 140,000 Africans were taken by southern colonies and about 30,000 were taken by northern colonies. The tobacco and slavery industry created an aristocratic Virginian planter class that lived off the bounty of the work of the people they held in slavery.[522]

At the time of the Federal Constitution, most people in slavery were located in the Upper South, in the Chesapeake Bay states. In 1790, Virginia alone had 42 percent of the enslaved people in the new nation. In just 60 years, by 1850, most slaves lived in the Deep South. That year, it has been calculated, the nation had perhaps one quarter of its wealth invested in 3.2 million enslaved people.[523]

Cotton Gin Starts the Cotton Boom

Eli Whitney invented the cotton gin in 1794, and cotton production soared because his machine could be used to easily clean field cotton by combing out seeds, stems, and other impurities. Before the cotton gin, combing cotton was a slow manual process taking many hours to produce small quantities of cotton ready to be baled. The cotton gin enabled slave workers to clean fifty pounds of cotton per day instead of one pound. It launched America's most important export industry on the hard labor of hundreds of thousands of enslaved field workers throughout the Deep South.

It is of some interest that Eli Whitney did not benefit from his invention because, before he could patent the cotton gin, planters stole the model and copied it. The cotton gin consisted of "a sieve, a rotating drum, a comb of hook-shaped wires, and a rotating brush." The device was invented in a few weeks. For the next decade after his invention, Eli Whitney fought for his rights in southern courts, but most of the money he collected went to pay his attorneys. Later, he was given credit, disputed by some, for creating a system for the mass production of goods called the American System of Manufactures. He is known for using interchangeable parts for rifles in his New England business. His production system allowed unskilled workers to turn out products equal in quality to those made by craftsmen. New manufacturing processes ushered in the American age of factory mass production.[524]

So much cotton was harvested and cleaned by enslaved workers using cotton gins that the nation's cotton production and exports increased dramatically. In 1802, cotton was 14 percent of all exported goods, and 18 years later it was 42 percent of exports. As the Civil War began, the cotton and slavery industry had pushed its exports to 61 percent of all goods exported from the United States. By 1860, about 830,000 slaves had been sent to work in cotton plantations in the Deep South and West. Throughout the nation during the Civil War there were about four million people in slavery.[525] There were a number of innovations to the cotton gin and cotton processing that increased productivity in the years before the Civil War. Also, new seed varieties were developed that produced larger cotton plants and multiple harvests, increasing production.

Cotton exports made the American cotton industry vital to world trade by the time of the Civil War. A nineteenth-century commentator wrote glowingly about the global trade in cotton, asserting that "Cotton with its commerce has become one of the many modern 'wonders of the world.'"[526] Sven Beckert, a historian today is one of several historians who are writing a new history of the cotton and slavery industry, particularly about its economic impact worldwide and how it was produced. He wrote in an article in 2014 for *The Atlantic* titled "Empire of Cotton:"

In England alone.... the livelihood of between one-fifth and one-fourth of the population was based on the industry; one-tenth of all British capital was invested in it and close to one-half of all exports consisted of cotton yarn and cloth. Whole regions of Europe and the United States had come to depend on a predictable supply of cheap cotton.... By the late 1850s, cotton grown in the United States accounted for 77 percent of the 800 million pounds of cotton consumed in Britain. It also accounted for 90 percent of the 192 million pounds used in France... and 92 percent of the 102 million pounds manufactured in Russia.[527]

The cotton industry has been the leading manufacturing industry for centuries. "By 1900, about 1.5 percent of the human population in the world–that is millions of men, women, and children– were engaged in the industry, either growing, transporting or manufacturing cotton." In America, the industry began with slavery, and, according to Professor Beckert, it was a capitalism organized by "violence and bodily coercion."[528] Professor Beckert wrote in his 2014 book, *Empire of Cotton: A Global History:*

> Too often we prefer to erase the realities of slavery, expropriation, and colonialism from the history of capitalism, craving a nobler, cleaner capitalism. We tend to recall industrial capitalism as male dominated, when women's labor largely created the empire of cotton. Capitalism was in many ways a liberating force, the foundation of much of contemporary life. We are invested in it, not just economically but emotionally and ideologically. Uncomfortable truths are sometimes easier to ignore.[529]

Cotton Creates Mass Migration of Slaves to Deep South

The mass migration of Virginians and others to the Deep South was one of the largest migrations of any people in history. It changed the demographics of the nation and created new slave states and slave societies that would rebel to protect their slave economies and culture. The early Confederate States in the Deep South could not have made a long and bloody civil war without the migration of millions of people, white and black. The mass migration is best described by maps showing the change in slave populations in 1790 and 1860, with each dot noting 200 slaves.

The mass migration involved the tragic forced separations of hundreds of thousands of people in the Upper South. One southern writer, Nehemiah Adams, asserted that forced separations were an "inevitable feature of slavery." There were few slave families which were not directly affected by the migration. The families and kin networks of friends and more distant relations were disrupted, leaving behind great suffering for often a death-like, forever-loss of a loved one who would never be seen again. It traumatized the persons who moved and those who were left behind to mourn and to live in constant fear of more family separations.[530]

Some white southerners tried to help their consciences about disrupting families by claiming that blacks were inferior human beings with no strong affections for loved ones. A physician said black women could easily be separated from their children, due to their natures. Some claimed shamelessly that "maternal attachments in slave mothers were short-lived." It was claimed that soon after separa-

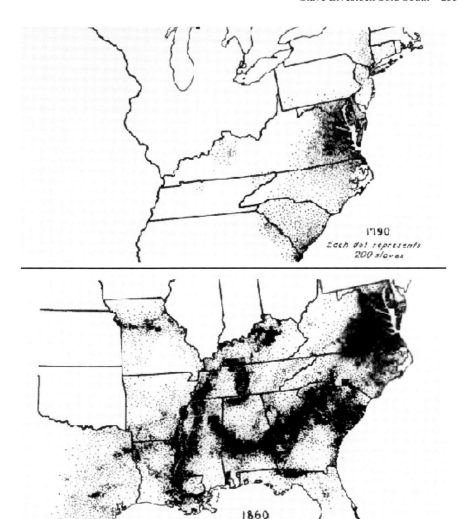

U. S. Department of Agriculture, Bureau of Agricultural Economics.   SCAL

Number of Slaves in the United States in 1790 and in 1860.

1. These two maps are the first and last of a group of six. Space does not allow of
     to be shown here.

2. The use of these two maps in a history lesson would clarify and simplify the s
     problem of 1860. This material in tabulated or verbal form would be formid

3. Only a section of each map is reproduced here.

Number of Slaves in U.S. in 1790 and 1860 (Each Dot = 200 Slaves) – *Image Original, U. S. Department of Agriculture* - **Source:** *Brinton, Willard Cope. Graphic Presentation. New York: Brinton Associates, 1939.*

tion, slave mothers forgot about their infants because by nature they were like hens that treat their chicks like strangers. For the separated persons sent to the Deep South, it changed their lives totally, for their work regimens, living and working environment, their shelter, clothing, food, relationships, family patterns and life expectancies. They were forced into gang labor systems with established production quotas enforced by predictable whippings. Careful bookkeeping could be used to track slave performance and assure expected output improvements. A terrible consequence of the dislocation of so many people held in slavery was that free blacks could be easily kidnapped and force into slavery far away from their homes.[531]

Professor Edward Baptist of Cornell University studied and analyzed the cotton and slavery industry in his 2014 book, *The Half Has Never Been Told: Slavery and the Making of American Capitalism.* His research supported an emerging new history of capitalism and the cotton industry as a whole. He showed that people sold from the Upper South were young, many were very young. In Virginia, during the decades of migration from 1820 to 1860, a person in slavery in the age range valuable for sale would have about a 50 percent chance of being "sold south." Of the people brought to New Orleans for sale from 1800 to1804, 84 percent were between the ages 11 and 24 years. In that period, one-third of the children sold in New Orleans were under age 13 years. From 1815 to 1820 the percentage of young children sold there remained high but dropped to 27.7 percent. The average age of slave children under the age of 13 years was 9 years, which was the age when slave girls were separated from their mothers and boys were considered ready for work. Infants in arms could be sold away from their mothers. Almost half of the slave children were sold separately from any family member. Slavery was a very cruel system.[532]

African Americans Picking Cotton: Savannah, GA – *Image Courtesy of Library of Congress*

Chapter 12

The Evolving History Of Slavery

Early Faux History: Slavery as Kind Help to Barbarians

A number of scholars in the first decades of the twentieth century wrote histories to excuse the Horror of Slavery and the many horrors that supported it. One line of southern history writing, called "retrogressionist history," contended that slavery had a "civilizing" effect upon slaves who, by their African nature, would return to "barbarism" if not kept under the control of whites. One slaver following this idea, George Fitzhugh, said that slaves, like wild horses, had to be "caught, tamed, and civilized." It was written that emancipation took a "child-like race out of the cradle."[533]

This approach to slavery and to segregation that followed was used by whites in the first four decades of the twentieth century to support the idea that slavery was beneficial to all, especially Africans and their descendants. Such southern history writing claimed that white control was essential to the survival of African Americans in "civilization." Virginia slavery was regularly presented to school children as a benign state of mutual benefit for slave and slaver. In 1902, Historian James C. Ballagh wrote in *A History of Slavery in Virginia* that the state's slavery was patriarchal and beneficial to enslaved people on small farms and large plantations.

He characterized Virginian slaves as the "playmate, pedagogue, brother, exemplar, friend and companion of the white from cradle to the grave." He wrote that a slave's pride in his white slaver's family far surpassed the pride of his slavers. He emphasized that it was the slave that set apart and "scorned the poor white people as 'po' white trash." A slave was a member of the slaver family and his slaver's goods were his own and he could take what he needed as the need arose. He fails to note that only a few slaves would be allowed access to the slavers' homes. He added a paternalistic caution that even good slaves would engage in petty theft, if left unchecked by what he called "indulgent masters." To some degree with such slavers, he wrote the "moral obliquity of the ordinary Negro in petty theft" would unfortunately arise.[534] Virginia slaves were spread more widely than those in the Deep South. They were on smaller farms, but membership in a slaver family is an extreme overstatement for most all enslaved Virginians.

History from the Southern View:
Reconstruction was "Criminally Stupid"

In 1933, Historian James Truslow Adams called Reconstruction "criminally stupid" and presented the southern history writer's unvarnished opinion of the Reconstruction Era in his book, *The March of Democracy: A History of the United States*. He wrote that "scalawags" got black voters to the polls, and the Ku Klux Klan and other racist groups were formed to intimidate black voters. Riders in white robes would appear in the night and frighten blacks "out of their wits." He justified violence against freed people as necessary to correct the damage done by Congress in Reconstruction. He claimed that the night riders were properly defending "white supremacy" to prevent black political control and the "plunder" of whites by former slaves. He wrote:

At first little violence was used, but when the method began to prove effective, as was shown by the big drop in Republican votes in 1870, Congress passed the Enforcement Act, imposing severe penalties for infractions of the new Constitutional Amendments, and the South then met force with force. Whatever Abolitionists and theorists like Charles Sumner might say, living in white Northern communities, whites will not consent to be ruled by blacks, and the South was fighting for white supremacy. The only way to combat Congressional legislation had to be violence when other methods failed, and there is no doubt violence was used, and racial bitterness much increased.

In 1871, Congress passed an even more rigid Enforcement Act, and in it gave the President power to suspend *habeas corpus* and to use the army to suppress the activities of the members of the Klan. The Congressional policy had been criminally stupid. No matter what its political faith, the white South could not be expected to submit supinely to be ruled and plundered by its former slaves. The [Negro] fanaticism of a Sumner could result only in arousing passion and delaying a solution of an extremely delicate and difficult problem.

Gradually, however, the whites regained control, and by 1877 throughout most of the South the [carpet-bag-Negro] regimes had ended, and the section had become solidly Democratic, the combined dishonesty and ignorance of the local Republicans making any two-party system impossible. The blacks were frankly intimidated, and [Negro] suffrage was nullified in one way and another.... The former slave learned to work for wages and almost a revolution in the agricultural condition of the section can be inferred from the reduction by almost a half, in little more than a dozen years, of the average size of Southern farms. The Old South of the "plantation" days with its romantic dreams had passed into history.[535]

This history of a "criminally stupid" Reconstruction saturated popular media, as well as academic science and history. These ideas provided the underpinning for disenfranchisement of blacks and a segregation system that forced separation of freed people from the mainstream of national life and culture. Like in slavery, the deprivations that were forced upon blacks after Reconstruction were used to prove their inferiority and support claims that blacks could not be "civilized" on their own.[536]

Slavery was a Profitable and Viable Industry Before the Civil War

The written history of slavery has changed and continues to evolve with a more deliberative and scientific process of discovery. For example, in 1962 Robert Evans, as a graduate student at the Massachusetts Institute of Technology, researched and evaluated what he called the "slave industry" and carefully calculated that it was a profitable industry in its last years, contradicting many accounts that slavery was in decline and might have faded away as an unprofitable industry in the years leading up to the Civil War. His research revealed slavery was an economic force that would not likely end on its own. Two college professors reviewed his graduate paper on the economics of slavery, and, while they had different reviews, both reflected evolving and more perceptive ideas of the time.[537]

Professor Thomas Govan of New York University reviewed and approved the economic analysis of the Evans paper, but he objected to calling slavery an "industry," when he insisted that it was merely a "social institution." Dr. Govan, like other historians, did not fully consider how Virginia slavery evolved from a social institution with workers used for local work production into a full-blown livestock commodity industry that turned young slaves, into profitable commodities to be "sold south" by the thousands each year for the 30 years leading up to the Civil War.

Dr. Govan fully credited Robert Evans' analysis of the economics of slavery. He found the research showed that slavery was profitable and "strong" in its last years before the Civil War. It would not have "withered and died," as some had contended. But Dr. Govan strongly objected to calling slavery an "industry."

> Slavery itself was not an industry; it was an institution, a social practice sustained by law and custom through which labor was procured, organized, controlled, and directed. Owners of slaves employed them as household servants, in agriculture, in manufacturing, in mining, in construction, and rented their services to others. The object was profit, slaves were sold and bought, but to call slavery itself an industry confuses the problem rather than helping to clarify it.[538]

On this key concept Professor Govan failed to take into account the thousands of young slaves sold as commodities to the slave trade for plantations in the Deep South. He thought that slavery was a stratified social system not not an industry subject to market forces. From the 1820s to the 1850s, the value of Virginia slaves doubled and thousands and thousands of slaves were sold to large plantations far away from local work in Virginia. Virginia's secession from the Union protected its livestock commodity markets in the Confederate states.

The slave livestock industry in Virginia cannot be ignored. Its importance and economic power should be understood, how it dominated American politics and culture in the early republic and how it led to a protracted and bloody civil war. The economics and politics of slavery fully supported secession. It was Virginia slavery that first paralyzed the morality of the nation when it created slavery as a social institution for local tobacco production. By the last three decades leading up to the Civil War, Virginia had a booming slave livestock industry. To approach slavery as only a social or cultural institution fails to account for the overproduction of slaves for local work in Virginia, and the major industry it created for selling people to the Deep South. It is of some interest that in the 1830s, the United States Department of Agriculture included slavery in its statistical analysis along with other agricultural industries.[539]

A second critique of the MIT paper of Robert Evans was by Professor John E. Moes at the University of Virginia. Professor Moes wrote to object to any idea that Virginians engaged in growing slaves like livestock for sale to the Deep South. He stated that the idea of Virginia being considered a slave livestock growing state was an unpleasant idea. He wrote that such an idea is unfair since slaves would increase on their own just by being together since slave couples lived together even though they could not legally marry.[540]

His opinion is generally confirmed by limited research today on forced childbearing practices. Economist Robert William Fogel was glib in writing that slavers "vigorously denied promoting promiscuity and practicing barnyard techniques to increase fertility." Slavers generally saw themselves as "devoted family men who promoted stable family lives among their slaves."[541] While most did encourage family relationships, some slavers did not. There appears to be no written records regarding intimate matters, forced or unforced. With the "perfect" submission required of every slave and the cruelty in the system needed to support it, any suggestion from a white in authority could be interpreted as a command and any turn away could be feared as "impudent" and subject to physical punishment or forced separation from loved ones.

Families and Their Infants in Slavery

With a booming slave livestock economy in Virginia, it is certain that childbearing would be encouraged as part of the servitude of women and maturing girls. Family groups provided the foundation for a natural increase in Virginians held in slavery and available for sale in the slave trade.

Fertility was of great value to slavers in Virginia as noted by Professor Thomas Dew. He said that Virginia's special emphasis on having parents in family settings produced more children than in other slave states, and allowed for 6,000 slaves from Virginia each year to be sold into the slave trade. Ex-President James Madison, who was considered a gentle master, was pleased to have one-third of his slaves under the age of five years. While he disapproved of "licentiousness," he said slave girls were having babies by age 15.[542]

The increase in the slave population was prized for commodity sales to the Deep South. Race mixing appears to have been common in Virginia since the 1700s and perhaps earlier. It is noted that Booker T. Washington's mother had sons by two different white fathers. Booker did not know his father and said nobly that his father too was a victim of slavery because slavery kept him from contact with his son. [543]

In the Malden Census in 1870, the census taker, who likely was white, gave about half of the black people listed an "M" for mulatto and the other half a "B" for black. Whites had no categories for skin color. The credibility of these notations is questionable, since they were wrongly recorded for Booker's family.

Research by Professor Herbert G. Gutman has shown that many of the slaves sold south had ancestors who were mixed race while living in the Upper South well before they were stolen away to the Lower South.[544] In Virginia, forced relationships are not proven by limited research to date, and most all commentators now and in the days of slavery have denied forced childbearing relationships. It is known that Virginia slaves were greatly encouraged to be in their own committed relationships and marriages, which in turn, gave them children.

Slaves themselves chose to live in families with extended kin networks throughout much of the South.[545] Their families were a precious adaptation to their lives in slavery. While Virginia slaves lived in committed unions as parents, they knew that their children were likely to be sold or leased away from home to harsh conditions in the Deep South, because they were more valuable there than for work near home in Virginia.

A high number of slave offspring meant higher profits for slavers in Virginia's livestock commodity industry. Without question any exploitation of intimate relations violates the most vital parts of humanity and can forever brand the physical, emotional, and spiritual identities of a person's life. Girls and women who may have objected to advances would have the specter of a forced sale south for them or for a loved one. By far most all slavers were honorable in regard to childbearing but some were not and that is the "element of savagery" essential to the cruelty of the system to keep enslaved people in "perfect" submission.

King Cotton Drives the American Economy

Professor Sven Beckert, Professor Edward Baptist and others have written a new history of cotton, slavery, and capitalism. They have broken important new ground. Their research and economic theories about slavery and its impact on capitalism and the industrialization of America's economy in the nineteenth century have stirred new ideas in economic history. Their approach is provocative and encourages comment and lively reviews.

Professor Baptist detailed the plantation system used on Deep South plantations to produce massive exports of cotton to New England, Britain, France, Russia and the world. He found that the cotton and slavery industry spurred growth in many support industries, from agriculture and transportation to manufacturing, shipping, and banking. Early life insurance in the South began as protection of slavers for the financial loss of slaves killed in dangerous occupations like coal mining. Professor Baptist asserted that supporting economic activities and mass slave migration spreading across the Deep South and into new western territories were effective to completely reorganize the American economy, South and North. The cotton industry led to industrialization primarily in the North, materially changing the economy, politics and demographics in the nation. He calculated that, while baled raw cotton was only 5 percent of the goods produced in America, in 1836, the cotton and slavery industry as a whole had indirect impacts that created or affected as much as 50 percent of the nation's goods and services.[546]

The cotton trade to northern textile mills began American industrialization and made mill owners the wealthiest people in the free states. By the 1840s, the northern "lords of the loom" were living in the land of abolitionism and were uncomfortable to admit that their wealth was produced by brutal slave labor.[547]

Professor Baptist found that, by 1850, the southern cotton and slavery industry was the key supplier for Britain's textile industry where hundreds of thousands of textile workers worked for Britain's world-wide sales of cotton fabric. Cotton fabric was the most popular commodity in the world. It made clothing which was more comfortable than wool, flax and other fabrics. Raw cotton became more than 60 percent of the nation's goods sold outside the United States.[548]

In 1832, there were 200,000 workers in northern states in some form of manufacture. This was an increase from 1820 of about 125,000 workers. In the 1830s there were 20,000 textile workers in cotton mills. One town, Fall River, Massachusetts, had 4,000 textile workers, many of whom were female. It was at the center of textile manufacturing in New England. The population of the North soared from 7.1 million in 1830 to 14 million in 1850. Over the same twenty years, the population in the South went from 5.7 million to 9 million. These different population numbers would matter in the Civil War.[549]

Antebellum cotton became the business of America, supported by the lives and slave work of over a million people. Professor Baptist found that, while these workers comprised only six percent of the American workforce, they were the true drivers of the American economy as a whole.[550] He credited slavery as a key force for America's westward expansion. He found the cost of expansion of slavery in eight years into the Deep South and West was equal to one-third of the national economic activity in the year 1830. He wrote broadly:

> Over eight years of seed time, the U.S. government, banks, private citizens, and foreign entities had collectively invested about $400 million, or one-third of the value of all U.S. economic activity in 1830, into expanding production of slavery's frontier. This includes the price of 250,000 slaves moved, 48 million new acres of public land sold, the costs of Indian removals and wars, and the massive expansion of the southwestern financial infrastructure.[551]

Professor Wilma A. Dunaway wrote in her 2003 book, *Slavery in the Mountain South,* that people held in slavery "made a much greater economic contribution to the Mountain South than scholars have previously acknowledged, especially to its antebellum development of town commerce, transportation networks, travel capitalism, manufacturing and extractive industries." The impact of the Kanawha Valley salt and slavery industry was remarkable in the southern Appalachian region, and, in 1850, it took over 3,000 people held in slavery to perform the grueling work of the salt furnaces and coal mines.[552]

Work Gangs, High Picking Rates, and "Whip Torture"

Professor Edward E. Baptist found that grueling labor organized carefully in work gangs greatly increased cotton production. He called it a "pushing system" to force up cotton production.[553] Work gangs were organized for specialized group tasks and performance was enforced by a new savage whip to discourage slacking. That motivation for workers, he called "whip torture." Other historians found that incentives were used to increase picking rates and that new varieties of cotton made higher picking rates easier to achieve, perhaps by four times the rates from early years of the industry.

Professor Kenneth Stamp wrote that slavers used incentives and competition between gangs and individual pickers. Some used profit sharing, sharecropping, early time off on Saturdays for the slave families' personal work, overtime pay, Saturday night dances, extra time to visit loved ones off the plantation, holiday and harvest celebrations, especially Christmas, a traditional three-to-five-day slave holiday. Some techniques to increase picking included humiliation. One slave was forced to eat the worms he failed to pick from tobacco leaves. Others were assigned to women's jobs and made to wear women's clothes. The incentives were part of the "persuasion doctrine," a substitute for corporal punishment.[554]

Many planters found such incentives ineffective in comparison to physical torture. Solomon Northrup, a free black who was kidnapped and forced into slavery for over a decade thought the opposite. After his self-emancipation, he wrote in 1853, in his book titled *Twelve Years a Slave,* that the kinder the slaver, the better work that was performed.[555] Whipping was preferred as punishment because it could inflict horrible pain publicly with or without scarring or maiming, as the slaver could choose. Whipping did not have to disable a slave worker for long, and it could be performed in a deliberate manner to have it seem more "necessary and just." In early Colonial America, whipping as punishment for whites and blacks was a common punishment. It fell out of favor for whites in the late 1700s. It was a slaver favorite until 1865. Whipping had a "dispiriting effect." Many slavers did not like to whip slaves themselves or use other violence against their slaves but nearly every slaver was able to have punishments inflicted and "few grown slaves escaped whipping entirely."[556]

Professor Baptist contended that daily cotton-picking rates, which increased fourfold in the forty years leading up to the Civil War, could best be explained by the pushing gang labor system enforced by "whip torture." Several historians questioned the value of "whip torture" on picking rates. They thought the best explanation for cotton's steadily increasing daily picking rates were new varieties of cotton plants grown in that period.

Professor Baptist characterized slave labor in cotton fields as being controlled, organized and worked with a crushing machine-like brutality. A cruel slaver, Bennett H. Barrow, wrote in the rules used for operation of his plantation, Highland, "A plantation might be considered as a piece of machinery.... and to operate successfully, all its parts should be uniform and exact, and its impelling force regular and steady."[557]

Slaver Barrow kept detailed records of whippings and injuries to workers from floggings, beatings and other punishments, which revealed little self-control and extreme cruelty. He would have a "general whipping frolic," where every slave in a field was whipped, including the drivers who were slaves. Slavers who were respected in their communities were thought to be humane to slaves, and they would show self-control in punishments. They also would have a commanding voice. These "respectable gentlemen" would be embarrassed to be known to actively sell slaves in the slave trade, unless the slave was a troublemaker or was sold as part of an estate sale or required by a slaver's last will and testament. Few slavers with high community standing would admit that they sold slaves to slave traders for profit or to pay debts. But slavers readily mortgaged slaves who would then be sold when debts had to be paid.[558]

Professor Kenneth M. Stampp wrote that slavery had in it an "element of savagery," and it attracted "fiends" who seemed to delight in brutality. "Neither law, nor social pressure, nor economic self-interest made Southern Gentlemen out of all slaveholders." He thought it was "pointless to catalogue the atrocities committed by psychopaths."[559]

Professor Baptist found the element of savagery in gang "pushing" systems which were enforced with a whip. Drivers who were lead slaves would force a relentless pace of picking and would readily whip slacking pickers.[560] Some overseers used whips and some left the whipping to drivers.

Detailed in Professor Baptist's 2014 book, *The Half Has Never Been Told:*

Slavery and the Making of American Capitalism, is how cotton was picked as fast as humanly possible by work gangs. On vast flat-land estates, cotton would be planted in large fields in straight rows, and fast slave workers would be selected to lead 15 or so workers in assigned rows, all in competition with other gangs to force the fastest picking possible. The gangs were ten to twenty workers in the field and other activities were organized as gang labor when possible. Slavers like Bennett H. Barrow used gang labor to create a mechanical-like process "uniform and exact, and its impelling force regular and steady." This mechanical "pushing" process assured the fastest picking possible--"backed by the lash, [it] proved an excellent mechanism for subordinating large numbers of slaves to the will of a small number of masters."[561]

Professor Baptist discussed a new long whip that was intended to improve production by cutting skin deeply with each lash. He asserted that the immediate and generous use of the torture of such a whip was a substantial cause for increased cotton production. He found also that unreasonable quotas were used to increase work production. Slackers in the field would be whipped in front of the work crews. The new whip was so brutal that people being whipped could not speak or think coherently. The cuts of the new whip were more horrible than those of the whips used in Virginia.

In the gang labor system, slackers could be easily identified and punished or threatened with punishment by whip-ready overseers and drivers in the field. There was another technique that allowed for a more deliberative-and scientific—approach to punishment. Slavers could purchase special ledgers printed by Thomas Affleck for a more organized and targeted approach to their pushing systems. They listed all slaves and recorded overall picking performances of individual workers and their gangs and leaders, and factors affecting production day-to-day, like weather and other matters that could slow production. The special ledgers would have different forms and displays to record picking amounts, age groupings, incentives paid and punishments inflicted, days and hours of work, weather, health, and other factors in production. They provided for more deliberative evaluations of performance and the need for incentives or whippings. With scientific reporting and information analysis, better performance could be encouraged and enforced in a more personal and deliberative way rather than just at the whim and caprice of overseers and drivers in the field who did not always function as part of a methodical process of "impelling force regular and steady." Methodical bookkeeping pushed higher and higher picking rates. Slavers could compare work progress, calculate honesty and dole out incentives and punishment on a day-to-day basis from field reports by overseers and others. Bookkeeping completed the mechanical nature of the work process. Quantification of factors affecting picking rates "complemented the driving force of the whip. Planters used their control to drive up the pace of labor, conduct experiments, distribute incentives and mete out punishment." [562]

Professor Baptist found this system of "whip torture" drove up cotton production which in turn made cotton America's leading business for manufacturing and export and made it the very foundation of the nation's industrialization, expansion and prosperity in the early nineteenth century.

Overseer on horseback watching African Americans pick cotton - *Image Courtesy of the Library of Congress*

Farm work in Virginia and other mountainous Upper South states could not be so tightly organized, controlled and punished or driven by incentives in a systematic way. The work there was more seasonal and many activities were specialized and performed at different speeds and times in mountain and valley terrain. But in flat-land cotton fields, all slave workers could be worked as functioning parts of a machine with whip torture being the "impelling force regular and steady," applied to workers who were doing the same work, in the same place, in the same times, pace and rhythms. They were called "hands" because picking and hoeing were the only skills needed in the mechanical process for cotton-picking with gang labor.[563]

Some conclusions in Professor Baptist's book have been questioned about how mighty the antebellum cotton industry became and about the details of brutal work conditions he found on some cotton plantations. It is accepted that in antebellum years, production of cotton increased dramatically with picking rates increasing about fourfold. It was reported by one slaver that the average daily picking rate for slave workers was observed to be 75 to 100 pounds for some varieties of cotton, but it was "at first" 150 pounds for Mexican varieties, and that average daily rate increased gradually to "several hundred pounds." Another account, with earlier cotton production in the 1830s, the quota for males on one plantation was 50 pounds. For older workers and children in these early years, the quota was 25 pounds. Because the plants would bloom in different levels at different times, each field would have periodic repeat harvests every season with six to ten pickings per field.[564]

Questions about the overall nature and impact of the cotton and slavery industry as presented in Professor Baptist's research appear in articles that can be read on the internet but for which their authors have chosen to refuse permission for any citation in other published works, limiting comment presumably for more research and new information. Such practice limits discussion. Fortunately, there are some reviews open to analysis and reuse.[565]

Researchers who questioned the brutal success of picking techniques contended that the increase in production was better explained by factors such as new varieties of cotton which had larger boll sizes, and may have been taller plants, and could be grown and picked more efficiently and perhaps more times on the same plants with more multiple picking cycles each harvest season. Today, the terms "high cotton" and "tall cotton" indicate a state of success or general well-being, but originally, they were likely specific references to bigger cotton plants and more lucrative harvests.

An extensive treatment of the subject of cotton varieties appears in *Creating Abundance: Biological Innovation and American Agricultural Development* by Alan L. Olmstead, a professor at the University of California at Davis, and Paul W. Rhode, a professor at the University of Arizona. Their book was published in 2008, six years before Professor Baptist's 2014 book. The two professors concluded "a stream of revolutionary biological innovations vastly increased both land and labor productivity." Specifically, they contended that Mexican and other varieties of superior cotton were responsible for the fourfold increase in the average daily picking rates by slave workers over the sixty years from 1800 to 1860. They found specifically that innovations in labor performance by those workers such as in punishing gang labor systems, and improved equipment could not fully explain the fourfold increase in daily picking rates.[566]

With any variety of cotton picked, it is stupefying that a person could in one day pick 50, or 100, or 150 or 200 pounds of the fluffy lightweight product that is field cotton. It would require many, many, many picks and bends and pulls and lifts to equal such very heavy weights. It is not surprising that people in slavery looked to a future in heaven instead one that included slavers and "perfect" submission on earth.[567]

Scholarly articles on this topic have created an interesting discourse.[568] They present questions about the sweeping new conclusions on the impact of the slave-based cotton industry on the national and world economies. Professor Baptist cited slave narratives for some of his conclusions including information that he thought showed individuals would be assigned quotas that would be increased once they were met, pushing slave workers to produce more and more cotton. Historians are careful to limit the use of ex-slave narratives for generalizations about slavery. They give voice to former slaves and are often used in context with other information sources.

Historians should use these narratives to help complete the story of slavery where data is scarce. Professor Wilma A. Dunaway, who has extensively studied plantation and other records for slavery in the southern Appalachian region, found that slave narratives taken as a group, generally provided more consistent and reliable information than plantation records. When read in combination and with caution, they can give an authentic voice to people who lived in slavery. In all, research with open conclusions that are widely shared adds greatly to the discourse on cotton capitalism.[569]

Slavery was a brutal labor system built on cruelty, and its extremes should be studied and detailed as part of its history as a system designed to use cruelty to produce "perfect" submission. The extremes of family separation and physical torture were used to support cotton-picking at high volumes. Slavery produced labor for a growing industry that provided great prosperity for persons who were not enslaved. All commentators should agree that "whip torture" was available and the threat of its use kept the lives of people under control and assured the organization of their work for cotton production at high levels.

It has been contended that Professor Baptist gave too much importance to actual whippings and slavery in the cotton industry. But to interested persons who are not economists, the issue is not complex, since all slavery in America was supported by an organized work system based on torture and the ever-immediate threat of torture, for "perfect" submission, including the sale of loved ones which caused a form of ongoing psychological whipping.[570] The impact of such whipping and the threat of whipping were effective enough throughout the South to brand in the brain of every person held in slavery the simple lesson that they were to be completely obedient and highly productive to survive and to see their loved ones survive. Regular whippings were not necessary when the clear threat of whipping was present. While it is an issue of economics as to the impact of the cotton industry on national and world economics, it should not be questioned that slavery created a crushing, brutal culture, and what Professor Baptist calls "whip torture" was real and used universally against people for the direct benefit of their slavers. New varieties of cotton would likely contribute to higher picking rates but without "whip torture" in some cruel form, the cotton and slavery industry would have collapsed as we know it. Torture and terror were mainstays in the industry, regardless of the picking techniques or cotton varieties that were used, and they appear to have had some substantial effect on dramatically increased production whether by the threat of whipping or its actual use. In that broad sense, "whip torture" can be called the foundation of the cotton and slavery industry and the foundation of all economic impacts that the industry created before the Civil War.

New provocative research and studies of slavery should be encouraged, conducted, published and discussed and, when needed, challenged. Historian Ira Berlin has written that history is not about the past. Instead, it is about the arguments we have about the past. Slavery can and should produce a lively discourse—and arguments--in a number of academic areas, which should in turn greatly increase the collective community understanding of slavery. Events described in written history without analysis of their antecedents and effects do not change ideas directly, but they can change how people see those events and what they can evaluate as a progression or other connection relevant in some way to their lives and their ideas about their lives. The procession of events may or may not challenge their life view.[571]

It is of some note that when the international magazine, *The Economist*, entered the discussion of slavery with an early negative review of Professor Baptist's book soon after it was published, the magazine immediately withdrew and disclaimed the review after it received considerable opposition to the review. Other reviews have taken opposing views, but no one seems to challenge the idea that "whip torture," broadly defined to include all "elements of savagery," was in fact the basis of slaver control to make human submission "perfect." In the harsh conditions of the cotton industry, "whip torture" could easily be a substantial primary cause, or a key contributing cause, of higher and higher levels of work production. It is interesting to see ongoing research in this area of study. Pertinent reviews that are open and available to all, in and outside of academia, are welcome.[572]

Chapter 13

Salt And Slavery Industry Is Built In The Kanawha Valley

Virginians Held in Slavery Build an Industry on the Western Frontier

King Salt was built on the hard labor of people who produced and shipped millions of barrels of salt from 1810 to 1865. Slave labor was less expensive and more controlled and dependable than free labor. Some free labor workers were available locally in the early years of the industry. But in the War of 1812, salt operations greatly increased, and local workers joined the Federal army, encouraging salt industrialists to exploit Virginia slavery.[573]

In Malden, the forced labor of slaves was used because the industry on the western frontier required factory systems with labor-intensive production processes.[574] Most any labor available, free or forced, had to be imported to the wilderness surrounding the Ruffner settlement. Forced work was well suited to an industry of hard and dangerous work. The coal industry in West Virginia after the Civil War had the same labor force problems in remote southern mountain valleys. The labor force there had to be recruited and supported with housing and new towns.

Slave labor could be readily forced into the wilderness for the new industry, using resident slaves and leased slaves. About half of the slaves were residents with slavers in the Kanawha Valley and about half were working under annual leases from slavers in central and southwestern Virginia. Slave leasing provided a flexible work force based on projected labor needs for the lease period. Salt industrialists could not attract and keep white or free black workers for wages as low as the cost of slave labor. Charleston lawyers arranged transactions for leased labor.

It is notable that the number of slaves in the industry tripled in the first decade of salt production, several years before the first factory systems were set up in Lowell, Massachusetts. The Kanawha Valley had the highest concentration of slaves in western Virginia. The number of persons reported as slaves in the census showed a substantial reduction in slave numbers just before the Civil War, likely resulting from reductions in numbers of leased slaves. The industry was in decline from strong competition and, also, in the lead up to the Civil War, leasing people far away from home could have been considered risky.[575]

Capital in the mountain region was invested in slaves, rather than manufacturing like in more prosperous regions. The percentage of the slave population to the free population grew from nine percent in 1810 to a peak of over 20 percent in 1850. That year, the industry in the Kanawha Valley alone had 1,500 leased slaves and about the same number of residents who were held in slavery. This concentration of people held in slavery for industrial production would made the frontier industry in the Kanawha Salines unique in the surrounding mountain economy. By 1860 the total number of slaves in Kanawha County dropped by about one-third to 2,184.

The salt and slavery industry began to decline in the 1850s with competition from salt operations in the free states of Ohio, Pennsylvania and New York. Salt industrialists in these states paid free worker wages, and they were competitive due to canals connecting established and new salt operations to the Ohio River.

Professor John E. Stealey, III, has written on the work of enslaved people in the Malden industry in his book, *The Antebellum Kanawha Salt Business and Western Markets* and in an article in *The Journal of Negro History*, "Slavery and the Western Virginia Salt Industry." The industry required thousands of workers, skilled and unskilled including factory workers, blacksmiths, barrel makers, boat builders, coal miners, river roustabouts and others. To support industry workers, enslaved and free, slaves would grow food, raise animals and do cooking, laundry, and cleaning. At peak production, the industry used about 3,000 slaves to work in or for the industry. As coal became an export industry, slaves were used more and more as miners. By 1850, with slave labor, coal became a major export commodity from the Kanawha Valley beginning the state's massive supply of fuel to America's industries by the end of the nineteenth century.[576]

The concentration of people held in slavery in the Kanawha Valley greatly exceeded other areas of western Virginia which had very few slaves. Professor Wilma A. Dunaway found in her study of the southern Appalachian region that the smallest populations of slaves were in western Virginia and eastern Kentucky. Throughout the Appalachian South about 20 percent of households had slaves whereas in the South as a whole, 29 percent of households had slaves. In West Virginia, only one in 16 households held people in slavery.[577] The highest concentration was in the Kanawha Valley for its salt factories. Professor Wilma A. Dunaway found that fewer than "15 percent of families owned slaves in forty West Virginia counties," and in Appalachian mountain counties "less than 8 percent of the residents held slaves."

Mountain people were becoming the poorest in the nation. Railroads were bypassing mountain terrain. Nearly half of all white households in the southern Appalachian region were landless people who had no slaves and fell below the poverty level. Wealth distribution was unbalanced in the mountain regions. Two percent of the population owned 29 percent of the wealth and three percent of the population owned half of the real property. Landless people included tenant farmers, coopers and blacksmiths.[578]

These mountain people would create a national sensation two decades after the Civil War with a family feud that, sadly, defined them and generations to follow as backward and different from middle class Americans—and a people to be lost and forgotten in the modern age.

Leased and Resident Slaves in Salt Production Industry

About one-half of all slaves working in the salt industry were leased. Slave leasing helped salt industrialists to adjust their slave force in the boom and bust cycles of salt markets and production limits. Resident slaves were a major continuing cost for industrialists. Slave leasing was suited to the salt industry and to other nonagricultural jobs. There were 1,500 slaves working under leases hundreds of miles away from their homes. Professor Wilma A. Dunaway found overall that about one in four slave workers were leased in the southern Appalachian region and of that number about 87 percent were leased to work in nonagricultural jobs.[579]

In the Kanawha Valley, because of the increased danger of escape, injury or death of a slave, the costs of leasing slaves to the salt industry were estimated to be 30 percent higher than for lease work elsewhere in Virginia. Higher leasing costs would have benefited leased slaves by making them more valuable and less subject to abuse and neglect. The high costs were due both to the dangers of the work and the short distance to freedom across the "River Jordan" into the Ohio Valley where the Underground Railroad could be counted on to move escaped slaves on to freedom in Canada. Slaves with loved ones back at their slaver's home were thought to be less likely to run away to Ohio. Runaways were a primary concern of slavers in the Kanawha Valley. A newspaper article in 1855 from Washington in the District of Columbia, called then "Washington City," stated that escapes by leased slaves from the Kanawha Valley were as high as twenty-five percent. The newspaper recommended that free men be hired or that the workers be made free. During the Civil War, people emancipated themselves and left the Kanawha Valley as early as 1862.[580]

There is little or no record or comment found about activities of the Underground Railroad in the Kanawha Valley before, during or after the Civil War. It was illegal and subversive to assist fugitive slaves. It was a Confederate slaver area and assistance to fugitive slaves could be dangerous if discovered. These concerns are not present after the Civil War and no one has commented on its activities in the Valley. No one is known to have stepped forward after the war to reveal their participation as a conductor or to disclose any special knowledge of activities of the Underground Railroad in the Kanawha Valley.

Historians in West Virginia have been silent on activities of the Underground Railroad in West Virginia, other than a doctoral student at West Virginia University who was the first African American to graduate with a doctorate degree in 1954. John Reuben Sheeler in his 1954 dissertation, *The Negro in West Virginia Before 1900,* extensively described slavery in western Virginia. He wrote that there were a number of established Ohio River crossing points for runaway persons at Parkersburg, Point Pleasant, Guyandotte near today's Huntington, and other locations north and south along the "River Jordan." The mass migration of slaves constantly moving from eastern Virginia through western Virginia to the Ohio River for shipment south made the passage of fugitive people less noticeable overland and on their river crossings. Being hidden in plain sight was also available in the Kanawha Valley where up to three thousand people held in slavery on a six-mile river plain had freedom to move about most anytime.[581] But there is no record known of such activities in the Valley. It is possible that fugitive from slavery going west to Ohio would stay away from the Kanawha Valley, depending on their place of escape. Slaves from Baltimore would likely follow the route of the B & O Railroad through Clarksburg to Parkersburg or Wheeling. Apparently, there were regular sanctuary places along that route. People escaping from central Virginia would likely follow the rivers to the Kanawha Valley either staying out of the Valley or going through the middle of it effectively concealed in plain sight by the numerous slaves who had free movement there with relative anonymity. Most would be helpful to runaway slaves on journeys to Freedom.[582]

Family connections discouraged runaways. The Underground Railroad made possible a quick ride from the Kanawha and across the "River Jordan" and then on to freedom in Canada. Virginia owned the Ohio River to its western shore because of language in its cession to the Congress which was established under the Articles of Confederation. Virginia ceded all territorial claims "beyond" the Ohio River, for what was called the Territory Northwest of the Ohio River. Later, the Northwest Territory would be in six states: Ohio, Indiana, Michigan, Wisconsin, Illinois, and the northeastern part of Minnesota.[583] Whites in Ohio generally did not want escaped blacks as neighbors. Slave catchers posed a constant threat of violence in Ohio.

The competition of salt industrialists for dependable and hard-working slaves would have made the personal opinions of leased slaves about their own work conditions and dangers important to their slavers who were far away from the work. Leased slaves could report on their work conditions and treatment when home for the Christmas holiday. Annual leasing terms were from January to Christmas, and a slave's return each Christmas would have given some voice for or against a return to any of the salt industrialists. Some slavers would provide in leases for extra visits by a slave to loved ones during the lease term.

Leasing slaves into the Kanawha Valley created hardships for the leased person and their families. The Kanawha Valley was far away from the homes of many leased workers in central and southwestern Virginia, forcing long separations from their families and kin networks. Washington Ferguson was leased on year-long leases that took him away from his wife, Jane, and her children. In Hales Ford, they were 225 miles away from Malden, so he could only see them on return trips at Christmas. Booker T. Washington wrote that his stepfather was with his family at Christmas holidays. Leased slaves separated from loved ones would have the misery of a year-long separation added to their hard labor under the lease.

As salt operations grew, the population of people held in slavery grew. The slave population in Kanawha County increased in each census from a low in 1800 of 231 slaves to a high in 1850 of 3,140 slaves. The census did not distinguish between resident and leased slaves. In 1810, as the industry was beginning to grow after the success of the first Ruffner well in 1808, the number of reported slaves was 352 in a population of 3,866. In 1820, the number of slaves in the county tripled to 1,073. In 1830, it grew by 70 percent to 1,717. In 1840 it was 2,560, and after the peak production year in 1846 in the next census the county's highest number of slaves were reported, 3,140.[584] It is notable that despite these increases in the slave population in Kanawha County, the overall slave population in western Virginia did not increase after 1820, when the population of people held in slavery was at most 12 percent of the total population and would decline to 7.8 percent by 1850, and even further after that census year. After the Civil War before 1900, the population numbers for blacks were never more than 4.5 percent of the state population, giving the state one of the lowest population percentages for blacks east of the Mississippi River. The population percentage in the 2010 Census was approximately 14 percent.[585]

It appears that slaves who were residents in the Kanawha Salines lived in multiple generation family groups, to some extent. Family groupings with non-abusive treatment of enslaved persons would have tied workers to their lives in Malden and would have discouraged resident slaves from running away. With family groupings, the lives of resident slaves would likely have been better with food, housing and clothing.[586]

Charts of the demographics of enslaved persons in the salt industry by age and gender indicate what may be family groupings. This seems true for Lewis Ruffner's slaves since they were housed in small, separate cabins in the family's slave quarters at Tinkersville. The general rule in the South was that slaves were housed in separate cabins. The 1870 Census reveals no large residential units and no new construction of cabins in Malden. Separate cabins, as revealed in the 1870 Census, would not have been built after the Civil War, because the salt industry and the Ruffner fortunes were in decline. There were thousands of slaves living and working in the Kanawha Valley in a compact river plain. A substantial number of slaves would have had some control over their day-to-day lives, especially workers who were skilled and favored for their hard work. Court records show that slaves generally could go about at large in the Kanawha Salines. The *Kanawha Banner* wrote in 1842 that streets were "thronged, at all hours of the night by blacks." Family groups there would be consistent with information on slave marriages in Virginia and the rest of the South.[587]

Free Blacks and Virginia Slavery

Free blacks formed a substantial black population in Kanawha County. In 1850, there were 212 free blacks of whom 54 lived in Charleston which was beginning to grow. It was common for free blacks to live in urban areas. Free blacks were often skilled laborers and they enjoyed a degree of superiority as free people. They were about ten percent of the black population across the Upper South. After the Nat Turner Rebellion, a number of Virginians wanted to force free blacks out of the state. In 1832, Virginia Episcopal Bishop William Meade called for deportation of free blacks.[588]

Some free blacks used their free status to become successful professionals in northern states. The great W. E. B. Du Bois came from a middle class family in Massachusetts and never knew the terror and hardship of slavery in his boyhood years. As the genius intellectual he was, W. E. B. Du Bois did not appear to understand or fully appreciate the struggles of the common African American. The editor of *The Negro World* wrote that W. E. B. Du Bois "looked down upon the masses and their infirmities 'from the height of his own greatness.'" This harsh judgment haunted W. E. B. Du Bois "until he drew his last breath," at age 95. A more appropriate judgment was made by his accomplished biographer, Professor

David Levering Lewis of Rutgers University, who wrote that W. E. B. Du Bois was an "avatar of a race whose troubled fate he was predestined to interpret and to direct." [589]

In the North, free blacks had few civil rights. Most could not vote or serve on juries, testify in court, join the militia, own dogs or carry guns. But they could own property, collect a wage, assemble as they wished and speak freely, and most importantly they could establish an independent, stable, and predictable family life. Free blacks formed communities and many were important in the life of Ohio communities, but generally they were encouraged to move on to Canada. Louisiana had a large population of free persons of color from the Caribbean and Africa. Three thousand free blacks from Haiti immigrated to New Orleans at different times. Under Spanish law before the Louisiana Purchase, slaves could buy their freedom and many did. In 1810, New Orleans, as well as in Mobile and Pensacola, had populations which included about thirty percent free persons of color. Virginia had a law requiring freed slaves to leave the state, but it was a law that was not enforced unless a free black might cause some difficulty. Many free blacks stayed in Virginia, more than those who left the state. Whites left the state in significant numbers to live away from slavery.[590]

Professor Kenneth M. Stampp in his 1989 book, *The Peculiar Institution: Slavery in the Ante-Bellum South,* found that slave labor had advantages that made it more economical than free labor, whether black or white free labor. The costs of slave labor were much less than free labor. Women and children and older workers could be exploited in slavery more than in free labor. Slaves worked longer hours with strict discipline. But slave labor required costly up-front investments and ongoing costs of maintenance and old age support for some slaves in family groups. He thought that the high valuation of slave labor during the decade before the Civil War was the best evidence of the continued profitability of slavery.[591]

In the salt and slavery industry, free labor was costly and difficult to procure. White labor and free black labor were about two times the cost of slave labor. White and free black workers would receive room and board plus wages. Salt industrialists favored slave labor "for the business in which [they] were engaged," slaves "were the best." A salt industrialist said that his few white workers required more supervision than all of his enslaved workers together.[592]

Despite regional differences in Virginia politics, terrain, heritage, people, values, and ideas about slavery in general, the western Virginia salt industrialists fully exploited slave labor to produce a lucrative product. The Kanawha Valley was an island of concentrated heavy industry and slavery in a mountain frontier with little other industry and few slaves. At the start of the Civil War, there were two areas with large populations of slaves in what would become West Virginia: the Kanawha Valley and today's Eastern Panhandle.

Industrial Danger at Salt Furnaces and Coal Mines

Industrial salt work was dangerous. The most compelling dangers for slaves were the hot furnaces in salt factories and pitch-black coal mines. Smoke-ridden air from factories built side by side in a river valley was very unhealthy. Factory work was round the clock, demanding, and repetitive. The arduous and dangerous work ran at least six days per week and at times round the clock. Slaves in common salt factory labor had piece-work goals whereas skilled laborers worked on a timed basis.[593]

Resident slaves would have been more skilled on the whole than leased slaves. They also would likely be protected from dangerous work at the furnaces, in coal mines and on boats. With a scarcity of labor, experienced and skilled slave workers would likely have been promoted to safer supervisory positions. Leased slaves would have had the worst jobs even if the required work was specifically barred by their leases. After David Ruffner's death in 1843, while his estate was being administered, a legal action was filed against Lewis Ruffner for the death of Ben, a slave killed in a coal mine roof fall. The claim was for $800.00 and made on the contention that Ben was leased to work in his father's salt works, not in a dangerous coal mine job.[594]

Death was so common in some jobs that slavers took out life insurance on the lives of their slaves. It was common for leased slaves and some resident slaves who worked in dangerous jobs to have such policies on their lives payable to their slavers, who wanted to protect their investments. By 1840, it was "common place" for slavers to insure the lives of slave coal miners. The annual premiums on a number of policies for $100.00 of coverage was one dollar for regular work and three to four dollars for coal mining work for the same coverage amount.[595]

Life insurance became popular for whites in northeastern cities and for slaves. A number of major life insurance companies prospered on sales of slave life policies but went out of business after the Civil War. Aetna Life had some slave life policies in Virginia, whereas New York Life's first 1,000 life insurance policies sold included 488 policies on the lives of slaves, or about half of the total. After two years, New York Life considered slave policies too risky and discontinued their sales in 1848. US Life had 173 policies. All three companies prospered after the War, as life insurance boomed a decade later into a $2.3 billion business on 800,000 policies nationwide.[596]

Coal production eventually grew into its own export industry. In 1836, nearly 1,000 slaves were mining two hundred thousand tons of coal to fuel 33 salt companies. By 1850, when coal became an independent export industry, there were as many as 2,000 slaves mining coal in the Kanawha Valley for twenty-five companies incorporated to produce coal. One of the largest was British-owned Winifrede Mining and Manufacturing. Coal companies set up housing for workers and had their own stores for free labor. The Winifrede store sold $57,632.00 in goods in less than a year. Another company store, for Western Mining and Manufacturing Company, transacted $15,000.00 annually in sales.[597]

Slaves were also used in the timber industry. It is reported that one major saw mill in the county had a 22-foot waterfall and could produce 30,000 to 40,000 board feet of lumber a day. Slaves worked in logging operations to transport timber and work in the sawmills. Western Virginia had fifteen sawmills which used the then modern technology of circular saws powered by steam.[598]

Enslaved people in Virginia were human property and could be forced to work or to be leased to any work the slaver chose for them. Salt factory work was dirty and was performed in polluted air from many factories crowded in a compact narrow river valley plain. It was essentially year-round work, but, due to lower water levels in the Great Kanawha River in different seasons, production might be stopped or delayed by dry weather. Production might also be stopped when planned production goals for the salt business trusts had been met. In general, salt operations had few scheduled idle periods other than for the Christmas holiday, from Christmas to New Years. That time was a universal slave holiday.

The labor of most slaves was in agricultural operations in central and southwestern Virginia counties where most of the slaves resided who were leased to the Kanawha Valley. Agriculture required its largest number of workers in peak harvest times. On the whole, agricultural labor was less demanding. It was seasonal work, subject to falling weather, with common peak production times and times of reduced work hours.

Agricultural work was safer and much cleaner than industrial work, and the work was in fresh air. But work in the Kanawha Salines had an advantage for a number of slaves. It was on a compact six-mile plain where as many as 3,000 slaves resided, many of whom could travel about at large. Any cruel treatment of slaves would be known and resisted readily, whereas slaves on secluded agricultural plantations and farms could be and were subjected to abuse and cruelty more often than those living in urban areas.

Slaves from across the southern Appalachian region, ranging generally from Virginia and Kentucky to the Deep South, reported in post-war narratives harsh punishment twice as often as other slaves, and they reported having cruel slavers five times more often than other slaves. Whippings were mostly for social control rather than work production. Public displays of punishment were used to destroy the dignity of slaves. A western Virginia slaver had his slaves eat worms if they did not work fast enough.[599]

It was accepted that slaves in cities were most always treated better than slaves on farms and plantations who were away from the eyes of peers who could judge how slavers treated their slaves. Half of all slaves in the South lived on farms instead of plantation estates. It was assumed that slaves were treated better on farms than on plantations, but that was not a proven fact. Slave narratives after the war show that people held in slavery on small farms were subjected to greater abuse than others. Slaves often did not want to be on small farms because the slavers might not afford to care for them and, when in debt, they would be sold. On farms and some plantations, slaves had "customary rights" to have their own small gardens and animals and to visit family off the farm or plantation. They were not rights at law but were respected rights of custom and expectation, and violation of those expectations caused discord between slaves and slavers. The general attitude of "proper" southerners was to disdain slavers who were cruel and slave traders unless they were rich. Wealthy men in the slave trade were leaders in a number of cities.[600]

In eastern Virginia, most slaves had agricultural work, but by the Civil War many slaves were being leased to factory work. With decline in the state's tobacco production and the new demands for slave labor in the Deep South, Virginia exported slaves as a regular and profitable business.

Wage Incentives Paid for Extra Work on Sabbath

Work on the Sabbath in the salt industry was illegal, technically, but was performed regularly and openly with little interference by government authorities. Reverend Henry Dans Ward, the rector of St. John's Episcopal Church in Charleston, chastised John Dickinson Lewis and other salt industrialists in his congregation to not have factory work performed on Sundays, but with no success. There was a clear benefit for having Sunday work not covered by slave leases.[601]

Salt industrialists offered incentive pay to slaves for any Sunday work in addition to their required work of six days under a lease.[602] Unlike in cotton fields where a variety of incentives were used, salt industrialists wanted their factory work to continue round the clock and wages were the best incentives to have workers continue working a seventh day. Other incentives and competitions may have been used but most salt industrialists used wages for Sabbath work. How much choice the workers had to refuse Sabbath work is unknown. Some commentators have claimed that the incentives of slavers in the cotton industry were well accepted by their cotton pickers and that their wide acceptance was some evidence of a mutual benefit. With a system of cruelty overlaying all interactions in slavery, it is difficult to understand how any choice by people who were held in slavery could ever be a free choice or the evidence of an acceptance of some benefit that slavers considered "mutual."

In the salt industry, this Sabbath incentive allowed slaves who wanted money to use for loved ones to be paid directly for their "extra work" outside the weekly pay due on the lease to the slaver. Slavers could use the same incentive for their resident slaves. Such incentives for Sabbath work were used across the South.[603] To increase production with positive incentives rather than punishments, salt industrialists encouraged competition games between work groups to build *esprit de corps* and profits.

The incentive pay would be paid to the slaves at Christmas. Importantly, such annual payments at Christmas discouraged slaves from running away during the year across the "River Jordan." It is unlikely that all leased slaves would be given their money to carry for the journey back to loved ones in eastern Virginia. They could be given store credits back home for purchases to share with their loved ones. Coal operators used a somewhat similar idea for store credits in their towns. They used "scrip" for store purchases in lieu of money wages. Scrip was a metal disc produced by coal operators for town currency. The Pioneer Coal Company on Campbells Creek was the first to use scrip in the Kanawha Valley.[604]

People Held in Slavery by Lewis Ruffner

In the 1850 Census for Kanawha County, Lewis Ruffner was reported to have 48 slaves, of whom 38 were males and 10 were females. He was living in Louisville. Tax records for 1851 show fewer numbers of slaves perhaps with the lower numbers reflecting the number of resident slaves for tax purposes while the higher number could have included leased slaves who were counted in the census along with resident slaves. That year, Lewis Ruffner's mother was living in the family home in Malden, and the family salt business was being managed by others. The next year, he had 27 slaves and in 1853 he had 32 slaves. It was listed that he had only 4 slaves in 1854. In the 1850 Census report, there were substantial numbers of slaves in generational groups. They were not all prime-of-life ages. There were nine children under age 15 and nine people who were over 50 years old. There were 13 who were between the ages of 20 and 29 years, and 13 who were ages 30 to 39 years. Professor Stealey thought these numbers tend to indicate age groupings of families. They also indicate that Lewis Ruffner used leased male slaves to supplement his resident work force.[605]

Lewis Ruffner's grandfather, Joseph Ruffner, owned three slaves at his death in 1803 before the first salt well was drilled. The slave numbers for other Ruffner families in the Kanawha Salines are all below those for the leading salt company, Dickinson & Shrewsbury, which had 232 slaves reported in the 1850 Census. Likely half of that number were leased slaves. According to the Bureau of the Census's *A Century of Population Growth of 1909*, in 1850 only 12 Virginia families had over 200 slaves, making this salt partnership a major slave-working business. How trustworthy those numbers are for slaver families in Virginia is not known because the data is not collected from the state as a whole, but it is calculated using sample counties.[606]

The demographics of slavery in the salt industry are difficult to know because slaves who were leased were recorded in census data along with resident slaves. Professor Stealey analyzed the slave census data for 1850 and 1860. When production was down in 1860 and leasing was greatly reduced, the numbers of male workers in 1860 are significantly lower than their numbers in 1850, whereas the female numbers more nearly approach the 1850 numbers.[607] He found those numbers show that leased slaves were more likely to be male slaves and that female slaves likely worked away from factories.

Professor Stealey finds the demographic numbers for slaves in the salt industry may support an analysis for family groupings but may also support a different analysis especially with so many leased slaves in the Kanawha Valley. It should be noted that slaves there were known by first names, and none were known to have used family names for newborns. Historian Herbert G. Gutman, in his study of slave marriages and naming customs, found that slaves used names to signify family bonds. Last names of former slavers were not used commonly unless a slave wanted to connect to a family or kin network at a farm or plantation. Washington Ferguson took the name of his slaver's Ferguson family in Hales Ford. He may have wanted to connect to family or a kin network there. Children were named for fathers but rarely for mothers. It appears that some slaves in Malden may have used first and last names, but official county records, such as death records, used only first names for slaves, with their slavers' names recorded with the slave's single name.[608]

The family grouping analysis for Lewis Ruffner's slaves seems appropriate in light of worker housing in Tinkersville, near his salt factory and farm. Housing at the former Ruffner slave quarters was in single-unit cabins, and it was integrated for white people and black people.[609] People in cabins with fireplaces would be responsible for their own cooking, cleaning and upkeep. Such single-unit housing may indicate family groupings. It is also possible that large-scale dormitory style housing was avoided to limit discord between slaves. It is unlikely that Washington Ferguson would have returned to Malden if he thought his wife and children could not live together when they arrived as a family with their own home.

Most slaves in the Kanawha Valley were salt production workers. The census data indicate there were no slave markets in the Kanawha Valley. Slaves there were not part of the eastern Virginia slave selling industry. Western Virginia's only major concentration of slaves was in the Kanawha Salines and they were working in salt and coal industries. Across the Appalachian region, 16 percent of slaves worked in some type of manufacturing mostly on plantations.[610] There were many slaves in the counties that would become the Eastern Panhandle after statehood. But the numbers from the rest of the territory that would become a new state show few slaves compared to eastern Virginia's population of enslaved people which was almost half a million souls in 1860.

In a respected museum in Cincinnati, Ohio, it has been displayed that the Kanawha Valley had a major slave market, but there has been no record or reference found to a slave market of any type in any record or publication for the Kanawha Valley. The numbers of slaves located in the area were too few and too valuable for work production in the salt factories for any mass marketing to take place. Granville Hall, a reporter for the Wheeling Conventions, wrote that there was what he called a formal slave growing farm located three miles east of Clarksburg near the home of an ex-governor of Virginia, where young people were "corralled, ranged and fed for the Southern market, almost as if they had been sheep or swine." The evidence of such a place is slight and no other such slave farms have been reported in the state. Almost half the slaves in the salt industry were leased from central and southwestern Virginia. Notably, there are no known newspaper advertisements for a slave market in the Kanawha Valley. There is a scattering of advertisements for the sale of specific slaves. Those few advertisements indicate there was no slave market in the Kanawha Valley, or anywhere in Western Virginia.[611] Many slaves walked in coffles on the James River and Kanawha Turnpike through the Kanawha Valley and their travel may have indicated a slave market was present, but no evidence of such market has been found by your author.

Slavery in the Kanawha Valley was changed by the Emancipation Proclamation. President Abraham Lincoln, with concern about freeing slaves in border states, carefully crafted the Emancipation Proclamation to leave border state slaves in bondage with loyal slavers in Maryland, Delaware, Kentucky, Missouri and western Virginia counties to be part of West Virginia. It has been estimated that the Emancipation Proclamation left almost ten percent of all slaves in bondage in the border states. A number of slaves left the Kanawha Valley after the Proclamation was announced. At the property of salt industrialist Rachel Grant Tompkins, it was said that President Lincoln's Emancipation Proclamation "emptied most of the slave cabins."

Washington Ferguson's status under the Emancipation Proclamation is interesting because he was freed by the terms of the Proclamation as a slave in eastern Virginia, but when he escaped to Malden, he returned to a border slave state. It is likely that he was able to work for wages with Lewis Ruffner like any freed worker. These wages would give him the funds he sent to young Booker's mother for the family's move to Malden after the war.[612]

It is not known if Lewis Ruffner's slaves left with the Emancipation Proclamation or at the end of the Civil War when all slaves were emancipated. It appears that the 1852 Christian believers stayed with the Ruffners during the war. The Ruffners and other salt industrialists were committed for five decades to supporting their businesses with labor of enslaved persons. In 1850, the eastern Virginia slave number is 22 times as many as the number in western Virginia. In eastern Virginia, in 1860, slaves represented about 31 percent of the population. In 1863, the State Auditor, Samuel Crane, filed with the state legislature a slave tax report showing Kanawha and Putnam counties had the highest numbers of slaves over the age of 12, who were taxable to slavers. He listed Kanawha County with 1,237 and Putnam County with 345. Eleven of the 32 counties listed in the report had fewer than 20 taxable slaves. Free blacks between the ages of 21 and 55 totaled 48 and all free blacks over 21 years of age totaled 143.[613]

In all, it may be asked: Was slavery "better" in Malden's salt industry than on a central Virginia farm? The easy answer is no, because there is no type of enslavement that can be "better." It is meaningless in the Horror of Slavery to compare the separate horrors of mistreated human beings. There are no sanctuaries for those who perpetrate horror on their neighbors. There may be redemption for future generations, when they appreciate what evil has been committed and they for themselves and their families accept a life commitment to help others to prevent present and future evils to humankind.

Chapter 14

Opposition To Slavery Silenced In South After The Nat Turner Rebellion

Ruffners use Slavery to Build Salt Industry

Joseph Ruffner, the first Ruffner in the Kanawha Valley, held people in slavery. Virginians with German heritage commonly had few or no slaves. Most German immigrants had a sentiment against slavery.[614] His oldest son, David Ruffner married the daughter of an immigrant German Mennonite minister whose faith community opposed slavery. It appears that David Ruffner was the first Ruffner to rely on a major slave work force for a business. His brothers became slavers for their salt interests.

No Ruffner publicly opposed slavery on religious or moral grounds. The family shared a belief in white superiority. As two leading Presbyterian ministers, Dr. Henry Ruffner and his son, Dr. W. H. Ruffner, regularly preached about the superiority of white people. As southerners and Virginians, the Ruffners thought religious and moral objections to slavery were the radical ideas of northern abolitionists. Brothers Lewis Ruffner and Dr. Henry Ruffner, and other Virginia leaders rejected abolitionism as radical and dangerous.[615] The dominant idea in the South was that abolitionists were the enemies of southern culture, not just slavery. For most southerners, there was no separation between southern culture and slavery.

While the Ruffners may have questioned slavery from time to time, they did not question the belief that blacks were inferior as a race and individually. It appears that Lewis Ruffner's ideas about race began to evolve during and after the Civil War. His observations of young Booker's family and other freed people influenced him to support their civil rights in Malden after the war. A German Mennonite heritage in their early years likely would have had the Ruffners view slaves as human beings which in turn should have led them to many questions about slavery and the evils it supported. But like all salt industrialists, the Ruffners were pragmatic entrepreneurs of the first and highest order. They relied on slave labor and likely believed that slavery made their factories possible, not just profitable. Slaves built and worked the salt industry for a half century with no known uprising or violent discord, and sadly with no benefit to their loved ones and future generations.

Frederick Douglass Speech: No Slave Celebrates July 4

The Horror of Slavery, especially in light of the ideas and values of the Declaration of Independence, is most eloquently reported by Frederick Douglass in his famous speech in 1852, "The Meaning of July Fourth for the Negro." The speech explains why slaves could not celebrate the Fourth of July. It was delivered in Rochester, New York, when he was asked to speak on the celebration of American liberty. Frederick Douglass calls out the tyrants of "Virginia and Carolina" for the evil of slavery and he warns all that slavery is a venomous reptile coiled at the nation's breast:

> The sunlight that brought light and healing to you, has brought stripes and death to me. This Fourth of July is yours, not mine. You may rejoice, I must mourn. To drag a man in fetters into the grand illuminated temple of liberty, and call upon him to join you in joyous anthems....

> What, to the American slave, is your 4th of July? I answer; a day that reveals to him, more than all other days in the year, the gross injustice and cruelty to which he is the constant victim. To him, your celebration is a sham; your boasted liberty, an unholy license;... your shouts of liberty and equality, hollow mockery; your prayers and hymns, your sermons and thanksgivings, with all your religious parade and solemnity, are, to Him, mere bombast, fraud, deception, impiety, and hypocrisy-a thin veil to cover up crimes which would disgrace a nation of savages. There is not a nation on the earth guilty of practices more shocking and bloody than are the people of the United States, at this very hour.

> Follow this drove to New Orleans. Attend the auction; see men examined like horses; see the forms of women rudely and brutally exposed to the shocking gaze of American slave-buyers. See this drove sold and separated forever; and never forget the deep, sad sobs that arose from that scattered multitude. Tell me, citizens, where, under the sun, you can witness a spectacle more fiendish and shocking. Yet this is but a glance at the American slave-trade, as it exists, at this moment, in the ruling part of the United States.

You...pride yourselves on your Democratic institutions, while you yourselves consent to be the mere tools and body-guards of the tyrants of Virginia and Carolina....You declare before the world, and are understood by the world to declare that you "hold these truths to be self-evident, that all men are created equal; and are endowed by their Creator with certain inalienable rights; and that among these are, life, liberty, and the pursuit of happiness; and yet, you hold securely, in a bondage which, according to your own Thomas Jefferson, "is worse than ages of that which your fathers rose in rebellion to oppose," a seventh part of the inhabitants of your country.

The existence of slavery in this country brands your... Christianity as a lie. It destroys your moral power abroad: it corrupts your politicians at home. It saps the foundation of religion... Oh! be warned! be warned! a horrible reptile is coiled up in your nation's bosom; the venomous creature is nursing at the tender breast of your youthful republic; for the love of God, tear away, and fling from you the hideous monster, and let the weight of twenty million crush and destroy it forever![616]

Last Chance to End Slavery in Virginia Without War

George W. Summers was a leading politician in western Virginia before the war. In 1832, he gave an important address speaking for emancipation.[617] He was a wealthy slaver in Charleston who ran for governor in 1851. He served in Congress from1840 to 1844. His brother, Lewis Summers, was an important judge who helped organize St. John's Episcopal Church, known during the war as a Confederate church.

He was best known locally as an early supporter of emancipation. He became a public proponent for emancipation in 1832, when he gave a stirring and well-respected speech for the end of slavery in Virginia. In 1831 and 1832, the Virginia House of Delegates considered and voted on an amendment to abolish slavery. It failed on a 58 to73 vote. Below is a map of the counties where delegates voted in the Virginia House of Delegates on the proposal to abolish slavery. The map shows the areas where abolitionist ideas form the general shape of what a generation later would become the State of West Virginia.[618]

George W. Summers was named by the General Assembly in early 1861 to serve as one of five peace commissioners to negotiate with federal officials before Virginia's decision on secession from the Union. A peace conference was held in Washington in February, and it was recommended that Congress pass

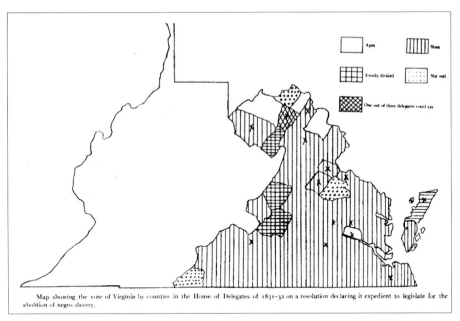

Map showing the vote of Virginia by counties in the House of Delegates of 1831–32 on a resolution declaring it expedient to legislate for the abolition of negro slavery.

Vote of Virginia House of Delegates 1831-32 on Resolution for the Abolition of Negro Slavery.
Image Permission from West Virginia University Press

an amendment to the Constitution to settle the sectional crisis before a bloody shooting war would begin. The proposal failed. He represented Kanawha County in the Richmond secession convention and voted no. He returned home frustrated and likely appalled at the pending war. He retired from political life. Unlike Lewis Ruffner, who became the area's leading Unionist and a state maker for West Virginia, George W. Summers was silent during the Civil War. He provided no leadership for the new state or on other political issues of the day. He died in 1868. Summers County in southern West Virginia was named for him in 1871.[619]

In today's Charleston's Elk City area, George W. Summers' stately home is "Glenwood," preserved beautifully as a restored plantation home. It is a furnished home museum next to Stonewall Jackson Middle School. The mansion house was built in 1852 by James Madison Laidley on 366 acres. It is a large, classic, two-story, red brick home in Federal style. It has a large slave quarters behind the mansion house. Glenwood and its plantation were sold to George W. Summers by James Madison Laidley, who was a salt industrialist and the uncle of his wife, Amasetta Laidley.

The Summers' plantation earlier had been owned by George Washington's niece, Betty Washington Lewis Lovell, the widow of attorney Joseph Lovell. He was a young attorney and salt industrialist who organized the Kanawha

Glenwood Estate, Home of George W. Summers and Amasetta Laidley
Image Courtesy of the Library of Congress

Salt Company, which was the first in a series of business combinations leading to the first business trust in America. The Summers' personal letters chronicle the family's life while he was away in Congress.[620]

Debate over Slavery Ends in Virginia after Nat Turner's Rebellion

Slavery was a ticking time bomb in the South especially in Virginia. In August 1831, Nat Turner led a bloody rebellion in eastern Virginia. At first, the rebellion convinced many people that slavery could not be controlled and should be abolished, but by the end of the decade that wholly changed as the sales of Virginians to the Deep South became more and more lucrative.

Nat Turner was an intelligent and educated enslaved man who had visions that he claimed came to him direct from God. Other slaves thought he was a prophet because he assured them that God told him how to put God's holy word into action. To start a slave rebellion in eastern Virginia in Southampton County, he announced that he was called by God to kill white children, women, and men in families who held slaves. Nat Turner, followed by as many as 50 slaves and free blacks killed whole families of white people in the area. It was a two-day massacre of nearly 60 whites.[621] The local response was swift and bloody. Black people known to have participated in the attacks were beheaded and their heads put on stakes along roads. Hundreds of black people not involved in the massacres were killed in the area of the uprising and elsewhere. Nat Turner hid from authorities for two months until he was captured and killed.

Nat Turner's Rebellion changed how slaves were treated after 1831 throughout the South. Soon after the rebellion, many Virginians were open to frank discussions about emancipation. The local slave economy had been stagnant before Virginians became very valuable for sale to the Deep South. Laws were passed to prevent slaves being taught to read, assemblies and meetings of slaves without a white present, and other personal liberties of enslaved people.

Many slavers believed that they would not be killed by their slaves, if they could turn them into Christians. Across the South in the 1840s and 1850s, slavers pushed Christian religion to be accepted by large numbers of slaves who were engaged primarily in agriculture. In the low country of South Carolina, slavers constructed plantation chapels, about one hundred in number. This effort made the number of Episcopal communicants in the Diocese of South Carolina, who were black, greater than the number who were white. In antebellum Macon, Georgia, with a society and culture more urban than in rural South Carolina, slaves earned wages and could contribute to their own selected churches. About six percent of all persons held in slavery resided in cities and larger towns.[622] Their lives were generally better in cities than in rural areas where most all slaves lived in restricted surroundings. Smaller towns did not have separate churches for slaves. Privileged slaves might have attended worship with their slavers.

There were four black congregations in Macon that were somewhat independent, two Baptist, one Methodist and one Presbyterian. The choice of churches in the South by slaves usually mirrored the choices of their slavers. The Macon congregations were associated with white congregations which encouraged their separate organizations. The black congregations had their own buildings with whites holding legal title. The black churches had their own ministers and services. The white Methodists wanted a separate building for their black congregation because they objected to "noisy" slave services. The black Methodist church in Macon had its own court to preside over behavior offenses by members. Throughout the South, more privileged slaves tended to join Methodist Episcopal churches and less privileged slaves joined Baptist churches, but with many exceptions. Most blacks left their slaver churches after emancipation in favor of churches organized by black leaders for black congregations.[623]

In western Virginia before the Civil War, there were very few Episcopal churches. In 1846, Bishop William Meade reported that in 42 counties west of the Allegheny Mountains, there were only seven Episcopal clergy to serve "260,000 souls." In 1848, Charleston's St. John's Episcopal Church reported to the Bishop in Richmond that it had 44 communicants, "of which one was colored." In 1849, the church reported 41 communicates and 18 baptisms including eight "colored" infants. The rector was Francis M. Whittle, who had recently graduated from seminary. He would become Bishop of Virginia during Reconstruction. Bishop Meade died during the war in 1862. Bishop Whittle agreed to the division of the Virginia diocese to create a diocese for West Virginia. St. John's Church was a leading parish for the push to create a new diocese after the war. It was where the new diocese was organized and where George W. Peterkin was elected in 1878, the first bishop of the new diocese. Prominent women leaders of the early St. John's Church were Sally Burns Quarrier, who always used her middle name and was the wife of Alexander W. Quarrier, and Betty Washington Lewis Lovell, who was the widow of attorney and salt industrialist, Joseph Lovell. Bishop Meade called Sally Burns Quarrier, the Mother of the Episcopal Church in western Virginia.[624]

Professor Thomas Dew Claims that Slavery Created a "Chivalrous" Aristocracy

Thomas Jefferson predicted that slavery would bring on terrible social evils. Slavery was inconsistent with the true ideals of democratic equality and liberty. He thought the state and nation should be constituted on those ideals. In direct opposition to this thinking were the "apologists" of slavery. Their leader was the prominent professor and then president of William & Mary College. Thomas Dew served as president from 1836 to 1846. His large portrait can be seen today in the Wren Building in line with the imposing portraits of other presidents of the institution.

He wrote an influential essay, "A Review of the Debates in the Virginia Legislature of 1831-32." It was said that he "pointed out the 'insuperable' difficulties of any plan of emancipation and deportation." He assured southerners that slave insurrections like the recent Nat Turner Rebellion would never be successful.[625] He helped calm and quiet southerners about slavery in general, and he set their resolve not to end slavery. He is recognized as the one scholar who stopped the rising tide of antislavery sentiment in Virginia after the Nat Turner Rebellion.

Thomas Dew articulated a defense of slavery that took full bloom from all quarters, "from the pages of history, from the teachings of Christianity, and from the writing of economists."[626] He wrote an essay about emancipation which was popular with southerners in the 1830s after the Nat Turner Rebellion. The viability and safety of slavery was openly discussed in Virginia at this time of uncertainty, and it would be the last time emancipation would be openly discussed until the war. He wrote to support what he saw as a glorious and heroic slave aristocracy that built the country from colony to rebellion to nationhood:

> [L]ooking backward upon actual rather than possible effects, both in politics and society, [slavery] produced a chivalrous, honorable, princely and hospitable aristocracy best fitted to rule a state and nation; while it conquered, civilized and Christianized a savage.[627]

He claimed that Virginian slavers whose leadership in the new nation was needed and successful, proved that slavery made their genius possible, available and valuable. After this defense of slavery as noble and chivalrous, any and all public discussions revealing antislavery sentiments were aggressively attacked in the South. Critics of his views were "voices in the wilderness," and their numbers began to drop significantly in the 1830s and 1840s.

President Dew claimed that slavery was a safe and effective social condition. His ideas were challenged in southern public discourse only with vehement opposition. Dr. Henry Ruffner's 1847 pamphlet proposing abolition of slavery in western Virginia was attacked as a great heresy of southern culture. In 1849, the Virginia General Assembly enacted a law with fine and imprisonment forbidding any person from maintaining "that owners have not right of property in their slaves."[628]

Willard Cope Brinton wrote that Professor Thomas Dew had overwhelming influence in the South, and he effectively cut off public debate on the subject of abolition in the South, ending any antislavery movement there.

> The anti-slavery tide was arrested at its flood, and began rapidly to ebb. The document which chiefly contributed to this result was an Essay upon Slavery, by Professor Dew of William & Mary College, in which the whole subject was treated with profound ability, and illustrated with great wealth of learning. In this essay the folly of a general emancipation without deportation and the impracticability of deporting so large a population were clearly demonstrated.... people at the time credited Dew with stopping the antislavery movement.[629]

By 1840, with Thomas Dew's defense of slavery, as noble and chivalrous accepted across the South, there were no discussions tolerated in Virginia on the abolition of slavery. It has been said that Dr. Henry Ruffner was effectively exiled from the South because of his daring free-thought in the 1847 pamphlet supporting emancipation of slaves in "West Virginia."[630]

The lack of meaningful political discourse in the South convinced John Brown that a violent military and political solution to end slavery was needed because economic and social forces could not be relied upon to put any limitations on slavery. Writer Calvin Colton in 1843 strongly objected to such "political abolition," which he believed could only be achieved with violence. Without economic and social forces leading to at least gradual emancipation, he thought violence would be certain. Gradual emancipation was a taboo subject in southern political debate in the thirty years leading up to the Civil War. After northern calls for abolition, Calvin Colton wrote in 1843, "scarcely an advocate of emancipation can be found in the slave States, where there were thousands, and tens of thousands before." He thought that the calls from abolitionists for a political end to slavery in the 1830s pushed slavers into an extreme defense of slavery, banning free speech and any fair political debate, which, in turn, pushed the issue to raw politics and violence.[631]

Slavery would have to become unprofitable to allow economic forces to push the nation toward abolition. But such an end to slavery by the economics of its industry would have taken decades, because, in John Brown's time, slavery was profitable and eastern Virginians were dependent on slavery for their prosperity. John Brown wanted immediate action for an immediate end to the Horror of Slavery.

America is Out of Step with the World

America was out of step with the rest of the world on slavery. In 1833, the British Parliament passed a law to outlaw slavery in all of its territories, leading to emancipation of 700,000 slaves in the Caribbean. By the time of Britain's abolition of slavery in 1833, slavers in America had been presidents for all but eight years of the almost half century of the existence of the nation's republic. The only American presidents who were not slavers in those early years were John Adams and his son, John Quincy Adams. The three-fifths representation clause in the Federal Constitution giving slavers extra representation for their male slaves, paid off in those early years both in the Electoral College and in the House of Representatives.

There was outrage in the South in response to the new British policy. Southerners felt under attack from northern abolitionists, new British policies, and guilt over their own sense of fair play for freedom and equality. The inconsistency of slavery and those basic ideas weighed heavily upon southerners and their shrinking body politic in the two decades before the Civil War.[632]

John C. Calhoun decried British abolitionism as a denial of natural rights and national honor. Southerners thought the abolition policy was just another scheme for Britain's imperial domination of the world economy. Southerners turned to the federal government to build a navy to challenge Britain's navy.[633]

The new British policy changed the order of business in the Western Hemisphere.[634] It threatened slavers who increasingly felt the condemnation of abolitionists in America, in Britain and around the World. Abolition was supported strongly by working people in Britain including textile workers who lost employment during the naval blockade imposed during the war by the North on cotton and other southern exports. Not all Britons favored abolition. Some had to be convinced, while some had a religious conversion to abolition.

John Newton was a slave trader and slave ship captain who became a priest in the Church of England and later wrote a poem about his deliverance by God while on a ship in a terrible sea storm. His poem, "Amazing Grace," became an anthem of the modern civil rights movement. The poem was likely written in 1772 and first published in 1779. It became a hymn in the 1830s when William Walker set it to the tune of "New Britain."[635]

> Amazing Grace, How sweet the sound
> That saved a wretch like me
> I once was lost, but now am found
> T'was blind but now I see
>
> T'was Grace that taught my heart to fear
> And Grace, my fears relieved
> How precious did that grace appear
> The hour I first believed....

Chapter 15

Americans Move West And The Malden Salt Industry Declines With New Competition

New Canals Bring Competition to Kanawha Salt

The salt and slavery industry began in 1810 when the scarcity of salt in the West was so extreme that it limited western agriculture expansion for many years. The industry became the mountain frontier's major salt producer, until Americans moved into the Midwest and then to western states. In turn, that migration west moved the center of the meat packing industry from Cincinnati to Chicago where Michigan salt producers could supply salt for meat packing on the Great Lakes much closer than Malden salt producers.

Salt, like cotton weaving, required factory systems with high labor and capital production costs. Salt, unlike cotton production, had a close margin of profit in the best of years. The added costs for transportation made Kanawha salt less competitive. Also, canals were built to open the Midwest to east coast products like salt. Salt producers could send on canals to the Ohio River salt that was produced in New York, western Pennsylvania and Ohio, greatly increasing competition against Kanawha salt. The industry in Malden began to decline after 40 years of industrial innovation and growth. The decline started after its peak production year in 1846 when 45 salt factories produced 3.2 million bushels of salt.[636]

The Kanawha salt and slavery industry had been built on its massive supply to the pork packing industry centered in Cincinnati. About one bushel or 50 pounds of salt was needed to pack 200 pounds of pork. Cincinnati's early growth and business success on the Ohio River made it the Queen City of the West.[637] Its early throne rested on the Kanawha salt and slavery industry which then dominated all markets for salt in the West.

In 1850, Kanawha salt sales began dropping. That year, three million bushels were produced. The 1860 census figures showed that Kanawha salt production dropped by one-third from three million bushels to two million bushels, with increased competition from New York, western Pennsylvania, and Ohio which began to overwhelm Kanawha salt sales. The Pennsylvania Canal, completed in 1840, allowed western Pennsylvania manufacturers to ship salt

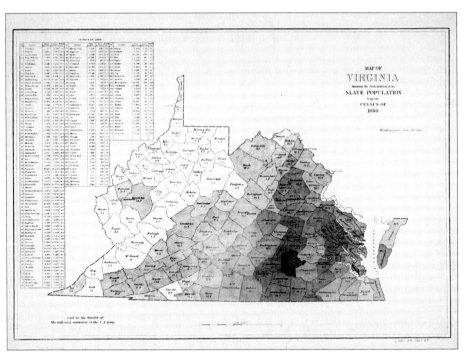

Map of Slave Population in Virginia, 1860 Census – *Image Courtesy of the Library of Congress*

west to the Ohio River with spectacular results. From 1850 to 1860, Western Pennsylvania production increased from 600,000 bushels to one million bushels. Likewise, salt production in Ohio increased from 550,000 to 1.7 million bushels, putting Kanawha salt production for the first time behind competing producers on the Ohio River.[638]

Kanawha salt production stayed steady during the war years from 1860 to 1867. There was some increase in production between 1868 and 1870. Production at 1.8 million bushels in 1869 was the highest salt production since 1854. The only year after 1870 with annual production numbers reported was the year 1875, and those numbers showed another decline of one-third from 1870 to only 967,465 bushels. These post-war production numbers indicate that perhaps there was no mass exodus of freed workers from the Kanawha Salines in the decade after the war, but that the industry was suffering from competition.

The 1860 Census shows there were 2,184 slaves in Kanawha County, and that number included children under twelve years of age. Three years later, the State Auditor slave tax report to the new West Virginia Legislature in 1863 shows only 1,237 slaves who were twelve years or older and thus taxable as property in Kanawha County. Rachel Grant Tompkins said that the Emancipation Proclamation encouraged her slaves to leave. Spicer Patrick a Kanawha

County member of the new state House of Delegates and its first Speaker, reported that his "efficient" slaves left in 1862 and the only ones left were "old and infirm." He had two older women slaves left to care for. When one of the women went to Ohio, she returned to him for support because she could not support herself in Ohio. Lewis Ruffner filed a notice in the Courthouse to acknowledge that he was sending children to Kentucky and that they were entitled to be freed when they reached an age of maturity in accordance with West Virginia law under the Willey Amendment. He stated that two of his slaves "were away from service," a euphemism for the fact that they had escaped or self-emancipated.[639]

The initial decline of the salt and slavery industry in the 1850s came from a number of factors other than new canal access to the Ohio River. There were newly opened local salt fields in the Ohio Valley, including the area around Point Pleasant in Mason County. Malden salt industrialists tried to control the marketing and production of salt in those fields in the Ohio Valley, with limited success. Salt was used as ballast for British ships and boats in the cotton and sugar cane trade, creating a strong import competition for salt on the Mississippi River. After the Civil War, railroads started an explosion of new development in the Midwest, carrying settlers and goods west.[640]

By the 1860s, Kanawha salt lost its fifty-year dominance in the industry. In 1861, a massive record-level flood in the Kanawha Valley took out many salt furnaces on the Great Kanawha River and with them most of the marginal salt producers.[641] In 1850, there were 33 salt companies operating in Malden, but by the 1860s the number had dwindled to fewer than 15. The Ruffners, Dickin-

Old Dickinson Salt Works in Kanawha Valley – *Image Courtesy of West Virginia State Archives*

sons, Lewises and Shrewsburys as major industrialists continued production. By 1875, there were no more than ten active producers. By 1890, only the J. Q. Dickinson Salt Works remained in operation. The Dickinson factory finally ended salt production in 1945.

Despite its long period of decline, Kanawha salt in this period maintained its national reputation for flavor and high quality in curing and packing meats.[642]

Women Salt Industrialists in Malden

In 1875, of the nine salt producers remaining in operation, two were women. They were "Ms. S. Dickinson." and "Ms. R. Tompkins." Their business operations could be seen as a challenge to male control, but it appears they became active after their husbands died. As married women before 1868, they would be barred by law from owning land and most business activity by custom, if not law. It was rare for women to be in businesses of their own.[643]

Married women in West Virginia could own property in their own names only after West Virginia's first Married Women's Property Act was enacted in 1868. English and Virginia common law barred married women from owning property. If they owned property, it would be held in a trust to be used for their benefit. By will, David Ruffner divided his estate into shares for each of his four children, two sons and two daughters. He gave the shares for his daughters to their husbands in trust. Joel Shrewsbury also made such provisions for inheritance by his female descendants.[644]

It is likely that Ms. S. Dickinson was Sally Lewis Dickinson, the widow of Henry Clay Dickinson, but it is not certain in the report of the remaining furnace operations. Ms. S. Dickinson operated the furnace named simply, "Malden." The other woman salt industrialist was Rachel Grant Tompkins, the widow of salt industrialist, William Tompkins. His estate was worth in today's money about $2.5 million, and she significantly increased the family estate. William Tompkins came to Malden as a blacksmith and became rich as a salt industrialist. He was the first industrialist in the western world to use natural gas to fuel his business operations.[645]

William Tompkins married well. His wife was the sister of Peter Grant, a successful principal partner in Armstrong, Grant & Company, the third company to operate major salt operations in the Kanawha Valley. Rachel Grant Tompkins was an effective businesswoman. She had a young nephew who would become General Ulysses S. Grant. Her father, Captain Noah Grant, was a revolutionary war officer who had participated in the Boston Tea Party. She was the sister of Jesse Root Grant, the father of General Grant. The family called the future general, "Hiram," which was his given name. The congressman who appointed him to West Point used the name "Ulysses Simpson Grant" in the paperwork by mistake. The cadet name was not changed at West Point, and the "S" was never corrected. His family nickname growing up was "Useless." At West Point he was called "Uncle Sam." His soldiers in the Civil War spoke of him as "Unconditional Surrender."[646] He saved the Union.

Rachel Grant Tompkins provided money to help her talented nephew get to West Point. The general got little help from his father, an Ohio abolitionist who once lived in the family household of John Brown. His father and mother boycotted his wedding because his bride used slaves in her household. His father, according to Rachel Grant Tompkins, was "not worth a hill of beans." She was a committed Confederate, but to save her property she would show federal troops a letter from General Grant directing that her property was not to be looted or destroyed. She wisely hid her cattle up a hollow over a mile from her home and farm.[647]

The Tompkins family lived near their salt operations at Burning Spring until 1845, when they built a classic Federal-style home up-river. They named the home "Cedar Grove," and it stands today in a town with that name. The Tompkins family built a small chapel in 1853, as a gift to a daughter, Virginia Tompkins. "Virginia's Chapel" stands today on a small hill across the road from their home. A slave cemetery was discovered on the grounds of the chapel. Virginia's Chapel is referred to as "The Old Brick Church" in a hymn written by Reverend H. Cummings in 1948 and published in the Golden Gospel Gems.[648]

Rachel Grant Tompkins was given all of her husband's property by his will. William Tompkins knew to trust the family's fortunes to her. She became a successful businesswoman. She favored tariffs on foreign salt which were supported by the Whig Party, to limit competition from other countries, like most other salt industrialists.[649]

She was equally skilled to men in the salt business at the time. She increased the family wealth and collected payments on debts owed to her husband, often with litigation. She once owned part of the lot where the African Zion Baptist Church would be located, as a result of a foreclosure sale. William Tompkins was known as a gentleman, and he let a number of debts and accounts remain unpaid. His great-granddaughter, a renowned West Virginia author, Mary Lee Settle, wrote that Rachel Grant Tompkins was "no gentleman," and she collected on each debt owed to the family. Historian George Atkinson wrote that she was "a lady of unusual good sense" and possessed "quite a business-like turn of mind." The Tompkins family joked that she once sued her son for taking an apple butter kettle off her back porch.[650]

The 1870s and early 1880s were a time of business stagnation in West Virginia.[651] The state had an agricultural economy. The industrial boom that was anticipated after the Civil War did not develop until railroads began to spread through northern and southern river valleys to create new coal and timber industries.

Kanawha Salt Remains Popular for Good Taste and Wins Awards in Europe

The popularity of Kanawha salt continued well after its early monopoly position was lost. Kanawha salt was famous for its strong flavor and for the long life of meats packed in it before the age of refrigeration. It was considered superior to all other salts. "Kanawha Red Salt" became a national brand because of its reddish color due to iron content. Historian and salt maker John P. Hale wrote in 1891 that Kanawha salt "has more lively, pungent and pleasant taste as a table salt than any other known." As a commercial salt, he wrote that it is free of "sulphate" of lime and it "penetrates and cures meats thoroughly to the bone" without common caking or crusting.[652]

It is reported that Kanawha salt earned awards in Europe. In 1851, Kanawha salt was recognized and awarded at the World's Fair in London. The fair was formally named the *Great Exhibition of the Works of Industry of All Nations*. Prince Albert sponsored the event with great success. The exhibition featured the impressive iron and plate glass Crystal Palace which was constructed for the exhibition. It drew millions of visitors. John P. Hale, a prominent Malden salt industrialist, attended the Fair. His Malden home is preserved by West Virginia State University in Malden. It is also reported that Lewis Ruffner's "dairy grade" salt was celebrated at the 1867 World's Fair in Paris called the *Exposition Universelle*.[653]

Industrial salt production in the Kanawha Valley ended in 1945, but a new system of salt production began in Malden in 2013 to produce gourmet salts for use at the table and for cooking. The new gourmet salt is being produced by great-great-grandchildren of Malden's last major salt industrialist, John Quincy Dickinson. Unlike the hot furnace-fired salt factories of old, Chef Nancy Payne Bruns and her brother, Lewis Payne, use a natural, solar evaporation process. Brine is pumped 350 feet from the ancient underground salt sea to drying tables for solar evaporation and processing. Under the brand name, "J. Q. Dickinson Salt-Works" at *jqdsalt.com*, 304-925-7918, they sell their gourmet salt in all 50 states and in the world beyond.

Today, the United States is one of the largest industrial salt producers in the world. Forty million metric tons are produced annually. Most of that production is used to remove ice on highways. Table salt is eight percent of the total, and J. Q. Dickinson Salt is a small but important part of the new age of American gourmet salts.[654]

Drawing of the Crystal Palace from the northeast during the Great Exhibition of 1851.
Image within Public Domain, c. 1852. Source: Dickinson Brothers' Dickinson's Comprehensive Pictures of the Great Exhibition of 1851.

John Brown Daguerreotype by Augustus Washington, c. 1846-47
Image in Public Domain, Courtesy of Wikimedia Commons

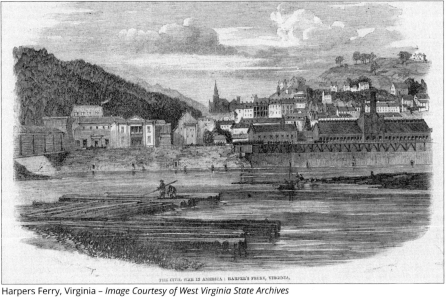

Harpers Ferry, Virginia – *Image Courtesy of West Virginia State Archives*

Chapter 16

John Brown Attacks Virginia Slavery

Harpers Ferry Raid Sparks a Violent End to Slavery

A powder keg exploded in Harpers Ferry, Virginia, on October 16, 1859. It destroyed the nation's peaceful acceptance of the horror that was slavery. John Brown from "Bloody Kansas" led 21 men on a raid at the federal munitions armory in Harpers Ferry. They included his two sons, Oliver Brown, and Watson Brown, and five black men, Dangerfield Newby; Osborne Perry Anderson; John A. Copeland, Jr.; Shields Green; and Lewis Sheridan Leary. Dangerfield Newby joined the raid to bring his wife and children out of slavery. He was freed with his mother and siblings by his father who was white. As a raider, his body was mutilated by vengeful whites.[655]

John Brown took his raid to Harpers Ferry because Virginia was a leading slave state with a large local slave population in an area he had seen before while surveying. Virginia created American slavery. The town had a federal armory with munition factories and major stores of weapons. John Brown thought the town had an accessible escape route into the Blue Ridge Mountains. John Brown wanted to start a slave uprising in Virginia.[656]

The raiders lost the battle but they implanted violence on the issue of slavery. John Brown's bold raid won many people in the North over to the idea that slavery had to end and that it deserved a violent end if necessary. No one could know how violent the end of slavery would be with the war deaths of over 600,000 soldiers. It is sobering and profound to realize the price of the war in human lives. Professor Ira Berlin wrote, "for every ten southern whites held in the Union and for every six slaves freed, one soldier died."[657]

Panic In The South And A Legendary Hero In The North

John Brown's raid spread panic and fear throughout the South. The raid confronted Northerners over their acceptance of the day-to-day quiet violence that was the reality of slavery for four million people. In the South, it reminded slavers of their panic in August 1831, when Nat Turner led a slave rebellion in eastern Virginia, where over 60 whites and hundreds of blacks were killed.[658]

In 1859, at Harpers Ferry, the response to John Brown's futile and incompetent raid was orderly, deliberate, lawful, and swift. He was charged by

John Brown, Northern Hero
Image Courtesy of West Virginia State Archives

authorities under Virginia law for treason against the Commonwealth. He was tried in state court in Charles Town soon after the raid. He was found guilty by a jury. He spoke eloquently at his trial. He was hanged six weeks after the raid, on December 2, 1859.[659]

Like the Nat Turner Rebellion, John Brown's raid at Harpers Ferry had important ramifications throughout the country. It heightened the bunker mentality of most southerners and helped solidify the resolve of many Northerners to oppose slavery aggressively in the fateful 1860 Presidential Election. Most importantly, it had many northerners accept violence in some form as a legitimate means to end the Horror of Slavery.[660] The northerners' response to the raid at Harpers Ferry drove millions of white southerners out of the Union.

John Brown's use of violence was a lightning rod alarm in the South. It was unlawful and contrary to all governmental and social controls in the American and Anglo-Saxon traditions for respect of law. Our nation's sentiment is to respect the law and use legal procedures as the only way to settle serious differences. Violence is not an option. The apparent sympathy of northerners for John Brown's raid, or at least their failure to universally condemn the violence of the raid, was the last straw for many southern slavers. The raid and the election of Abraham Lincoln ended political maneuvering and compromises that had controlled American politics for 72 years since the signing of the Federal Constitution. That document approved slavery by delicate references without using the words "slave" or "slavery." John Brown's use of violence set aside all delicacies and made the hard lines needed for both sides to begin a shooting war.

The legend of John Brown grew in the North. It was reported that John Brown kissed a slave baby on his way to the gallows. The kiss likely never happened. Blacks, women, and children were barred from contact with John Brown, and they were not allowed in the area of the hanging.[700] But the kiss was reported widely and sparked poems, paintings and commentary. A poem of John Greenleaf Whittier, a well-known Quaker abolitionist, "The John Brown Kiss," romanticized the symbolic kiss.

> John Brown of Osawatomie
> They led him out to die;
> And lo!-- a poor slave-mother
> With her little child pressed nigh.
> Then the bold blue eyes grew mild,
> And the old harsh face grew mild,
> As he stooped between the jeering ranks
> And kissed the Negro's child![661]

Northerners wanted to believe the kiss happened, because for them it summarized the events of his death more fairly than his use of violence. For southerners, such a kiss was a kiss of violent death. The Metropolitan Museum of Art in New York City has one of several paintings of the tender iconic kiss of John Brown, painted from 1882 to 1884 by Thomas Hovenden. He titled the paintings *The Last Moments of John Brown.* He memorialized a gallant older gentleman kissing a black baby as he walked down steps in house shoes on the way to the gallows. An article in *The New York Times* on May 18, 1884, broadly called the Hovenden painting the most significant and striking "historical work of art ever executed in the republic."[662] It hangs near the landmark, giant-size 1851 painting by Emanuel Leutze *Washington Crossing the Delaware.*

The Last Moments of John Brown by Thomas Hovenden
Image Courtesy of the Metropolitan Museum of Art

At the place of John Brown's hanging in Charles Town, the scene was impressive with hundreds of Virginia soldiers stationed around the gallows, including a corps of cadets from Virginia Military Institute. There were a number of people who would be important to the Civil War and the vengeful peace that followed. It was John Brown himself, serenely calm and composed, who brought reverence and awe to the frightful proceedings. Oswald Garrison Villard, a journalist and newspaper publisher, who helped W. E. B. Du Bois organize the National Association for the Advancement of Colored People, the NAACP, wrote years later that John Brown's serenity and calmness of spirit controlled the hanging ceremony.

> There were fifteen hundred soldiers present to see that this one old man was hanged. But, watch him as they might, they could detect no sign of flinching. With alacrity the despised Abolitionist climbed down from the wagon and ascended the scaffold to take one last, longing glance at the Blue Ridge Mountains which had to him spelled liberty for the enslaved these many long years.... John Brown was a wonderfully dignified and impressive figure on the scaffold, because of the serenity and calmness of his spirit. The solemnity of it all moved everyone, from the boyish cadets to the oldest soldiers. The most deeply religious man among the troops, 'Stonewall' Jackson, was shaken like the rest, and 'sent up a fervent petition' to Heaven that John Brown might be saved.... While the three companies that had been his escort deployed slowly into place, he stood erect as a soldier of the Lord. As if to test his courage to the end, they were a long twelve minutes filing into place, while John Brown showed Virginia how a brave man could die.[664]

Robert E. Lee Predicts "The Last of John Brown"

Robert E. Lee was present at the hanging as a Colonel of the United States Marines and commander of federal troops in the raid that repelled John Brown's attack. The future Confederate General was with his wife at Capon Springs, Virginia, when he was called to command troops at Harpers Ferry. The Lees were there for treatment of her arthritis. There were many springs in Virginia that were visited for health reasons. The future Confederate General, then in the Union army, was reported to say before the hanging that it would be "the last of John Brown."[665] He was wrong.

John Brown's legend of reckless courage in a battle against evil was adopted by Union troops. The power of John Brown's message to end slavery at all costs remained during the Civil War as a symbol of courage and purpose for northerners. Early in the war, soldiers from the 12th Massachusetts Regiment sang a hallmark tune in the North, commemorating John Brown's death and his commitment to end slavery.

> John Brown's body lies a-mouldering in the grave,
> John Brown's body lies a-mouldering in the grave,
> But his soul goes marching on.
>
> Glory, glory, hallelujah,
> Glory, glory, hallelujah,
> His soul goes marching on....
>
> John Brown died that the slaves might be free,
> John Brown died that the slaves might be free,
> His soul goes marching on....

Julia Ward Howe used the tune and words of the marching song to create her epic classic, "Battle Hymn of the Republic." Her song is sung today as an anthem for aggressive action to pursue a Christian duty. "Mine eyes have seen the glory of the coming of the Lord....He hath loosed the fateful lightning of his terrible swift sword, His truth is marching on," and, "As [Christ] died to make men holy, let us die to make men free, While God is marching on."[666]

VMI Cadets Led by Thomas Jackson--Later "Stonewall" Jackson

There were many important persons at the hanging of John Brown. One of the founders of Virginia Military Institute, VMI, John T. L. Preston, wrote a letter describing the mystery of John Brown from the perspective of a southerner.

The culprit still stood ready until the sheriff, descending the flight of steps, with a well-directed blow of a sharp hatchet, severed the rope that held up the trap-door, which instantly sank beneath him, and he fell about three feet; and the man of strong and bloody hand, of fierce passions, of iron will, of wonderful vicissitudes, the terrible partisan of Kansas, the capturer of the United States Arsenal at Harpers Ferry, the would-be Catiline of the South, the demi-god of the abolitionists, the man execrated and lauded, damned and prayed for, the man who in his motives, his means, his plans, and his successes, must ever be a wonder, a puzzle, and a mystery –John Brown– was hanging between heaven and earth.[667]

A federal army lieutenant in the siege named J. E. B. Stuart tried to per-
suade John Brown to surrender peacefully. "Jeb" Stuart remembered him from
Kansas and would become one of the Confederacy's most colorful cavalry
commanders. More notably at the hanging was Thomas Jackson, a native of
Harrison County later nicknamed, "Stonewall," who was the faculty commander of the VMI cadets at the hanging. He was an instructor who was considered by his students to be eccentric, withdrawn, and too religious. He taught
a Sunday School class for slaves because he believed they had souls to save.
He taught Bible lessons and verses but not the mechanics of reading and writing. Literacy undercut the servile condition slavers expected of their human
property. After the Nat Turner Rebellion, a person teaching a slave to read
could be punished with a $50.00 fine and two months in jail. It was common to
teach slaves to read until the 1800s. Young members of a slaver family would
teach favorite slaves to read. In the South about ten percent of slaves could
read to some extent and about two percent could write.[668] Thomas Jackson
treated slaves decently and learned their names. He would raise his hat courte-
ously to older slaves, and he checked on their school when he was away at war.
They "reverenced and loved him." He was called "the black man's friend."[669]

Thomas Jackson grew up at Jackson's Mill south of today's Clarksburg.
He was an orphan in the wealthy and influential Jackson family. The Jacksons
were Scot immigrants from Ulster. His great uncle, John George Jackson, in
1800 married Mary "Polly" Payne, the sister of Dolly Madison possibly at
Montpelier, the large Madison estate in central Virginia. The Madison marriage established the Jackson family's political prominence on the Virginia
frontier throughout the nineteenth century. John George Jackson would later
be a Congressman and important federal judge appointed by his brother-in-
law, President James Madison. One of the general's uncles was a successful
fur trader in Wyoming and gave the Jackson name there to the Jackson River
and Jackson Hole. West Virginia' sixth governor, from 1881 to 1885, was Jacob Beeson Jackson, a member of the Jackson family.[670]

General "Stonewall" Jackson was a brilliant strategist, and became General Lee's best field commander. He was called "Stonewall" for his immovable
stance and the solid positioning of his troops at the first Battle of Bull Run.
He looked as immovable as a stone wall. Some have said his nickname was
actually intended as a criticism about his failure to move freely in battle, but
his present-day recognition as a military strategist denies criticism of most
any action that he took or did not take in battle. General Jackson died at Chan-
cellorsville on May 10, 1863, two months before Gettysburg. If he been a
general at Gettysburg, the history of the war -- and the world -- may have been

different. He was shot by Confederate soldiers who mistook him at night for a Union spy. The words reported to be his last do not reveal the violence of the Civil War that took him: "Let us go over the river and rest in the shade of the trees."[671]

Stonewall Jackson is a native son of West Virginia, his boyhood state. He and Booker T. Washington are among West Virginia's most enduring and best-known celebrities. A high school in Charleston was named for Stonewall Jackson in 1940. It now has his name as a middle school. There is a "Stonewall Jackson State Park and a resort named "Stonewall Resort," not far from his family home place which is called "Jackson's Mill" near Weston. It is maintained by West Virginia University as a historic site with housing facilities for 4H camps and a conference center.

The statue of Stonewall Jackson at the Capitol, and a bust of him inside the building, are the only memorials to a Confederate at the Capitol. A few blocks away there is a grand memorial to the Confederate Kanawha Riflemen in Ruffner City Park. The Jackson statue was designed by Moses Ezekiel for the Daughters of the Confederacy and dedicated in 1910. There are three other Civil War-era statues.

The most prominent statue on the Capitol grounds is the tall riverside statue of Abraham Lincoln produced by sculptor Bernard Wiepper from a small 1933 statue by sculptor Fred Martin Torrey. President Lincoln's late-night concerns are portrayed showing him walking in his bed gown and slippers in a pensive mood the night of December 31, 1862, when he had to approve the final Emancipation Proclamation and the West Virginia statehood bill. The sculpture is named *Abraham Lincoln Walks at Midnight.* The small Torrey statue was displayed at the 1939 Chicago World's Fair. Two generations later, the large Wiepper statue was dedicated with a major ceremony.[672]

There are two memorials for Union soldiers: the Union Soldiers, Sailors and Marines monument and the Grand Army of the Republic Home Guard monument. The latter was sculpted by Henry K. Bush-Brown. A stately memorial to Booker T. Washington is on the Capitol grounds. The bust was sculpted by Bill Hopen. The bust and memorial are displayed with great honor after they were relocated from Malden to the Capitol grounds in 1985 after vandals damaged the bust.

There are two memorials on the Capitol grounds for modern day soldiers. A large and stately veterans' memorial commemorates the soldiers from West Virginia who died in service in the two World Wars, Korea and Vietnam. The memorial is a grand work of memorial art designed by P. Joseph Mullins, himself a veteran. He sculpted five lifelike statues of soldiers. Four soldier statues

Booker T. Washington Monument on State Capitol Grounds Charleston, West Virginia
"Booker T. Washington Monument" photograph by Christopher Taylor ©2018

represent men in the four wars. That memorial was dedicated on November 11, 1995. There is a fifth statue of a woman soldier which stands guard holding a flag nobly near the monument. That statue was dedicated on November 11, 2011. Also honored with statues near the Culture Center are police officers and firefighters, and there is a statue of a coal miner sculpted by Burl Jones.[673]

Inside the Capitol are several memorials including busts for Stonewall Jackson, Anna Jarvis of Grafton, the founder of Mother's Day in America, and long serving West Virginia Congressman Cleveland Bailey. There is a recently installed plaque for John Fitzgerald Kennedy with a poem of St. Francis. President Kennedy was much loved in the Mountain State. During his election campaign, he and his family were dismayed at the poverty they discovered and the genuine warmth of the people they met in their many travels around the state. The state's Presidential Primary in 1960 with Herbert Humphrey is thought to be the turning point for John F. Kennedy's election. Winning a predominantly Protestant state like West Virginia, by a large margin, proved that his religion as a Roman Catholic was of little concern to Protestant voters nationwide. That primary had the second known televised debate between major party presidential candidates, on WCHS in Charleston. John F. Kennedy's debates with Richard Nixon in the general election campaign would be landmarks in television and political history. John F. Kennedy is often remembered for his remarks as president on the rain-swept Capitol steps for the State Centennial Celebration on June 20, 1963,

> The sun may not always shine in West Virginia, but the people always do.[674]

Inside the Capitol, there are large portraits of each governor lining the marble hallways of the ground floor. They are moved each time another governor is elected. Two governors have been imprisoned and their portraits remain in line to recognize their previous government service to the state.

The grandest of all memorials is an imposing statue of Senator Robert C. Byrd in the rotunda. It was sculpted by Bill Hopen and placed in 1997. Senator Byrd encouraged construction of the Appalachian Highway system and other federal projects in the state. He was in the United States Senate from 1959 to 2010 and served long enough to regret openly and apologize formally for his former membership in the Ku Klux Klan and his leadership in the 1960s to oppose the Civil Rights Acts. After decades of service to the state, the longest tenure in the history of the United States Senate, 51 years, and his late conversion to support civil rights, Senator Byrd became a foundation figure in the state's history. He was beloved like a "Grandpa" by most white West Virginians. He made mistakes, but, some would say, like family, "he loved us and we loved him." [675]

The West Virginia Capitol is a beautiful domed building which architect Cass Gilbert copied from a design of Jules Hardouin-Mansart that he had copied from his famous great-uncle, the accomplished French architect, Francois Mansart. Jules Hardouin-Mansart was commissioned by King Louis XIV to design a chapel for his national home for disabled soldiers, giving it the name used today, Dome des Invalides. Construction began in 1677, and the keys to the royal domed chapel were turned over to Louis XIV in 1706. It is a prominent landmark in the middle of Paris where Napoleon's tomb rests. All persons visiting Paris should see the Dome des Invalides.

The structural design of the Paris dome was used to give the Capitol dome a

Dome des Invalides in Paris, France
"Cathédrale Saint-Louis-des-Invalides"
– Image *Courtesy* of Daniel Vorndran / DXR.
Licensed under CC BY-SA 3.0[676]

"West Virginia State Capitol"
– *Image Courtesy of Christopher Taylor ©2018*

five-story separation between the outside dome and the inside shell ceiling. The exterior Capitol dome decoration is copied from the Paris landmark with small, helmet-like windows and gold covered linear garlands spread on large vertical colored panels. The interior dome ceiling has below it a floor structure copied from the Paris landmark with a cut out circle to create a well in the main floor exposing the ground floor below. In Paris, the ground floor well is the location of Napoleon's tomb.

Architect Gilbert designed the overall exterior look of the Capitol dome to be in levels similar to the Paris dome. The Capitol dome uses colonnades for bands at different levels. It has a smooth cylindrical shape whereas the Paris dome has ridges. The porticos are different with the Capitol portico using an imposing three story Greek Parthenon design with massive columns whereas the Mansart design used more of a Palladian design with a small second story portico set between modest double columns above a first-floor entrance set between similar columns. The lanterns atop the domes are very similar with the Capitol lantern having a colonnade and the Paris dome using four arches.

Cass Gilbert is not known to have given credit to the dome and chapel designs from Paris which he used for his work on the West Virginia Capitol.[677] While working to finish the Capitol dome, Cass Gilbert won the important competition to design a United States Supreme Court Building across from the Nation's Capitol. The West Virginia Capitol was dedicated on June 20, 1932. Cass Gilbert died as one of the greatest architects of his day on May 17, 1934. The construction of his design for the United States Supreme Court building was completed on April 4, 1935.

John Wilkes Booth Attends the Hanging of a Hero

John Wilkes Booth attended the hanging of John Brown. He would be the assassin of Abraham Lincoln six years later. Because John Brown used violence to turn human events, John Wilkes Booth celebrated him as a hero, saying, "John Brown was a man inspired the grandest character of the century." One writer stated that two men were "up-front" observers at the hanging because they wore VMI cadet uniforms: John Wilkes Booth and the prominent Virginia planter and pro-secessionist pamphleteer, Edmund Ruffin. With Thomas Jackson in command of the cadets, that seems unlikely.[678]

On April 11, 1865, as the Civil War was ending, John Wilkes Booth resolved to kill the president over voting rights and citizenship for blacks after the war. He heard the president give a speech where he proposed that male slaves should have the right to vote. Women, white and black, would not get the right to vote in every state until 1920 when the right was guaranteed under the 19th Amendment to the Federal Constitution. President Lincoln proposed only a limited right to vote for black males, and then only for "the very intelligent" and "those who serve our cause as soldiers."[679]

Black suffrage was a radical idea. Most all whites opposed black suffrage. In the North, outside New England, black men were not allowed to vote generally. In 1865, three state referendums were held to give black men the right to vote. They were defeated in Connecticut, Wisconsin and Minnesota. The greatest criticism of Booker T. Washington's leadership is that he failed to demand publicly that blacks be guaranteed the right to vote, among other important civil rights. Disenfranchisement did not begin immediately in all southern states after federal troops withdrew from the South in 1878. There were ten blacks elected to Congress during Reconstruction and ten were elected after Reconstruction. Blacks voted in large numbers for more than two decades after Reconstruction ended. As voters, blacks were hated and cajoled, intimidated and courted by Democrats and Republicans, but they could never be ignored so long as they voted.[680]

At the president's April 11 speech, John Wilkes Booth raged, "That means N----r citizenship," and he urged his associate, Lewis Paine, to shoot Lincoln. Paine refused and Booth turned to another companion stating, "Now, by God, I will put him through....That will be the last speech he will ever make." It was the last speech the president gave. He was assassinated on April 14, 1865. John Wilkes Booth despised the president, claiming he was a tyrant who would be king if he could. The president was unpopular with Radical Republicans in Congress at the time for his Second Inaugural Address where he proposed a policy for reconciliation with former Confederates, with "malice toward none." Many northerners wanted policies that were more vengeful and punishing toward rebellious southerners. The lessons of post-Second World War with the great success of the $13 billion Marshall Plan, transforming a vanquished foe into a helpful friend teach us that President Lincoln's policies to rebuild the South would have helped heal the wounds of war and could have brought back each Confederate state as a Prodigal Son of the nation.[681]

John Wilkes Booth's moment of infamy killing President Lincoln was perhaps the single most consequential event in American history. Abraham Lincoln's death ended any hope of rebuilding the Confederate South for the benefit of the nation. Without President Lincoln, there was no political force to challenge the northern Radical Republicans who would use soldiers to impose a new social order in the South while providing no help to rebuild its economy. Southerners thought the new social order of Congressional Reconstruction was punishment to a vanquished foe.

There is no doubt that President Abraham Lincoln was fully committed to heal the wounds of war and rebuild the South. His ideas for Reconstruction are revealed in the words of his immortal Second Inaugural Address delivered on March 4, 1865, a month before his death.[682] The speech is memorialized on a chamber wall of the Lincoln Memorial. His analysis was cutting, courageous and moral. He said the Civil War was God's judgment on the nation for the offense of forcing unpaid slave labor for 250 years and as recompense for every drop of blood drawn from whipping slaves with a drop of blood drawn from the sword of war.

> The Almighty has His own purposes....If we shall suppose that American slavery is one of those offenses which, in the providence of God, must needs come, but which, having continued through His appointed time, He now wills to remove, and that He gives to both North and South this terrible war as the woe due to those by whom the offense came, shall we discern therein any departure from those divine attributes which the believers in a living God always ascribe to Him? Fondly do we hope, fervently do we pray, that this mighty scourge of war may speedily pass away. Yet, if God wills that it continue until all the wealth piled by the bondsman's two hundred and fifty years of unrequited toil shall be sunk, and until every drop of blood drawn with the lash shall be paid by another drawn with the sword, as we said three thousand years ago, so it must be said "the judgments of the Lord are true and righteous altogether."

> With malice toward none, with charity for all, with firmness in the right as God gives us to see the right, let us strive on to finish the work we are in, to bind up the nation's wounds, to care for him who shall have borne the battle and for his widow and his orphan, to do all which may achieve and cherish a just and lasting peace among ourselves and with all nations.[683]

These are the words of a man on a mission to reunite the nation and set it on a new course of freedom and equality for all. His early death is the nation's greatest loss. He made the ultimate sacrifice for the idea of equality of all people, an equality for freed people he wanted to help secure by the right to vote.

John Brown's Fort is Saved by His Wife's Attorney

A less well-known figure at the hanging of John Brown was Hector Tyndale. He was a young Philadelphia attorney who accompanied John Brown's wife, Mary Ann Day Brown, to Charles Town, so she could see him before he died.[684] She went there after she received a letter from Governor Henry A. Wise informing her that the remains of her husband and their three sons would be given to her by Major General William B. Taliaferro, who was to be in command at the hanging. The commander's last name is the same name that Jane Ferguson chose for Booker and which he used as a middle name.

Governor Wise sent a telegram to advise jail authorities that only Mrs. Brown could see her husband before the hanging. Hector Tyndale was not allowed to go into the jail with her. He was detained, and Mrs. Brown went alone to see her husband, escorted by marching soldiers.

Hector Tyndale returned to Harpers Ferry as a major in the 28th Pennsylvania Infantry. On February 7, 1862, many buildings were burned at Harpers Ferry, but he ordered the small brick fire station to be left standing. It was where John Brown was captured and is now known and revered as "John Brown's Fort."[685]

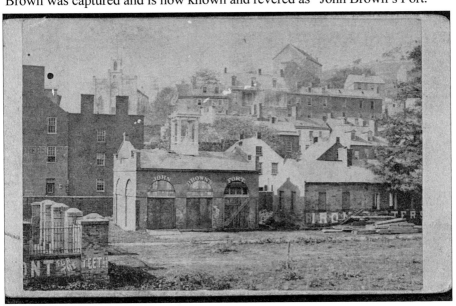

John Brown's Fort – *Image Courtesy of the Library of Congress*

John Brown's fort has been moved several times. It was dismantled and shipped as a private sideshow exhibit for the Chicago World's Fair in 1893.[686] It is now enshrined as the centerpiece of the Harpers Ferry National Historic Park. The park and the fort are sobering monuments to be visited as a pilgrimage to the past and a place to renew personal commitments to liberty, equality, and social justice.

Violence for Social Justice

John Brown's pursuit of social justice through violent means makes him one of America's most controversial figures. The American judicial system had the goal and tradition of treating all white people equally before the Civil War. It protected their individual rights and provided ready access to courts for speedy redress of grievances by whites against the government and private persons. In a system of socially just laws and procedures, John Brown's violence may be called "un-American," but the American system of slavery may also be called "un-American." It was outside the bounds of the nation's founding ideas and individual morality. Slavery denied civil rights and social justice to four million Americans in the South until the end of the Civil War and to millions more during the Jim Crow segregation period after the war. Cruelty against enslaved people in the South, especially the Deep South, was made legal and institutionalized since the 1660s in colonial Virginia.[687] Early in Virginia, by custom, the Christian baptism of a person held in slavery automatically emancipated the person. The law was changed to prevent automatic emancipation stating "An act declaring that baptisme of slaves doth not exempt them from bondage." While Christian baptism could save the soul of a person held in slavery, it could not change the personhood of that soul.[688]

In the 1960s, Malcolm X justified his early calls for violence to end racist treatment of blacks during the modern civil rights movement. He used a theory of self-defense and the failure of courts to protect blacks' civil rights and safety. Malcolm X proposed fierce self-defense for whites as well as blacks when they are denied protections of the courts.

> They called me the "angriest Negro in America." I wouldn't deny that charge. I spoke exactly as I felt. "I *believe* in anger. The Bible says there is a *time* for anger. They called me a "teacher, a fomenter of violence." I would say point blank, "That is a lie." I'm not for wanton violence, I'm for justice. I feel that if white people were attacked by Negroes--if the forces of law prove unable, or inadequate, or reluctant to protect those whites from those Negroes--then those white people should protect and defend themselves from those Negroes using arms if necessary. And I feel that when the law fails to protect Negroes from whites' attack, then those Negroes should use arms, if necessary, to defend themselves."[689]

Societies are created by attitudes of mutual respect and trust, and standards of conduct within a society are created by mutual consent, the same consent our society relies on from "We the People." Violence confuses the moral judgments of a community about its minorities, and can prompt violence and destruction instead of moral clarification. That was the great gift of understanding about violence by Reverend Dr. Martin Luther King, Jr. But it cannot be denied that John Brown focused the nation on the day-to-day violence that was slavery for the people who were enslaved at birth. When the Founding Fathers excluded people held in slavery from "We the People," they left them to languish as property not human beings, and, there, began the quiet violence and cruelty that would be a path to the Civil War. Slavery was followed by Jim Crow segregation and the confusion and inconsistencies of the nation, and in its history writers for over a century, about the true nature of that violence and cruelty, until the ideas of separation and white superiority were overthrown by truth and justice.[690]

Chief Justice Roger Taney, who was himself a slaver, wrote in the *Dred Scott* decision that slaves were never intended to be included in "We the People." They were regarded as an inferior race and they were considered as property, "held, and bought and sold as such."

> They had for more than a century before been regarded as being an inferior order, and altogether unfit to associate with the white race…; and so far inferior, that they had no rights which the white man was bound to respect; and that the negro might justly and lawfully be reduced to slavery for his benefit.…[691]

John Brown is a reminder that when social justice and decent treatment of individuals are outside of the control of electoral processes and the courts, violence becomes a law unto itself. When social justice and civil rights are denied year after year in electoral institutions of government, executive and legislative, the courts must rise up to create and enforce standards for liberty, equality and social justice upon the jurisdictions of all branches and levels of government. Law must direct the morality of community when electoral processes do not treat minorities fairly. The law must be just for all. It is the duty of courts to protect individuals and minorities in order to preserve the rule of law in order to deny to all that violence can possibly be a reasonable substitute for the rule of law. James Madison envisioned this role for federal court review of state and federal law and actions to protect minority rights guaranteed under the Federal Constitution against the will and whim of electoral majorities. This doctrine is called "judicial review." This may be James Madison's greatest contribution to American government and to a more just world order.

The depth of affection of black people for John Brown rises in part out of his complete personal lack of race-prejudice. He considered people held in slavery to be his equals in all respects, with no paternalism or political theory. Unlike other white people, including most abolitionists, John Brown saw no barriers to living with black people as equals. Some abolitionists would espouse emancipation as a political doctrine, but they did not accept black people as social equals. The dominant belief of most white Americans was that black people were not equals because, as a race and individually, they could not be equals under God's plan for humankind. John Brown refused to believe that blacks were inferior in any way.[692] He was comfortable being with black people and sharing his life with them, and for that model of living he must be respected as a man.

The hanging of John Brown marks the end of the Horror of Slavery as an accepted part of American life. He introduced violence into the politics of the issue, but his raid did little to challenge the idea of white superiority that continued beyond the end of slavery. Segregation replaced slavery after the Civil War. Blacks went from being chattel property to an underclass of personal servants. The bonds of slavery were replaced by bonds of separation, poverty, and deprivation.

Hanging day for John Brown was December 2, 1859. That day for many Americans has been known as "Martyr Day." Booker T. Washington wrote letters to support a 50-year anniversary celebration of John Brown's raid, but he seemed to have little enthusiasm for the cause. The celebration could be seen as a celebration of violence used to promote social justice. In 1909, violence for purpose involved unionization fights. Powerful industrialists, including some who were major contributors to Tuskegee Institute wanted to limit discord and discourage union membership without violence. Booker T. Washington pragmatically agreed with his patrons.[693]

John Brown achieved sainthood for many, despite his fundamental disrespect for law and due process. He focused all Americans on the unholy contradiction of their ideas of equality and liberty and the acceptance of the cruel enslavement of four million people. His last words addressed the contradiction and warned clearly of the bloody war to come, with no regret for his work in the cause he saw as just and necessary.

"I, John Brown am now quite *certain* that the crimes of this *guilty land*: *will* never be purged *away*: but with Blood. I had *as I now think*: *vainly* flattered myself that without *very much* bloodshed; it might be done." [694]

Uncontrolled bloodshed was unthinkable in the North and South until it happened for the four years of the war. The war presented new issues for the nation, for its troubled president, Abraham Lincoln and for many loyal Union slavers like Lewis Ruffner.

The raid put the political and social system of the South under great stress, from "outside criticism, internal incoherence, and uneasiness." Some commentators have speculated about the possibility, no matter how slight, of ending slavery without the violence of an all-out war.[695] The economics of slavery in the political environment of mid-nineteenth century America made the war as "inevitable" as it could be in that time, but "if" the economics of slavery had been different or changed, or stronger leadership in Virginia and elsewhere in the South or North had emerged, an all-out war may not have been required especially for the gradual emancipation of all slaves. History shuns "what if" speculation but leadership studies call out for "what ifs" to be studied for alternatives and other possibilities that different leadership may have produced in its own time, place and people.

In the limited view of flat hindsight, it appears slavery could not have continued into the twentieth century. If it did so, we would have been a very different people going into the First World War which America fought to save democracy, if not for social justice. The booming economy of the cotton and slavery industry and the nation's business dependence on slavery-based profits did not allow for a peaceful negotiated end to slavery at the time of the Civil War. If slavery had become unprofitable, it could have been abolished, step-by-step.

The cotton boom made slavery possible. The war carnage was unthinkable until it happened. James Buchanan was president. He was a caretaker and ineffective leader for the nation as emotions and complicated loyalties boiled over in the lead-up to the presidential election of 1860. Leadership was fractured and ineffective in all positions on the issue of slavery, at least in flat hindsight. Slavery was the only issue of the day. Southerners had a bunker mentality, with enemies real and imagined in the North and in the world at large, as they started to hear more and more objections about their slave societies.

In Virginia, slavery was the early foundation of the state economy. It created a dominant slave society in eastern Virginia. Again, with the limited view of flat hindsight, it seems, at least, that a violent end of slavery was inevitable in the nineteenth century, in light of the combination of cheap labor, and aristocratic slave culture, and Virginia's ongoing commodity slave sales to Confederate states. If Virginia did not have those lucrative sales, gradual emancipation would have been a subject of open debate there for the first time since Nat Turner's Rebellion in 1832.

Cotton made slavery profitable, too profitable. It would have become unprofitable especially in Virginia, if cotton plantations had experienced overpopulation of slaves in the 1850s, cutting off the markets for sales of people in eastern Virginia. The Civil War would likely have never happened, at least when it did, without the dependence of Virginians on slavery and their need to protect their market states in the Deep South. Without those markets in the Confederacy, Virginia would have likely remained in the Union, making the Civil War little more than the 1832 nullification protest in South Carolina and other southern states. President Andrew Jackson crushed the nullification protest by the force of his will and with a clear threat to destroy protesters, as only "Old Hickory" could and would do as Commander-in-Chief.

In the 1832-33 Virginia General Assembly session, Western Virginia delegates voted to oppose South Carolina's nullification protest. The counties they represented give an early indication of the shape of a new state to be formed three decades later during the Civil War.[696]

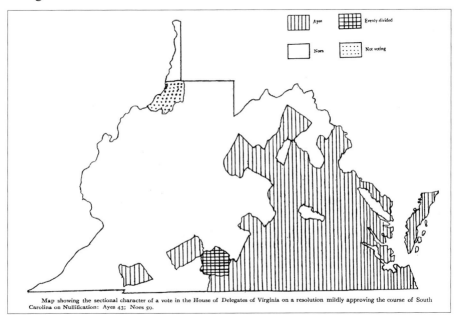

Map showing the sectional character of a vote in the House of Delegates of Virginia on a resolution mildly approving the course of South Carolina on Nullification: Ayes 43; Noes 59.

Vote in Virginia House of Delegates on Resolution Mildly Approving South Carolina's Leadership on Nullification (Ayes 43, Noes 49) – Image Permission from *West Virginia University Press*

The business of slavery pushed the nation into war. By 1860, political parties were hardened on the issue of slavery along new regional lines. In the November election of 1860, Abraham Lincoln won the Electoral College vote as a northern candidate in a fractured field of four candidates. His election triggered the formation of the Confederacy. Six weeks after his election, on December 20, 1860, South Carolina passed a "Resolution to Call the Election of Abraham Lincoln as U. S. President a Hostile Act" and then voted to secede from the Union.[697] The Confederacy started twelve months after John Brown was hanged for treason.

Regardless of speculation about a peaceful end to slavery, after the raid at Harpers Ferry, the issue of slavery, and violence to end it, became the key subject of all political and social discourse in a nation deeply divided over the institutional enslavement of human beings. That time in America was only seven generations ago and during the experience of the great-great-grandparents of the author and many others who read this work. Segregation was parented by slavery from the idea of white superiority.[698] Established race discrimination was in the experience of the author and many other Americans.

From our collective national memory, we should acknowledge the benefit and joy of being good neighbors to all people from all places, births, backgrounds, genders, faiths, cultures, orientations, identities, hopes, and dreams for themselves, and their families in a land of good neighbors for all. This was the boyhood dream of Booker T. Washington. It should be the enduring "American Way."

John Brown Hanging - Image *Courtesy Library of Congress*

Chapter 17

Virginia Joins The Confederacy And Protects Its Markets For Slaves

Seven Agricultural States Start the Confederacy

John Brown's raid was the first major event leading to the Civil War. The second was the election of President Abraham Lincoln. The war started with a Confederate attack on April 12, 1861, at Fort Sumter in Charleston, South Carolina. Abraham Lincoln was inaugurated on March 4, 1861, five weeks before the attack. The attack was jurisdictional to expel federal troops from territory claimed by the Confederacy after secession of the first seven Confederate states, before Virginia officially joined the Confederacy in May.

Virginians met in convention in February to consider secession from the Union. The early sentiment against secession was strong. On April 4, 1861, a resolution to secede from the Union was defeated by an overwhelming two-to-one vote of 90 opposed and 45 in favor. Eight days later, after President Abraham Lincoln called for 75,000 volunteer troops to join the federal army for 90 days, the sentiment in eastern Virginia changed dramatically. On April 17, 1861, two weeks after rejection of the resolution to secede, the Convention passed a resolution for secession by a vote of 88 to 55 which was to become official only after it was approved by a majority vote in a statewide referendum. On May 23, 1861, voters in the referendum approved secession with 125,950 voting for and 20,373 voting against. It was said that many western Virginia votes were not counted in the tally. After its convention vote in April, Virginia was followed into the Confederacy by three states, each strategically essential to the rebellion: Arkansas, North Carolina, and Tennessee.[699]

South Carolina was the first state to leave the Union on December 20, 1860. That state had led the Southerners in the confrontation with President Andrew Jackson in 1832 and 1833 over a state's right to nullify federal laws it opposed or wanted to disregard. South Carolina conceded to a president who was a slaver and had the absolute will to crush any rebellious act.

President Jackson predicted total destruction in a civil war by this warning to South Carolina leaders, stated in no uncertain terms:

Disunion by armed force is *treason*. Are you really ready to incur its guilt?....On your unhappy state will inevitably fall all the evils of the conflict you force upon the government of your country. It cannot accede to the mad project of disunion, of which you would be the first victims. [As president, I] ...Declare that you will never take the field unless the star-spangled banner of your country shall float over you; that you will not be stigmatized when dead, and dishonored and scorned while you live, as the authors of the first attack on the Constitution of your country. Its destroyers you cannot be.[700]

The nullification movement in South Carolina and its region ended peacefully in 1833, and claims of states' rights to openly nullify federal law were settled, but the idea of states' rights would continue and have full bloom in the Confederacy. President Jackson's prediction that treason would lead to dishonor did not come true for the rebellion lead by Virginia in 1861.

Of the first seven states to join the Confederacy only South Carolina and Georgia were states at the time of the Federal Constitution in 1787. The other Confederate states were territories except for Texas, which was part of Mexico. In order of secession, the six states joining South Carolina before Virginia voted to secede in convention on April 17, 1861, included: Mississippi (January 9, 1861), Florida (January 10, 1861), Alabama (January 11, 1861), Georgia (January 19, 1861), Louisiana (January 26, 1861), and Texas (February 1, 1861). Virginia's overwhelming importance to the Confederacy is evidenced by the immediate move of the Confederate capital to Richmond in May 1861.

These first seven agricultural states were not capable of maintaining all-out war against the industrialized North. They needed resource-rich Virginia to join the Confederacy to give them any chance of success. Virginia was the leading manufacturing state for strategic materials needed for the Confederacy, other than for iron, and, for iron, Virginia produced nearly 40 percent of the South's needs early in the war.

Virginia's large population with a number of urban centers was about one and one-half million people, of which almost one-third, or one-half million people were held in slavery and valued by some to be almost one-third of Virginia's overall wealth. The slave livestock industry made the idea of ending slavery a financial nightmare for eastern Virginians. Thomas Dew, the best-known apologist for slavery as a romantic ideal, earlier wrote that, if slavery were to end, Virginia would be a "desert."[701]

The map that follows shows the votes by counties on the secession referendum and it has a shape similar to the western boundaries of the new state.

Map 49: Results of the Virginia Referendum on Secession in the Counties that Became the State of West Virginia—May 23, 1861

County Votes on Secession Referendum May 23, 1861. – *Image permission by West Virginia University Press, Source: Frank S. Riddle. A Historical Atlas of West Virginia, 2008.*

Three States Follow Virginia To Rebellion

The Civil War was never a war of true equals, but the addition of Virginia to the Confederacy, along with three other strategically located states that followed Virginia into rebellion, made the Civil War a winnable war for the South. Those states included two key Mississippi Valley states, Arkansas and Tennessee, and a key coastal state, North Carolina, which divided the Coastal Confederacy between Virginia and South Carolina. Importantly, four slave border states did not secede along with counties in northwestern Virginia, soon to be made into a new state. The four border slave states were Missouri, Kentucky, Maryland, and Delaware.

With some luck and the brilliant leadership of two generals from Virginia, Robert E. Lee and Thomas "Stonewall" Jackson, the Civil War could have been won for the South. Victory for Robert E. Lee at Gettysburg would likely have forced a compromise truce because northerners were growing tired of the war and its overwhelming casualties. A week after Gettysburg there was a murderous anti-conscription riot in New York City, which lasted for four days with citywide mayhem directed against black adults and children. It is considered the largest insurrection in American history.[702]

With Virginia in the Confederacy, the war became a four-year death fight. The death toll was over 600,000 soldiers, many of whom are in unmarked graves, some in mass graves. There is a mass grave for 95 Confederate soldiers in Lewisburg, West Virginia. In Salisbury, North Carolina, there is a cemetery where the bodies of people who are known are buried in 85 separate graves, while there are 12,027 unidentified bodies, of which 11,700 "are buried in trenches, not graves."[703]

Western Virginians who resided in the rural areas north of the Great Kanawha River and Gauley River were mostly loyal to the Union, whereas in the Kanawha Valley the population was split generally with the Confederacy supported widely in Charleston and Malden and in the more rural areas south of the Great Kanawha River. Eastern Virginians largely supported the Confederacy and contributed vast resources to destroy the Union. The purpose was to protect an aristocratic culture and economy supported by a slave livestock industry. Poet Maggie Anderson reminds us of turbulent times in her book, *Years That Answer*, with a quote from Zora Neale Hurston in *Their Eyes Were Watching God*:

> There are years that ask questions
> and years that answer.[704]

Virginia's Capital Becomes Capital of the Confederacy

Virginia's importance in the Civil War is revealed by the move of the Confederate capital to Richmond after Virginia joined the Confederacy. This grand act acknowledged Virginia's strategic importance for resources and leadership.

Virginia was the power center of the Confederacy. It had factories and a large white population for soldiers and their support. It would provide two of the most effective generals of the Civil War, Robert E. Lee and Thomas "Stonewall" Jackson . Only with Virginia's vast man-power and resources could a political disturbance of a few months in the Deep South become an all-out, four-year war.[705]

The value paradox of slavery and freedom is presented clearly by Virginia's role in American history.[706] In the 1620s, Virginia servitude was used to start the first profitable commerce in the colonies to produce tobacco. About 200 years later, Richmond became the Upper South's center for slave-trading after Congress banned importation of African slaves effective in 1808. Slave exports to the Deep South made slavery a major livestock industry in Virginia and the evil of the Virginia slave trade is obvious to us today. Vehement attacks by slavers on any criticism of slavery reinforced their dependence on a slave culture in Virginia that pushed the Commonwealth to join the Confederacy.

The Virginia Statehouse was designed by Thomas Jefferson and a French architect, Charles-Louis Clerisseau. It was modeled from *Maison Carree* an ancient Roman structure in Nimes, France.[707] Its design and placement on a high hill bring to mind symbols of the contradictions in American ideas and American life in the time of the Civil War. It has a portico projecting out majestically over the hill, in the noble style of the Greek Parthenon, announcing the Commonwealth's belief in fundamental democracy.

The Jefferson Capitol is an imposing structure built during the Revolutionary War in 1780, and it evokes warm memories of Thomas Jefferson 's eloquence in the Declaration of Independence four years before. His immortal words have imprinted liberty and equality on all social and political ideals of America life. They should be repeated often as a commitment of the heart to the best of American ideas:

> We hold these Truths to be self-evident, that all Men are created equal, that they are endowed by their Creator with certain unalienable Rights, that among these are Life, Liberty, and the pursuit of Happiness.[708]

This statement is one of the most glorious and enduring statements for freedom, equality, and social justice in the history of the world. Thomas Jefferson 's spirited and eloquent gift of inspirational ideas is perfectly expressed in the Capitol's classic Roman and Greek design. But today, when the majestic statehouse building is remembered with those words of inspiration, its role as the former Confederate Capitol makes it a heresy of those great ideas. How could this building built to announce the glory of the best hopes of America serve as the Capitol of an aristocratic nation dedicated to protecting slavery and its attendant horrors?

Virginia Capitol in Richmond in April, 1865 – *Image Courtesy of the Library of Congress*

The Virginia Capitol introduces another interesting moment in history. It stands above and faces the square federal courthouse shown in the photograph above to the right of the Capitol, where in 1807 Aaron Burr was tried and acquitted of treason against the United States. He was elected Thomas Jefferson's vice president and became the president's bitter political enemy. While Vice President, Aaron Burr murdered a defenseless Alexander Hamilton in a New Jersey duel on July 11, 1804. Alexander Hamilton thought it was immoral to shoot a man in a duel. He shot first and away into trees. Vice President Aaron Burr then shot to kill. The murder of a defenseless man destroyed Aaron Burr's public reputation and career. He apparently escaped criminal prosecution on the technicality that his victim died in New York rather than New Jersey. Aaron Burr showed little remorse for the death of Alexander Hamilton. Alexander Hamilton wanted to make a statement against duels. His 19-year-old son, Philip Hamilton, died in a duel two years before, after his father advised him to "reserve his fire... [and] discharge his pistol in the air" in order to maintain proper reputation and honor. The Hamiltons were men of high honor and courage, easily challenged to deadly duels.[709]

Aaron Burr's treason trial was for allegations that he tried to establish his own nation in the West in 1806 and 1807. Little evidence of overt treasonous acts was produced despite President Jefferson doing all he could do to have the charges proved. It was a political event. One commentator called the Aaron Burr trial "one of the choice comedies of American justice and politics."[710] As part of his adventures in the West, Aaron Burr was hosted at the elegant mansion of Harman Blennerhassett and Margaret Agnew Blennerhassett on their Virginia island in the Ohio River near today's Parkersburg. Harman Blennerhassett was jailed and released only when Aaron Burr was acquitted. The Blennerhassetts were ruined by the escapade. Blennerhassett Island today has a reconstructed mansion and grounds. It is an important and fascinating state park on an island in the Ohio River near today's Parkersburg.

Other than for the treachery of General Benedict Arnold, it seems that, in America, it is difficult to prove treason either presently or in the past, whether it is for designs to create a nation in the West or for Confederate leaders who have been glorified as heroes for taking up arms to destroy the Union. For that, America may be a nation of extreme forgiveness, romance, and selective, fuzzy memory.

Names for War and Its Battles Vary in North and South

The region known as the "South" includes slave states which are south of the Mason-Dixon Line . That is the southern border of Pennsylvania which was surveyed in 1767. After the Civil War, places in the southern region were expected to observe faithfully Jim Crow social codes of separation and subjugation of blacks. The White House is below the Mason-Dixon Line and southerners expected presidents to obey the racist Jim Crow social codes observed in the rest of the South. When Booker T. Washington had dinner with President Theodore Roosevelt and his family at the White House on October 16, 1901, it caused outrage in the South because no black of any standing was ever allowed to eat at table with any white person south of the Mason-Dixon line. The same dinner above the Mason-Dixon Line would have been of no consequence to southerners.

Names reflecting social codes are important. The names given to "the war" once divided supporters of the South and North. The public message from southern supporters after the Civil War, and perhaps today, has been that the war is properly called the "War Between the States" because they claim that it was fought over the sovereign rights of states against an overreaching federal government.

The United Daughters of the Confederacy, UDC, pushed that name as part of its post-War propaganda campaign to glorify southern leaders, culture, the secession of Confederate states from the Union and the alleged true purpose of the War to protect states' rights. The UDC began in Nashville, Tennessee, and was popular in Richmond. It was so successful at the beginning of the twentieth century that it had 200,000 people attend its June 3, 1907 dedication of a monument in Richmond to Jefferson Davis . It put up many monuments in the early part of the century to heroes of the Confederacy. They even put up a monument to Henry Wirz, the commander of the Confederate prison in Andersonville, Georgia, who was hanged as a war criminal for the many thousands of prisoners who died under his command and care during the war.

Southerners used terms like the "War for Southern Independence" or the "War of Northern Aggression." Southern sympathizers also romanticized the South by naming the Civil War the "Lost Cause of the Confederacy." Northerners saw it as a "Civil War" to keep the nation unified and later to end slavery. Southerners were more likely to use a genteel name signifying states' rights, such as the "War Between the States," or the "War of Rebellion."[711]

The name "War Between the States" became the prominent name for the war with states' rights advocates after the war. It helped them argue that jurisdictional issues, not slavery, were the cause of the war between the North and South. Southern states claimed to be sovereign in their jurisdictions and superior to the federal government. This argument can be technical and ignores the fact that states' rights doctrines have been most prominently used to deny federal civil rights following a direct tradition from slavery and Jim Crow segregation. Other jurisdictional issues may be involved in a federal system, but "the war" by any name was fought over the rights of states to enslave people. Slavery was incorporated in the Federal Constitution under the leadership of Virginians to encourage ratification by all the states, North and South. The states' rights argument was used successfully for over a century to pull many judges and historians along to ignore obvious racial degradations. Thus, "the war" can properly be called, as some northerners did following the war, the "Slaveholders' Rebellion" because it was fought over slavery and was a treasonous rebellion, not a hypothetical sovereignty fight over federal versus states' rights. In eastern Virginia, it was clearly a "Slaveholders' Rebellion."

Battle names also were different for the two sides. The North used names of waterways, rivers and creeks and other natural features, while southerners used the names of towns nearby.[712] The Battle of Antietam in the North was called the Battle of Sharpsburg in the South. Similarly, Bull Run and Manassas are different names for the same battles fought not far from the nation's capital.

Chapter 18

War-Time Dilemma Over Emancipation

Emancipation Dilemma for President Lincoln and Loyal Slavers

President Abraham Lincoln and Lewis Ruffner struggled in the Civil War over the emancipation of slaves. President Abraham Lincoln's anguish was over how he could emancipate slaves in the Confederate South without creating discord in the border slave states that remained loyal to the Union. He favored compensation for emancipated slaves. His proposals to Congress on the issue were rejected. The border states were Maryland, Delaware, Missouri, Kentucky and loyal northwestern counties in Virginia. They were vital to the war effort. The borders states surrounded the nation's capital. They insulated the North from southern advances. They created platform territories for Union armies to be mustered and supplied. They provided men and resources to support the Union cause on the Atlantic Coast and along the Ohio and Mississippi rivers. As Union states, they kept resources away from the Confederacy. President Lincoln needed a solution to this dilemma. He found the solution in his skills as a lawyer, as he crafted drafts of the Emancipation Proclamation.

In his 1860 election campaign, Abraham Lincoln accepted slavery as a historic and institutional fact of the disparate human conditions in America. In the second year of his presidency, his public position on slavery began to evolve toward abolition. He did not publicly support the abolition of slavery before his election as president. At an important election speech at Cooper Union in New York on February 27, 1860, he said the institution of slavery was wrong. He hated enslavement of human beings but, as a public servant, he fully accepted slavery as included in the Federal Constitution and as a part of American society and culture.

For Lewis Ruffner, emancipation presented a personal financial problem. He was a loyal Unionist with a substantial investment in slaves when the salt and slavery industry was in decline. He wanted compensation for emancipation of his slaves. He needed workers for his salt and coal businesses. He knew early in the Civil War that emancipation could adversely affect his businesses. This may have been a reason for him to be a delegate to the Wheeling Conventions. The conventions could abolish slavery with a restored Virginia government loyal to the Union or they could create a new state, perhaps a new free state, with or without compensation for his slaves. He needed a good resolution of this financial dilemma.

Lewis Ruffner was almost alone in the Ruffner family as a public Union supporter. His brother, Dr. Henry Ruffner, in 1856 gave a publicized Fourth of July Speech extolling the Union and the many advances the nation made in unity with a mix of many different white immigrants, who together made the "American mold" and established a "national character." During the Civil War, Dr. Ruffner was silent, likely because his sons and nephews were Confederate soldiers. Six young Ruffners joined the elite Confederate Corps of the Kanawha Riflemen organized earlier by David Lewis Ruffner, who was Dr. Henry Ruffner's second son. David Lewis Ruffner was a teacher at Mercer Academy in the 1850s.[713]

Quakers Urge Emancipation to be the Purpose of the War

Emancipation for President Abraham Lincoln, at first, was just one more almost impossible political issue to manage. The war made the president a more spiritual person with an evolving wisdom and sense of responsibility. Notably, he was one of the first major politicians in America to announce allegiance to God in his political speeches.[714] When he first used references to God, they were for political purposes. He understood that religion was an untapped motivator for voters. As the war went on, it became a motivator of his spiritual self.

Religion had not been at the center of his young life. His ancestors had been Quakers and his Baptist parents were antislavery. They lived in Virginia and Kentucky and then moved to Indiana, a free state. His mother, Nancy Hanks, was born in western Virginia near Antioch in today's Mineral County, West Virginia.[715] Nancy Lincoln died when Abraham was nine years old. His home life was hard with physical labor at an early age, much like what other children had to perform on the frontier. He became a very successful, well-to-do railroad attorney, but he appealed to the common man for votes to win elections. He used a down-home image of his youth, as a log splitter who was born in a log cabin.

A fateful day for the president's dilemma over emancipation was June 20, 1862, when a committee of Quaker representatives, three men and three women, met with the president to ask him to order the immediate emancipation of all slaves. The president considered their ideas. His ancestors had been Quakers. They had a record of leading opposition to slavery. They did not fade as a faith group in their opposition during the antebellum years. Formal Quaker peace committees have been regularly sent to leaders in violent conflicts, to seek an end to hostilities. The Quaker committee advised the president that they supported his work to prosecute the Civil War as required by the Federal Constitution, and they asserted that he had a duty to conduct the war only for a just purpose. They thought the rebellion was treason, and they wanted emancipation to become the nation's purpose for the war. They said that this purpose would free the slaves and save the nation from destruction.[716]

President Lincoln explained the problem in terms of enforcement. He responded from his experience as a successful railroad attorney. He would make many legal points about why he had little power to turn the Civil War into a war to end slavery. The president's authority to enforce emancipation was limited by law and the Federal Constitution. He could not emancipate slaves in the South because the Confederacy did not recognize the Constitution, nor would it recognize any authority he might have in a war against what they considered to be their own country. A mere edict would not suffice. Further, it could be an unconstitutional act for him alone as president to outlaw slavery when it was legal in five border states that were still loyal and important to the Union. Those slave states were essential to Union victory. Any uproar in those states over emancipation could turn the tide against the Union.[717]

Many people today, think of the Civil War as an obvious win for the North, primarily based on its greater population, army, soldiers, financial and manufacturing resources, and eventual purpose. But in the North, as the war went on and on, there was a growing exhaustion over the costs and high death toll for a war fought in the southern states. The growing discontent in the North could have brought the war to an earlier end by attrition, like it did for mighty Britain in the Revolutionary War after Yorktown. With losses by the North at Antietam or Gettysburg, in northern territory, the South may have been able to bargain for peace for the sake of peace, based on exhaustion in the North for the war. That result would have left the Union divided into two nations with a shared heritage and ethnicity--ready for new squabbles, disputes, and armed conflicts, at least in their next generations.

To the Quaker committee, the president would have acknowledged their moral high ground and that he struggled with the moral and political problems presented by slavery, since so many Unionists wanted to end slavery. He would have likely admitted that he needed Divine assistance. His legal authority to end slavery by presidential order was questionable. The Quaker committee encouraged the president to work on the dilemma and find a solution. The president knew that northerners had "moral disgust" for slavery and for the people who supported it. Before the war, the overriding sentiment in the North had been to ignore slavery. After John Brown's raid, that sentiment turned and many northerners were ready at all costs to end slavery.[718] But as the war dragged on, the resolve of many northerners to finish the war waned.

The president took to heart the Quaker committee's concerns, and four weeks later, in July 1862, he sketched a draft preliminary executive order he called the "Emancipation Proclamation" to order that slaves in the Confederacy would "thenceforward and forever, be free." He wrote that it was his purpose to recommend to Congress "a practical measure for tendering pecuniary aid to states for full or gradual emancipation of their slaves when they have accepted or will accept "the authority of the United States." His drafting was very artful and precise, because he had proposed compensation for emancipation to Congress a number of times and each proposal was rejected. His draft was shared with his cabinet members on July 22, 1862. They were strongly divided over it. Most opposed the proposal and one member was ready to resign over it. The president had little support at first in his cabinet on emancipation.[719]

Cabinet Meeting on Abraham Lincoln's Emancipation Proclamation – *Image Courtesy of West Virginia State Archives*

A month after his meeting with the Cabinet, on August 22, 1862, the President wrote to Horace Greeley, the influential editor of the *New York Tribune*, about his intention to preserve the Union, with or without emancipation. He acknowledged his "oft-expressed *personal* wish that all people everywhere, could be free," but wrote that his official duty was to preserve the Union. "If I could save the Union without freeing *any* slave, I would do it; and if I could save it by freeing *all* the slaves, I would do it; and if I could do it by freeing some and leaving the others alone, I would also do that." [720]

Emancipation at least moved up to be his second priority. President Lincoln knew he could not free slaves in loyal border states. Emancipation of slaves in those states would be seen as a punishment to slavers loyal to the Union. It could cause economic and political upheaval. The president was also concerned that emancipation by an executive order, even in time of war, would be a lightning rod for and against slavery. There were no opinion polls to gauge popular sentiment in the North or the South.

With the skill of an experienced lawyer, he narrowly crafted an executive order that he named the "Preliminary Emancipation Proclamation." He wanted to publicize the executive order as a trial balloon before a final proclamation would take effect on New Year's Day 1863. He based emancipation on his war powers, to end slavery for disloyal slavers because its existence aided and abetted them in their treason against the United States. It was like Lord Dunmore's 1774 Emancipation Proclamation to free slaves to fight for King George. It applied only to those slaves who were bound to rebels against the king, not the slaves of loyal subjects. [721]

The president wanted to assess sentiment for the proposal and revise it as needed before it would become official. This approach brilliantly allowed him to leave slavery in place while he measured opposition to emancipation in the border states loyal to the Union. It was conceptually consistent with his goals to win the war based upon established war powers as Commander-in-Chief. He earlier used his war powers to suspend *habeas corpus* protections against incarceration without judicial due process, to have state legislators and a sitting Congressman arrested and detained in Baltimore for haranguing against the Union and his leadership. The Supreme Court found his suspension of *habeas corpus* was unconstitutional in a decision written by Chief Justice Roger B. Taney. To the continuing alarm of constitutional scholars today, President Lincoln officially ignored the decision. He delayed announcement of the preliminary executive order until the Union won a decisive victory, and the outcome of the war would be more certain. For some abolitionists, it was too limited to be celebrated since as many as 450,000 people remained enslaved in the border states. [722]

He waited patiently into the autumn of 1862 to announce the Preliminary Emancipation Proclamation. His opportunity came after the North won an apparent victory at the Battle of Antietam near Sharpsburg, Maryland. This victory for the Union came on September 17, 1862, which happened to be the 75th Anniversary of public signing of the secret Federal Constitution in Philadelphia in 1787. The battle was a bloody legacy with some 23,000 casualties including 3,650 dead in one day. It is the bloodiest one-day battle in American history. It is viewed today by some military strategists as a draw on the battlefield. General George McClellan widely claimed victory and was popular with his troops.[723] His failure to pursue and crush the Confederate Army in retreat disappointed President Lincoln. It may have extended the war for two more years.

General Robert E. Lee's plan to end the war with a major victory in the North was lost because of the extreme loss of Confederate soldiers who could not be replaced. That made Antietam a major blow to the Confederacy because it desperately needed to win in Pennsylvania, so its army could march on Washington and depress northern hopes for an early end to the war. General Lee retreated to Virginia. Some thought that the Civil War could have ended for the Union after this battle in 1862, if General McClellan's army had aggressively pursued General Lee's army before its swift Potomac River crossing back to Virginia. The Confederate army escaped overnight, and it would take the Union army weeks to move across the Potomac River and back into Virginia. Of course, some think that the South could have ended the war almost a year later at Gettysburg, if Robert E. Lee had won that battle and marched on to Washington. There were 50,000 soldiers killed, wounded or lost, in three days of battle at Gettysburg. General McClellan was replaced by President Lincoln a month and a half after Antietam and a few days after the mid-term Congressional elections. Union generals were slow to engage the enemy until General U. S. Grant took charge with support from his lead generals, William Tecumseh Sherman and Philip Henry Sheridan.

At Antietam, General Lee had the smaller army and lost 60 percent of the casualties. He was in no way ready to march on Washington after Antietam in the autumn of 1862. His plan to march to Washington would have to wait until the next summer when he would return to eastern Pennsylvania. No one in the small town of Gettysburg could know it would host one of the most consequential battles of all time—a battle which would secure the unity of the nation and make casualties of 50,000 American soldiers in three days.[724]

On November 19, 1863, to commemorate the large number of men buried in the new cemetery at Gettysburg, President Lincoln gave one of the most beloved addresses in American history. He followed an orator who spoke for two hours. The president's speech consisted of 272 words, and it took him two minutes to deliver. He concluded by announcing an anthem for the North.

It is for us, the living, rather, to be dedicated here to the unfinished work which they who fought here have thus far so nobly advanced....that from these honored dead we take increased devotion to that cause for which they gave the last full measure of devotion; that we here highly resolve that these dead shall not have died in vain–that this nation, under God, shall have a new birth of freedom and that government of the people, by the people and for the people, shall not perish from the earth.[725]

Vincent Wilson, Jr., wrote that Americans can fully understand the president's message to keep the nation's experiment in free government alive and flourishing. It is a duty passed on, as stated in his immortal words, from the honored dead who gave the "last full measure of devotion."

No American reading the Gettysburg Address can miss Lincoln's message—his emphasis on continuity, on challenge, and on sacrifice and devotion: by acknowledging the supremacy of what the soldiers did, he touched the very nerve of democracy and free government. And he saw the outcome of the battle as no golden victory, but as an opportunity, purchased at great human cost, for the living, in their turn, to resolve to do--simply to do their part to continue to keep the experiment in free government alive.[726]

A few days after Antietam, President Lincoln announced to his cabinet that he was ready to announce the Preliminary Emancipation Proclamation which they had reviewed and declined to approve two months before in July. He informed cabinet members that he had prepared a new draft of the preliminary executive order in what he considered final form, and that he was determined to make only minor changes that were helpful. He refused to make significant changes. Cabinet members had been divided on the emancipation issue, morally and politically. He chose not to consult them in his final deliberations. On September 22, 1862, five days after Antietam, he announced to the public the Preliminary Emancipation Proclamation. The cabinet members publicly supported the Proclamation.[727]

After the Preliminary Proclamation was announced, there was little surprise or discord in the border slave states. The executive order announced a policy for slavers loyal to the Union throughout the Civil War to be compensated for emancipation of their slaves. The document proclaims that the president intended to see that

[All] citizens of the United States who shall have remained loyal thereto throughout the rebellion, shall be compensated for all losses by acts of the United States including the loss of slaves.[728]

The Preliminary Emancipation Proclamation also announced the intention of the president to seek to have Congress provide financial assistance to slave states that "may voluntarily adopt, immediate, or gradual abolishment of slavery within their respective limits."[729] Such assurances of the president's support would have at first relieved many loyal slavers, like Lewis Ruffner, who were concerned over what appeared to be the inevitable abolition of slavery--if the Union won the war. Compensation was unpopular with Radical Republicans who controlled Congress.

Emancipation Brings Best Hope for Equality

In an address to Congress on December 1, 1862, President Lincoln made clear that emancipation had become the purpose for winning the Civil War.

In giving freedom to the slave, we assure freedom to the free--honorable alike in what we give, and what we preserve. We shall nobly save, or meanly lose, the last best hope of earth. Other means may succeed; this could not fail. The way is plain, peaceful, generous, just-- a way which, if followed, the world will forever applaud, and God must forever bless.[730]

On New Year's Day 1863, President Lincoln issued the final version of the Emancipation Proclamation using his war powers to emancipate slaves in the areas of rebellion as originally planned. Cabinet members supported the Proclamation.[731] President Lincoln's final document listed the states in rebellion and exempted the counties to be designated for the new state in western Virginia. The president announced in the Emancipation Proclamation:

Now therefore, I, Abraham Lincoln, President of the United States, by virtue of the power in me vested as the Commander-in-Chief of the Army and Navy of the United States in time of actual armed rebellion against authority and government of the United States and as a fit and necessary war measure for suppressing said rebellion, do, on this day ... order and declare that all persons held as slaves within said designated States and parts of states, are, and henceforward shall be free....

And upon this act, sincerely believed to be an act of justice, warranted by the Constitution, upon military necessity, I invoke the considerate judgment of mankind, and the gracious favor of the Almighty God.[732]

Importantly, the final executive order made an approving general reference to the Preliminary Emancipation Proclamation, but it did not repeat the assurances of compensation for loyal slavers. Well after the final Proclamation was in effect, President Lincoln discussed a plan with Frederick Douglass to form an elite band of black scouts to go through the Confederate South to "carry the news of emancipation" and to urge slaves to come to Union territory. Because the war going well for the Union, the plan was not implemented by the president.[733]

The decision to emancipate slaves in Confederate states was one of the boldest acts of any leader in history. It cut off the Confederacy from all possible allies, even Britain and its giant cotton textile industry that was dependent on southern cotton.[734] It would end the primary dynamic of American politics since the Revolutionary War, and, finally, it would start making the ideas of liberty, equality, and social justice to apply to all people at law, if not in fact.

CHARLES SUMNER,
"The Abolitionist."

ABRAHAM LINCOLN.

HARRIET BEECHER STOWE,
Author of "Uncle Tom's Cabin."

"WITH CHARITY FOR ALL AND MALICE TOWARD NONE"

Abraham Lincoln, Charles Sumner, & Harriet Beecher Stowe - *Image Under Public Domain. Source: Henry Davenport Northrop, Joseph R. Gay, and I. Garland Penn, The College of Life or Practical Self-Educator: A Manual of Self-Improvement for the Colored Race.*

By his Excellency the Right Honourable JOHN *Earl of* DUNMORE, *his Majesty's Lieutenant and Governour-General of the Colony and Dominion of* Virginia, *and Vice-Admiral of the same:*

A PROCLAMATION.

AS I have ever entertained Hopes that an Accommodation might have taken Place between *Great Britain* and this Colony, without being compelled, by my Duty, to this most disagreeable, but now absolutely necessary Step, rendered so by a Body of armed Men, unlawfully assembled, firing on his Majesty's Tenders, and the Formation of an Army, and that Army now on their March to attack his Majesty's Troops, and destroy the well-disposed Subjects of this Colony: To defeat such treasonable Purposes, and that all such Traitors, and their Abetters, may be brought to Justice, and that the Peace and good Order of this Colony may be again restored, which the ordinary Course of the civil Law is unable to effect, I have thought fit to issue this my Proclamation, hereby declaring, that until the aforesaid good Purposes can be obtained, I do, in Virtue of the Power and Authority to me given, by his Majesty, determine to execute martial Law, and cause the same to be executed throughout this Colony; and to the End that Peace and good Order may the sooner be restored, I do require every Person capable of bearing Arms to resort to his Majesty's S T A N- DARD, or be looked upon as Traitors to his Majesty's Crown and Government, and thereby become liable to the Penalty the Law inflicts upon such Offences, such as Forfeiture of Life, Confiscation of Lands, &c. &c. And I do hereby farther declare all indented Servants, Negroes, or others (appertaining to Rebels) free, that are able and willing to bear Arms, they joining his Majesty's Troops, as soon as may be, for the more speedily reducing this Colony to a proper Sense of their Duty, to his Majesty's Crown and Dignity. I do farther order, and require, all his Majesty's liege Subjects to retain their Quitrents, or any other Taxes due, or that may become due, in their own Custody, till such Time as Peace may be again restored to this at present most unhappy Country, or demanded of them for their former salutary Purposes, by Officers properly authorised to receive the same.

GIVEN under my Hand, on Board the Ship William, *off* Norfolk, *the* 7th *Day of* November, *in the* 16th *Year of his Majesty's Reign.*

D U N M O R E.

G O D   SAVE   THE   K I N G.

Proclamation by Royal Governor of Virginia, the Earl of Dunmore - *Image Courtesy of the Library of Congress*

Chapter 19

Success And Criticism
Of Emancipation Proclamation

Emancipation Proclamation Wins the War

The Emancipation Proclamation was a great success as a military strategy and a diplomatic *coup d'etat*. It energized people in the North to fight for a moral cause, and it did not increase opposition in Confederate states since what was proclaimed in Washington was given no more credit than the musings of a foreign monarch. It secured Great Britain's neutrality, because its working classes firmly supported emancipation. Even out-of-work textile workers supported emancipation. They were unemployed because of the cotton embargo, but opposed slavery. The cotton embargo enforced by a Naval blockade intercepted Confederate cotton exports reducing 166,000 British factory workers to part-time work and 247,000 to unemployment.[735] For slaves in the Deep South, there were no universal effects. Many slaves had no alternatives to remaining in the place of their birth and loyal to the lives they had accommodated with slaver families whose men, ironically, were away fighting a war to continue their enslavement. Slaves self-emancipated when Union army officials were helpful to them.

In the five loyal border slave states, there were hundreds of thousands of slaves who were left in bondage by the proclamation. Slavers like Lewis Ruffner thought, or hoped, they would be paid compensation for their slaves on account of their loyalty to the Union. Their apparent appeasement on the compensation issue, whether fair or not, limited early discord over the preliminary proclamation.[736]

The president's anguish over the Emancipation Proclamation was just one of many pressures of his office, pressures that would have been crushing to other leaders. His careful review of all effects of the Proclamation demonstrated a brilliance in political and military leadership and complete dedication to duty. He could not celebrate his successes. His life was like the Old Testament story of the suffering of Job. President Lincoln and his wife, Mary Todd Lincoln, lost a son, Willie, while living in the White House, so the president knew grief in every part of his being. It was the second young son they had lost. As president, he felt the pain and responsibility of Union defeats and the burden of thousands of deaths on both sides. He genuinely sympathized with the families of lost soldiers. There were thousands and thousands of deaths and casualties to mourn.

Many black soldiers were killed for the Union in the Civil War. A stirring memorial stands on Boston Commons across from the Old Statehouse on Beacon Hill to commemorate the valiant, black 54th Massachusetts Regiment Volunteer Infantry and their white commander Colonel Robert Gould Shaw. With 1,000 troops volunteering in a few weeks, it was one of the first regiments organized for African Americans. It would be one of the first black regiments to fight in the war. On July 18, 1863, at Fort Wagner, leading to Morris Island near Charleston, South Carolina, the Regiment made a direct, courageous assault on the fort, suffering over 200 killed and many more wounded and lost. The numbers of casualties from all regiments are not known. The Confederates buried 800 bodies in a mass grave. There were only 315 soldiers left in the 54th Regiment. The commander, Colonel Robert Gould Shaw, and two captains were buried in a single grave with the black soldiers who died with them on the battlefield. His family erected a monument to him at Moravian Cemetery on Staten

Boston Parade March on May 28, 1863 by Massachusetts 54th Regiment shown on the *Memorial to Robert Gould Shaw and the Massachucsetts Fifty-Fourth Regiment*, a relief sculpture by Augustus Saint-Gaudens-- *Image Courtesy of the Library of Congress*

Island. Confederates thought a common grave for white officers with black soldiers was an insult, but Colonel Shaw would likely have felt honored by burial with his brave men. Sergeant William Harvey Carney became the first African American voted by Congress for the Medal of Honor for his bravery in going onto the battlefield to seek and retrieve the regiment's flag.[737] The story of this great Regiment is told in the film *Glory*, with a story focus on Colonel Shaw.

The 54th Regiment's Memorial contains a great work of art. It is a relief sculpture depicting the regiment's proud march on May 28, 1863, down Beacon Street before the bloody assault less than two months later at Fort Wagner on July 18, 1863. The large bronze relief by Augustus Saint-Gaudens titled *Memorial to Robert Gould Shaw and the Massachusetts Fifty-Fourth Regiment*, shows Colonel Shaw riding a horse with one leg in the air, traditionally signifying that he died of wounds in battle. This heroic regiment helped start the recruitment of slaves to the Union army. Black soldiers would become ten percent of the Union's troops.[738] Acclaimed as a great work of art, the memorial displays a salute to the brave black soldiers by Charles W. Eliot:

The black rank and file volunteered when disaster clouded the Union Cause. Served without pay for eighteen months till given that of white troops. Faced threatened enslavement if captured. Were brave in action. Patient under heavy and dangerous labors. And cheerful amid hardships and privations. Together they gave to the Nation and the World undying proof that Americans of African descent possess the pride, courage and devotion of the patriot soldier.[739]

The 54th Massachusetts Regiment's bravery proved in the North that black soldiers could be relied upon for valiant service, and it showed the South that black soldiers joining Union ranks would swell the Union's fighting force, which was already greater than what the Confederacy could muster by conscripting old and very young white men to fight for its cause. The 200,000 black soldiers who fought in the Civil War were affected by their service like the 367,000 "dough boys of African descent" in the First World War, which war W. E. B. Du Bois called the "jealous and avaricious struggle for the largest share in exploiting darker races." In the Civil War, black soldiers fighting for the Union, included about one in five of all military age black men in America, they were ten percent of the Union troops. They expected freedom and citizenship rights for their service. Abraham Lincoln agreed and announced in his last speech that black soldiers had earned the right to vote. He was assassinated for that idea.[740]

President Lincoln's main concern was the grinding, slow progress of the war. The early years of the war went poorly for the Union. It was an invading army with little success and considerable impatience at home. The president's generals could not contain or defeat the enemy, time after time. He dismissed from command General George McClellan for poor results, and the general responded by running against the president in his reelection bid in 1864. It was a difficult race against the general, who pushed for early compromise without victory as a way to end what had become an unpopular war.[741]

Military defeat of the Union in the Civil War was a strong possibility before General Ulysses S. Grant won in the West to secure control of the Mississippi River. When he took over the Union Army in the East, he was more than ready to wreak havoc in eastern Virginia because he thought eastern Virginia had special responsibility for its treason in making the Civil War an all-out fight to the death for both sides.[742] General Grant wrote in a letter to his sister about his personal interest in revenge and punishment of eastern Virginia's treason:

The conduct of eastern Virginia has been so abominable through the whole contest that there would be a great deal of disappointment here if matters should be settled before she is thoroughly punished. This is my feeling and I believe it universal. Great allowance should be made for South Carolinians; for the last generation have been educated from their infancy to look upon their government as oppressive and tyrannical and only to be endured till such time as they might have sufficient strength to strike it down. Virginia and other border States have no such excuse, and are therefore traitors at heart as well as in act."[743]

General Grant took great care and ceremony to show respect for General Robert E. Lee and his Virginia men at Appomattox Court House. He knew it was important to have General Lee and his troops feel that they were being treated well in the surrender, because he understood clearly that the enemy would become American citizens and neighbors. He was in tune with President Lincoln's "malice toward none" approach announced in the Second Inaugural Address in early March before General Lee's surrender on April 9, 1865, at Appomattox.

Defeat of the Union would have created a paralyzing crisis, encouraging intrigues by European powers as they would be free to pursue their interests in North America. It was earlier believed throughout Europe that Americans could never unify as a nation. It was assumed to be just a matter of time before the independent states would begin bargaining separately with European powers to serve their provincial interests. The union of states created by the Federal Constitution as one country was completed in fact by unifying patriotism of all Americans in the War of 1812. The Civil War eliminated all exceptions to unification. It is said that before the Civil War, the term "the United States" was considered to be a plural term, whereas after the war the usage became singular. Thus, the Civil War changed the conceptualization of the nation as a unity instead of a collection of states, and the phrase "the United States are" became the phrase, "the United States is."[744]

Lack of unity destroyed the Roman Empire and would have destroyed the United States of America. It was the first republican nation in the almost two centuries following Julius Caesar's overthrow of the Roman Republic. Only Virginia slavery, born of the tobacco industry and later used for booming cotton plantations in the Deep South, could possibly destroy America's national unity.[745]

The leadership of President Abraham Lincoln is unparalleled in American history. He was energized and directed by principles of morality and decency, and he applied them in ways to make effective, strategic policy. He was visionary but pragmatic when needed to solve an immediate problem. Anguish by a leader over moral public policy can at times bring on great vision and success. The anguish of President Lincoln over slavery clearly contributed to his improving leadership in office to become the nation's greatest president and a leader of inspiration for the Ages.

450,000 People in Border States are Left in Slavery

The Emancipation Proclamation left in slavery an estimated 450,000 slaves in the five border states.[746] President Lincoln's approach to end the war has been criticized. Reviews of his decision to outlaw slavery selectively, only in the Confederate South, tend to be technical, focusing on his clever drafting of the Emancipation Proclamation rather than its high purpose to win the Civil War and assure that all slaves could be set free.

Abolitionists objected to leaving slavery in place in the border states. Some recent purists also would prefer that his approach had been more of a marching moral crusade than a careful device to win the war. Critics would prefer a ringing proclamation to the tune of "Battle Hymn of the Republic" to better seal the president's heroic stature for the ages.

Instead, President Lincoln wanted to win the Civil War, or, more appropriately, in his mind he did not want to lose the war over emancipation. He used legal skill, careful language, and a surgical approach to emancipation, with great tactical success. His approach was too limiting to some who would prefer a pure moral victory without footnotes for slaves in border states. Such cool reviews safely rely on flat hindsight, like some reviews of the leadership of Booker T. Washington a half-century later and the critiques today of George Washington, Thomas Jefferson, James Madison, Alexander Hamilton and the other early leaders of the republic who believed in white superiority, fully in step with most all other whites in their day and for another two hundred years.

These men of greatness and other leaders deserve to be judged across the ups and downs, hills, valleys and mountains of real people in their own times, as they struggled with social change and new ideas and values. Leadership in those different times should be judged in light of the situational circumstances, struggles, and mountains they had to climb for those ideas. Not all steps are forward, but the most important ones should be.

The Final Emancipation Proclamation fairly should be revered as a master stroke of moral public policy in uncertain times. It posed a high risk of failure for the Union. It applied for the first time the founding idea of freedom to about 90 percent of the enslaved people in America, at a time and in a way needed to win a war to secure freedom for 100 percent of the enslaved people in America.

Father Abraham Stops the Whip Torture--Forever

The most exposing and favorable analysis of Abraham Lincoln comes from a story of Memphis Tennessee Garrison, a well-known civil rights activist in southern West Virginia, who knew first-hand the evil of slavery. She remembered from her childhood that when she touched the large welts and scars on her grandfather's back, he told her that, because of Abraham Lincoln, she would never be whipped. Memphis Tennessee Garrison wrote:

Before my grandfather went to war, he tried to run away as a young [slave]. Of course, he was severely beaten, and he bore the marks. I used to look at them and rub my fingers across them, and I'd want to know what those welts were on his back. I'd see Momma rub his shoulder, and he would be stiff. He was an old man then. I'd want to know. "What's that for, Granddaddy?"

"That was by a bullwhip." He would say. "You ain't gonna feel it. You'll never feel it. Thank God for Abraham Lincoln." Abraham Lincoln was his great savior, and that's why I don't care what others interpret Abraham Lincoln as being and doing. I've only got to think about those ridges on my Granddaddy's back and they can't do anything when it comes to what I think about Abraham Lincoln. Anything that saved me and those of us who've come on from that, that's enough.[747]

That is enough, and perfectly said by someone who knew the reality of her family's suffering and who knew who was the person most responsible for ending that suffering. It is a valid, simple analysis of the leadership of "Father Abraham" as he would be known by many after the Civil War and his tragic death. History by flat hindsight does not account for the full reality of emancipation and other

Abraham Lincoln, "Father Abraham," 16th U.S. President – *Image Courtesy of West Virginia State Archives*

events affecting the ideas of liberty and equality.

Whipping enslaved people in Virginia was authorized by custom and law. Lashes would be cut on the bare backs of men and women. Lashes authorized by law could be any number up to 39 with no prior court approval. Slavers used whippings to assure absolute control over their slaves. As a small child, Booker saw his uncle strapped to a tree and whipped on their farm in Franklin County, Virginia. It was a deliberate lesson about obedience enforced by terror presented to him and others on the farm and in the neighborhood.[748]

For Booker's uncle and Memphis Tennessee Garrison's grandfather, whippings were permanent reminders of their spirit of freedom and its horrible punishment in slavery. A simple oval sign in Malden reads, "1863 Kanawha Salines, Remember here the enslaved African Americans who were abused, chased and beaten because God's Spirit of Freedom was manifest in them."[749]

Abraham Lincoln's First Inauguration - *Image Courtesy of the Library of Congress*

Chapter 20

Statehood For Western Virginia

Lewis Ruffner's Dilemma over Compensation for Emancipation

The dilemma for loyal slavers like Lewis Ruffner over emancipation was much more manageable and personal than the dilemma of President Lincoln over the loss of border states to the Confederacy. The Ruffner family fortune was built on slave labor, and emancipation meant loss of capital unless compensation were paid. He jeopardized his life, family and fortune for the Union and he wanted compensation for emancipation for his loyalty to the Union.

There was precedent for compensation. President Lincoln used compensation to free slaves in the District of Columbia early in the war. Slavers there were paid $300.00 per person.[750] The president promised to ask Congress for compensation for loyal slavers in the Preliminary Emancipation Proclamation. The cost would have been substantial for 450,000 enslaved people in border states. At the rate of $300.00 each for 450,000 freed persons, the cost would have been $135 million. At $500.00 per freed person the cost would have been $225 million, a mere fraction of the value of their labor for the nation, but likely considered too costly for a rebuilding nation. Lewis Ruffner supported emancipation but wanted compensation to help carry on his businesses after the Civil War. As a major salt industrialist during and after the Civil War, he needed workers in his salt operations and coal mines, and with emancipation, he would have to pay wages to freed people to work in an industry already in decline.

Abolitionists and others in the North opposed compensation for any slaver, as both symbolic and some justice for the uncompensated labor that built up family fortunes in the South. It was a new world on many levels. Salt industrialists would have had little loss of glory to romanticize after the Civil War. Most slavers in Malden were Confederates. They only lost their investments in the people they held in slavery, which in comparison to the losses of major Confederate slavers in the rest of Virginia and the South was a fortunate result of the war. All salt industrialists would have been thankful that their homes and businesses were spared the destruction which the Union wreaked on the rebellious Confederate South.

Lewis and Viola Ruffner were one of four leading salt families in town.

They were practical, tough business competitors who survived many cycles of boom and bust in their industry. The Ruffners and other slavers in Malden had economic losses with emancipation, but they retained their businesses and few if any were bankrupted by loss of their investments. Despite his undying support of the Union with no compensation, Lewis Ruffner was treated the same as the disloyal Confederate slavers. He might have felt unappreciated at some point, but that would be inconsistent with the grit of the Ruffner family. There is little record found that Lewis Ruffner objected to his personal economic loss, other than for a resolution in the last statehood convention in Wheeling when he proposed the new state to pay loyal slavers for emancipation of their slaves.

Delegate Lewis Ruffner and the Wheeling Conventions

With war looming in the spring of 1861, Lewis Ruffner returned to politics to boldly support the Union. He aggressively opposed secession, against the wishes and warnings of his family and friends, most all of whom were Confederates. Lewis Ruffner never wavered in his allegiance to the Union. His patriotism for the Union as a slaver was courageous and remarkable. Like other leaders of his family, he was fearless, strong-willed, free-thinking, and pragmatic.

Lewis and Viola Ruffner returned to Malden from Louisville, Kentucky in 1857. He had been a sales agent for Kanawha salt interests for twelve years. They moved into his parents' home place and farm, where Lewis' mother, Anna Brumbach Ruffner had died five years before. The home was a sizable but modest two-story frame house on the property of the family's first salt factory, near their coal mines on Campbells Creek. It was on a small riverside knoll, surrounded by flat-land farm operations.

Lewis Ruffner was elected delegate for Kanawha County to the Wheeling conventions. These conventions first established a restored Virginia government loyal to the Union, and then formed a new state with permission from the restored government. The restored government could give permission for the creation of a new state under the requirements of the Federal Constitution.[751]

The First Wheeling Convention convened on May 12, 1861, and adopted a resolution declaring the Richmond secession convention and its proceedings to be illegal, in violation of the Federal Constitution. In the earlier referendum on secession, more votes in eastern Virginia were for secession, whereas in northwestern Virginia, more votes were against secession. A resolution of the Wheeling Convention stated that the ruling power of the Commonwealth in eastern Virginia was subversive and destructive to the interests of western Virginians and that western Virginians could rightfully form a separate, restored Virginia state government loyal to the Union.[752]

The Second Wheeling Convention convened on June 4, 1861, and formally established the restored and loyal government of Virginia. Senators and congressmen were elected to replace former senators and congressmen who had defected to the Confederacy. On June 20, 1861, Francis Harrison Pierpont of Marion County was elected governor of the restored and loyal government of Virginia. He was a descendent of Morgan Morgan, the first settler in today's West Virginia. He was also an early partner of James Otis Watson, of Fairmont, whose family's coal companies in 1903 would form one of the state's largest corporate coal producers of the twentieth century, Consolidated Coal Company. After West Virginia became a state with its capital in Wheeling, Frances Harrison Pierpont made his state capital in Alexandria, a town which the Union controlled for the rest of the war. He was never elected governor of the new state, but he served in the West Virginia Legislature.[753]

The Wheeling convention met again in September 1861, and approved a referendum proposing a convention to create a new state in western Virginia separate from eastern Virginia. The restored Virginia government consented to the creation of a new state from territory in its borders. Consent of the home state or mother state was required by the Federal Constitution. Virginia had given permission in 1789 for Kentucky to be carved out of its vast western frontier. But it seemed certain that eastern Virginians would not consent to the rough carving out of a new state, taking away some 40 percent of the state's territory. Territories and states with consent of the home state come into the Union on equal footing with the original States.[754] The process in Wheeling for consent by Virginia bestowed only by the restored Virginia government there has tainted the statehood movement since its beginnings.

Support for a new state was prominent in more urban and developed areas. It was led by people in the Northern Panhandle and in counties along the Ohio River and the Baltimore & Ohio Railroad, known as the B & O Railroad, which extended in the 1850s in two directions west from Clarksburg to Wheeling and to Parkersburg. It would be called "Lincoln's Lifeline" because of the railroad's strategic importance during the war. Virginia and Maryland Confederates destroyed its bridges north and west of "Washington City,' disrupting communications and the transportation of troops and supplies for the Union early in the war. Maryland like Virginia was a slave exporting state before the war. Western Virginians protected the railroad in the western mountains. Support was also strong in counties along mostly navigable westward flowing rivers, including the Ohio, Great Kanawha, Little Kanawha, and Monongahela Rivers. The restored government could be counted on to approve the creation of a new state out of Virginia territory. The statehood referendum was scheduled for October 24, 1861.[755]

The initial working name for the new state was "Kanawha." This state name would be consistent with the naming of 15 states that share their names with rivers like Alabama, Arkansas, Colorado, Connecticut, Delaware, Illinois, Iowa, Kansas, Kentucky, Minnesota, Mississippi, Missouri, Ohio, Tennessee, and Wisconsin. The name was changed in the statehood convention because there remained a strong civic pride in being Virginians. The name "Kanawha" was called provincial, since it was known nationwide as the Kanawha Salines for the Kanawha Valley's salt and slavery industry. The name also was used for a county and two major rivers. Delegate W. T. Willey of Monongalia County joked that "Kanawha" was hard to spell and that "in this case I think the rose would smell sweeter by some other name (Laughter)...." [756]

The name "Kanawha" was rejected by the delegates. The name "West Virginia" was selected by a vote of 30 to 14. That name had been publicized nationwide by Dr. Henry Ruffner in his 1847 pamphlet proposing an end to slavery in the part of Virginia that he named "West Virginia."[757] The rivalry between Wheeling and the Kanawha Valley may have been a factor in the debate. They were the two largest urban areas in the western and northern parts of the new state. Wheeling would be the Republican stronghold while Kanawha County and the areas south would be controlled by traditional conservative Democrats and Confederate supporters. They would be the chief city rivals in the nineteenth century. Their rivalry would become a serious matter in the next decade when conservative Democrats would win control of many state offices and have the Legislature move the state capital from Wheeling to Charleston in 1870. The capital would move between those two cities three times.

It is noted that there have been two state capitols on Capitol Street in Charleston. The first was built by investors led by John P. Hale, an early mayor of Charleston. A second capitol was constructed by expanding the first capitol. The second capitol caught fire on January 3, 1921 and could not be saved because of exploding ammunition stored in the attic for the state militia. Some of the ammunition had been seized two years before from a railroad shipment intended for coal miners to use in their union activities in Boone County. Today's majestic state capitol was constructed up-river one mile at the former home and farm of Joseph Ruffner and Anna Heistand Ruffner, they called "Rosedale."[758]

On October 24, 1861, the referendum vote approved the creation of a new state with votes totaling 18,408 for and 781 against statehood.[759] It is doubted

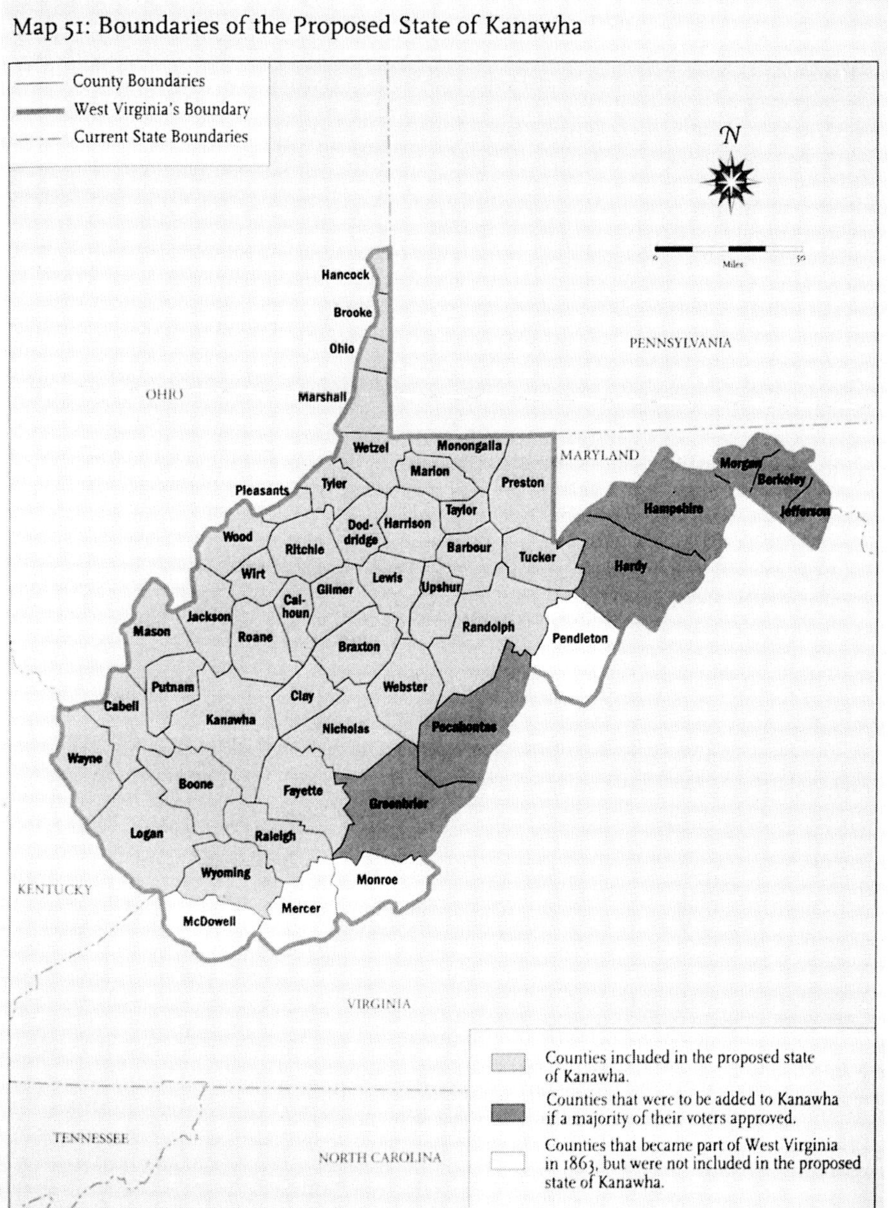

Map 51: Boundaries of the Proposed State of Kanawha

— County Boundaries
▬▬ West Virginia's Boundary
—·—· Current State Boundaries

Counties included in the proposed state of Kanawha.

Counties that were to be added to Kanawha if a majority of their voters approved.

Counties that became part of West Virginia in 1863, but were not included in the proposed state of Kanawha.

Boundaries of the Proposed State of Kanawha – *Image permission by West Virginia University Press, Source: Frank S. Riddle. A Historical Atlas of West Virginia, 2008.*

that these numbers fairly represent overwhelming sentiment for a new state when voice voting was required. Such universal, complete support for a new state seems impossible. These vote totals reveal more about power elites and less about individual choice and minority interests. The numbers suggest that active dissent was discouraged. There was dislocation of voting-age males for military service and others because of the war. In many counties which were proposed for the new state, Confederate men may have chosen not to voice vote for or against statehood. No woman had a right to vote. Public voice voting was used before the time of secret ballots. Further, the integrity of the vote counting systems is not known. With public voice voting and war fever high, it took great courage to vote against an area majority seeking statehood in most parts of western Virginia. It took the same courage earlier in eastern Virginia counties to vote against secession.

On November 26, 1861, the statehood convention was convened in Wheeling, and delegates met for eighty-five days into February in formal session to work out a new system of government under a new Constitution. The convention proposed a detailed state constitution to be approved by Congress and the president. The institutions of government were established, boundaries were considered, and the question of compensation to loyal Union slavers for emancipation was debated but never resolved or included in the new state constitution. The proposed state constitution continued slavery with no limitations.

Jeopardy of Lewis Ruffner as Major General of Militia

Lewis Ruffner put himself, his family, and his businesses in jeopardy by being a delegate to the Wheeling conventions. He was a well-known slaver and leading Unionist in the Kanawha Valley. On May 7, 1862, he increased that jeopardy by accepting from the restored Virginia government a commission as major general of the Fifth Division of Virginia Militia. General Ruffner continued as a major general after West Virginia was made a state. This wartime commission put him in special jeopardy because he was a high-ranking military officer and the winds of war were uncertain in the first years of the Civil War.[760]

In September 1862, four months after General Ruffner's commission, a Confederate army under General W. W. Loring took over the Kanawha Valley. General Loring issued a stern warning on September 15, 1862 to citizens to remain quietly in their homes.

The army of the Confederate States has come among you to expel the enemy, to rescue the people from the despotism of the counterfeit State government imposed on you by Northern bayonets, and to restore the country once more to its natural allegiance to the State. We fight for peace and the possession of our own territory.[761]

The latter part of the Confederate warning seemed specially directed to General Ruffner when the order says that persons supporting the "pretended State government" in Wheeling would "be dealt with as their obstinate treachery deserves." It is not known if the General remained in the Kanawha Valley after federal troops withdrew. He owned property in Kentucky that would be a safe haven if needed. The warning to Union sympathizers was issued in no uncertain terms:

> We do not intend to punish those who remain at home as quiet citizens in obedience to the laws of the land, and to all such, clemency and amnesty are declared; but those who persist in adhering to the cause of the public enemy and the pretended State government he has erected at Wheeling will be dealt with as their obstinate treachery deserves.[762]

Any time Confederates might take over the Kanawha Valley, General Ruffner would be subject to capture and all his property could have been commandeered for the Confederate war effort. Fortunately, once General Loring left, Union forces controlled the Kanawha Valley until the war ended.

General Loring found in the Kanawha Valley that he could use "its magnificent crop of growing corn and its salt." The saltworks were in good condition, but he said there were no workers in the Valley to produce salt, as the general had planned for them to do for the "whole Confederacy." He wrote that the workers who normally operated the salt furnaces had been "carried off by the enemy."[763] General Ruffner may have moved the salt workers and people he held in slavery to his Kentucky property.

The jeopardy that Lewis Ruffner accepted as a major general of militia was day-to-day, even when the Union army controlled the area, because there were marauding Confederates everywhere, and he was a military official. They might shoot him, or capture him or set fire to his factory buildings or barns. After the statehood convention, Anderson "Devil Anse" Hatfield organized a confederate militia he called the "Logan Wildcats."[764] He was a major land owner in Logan County, who would later be famous for the feud between his family and the family of Randolph McCoy. No activity of his men is known in or near Malden or in the Kanawha Valley. Today's Logan High School team name is the "Logan Wildcats."

The capture of General Ruffner, a man in his mid-sixties, could mean death for him in a prison camp. The prison camp at Andersonville, in central Georgia, was a death trap for thousands of captured Union soldiers. Walt Whitman wrote that "not Dante's pictured hell and all its woes, its degradations, filthy torments, excell'd" that prison's horrors."

The prison camp was in rural Macon County. It was used to hold as many as 32,000 men. Thousands of men died from starvation and disease. In the summer heat of 1864, the death rate rose from 300 per month to 3,000 per month for three months. That summer about one-third of the prisoners died in heat and squalid conditions. Another writer contended that twenty-nine percent of the men who entered the camp died there. Men hoped for prisoner exchanges but they failed to help many men. The camp had few buildings for prisoner shelter. There were some flimsy wooden barracks but they could house only a small percentage of the prisoners. At best, prisoners had tents or remnants of tents for shelter from the hot Georgia sun. There was a stockade fence around an open area with a stream running through it. The men had no sanitation or proper food, water or clothing. Prisoners used clothing they removed from corpses. Security was simple. There was a "No Man's Land" on the perimeter of the camp next to the fences, and any prisoner seen in that area was shot, no questions asked.[765]

Not all persons in the camp at Andersonville were soldiers. A young Jewish merchant in Charleston, Moses Frankenberger, was arrested for refusing to give over his store inventory to the Confederate cause. He was sent to Andersonville. He survived and would become very successful in his store, which

Andersonville Prison Camp – *Image Courtesy of the Library of Congress*

continued for a century as one of West Virginia's most prominent retail clothing stores. The Frankenberger name is enshrined on Capitol Street today where the store was located, as part of the city's remarkable preservation of late nineteenth century Charleston street fronts.

After the Civil War, for the deaths of thousands of prisoners at Andersonville, Captain Henry Wirz, the commanding Confederate officer of the camp, was hanged. At his trial, there were over two thousand pages of testimony that he had been seen to shoot men, knock down sick men, cripple men and stamp upon them, and run-down men with hounds. Confederate surgeons testified to confirm that men under Wirz's control suffered from preventable "scurvy, diarrhea, gangrenous sores and lice." He was one of a few soldiers convicted of capital war crimes. He was hanged in Washington on November 10, 1865 and was buried next to one of the accomplices in the assassination of President Abraham Lincoln.[766]

A prisoner at the camp for fifteen months, John McElroy, in his 1879 book, *Andersonville: A Story of Rebel Military Prisons,* detailed the horrors of the camp. He blamed top Confederates for the conditions allowed to continue at Andersonville after they became notorious. He contended that in the last years of the war, in 1864 and 1865, more Union troops died behind Confederate lines with starvation and disease than in front of them in battle. He wrote that 45,613 men were delivered to the prison camp and of that number 12,912 died there. He wrote that the three main causes of death were improper and insufficient food, un-heard of crowding together, and utter lack of shelter.[767]

Southerners claimed Captain Wirz was a scape goat. A monument to Henry Wirz was erected near the camp by the United Daughters of the Confederacy.[768] The camp site is now the Andersonville National Historic Site and located there is the National Prisoner of War Museum.

Kanawha Industries and Population Base
Move State Boundaries South

The Kanawha Valley's location, industry and population were important for the success of statehood. The salt and slavery industry built a large population base for state makers to justify moving the southern border well below the Great Kanawha River to the southern river boundaries of the Big Sandy River and Tug Fork River. The Eastern Panhandle boundaries were set along the Potomac River to include the Baltimore & Ohio Railroad in the new state for economic benefits and strategic military objectives.[769]

It is very unlikely that the state's distant southern river boundaries would have been used without a large population base and major business interests in the Kanawha Valley. The new state included a number of southern counties that voted for secession, including: Boone, Raleigh, Logan, Wyoming, Mc-Dowell, Mercer, and Monroe. The votes for statehood in some Confederate counties were questionable when they were under the control of Union forces. Without those southern counties, the new state would have been very different. Wheeling, as a more centered major population area and economy, might have been unchallenged as the new state capital. Also, Virginia, not West Virginia, would have enjoyed the coal boom in the southern counties, which transformed the economy of West Virginia in a few decades after the war, to make the new state a "Coal State" for over 150 years.[770]

Constitution for a New Slave State Sent to Washington

Reverend Gordon Battelle, a Wheeling abolitionist and Methodist Episcopal minister, was a leader for the proposed state constitution to ban slavery. He moved a resolution in the convention to prevent slaves coming into the new state for permanent residence. It was approved on a vote of 48 to one, but his more important proposal was tabled without debate, to set slave children free after July 4, 1865. In short, under the new constitution, slavery was to continue in West Virginia with business as usual. The referendum was approved on April 3, 1862, by public voice voting reported to be 18,682 for and 514 against statehood. These numbers signal that the vote was more of a directed plebiscite than a free and fair referendum of choice.[771] The West Virginia Legislature would abolish slavery in February 1865 in the time that Congress was proposing the Thirteenth Amendment to abolish slavery nationwide, as the Civil War was coming to an end in eastern Virginia.

After the referendum votes were tallied, the state constitution was forwarded to Washington for review and approval by Congress and President Lincoln.[772] The state constitution was soundly criticized for failing to address slavery and for proposing the admission of a new slave state. Virginia's alleged permission for a new state by what many considered to be no more than a rump government in Wheeling was also strongly criticized, since Virginia would lose about 40 percent of its territory. The statehood bill had a difficult, slow path to passage in Congress. These concerns would be shared by President Abraham Lincoln.

Many West Virginians think that their state joined the Union as a free state. It did not. The new state constitution proposed in Wheeling allowed slavery to continue. It was silent on existing slavery, and that slowed movement of the statehood bill through a Congress controlled by Radical Republicans. The proposed state constitution was also silent on the issue of compensation to loyal slavers. The compensation issue was very controversial in the state and the nation. It was important to Lewis Ruffner and other loyal slavers at the Wheeling conventions, but they failed to gain support for state compensation. Most delegates in Wheeling agreed that slavery issues might sink the statehood movement. Delegate Battelle was directly admonished by Delegate Hiram Haymond of Marion County "to never mention slavery here again."[773]

In Congress, the statehood bill was supported by Waitman T. Willey of Morgantown, one of two senators elected by the restored Virginia government. The bill was opposed by the other elected senator, John S. Carlile of Harrison County. Senator Carlile was popular as an early leader who pushed for a convention to be held in Wheeling to reject secession from the Union. But, at some point, and historians do not know why, he became a strong public opponent of statehood.

Senator Willey took up the statehood cause and was able to maneuver the statehood bill through both Houses of Congress, despite Senator Carlile's opposition. To secure passage by the Republican majority, Senator Willey added an amendment that carries his name, which provided for emancipation of the children of slaves by age 25 years.

> The children of slaves born within the limits of this State after the fourth day of July, eighteen hundred and sixty-three, shall be free, and all slaves within the said State who shall, at the time aforesaid, be under the age of ten years, shall be free when they arrive at the age of twenty-one years and all slaves over the age of ten years shall be free when they arrive at the age of twenty-five years; and no slave shall be permitted to come in to the State for permanent residence therein. Section 7, Article XI, Constitution of 1863.[774]

In Congress, the amended bill passed both Houses despite keen opposition from Democrats, the minority party. The vote in the House of Representatives was generally along party lines with 96 in favor to 55 against statehood. The vote in the Senate was close at 23 in favor and 17 opposed. The six-vote difference in the Senate would have been reversed if only three more senators had voted against statehood. Like close votes on ratification of the Federal Constitution, the Senate's vote shows that in times of great change a very few people may hold the fate of millions of people in their hands. When the statehood bill was approved, it required a new state constitutional convention and state referendum to approve the constitution with the Willey Amendment added. President Lincoln postponed his decision on signing the statehood bill until the very last day allowed under the Constitution, New Year's Eve, which was the day before the final Emancipation Proclamation was to be issued and take effect.[775] For Abraham Lincoln, New Year's Eve in 1862 was a time of strategy and decision--and no turning back.

Statehood Bill Complicates Emancipation Issue for President Lincoln

The statehood bill complicated the slavery issue for the president. The taking of a large portion of Virginia's territory looked like a fraud on eastern Virginia, set up only by what opponents called a "rump government" in Wheeling. At best, it was a clever legal manipulation of the Federal Constitution to get approval of the home state to be divided for a new state. Also, the referendum to create a new state was suspect since it was voted by voice voting while Union forces controlled many Confederate-leaning counties. The political liability of accepting a new slave state under the cloud of its creation was understood clearly by the president. He may also have seen that the dismemberment of Virginia would run counter to his plans for a friendly recon-

Abraham Lincoln Walks at Midnight by Bernard Wiepper – *Image Courtesy of West Virginia State Archives*

struction of the Confederate states after the Civil War.[776]

President Lincoln wrote a number of questions about the statehood bill. He questioned the legal twists, turns and technicalities to have the home state of Virginia to approve statehood and the taking of such a large portion of its territory. He in general terms agreed with the Willey Amendment to assure early emancipation of slave children and ultimately of all people held in slavery.[777] On New Year's Eve, the president met with representatives supporting the new state and declined to tell them how he would act on the bill. They had to wait to know his late-night decision, until the next morning.

He signed the bill on the requirements that the statehood convention would reconvene, and it would adopt the terms of the Willey Amendment and present the new state constitution to voters for another referendum. The statehood convention reconvened in Wheeling on February 12, 1863, and it approved the Willey Amendment and presented the revised constitution to a referendum of voters on March 26, 1863. The vote was 23,321 in favor to 472 against.[778] This was the same month in Malden that people held in slavery organized the "African Zion Baptist Church" formally as a black Baptist church, with the encouragement of Lewis Ruffner.

On April 20, 1863 President Lincoln issued a statehood proclamation and West Virginia became a state 60 days later on June 20 1863.

Lewis Ruffner Seeks Compensation for Loyal Slavers

While supporting the Willey Amendment and emancipation of child slaves, Delegate Lewis Ruffner offered a resolution to have slavers compensated, who were loyal to the Union, for "the actual value of such slaves at the time of emancipation, if they have not forfeited that right by disloyal acts."[779] Delegate Ruffner knew that slavery would end if the Union won the war, whether or not his slaves were released during the war by the fine print in the president's two proclamations, both preliminary and final.

On August 24, 1863, while he was serving in the new West Virginia Legislature, Lewis Ruffner signed a paper filed at the county courthouse to clarify the rights of slave children he was relocating to Kentucky. He acknowledged, for all purposes and to all people, that each named child was entitled to be emancipated when they were the years set out in the West Virginia Constitution, wherever they may be living at those ages. In the paper on file, he notes that two people had left his slavery. One young man held in "Service" was "with the Federal army" at Camp Piatt nearby. The other person was an 18-year-old girl who was "in Ohio escaping from Services."[780] Lewis Ruffner may have also moved his persons held in "Service" to Kentucky when Confederates took over the Kanawha Valley and found no slaves who could be used to produce salt for the Confederacy.

Lincoln's stated commitment in the Preliminary Emancipation Proclamation to seek to have loyal slavers compensated was lost in the final version. For most slavers, emancipation was a foregone conclusion, so long as the Union won the war. In 1863 and 1864, the war was in doubt. The compensation issue was not addressed by the president or Congress, because it was too controversial, despite assurances in the preliminary proclamation. Radical Republicans opposed compensation generally. The issue of compensation was left unaddressed, just as the Wheeling conventions had done.

In the February 1863 Wheeling Convention, Delegate Lewis Ruffner raised eyebrows, and the hackles of some delegates, by arguing that opposition to compensation for loyal slavers was a form of abolitionism and, worse, the delegates who opposed compensation were as bad as abolitionists.

> I look upon the stand taken by the members opposing this proposition as abolition in its sentiment. No class in the community except abolitionists outright ask for the abolition of slavery without compensation; and gentlemen who advocate their ground taken here in opposition place themselves in that category according to my conception.[781]

Delegate Moses Tichenell of Marion County quickly moved to "call the gentleman to order," saying that Delegate Ruffner's remarks made a "slander on me to call me an abolitionist in this hall."[782] Delegate Ruffner responded that he did not intend to be name calling, but the effect of the Willey Amendment with no compensation to loyal union slavers was the same as abolitionism, since only abolitionists at the time actively opposed compensation. The original statehood constitution as proposed to Congress was intentionally silent on the issues of slavery and compensation to loyal slavers. As one delegate said, such a matter could be taken up "in its own time and our own way." Delegate Ruffner added in debate:

> I favor and have always favored emancipation; but I propose not to do it under coercion, which is now brought upon us by Congress and the President, unless it is clearly understood we are to be compensated for our property. Notwithstanding, sir, the possessors of this odious---as the matter now stands--description of property, we are as much entitled to protection as any other class of people who own property.[783]

Finding little support for his proposal, Delegate Ruffner withdrew the resolution without a vote. The state constitution, with the Willey Amendment added, was passed with no reference to compensation. This allowed statehood to proceed and the compensation issue to be dealt with by the Legislature "in its own time and our own way."[784] The new Legislature declined to compensate slavers for emancipation-- loyal or rebellious. On July 28, 1868, the Fourteenth Amendment to the Federal Constitution was ratified, putting the issue to rest forever by its ban on compensation for emancipation by state or local governments or by the federal government.

On April 20, 1863, President Lincoln signed the final statehood bill making West Virginia a new state 60 days later on June 20, 1863, exactly one year to the day that he met and prayed with the Quaker committee over emancipation.

Coincidentally, West Virginia statehood day is one day after another notable date for nationwide celebration. On June 19, 1865, the last slaves in the Confederate states were freed by federal troops in Texas. This day is named "Juneteenth," and each year on the 19th day of June, the end of slavery is recognized and memorialized throughout the nation. "Juneteenth" is a holiday in some states, and a day of commemoration in others. It has been celebrated recently without great fanfare at the State Capitol pursuant to House of Delegates Resolution No. 19 passed in 2008.[785]

Slavery in West Virginia was finally abolished 20 months after statehood by a bill passed by the Legislature on February 3, 1865. At this time, Congress approved the Thirteenth Amendment to abolish slavery nationwide, and sent the amendment to the states for ratification. House Bill No. 25 was passed by the House of Delegates on February 1, 1865, and it passed the Senate two days later with only one vote against the bill. That vote was cast by Ritchie County Senator Daniel Haymond, who earlier attempted to amend the bill to require compensation for emancipation of slaves. After his amendment was defeated, he voted against the bill.[786]

During debate in the West Virginia House of Delegates on House Bill No. 25, Delegate Spicer Patrick from Kanawha County, who was the new state's first House Speaker in 1863 and a prominent member of St. John's Episcopal Church in Charleston, stated that all of his slaves left in 1862 except for two older women. He added that after one of those women went to Ohio to live, she returned to him for support because she could not support herself there.[787]

The year 1862 was the year that the Preliminary Emancipation Proclamation was announced on September 22, 1862. It may have been the time when the people held in slavery by Rachel Grant Tompkins self-emancipated from her slave quarters after annoucement of the "Emancipation Proclamation."[788]

There was little debate or discussion on compensation to loyal slavers as part of the state abolition bill. It was said that the issue was no longer important because the only slaves left in the state were "old and infirm," and they would have to be cared for humanely. Lewis Ruffner was not a delegate in the Legislature at the time. He had some workers remaining in his salt works who technically would have continued to be slaves, perhaps indicating some approval by them of their work arrangements with Lewis Ruffner, but that is not known. By 1865, he likely had given up on compensation for any emancipated slave remaining in what he called his "Service."

At this time, Congress was debating and voting to send the Thirteenth Amendment to the states for ratification to abolish slavery. The Thirteenth Amendment was ratified on December 6, 1865, 10 months after the West Virginia statute. The state statute and the new federal constitutional amendment used language similar to what was used in the 1787 Northwest Ordinance banning slavery in the territory northwest of the Ohio River. Congress under the Articles of Confederation approved its abolition provisions, with no states opposing the measure in July while the delegates to the constitutional convention in Philadelphia were taking secret votes on compromises to legalize slavery.[789]

In flat and selective hindsight, there are many questions. If emancipation language such as the language used for gradual emancipation in the Willey Amendment had been used for the Federal Constitution, in any number of alternative possibilities for generational emancipation, would there have been a divided nation or a Civil War--either or both? Would alternative compromises for emancipation been debated if slavers had not been managing the compromises of the Convention in secret? Would such compromises have split the Philadelphia convention for and against slavery or would ratification have been denied with any emancipation alternative included? Why did no delegate propose a gradual emancipation clause? Was unity the only consideration? The unity of the republic was at stake, but so were the lives of millions of people held in slavery.

Chapter 21

Civil War Ends Slavery But The Idea Of White Superiority Lives On With Segregation And White Supremacy

Southern View: The War was a War of Aggression Against Virginia

Many southerners adopted the view that it was the North's tyrannical oppression of the South that caused the war--not slavery. John Richard Dennett, a journalist for the *Nation*, published the following interview taken in Richmond soon after the war from a bitter Virginian that echoes that southern viewpoint.

The interviewed Virginian has a traditional view of state sovereignty and a self-righteous view of the South's secession and treason against the nation formed by slavers to protect slavery. It foreshadows the myths of a lost glory caused by an overreaching federal government which provoked the war in order to destroy Virginia's identity and culture and the whole of southern society. It ignores that southerners readily pushed for federal intervention to enforce the fugitive slave act and to build a strong navy to protect its cotton, rice, sugar cane and tobacco exports when threatened by Britain. The themes of states' rights and federal overreach would be used for a century after the Civil War to support segregation and the denial of fundamental civil rights to African Americans. It took a full one hundred years for Americans, and their written history, to begin to admit that the Civil War was caused by and was all about slavery and southern slave societies.

The people of the South feel that they have been most unjustly, most tyrannically oppressed by the North. All our rights have been trampled upon. We knew that we had a perfect right to go and leave you. We were only carrying out the principles of the Revolution. It was our deliberate opinion that we ought to go out from the old Union. We could no longer give to the general Government the consent of the governed, and the general Government could therefore no longer have any just power over us. But aside from that, our right to secede was perfect. Mr. Calhoun demonstrated that. Mr. Webster's speeches in reply are powerful appeals to sentiment and imagination but the argument of Mr. Calhoun is irresistible. And even Mr. Webster allows that one party to a compact having violated it, the other is released from all obligation. Now the North has repeatedly violated the constitutional guaranties of slavery.... And yet it is the fashion to call us traitors!....It was not slavery that caused this war, for it was not the South that began it. We endured the encroachments of the North upon our rights, and then quietly availed ourselves of the reserved right of secession. We fired upon Sumter. True; but not till Sumter had become a South Carolinian fort, in which you maintained our enemies. Few men at the South owned slaves. We wanted to leave you....You see Mr. Lincoln had issued his proclamation calling for seventy-five thousand men. We all, whether we owned slaves or not, believed that coercion was mere tyranny, and that we ought not to submit to it.[790]

Cultural, philosophical, political and other factors would have been important to Virginia voters in the referendum for secession. But it seems likely that a public movement for secession began in order to protect slavery and its essential slave commodity markets in the Deep South. A vote of 90 to 45 to refuse secession was passed in the Virginia secession convention on April 4 1861, and, after Fort Sumter was attacked on April 12, the convention vote on April 17, switched in favor of secession. Those markets were to be protected because they made slavery profitable in eastern Virginia. The markets stabilized and supported the investments of eastern Virginians in slaves. Without those markets there would have been an overpopulation of slaves in eastern Virginia, leading to a financial crisis there and throughout the Upper South. As Professor Thomas Dew so eloquently stated, Virginia without slavery would be a "desert."[791]

Economic factors should never be ignored in the history of political events. Slavery was spread widely across the eastern part of Virginia, east of the Allegheny Mountains, where almost a half million people were enslaved. The slave investments there were too valuable to lose. The movement to protect slavery carried the day in the secession vote with majorities in eastern counties where the slave trade was the highest. The movement by eastern Virginians to secede had the effect of imposing secession on western mountain counties where slavery was at the lowest rate in the South and loyalty to the Union was high. Secession gave validity to the birth to the new state of West Virginia. The claims in the Virginian's interview about "overreaching government" can be applied to Virginia's government which was controlled by and for eastern Virginians since colonial times.[792]

Malden Spared Devastation Of War

By the end of the war, the Confederate South was ravaged economically, socially and politically. However, in Malden, and in most of West Virginia where few battles were fought, there was little burning, looting or commandeering of private goods.

The major impact of the war in West Virginia was emancipation at the end of the war in the several counties with substantial numbers of people held in slavery, including in Kanawha County and its salt and coal industries. Many freed people left the salt factories and coal mines in the area. Slavery was not wide-spread in the state. In 1860, there were 12,771 enslaved persons in 49 of the 55 counties to be joined in the new state, likely the lowest number for any region in the South. Almost one-sixth of the new state number lived in Kanawha County, where there were 2,180 slaves and 180 free blacks. A report of the state auditor to the new state legislature in 1863 listed counties with slaves over the age of 12 years and subject to taxation. The report showed that Kanawha County could levy tax on 1,237 slaves over that age, constituting over one third of all taxable slaves remaining in the state. There were only 6 counties with more than 100 slaves over the taxable age of twelve years. The total of taxable slaves over the age of twelve years was reported to be 3,268.[793]

State Auditor Slave Tax Report 1863

County	No.	Tax.	County	No.	Tax.
Wood, ---	93	$111.60	Cabell, ---	177	$212.40
Wetzel, ---	6	7.20	Wayne, ---	77	92.40
Preston, ---	44	62.80	Mason, ---	249	298.80
Taylor, ---	69	82.80	Tucker, ---	14	16.80
Brooke, ---	6	7.20	Roane, ---	37	44.40
Doddridge, ---	20	24.00	Pleasants, ---	8	9.60
Tyler, ---	13	15.60	Jackson, ---	41	49.20
Marshall, ---	15	18.00	Lewis, ---	24	19.20
Ohio, ---	23	27.60	Barbour, ---	66	79.20
Upshur, ---	34	40.80	Calhoun, ---	5	6.00
Hancock, ---	2	2.40	Marion, ---	42	60.40
Monongalia, ---	63	75.60	Gilmer, ---	28	33.60
Wirt, ---	17	20.40	Nicholas, ---	77	92.40
Harrison, ---	304	364.80	Randolph, ---	110	132.00
Ritchie, ---	13	15.60	Clay, ---	9	10.80
Putnam, ---	345	414.00	Kanawha, ---	1237	1,484.40

State Auditor Slave Tax Report 1863[794]

The percentages of slaves in the state and in Kanawha County were low compared to the rest of the South especially eastern Virginia, at 13.5 percent in Kanawha County and 3.4 percent statewide. Those numbers apparently did not present a significant threat to existing power structures or cause alarm to whites sufficient to encourage their use of terror to deny voting rights and other civil rights of freed people. There was little organized violence against blacks in West Virginia, although in Malden, in 1869, there was a violent race riot that rocked the town and left Lewis Ruffner permanently disabled.[795]

Economic differences between the devastated Confederate South and the spared Kanawha Valley were stark. The differences after the war gave time and hope to some that Malden and the Kanawha Valley could be part of a new social order that would include freed people as full citizens. Young Booker's family and church community acted on that hope. The hope was dim in the first five years after the war because of marauding night riders who pledged to suppress black people in the area. They shot at black people on the streets of Malden and elsewhere until at least 1870, the year after Washington and Jane Ferguson purchased their family home in Malden.[796]

The poverty of spirit and resources and the deaths of so many Confederate soldiers touching most every southern family led to a romanticized glory for slave times. Slavery primarily benefited wealthy aristocrats, but the glory was romanticized for all southerners because they lived with family deaths in the cultures of slave societies. Historians popularized a white supremacist history, claiming that slavery was a benign institution which blacks needed for their own protection from their special instincts to return to the barbarism of their African culture. Slave times became the romanticized culture of the South, and the Confederate battle flag, with an "X" shaped cross lined with stars on a field of red, called the "Stars and Bars," became a prominent and enduring symbol of pride for the "Old South."[797] The flag has now fallen out of favor in the general population, identified as a symbol of lost glory for the time of slavery in the South. A new symbol is needed for southern culture after the war, such as a steamboat floating beside trees with Spanish moss. Such possibilities are endless.

The fantasy of the glory of the "Old South" was taken to heart by rich and poor.[798] Segregation separated blacks and whites in the decades following Reconstruction, and the wall between the races continued racist culture and economic stagnation, with what President Abraham Lincoln could have called malice toward all.

Booker's Family are Courageous Social Pioneers
for Equality and Community Respect

The story of the Ruffners and Fergusons working together to change the social order of Malden after the Civil War is told in the companion book to this work: *Booker T. Washington's Boyhood American Dream: The Climb of the Black Middle Class Up from Slavery.* The Fergusons were employed by the Ruffners and gained their respect. Together they worked in Malden to defeat white domination and the idea of white superiority.

The Fergusons integrated housing in Malden and helped start the movement for a black middle class that impressed upon young Booker how the lives of all freed people could be improved with education and fair opportunity to work at jobs valuable to local economies. The success of his boyhood heroes would give him the idea that self-determination, fueled by hope and belief in what we call today the "American Dream," should inspire all people to work hard and help their families and communities grow and prosper, not for themselves but for future generations. The striving to move their families into the middle class defined them as being part of an American middle class open to all people.

The Ferguson's home purchase was not for the comfort or convenience of the family. It created a great financial burden on four family members to work to pay a $500.00 mortgage for the purchase price. The new home's location put the Fergusons in Malden alone, surrounded by white families, a mile away from their church and their friends in the safe and protective community at Tinkersville. They had lived there since Jane Ferguson brought her young family to Malden at the end of the war. The new home was a mile away from their day-to-day work at the Ruffners' home, and at the salt factory and coal mines. Worse, the home was located where blacks were banned from living by the local Ku Klux Klan society. Home ownership by blacks was unthinkable to the night riders who, at first, had the full support of the white community. But young Booker's parents and friends were fully committed to changing their community and making it a welcoming home to all.

Young Booker's family and heroes had to navigate uncertain times under the suspicious eyes of people who wanted to protect white privilege, whether they appeared in secret marauding bands at night or when they were employers or next-door neighbors. Freed people had to use courage, hard work and their Christian faith to be leaders in their community. At first, those personal qualities were the only resources they had to bring to the fight against white supremacy.

The Ferguson family and the Ruffner family were pioneer stock, both equal to the tasks of turning the wilderness of their times and the uncertainty of their lives into a new social order.[799] Before the war, the Ruffners were industrial pioneers on the American frontier in a wilderness where they applied their talents in engineering, religion and public service to build an industry, a town and a new state exploiting the hard labor of enslaved families.

The Ferguson family and their friends were modern social pioneers. Their wilderness was race prejudice, fed by suspicion, fear and violence. Their wilderness was in a society that claimed inferiority for their race and their personhood. They had to demand new core social values and expressions in a society where they were citizens, but were known as subservient slaves. Appropriate and predictable interactions had to be established between blacks and whites. Most all social interactions were complicated after slavery. New sets of interactions were required for how and when to communicate, how to address and be addressed with first or last names, and where to work, live, worship, and play, and with whom. Shaking hands, doffing hats, and even walking on a sidewalk at first were social experiments.[800] Freed people needed courage and skill to bridge over to a new status for equal civil rights. The Fergusons modeled important values of hard work, individualism, and good citizenship to conquer the wilderness of their new social lives in a white-dominanted society.

The force of their success had a major impact on young Booker. He was an eager, bright-eyed nine-year-old boy on arrival in Malden. He could see that everything in his world was new. West Virginia, as a state, was two years old. His family had their own home for the first time in the former Ruffner slave quarters. They had meals together for the first time. They had decent pallets to sleep on instead of rag piles. He learned to spell his name by associating a sound with each letter as he wrote it with a stick in dirt. For the first time, it was not illegal for someone to teach him to read so he could understand the music in those sounds and letters.[801] He was in a new world and he was watching it unfold before him.

Young Booker was thirteen years old when his family moved to town from the protective community in the Ruffners' former slave quarters at Tinkersville. He was pleased to leave problems with close quarters, flooding, sanitation, and racial mixing that he saw in Tinkersville.[802] He observed his family endure fear and violence surrounding their new home in town. But courageously, like Rosa Parks staying in her bus seat a century later, young Booker's family continued with their home purchase and became leaders by the example of their self-determination, courage, and good citizenship. As one of the first black families to live in a home in town, they integrated Malden and helped open it to other freed families. Just a decade later, Amanda Ferguson Johnson and her husband, Benjamin Johnson would own a nice two-story brick home on main street, among other freed families living in Malden.

Surrounded by white family homes, his family did what good families do. They were good neighbors. They worked hard. They educated and protected their children. They were day-to-day good citizens. But the move to Malden for the purpose of integrating the town was unparalleled sacrifice and community leadership. Their pioneering home purchase made them a family to be recognized in history for leading the climb up of freed people in Malden to the middle class.

The Ferguson's home purchase fairly marks the beginning of the black middle class in West Virginia and less directly in America through the life work of Booker T. Washington. By their example as leaders in their church and community, his parents and their friends created a legacy of leadership which directly influenced young Booker to use the idea of the American Dream and the values of the American middle class to serve as a path for blacks to earn equality and respect nationwide.

Because of the Horror of Slavery and re-enslavement with sharecropping on cotton and other plantations and the establishment of Jim Crow segregation, such common values and activities were denied to many

Amanda Ferguson Johnson – Beloved Sister of Booker T. Washington
– Anna Evans Gilmer Collection

freed people because whites considered any help to them to be radical and dangerous.[803] In Malden, this was true for some whites in the first five years after the war, but, in the Confederate South, white domination would be the controlling social legacy for over a century.

The Fergusons did not work alone for a new social order. They were part of a movement flowing from the family's church, the African Zion Baptist Church. It was the center of a new black Christian community. When Jane Ferguson and her children arrived in Malden in 1865, the formal organization of the church was two years old, after it had been chartered as the state's first Baptist church during the war by enslaved people living in the Ruffner slave quarters. The church began as a community of Christian believers nine years before the Civil War. They were in violation of the Virginia statute banning assemblies by slaves. The church encouraged new social relationships and aided members as they integrated housing in their town. They celebrated the success of the Ferguson family's home purchase in the center of Malden. Young Booker was an active member of the church and attended school there before state schools for blacks were established in 1867.

The African Zion Baptist Church was aptly named. The term "African" was used because of pride in the race and the exclusive control of the church by people held in slavery. "Zion" came from scripture about God's plan for the Israelites after they escaped from slavery in Egypt. God told those freed people that Zion was the Promised Land, and God had placed there a foundation stone for them to establish a "royal priesthood" to build a "holy nation." Church leaders accepted that duty as a special covenant with God, and it would become a covenant fulfilled by a legacy of national black leaders from West Virginia before and during the modern civil rights movement.

As the first black Baptist church formally organized in the new state of West Virginia, its members envisioned themselves as a community of leaders, both during slavery and in Freedom. The covenant for leadership to build a "holy nation" launched Booker T. Washington's career and his gospel for expansion of the American Dream to include the ten million African Americans living in America when his national leadership began in 1895.

Lewis and Viola Ruffner grew to respect the long suffering and determined members of Booker's family and other members of the African Zion Baptist Church. Many of them lived in the Ruffner slave quarters and had been held in slavery by the Ruffners. Young Booker's family and others in their church community were model citizens, and the Ruffners became their neighbors and then their friends and then their champions. Elsewhere in the South, it was a time of separation, terror, despair and segregation.

The Ruffners had been pioneers on the western frontier in the nineteenth century. They created some of the first factory systems at the beginning of the Industrial Revolution. The concept of industry was so new that they were called "salt makers" instead of salt industrialists. They made many innovations and improvements in industry, education and the life of the Kanawha Valley. The family questioned slavery but not the idea of white superiority. But, after the Civil War, Lewis and Viola Ruffner could observe the growing talents and work ethic of young Booker and his family. The Ruffners knew that freed people deserved better, equal lives in their community.

Viola Ruffner, as a "Yankee" lady, likely encouraged her husband and others to respect and appreciate blacks in Malden, so they could have education and fair economic opportunities. Young Booker showed great promise. Viola Ruffner cherished him like a favorite grandchild as she saw him grow into a fine young man. He was a bright, dutiful young man the Ruffners knew could succeed if he had a good education and genuine opportunities in his future.

Lewis and Viola Ruffner also could see that no successful Ruffner was superior to the gifted, sincere, and hard-working black youth living in their home. Such a judgment would be remarkable because Lewis Ruffner's family members were more talented and successful in many fields than any other family known to this author in the nineteenth century. There were five Ruffners who excelled.

First, Lewis Ruffner's father, David Ruffner, invented percussion drilling for the western world, and he established and directed a new industry on the frontier at the very beginning of the Industrial Revolution. He started the coal industry, along with the area's first Presbyterian churches, and the first major academy for men and women students together, all in what was then a wilderness in the Kanawha Valley.

Second, Dr. Henry Ruffner, Lewis Ruffner's brother, was a Latin and Greek scholar, a nationally published free-thinking author of social and political commentary, fiction, and theology. He was the leading educator in Virginia before the Civil War pushing for free public education, which he proposed to be funded by property taxes, a visionary and very controversial proposal in its day. Thomas Jefferson and Dr. Henry Ruffner do not get the credit they deserve for their early work for universal public school education. Henry Ruffner was president of a leading college in Virginia in 1836. He wrote the only national treatise by a southern slaver proposing abolition of slavery in any part of the South.

Third, Lewis Ruffner's career was in and for Malden. He was a respected no-nonsense town leader before and after the Civil War. He had been the Kanawha Valley's leading slaver who was loyal to the Union. He was a successful salt industrialist, state legislator and local government official. He was a state maker in the Wheeling Conventions and was a powerful delegate in the first two years of the new state legislature in Wheeling. He became a major general of militia during the war. After the war, Lewis Ruffner and other leaders had to decide about how best to proceed with the rights of hundreds of freed people who elected to stay in their community and work in their industry operations. Town leaders ultimately made their decisions relying on well-established pioneer values supporting respect of the individual and basic rights to social justice, which fundamentally means a fair opportunity to succeed or fail for all.

Fourth, Dr. William H. Ruffner, son of Dr. Henry Ruffner and friend of Viola Ruffner, was Virginia's leading educator after the war. He was its first state public school superintendent and greatest advocate in the South for free public schools for all children, white and black as mandated by Congress for Reconstruction. In just his first year, Dr. W. H. Ruffner had 130,000 students, white and black, in 2,900 segregated free public schools. Historian Eugene D. Genovese wrote that the passion for learning by adult and young freed slaves was "the most moving chapter in American social history." W. E. B. Du Bois wrote that the "thirst of the black man for knowledge...gave birth to the public free-school system of the South."[804]

W. H. Ruffner fought for equal funding of schools for black students and white students, despite strong opposition around the Commonwealth. His public school system was the first in the Confederate South and he worked hard for good schools for black students. W. H. Ruffner was an accomplished writer in Reconstruction. Of his philosophy for public education for blacks, he wrote

> The Negro is our brother and our ward: and will hold us responsible for his training and for his end, temporal and eternal. He may, by suitable effort, become a blessing and an ornament to the earth...

He was president of today's Longwood University, and he helped establish and organize Virginia Tech and other colleges in Virginia. W. H. Ruffner pioneered a system of comprehensive higher education for Virginia that is greatly respected today. He favored co-education and respect for all individual religious beliefs. His geologic surveys of the State of Washington are renowned and still in use. Like his father, he was a true Renaissance Man. [805]

Fifth, the youngest of the five brilliant Ruffners was Ernest Howard Ruffner. He was the son of Lewis and Viola Ruffner. He graduated from West Point in 1867, first in his class. He became a leading federal engineer on the Ohio River and, in 1901, he was in charge of the important new federal lock and dam system on the Great Kanawha River after its completion in 1898. The system cost Congress about $3.4 million and it took 25 years to complete Its success was notable. It opened the Kanawha coalfields with reliable river transportation. At the time of his death in 1937, at age 91 years, Ernest Howard Ruffner was living in Cincinnati in the home that was the birthplace of President William Howard Taft, the last president that Booker T. Washington would counsel. It can be toured today as a national monument to President Taft.[806]

It is most likely that young Booker and his courageous family and their friends convinced the Ruffners that social change was deserved, and that it should begin with their family helping freed people to build a better community life in Malden. In his formative years, young Booker observed heroes establishing middle class values in Malden as part of a visionary plan to benefit future generations instead of their own immediate needs and pastimes. He saw them embracing hope to fuel their dreams of better lives for their families. His heroes in Malden included his parents, particularly his mother, Jane Ferguson, who encouraged his education and sophistication in the social graces and manners of the day at the Ruffner home. Other heroes were his pastor, Lewis Rice, who started a secret faith community in 1852, and his first teacher, William Davis, who would lead the education of black youth in the Kanawha Valley for over 40 years. Their lives of service and determination inspired the path for young Booker's national leadership. The success of these heroes in creating a middle class in Malden in the first generation after slavery is iconic for the era of Reconstruction. Unfortunately, it was not duplicated in the Confederate South.

For their struggle to improve the lives of future generations, Booker T. Washington would see them as the new "middle class" which he envisioned for the whole nation. His heroes directed him to a gospel for expansion of the American Dream to hard-working blacks who were committed to improving

Lewis Rice, Pastor of African Zion Baptist Church (L) – William Davis, First teacher of Booker T. Washington at School of African Zion Baptist Church (R) – *First Baptist Church of Charleston Collection*

the lives of their families. The term "American Dream" would not have been used by Booker T. Washington. It became a popular term in the mid twentieth century, capturing in essence his polestar belief that, in America, all people should have the opportunity to achieve anything in life for which they have the will, talent and determination to achieve.[807]

The life of Booker T. Washington embodied the American Dream, and he fought against any exception applied to any American for any reason. The idea of white superiority was his archenemy. It created a clear, overwhelming racist exception for black Americans, and he dedicated his life to fighting that racist idea and all exceptions to the American Dream. It would take almost a century to extend the American Dream to African Americans.

Television Journalists Upend White Supremacy

The majority idea of white superiority survived in America for three and a half centuries. It survived colonial times and the Revolutionary War despite the best ideas of the Founding Fathers for equality, freedom, and social justice. The idea reigned supreme in the closed-door constitutional convention in Philadelphia. It survived the years of the African slave trade after the Revolutionary War and the depression years before the slave livestock industry in Virginia boomed with huge profits on the sales of slaves to Deep South states.

The idea of white superiority survived Virginia's second rebellion making the Civil War the bloodiest event in American history. It won against Reconstruction ideas of equality and due process of law. It created separation of the races during segregation days. The United States Supreme Court protected the idea of white superiority by allowing private businesses and persons to discriminate in public accommodations as long as there was no government action directly involved. Discriminatory state action was sanctioned so long as it met the requirements of the judicial doctrine of "Separate but Equal," which generally was a sham. Black facilities and opportunities were separate and anything but equal. The blessing by the Supreme Court for white supremacy let bloom and blossom Jim Crow social codes that spread across the South as fast and full as wildflowers in the spring, all enforced with violence, terror, separation and subjugation of blacks. Jim Crow segregation codes could deny civil rights and voting rights only with acceptance by whites that they were superior to African Americans. These codes were enforced with terror and violence as Booker T. Washington took the national stage in 1895.

The majority idea of white superiority also survived Booker T. Washington's best attempts to overcome it publicly by proving the worth of African Americans by his example and his work for education and economic opportunity. Unknown to the public, he worked secretly to crush the idea of separation and racial superiority by encouraging and financing lawsuits to challenge segregation laws around the country. One writer noted he was not "wholly the conservative and conciliatory figure he appeared to be," because "Washington waged an under-cover war against segregation and disfranchisement."[808] Selective law suits to gain civil rights would be an important tactic later used in the modern civil rights movement by the National Association for the Advancement of Colored People, the NAACP, to win civil rights cases for integrated schools, open public accommodations, and new legislation for fair housing, voting, employment and other civil rights. Booker T. Washington did not succeed in his "undercover war."

The lost glory of the Old South became the dominant and charming theme of American culture, in the first part of the twentieth century, empowering the Ku Klux Klan to push for extreme prejudice against blacks, immigrants, Catholics, and other minorities. It was a popular culture encouraged by white Protestants in the Prohibition movement and by the writers of United States history. Motion pictures romanticized slave times in the Old South where slaves were portrayed as happy servants living in luxurious homes until the Civil War, when the Yankees attacked and "ruined" the lives of their slaver families. The idea of white superiority even survived early mass action in the modern civil rights movement until the movement's step-by-step changes brought on school integration in 1954, in *Brown v. Board of Education.* There the Court overturned the idea that "separate" could ever be "equal." Integration across the nation began chipping away at the fortress of racism and segregation leading to passage of modern federal civil rights laws a decade later, outlawing discrimination in public accommodations, employment, housing, and voting rights.

Government-sponsored white supremacy was slow to die. The Supreme Court in *Brown v. Board of Education* allowed local schools to use "all deliberate speed" to integrate schools. That terminology was used to delay integration of many public schools for over a decade. Writer James Baldwin thought the delay showed weak support among whites for equal opportunity and that the decision would be "tokenism" in the long run with little change in race policy over time. The delay encouraged resistance by local authorities, surprisingly in northern and border state cities as well as cities in the Deep South. Reinhold Niebuhr thought that the delay in public school integration was wise. A reorientation of life in America was required, and some time for adjustment was needed. He thought that it deflected any possible incipient revolt against the decision. He also thought a step-by-step progression from "Separate But Equal" was appropriate to prepare the nation for the full import of the court decision.[809]

In the end, white supremacy was finally dethroned by television journalists in a new media that could report the horror of race violence in the South visually by film and photographs. Television reports carried race terror into the living rooms of most American families. Viewers were shocked and many sympathized with the people they saw to be regular parents and students, who happened to be black, being attacked simply because they wanted their students to attend decent schools. That impression from television for millions of Americans began the end of mainstream social respectability for racist ideas. The essential evil behind the idea of white superiority was exposed for all to see. Reverend Dr. Martin Luther King, Jr., and others in the modern civil rights movement worked to produce such television images to overcome and defeat white domination.[810] As a belief, the idea of white superiority became, at least publicly, officially unacceptable in the expression of American values.

In their homes, many white families realized the fundamental inconsistency of their family ideas of equality and social justice which were not applied to black people. The truth seen on television knocked white supremacy to its knees, and it could not rise up because children and adults were asking questions in homes, schools and offices about fairness, the Golden Rule, and what it means to be in a country that seeks to lead the world in its best ideas of equality and freedom. Under the weight of truth displayed nationwide by professional journalists, the idea of white superiority lasting three and a half centuries was overturned in one generation.

A Glorious Celebration Of Freedom in a Slave Market

It is appropriate to end a discussion of slavery remembering the day in history when federal troops marched into Charleston, South Carolina, where thousands of people had been sold at public slave auctions. Leading the Union troops was a regiment of black soldiers, recruited from escaped slaves in the local area.[811] They were the first Union soldiers to enter the city. The joy and wonderment of these soldiers who had been held in slavery nearby, themselves then standing triumphant, bold, and free in a city that prospered on the terror of slave market auctions, would have been great reward for their service to the Union.

This historic moment of wonder gives credit to all who worked to end slavery and segregation in America. For those soldiers, it would have been one of the most gratifying experiences of any life, anytime, anywhere.

Conclusion:

America's Story Of People Coming Up From Slavery Continues In Book II With Jane Ferguson Bringing Her Three Young Children To Malden

The remarkable story of the Ferguson and Ruffner families after the Civil War is presented in a companion book, *Booker T. Washington's Boyhood American Dream: The Climb of the Black Middle Class Up from Slavery.* The second book has new resource materials on Booker T. Washington's boyhood, his heroes and his family's community which was centered in their church, the African Zion Baptist Church. This small church establish by slaves was unique in its history and its legacy. It was formed independently before the Civil War by slaves for slaves, and solely controlled by slaves. It was the first organized black Baptist church in West Virginia, and it had the second school in the state for freed people--children and adults. day and night. Its early church organization and school were repeated after the Civil War throughout the South as freed people established their own communities and social institutions.[812]

The community of heroes in the Malden church directly challenged and overcame the idea of white superiority by increasing their participation in the community at large. As good neighbors, they were able to end the evil of separation. The day-to-day contacts of families in Malden, including contacts between the Ferguson and Ruffner families, were important to the social changes they worked to achieve. The personal contacts of the Fergusons with white neighbors in town caused whites to see that separation of the races was an idea wholly foreign to their core frontier values for equality and fair play.

The Fergusons accepted the mission to prove they were worthy neighbors who should not be separated from whites. Separation is the well spring of suspicion and hatred leading to violence. It denies neighborly relationships. Many people believe that separation from God is darkness and despair. To say that God is love is to say that God is the substance of relationship, and for many believers who think God is the substance of relationship, separation of people by race and other generalized qualities is the ultimante evil, a heresy of faith. The acceptance of the Fergusons by white neighbors helped to defeat the idea of white superiority. Tragically, white domination would not be rejected by the nation, in the North or South, for another century. In the South, white domination was enforced by violence, brutality, exploitation and segregation.

C. Vann Woodward wrote about the terror that created the South's wall of separation. He stated that lynchings in the 1880s and early1890s "attained the most staggering proportions ever reached in the history of that crime."[813]

> The fanatical advocates of racism, whose doctrines of total segregation, disenfranchisement and ostracism eventually triumphed over all opposition and became universal practice in the South, were already at work and already beginning to establish dominance over some phases of southern life.[814]

The legacy of Booker T. Washington and his church community in Malden is the black middle class rising up from slavery. Young Booker observed his heroes building a black middle class. They were people of honor and vision, committed at all costs, to improving the lives of their children and grandchildren. Those heroes were vital to young Booker's adult career path and goals. They saw social respect and acceptance by the white majority as a major step for them and their families to realize liberty, equality, and the pursuit of happiness. His plan for the South is criticized for reliance on help from whites, but it is easily understood from his boyhood experiences. His acceptance of white control is also difficult to understand, given the valiant independence of his family and their church and church community.

His boyhood heroes did not doubt their mission. They lived their lives for it, and had their children and grandchildren live and work to improve the lives of future generations. They readily proved their entitlement to full citizenship, which was unfairly required by the idea of white superiority. They nurtured each other through family and kin networks and lived middle class community values in Malden, Charleston and beyond, much like they did during slavery, without the terror of forced separations. The best markers for the beginning of the church community's legacy for a middle class can be summarized:

(1) Establishment of the African Zion Baptist Church as an independent social institution starting in 1852 and continuing until its Christian believers formally organized as the first black Baptist church in the new state, all while they were held in slavery;

(2) Covenant of church members to join together to create a "royal priesthood" of leaders to build a "holy nation;"

(3) Church community's early school to educate children and adults for full participation in society, the second school for blacks in the state; and

(4) The 1869 purchase by Jane and Washington Ferguson of Booker's family home to integrate Malden four years after they were slaves.

That home purchase was likely directed by Jane Ferguson, for the purpose of seeking community-wide acceptance of her children and other freed children as neighbors and deserving citizens. She was ambitious for her children to succeed in the new world of Freedom. She encouraged in them strong character, honesty, thrift, and the self-confidence needed to be helpful to others and self-reliant in dark days of despair. Most importantly, she encouraged them in her own hope for her family to live in a "holy nation."[815]

In *Up from Slavery*, Booker T. Washington remembered that in Hale's Ford at their slaver's farm his mother cried when a Union soldier came to announce they were free. She hugged her children and said she always dreamed that they would be free, and now they were free. It cannot be imagined what joy and personal affirmation Jane Ferguson realized in that moment of joy, hope and determination to help her children enjoy the fruits of their freedom. She would die in 1874, in the summer before young Booker would finish his studies at Hampton Institute, well before her dreams would be fulfilled.

Young Booker saw great possibilities for a black middle class supported by the American Dream unfurl over his hometown like a flag. He was confident that he could fly the same flag across the Confederate South. His leadership today is recognized in most all-American history texts with no reference to his legacy for a black middle class. Many have criticized his self-imposed limitations to accommodate a racist white power structure by giving up on political and social rights needed to achieve "someday" equality, liberty, democracy and social justice.

An evaluation of Booker T. Washington's leadership must account for his special time in American history. He was an important transititonal figure. His story begins with slavery in Virginia, and extends through the dark times of Jim Crow lynchings and terror. It ends with him recognized as one of the most celebrated national black leaders in history. His legacy is properly debated today. The standards to be applied to his leadership are appropriate for evaluation of today's leaders. He was not an agitator for immediate change. He worked in the white power structure of the Confederate South, not in the North where writers and journalist agitators were protected and few had major institutions to support, manage and protect. He became the vulnerable head of the most prominent black institution in America, which, at age 25, he started in the Deep South. A decade before he arrived in South Alabama at Tuskegee, most all black schools and churches in the area were burned to terrorize and intimidate freed persons into subjugation.[816] He walked into the mouth of a lion and came out a hero to millions who desparately needed a hero to survive.

The commitment to duty that young Booker observed in his boyhood heroes took him south to Tuskegee. His bond to public service in the South put him there during dark times of violence and terror. In 1881, he was called by local citizens to start a school in Tuskegee, like his acclaimed alma mater, Hampton Institute. His Alabama school would also limit his role for social change to a slow and peaceful buildup to a new social order, while accommodating the white power structure which was supported by terror. He rejected public agitation against the entrenched racist social order for change. He believed that whites across the South would change with greater economic equality and interactions between the races, as happened for his boyhood heroes in Malden. He was wrong. The circumstances were different. The ratio of numbers of freed slaves to whites in the South and in Malden were very different. The heritage and values were different for the aristocratic South and equalitarian Malden. Jim Crow segregation was "glove to fist" in the South.

Inflexibility was an early limitation in his career. His short life of 59 years limited the time of his service and the natural evolution of his leadership with changing times.[817] If he had lived to be 95 years old as did Frederick Douglass and W. E. B. Du Bois, he would have lived to see his plan to attack segregation with law suits succeed for the National Association for the Advancement of Colored People, NAACP. he would have seen the Tuskegee Airmen gain respect for African American servicemen and he would have seen an integrated military for the United States enter the Korean War. He would have responded to these changes in changing times and with mass action in the modern civil rights movement likey started by a Lincoln Memorial concert by Marion Anderson, and with mass action led by A. Philip Randolph, NAACP, and others.

Booker T. Washington's leadership is sometimes dismissed when cast about on a flat landscape of judgments made in isolated hindsight about his leadership failures and successes. Other great leaders may come under similar criticism and be unfairly dismissed in hindsight like the leaders of the Revolution against King George who, as slavers, led an "all-in" treasonous rebellion to create the first national republic in almost two thousand years. Two hundred fifty years later, from the safe, comfortable present day that they made possible for us, we should carefully review our judgments of them for failure to directly challenge the idea of white superiority in their day and time. These men of accomplishment and lovers of freedom and equality for whites, when viewed in flat hindsight may not at first measure up to visionary free-thinkers, writers, and agitators today who can safely position themselves on the right side of a history written for the future with no institution to protect and no specific social goals to achieve. Articulate critics can and should be celebrated as the years pass. But pioneer leadership is always situational to its own time, and it is neither perfect nor a blueprint for other situations and times of social change.

John P. Hale wrote, "Pioneer history does *not* repeat itself." Socrates reminded the ages in Plato's *The Republic,* after he approved of slavery for non-Greeks, that people should not expect the "actual State will in every respect coincide with the ideal."[818]

Booker T. Washington was followed a generation later by giants of the modern civil rights movement. A. Philip Randolph was an important labor leader in Harlem during the Great Depression and leading up to the Second World War. He lifted up the movement using mass action and threats of mass action to successfully attack race discrimination and segregation. The first mass action may have occurred on April 9, 1939, when Marian Anderson, recognized as one of the world's greatest opera singers, performed before thousands at the Lincoln Memorial in Washington after she had been denied use of a local theatre by the Daughters of the American Revolution because of her race. First Lady Eleanor Roosevelt publicly resigned from the organization and the concert was a historic success. The thousands of people who came to the Mall for the concert were in effect protesting racial discrimination.[819] Marion Anderson's historic success may encouraged A. Philip Randolph two years later to threaten President Franklin Roosevelt with a mass protest march on Washington if he refused to integrate the armed forces and ban race discrimination for employment in federal military contracts. The president was preparing for a possible war with Germany and thousands of jobs were at stake. It was six months before Pearl Harbor, and, with mediation by Eleanor Roosevelt, the president agreed to ban job discrimination but declined to integrate the armed forces at such a difficult time against opposition of top military leaders.

A. Philip Randolph agreed to the compromise, and one of the most important marches on Washington never happened. He would be the honorary leader of the August 28, 1964 March on Washington For Jobs and Freedom, where Reverend Dr. Martin Luther King, Jr., delivered the immortal "I Have a Dream" speech at the Lincoln Memorial, the location of Marian Anderson's courageous concert. His speech at the place of her heroic stand against race prejudice changed America, forever.[820]

During the Second World War, the Tuskegee Airmen proved on a statistical basis the high abilities of many black servicemen. Several airmen began their training at today's West Virginia State University. Their success proved black soldiers had the talent and courage to serve alongside white soldiers. President Harry Truman ordered integration of the armed services during his reelection campaign in 1948, and it is believed to have secured to him reelection in one of the most heralded election upsets in history.

One of the "royal priesthood" of leaders from the Kanawha Valley in the modern civil rights movement was Reverend Dr. Mordecai Wyatt Johnson, President of Howard University. He was named president while he was serving in the pulpit of First Baptist Church of Charleston. He established Howard University as the leading African American academic institution and set the mission of its law school to train top level graduates who could successfully attack segregation one case at a time. The National Association for the Advancement of Colored People, NAACP, was successful in selecting and winning segregation court cases with Howard University law graduates. Its success after the Second World War created what Historian C. Vann Woodward called the "Second Reconstruction." The greatest victory was by Howard Law graduate, Thurgood Marshall, in the landmark 1954 case of *Brown v. Board of Education,* shocked the nation and the world. Some historians see this decision to force integration of public schools to be one of the most important national policy changes since the Magna Carta.[821]

The Supreme Court decision in *Brown v. Board of Education* today seems inevitable but it was not. The decision dismantled the walls of separation which the Court had erected for over three generations. It swept away segregation in public schools and crushed the idea of state sovereignty over federal civil rights. It approved new research that showed very young black children in segregated schools had low self-esteem and developed psychological limitations as a result of their separation from white peers.

The second modern leader of the "royal priesthood" at First Baptist of Charleston was an early civil rights activist, Reverend Vernon Johns. After he delivered brilliant sermons, he would don coveralls and sell produce out of the back of a truck. He believed in helping common people and disdained the elitism of W. E. B. Du Bois and the accommodation theory of Booker T. Washington. He followed Reverend Dr. Mordecai Wyatt Johnson in the pulpit of First Baptist and left there to be the minister of the prominent Dexter Avenue Baptist Church in Montgomery, Alabama. He was succeeded there by the Reverend Dr. Martin Luther King, Jr., as he began his career after college graduation in Boston. The third member of the "royal priesthood" was a youth member of First Baptist Church of Charleston, Reverend Leon Sullivan. He, led the international business boycott of South Africa to peacefully end modern slavery there.

Reverend Dr. King began his civil rights career at Dexter Avenue Baptist Church with the Montgomery bus boycott which was started by Rosa Parks in 1955. For over a decade, he valiantly led protests and boycotts to challenge Jim Crow laws, that led to new federal laws enacted after the assassination of President John Fitzgerald Kennedy. The new civil rights laws protected voting rights and banned race discrimination in employment, housing, and public accommodations. Reverend Dr. King was the first national black leader to come out of the South after Booker T. Washington. With his success, he was martyred on April 4, 1968.

Booker T. Washington is one of the most important transitional figures in American history. He encouraged blacks to improve their lives with hard work and to create new opportunities for their families to join in the full life of America. His leadership for change was based on hope, optimism, and self-determination that few other freed persons could know in their own lives day-to-day after the Civil War. It was based on his life with boyhood heroes in Malden. He intended his life work to be a model for the value and worth of all African Americans despite times of terror. In the Confederate South, he gave hope to ten million blacks, where there was no hope.[822] He gave value where proof of value was demanded by the idea of white superiority. He publicly challenged segregation as well as it could be challenged openly in the South without violence. The rest he challenged secretly in lawsuits he funded regularly against segregation. His attacks on Jim Crow social codes have been called a personal "war" against segregation. He helped his friends and family. He tangled readily with his critics. He was on a path to expand the American Dream, a path that he refused to leave in his twenty years of leadership. He died at age 59 without questioning the path or the boyhood heroes in Malden who put him on that path. His leadership, good and bad, should be respected for its time and place.

The overwhelming, evil power of separation in human relationships was underestimated by Booker T. Washington. The Jim Crow segregation system nurtured hate and deprivation of blacks. He envisioned blacks and whites interacting on a regular basis in the South, and he thought their economic interactions would eventually promote neighborly relationships like in Malden, especially when blacks became skilled and full partners in the economy of the South.

But he was assuming a conclusion from the success he saw in his boyhood heroes in the small town of Malden. It was a very different place from the aristocratic South where separation was complete and stratified in all social interactions. Malden had hundreds of freed people whereas the Confederate South had millions of freed people. The economic class separation, enforced with strict racist social codes, made it impossible for blacks in the South to interact fairly with whites and overcome ideas of white superiority. Individual blacks working hard for success were degraded by racist generalizations, regardless of their ability or value to the community. Denials of social and political rights were supported by claims of dominant whites that the poverty, illiteracy, and deprivations they saw blacks suffering were a matter of nature running its course. Worse, some saw the results of degradation as part of a Divine plan for mankind.

Segregation, through the deprivations of separateness, continued white domination in America into the mid-twentieth century, well after Booker T. Washington's death in 1915. Those deprivations had been used in slavery and supported in minstrel shows, as some would use them today to try to prove status by statistics. The idea of white superiority was overcome as the nation's majority belief after integration of the races changed in public schools and as demands for equal civil rights to employment, housing and public accommodations increased.

These gradual changes reset the national character with ideas that were stated as ideals of the republic and which required work to fulfill for liberty, equality, and social justice for all. Official institutional morality in America changed, and that has encouraged individuals to assess their own prejudices against blacks and other peoples who are in some way different from the mainstream of Americans. The nation is no longer officially race-prejudiced in its institutions but many vestiges and results of current discrimination remain. Individual morality continues to be a checkered fabric of racism. Race prejudice is today around many dark corners and is applied quietly to blacks and any other minority group which is perceived as somehow different. Code words are used for the "good old days," when white power was unchallenged. Most sources of discrimination are indirect for racism in institutions and they remain in the heads and hearts of millions of people, who may be aware or unaware of deep seeded prejudice. African Americans still today suffer from special prejudice due to what writer and free thinker James Baldwin called the history of African peoples written in the color of their skin.[823]

The institutions of government and society have accepted and support fully the morality of non-discrimination, but individual racism and, with it, consequential institutional racism lingers. The conflicting ideas of equality and white superiority continue to present race issues for millions in the story of America. They confront the individual value systems of Americans with questions about how the nation's founding ideas for whites can be applied to all neighbors, in light of centuries of slavery and degradation for millions of

African Americans. A history of racism should challenge people to ask, "Who are our neighbors that we today may be excluding from the mainstream of the America which we exalt and love as our home?" Instead, many accept the din of celebration for the "good old days."

The advance of human rights is an ongoing process for many white-centered organizations. For example, the national Episcopal Church in America has accepted responsibility for the strong support of its southern dioceses for slavery before the Civil War. Like the Ruffners, the church changed. It has become a leading denomination supporting human rights and inclusion of all people in the life, ministries and sacraments of the Church, including the sacrament of holy marriage.

St. John's Episcopal Church in Charleston was a slaver church before the Civil War, but since the 1970s in the time of Rector Thomas Morris and, after 1974 with Rector Jim Lewis , the church has been a leader in the state and the national Episcopal Church for human rights and social justice for poor, homeless and excluded people. It includes women and men, people who are lesbian, gay, bi-sexual and transgender, and families and friends, all in the full life of the church without separation or judgment. In 1977, Reverend Lewis was a pioneer the national church when he blessed the unions of two couples, one lesbian and one gay, to the great consternation of the St. John's congregation at the time, some four decades before the national Episcopal Church began conducting marriages for people of the same gender in all its dioceses.

At the time, St. John's Church centered many social justice programs and agencies. Three major programs are notable, originating from the broader church community started while Reverend Jim Lewis was rector. He famously stirred swirling energies for new approaches to social justice. He was a early activist in Charleston for social justice. He was ably assisted by Virginia Adams, who helped organizers in and out of the church begin new programs. First, they had Judy Teel start Manna Meal in the late 1970s. It is Charleston's largest downtown free meal program. It started with soup first provided by Virginia Adams, and then Harriett Beury, Maggie McCoy, Jane McCabe and others. It is located in the church now as an independent organization supported by community wide fundraising. In 2018, Manna Meal served 110,000 cooked meals, for breakfast and lunch, to an average of 750 different people. Second, West Virginia Health Right is a free medical and dental clinic headquartered on Washington Street in Charleston, which was started by Patricia White from initial meetings at St. John's Church, and today serves over 25,000 patients from 34 counties. Third, former Catholic nuns, Patricia Hussey and Barbara Ferraro, established Covenant House in 1981, as a social service agency located next to St. Johns Church, to help homeless, poor and needy people. It now has a new location on Shrewsbury Street. It helped begin hospice care in Charleston and collaborates with other social service agencies including West Virginia Health Right and others on HIV and hepatitis prevention programs. In 2018, Covenant House had 32,300 in-person visits to its facility, and it had 28,600 phone contacts. Its service group contacts in 2018 included 10,000 people who were people of color and 23,000 whites.[824]

All three of these major social justice organizations were started by women in a time when women were not leaders of major organizations. The national debate at the time was over a woman's place in the kitchen versus their leadership in society. In the time before gender equality was important in America, the Young Women's Christian Association, YWCA, across the street from St. John's Church, under the continuing leadership of Debby Weinstein, began many social service programs, including the Sojourners Shelter for Homeless Women and Children. Also, at the time, a leading community and state activist for social justice was Florette Angel who, as the legendary head of the West Virginia Section of the National Council of Jewish Women, was an inspirational leader encouraging new social service programs and new roles for women as community leaders. In all, St. John's Episcopal Church was at the center of swirling commitments to help people with very basic human needs. It had a white congregation and a slaver heritage that was transformed into a critical mass of hope and energy for fundamental social justice. People, churches and communities can lead for change.

Notably in 1983, with the place of women in the National Episcopal Church and otherwise outside the kitchen being tested, the Reverends Mary Adelia McLeod and Mac McLeod were called from Alabama to be co-rectors of St. John's Church following Reverend Jim Lewis. Opposition was strong in the National Episcopal Church against the ordination of women and their leadership. After a decade of service at St. John's Church, Mary Adelia McLeod was elected on June 5, 1993 as the Bishop of the Diocese of Vermont. Her election to lead a state diocese was the first for a woman in the history of the national Episcopal Church and it was one of the two firsts in the history of the British Anglican Church going back to Henry VIII. Bishop McLeod, a woman of genteel southern grace and charm, did not celebrate or publicize her historic election. She and her husband Mac McLeod wanted her service as bishop to be quiet, firm proof that qualified people could assume high positions in the church even though they happen to be women. The McLeods shunned national attention. Bishop McLeod realized their approach was successful, when a small Vermont boy during a communionm service looked up at her from the alter rail and asked, "Can boys be bishops too?" She paused, smiled and quietly replied, "Yes."[825]

Almost twenty years into the twenty-first century, many young African Americans have a sense of entitlement not known in prior generations as they can see their lives and the lives of their peers begin to bloom with their unique culture and talents for music, arts, plays, writing, sports, businesses, and foods being exalted, and not just accepted. Of course, young whites are able to enjoy the same entitlement their ancestors in America realized for centuries, but entitlement is spread widely today and is now being enjoyed by more and more Americans. The entitlement of all enriches all. It is less a matter of earned status than the status of humanity. Most all young people today can see America as the home that they love with fewer and fewer reminders of a history of oppression, but the reminders and barriers are present, and they need to be studied and challenged. Slavery should be included in the regular study of politics, economics and social history. The history must be told, and, for many, young and old, it can be a painful telling. That pain should be appreciated and respected by those whose families did not suffer in that history, and perhaps prospered by it.

Television journalism brought to American homes a close and personal experience of the horror and brutality of racism and segregated lives. It changed the ideas of most white youth and many adults who readily rejected white domination. Those ideas of hope and purpose must be kept alive and meaningful to the generations of leaders to follow. The solid high wall that was segregation should not become a barrier hedgerow of technical, porous, and thorny separation. Open garden paths are needed between good neighbors.

The ideas of hope, self-determination and social justice, and the struggles to support them, should be taught to future generations. Suffering ancestors may become more distant in memory and lovingly assigned to history, but they should never be forgotten for their sacrifices and guidance through dark times of slavery and segregation. Such teachings may be the only fundamental checks on majority-rule government which at times can become uninterested in protecting the rights of any minority.[826]

African Americans are today one of the world's largest population groups, with over 70 million people. Many, like the "royal priesthood" of the African Zion Baptist Church, are becoming race proud leaders in the social, educational, and governmental institutions of America and in wider world affairs and culture. But racism and religious hatred is not gone from millions of individuals around the world. Like in the twentieth century, racism and hatred can be easily manipulated in religion, politics and society for evil ends in any society. That happened in Germany. Leaders pandering on the concerns and separations of people like to promote high walls of fear and suspicion to those who hold conscious racist ideas and to those who have unconscious unformed ideas of racism and separation. Also, there are many places of separation of people who have legal entitlement to share in the American Dream, but who cannot share because of the overwhelming separation caused by poverty, loss of hope, and despair. Their reality is not about ideas as much as it is about raw survival. A person's commitment to work for America's best ideas requires a present commitment to end social injustice, poverty and despair. That mission was shared by Booker T. Washington and Reverend Dr. Martin Luther King, Jr. and the giants of the modern civil rights movement. It should be the mission of today's leaders and followers. When America's leadership relies on its best ideas, it can be a beacon for what some would say should be the "Hope of the World."[827]

Booker T. Washington promoted policies that would allow blacks to strive for middle class success that we today include in the "American Dream." Some people see that goal as insubstantial and wrong-headed, too narrow, and limiting as raw class consciousness. But the broad American middle class can include all Americans. For Booker T. Washington, it was an unquestioned path to freedom and equality defined by hope, purpose and self-determination, not finances or social status. He had an educational institution to support, and he saw the values of the American middle class to be uplifting for freed people, for all people.

He was certain that if blacks had education and fair opportunities for good jobs, they would compete well and improve the lives of their families and communities. Many changes in the twentieth century may be a legacy of that idea. He thought blacks had to become major contributors to the national and local economies to have political and social equality. *Up from Slavery* was written to announce to all people this path to success. Its simple message was "If I could make it 'up' from the degradation of slavery, then any one in America, can make it 'up' from any despair or separation." His vision took many more generations than he could think would be needed. He misjudged the depth of fear, hate and separation in the South, and the almost religious belief nationwide in the idea of white superiority. He died an early death on November 14, 1915, a victim of his own hope and self-determination which he took as gospel from the struggling, hard-working, proud heroes of his youth.

He worked to fulfill the dreams of his boyhood heroes. His fight was to forever end the depreciating exceptions to the American Dream applied uniformly to African Americans and other minority peoples by the dominant majority idea of white superiority. He believed in equality as something earned at first, and not bestowed as an entitlement. He worked to provide all African Americans--the poor, talented, and untalented--with education and fair opportunity to earn their way into the broad American middle class, fulfilling what he considered to be the true American Dream and only path to lasting equality and social justice.

In the twentieth century, the American Dream evolved and expanded to include more and more peoples especially immigrant minorities. But it took many, too many, years to end the footnoted exceptions to the American Dream which were applied to African Americans. As recent as a decade ago, the parents of black children could not with any confidence encourage their children in the American Dream, because the ultimate symbolic success for the American Dream is to be president of the United States. Black parents were shackled with the real limitations of their own lives. They could not truthfully assure their children that, in their futures, they would become entitled to share fully in the American Dream. Their own entitlement was elusive through the twentieth century. Parents saw improvements in civil rights step-by-slow-step, and they could hope for more progress, but in their life times they had been barred from realizing the equality of personhood and the affirming social justice that flows from it.

Then in 2008, the universal exceptions to the American Dream were swept away. The history of America was forever changed by the election of Barack Hussein Obama II as President of the United States. He was an African American with a heritage and names that came directly from Africa. The election, almost a century after the death of Booker T. Washington, required the work, unity and resolve of a strong black middle class. That election, and the establishment of the black middle class which made it happen, have now expanded the American Dream to all children, with no depreciating footnotes for "someday." But the inaugural celebration of that great event is now a matter of history and perspective, while prejudice remains.

The twenty-first century belongs to youth, all youth, and they will judge us for our dreams, effort, and inconsistencies, perhaps with more hope and fewer scars than any Americans before, but also perhaps more harshly than generations before them--because we should have known better after the experience of World War II. That could be a first step to an awaking to make our national creed for liberty, equality and social justice available to all, to everyone. But nothing is certain. New ideas and harsh judgments are not always improvements pushing us to goals of equality and social justice. The work of individual commitment to social justice must continue in earnest.

Despite great hopes and confidence in future progress--an important American value--dark despair can sometimes overwhelm just before dawn. James Baldwin wrote his classic, *The Fire Next Time*, during gloomy and difficult days for civil rights when statutory civil rights reforms in 1962 and 1963 seemed generations away. He reported that Attorney General Robert F. Kennedy predicted an African American would be elected president forty years after enactment of the federal voting rights law. As it turned out, the election happened exactly as predicted. But in the overwhelming gloom of his day in the early 1960s, James Baldwin was discouraged after a slow start to integration following the 1954 decision in *Brown v. Board of Education* and before new federal civil rights statutes were enacted. He took the Attorney General's prediction to be gratuitous and yet another indication that whites felt generous at giving blacks opportunities to become equal to whites, when their humanity entitled blacks to full equality and not the airs of generosity—a reasonable assessment when James Baldwin made it.[828] But the civil rights statutes were enacted several years later, after Reverend Dr. Martin Luther King's "I Have a Dream" speech and the 1963 assassination of President John F. Kennedy. America continued to move slowly toward change, which is the story--the history--of America.

Today, reminders of racism force upon many African Americans, who are about fourteen percent of the nation's population, a filter for their view of history and community and their present safety and well-being.[829] Many have a special fear for the safety and well-being of people in their communities and especially for their youth in contacts with authorities in general and with individuals who may have race prejudice. Many African Americans still experience disappointments in the high promise of equality, and they can identify many categories of obvious disparities in the lives of people in America's two prominent races. They can point to statistics revealing many disparities between the races and in our ideals when compared to the reality of the lives of many in their communities.[830]

When African Americans reveal their concerns and fears, and protest the same debilitating apathy that allowed people to suffer in slavery for three and a half centuries, they should be respected for their voice and the reminders of the extreme sacrifices of their families. All people should be celebrated for the many expressions for their own commitments to family and community and for the love they share for their nation home, our shared home--America. In their families, there are ever-present reminders of sacrificing ancestors who loved and helped build up America for the benefit of others. After all, it is African American parents who must try to explain to their children the unexplainable sacrifices of their family and race while many other parents may not readily understand or grasp the continuing concern because of their own family's generations of entitlement to equality and social justice.[831]

We all in America can benefit by reassessing that story and the filters we apply to history and human rights. In our nation, we can proudly acknowledge significant--if imperfect--progress in spreading entitlements at law for basic civil rights to all citizens because, yes, African Americans can be president of the United States, and yes, all people who love each other can be secure together in marriage protected by law, and, yes, always and forever, boys can be bishops too.[832]

This spirit of hope and neighborly respect is the legacy of Booker T. Washington's boyhood heroes, his family and their friends in the community of the African Zion Baptist Church. They fulfilled an inspirational covenant with God in the darkest hours of the republic to start a "royal priesthood" to build a "holy nation." The covenant to build a "holy nation" in the Zion of their day for the benefit of the Zion of our day is explored, detailed, and celebrated in the second part of this work, *Booker T. Washington's Boyhood American Dream: The Climb of the Black Middle Class Up from Slavery.*

Please read on.

Appendix

List of Documents

Ruffner Family Tree 374

Henry Ruffner Pamphlet 1847: 375

West Virginia Statute Abolishing Slavery 1865 413

Preliminary Emancipation Proclamation 414

Final Emancipation Proclamation 416

Thirteenth Amendment... 418

Fourteenth Amendment 419

Ruffner Family Tree

RUFFNER FAMILY TREE
Revised December 2019

IN VALLEY OF VIRGINIA--LURAY

*Peter Ruffner---*Mary Steinman
|1713-1778| |1714-1798|

CHILDREN IN LURAY
*Joseph Ruffner   Reuben R. Ruffner
Benjamin Ruffner   Tobias Ruffner
Catherine Ruffner   Elizabeth Ruffner
Peter Ruffner (Jr.)   Emanuel Ruffner

IN KANAWHA VALLEY--CHARLESTON

*Joseph Ruffner---*Anna Heistand
b.|09/25/1740| b.|10/15/1742|
d.|03/23/1803| d.|08/29/1820|

CHILDREN IN LURAY
Esther Ruffner   *Samuel Ruffner
*David Ruffner   Eve Ruffner
*Joseph Ruffner II   *Daniel Ruffner
*Tobias Ruffner   *Abraham Ruffner

*David Ruffner----*Anna Brumbach
b.|06/18/1767| b.|11/11/1766|
d.|02/01/1843| d.|11/22/1852|

CHILDREN IN MALDEN
*Henry Ruffner
*Ann Eve Ruffner
*Susan B. Ruffner
*Lewis Ruffner

*Dr. Henry Ruffner----*Sarah Lyle
b.|01/16/1790| b.|1787|
d.|12/17/1861| d.|1849|

CHILDREN IN LEXINGTON
*William Henry "W. H." Ruffner
*David Lewis Ruffner
Julia Elizabeth Stuart Ruffner
Anna Brumbach Ruffner

*Dr. Henry Ruffner ----*Laura J. Kirby
2nd Marriage   b.|1828|

*Lewis Ruffner-----*Elizabeth Shrewsbury
b.|10/01/1797| b.|10/01/1804|
d.|11/19/1883| d.|01/05/1843|

CHILDREN IN MALDEN
Madeline Eloise Ruffner   Lewis Ruffner, Jr.
David Henry Ruffner   Julia L. Ruffner
Sarah Ann Ruffner   Henrietta Ruffner
Joel Shrewsbury Ruffner

*Lewis Ruffner ----*Viola Knapp
2nd Marriage   b.|1812| d.|1903|

CHILDREN IN MALDEN
*Ernest Howard Ruffner
b.|06/24/1845| d.|05/24/1937|

*Stella Blanche Ruffner

*Detailed Information is Provided in the Text.

Henry Ruffner Pamphlet 1847:

X FOR GENERAL CIRCULATION.

ADDRESS

TO THE

PEOPLE

OF

WEST VIRGINIA;

SHEWING THAT

SLAVERY IS INJURIOUS TO THE PUBLIC WELFARE, AND
THAT IT MAY BE GRADUALLY ABOLISHED, WITH-
OUT DETRIMENT TO THE RIGHTS AND IN-
TERESTS OF SLAVEHOLDERS.

BY A SLAVEHOLDER OF WEST VIRGINIA.

LEXINGTON:

PRINTED BY R. C. NOEL,

1847.

CORRESPONDENCE.

LEXINGTON, VA., SEPT. 1st, 1847.

Dear Sir:

The undersigned believing that the argument recently delivered by you in the Franklin Society, in favor of the removal of the negro population from Western Virginia, was not only able but unanswerable; and that its publication will tend to bring the public mind to a correct conclusion on that momentous question; request that you will furnish us with a full statement of that argument for the press.

We cannot expect that you will now be able to furnish us with the speech precisely as it was delivered, nor is it our wish that you shall confine yourself strictly to the views then expressed. Our desire is to have the whole argument in favor of the proposition, presented to the public, in a perspicuous and condensed form. And believing that your views were not only forcible but conclusive, and that they were presented in a shape, which cannot give just cause of offence to even those who are most fastidious and excitable on all subjects having any connexion with the subject of slavery, we trust that you will be disposed cheerfully to comply with our request above expressed.

Very Respectfully,

Your ob't serv'ts,

S. McD. MOORE,
JOHN LETCHER,
DAVID P. CURRY,
JAMES G. HAMILTON,
GEORGE A. BAKER,
J. H. LACY,
JOHN ECHOLS,
JAMES R. JORDAN,
JACOB FULLER, Jr.,
D. E. MOORE,
JOHN W. FULLER.

The Rev. HENRY RUFFNER, D. D.

LEXINGTON, VA., September 4th, 1847.

To Messrs. Moore, Letcher, &c.,

GENTLEMEN:

Though long opposed in feeling to the perpetuation of slavery, yet like others I felt no call to immediate action to promote its removal,

4

until the close of the important debate in the Franklin Society, to which your letter alludes. The arguments delivered by several of yourselves, and the results of my own examination of facts, so impressed my mind with the importance of the subject to the welfare of the country, that I proceeded immediately to write out an argument in favor of a gradual removal of slavery from my native soil, our dear West Virginia; and intended in some way to present it to the consideration of my fellow-citizens. Some months ago you privately signified a desire that it might be printed, and have now formally made the request.

I cheerfully comply, so far as this, in the first instance, that I will prepare for the press an Address to the Citizens of West Virginia, comprising the substance of the argument as delivered by me, enriched and strengthened by some of the impressive views exhibited by several of yourselves. Within the limits of a moderately sized pamphlet, it is impossible to introduce every important consideration bearing on the subject, or to do more than present the substance of the prominent facts and reasons which were more fully exhibited and illustrated by the debaters in the Society.

As we are nearly all slaveholders, and none of us approve of the principles and measures of the sect of abolitionists, we think that no man can be offended with us for offering to the people an argument, whose sole object is to show that the prosperity of our West Virginia —if not of East Virginia also,—would be promoted by removing gradually the institution of slavery, in a manner consistent with the rights and interests of slaveholders.

To the Great Being who rules the destinies of our country, I commit the issue of this important movement.

Yours,

HENRY RUFFNER.

ADDRESS

TO THE

CITIZENS OF WEST VIRGINIA.

FELLOW-CITIZENS,

Now is the time, when we of West Virginia should review our public affairs, and consider what measures are necessary and expedient to promote the welfare of ourselves and our posterity. Three years hence another census of the United States will have been completed. Then it will appear how large a majority we are of the citizens of this commonwealth, and how unjust it is that our fellow citizens of East Virginia, being a minority of the people, should be able, by means of their majority in the Legislature, to govern both East and West for their own advantage. You have striven in vain to get this inequality of representation rectified. The same legislative majority has used the power of which we complain, to make all our complaints fruitless, and to retain the ascendancy now when they represent a minority of the people, which they secured to themselves eighteen years ago, while they yet represented the majority.

You have submitted patiently, heretofore, to the refusal of the East to let West Virginia grow in political power as she has grown in population and wealth. Though you will not cease to urge your claims, you will, if necessary, still exercise this patient forbearance, until the next census shall furnish you with an argument, which cannot be resisted with any show of reason. Then—as it seems to be understood among us—you will make a final and decisive effort to obtain your just weight in the government.

That will be a critical period in your public affairs. A great end will then be gained, or a great failure will be experienced. Are you sure of success? Can you be sure of it, while the question of representation stands alone, and liable to unpropitious influences, even on our side of the Blue Ridge? We propose to strengthen this cause, by connecting with it another of equally momentous consequence—in some respects even more—to our public welfare. United they will stand ; divided they may fall.

You claim the white basis of representation, on the republican

6

principle that *the majority shall rule.* You deny that slaves, who constitute no part of the political body, shall add political weight to their masters, either as individual voters or as a mass of citizens. But the slaveholding interest, which is supreme in the East, is also powerful in some parts of the West. Let this be considered as a *perpetual* and a *growing* interest in our part of the State, and it may throw so much weight on the side of the Eastern principle of representation, when the hour of decision comes, as to produce a compromise, and to secure to the East a part at least of what she claims on the ground of her vast slave property. But let all the West, on due consideration, conclude that slavery is a pernicious institution, and must be gradually removed; then, united in our views on all the great interests of our West Virginia, we shall meet the approaching crisis with inflexible resolution; and West Virginia can and must succeed in her approaching struggle for her rights and her prosperity.

The more you consider the subject, the more you will be convinced that both these questions—the white basis and slavery—are of vital importance, and so intimately connected, that to insure success in either, we must unite them in our discussions both among ourselves and with East Virginia. On both should our views and our policy be firmly settled, when the crisis of 1850 shall arrive.

It is not the object of this address to discuss the question of representation. We leave that subject to the abler management of those who have heretofore conducted the discussion. Yet as the success of the great measure which we shall advocate in this address, will depend much upon our obtaining a just share of representation in the Legislature, we call your attention to some facts, for the purpose of showing, that West Virginia has heretofore suffered incalculably from her weakness in the Legislature. We remind you of these things, not to excite resentful feelings, but to confirm you in your purpose to adhere inflexibly to your just claim of representation on the white basis, *without compromise.* We shall refer to two facts only, out of many that might be mentioned.

Fifty years ago, when the country beyond the Ohio began to be opened for settlement, Virginia had already been for years in full and undisputed possession of her extensive territory on this side. The country between the Alleghany and the Ohio, containing eighteen millions of acres, much of it excellent soil, and abounding in mineral wealth, was an almost unbroken wilderness, and almost inaccessible to emigrants, for want of roads through the mountains. The feeble and detached settlements applied, and for thirty years continued to apply, *almost in vain,* for legislative aid to open wagon roads from the Eastern settlements into their valleys. Let the Acts of Assembly for these thirty years of our infancy in West Virginia, be examined, and they will show how little, how *very* little, our Eastern mother was willing to do to promote the growth of her nurseling in the mountains. A few thousand dollars out of her rich treasury—very few indeed—and now and then some arrearages of taxes due from the poor settlers in the wilderness, was all that the

7

government could be prevailed on to advance, for the purpose of opening this extensive territory for settlement, and to accommodate its secluded inhabitants.

Now can any man doubt, that if the Legislature had, in the prosperous days of East Virginia, from 1794 to 1824, appropriated only ten or twelve thousand dollars a year to make good wagon roads through the mountain districts, that West Virginia would have increased in population and wealth far more than she did, or could do without roads? May we not affirm, that if East Virginia had pursued that just and enlightened policy, West Virginia would 20 years ago have been more populous than she was by 100,000 souls, and more wealthy in a still greater proportion? No man who has seen the effect of some lately-constructed roads, in promoting population and wealth, can doubt it. And what shows more conclusively the blindness or illiberality of this Eastern policy towards the West, is, that the public treasury would have been remunerated, fourfold at least, by the additional revenue which this early outlay for roads—had it been made—would have produced from the taxpayers of West Virginia. Here we have one notable instance of what West Virginia has suffered from her dependence on an Eastern Legislature. Though her growth in spite of Eastern neglect, has enabled her of late years to get some valuable improvements made, she is still dependent for every boon of this kind, upon the will of those Eastern people who are now a minority of the Commonwealth.

The other instance to which we intended to refer, is of still greater importance than the former. Many of you remember that in 1832, when a negro insurrection in Southampton county had filled nearly all Virginia with alarm, and made every white man think of the evils of slavery, a resolution was introduced into the Legislature, to adopt a system of gradual emancipation, by which the State might, in the course of 50 years, get rid of the evils of slavery.

Whatever may be thought of such a measure in reference to East Virginia, where the slaves are more numerous than the whites; there can be no rational doubt that in West Virginia, the measure, had it been carried 15 years ago, would by this time have wrought a most happy change in the condition and prospects of the country: and so the people of West Virginia then thought, for they were generally and warmly in favor of it, and zealously advocated it through their able and patriotic Delegates. But in spite of their efforts, it was rejected by the all powerful Eastern majority, though several Eastern Delegates joined the West in its support.

We do not censure our Eastern brethren for opposing this measure so far as their part of the State is concerned. But still, we of West Virginia must deem ourselves not only unfortunate, but aggrieved, when an Eastern majority in the Legislature debars us from obtaining measures conducive to our welfare, because these same measures may not suit the policy of East Virginia.

Though defeated for the time, the friends of gradual emancipation

8

were not in despair. There was a general acknowledgment of the evils of slavery; and strong hopes were entertained that, in a few years, a decided majority of the Legislature would be for ridding the country of this deleterious institution. But these hopes were sadly disappointed. East Virginia became more and more adverse, not only to emancipation in any mode or form, but to any discussion of the subject. Even in our West Virginia, though we believe no material change of sentiment has taken place, little has since been said, and nothing done, to effect an object so important to the welfare of the country.

This long silence and apparent apathy on our part, is also in some degree owing to our conscious inability to do any thing requiring Legislative action, unless East Virginia be pleased to aid us, and this we have felt certain she would not do, at any time since the debate of 1832.

But this unfavorable change of sentiment in Virginia, is due chiefly to the fanatical violence of those Northern anti-slavery men, who have been usually called ABOLITIONISTS.

The excitement in Great Britain on the subject of West Indian slavery, was caught by some enthusiasts in this country, and from that day to this some thousands of these people have been smitten with a sort of moral insanity. A malignant rage against slave-holders—denoted by bitter denunciations and unprincipled calumnies—has characterized their proceedings. Many other anti-slavery men, led on by indiscreet zeal, but actuated by purer motives, contributed to swell the torrent of denunciation, and to alarm the Southern people by incessant attempts to disturb their domestic relations, and to drive them into an immediate abolition of slavery. Southern men of all parties were indignant at this unjustifiable interference with their domestic concerns: they knew also that as the principles of the abolitionists were erroneous, so the measures which they insisted on our adopting, were rash and dangerous.

The friends of gradual emancipation soon saw that of all the ill winds that would blow upon their cause, this storm of abolitionism was the worst. They had to postpone all efforts to effect their object, until this tempest of fanaticism should spend its violence, or become less alarming. It has raged during 15 years: and now the abolitionists may boast, if they will, that they have done more in this time to rivet the chains of the slave, and to fasten the curse of slavery upon the country, than all the pro-slavery men in the world have done, or could do, in half a century. They have not, by honorable means, liberated a single slave: and they never will, by such a course of procedure as they have pursued. On the contrary, they have created new difficulties in the way of all judicious schemes of emancipation, by prejudicing the minds of slave-holders, and by compelling us to combat their false principles and rash schemes, in our rear; whilst we are facing the opposition of men, and the natural difficulties of the case, in our front.

9

But, fellow-citizens, shall we suffer this meddlesome sect of abolitionists to blind our eyes to the evils of slavery, and to tie up our
hands, when the condition of the country and the welfare of ourselves and our children, summon us to immediate action? We all
agree that the abolitionists shall not interfere with any policy that
we may choose to adopt, in reference to our domestic relations. We
repudiate all connection with themselves, their principles and their
measures. All that we ask of them, is that they stand aloof, and let
us and our slaves alone. One thing we feel certain of, that we
can and do provide better for the welfare of our slaves, than they
ever did or ever will. What have they ever done, to better the condition of the slaves whom they have enticed away from their masters? We venture to affirm, that the majority of the poor fellows
who have thus been lured away, have regretted the ease and plenty
which they left behind them. We are not sure that those even, who
have been paraded, as abolition lions, from city to city, to tell horrible stories—the more horrible the better—about the cruelty of slaveholders—have long enjoyed as much comfort in their lying occupation, as many a contented inmate of our Southern negro-quarters has
enjoyed in his slavery.

But what of all these abolition manœuvres? They are of such
a character, that they disgrace the party which employs them, and
disable that party to do as much mischief as they otherwise could.

Having failed in their first mode of action, by denunciatory pamph-
lets and newspapers and by petitions to Congress, the most violent
class of abolitionists have now formed themselves into a political
party, aiming to subvert the Federal Constitution, which guaranties
the rights of slaveholders, and to destroy the Federal Union, which
is the glory and safeguard of us all. Thus they have armed against
themselves every American patriot: and what is most remarkable,
they have met, from the opposite extreme, those Southern politicians
and ultra-proslavery men—called chivalry and nullifiers—who so often predict and threaten a dissolution of the Union. Thus it is that
extremes often meet.

Now when the ultraists on both sides have shown their colors, we
may leave them to the management of the uncorrupted classes of
American citizens, *who will doubtless give a good account of them
all*—whilst we of West Virginia steer our course in the safe middle way, and seek to remove the plague of slavery from our limits,
without incurring the charge of ultra-abolitionism on the one hand,
or of ultra *proslaveryism*—or whatever it may be called—on the
other. Against the one party we affirm the right of slaveholding,
under present circumstances; against the other party, we affirm the
expediency of removing slavery from West Virginia, and from every
other State or portion of a State, in which the number of slaves is
not too large.

At the same time we avow the principle, that every State, and
every great division of a State, ought, in a domestic matter of such

2

10

importance to judge and act for itself. We disclaim all intention to interfere with slavery in East Virginia. We leave it to our brethren there, to choose for themselves, whether they will let the institution remain as it is, or whether they will modify it or abolish it, in one way or in another. Their slave population is relatively eight times as large as ours. The same remedy may not be expedient in such different stages of a disease. All that we ask of our Eastern brethren, in regard to this matter, is, that if West Virginia shall call for a law to remove slavery from her side of the Blue Ridge, East Virginia shall not refuse her consent, because the measure may not be palatable to herself.

Heretofore no such scheme for West Virginia only has been proposed among us ; and no State has abolished slavery in one part of her territory and retained it in another. For this reason some persons may at first thought consider such a scheme as unfeasible. A State composed partly of free, and partially of slaveholding territory, may seem to present a political incongruity, and to be incapable of conducting its public affairs harmoniously. To relieve the minds of those who may feel apprehensions of this sort, we offer the following suggestions.

1. Free States and slaveholding States have, during 58 years, lived peaceably and prosperously under one Federal government. Sectional jealousies and occasional jars have occurred, but without evil consequence.

2. Nothing in the nature of the case need create difficulty, except the framing of laws that may affect the rights and interests of slaveholders. But an amendment of the constitution could easily provide for the security of slaveholders in East Virginia against all unjust legislation, arising from the power or the anti-slavery principles of the West.

3. After such an emancipation law as we propose, should be passed for West Virginia, no immediate change would take place in the institution of slavery among us ; except that masters would probably choose to emancipate or remove from the State, a larger number of slaves than heretofore. As only the next generation of negroes would be entitled to emancipation, the law would not begin its practical operation for 21 years at least, and then it would operate gradually for 30 or 40 years longer, before slavery would be extinguished in West Virginia. So that for many years the actual slave interest among us would not be greatly diminished.

4. There is, and long has been, in different parts of Virginia, every degree of difference, from the least to the greatest, between the slaveholding and non-slaveholding interests of the people. In some parts, the slaves are two or three times as numerous as the whites, and the slaveholding interest overrules and absorbs every thing. In other parts, not one man in a hundred owns a slave, and the slaveholding interest is virtually nothing. In West Virginia at large, the slaves being only one-eighth of the population, and the slaveholding

11

population less than one-eighth of the whites, the free interest predominates nearly as much as the slave interest predominates in East Virginia : so that we have in practical operation, if not in perfection, that political incongruity of slave interest and free interest, which is feared as a consequence of the measure that we propose.

5. By allowing West Virginia her just share of representation, and, if she call for it, a law for the removal of slavery, East Virginia will do more to harmonize the feelings of the State, than she ever has done, or can do by a continued refusal. West Virginia being then secured in her essential rights and interests, will not desire a separation, nor be disposed to disturb the harmony of the Commonwealth. So far from aiding the designs of the abolitionists, either in Congress or in our Legislature, both her feelings and her interests will make her more than ever hostile to that pernicious sect.

6. If East Virginia apprehend, that the delegates from the free counties would often speak more freely about slavery matters, than she would like to hear in her central city of Richmond ; let her agree to remove the seat of government to Staunton, near the centre of our territory and of our white population, and she will be free from all annoyance of this sort. West Virginia would then appear no more like a remote province of East Virginia, and be no longer subject to the disadvantage of having all measures affecting her interest, acted upon by a Legislature deliberating in the heart of East Virginia, and exposed to the powerful influence of a city and a people, whose bland manners and engaging hospitalities, are enough to turn both the hearts and the heads of us rough mountaineers, whether we be legislators or not.

Having thus removed some grounds of misapprehension and prejudice respecting our views, we shall now proceed, fellow-citizens, to lay before you some facts and arguments, which prove the expediency of abolishing slavery in West Virginia, by a gradual process, that shall not cause any inconvenience either to society in general, or to slaveholders in particular.

We use no theoretical or abstract arguments. We ground our conclusions upon facts and experience. Though the history of other ages and countries would furnish us with useful illustrations, we have not room in this address to extend our observations much beyond our own age and country. Nor is it necessary that we should ; for within these limits we have abundant materials for argument,— far more than we shall be able to use on the present occasion.

No where, since time began, have the two systems of slave labor and free labor, been subjected to so fair and so decisive a trial of their effects on public prosperity, as in these United States. Here the two systems have worked side by side for ages, under such equal circumstances both political and physical, and with such ample time and opportunity for each to work out its proper effects,—that all must admit the experiment to be now complete, and the result decisive. No man of common sense, who has observed this result, can doubt

12

for a moment, that the system of free labor promotes the growth and prosperity of States, in a much higher degree than the system of slave labor. In the first settlement of a country, when labor is scarce and dear, slavery may give a temporary impulse to improvement: but even this is not the case, except in warm climates, and where free men are scarce and either sickly or lazy: and when we have said this, we have said all that experience in the United States warrants us to say, in favor of the policy of employing slave labor.

It is the common remark of all who have travelled through the United States, that the free States and the slave States, exhibit a striking contrast in their appearance. In the older free States are seen all the tokens of prosperity :—a dense and increasing population ;—thriving villages, towns and cities ;—a neat and productive agriculture, growing manufactures and active commerce.

In the older parts of the slave States,—with a few local exceptions,—are seen, on the contrary, too evident signs of stagnation or of positive decay,—a sparse population,—a slovenly cultivation spread over vast fields, that are wearing out, among others already worn out and desolate ;—villages and towns, " few and far between," rarely growing, often decaying, sometimes mere remnants of what they were, sometimes deserted ruins, haunted only by owls ;—generally no manufactures, nor even trades, except the indispensable few ;—commerce and navigation abandoned, as far as possible, to the people of the free States ;—and generally, instead of the stir and bustle of industry, a dull and dreamy stillness, broken, if broken at all, only by the wordy brawl of politics.

But we depend not on general statements of this sort, however unquestionable their truth may be. We shall present you with statistical facts, drawn from public documents of the highest authority. We shall compare slave States with free States, in general and in particular, and in so many points of view, that you cannot mistake in forming your judgment of their comparative prosperity.

Density and increase of population are, especially in the United States, both an element and a criterion of prosperity. The men of a State are its first element of power—not only military power, and political power—but what is of more importance, *productive* power. The labor of men produces wealth, and with it the means of all human comfort and improvement. The more men there are on a square mile, the more power there is on that square mile, to create every thing that conduces to the welfare of man. We know that the natural resources of every country are limited ; and that whenever there are men enough in a country, to improve all its resources of wealth to the best advantage, increase of population becomes an evil. But no State in this Union has yet approached that point ; no slave State has advanced half way to it. England still prospers with more than 250 inhabitants to the square mile ; Virginia languishes with only 20, though she is by nature almost as richly endowed as England. Massachusetts thrives with 100 inhabitants to the square mile;

13

Virginia, considering her natural advantages, ought to thrive as well with a much larger number; and so she would, if she had the same quality of men on her soil.

Without further preface, we proceed to compare

1. *The progress of population in the free States and the slave-holding States.*

It has so happened that, from the beginning, these two classes of States have been nearly equal in number and in natural advantages; only the slaveholding States have always had the larger share of territory, with a soil and climate peculiarly adapted to the richest products of Agriculture.

At the first census in the year 1790, these two classes of States were about equal in population: the free States had 1,968,000 inhabitants, and the slave States 1,961,000; so that they started even in the race of population; for the superior extent of the slave States gave them an advantage in the race, far more than equivalent to their small inferiority of numbers.

Twenty years later, it was found that the free States had gained 276,000 inhabitants more than the slave States; though Louisiana with her population, had in the mean time been added to the latter.

The free States continued to run ahead, gaining more and more on the slave States at each successive census, up to the last in 1840, when they had a population of 9,729,000, against 7,320,000 in the slave States.

This result is more surprising, when we consider that in 1790, the slave States had a territory embracing 220,000 square miles, against 160,000 square miles in the free States; and that as new States and Territories were added to the old, the class of slave States still gained in Territory, as they continued to fall behind in population. In 1840, the slaveholding Territory, actually inhabited, contained an area of 580,000 square miles, at least; while the inhabited free Territory, contained about 360,000 square miles. The slave country was therefore less than half as thickly peopled as the free country.

Some advocates of slavery apologize for this result, by ascribing it to foreign emigration, which, they say, goes almost wholly to the free States. We deny that it goes *almost wholly* to the free States: but if it did; what are we to infer from the fact? That slavery does not check the growth of States? No; but on the contrary, that it checks their growth in various ways; partly by repelling emigrants, who would come from the free States and from foreign countries—which it does: and partly by driving out free laborers from the slave States into the free States—which it does, also.

But this general comparison between the two classes of States, does not truly measure the effect of slavery in checking the growth and prosperity of States; because, in the first place, it takes in the new thinly peopled slave States, where slave labor operating on new soils of the best quality, has not had time to do its work of impoverishment and desolation; and because, in the second place, it takes in some States, both old and new, in which the slaves are com-

14

paratively few, and a predominance of free labor counteracts the destructive tendencies of slavery. Such are the old State of Maryland and the new State of Missouri; besides others—as Kentucky and Tennessee—in which slavery, though deeply injurious, is itself held in check by a free laboring population.

We will therefore take the old free States, and compare them with the old slave States of Virginia, the Carolinas and Georgia, in which slave labor predominates.

New England and the middle States of New York, New Jersey, and Pennsylvania, contained in 1790, 1,968,000 inhabitants, and in 1840, 6,760,000; having gained, in this period, 243 per cent.

The four old slave States had in 1790, a population of 1,473,000; and in 1840, of 3,279,000, having gained, in the same period, 122 per cent, just about half as much in proportion, as the free States. They ought to have gained about twice as much; for they had at first only seven inhabitants to the square mile, when the free States not only had upwards of twelve, but on the whole much inferior advantages of soil and climate. Even cold, barren New England, though more than twice as thickly peopled, grew in population at a faster rate than these old slave States.

About half the territory of these old slave States is new country, and has comparatively few slaves. On this part the increase of population has chiefly taken place. On the old slave-labored lowlands, a singular phenomenon has appeared: there, within the bounds of these rapidly growing United States,—yes, there, population has been long at a stand; yes, over wide regions—especially in Virginia—it has declined, and a new wilderness is gaining upon the cultivated land! What has done this work of desolation? Not war, nor pestilence; not oppression of rulers, civil or ecclesiastical;—but *slavery*, a curse more destructive in its effects than any of them. It were hard to find, in old king-ridden, priest-ridden, overtaxed, Europe, so large a country, where within twenty years past, such a growing poverty and desolation have appeared.

It is in the last period of ten years, from 1830 to 1840, that this consuming plague of slavery has shown its worst effects in the old Southern States. Including the increase in their newly settled, and Western counties, they gained in population only 7½ per cent; while cold, barren, thickly peopled, New England gained 15, and the old middle States, 26 per cent. East Virginia actually fell off 26,000 in population; and with the exception of Richmond and one or two other towns, her population continues to decline. Old Virginia was the first to sow this land of ours with slavery; she is also the first to reap the full harvest of destruction. Her lowland neighbors of Maryland and the Carolinas, were not far behind at the *seeding*; nor are they far behind at the ingathering of desolation. Most sorry are we for this fallen condition of "The Old Dominion," and of her neighbors; but such being the fact, we state it, as an argument and a warning to our West Virginia. It demonstrates the ruinous effects of slavery upon the countries in which the longest and most complete trial of it has been made.

15

There are certain drugs, of which large doses are poisonous, but small ones are innocent or even salutary. Slavery is not of this kind. Large doses of it kill, it is true; but smaller doses, mix them as you will, are sure to sicken and debilitate the body politic. This can be abundantly proved by examples. For one, let us take the rich and beautiful State of Kentucky, compared with her free neighbor Ohio. The slaves of Kentucky have composed less than a fourth part of her population. But mark their effect upon the comparative growth of the State. In the year 1800, Kentucky contained 221,000 inhabitants, and Ohio, 45,000. In forty years, the population of Kentucky had risen to 780,000; that of Ohio to 1,519,000. This wonderful difference could not be owing to any natural superiority of the Ohio country. Kentucky is nearly as large, nearly as fertile, and quite equal in other gifts of nature. She had greatly the advantage too in the outset of this forty years race of population. She started with 5½ inhabitants to the square mile, and came out with 20; Ohio started with one inhabitant to the square mile, and came out with 38. Kentucky had full possession of her territory at the beginning. Much of Ohio was then, and for a long time afterwards, in possession of the Indians. Ohio is by this time considerably more than twice as thickly peopled as Kentucky; yet she still gains both by natural increase and by the influx of emigrants; while Kentucky has for twenty years been receiving much fewer emigrants than Ohio, and multitudes of her citizens have been yearly moving off to newer and yet newer countries.

In Tennessee the proportion of slaves is about the same, and the effects are about the same, as in Kentucky. Missouri is too new a country to afford instruction on this subject; but her physical advantages are drawing such a multitude of free emigrants into her, that her small amount of slavery must, ere long, give way and vanish before "the genius of universal emancipation."

Maryland has comparatively few slaves, and these are found chiefly about her old tide water shores, where like the locusts, they have eaten up nearly every green thing. On the whole, the slaves of Maryland have composed between a fourth and a fifth part of her population. Her progress under this dead weight, has been much slower than that of her neighbor Pennsylvania; and would be completely stopped, if this free neighbor did not send a vivifying influence into her upper counties and her city of Baltimore.

Our own West Virginia furnishes conclusive evidence, that slavery, in all quantities and degrees, has a pernicious influence on the public welfare. But we reserve this example to a subsequent head of the argument, where we can present it in a more complete form.

We have now seen how slavery, when in full operation, first checks, and then stops, the growth of population; and finally turns it into a decline. We have seen also that slavery, when in partial operation, or mixed with a larger proportion of free labor, hangs like a dead weight upon a country, and makes it drag heavily onwards in the march of population.

Increase of population depends upon increase in the means of

16

living. Whenever the three great branches of productive industry, Agriculture, Manufactures and Commerce, or any of them, continue to yield increasing products, the population will increase at the same rate; because then industry produces a surplus beyond the present wants of the people, and more families can be supported. This is the general rule. The only exceptions to it are partial and temporary in their occurrence. Population may increase to a small degree, while the yearly products of industry are stationary; but then it can be, only by allowing to each individual a reduced share of products. In this case poverty and misery increase with the population, and must soon stop its progress. In this country, where emigration to new territories is so easy, the people are sure to relieve themselves by emigration, whenever the means of living begin to fail in their native place. Without some pressure of this sort, attachment to their native land is ordinarily sufficient to prevent men from emigrating. Some may emigrate without any feeling of necessity; but as many, if not more, will not emigrate, until want pinches them sorely.

We may lay it down as a general rule, therefore, that the quantity of emigration from a State is a pretty accurate index of its comparative prosperity. If few leave it, we may justly infer that its industry is thriving—sufficiently so to support the natural increase of its population, and to make nearly all contented at home. But if a large and perpetual stream of emigrants is pouring out of it in search of better fortune elsewhere;—it is an infallible symptom of one of two things; either that the country has no more natural sources from which industry may draw increasing products,—or that the people are defficient in enterprise and skill to improve the resources of their country.

Let us apply this rule to Virginia, and how will she appear? We take it for granted, that the people of Virginia multiply as fast, naturally, as the people of other States—that is, at the rate of 33½ per cent in ten years; so that if none emigrated, the number would be increased by one third in that period of time.

Compare this natural increase with the census returns, and it appears that in the ten years from 1830 to 1840, Virginia lost by emigration no fewer than 375,000 of her people, of whom East Virginia lost 304,000 and West Virginia 71,000. At this rate Virginia supplies the West every ten years with a population equal in number to the population of the State of Mississippi in 1840!

Some Virginia politicians proudly—yes, *proudly*,—fellow-citizens,—call our old Commonwealth, *The Mother of States!* These *enlightened* patriots might pay her a still higher compliment, by calling her *The Grandmother* of States. For our part, we are grieved and mortified, to think of the lean and haggard condition of our venerable mother. Her black children have sucked her so dry, that now, for a long time past, she has not milk enough for her offspring, either black or white.

But, seriously, fellow-citizens, we esteem it a sad, a humiliating, fact, which should penetrate the heart of every Virginian, that from

17

the year 1790 to this time, Virginia has lost more people by emigration, than all the old free States together. Up to 1840, when the last census was taken, she had lost more by nearly 300,000. She has sent—or we should rather say, she has driven from her soil—at least one third of all the emigrants, who have gone from the old States to the new. More than another third have gone from the other old slave States. Many of these multitudes, who have left the slave States, have shunned the regions of slavery, and settled in the free countries of the West. These were generally industrious and enterprising white men, who found by sad experience, that a country of slaves was not the country for them. It is a truth, a certain truth, that *slavery drives free laborers—farmers, mechanics, and all, and some of the best of them too—out of the country, and fills their places with negroes.*

What is it but slavery that makes Marylanders, Carolinians, and especially old Virginians and new Virginians—fly their country at such a rate? Some go because they dislike slavery and desire to get away from it: others, because they have gloomy forebodings of what is to befal the slave States, and wish to leave their families in a country of happier prospects: others, because they cannot get profitable employment among slaveholders: others, industrious and high-spirited working men, will not stay in a country where slavery degrades the working man: others go because they see that their country, for some reason, does not prosper, and that other countries, not far off, are prospering, and will afford better hopes of prosperity to themselves: others, a numerous class, who are slaveholders and cannot live without slaves, finding that they cannot live longer with them on their worn out soils, go to seek better lands and more profitable crops, where slave labor may yet for a while enable them and their children to live.

But you know well, fellow-citizens, that this perpetual drain of our population, does not arise from a failure of natural resources for living in Virginia. How could it, while so much good soil is yet a wilderness, and so much old soil could be fertilized; and while such resources for manufactures and commerce lie neglected?

Had Virginia retained her natural increase, or received as many emigrants as she sent away, from the year 1790 to the present time, she would now have had three times her actual population; and, had all been free-men, each laboring voluntarily, and for his own benefit, all could have prospered in her wide and richly-gifted territory.

The true cause of this unexampled emigration is, that no branch of industry flourishes, or can flourish among us, so long as slavery is established by law, and the labor of the country is done chiefly by men, who can gain nothing by assiduity, by skill, or by economy. All the older slaveholding States have proved this by sad experience. We shall make good the assertion by setting before you,

2. *A comparative view of the Agriculture, the Manufactures*

3

18

and the Commerce, of the old free States, and the old slave
States,—especially Virginia.

Thus we shall lay open the immediate causes of the vast emigration from our State, and of the slow growth of West Virginia and
Kentucky, in comparison with the neighboring free countries.

You will observe also, how every class of facts that bear at all upon
the subject, lead uniformly to the same conclusion; how every line
of inquiry always points to slavery, as the original cause of inferior
prosperity or of positive decline.

In our statements we always go upon the best evidence which can
be had,—generally official documents.

We begin with

The Agriculture of the old States.

The census of 1840 embraces returns of the number of live stock
in each State;—the estimated quantities of grain and other crops
raised the preceding year;—the value of poultry, of the products
of dairies, orchards and market gardens;—the quantities of fire-
wood, lumber, tar, &c., sold in each State;—together with the number of persons employed in agriculture.

The plan was to obtain a complete view of the agriculture of the
United States. Many errors undoubtedly exist in these returns,
partly from wrong estimates of the farmers, partly from the negligence
of the Deputy Marshals who took the census. Some blunders of
the latter are manifest upon the face of the returns; but these may
sometimes be corrected, if not perfectly, yet sufficiently for all useful purposes.

Be it observed, that what we want to know on the present occasion, is not the quantity to a bushel, nor the value to a dollar, of
the agricultural products of each State; but such a comparative view
of what the lands of the several States produce, in quantity and in
value, that we may form a substantially correct judgment of the relative productiveness of their agricultural industry. This we can do
beyond a reasonable doubt, by a judicious use of the census. Persons acquainted with this sort of investigations know, that although
each farmer in reporting his crops might commit some error, yet
when all the reports came to be summed up, the errors would tend
to balance one another; and that, as the same sorts of errors would
probably be committed in all the States, the returns might, on the
whole, be comparatively right, though each one was positively wrong.
Thus, if the returns for Virginia should be one-fourth below the
truth, and those for New York one-fourth below the truth; each
would be erroneous in itself, yet the two would truly represent the comparative products of agriculture in these States: and this is all that
we want in the present argument. But again, suppose that the errors
did not tally so exactly;—for example, that the returns for Virginia
were one-fourth below the truth, but for New York only one-fifth be-

19

low the truth ; yet if it appeared by the returns, that the agriculture of Virginia was only half as profitable as that of New York ; though the result would not show accurately *how much* less profitable our agriculture was, than that of New York ; yet it would truly show the fact, that it was *much* less profitable ;—and this degree of truth is sufficient for our argument.

Now if any man deny that this sufficient degree of truth can be deduced from the census ; he is bound to sustain his denial, by convicting the census of a greater amount of error than we have made allowance for ;—and that too, *in the very same returns that we use in our calculations.* But no man alive can do this ; for these returns are incomparably *the best evidence that exists on the subject,* and are substantially confirmed by the agricultural census of New York—(since made)—so far as that State is concerned ; and in fact, generally confirmed by all sorts of evidence, so far as any exists.

In the returns of hemp and flax raised in Virginia, there is an evident blunder of the Deputy Marshals in the counties of Bedford, Prince William, Lee and Lewis: where *hundred weights* reported, seem to have been set down as *tons.* With this exception, no great error appears. We have made the correction in our calculations ; but enormous as the error seems to be, it might stand without materially varying the comparative results.

By estimating the value of the yearly products of each State, and dividing the same by the number of persons employed in making those products, we find the average value produced by each person : and by comparing the results of the calculation for the several States, we discover the comparative productiveness of Agricultural labor in the States. This is what we want for our argument.

Professor Tucker, late of the University of Virginia, in his useful book, on The Progress of Population, &c., has given in detail a calculation of this sort. He was certainly not partial to the North in his estimates. We have carefully examined them ; and think that his valuations of products are in some particulars erroneous. We think, also, that he has omitted some elements necessary to an accurate result. We have therefore in our own calculations arrived at results somewhat different from his ; yet so far as our argument is concerned, the difference is immaterial. We can therefore assure you, fellow-citizens, that no sort of calculation, founded on any thing like truth or reason, can bring out a result materially different from ours.

We have not room here for the particulars that enter into the calculations : we can only give the results themselves.

The general results, according to both Mr. Tucker and ourselves, are as follows :

In New England, agricultural industry yields an annual value, averaging about one hundred and eighty dollars to the hand, that is, for each person employed.

In the middle States of New York, New Jersey and Pennsylvania,

20

the average is about two hundred and sixty-five or two hundred and seventy-dollars to the hand.

And in the old slave States, South of the Potomac, the average is about 130 dollars to the hand. This, according to our calculation, is rather above the average for East Virginia, but below that for West Virginia. The average for all Virginia is about 138 dollars.

Thus it appears by the best evidence which the case admits of, that the farmers of the middle States, with their free labor, produce more than twice as great a value to the hand, as the farmers and planters of the old slave States; and that even the New Englanders, on their poor soils and under their wintry sky, make nearly forty per cent more, to the hand, than the old Southerners make in the "sunny South," with the advantage of their valuable staples, cotton and tobacco.

In Maryland, the result is intermediate between the average of the North and that of the South: and this agrees strikingly with her condition as a half-slave State; for lower Maryland is cultivated by negroes, and has a languishing agriculture, as well as a stationary population: but upper Maryland is cultivated by free labor, and has a thriving agriculture with a growing population.

These results, founded on the best evidence, and confirmed by general observation, are for substance undubitably correct, and cannot be overthrown.

Now it is admitted on all hands, that slave labor is better adapted to agriculture, than to any other branch of industry; and that, if not good for agriculture, it is really good for nothing.

Therefore, since in agriculture, slave labor is proved to be far less productive than free labor,—*slavery is demonstrated to be not only unprofitable, but deeply injurious to the public prosperity.*

We do not mean that slave labor can never earn any thing for him that employs it. The question is between free labor and slave labor. He that chooses to employ a sort of labor, that yields only half as much to the hand as another sort would yield, makes a choice that is not only unprofitable, but deeply injurious to his interest.

Agriculture in the slave States may be characterized in general by two epithets—*extensive—exhaustive*—which in all agricultural countries forebode two things—*impoverishment—depopulation.* The general system of slaveholding farmers and planters, in all times and places, has been, and now is, and ever will be, to cultivate much land, badly, for present gain—in short, to kill the goose that lays the golden egg. They cannot do otherwise with laborers who work by compulsion, for the benefit only of their masters; and whose sole interest in the matter is, to do as little and to consume as much as possible.

This ruinous system of large farms cultivated by slaves, showed its effects in Italy, 1800 years ago, when the Roman empire was at the height of its grandeur.

Pliny, a writer of that age, in his Natural History, (Book 18, ch.

21

1—7,) tells us, that while the small farms of former times were cultivated by freemen, and even great commanders did not disdain to labor with their own hands, agriculture flourished, and provisions were abundant : but that afterwards, when the lands were engrossed by a few great proprietors, and cultivated by fettered and branded slaves, the country was ruined, and corn had to be imported. The same system was spreading ruin over the provinces, and thus the prosperity of the empire was undermined. Pliny denounces as the worst of all, the system of having large estates in the country cultivated by slaves, or indeed, says he, "*to have any thing done by men who labor without hope of reward.*"

So Livy, the great Roman historian, observed, some years before Pliny, (Book 6, ch. 12,) that "innumerable multitudes of men formerly inhabited those parts of Italy, where, in his time, none but slaves redeemed the country from desertion ;"—that is, a dense population of free laborers had been succeeded by a sparse population of slaves.

In further confirmation of our views of the unproductiveness of slave labor, when employed in agriculture, we call your earnest attention, fellow-citizens, to an address delivered to the Agricultural Clubs of Mecklenburg, Va., and Granville, N. C., on the 4th of July last, by James Bruce, Esq.

Mr. Bruce is an intelligent gentleman, and one of the largest slave-holders of Virginia. His opinion of slave labor is therefore entitled to great weight.

We have room for only a few extracts from his Address. After an estimate of the value of slave labor on the exhausted soil of Virginia, compared with its value in cultivating sugar and cotton on the exuberantly fertile bottoms of Louisiana, he says; "This calculation makes the average product of slave labor in Virginia a little over 22 dollars [a year, for each slave.] Thus we see that the profits of slave labor in Louisiana are more than four times greater than in Virginia. The inference seems to be very clear, if there be the remotest approach to accuracy in these calculations, that a large portion of our negroes should be sent to the South West.——I doubt whether every man who owns more than ten working hands, would not be better off by the sale or removal of all beyond that number. But, it may be said, shall we part with so large a portion of our labor, and leave our lands to waste? *Certainly if the labor be unproductive, it is folly to keep it. The slave adds nothing to the moral and physical strength of the country, and if his labor be profitless, of course he is a nuisance, and the sooner we rid ourselves of him the better. His place will soon be supplied with a better population,* and in the meantime the poorer lands will be thrown out of cultivation. The poorer lands in cultivation scarcely produce returns beyond the support of the laborers who cultivate them.——But, gentlemen, (continues Mr. Bruce) there is another view of this question, which should urge us to immediate removal. *All look to the period when the negro must leave Virginia and*

22

North Carolina. There is now a demand for this population, and the new States of the South are anxious to receive it. *The time is approaching when this demand may cease,*^{*} *and when their doors may be closed against the admission of our slaves.* Is it prudent to lose the present opportunity ? Is it not better to commence the work at once, and to do now what we may be unable to do, when the emergency becomes more pressing ?"

" Suppose (says Mr. Bruce again) all this *dead capital,* now invested in slaves, were to become an active monied capital, how many manufactories might be built ? How many improvements might be made ? Capital would attract labor,† labor for our workshops and our fields. *We should soon have a dense population, which would give schools to our children, a market to our farmers, and those railroads which we now clamor for, but which our poverty and a sparse population places far beyond our reach.*"

Every sentence in these extracts contains an important truth; and especially do the lines that we have marked with *Italic letters* deserve the maturest consideration of every citizen of Virginia.

Agriculture, according to Mr. Bruce, cannot flourish among us, because slave labor is unproductive, and keeps down the population, —also because it prevents the growth of manufactures, and thereby deprives our farmers of a home market, the most valuable of all;—also because it disables the country to construct railroads and canals, to facilitate trade and travel; and finally, we may add, because it destroys the spirit of industry and enterprise in the white population, and thus prevents them from doing what is yet in their power to do for the improvement of the country.

Thus it comes to pass that lower Virginia with stores of fertilizing marl on her extensive shores, still goes on to impoverish probably ten times as much land as she fertilizes;—that the valley, though full of limestone and fertile subsoil, is on the whole becoming more exhausted by a too wide-spread and shallow cultivation;— and that West Virginia in general,—to mention but one of many particulars,—still leaves unoccupied the cheapest and the best sheepwalks in the United States, and confines her husbandry to a few old staple products; while New York and Vermont, in their snowy climate, gain millions of dollars annually by sheep-husbandry.

In 1840, Vermont had 160 sheep to the square mile, and New York, in her Northern districts, nearly as many: whilst Virginia had only 20 to the square mile,—few of them fine-wooled sheep, and these few chiefly on her Northern border, near free Pennsylvania.

No doubt sheep could be kept among our mountains, at one third

---

*We will add to Mr. Bruce's remark, that the time is not distant, when the Southern demand for slaves *must* cease, and the surplus of this population in old Virginia be diffused over West Virginia—as we may show before we close this address.

†He means free labor; and thus suggests his opinion of the superior productiveness of free labor, for which he would make room by removing the slaves.

23

of what they cost in those cold Northern countries, where they must be stabled and fed during the five snowy months.

Suppose that the mountains of Virginia were as well stocked with improved breeds of sheep as those North countries; they would now be pastured by six millions of those useful animals; whose yearly product of wool and lambs would be worth seven or eight millions of dollars; and the keeping of them would furnish profitable occupation for 12,000 families of free citizens. Then how changed would be the scene! Our desolate mountains enlivened with flocks; and ten thousand now silent nooks and dells, vocal with the songs of Liberty,—"The Mountain Nymph, sweet Liberty"!—Why is it not so in our mountains?—They who keep slaves cannot keep sheep. The occupation requires care; but what do slaves care? Poor wretches! what should make them care?

A few significant facts will conclude this sketch of our slave-system of agriculture. The towns and cities of lower Virginia are supplied with a great part of their hay, butter, potatoes, and other vegetables, not from the farms of Virginia, but from those of the free States. And even our great pastoral valley imports cheese in large quantities from the North.

Next we shall notice briefly

The Influence of Slavery on Manufactures.

It matters not to our argument, whether a high tariff or a low tariff be thought best for the country. Whatever aid the tariff may give to manufactures, it gives the same in all parts of the United States. Under the protective tariffs formerly enacted, manufactures have grown rapidly in the free States; but no tariff has been able to push a slaveholding State into this important line of industry. Under the present revenue tariff, manufactures still grow in the North; and the old South, as might be expected, exhibits no movement, except the customary one of emigration. We hear indeed, once in a while, a loud report in Southern newspapers, that "The South is waking up," because some new cotton mill, or other manufacturing establishment, has been erected in a slave State: a sure sign that in the slave States an event of this sort is extraordinary. In the free States it is so ordinary, as to excite little attention.

Even the common mechanical trades do not flourish in a slave State. Some mechanical operations must, indeed, be performed in every civilized country; but the general rule in the South is, to import from abroad every fabricated thing that can be carried in ships, such as household furniture, boats, boards, laths, carts, ploughs, axes and axehelves, besides innumerable other things, which free communities are accustomed to make for themselves. What is most wonderful, is, that the forests and iron-mines of the South supply, in great part, the materials out of which these things are made. The Northern freemen come with their ships, carry home the timber and pig-iron, work them up, supply their own wants with a part, and then sell the rest at a good profit in the Southern markets.—

21

Now, although mechanics, by setting up their shops in the South, could save all these freights and profits; yet so it is, that Northern mechanics will not settle in the South, and the Southern mechanics are undersold by their Northern competitors.

Now connect with these wonderful facts another fact, and the mystery is solved. The number of mechanics in different parts of the South, is in the inverse ratio of the number of slaves: or in other words, where the slaves form the largest proportion of the inhabitants, there the mechanics and manufacturers form the least. In those parts only where the slaves are comparatively few, are many mechanics and artificers to be found; but even in these parts they do not flourish, as the same useful class of men flourish in the free States. Even in our Valley of Virginia, remote from the sea, many of our mechanics can hardly stand against Northern competition. This can be attributed only to slavery, which paralyzes our energies, disperses our population, and keeps us few and poor, in spite of the bountiful gifts of nature, with which a benign Providence has endowed our country.

Of all the States in this Union, not one has on the whole such various and abundant resources for manufacturing, as our own Virginia, both East and West. Only think of her vast forests of timber, her mountains of iron, her regions of stone coal, her valleys of limestone and marble, her fountains of salt, her immense sheepwalks for wool, her vicinity to the cotton fields, her innumerable waterfalls, her bays, harbors and rivers for circulating products on every side;—in short every material and every convenience necessary for manufacturing industry.

Above all, think of Richmond, nature's chosen site for the greatest manufacturing city in America—her beds of coal and iron, just at hand—her incomparable water-power—her tide water navigation, conducting sea vessels from the foot of her falls,—and above them her fine canal to the mountains, through which lie the shortest routes from the Eastern tides to the great rivers of the West and the South West. Think also that this Richmond in old Virginia, "the mother of States," has enjoyed these unparalleled advantages ever since the United States became a nation;—and then think again, that this same Richmond, the metropolis of all Virginia, has fewer manufactures than a third rate New England town;—fewer—not than the new city of Lowell, which is beyond all comparison,—but fewer than the obscure place called Fall River, among the barren hills of Massachusetts:—and then fellow-citizens, what will you think,—what *must* you think—of the cause of this strange phenomenon? Or, to enlarge the scope of the question: What must you think has caused Virginians in general to neglect their superlative advantages for manufacturing industry?—to disregard the evident suggestions of nature, pointing out to them this fruitful source of population, wealth and comfort?

Say not that this state of things is chargeable to the *apathy* of Virginians. That is nothing to the purpose, for it does not go to the bottom of the subject. What causes the apathy? That is the

25

question. Some imagine that they give a good reason when (leaving out the apathy) they say, that Virginians are devoted exclusively to agriculture. But why should they be, when their agriculture is failing them, and they are flying by tens of thousands from their worn out fields to distant countries? Necessity, we are told by these reasoners, drive the New Englanders from agriculture in their barren country, to trade and manufactures. So it did : Necessity drives all mankind to labors and shifts for a living. Has necessity, the mother of invention, ever driven Virginians to trade and manufactures? No; but it drives them in multitudes from their native country. They cannot be driven to commerce and manufactures. What is the reason of that? If a genial climate and a once-fertile soil wedded them to agriculture, they should have wedded them also to their native land. Yet when agriculture fails them at home, rather than let mines, and coal beds, and waterfalls, and timber-forests, and the finest tide rivers and harbors in America, allure them to manufactures and commerce, they will take their negroes and emigrate a thousand miles. This remarkable fact, that they will quit their country rather than their ruinous system of agriculture, proves that their institution of slavery disqualifies them to pursue any occupation, except their same ruinous system of agriculture. We admit that some few individuals should be excepted from this conclusion : but these few being excepted, we have given you the conclusion of the whole matter; and as Lorenzo Dow used to say—

You cannot deny it.

But many Virginians, from the rarity of manufactures among them, are apt to conceive so largely of those that they see or hear of in our State, that they can hardly be persuaded of the exceeding deficiency of Virginia in this branch of industry. Therefore, in order to establish the truth of all that we have said on this subject, we shall give you from the census of 1840, a comparative view of the manufactures of some of the Free States, and of Maryland and Virginia. We go no farther South in our comparison, but remark what is well known to be true, that the farther South, and the larger the proportion of slaves, the fewer are the manufactures of the country.

We begin with IRON-MAKING, which, although an agricultural operation according to the political economists, is however commonly classed with manufactures. In the returns of the census for Virginia, there is an evident blunder ; one furnace in Brunswick county being reported to have made 5000 tons of cast metal. We have reduced this to 500 tons; which cannot be below the truth. With this exception, the returns for Virginia are probably correct. Those for some of the Northern States are certainly defective—but we take them as they are.

We put together the three New England States of Vermont, Massachusetts and Connecticut, which are in size and resources for iron-making, equal to about one-third of Virginia. New York is inferior to Virginia in iron mines, and Pennsylvania about equal.

3

26

New Jersey and Maryland are not half so richly furnished with ore-beds as our State.

Putting cast iron and bar iron together for brevity's sake, we find by the census that the three New England States made about 33,-000 tons a year; New York 82,000 tons; New Jersey 18,000 tons; Maryland 19,000 tons; Pennsylvania 186,000 tons; Virginia 20,-000 tons; and young Ohio, with less than half the resources of Virginia, 43,000 tons. The two Carolinas together made 4,000 tons. If we value the cast iron at thirty dollars a ton, and the bar iron at fifty dollars, exclusive of the value of the pig metal used in making it, then Pennsylvania, the only State that has resources for iron-making equal to those of Virginia, made iron to the value of about 7,400,000 dollars a year, and Virginia, to the value of 720,000 dollars,—less than one-tenth.

Next, in order to save room, we put together the values of the manufactures of *Cotton, Wool, Leather*, and articles manufactured out of iron and steel, such as *Cutlery, Hardware, &c.* We also put together the three New England States of Massachusetts, Connecticut and Rhode Island, which are in size equal to about one-fifth of Virginia, and in natural resources for manufactures, to about one-tenth.

The total value of these four manufactures was.—In the three New England States, fifty millions of dollars; in New York, twenty-one millions; In little New Jersey, six millions; In Pennsylvania, sixteen millions; In Maryland, three and a half millions; and in Virginia two and three-fourth millions: So even half-slaveholding Maryland, a comparatively small State, beats Virginia in these manufactures: and as to the wholly free States, why, you see how the comparison stands.

To give a clearer idea of the comparative amount of these manufactures, we divide the total value in the several States by their population; and thus find how much it makes on the average for each individual. In the three New England States, the average is forty-five dollars a head; in New York, nine dollars; in New Jersey, sixteen; in Pennsylvania, nine; in Maryland seven and a half; and in Virginia two and a fourth.

If we had taken into the calculation all the various kinds of manufacture, the result of the comparison would not be materially different. We may say therefore that the old Free States have in general about seven or eight times as large a proportion of manufactures, as our old State of Virginia has, notwithstanding her superior resources for that branch of industry.

The last census gave also the cost of constructing new buildings in each State, exclusive of the value of the materials. The amount of this is a good test of the increase of wealth in a country. To compare different States in this particular, we must divide the total cost of building by the number of inhabitants, and see what the average will be for each inhabitant. We find that it is in Massachusetts, $3 60 cents; in Connecticut, $3 50 cents; in New York,

27

$3 00; in New Jersey, $2 70 cents; in Pennsylvania, $3 10 cents; in Maryland, $2 30 cents; and in Virginia, $1 10 cents.

The census enables us also to find what proportion there is between the number of persons employed in agriculture, and the number employed in mechanical trades and manufactures. By calculation we find, that for every 100 persons employed in agriculture, there are employed in manufactures and trades, the following numbers, viz: in Massachusetts, 98; in Connecticut, 49; in New York, 38; in New Jersey, 48; in Pennsylvania, 51; in Maryland, 20; and in Virginia, 17.

All these successive comparisons, that we have made between the principal old free States and Virginia, coincide in their general results; and thus prove each other to be approximately correct,—sufficiently so to answer the purpose of our present argument. The reader must have observed also, how uniformly half-slaveholding Maryland serves as an intermediate stepping-stone, as we descend from the high level of Northern prosperity, to the low ground of Virginia depression.

Surely we need say no more to satisfy every one of you, fellow-citizens, that trades and manufactures do not flourish in Virginia; that they are indeed in a very low state; though nature has done every thing that nature can do, to make them easy and profitable to our people.

———————————————

Let us now turn to the third great branch of productive industry,

Commerce and Navigation.

The Northern people derive much of their wealth from commerce and shipping. But the slave States are more deficient in these, than they are in manufactures. They only make cotton and tobacco for Northern men and foreigners to buy and ship. We have mentioned, in general terms, the excellent facilities which our State possesses for commercial pursuits. We may say, that her bay and tide-rivers all make one great haven, 500 miles long, situated midway between the Northern and Southern extremes of our Atlantic coast. Norfolk is the natural centre of the foreign and coasting trade of the United States. It ought to have commanded the trade of North Carolina, of all the countries upon the waters of the Chesapeake, and of half the Great West. It ought to have been the second, if not the first, commercial city in the United States.

Norfolk is an ancient borough, and once stood in the first rank of American seaports. But its trade declined, its population was long at a stand, and nothing but the public Navy Yard has kept it up. Meanwhile, Northern towns have grown up to cities, and Northern cities to great and wealthy emporiums; until our Virginia seaport, once their equal, would cut a poor figure among their suburbs. Oh

28

that Norfolk were as prosperous, as her citizens are kind and hospitable!

This sketch of the natural advantages of Norfolk, compared with its condition, is a good index of the commercial history of Virginia. In fact the commerce of our old slave-eaten Commonwealth, has decayed and dwindled away to a mere pittance in the general mass of American trade.

The value of her exports, which twenty-five or thirty years ago, averaged four or five millions of dollars a year, shrunk by 1842, to 2,820,000 dollars, and by 1845, to 2,100,000 dollars.

Her imports from foreign countries, were, in the year 1765, valued at upwards of 4,000,000 of dollars: in 1791, they had sunk to 2½ millions; in 1821, they had fallen to a little over one million; in 1827, they had come down to about half this sum; and in 1843, to the half of this again, or about one-quarter of a million; and here they have stood ever since,—at next to nothing.

So our great Virginia, with all her natural facilities for trade, brings to her ports about one five-hundredth part of the goods, wares and merchandize, imported into the United States.

Shall we be told that the cause of this decline of Virginia commerce, is the growth of Northern cities; which by means of their canals and railroads and vast capital, draw off the trade from smaller ports to themselves? And what then? The cause assigned is itself the effect of a prior cause. We would ask those who take this superficial view of the matter: Why should the great commercial ports be all outside of Virginia, and near or in the free States? Why should every commercial improvement, every wheel that speeds the movements of trade, serve but to carry away from the slave States, more and more of their wealth, for the benefit of the great Northern cities? The only cause that can be assigned, is, that where slavery prevails, commerce and navigation cannot flourish, and commercial towns cannot compete with those in the free States. They are merely places of deposit, for such country produce, as cannot be carried directly to the Northern markets. Here Northern and foreign ships come to carry away these products of slave labor—and this constitutes nearly all the trade of Southern ports.

No State has greater conveniencies for ship navigation and ship building, than Virginia. Yet on all her fine tide waters, she has little shipping; and what she has, is composed almost wholly of small bay craft and a few coasting schooners. The tonnage of Virginia —that is, the number of tons that her vessels will carry—is shamefully small, compared with that of the maritime free States. Maine and Massachusetts, with about an equal population, have about fifteen times as much; little Rhode Island has considerably more; New York has at least twelve times as much; Pennsylvania, with her one sea port, has more than twice as much; and so has half-slaveholding Maryland.

As to ship building, Virginia, that ought, with her eminent advan-

29

tages for the business, to build as many ships as any State in the Union, does less at it than the least of those free States. All that she builds in a year on her long forest-girt shores, would carry only eight or nine hundred tons—that is, about as much as one good packet ship of the North. Maine and Massachusetts build thirty-five times as much; little Rhode Island builds twice as much; New York twenty times as much; Pennsylvania twelve times as much; and Maryland seven times as much; and what would astonish us, if we did not know so many like facts, is, that much of the ship timber used in the North, is actually carried in ships from our Southern forests, where it might rot before Southern men would use it for any such purpose. We do not blame our Southern people for abstaining from all employments of this kind. What could they do? Set their negroes to building ships? Who ever imagined such an absurdity? But could they not hire white men to do such things? No: for in the first place, Southern white men have no skill in such matters; and in the second place, Northern workmen cannot be hired in the South, without receiving a heavy premium for working in a slave State.

Here we close our general review of the effects of slavery upon the population and the productive industry of States.

We shall now advert briefly to the effects of slavery upon

Common Schools and Popular Education.

There are two ways of estimating the degree of general education and intelligence among a people: the one is, to judge by the number of children going to school; and the other, to judge by the number of grown people who are unable to read or write. The last census contains returns of all these things.

1. The number of scholars that attended school during some part of the year, was in New England and New York, one to every four and a half white persons; in New Jersey and Pennsylvania, one to every nine; in Maryland, one to every nineteen; in Virginia, one to every twenty-one; and in the Carolinas, one to every twenty-seven.

2. In respect to the number of grown white persons unable to read or write, we have to remark, that the returns of the census for all the States, are somewhat defective; for the Southern States exceedingly so, on account of the great numbers of this class of persons, and their reluctance to confess their ignorance. The school systems in the North have made the number very small, excepting the foreign emigrants, who brought their ignorance with them. In the South, not only is the number known to be very large, but they are chiefly natives. Hence it is only in the South, that the defects

30

in the returns prevent us from forming an accurate judgment of the amount of popular ignorance, resulting from the want of an efficient school system. In the returns for Virginia, there are eight or ten counties in which few or none of this class were returned ; and in many other counties, the numbers returned are evidently far short of the truth. We ought certainly to add one-third to the total return, to bring it near the truth. The number returned for Virginia, is 58,787 : the actual number could not have been under 80,000. But to be sure of not exceeding the truth, we put it 70,000. We also put North Carolina at 60,000, and South Carolina at 24,000 ; which exceed the returns, but certainly fall short of the actual numbers.

By examining the census, we find that the adult part of the population is about one-half of the whole. We compare the numbers of white adults who cannot read, with the total number in each State : and find that in New England, these illiterates are as one, to one hundred and seventy : in New York, as one to fifty-three ; in New Jersey, as one to fifty-five ; in Pennsylvania, as one to forty-nine ; in Maryland, as one to twenty-five ; in Virginia, as one to five and a half; in North Carolina, as one to four and a half; and in South Carolina, as one to five and a half.

We give these only as approximations to the truth ; but they are sufficiently near to show, beyond any manner of doubt, that slavery exerts a most pernicious influence on the cause of education. This it does by keeping the white population thinly scattered and poor, and making the poorer part of them generally indifferent about the education of their children.

A similar difference between the free States and slave States, appears in the West, when we compare Ohio with Kentucky and Tennessee. Four times as large a proportion of children attend school in Ohio, as in the other two States ; while the proportion of illiterates is only one-fourth as great. On the whole, the evidence on this subject is complete and unquestionable. The people in the slave States are not, and cannot be, half as well accommodated with schools, as in the free States ; and slavery inflicts on multitudes of them the curse of ignorance and mental degradation through life.

Having thus briefly, yet we believe sufficiently, established the proposition that *slavery is pernicious to the welfare of States ;* we shall conclude the argument by establishing the particular proposition, that *slavery is pernicious to the welfare of West Virginia.* This being contained in the general proposition, does not need any separate proof; yet, lest some people should imagine that West Virginia is an exception, and has not suffered from slavery, we shall demonstrate to you the contrary by plain facts—facts derived from actual experience—the very best evidence which the nature of the case admits of. We compare the past progress and present condition of West Virginia, with the past progress and present condition of the countries adjacent to her.

31

Fellow-citizens, has it occurred to you to notice the fact, that West Virginia is almost as large as the State of Ohio? If the counties of Allegany and Washington, in Maryland, were added to her, she would be larger than Ohio.—" Oh, but Ohio is a much better country than West Virginia."—About half the State of Ohio is better, we grant—that is, it is a better farming country ;—but the other half is not so good. About one third of Ohio consists of dismal swamps and poor hills. In mineral wealth our country is decidedly superior. Taking every thing except slavery into consideration, we say that West Virginia ought now to have had more than two thirds as much population and wealth as Ohio. Our great valley is a comparatively old country, and naturally not much inferior to the best parts of Ohio. But instead of two-thirds, we have not more than one-fourth of her population and wealth. In proportion to our natural resources and actual population, we do not grow even one-third as fast as Ohio, and our lands in proportion to quality, are not on the whole more than half as valuable.

But West Pennsylvania furnishes a comparison free from all reasonable objection or doubt ; for it is a country in the same range of mountains, and similar in every respect, except that it has a harsher climate. Some say that it is on the whole less fertile. It is not so large by 5,500 square miles ; containing 33,000, while West Virginia contains 38,500 square miles.

Let us see

1. The comparative growth and population of West Virginia and West Pennsylvania.

In 1830, West Virginia contained 378,000 inhabitants.
In 1840,   "   "   "   432,000   "
The increase was 54,000, or 14¼ per cent.
In 1830, West Pennsylvania contained 593,000 inhabitants.
In 1840,   "   "   "   815,000   "
The increase was 222,000, or 37¼ per cent.

West Virginia increased in these ten years, about one and a half to the square mile, and ended with a population of eleven and a half souls to the square mile.

West Pennsylvania increased in the same time, about seven to the square mile, and ended with a population of nearly twenty-five to the square mile.

The *Great Valley* of Virginia, between the Blue Ridge and Allegany, and from Montgomery county to the Potomac river, has an area of 10,100 square miles. The same Valley with no material change of character, extends from the Potomac to the Susquehanna river, containing an area of 5,100 square miles, in the counties of

32

Cumberland, Franklin, Perry, Huntingdon and Bedford, in Pennsylvania, and Washington, in Maryland; which last, though a few slaves remain in it, is a county of free labor. But it might be omitted, with no sensible change in the result of our comparison.

The Virginia section of the Valley contained,

> In 1820, a population of 154,000,
> In 1830,   "   " 174,300,
> In 1840,   "   " 175,500.

The Northern section of the Valley, on half the space, contained,

> In 1820, a population of 129,600,
> In 1830,   "   " 155,500,
> In 1840,   "   " 179,500.

The Virginia section increased moderately, the first ten years; but scarcely at all, the second ten. The total increase in twenty years, was less than fourteen per cent.

The Northern section kept on, all the time, increasing at a good rate; and gained in the twenty years, thirty-eight and a half per cent, nearly three times as much as the Virginia section.

Yet the Virginia section was at last only half as thickly peopled as the other, and ought therefore to have grown twice as fast. Instead of that, it came almost to a full stop, the last ten years: in fact the newer mountain counties, where there are almost no slaves, and they only, increased a little: the other and richer counties, where slaves were numerous, and had been gaining on the white population— these counties have increased very little for twenty years; some of them have rather declined. The land has already got slave-sick, and is spewing out its inhabitants.

What a pity that so rich and so lovely a land, should be afflicted with this *yellow* fever and this *black* vomit.

But let us return to the general comparison.

The AGRICULTURE of West Pennsylvania is much better conducted, and much more prosperous, than that of West Virginia. We have calculated its productiveness from the census tables, in the manner before described; and we find that the farming industry of West Pennsylvania yields the annual value of two hundred and twelve dollars to the hand; that of West Virginia, one hundred and fifty-eight dollars to the hand. This result is substantially correct; for the lands of West Pennsylvania are much more highly valued, than those of similar natural qualities in West Virginia. This is true, both in the Great Valley, and West of the Allegany. Mark that fact, fellow-citizens; it is worthy of deep consideration; it is full of meaning. Lands in West Virginia are much cheaper than similar lands in

33

the free country North of Virginia. Yet rather than buy and cultivate these good cheap Virginia lands, Northern farmers go farther,
pay more, and fare worse;—so they do, and so they will. They
look upon all Virginia as an *infected country* ;—and so it is.

Next, the *Iron-making Business.*

West Virginia had, in 1840, as good natural resources, in every
respect, for making iron, as West Pennsylvania. Yet, according to
the census of 1840, (when no stone-coal was used in iron furnaces,)
West Virginia made only 14,660 tons of cast and of bar iron, a
year; when West Pennsylvania, made 116,530 tons. The value of
the West Virginia iron was 515,000 dollars, that of West Pennsylvania iron was 4,763,000 dollars. The West Virginia iron masters made seventy per cent on their capital, and 390 dollars worth
to the hand—chiefly slaves. The West Pennsylvania iron-masters
made 109 per cent on their capital, and 720 dollars worth to the
hand :—all free laborers.

There is no sign of material error in the census returns, from
which we derive these results ; and no error can be supposed, which
would materially change them.

The iron business has since increased in West Virginia ; it has
increased vastly more in West Pennsylvania.

Next, *Manufactures.*

If to the value of the cast and the bar iron of each country, we
add the value of the manufactures of iron and steel, of wool, cotton
and leather, we get a total of 770,000 dollars in West Virginia, and
about six millions of dollars in West Pennsylvania.

The cost of constructing new buildings, amounted, in West Virginia, to about one-fourth of what it did in West Pennsylvania ; indicating an increase in wealth and population at the same comparative rate.

Manufactures make towns, and towns make good markets for farmers ; the larger the towns the better the markets, and the more valuable the lands near them. The Pennsylvania towns are larger and
more numerous than the Virginia towns, both in the Valley and West
of it. The boast of our West Virginia is the good city of Wheeling. Would that she were six times as large, that she might equal
Pittsburg, and that she grew five times as fast, that she might keep
up with her.

We glory in Wheeling, because she only, in Virginia, deserves to
be called a manufacturing town. For this her citizens deserve to be
crowned—not with laurel—but with the solid gold of prosperity.
But how came it, that Wheeling, and next to her, Wellsburg—of

5

34

all the towns in Virginia—should become manufacturing towns?—Answer: They breathe the atmosphere of free States, almost touching them on both sides.—But again; seeing that Wheeling, as a seat for manufactures, is equal to Pittsburg, and inferior to no town in America, except Richmond; and that moreover, she has almost no slaves:—why is Wheeling so far behind Pittsburg, and comparatively so slow in her growth?—Answer: She is in a country in which slavery is established by law.

Thus it appears, fellow-citizens, by infallible proofs, that West Virginia, in all her parts and in all her interests, has suffered immensely from the institution of slavery.

The bad policy of the Legislature in former times, in respect to roads and land surveys west of the Allegany, did great injury to the country. But after allowance is made for this, a vast balance of injury is chargeable to slavery, and to nothing else. In the Great Valley, where the other causes had little or no operation, the effects of slavery are most manifest and most pernicious. In those parts West of the Allegany, upon the Ohio and its navigable waters, where want of roads and disputed land titles did least injury—there too the corrosive touch of slavery has also shown its cankerous effects.

Here, fellow-citizens, we conclude the general argument; not because we have exhausted our materials—far from it—but because you will think we have said enough for the present. We shall now, by way of appendix to the argument, lay down three propositions, to show the necessity of immediate action, to deliver our West Virginia from the growing evils of slavery.

1. *Comparatively few slaves in a country, especially one like ours, may do it immense injury.*

This has been already proved; but we wish to impress it on your minds. We shall, therefore, explain by examples, how a few slaves in a country may do its citizens more immediate injury, than a large number.

When a white family own fifty or one hundred slaves, they can, so long as their land produces well, afford to be indolent and expensive in their habits; for though each slave yield only a small profit, yet each member of the family has ten or fifteen of these black work-animals to toil for his support. It is not until the fields grow old, and the crops grow short, and the negroes and the overseer take nearly all, that the day of ruin can be no longer postponed. If the family be not *very* indolent and *very* expensive, this inevitable day may not come before the third generation. But the ruin of small slaveholders, is often accomplished in a single life-time.

When a white family own five or ten slaves, they cannot afford to be indolent and expensive in their habits; for one black drudge can-

35

not support one white gentleman or lady. Yet, because they are slaveholders, this family will feel some aspirations for a life of easy gentility ; and because field work and kitchen work are negroes' work, the young gentlemen will dislike to go with the negroes to dirty field work, and the young ladies will dislike to join the black sluts in any sort of household labor.—Such unthrifty sentiments are the natural consequence of introducing slaves among the families of a country ; especially negro-slaves. They infallibly grow and spread, creating among the white families a distaste for all servile labor, and a desire to procure slaves who may take all drudgery off their hands. Thus general industry gives way by degrees to indolent relaxation, false notions of dignity and refinement, and a taste for fashionable luxuries. Then debts slyly accumulate. The result is, that many families are compelled by their embarrassments to sell off and leave the country. Many who are unable to buy slaves, leave it also, because they feel degraded, and cannot prosper where slavery exists. Citizens of the Valley ! Is it not so ? Is not this the chief reason why your beautiful country does not prosper like the Northern Valleys.

2. *Slavery naturally tends to increase from small beginnings, until the slaves out-number the whites, and the country is ruined.*

How this comes to pass, is partly explained in the preceding remarks.

The tendency of a slave population to gain upon the whites, may be counteracted by local causes, permanent or temporary. One permanent cause is the vicinity of a free State ; a temporary cause occurred ten or twelve years ago, when the high price of negroes in the South, caused many to be sold out of our Valley. The tendency is stronger also in a planting country, than it is in a farming or grazing country ; yet so strong is the tendency itself, that it overcomes this check in West Virginia ; for with the temporary exception just alluded to, the slave population has been steadily gaining on the white, in all parts except the vicinity of the free States.

We have examined the census of counties for the last thirty or forty years, in Maryland, Virginia and North Carolina, with the view to discover the law of population in the Northern slave States. The following are among the general results.

When a county had at first comparatively few slaves, the slave population—except near the free borders—gained upon the whites, and most rapidly in the older parts of the country.

The population, as a whole, increased so long as the slaves were fewer than the whites, but more slowly as the numbers approached to equality. In our Valley, a smaller proportion of slaves had the effect of a larger one in East Virginia, to retard the increase of population.

When the slaves became as numerous as the whites in the Eastern and older parts of the country, population came to a stand ; when they outnumbered the whites, it declined. Consequently, the slave

37

the slave population; for cotton and sugar are the only crops in which the slaves can be profitably employed; and the production of sugar cannot increase faster than that of cotton. There will be no stoppage for want of good land; Texas has enough to produce ten times the quantity of the present annual crop.

But the consumption of cotton cannot increase at the same rate. The population of the countries that consume our cotton, does not double itself in less than 60 years; how then can they double their consumption in 18 years, or even twice that period? Therefore the price of cotton must fall, and the Southern demand for Virginia negroes must cease.

2. Good policy will require the Southern States, ere long, to close their markets against Northern negroes. The natural increase of their present stock of slaves, will increase the production of cotton as fast as the market will bear. Their short crops have always brought them more money than their full crops; showing that it is their interest to restrict the quantity within certain limits. A small excess in the quantity causes a ruinous fall in the price. Suppose the average profit to the planters to be now two cents to the pound; then a fall of one cent takes away half the profit and half the value of their slave labor; and a fall of two cents would ruin the business. Good reason, therefore, had Mr. Bruce to apprehend that the Southern slave market might, ere long, be closed; and to urge Virginians to hasten the removal of their negroes to the South.

But whether it be closed or not, one thing is evident,—that the value of slaves in the market must decline more and more. What then?

3. When the Southern slave market is closed, or when, by the reduced profits of slave labor in the South, it becomes glutted;— then the stream of Virginia negroes, heretofore pouring down upon the South, will be thrown back upon the State, and like a river damned up, must spread itself over the whole territory of the commonwealth. The head spring in East Virginia cannot contain itself; it must find vent; it will shed its black streams through every gap of the Blue Ridge and pour over the Alleghany, till it is checked by abolitionism on the borders. But even abolitionism cannot finally stop it. Abolitionism itself will tolerate slavery, when slaveholders grow sick and tired of it.

In plain terms, fellow-citizens, Eastern slaveholders will come with their multitudes of slaves to settle upon the fresh lands of West Virginia. Eastern slaves will be sent by thousands for a market in West Virginia. Every valley will echo with the cry "Negroes! Negroes for sale! Dog cheap! Dog cheap!" And because they are dog cheap, many of our people will buy them. We have shown how slavery has prepared the people for this: how a little slavery makes way for more, and how the law of slave-increase operates to fill up every part of the country to the same level with slaves.

And then, fellow-citizens, when you have suffered your country to be filled with negro-slaves instead of white freemen; when its

38

population shall be as motley as Joseph's coat of many colors,—as ring-streaked and speckled as father Jacob's flock was in Padan Aram;—what will the white basis of representation avail you, if you obtain it? Whether you obtain it or not, East Virginia will have triumphed; or rather *slavery* will have triumphed, and all Virginia will have become a land of darkness and of the shadow of death.

Then by a forbearance which has no merit, and a supineness which has no excuse, you will have given to your children for their inheritance, this lovely land blackened with a negro population— the offscourings of Eastern Virginia,—the fag-end of slavery—the loathesome dregs of that cup of abomination, which has already sickened to death the Eastern half of our commonwealth.

Delay not then, we beseech you, to raise a barrier against this Stygian inundation,—to stand at the Blue Ridge, and with sovereign energy say to this Black Sea of misery, "Hitherto shalt thou come, and no farther."

To show that the extinction of slavery among us is practicable without injustice or injury to any man, we present you the following

Outlines of a Scheme for the Removal of Slavery.

1. *Let the farther importation of slaves into West Virginia be prohibited by law.*

The expediency of this measure is obvious.

2. *Let the exportation of slaves be freely permitted, as heretofore; but with this restriction, that children of slaves, born after a certain day, shall not be exported at all after they are five years old, nor those under that age, unless the slaves of the same negro family be exported with them.*

When the emancipation of the after-born children of slaves shall be decreed, many slaves will be exported, from various motives. The restriction is intended to prevent slaveholders from defeating the benevolent intentions of the law, by selling into slavery those entitled to freedom, and old enough to appreciate the privilege designed for them. Young children are allowed to be taken away with their parents and older brothers and sisters, but not to be sold off separately to evade the law.

3. *Let the existing generation of slaves remain in their present condition, but let their offspring, born after a certain day, be emancipated at an age not exceeding 25 years.*

By this measure slavery will be slowly but surely abolished, without detriment or inconvenience to slaveholders. No pecuniary loss can be sustained, except at the option of the slaveholders, who, if they think that the measure will diminish the value of their slaves in West Virginia, can sell them for exportation or take them away,

39

with the certainty of making more out of them in that way, than they could by keeping them and their children as slaves in West Virginia. If they choose to stay and submit to the operation of the emancipation law, they have the certainty of gaining more by the rise in the value of their lands, than they will lose in the market value of their slaves, in consequence of the emancipation law.

Undoubtedly such a law would immediately attract emigrants by thousands from the North,—farmers, manufacturers and laborers; who would bring their capital, their skill, and their industry, to enrich the country,—to improve its agriculture, draw out the wealth of its mines, and make its idle waterfalls and coal beds work up its abundant materials of manufacture. Before the law would emancipate a single negro, it would already have added more to the value of the lands and town property of West Virginia than all her slaves are worth. If any man among us have many slaves and little or no land, he can easily profit by the law as well as others; let him sell negroes and buy land.

Will any man argue, that the rights of slaveholders will be violated, because those rights extend to the offspring of their slaves?

Now the slaveholder's right of property extends to the offspring of his slaves, so far as this, that when the offspring comes into existence, the law at present allows him to claim it as his. But when the law of the land shall in this particular be changed, his right is at an end; for it is founded solely on human law. By nature all men are free and equal; and human laws can suspend this law of nature, only so long as the public welfare requires it; that is, so long as more evil than good would result from emancipation. When the law of slavery is changed for the public good, all that the slaveholder can claim, is that in some way, he shall be compensated for the property acquired by sanction of law, and taken away by a change of the law. By our scheme nothing is absolutely taken from the slaveholder. It gives him an option, to remove without loss a nuisance which he holds in the country, or to submit, with a very small loss of value, to another mode of abating that nuisance. We say that the people have a right to remove this pest; and that our scheme gives slaveholders double compensation for what they will suffer by the measure. We have no doubt that before ten years, nearly every slaveholder would acknowledge himself doubly compensated.

4. *Let masters be required to have the heirs of emancipation taught reading, writing and arithmetic: and let churches and benevolent people attend to their religious instruction.*—Thus an improved class of free negroes would be raised up. No objection could be made to their literary education, after emancipation was decreed.

5. *Let the emancipated be colonized.*—This would be best for all parties. Supposing that by exportation, our slave population should in twenty-two years be reduced to 40,000. Then about 1000 would go out free the first year, and a gradually smaller number each successive year. The 1000 could furnish their own outfit, by laboring

40

a year or two as hirelings; and their transportation to Liberia would cost the people of West Virginia 25,000 dollars: which, as population would by that time have probably reached a million, would be an average contribution of two and a half cents a head. This would be less and less every year.—So easy would it be to remove the *bugaboo* of a free-negro population, so often held up to deter us from emancipation. Easy would it be, though our calculations were not fully realized.

Finally, in order to hasten the extinction of slavery, where the people desired it, in counties containing few slaves: *the law might authorize the people of any county, by some very large majority, or by consent of a majority of the slaveholders to decree the removal or emancipation of all the slaves of the county within a certain term of years*, seven, ten or fifteen, according to the number of slaves.

This as an auxiliary measure, would be safe and salutary; because the only question then in a county, would be the question of *time*, which would not be very exciting. But it would be inexpedient as the chief or only measure; for then the people of the same county or of neighboring counties, might be kept embroiled on the subject for years, and the influence of East Virginia, operating on counties here and there, might defeat the whole measure, by a repeal of the law. Let us move as a body first, and determine the main point. Then the counties might decide the minor point for themselves. Let West Virginia determine to be free on a general principle. Then let the counties, if they will, modify this principle, for more speedy relief.

Now, fellow-citizens, it is for you to determine whether the slavery question shall be considered, discussed and decided, at this critical, this turning point of your country's history: or whether it shall lie dormant until the doom of West Virginia is sealed. May heaven direct your minds to the course dictated by patriotism, by humanity and by your own true interest.

A SLAVEHOLDER OF WEST VIRGINIA.

☞ Gentlemen friendly to the cause, are requested to aid in the sale and circulation of this Address. The expense of printing this large edition is considerable, and much of it must, at all events, fall on a few individuals.

ERRORS OF THE PRESS.

Page 16, line 1 (in some copies) for "protective" read "productive."
"   25   "   6 for "drive" read "drove,"
"   "   "   21 for "their" read "this,"
"   28   "   22 for "drawn" read "draw,"

West Virginia Statute Abolishing Slavery 1865

ACTS OF THE LEGISLATURE
OF
WEST VIRGINIA AT ITS THIRD SESSION
1865

CHAPTER. 10 – An ACT for the Abolishment of Slavery in this State.

Passed February 3, 1865

Be it enacted by the Legislature of West Virginia:

1.All persons held to service or labor as slaves in this state, are hereby declared free.

2.There shall hereafter be neither slavery nor involuntary servitude in this State, except in punishment for crime, whereof the party shall have been duly convicted.

Preliminary Emancipation Proclamation

September 22, 1862

A Transcription

By the President of the United States of America [Abraham Lincoln]:

A Proclamation.

I, Abraham Lincoln, President of the United States of America, and Commander-in-Chief of the Army and Navy thereof, do hereby proclaim and declare that hereafter, as heretofore, the war will be prosecuted for the object of practically restoring the constitutional relation between the United States, and each of the States, and the people thereof, in which States that relation is, or may be, suspended or disturbed.

That it is my purpose, upon the next meeting of Congress to again recommend the adoption of a practical measure tendering pecuniary aid to the free acceptance or rejection of all slave States, so called, the people whereof may not then be in rebellion against the United States and which States may then have voluntarily adopted, or thereafter may voluntarily adopt, immediate or gradual abolishment of slavery within their respective limits; and that the effort to colonize persons of African descent, with their consent, upon this continent, or elsewhere, with the previously obtained consent of the Governments existing there, will be continued.

That on the first day of January in the year of our Lord, one thousand eight hundred and sixty-three, all persons held as slaves within any State, or designated part of a State, the people whereof shall then be in rebellion against the United States shall be then, thenceforward, and forever free; and the executive government of the United States, including the military and naval authority thereof, will recognize and maintain the freedom of such persons, and will do no act or acts to repress such persons, or any of them, in any efforts they may make for their actual freedom.

That the executive will, on the first day of January aforesaid, by proclamation, designate the States, and part of States, if any, in which the people thereof respectively, shall then be in rebellion against the United States; and the fact that any State, or the people thereof shall, on that day be, in good faith represented in the Congress of the United States, by members chosen thereto, at elections wherein a majority of the qualified voters of such State shall have participated, shall, in the absence of strong countervailing testimony, be deemed conclusive evidence that such State and the people thereof, are not then in rebellion against the United States.

That attention is hereby called to an Act of Congress entitled "An Act to make an additional Article of War" approved March 13, 1862, and which act is in the words and figure following:

"Be it enacted by the Senate and House of Representatives of the United States of America in Congress assembled, That hereafter the following shall be promulgated as an additional article of war for the government of the army of the United States, and shall be obeyed and observed as such:

"Article-All officers or persons in the military or naval service of the United States are prohibited from employing any of the forces under their respective commands for the purpose of returning fugitives from service or labor, who may have escaped from any persons to whom such service or labor is claimed to be due, and any officer who shall be found guilty by a court martial of violating this article shall be dismissed from the service.

"Sec.2. And be it further enacted, That this act shall take effect from and after its passage."

Also to the ninth and tenth sections of an act entitled "An Act to suppress Insurrection, to punish Treason and Rebellion, to seize and confiscate property of rebels, and for other purposes," approved July 17, 1862, and which sections are in the words and figures following:

"Sec.9. And be it further enacted, That all slaves of persons who shall hereafter be engaged in rebellion against the government of the United States, or who shall in any way give aid or comfort thereto, escaping from such persons and taking refuge within the lines of the army; and all slaves captured from such persons or deserted by them and coming under the control of the government of the United States; and all slaves of such persons found on (or) being within any place occupied by rebel forces and afterwards occupied by the forces of the United States, shall be deemed captives of war, and shall be forever free of their servitude and not again held as slaves.

"Sec.10. And be it further enacted, That no slave escaping into any State, Territory, or the District of Columbia, from any other State, shall be delivered up, or in any way impeded or hindered of his liberty, except for crime, or some offence against the laws, unless the person claiming said fugitive shall first make oath that the person to whom the labor or service of such fugitive is alleged to be due is his lawful owner, and has not borne arms against the United States in the present rebellion, nor in any way given aid and comfort thereto; and no person engaged in the military or naval service of the United States shall, under any pretence whatever, assume to decide on the validity of the claim of any person to the service or labor of any other person, or surrender up any such person to the claimant, on pain of being dismissed from the service."

And I do hereby enjoin upon and order all persons engaged in the military and naval service of the United States to observe, obey, and enforce, within their respective spheres of service, the act, and sections above recited.

And the executive will in due time recommend that all citizens of the United States who shall have remained loyal thereto throughout the rebellion, shall (upon the restoration of the constitutional relation between the United States, and their respective States, and people, if that relation shall have been suspended or disturbed) be compensated for all losses by acts of the United States, including the loss of slaves.

In witness whereof, I have hereunto set my hand, and caused the seal of the United States to be affixed.

Done at the City of Washington this twenty-second day of September, in the year of our Lord, one thousand, eight hundred and sixty-two, and of the Independence of the United States the eighty seventh.

[Signed:] Abraham Lincoln
By the President

[Signed:] William H. Seward
Secretary of State

U. S. National Archives and Records Administration
Preliminary Emancipation Proclamation, September 22, 1862; Presidential Proclamations, 1791-1991; Record Group 11; General Records of the United States Government, National Archives.

Final Emancipation Proclamation

January 1, 1863
A Transcription
By the President of the United States of America [Abraham Lincoln:
A Proclamation.

Whereas, on the twenty-second day of September, in the year of our Lord one thousand eight hundred and sixty-two, a proclamation was issued by the President of the United States, containing, among other things, the following, to wit:

"That on the first day of January, in the year of our Lord one thousand eight hundred and sixty-three, all persons held as slaves within any State or designated part of a State, the people whereof shall then be in rebellion against the United States, shall be then, thenceforward, and forever free; and the Executive Government of the United States, including the military and naval authority thereof, will recognize and maintain the freedom of such persons, and will do no act or acts to repress such persons, or any of them, in any efforts they may make for their actual freedom.

"That the Executive will, on the first day of January aforesaid, by proclamation, designate the States and parts of States, if any, in which the people thereof, respectively, shall then be in rebellion against the United States; and the fact that any State, or the people thereof, shall on that day be, in good faith, represented in the Congress of the United States by members chosen thereto at elections wherein a majority of the qualified voters of such State shall have participated, shall, in the absence of strong countervailing testimony, be deemed conclusive evidence that such State, and the people thereof, are not then in rebellion against the United States."

Now, therefore I, Abraham Lincoln, President of the United States, by virtue of the power in me vested as Commander-in-Chief, of the Army and Navy of the United States in time of actual armed rebellion against the authority and government of the United States, and as a fit and necessary war measure for suppressing said rebellion, do, on this first day of January, in the year of our Lord one thousand eight hundred and sixty-three, and in accordance with my purpose so to do publicly proclaimed for the full period of one hundred days, from the day first above mentioned, order and designate as the States and parts of States wherein the people thereof respectively, are this day in rebellion against the United States, the following, to wit:

Arkansas, Texas, Louisiana, (except the Parishes of St. Bernard, Plaquemines, Jefferson, St. John, St. Charles, St. James Ascension, Assumption, Terrebonne, Lafourche, St. Mary, St. Martin, and Orleans, including the City of New Orleans) Mississippi, Alabama, Florida, Georgia, South Carolina, North Carolina, and Virginia, (except the forty-eight counties designated as West Virginia, and also the counties of Berkley, Accomac, Northampton, Elizabeth City, York, Princess Ann, and Norfolk, including the cities of Norfolk and Portsmouth[)], and which excepted parts, are for the present, left precisely as if this proclamation were not issued.

And by virtue of the power, and for the purpose aforesaid, I do order and declare that all persons held as slaves within said designated States, and parts of States, are, and henceforward shall be free; and that the Executive government of the United States, including the military and naval authorities thereof, will recognize and maintain the freedom of said persons.

And I hereby enjoin upon the people so declared to be free to abstain from all violence, unless in necessary self-defence; and I recommend to them that, in all cases when allowed, they labor faithfully for reasonable wages.

And I further declare and make known, that such persons of suitable condition, will be received into the armed service of the United States to garrison forts, positions, stations, and other places, and to man vessels of all sorts in said service.

And upon this act, sincerely believed to be an act of justice, warranted by the Constitution, upon military necessity, I invoke the considerate judgment of mankind, and the gracious favor of Almighty God.

In witness whereof, I have hereunto set my hand and caused the seal of the United States to be affixed.

Done at the City of Washington, this first day of January, in the year of our Lord one thousand eight hundred and sixty three, and of the Independence of the United States of America the eighty-seventh.

By the President: ABRAHAM LINCOLN

WILLIAM H. SEWARD, Secretary of State.

U. S. National Archives and Records Administration
Emancipation Proclamation, January 1, 1863; Presidential Proclamations, 1791-1991; Record Group 11; General Records of the United States Government; National Archives. Transcript of 13th Amendment to the U.S. Constitution: Abolition of Slavery (1865)

Thirteenth Amendment

Section 1.

Neither slavery nor involuntary servitude, except as a punishment for crime whereof the party shall have been duly convicted, shall exist within the United States, or any place subject to their jurisdiction.

Section 2.

Congress shall have power to enforce this article by appropriate legislation.

U. S. National Archives and Records Administration

The House Joint Resolution proposing the 13th amendment to the Constitution, January 31, 1865; Enrolled Acts and Resolutions of Congress, 1789-1999; General Records of the United States Government; Record Group 11; National Archives.

Transcript of 14th Amendment to the U.S. Constitution: Civil Rights (1868)

Fourteenth Amendment

Section 1.

All persons born or naturalized in the United States, and subject to the jurisdiction thereof, are citizens of the United States and of the State wherein they reside. No State shall make or enforce any law which shall abridge the privileges or immunities of citizens of the United States; nor shall any State deprive any person of life, liberty, or property, without due process of law; nor deny to any person within its jurisdiction the equal protection of the laws.

Section 2.

Representatives shall be apportioned among the several States according to their respective numbers, counting the whole number of persons in each State, excluding Indians not taxed. But when the right to vote at any election for the choice of electors for President and Vice-President of the United States, Representatives in Congress, the Executive and Judicial officers of a State, or the members of the Legislature thereof, is denied to any of the male inhabitants of such State, being twenty-one years of age, and citizens of the United States, or in any way abridged, except for participation in rebellion, or other crime, the basis of representation therein shall be reduced in the proportion which the number of such male citizens shall bear to the whole number of male citizens twenty-one years of age in such State.

Section 3.

No person shall be a Senator or Representative in Congress, or elector of President and Vice-President, or hold any office, civil or military, under the United States, or under any State, who, having previously taken an oath, as a member of Congress, or as an officer of the United States, or as a member of any State legislature, or as an executive or judicial officer of any State, to support the Constitution of the United States, shall have engaged in insurrection or rebellion against the same, or given aid or comfort to the enemies thereof. But Congress may by a vote of two-thirds of each House, remove such disability.

Section 4.

The validity of the public debt of the United States, authorized by law, including debts incurred for payment of pensions and bounties for services in suppressing insurrection or rebellion, shall not be questioned. But neither the United States nor any State shall assume or pay any debt or obligation incurred in aid of insurrection or rebellion against the United States, or any claim for the loss or emancipation of any slave; but all such debts, obligations and claims shall be held illegal and void.

Section 5.

The Congress shall have the power to enforce, by appropriate legislation, the provisions of this article.

U. S. National Archives and Records Administration

The House Joint Resolution proposing the 14th amendment to the Constitution, June 16, 1866; Enrolled Acts and Resolutions of Congress, 1789-1999; General Records of the United States Government; Record Group 11; National Archives.

Endnotes

1   Fawn Valentine, West Virginia Quilts and Quiltmakers (Athens, OH: Ohio University Press, 2000), 272.

2   Charles H. Ambler, A History of West Virginia (New York: Prentice- Hall Inc., 1933), 48-50.

3   Barbara Beury McCallum, "Minnie Cooper," Hodge Podge, January – March 1991.

4   Wilma Dunaway, Slavery in the American Mountain South (New York, Cambridge University Press, 2003), 236.

5   Louis R. Harlan, Booker T. Washington the Making of a Black Leader 1856-1901 (New York: Oxford University Press, 1972), Preface.

6   William Tiernan, "Putting Booker T. Back Together Again" The Charleston Gazette (Charleston, WV) August 16, 1979. Sandy Wells, "Malden Sisters Amass Wealth of Facts About Town," The Charleston Gazette (Charleston, WV) March 07, 1991.

7   Division of Christian Education of the National Council of the Churches of Christ in the United States of America, The Holy Bible, New Revised Standard Version (New York: Oxford University Press,1989), 251.

8   Arthur M. Schlesinger Jr., The Age of Jackson (Boston, MA: Little Brown and Company, 1945), 427.

9   Seema Sohi, "Immigration Act of 1917 and the 'Barred Zone' in Xiaojian Zhao and Edward J. W. Park, Asian Americans: An Encyclopedia of Social, Cultural, Economic, and Political History, vol. 1, A-F (ABC-CLIO, 2013), 534-537.; Shiho Imai, "Gentlemen's Agreement," Densho Encyclopedia, https://encyclopedia.densho.org/Gentlemen's%20Agreement/, accessed January 7, 2019.

10   Kathleen Gerson, "Children of the Gender Revolution," Judith Lorber, Gender Inequality: Feminist Theories and Politics, Fifth Edition (NY: Oxford University Press, 2012), 55-56; quoting Andrew Hacker, Two Nations: Black and White, Separate, Hostile, Unequal. (NY: Scribner, 2003), 22.

11   Henry Louis Gates Jr., Colored People, A Memoir (New York: Vintage Books, 1995), 27-28.

12   William Rhee and Stephen C. Scott, "Geographic Discrimination: of Place, Space, Hillbillies, and Home," West Virginia Law Review 2, vol.121 (Winter 2018): 561-562

13   James Truslow Adams, The Epic of America (New York: Little, Brown and Company, 1931).

14   Charles Sellers, The Market Revolution: Jacksonian America 1815-1846 (New York, NY: Oxford University Press, 1991), 238.

15   Calvin Colton, The Junius Tracts, No.VII: Labor and Capital (New York, NY: Greeley & McElrath, 1844) 15.

16   Ronald D. Eller, Miners, Millhands, and Mountaineers: Industrialization of the Appalachian South 1880-1930 (Knoxville, TN: The University of Tennessee Press, 1982), 8.

17   Gerson, "Children of the Gender Revolution," Judith Lorber, Gender Inequality: Feminist Theories and Politics, 39.

18   Booker T. Washington, Up from Slavery: An Autobiography (New York City, NY: Doubleday & Company, 1901), 219.

19   Thomas D. Morris, Southern Slavery and the Law, 1619-1860 (Chapel Hill, NC: The University of North Carolina Press, 1996), 190.; Eugene D. Genovese, Roll, Jordan, Roll: The World The Slaves Made (New York, NY: Pantheon Books, 1974), 35-36.

20   H.G. Wells, The Outline of History

(Garden City Publishing Company, 1920), 472.; Todd S. Purdum, An Idea Whose Time Has

Come (NY: Henry Holt and Company, LLC, 2014), 113.; Edmund S. Morgan, American Slavery, American Freedom, The Ordeal of Colonial Virginia (New York: W.W. Norton & Company Inc., 1975), 386-387.

21   C. Vann Woodward, The Strange Career of Jim Crow (New York, NY: Oxford University Press, 1974), 11.

22   Thomas Jefferson, The Declaration of Independence [Original Manuscript] (Philadelphia, PA: 1776).

23   Jeff Nilsson, "The Debt and Death of Thomas Jefferson," The Saturday Evening Post (July 2, 2015), accessed January 7, 2019,

https://www.saturdayeveningpost.com/2015/07/the-debt-and-death-of-thomas-jefferson-2/.; Ken Burns, "Jefferson: A Film by Ken Burns" (The American Experience Lives Film Project, Inc., 1996).

24   Thomas Jefferson, Notes on the State of Virginia (London, UK:1787), 143-151.

25   Webster's Unabridged Dictionary of the English Language (New York City, NY: Random House 1989),1339.

26   Thomas Jefferson, Notes on the State of Virginia, 146-155.

27   Paul Finkelman, Slavery and the Founders: Race and Liberty in the Age of Jackson (Armonk, NY: M. E. Sharpe, 1996), 110-112.

28   "The Voyage Made by M. John Hawkins, Esquire, 1565," American Journeys Collection: Wisconsin Historical Society Digital Library and Archives, Document No. AJ-130, accessed November 14, 2018, http://www.americanhttp://www.americanjourney.org/pdf/AJ-030.pdf.; "Early Times: Adventurers and Slavers," The National Archives (UK), Exhibitions: Black Presence, accessed November 26, 2018, http://www.nationalarchives.gov.

uk/pathways/blackhistory/early_times/adventurers.htm; "John Hawkins' Coat of Arms," The National Archives (UK), Exhibitions: Black Presence by permission of The college of Arms, London (1568), accessed November 26, 2018, http://www.nationalarchives.gov.uk/pathways/blackhistory/early_times/docs/hawkins.htm.; "The First Africans," Jamestown Rediscovery: Historic Jamestowne, accessed November 26, 2018, https://historicjamestowne.org/history/the-first-africans/.; John W. Wayland, A History of Virginia for Boys and Girls (New York, NY: The MacMillan Company, 1922), 43.; Morgan, American Slavery, American Freedom, The Ordeal of Colonial Virginia, 386.; Ira Berlin, Generations of Captivity: A History of African-American Slaves (Cambridge, MA: Harvard University Press, 2003), 63.

29   J. Russell Major, Civilization in the Western World, Renaissance to 1815 (Philadelphia, PA: J. B. Lippincott Company, 1966), 281.; Berlin, Generations of Captivity: A History of African-American Slaves, 55.

30   Office of the Surgeon General, U.S. Department of Health and Human Services, The Health Consequences of Smoking--50 Years of Progress: A Report of the Surgeon General, Executive Summary, (Rockville, MD: U.S. Department of Health and Human Services, 2014), 15.; "The Toll of Tobacco in West Virginia," Campaign for Tobacco Free Kids, https://www.tobaccofreekids.org/problem/toll-us/west_virginia, (accessed August 6,2018).

31   B. Jowett, Plato's The Republic (NY: Vintage Books, N.D.), 312.

32   Ambler, A History of West Virginia, 66.

33   Berlin, Generations of Captivity: A History of African-American Slaves,15-17.; Kenneth Stampp, The Peculiar Institution: Slavery in the Ante-Bellum South (New York, NY: Vintage Books, 1989), 29.

34   Herbert G. Gutman, The Black

Family in Slavery and Freedom 1750-1925(New York, Random House Inc.:1976), 301.

35   Viola Ruffner to Gilson Willetts, May 29, 1899, in Willetts, "Slave Boy and Leader of His Race." New Voice, XVI (June 24, 1899), 3. Cited in Louis Harlan, "Booker T. Washington's West Virginia Boyhood," West Virginia History 2, Vol. 32 (January 1971): 74.; Booker T. Washington, Up from Slavery (NY: Bantam Pathfinder Edition, 10th Printing, 1901), 30.

36   Woodward, The Strange Career of Jim Crow, 50.

37   Washington, Up from Slavery, 219.; Maria Young, "Founding Father," Charleston Gazette-Mail, June 16, 2019.

38   Henry Ruffner, Address to the People of West Virginia (Lexington, KY: R. C. Noel, 1847), 39.; Mark and Pam Flasch, Peter Ruffner and his Descendants, vol. 2, The Descendants of Peter the Pioneer's first child: Joseph Ruffner (Ruffner Family Association, 2007), 50.

39   Charles Hedrick, History of the Ruffner Family of Kanawha (1884), 11.

40   "The Malden Riot," in the West Virginia Journal, ed. G. W. Atkinson (Charleston, WV, December 15, 1869).

41   Webster's Unabridged Dictionary of the English Language (New York City, NY: Random House 1989), 767.; Sellers, The Market Revolution: Jacksonian America 1815-1846, 389.; Ken Fones-Wolf, Glass Towns: Industry, Labor, and Political Economy in Appalachia, 1890-1930s (Urbana and Chicago, IL: University of Illinois Press, 2007), 96, 99.

42   Louise McNeill, Hill Daughter: New & Selected Poems (Pittsburgh PA: University of Pittsburgh Press, 1991), with Maggie Anderson, 127.

43   Bill Case, State Papers & Public Addresses of Bob Wise: Thirty-third Governor of West Virginia, 2001-2005 (Beckley, WV: Central Printing Company, N.D.), 19.

44   Henry Louis Gates Jr., In Search of Our Roots (New York: Crown Publishers, 2009), 263.

45   Gates, Jr., In Search of Our Roots, 263.

46   Eller, Miners Millhands, and Mountaineers: Industrialization of the Appalachian South 1880-1930, 9.

47   Eller, Miners Millhands, and Mountaineers: Industrialization of the Appalachian South 1880-1930, 10.

48   Stampp, The Peculiar Institution: Slavery in the Ante-Bellum South, 151, 401.

49   Thomas Miller and Hu Maxwell, West Virginia and Its People, Vol. 3 (New York: Lewis Historical Publishing Company, 1913), 197.; Samuel Eliot Morrison, The Oxford History of the American People (New York: Oxford University Press, 1965), 512.; Nullification Crisis: United States History [1832-1833]," Encyclopedia Britannica, December 11, 2018, accessed January 7, 2019, https://www.britannica.com/topic/nullification-crisis.

50   Stephen W. Berry II, All That Makes A Man: Love and Ambition in the Civil War South (New York City, NY: Oxford University Press, 2003), 18.

51   McNeill, Hill Daughter: New & Selected Poems, 38.

52   Granville Hall, The Rending of Virginia: A History (Chicago, IL: Mayer & Miller, 1902), 29.

53   Frederick Law Olmsted, A Journey in the Seaboard Slave States, With Remarks on Their Economy (New York, NY: Dix & Edwards, 1856), 109.

54   Charles H. Ambler and Festus P. Summers, West Virginia the Mountain State, second edition (Englewood Cliffs, NJ: Prentice-Hall: 1958), 13-21.

55   John Long, The Indian Captivity Narrative of Charles Johnston (Blacksburg, VA: The Smithfield Review, Volume XI, 2007),

5-16.

56   David Hackett Fisher and James C. Kelly, Bound Away: Virginia and the Westward Movement (Charlottesville, VA: University Press of Virginia, 2000), 119.

57   James Morton Callahan, History of West Virginia (West Virginia: Semi-Centennial Commission, 1913), 16.; Fisher and Kelly, Bound Away: Virginia and the Westward Movement, 118-121.

58   Fisher and Kelly, Bound Away: Virginia and the Westward Movement, 130-131.

59   Miller and Maxwell, West Virginia and Its People, Vol. 3, 195.; Leo Damrosch, Tocqueville's Discovery of American (New York, NY: Farrar, Straus and Giroux, 2010), 126-128.; Alexis De Tocqueville, Democracy in America, ed. Richard Heffner (New York: Mentor Books, 1956).; Gutman, The Black Family in Slavery and Freedom, 336-337.

60   Alexis De Tocqueville, Democracy in America, ed. Richard Heffner (New York: Mentor Books, 1956), 43; "Mayflower Compact," Encyclopedia Britannica, Encyclopedia Britannica Online, Encyclopedia Britannica Inc., accessed August 25 2017 https://www.britannica.com/topic/Mayflower-Compact>.

61   Vincent Wilson, Jr., The Book of Great American Documents (Brookeville, MD: American History Research Associates, 2017), 5-10.

62   De Tocqueville, Democracy in America, 41-42.

63   De Tocqueville, Democracy in America, 41-42.; Robert Prichard, A History of the Episcopal Church (Harrisburg, PA: Morehouse Publishing, 1991),113.

64   Carter G. Woodson, "Freedom and Slavery in Appalachian America," in Blacks in Appalachia, ed. William H. Turner and Edward J. Cabbell (Lexington, KY: University Press of Kentucky, 1985), 32.

65   Dr. Henry Ruffner, Union Speech of Fourth of July 1856 in the Kanawha Salines (first printed Cincinnati, OH: Applegate & Co. 1856).

66   Thomas C. Miller ed. and Hu Maxwell, West Virginia and It's People, Vol.1 (New York: Lewis Historical Publishing Company, 1913),189; Prichard, A History of the Episcopal Church, 189.

67   Ella Lonn, Foreigners in the Confederacy (Chapel Hill, NC: The University of North Carolina Press, 1940), 416-438

68   Prichard, A History of the Episcopal Church, 113.

69   Prichard, A History of the Episcopal Church, 113.; Nehemiah Adams, A South-Side View of Slavery; or, Three Months at the South in 1854 (Port Washington, NY: Kennikat Press, Inc., 1969), 195-196

70   Genovese, Roll, Jordan, Roll: The World The Slaves Made, 161-168.

71   Olmsted, A Journey in the Seaboard Slave States, With Remarks on Their Economy, 118-121.

72   Dunaway, Slavery in the American Mountain South, 166.

73   Carter G. Woodson, The Education of the Negro Prior to 1861 (NY: Arno Press and the New York Times, 1968), 187-188.; Rachel Erdman, "Project on Slavery, Racism, and Reconciliation," From the Mountain, The University of the South School of Theology (Fall 2018), 20-25.

74   Noah Adams, Far Appalachia: Following the New River North (New York City, NY: Dell Publishing, 2001), 60.; Todd J. Wilkinson, "Hillbillies and Rednecks," Scottish Tartans Authority, accessed September 26, 2017 from http://www.tartansauthority.com/global-scots/us-scots-history/hillbillies-and-rednecks/; Erik Devany, "How the Irish and the Scots Influenced American Music," London Celtic Punks Web-Zine, accessed September 26, 2017 from https://londoncelticpunks.wordpress.com/2016/02/28/how-the-irish-and-the-scots-influenced-american-music/.;

Wess Harris, Written in Blood: Courage and Corruption in the Appalachian War of Extraction (Gay, WV & Oakland, CA: Appalachian Community Services & PM Press, 2017), 230.; Rosemary V. Hathaway, "Hillbilly or Frontiersmen? A Brief Cultural History of the West Virginia Mountaineer," West Virginia Humanities Council (MacFarland-Hubbard House, Charleston WV: June 24, 2018).

75   B. Kennedy, "Ulster-Scots and the United States Presidents, Ulster-Scots Agency, accessed August 25, 2017 https://www.ulsterscotsagency.com/fs/doc/new_range_of_ulster-scots_booklets/US_and_USA_Presidents_BK3_AW_6.pdf

76   Ambler and Summers, West Virginia: The Mountain State, second edition,125.; Oscar Doane Lambert, West Virginia and Its Government (Boston, MA: D. C. Heath and Company, 1951), 87-88.; Mary M. Schweitzer, "The Ratification Paradox in the Great Valley of the Appalachians" in Eliga H. Gould's Empire and Nation, Part II, Society, Politics, and Culture in the New Nation (Baltimore, MD: Johns Hopkins University Press, 2005), 115-118.; Miller and Maxwell, West Virginia and Its People, 196-197.; Howard Zinn, Writings on Disobedience and Democracy (New York City, NY: Seven Stories Press, 1997), 524.

77   De Tocqueville, Democracy in America, 219.

78   Ambler, A History of West Virginia, 54.

79   Lambert, West Virginia and Its Government, 87.

80   Miller and Maxwell, West Virginia and Its People, 197.

81   De Tocqueville, Democracy in America, 49.

82   De Tocqueville, Democracy in America, 50-51.

83   Frederic Bancroft, Slave Trading in the Old South (New York, NY: Frederick

Ungar Publishing Co., 1931), 13.; Thomas Jefferson, Notes on the State of Virginia (London, 1787),146.; Olmsted, A Journey in the Seaboard Slave States, With Remarks on Their Economy, 259-264.

84   Ambler, A History of Education in West Virginia from Early Colonial Times to 1949, 163.

85   Rodger Cunningham, Apples on the Flood: The Southern Mountain Experience (Knoxville, TN: University of Tennessee Press, 1987), 90-91.

86   G. F. R. Henderson, Stonewall Jackson and The American Civil War (New York, NY: Da Capo Press, Inc., 1943), 4.; James G. Legburn, Scotch-Irish: A Social History (Chapel Hill, NC: The University of North Carolina Press, 1989), 117.

87   Klaus Wust, The Virginia Germans (Charlottesville, VA: The University Press of Virginia, 1969), 97.; Eller, Miners Millhands, and Mountaineers: Industrialization of the Appalachian South 1880-1930, 8.

88   Callahan, History of West Virginia, 22.; Ambler, A History of West Virginia,107.

89   Lori Henshey, "Vandalia Colony," e-WV: West Virginia Encyclopedia, July 13, 2018, accessed May 3, 2019, https://www.wvencyclopedia.org/articles/857.

90   Alain Locke, "The American Temperament," The North American Review 194, no. 669 (1911): 268, accessed July 7, 2017, http://www.jstor.org/stable/pdf/25106997.; A History of West Virginia,107, 119-120.; John E. Stealey, III, "Marker Dedication Bee Line March, July 4, 2012," Good News Paper (Fall 2012):18-19.

91   George Washington, The Diaries of George Washington, 1748-1799, Volume I (Boston, MA: Houghton Mifflin Company, 1925), 444- 446.

92   "President Clinton: Celebrating

America's Rivers" American Heritage Rivers, July 30, 1998, accessed September 26, 2017 from https://clintonwhitehouse2.archives.gov/CEQ/Rivers/.

93   Charles H. Ambler, George Washington and the West (Chapel Hill, NC: University of North Carolina Press, 1936), 18, 70, 132, 173.; Roy Bird Cook, Washington's Western Lands (Strasburg, VA: Shenandoah Publishing House, Inc., 1930), 70.

94   James Evelyn Pilcher, The Surgeon General of the Army of the United States of America (Carlisle, PA: The Association of Military Surgeons, 1905), 23, 411, 444.

95   "Opening the Door West: The Story of How the Ohio Company of Associates Began the First Organized American Settlement on the Old Northwest Territory" (Reedsville OH: Shelbourne Films mmlll).

96   Washington, The Diaries of George Washington, 1748-1799, Volume I, 403, 408, 411, 415, 444.

97   Washington, The Diaries of George Washington, 1748-1799, Volume I, 402-405, 426-431.

98   D. C. Gallaher, Genealogical notes of the Miller- Quarrier- Shrewsbury- Dickinson- Dickenson Families and the Lewis, Ruffner, and Other Kindred Branches with Historical Incidents, etc. (Charleston, WV: 1917), 60-63.; George W. Peterkin, A History and Record of the Protestant Episcopal Church in the Diocese of West Virginia and Before the Formation of the Diocese in 1878 in the Territory now Known as the State of West Virginia (Charleston, WV: The Tribune Company Printers, 1902), 636-639.; Joseph C. Jefferds, Jr., A History of St. John's Episcopal Church: Charleston, West Virginia (Charleston, WV, 1976), 14.

99   Washington, The Diaries of George Washington, 1748-1799, 447.; Ambler, George Washington and the West, 173; Kanawha County Land Book, 1797, Kanawha County Clerk's Office, Charleston, West Virginia.

100   Cheryl Wintz Withrow, The Course of History in the Kanawha Valley (Charleston WV: Charleston Blueprint, 2003), 18-20.

101   Withrow, The Course of History in the Kanawha Valley, 18-20.

102   Allen W. Eckert, The Frontiersmen: A Narrative (Boston, MA: Little, Brown and Company,1967), 253-264.

103   Ken Burns, "The Civil War: A Film by Ken Burns" (American Documentary Inc.1990).

104   William Blackstone, Thomas McIntyre Cooley, and James De Witt Andrews, Commentaries on the Laws of England: In Four Books. 3rd ed. Whitefish, MT: Kessinger, 2010.

105   Ron Chernow, Washington: A Life (New York, NY: Penguin Books, 2010), 815-816.

106   Virgil A. Lewis, History of the Battle of Point Pleasant (West Virginia) (Charleston, WV: The Tribune Printing Company, 1909; reprinted by J. C. Carrier Co., Virginia, 1974), 9-10; Virgil Lewis, History of West Virginia (Philadelphia, PA: Hubbard Brothers Publishers, 1889), 113- 114; Reuben Gold Thwaits and Louise Phelps Kellogg ed., Documentary History of Lord Dunmore's War 1774 (Madison, WI: Wisconsin Historical Society, 1905), 103.

107   Thwaits and Kellogg ed., Documentary History of Lord Dunmore's War 1774, xvii- xviii.

108   Morgan, American Slavery, American Freedom, The Ordeal of Colonial Virginia, 377.

109   David S and Jeanne T. Heidler, "Manifest Destiny," Encyclopedia Britannica, accessed January 1, 2017, https://www.britannica.com/event/Manifest-Destiny.

110   Wayland, A History of Virginia for Boys and Girls, 140.

111   Conley, Beacon Lights of West Virginia History, 155.; Ruth Woods Dayton,

Greenbrier Pioneers and Their Homes (Charleston, WV: West Virginia Publishing Company, 1942), 35.

112 Joyce Mott, "Greenbrier County," e-WV: The West Virginia Encyclopedia, 31 May 2013 https://www.wvencyclopedia.org/articles/2168.

113 Miller and Maxwell, West Virginia and Its People, 104.

114 Dayton, Greenbrier Pioneers and Their Homes, 34-37.; Miller and Maxwell, West Virginia and Its People,104; Virgil A. Lewis, History of the Battle of Point, 31-34; Phil Conley, Beacon Lights of West Virginia History, 157-158.

115 John T. Hriblan, II., The Historic Midland Trail [Map]. 1 inch to 50 miles. Morgantown, West Virginia: Institute for the History of Technology and Industrial Archaeology, a part of West Virginia University, n. d.; Otis K. Rice, The Allegheny Frontier West Virginia Beginnings, 1730-1830 (Lexington: The University Press of Kentucky, 1970), 333.

116 John P. Hale, Trans-Allegheny Pioneers (Radford, VA: Roberta Ingles Steele, 1971), 282.; Ken Sullivan, "Joseph Lawton Beury," e-WV: West Virginia Encyclopedia, September 25, 2012, accessed October 31, 2017, https://www.wvencyclopedia.org/articles/476; Noah Adams, Far Appalachia, Following the New River North (New York, New York: Dell Publishing, 2001), 168; "Joseph Buery," National Park Service: New River Gorge, February 26, 2016, accessed October 31, 2017, https://www.nps.gov/neri/learn/historyculture/buery.htm; "How West Virginia Coal Fields Grew," Coal Trade Journal 50 no. 25 April 16, 1919 (New York): 384.; "Adventures on the Gorge: Rafting and Ziplines [Brochure]," AOTG-WV.com, n.d.

117 W. S. Laidley, History of Charleston and Kanawha County, West Virginia and Representative Citizens (Chicago, IL: Richmond-Arnold Publishing Co., 1911), 128.

118 Stan Cohen with Richard Andre, Kanawha County Images: A Bicentennial History 1788- 1988, Vol. 1 (Charleston, WV: Pictorial Histories Publishing Company and Kanawha County Bicentennial, Inc., 1987), 35; Roy Bird Cook, Washington's Western Lands (Strasburg, VA: Shenandoah Publishing House, Inc., 1930), 70-71; George W. Atkinson, History of Kanawha County (Charleston, WV: Office of the West Virginia Journal, 1876), 200.; Edgar B. Sims, Making a State (Charleston, WV: Matthews Printing and Lithographing Company, 1956), 130-131.

119 Hale, History of the Great Kanawha Valley, Vol. 1, 154-168, 213.; Gallaher, Genealogical notes of the Miller- Quarrier- Shrewsbury- Dickinson- Dickenson Families and the Lewis, Ruffner, and Other Kindred Branches with Historical Incidents, etc., 90-92.

120 Hale, Trans-Allegheny Pioneers, 185-186.

121 Hale, Trans-Allegheny Pioneers, 194-195.

122 Hale, History of the Great Kanawha Valley, Vol. 1, 193.; Lewis, History of the Battle of Point Pleasant, 44, 50.; J.T. McAllister, "The Battle of Point Pleasant," The Virginia Magazine of History and Biography, IX (1902), 405-406; Callahan, History of West Virginia, 28.; Joy Gregoire Gilchrist-Stalnaker, "Lewis County," e-WV: West Virginia Encyclopedia, December 16, 2015, https://www.wvencyclopedia.org/articles/1362.; Dayton, Greenbrier Pioneers and Their Homes, 37.

123 Joseph Doddridge, Logan, The Last Of The Race Of Shikellemus, Chief of the Cayuga Nation (Parsons, WV: McClain Printing Co., 1971), 4.; Callahan, History of West Virginia, 29.

124 Hale, Trans-Allegheny Pioneers, 227.

125 Lewis, History of the Battle of Point Pleasant, 36-39, 40-66.; Callahan, History of West Virginia, 33, 102.

126 Lewis, History of the Battle of Point

Pleasant, 55.

127   Hamilton's America: A Documentary Film. Directed by Alex Horwitz. United States: PBS, 2016. Television. http://www.pbs.org/wnet/gperf/hamiltonfullfilm/5801/.

128   David S. Kidder and Noah D. Oppenheim, The Intellectual Devotional: American History (New York: Modern Times, 2007), 37, 55; Ralph Waldo Emerson, "Concord Hymn" (1837).

129   Wayland, A History of Virginia for Boys and Girls, 138.; Eric Foner, Gateway to Freedom: The Hidden History of the Underground Railroad (New York, NY: W. W. Norton & Company, 2015), 33-34.

130   Proclamation made by Lord Dunmore (November 7, 1775), (Accessed June 06, 2017) Manuscript/Mixed Material Retrieved from University of Maryland-Baltimore County; http://www.umbc.edu/che/tahlessons/pdf/Fighting_for_Whose_Freedom_Black_Soldiers_in_the_American_Revolution_RS4.pdf

131   Christopher Klein, The Ex-Slaves Who Fought with the British, History.com, May 24, 2016, accessed August 10, 2018,

https://www.history.com/news/the-ex-slaves-who-fought-with-the-british/.

132   Hale, Trans-Allegheny Pioneers, 192.

133   Lewis, History of the Battle of Point Pleasant, 95.

134   Hale, Trans-Allegheny Pioneers, 225.

135   Chief Logan to Lord Dunmore, 1774, 1774, (Accessed June 06, 2017) Manuscript/Mixed Material, Retrieved from the Library of Congress, https://www.loc.gov/item/mtjbib008956/.

136   Lewis, History of the Battle of Point Pleasant, 67-69.

137   Miller and Maxwell, West Virginia and Its People, Vol. 1, 68, 113-115.

138   Miller and Maxwell, West Virginia and Its People, Vol. 1, 113-115.

139   H.G. Wells, The Outline of History,

8, 1087.; Dunaway, Slavery in the American Mountain South, 47.

140   Ambler, West Virginia Stories and Biographies, 78-80; Phil Conley, Beacon Lights of West Virginia History, 171.

141   Miller and Maxwell, West Virginia and Its People, Vol. 1, 113-116.

142   George Washington Papers, Series 4, General Correspondence: Fairfax County, Virginia, Citizens, July 18, 1774, Resolutions and Abstract. 1774. Manuscript/Mixed Material. Retrieved from the Library of Congress, accessed August 16, 2017, https://www.loc.gov/collections/george-washington-papers/articles-and-essays/fairfax-resolves/.

143   Lewis, History of the Battle of Point Pleasant, 121.

144   Lewis, History of the Battle of Point Pleasant, 121-122.

145   Lewis, History of the Battle of Point Pleasant, 122.

146   Virgil A. Lewis, History and Government of West Virginia, 23.; Lewis, History of the Battle of Point Pleasant, 122.

147   Major, Civilization in the Western World, Renaissance to 1815, 139-282.

148   Alexander Scott Withers, Chronicles of Border Warfare. Ed Reuben Gold Thwaites (Cincinnati, OH: Stewart & Kidd Company, 1912), 28-37.; State Superintendent of Schools, History of Education in West Virginia (Charleston, WV: Tribune Printing Company, 1907), 24.; John Alexander Williams, Appalachia: A History (University of North Carolina Press, 2002), 68; Frank S. Riddle, A Historical Atlas of West Virginia (Morgantown, WV: West Virginia University Press, 2008), 86-87.

149   Sullivan, The West Virginia Encyclopedia, 572- 573; Livia Nye Simpson-Poffenbarger, The Battle of Point Pleasant: A Battle of the Revolution, October 10th, 1774 (Point Pleasant, WV: State Gazette Publisher, 1909) 36.

150 Andrew Delbanco, The War Before the War: Fugitive Slaves and the Struggle for America's Soul from the Revolution to the Civil War (New York, NY: Penguin Press, 2018), 66.

151 Allen Weinstein and David Rubel, The Story of America (New York: DK Publishing, 2002), 116; "Constitution of the United States," in The World Book Encyclopedia 2000 Vol. 4, Ci - Cz (Chicago, IL: World Book, Inc, 2000), 999.

152 Wilson, Jr., The Book of Great American Documents, 45-46.

153 Wilson, Jr., The Book of Great American Documents, 45-46.

154 Hillary Hughes, "First in War, First in Peace, and First in the Hearts of His Countrymen," Mountvernon.org, accessed January 2, 2019, https://www.mountvernon.org/library/digitalhistory/digital-encyclopedia/article/first-in-war-first-in-peace-and-first-in-the-hearts-of-his-countrymen/.

155 William P. Kladky, "Constitutional Convention," George Washington's Mount Vernon, accessed October 04, 2017, http://www.mountvernon.org/digital-encyclopedia/article/constitutional-convention/; Theodore J. Crackel, "George Washington and the Constitution," The Gilder Lehrman Institute of American History: The Constitution, accessed October 04, 2017, https://www.gilderlehrman.org/history-by-era/early-republic/essays/george-washington-and-constitution.

156 Catherine Drinker Boven, Miracle at Philadelphia (Boston, MA: Little Brown and Company, 1966), 29.

157 Wilson, Jr., The Book of Great American Documents, 29.

158 Jessie Kratz, "The Compromise of 1790," National Archives, May 31, 2015, accessed January 11, 2019, https://prologue.blogs.archives.gov/2015/05/31/the-compromise-of-1790/.

159 Hamilton's America: A Documentary Film. Directed by Alex Horwitz. United States: PBS, 2016. Television. http://www.pbs.org/wnet/gperf/hamiltonfullfilm/5801/.

160 "Shays's Rebellion," Encyclopedia Britannica, accessed February 13, 2019, https://www.britannica.com/event/Shayss-Rebellion; David P. Szatmary, Shays' Rebellion: The Making of an Agrarian Insurrection (Amherst, MA: The University of Massachusetts Press, 1980).

161 The Constitution of the United States of America (Bedford: Massachusetts, ND), 1.

162 Boven, Miracle at Philadelphia, 392.; H.G. Wells, The Outline of History, 1117.

163 Bancroft, Slave Trading in the Old South, 13.; Allan Kulikoff, Tobacco and Slaves: The Development of Southern Cultures in the Chesapeake, 1680-1800 (Chapel Hill, NC: The University of North Carolina Press, 1986), 48.; Ira Berlin, The Making of African America: The Four Great Migrations (New York, NY: Penguin Books, 2010), 113.

164 Matthew Spalding, "Slave Trade," The Heritage Guide to the Constitution, accessed October 02, 2017, http://www.heritage.org/constitution/#!/articles/1/essays/60/slave-trade.

165 Don Nardo, ed., The Creation of the U.S. Constitution (Detroit, MI: Thomson Gale, 2005), 140-152.

166 Nardo, The Creation of the U.S. Constitution, 105, 140-142.

167 Nardo, The Creation of the U.S. Constitution 104.; James Curtis Ballagh, A History of Slavery in Virginia (Baltimore, MD: The Johns Hopkins Press, 1902), 34, 39.; Edward E. Baptist, The Half Has Never Been Told: Slavery and the Making of American Capitalism (New York, NY: Basic Books, 2014), 11.

168 Berlin, Generations of Captivity: A History of African-American Slaves, 13.

169 Pauline Maier, Ratification: The People Debate the Constitution, 1787-1788 (New York, NY: Simon & Schuster, 2010),

284.; Delbanco, The War Before the War: Fugitive Slaves and the Struggle for America's Soul from the Revolution to the Civil War, 77-78.; Finkelman, Slavery and the Founders: Race and Liberty in the Age of Jackson, 30-31.

170 "Chapter 10- An ACT for the Abolishment of Slavery in this State," Acts of the Legislature of West Virginia at its Third Session, Commencing January 17th 1865 (Wheeling, WV: John F. M'Dermot, Public Printer, 1865), 6.; "House Bill No. 25," Journal of the House of Delegates Third Legislature of West Virginia: Regular Session 1865 (Charleston, WV), 1865.

171 United States, Charles Thomson, United States Continental Congress, and Continental Congress Broadside Collection, An ordinance for the government of the territory of the United States, North-west of the river Ohio, [New York, 1787], Library of Congress, accessed October 02, 2017, https://www.loc.gov/item/90898154.

172 Wilson, Jr., The Book of Great American Documents, 32.

173 Wilson, Jr., The Book of Great American Documents, 36.

174 Delbanco, The War Before the War: Fugitive Slaves and the Struggle for America's Soul from the Revolution to the Civil War, 77-78.; Matthew Karp, This Vast Southern Empire: Slaveholders at the Helm of American Foreign Policy (Harvard University Press, 2016), 5.; Wilson, Jr., The Book of Great American Documents, 25, 41.

175 Nardo, The Creation of the U.S. Constitution 104.

176 Wilson, Jr., The Book of Great American Documents, 29.

177 Jeffrey Rosen and David Rubenstein, "Why did Jefferson Draft the Declaration of Independence," National Constitution Center, April 13, 2015, accessed February 7, 2019, https://constitutioncenter.org/

blog/why-did-jefferson-draft-the-declaration-of-independence.; Wilson, Jr., The Book of Great American Documents, 13.

178 Don Nardo, The Atlantic Slave Trade (Detroit, MI: Lucent Books, 2008), 74.

179 Ken Burns, "Thomas Jefferson: A Film by Ken Burns" (The American Lives Project Inc., 1996).

180 Eric Saul, ed., "United States Abolition and Anti-Slavery Timeline," American Abolitionists and Antislavery Activists: Conscience of the Nation, accessed May 21, 2019, http://www.americanabolitionists.com/us-abolition-and-anti-slavery-timeline.html.

181 Conley, Beacon Lights of West Virginia History, 192.; Gutman, The Black Family in Slavery and Freedom, 328.

182 Berlin, Generations of Captivity: A History of African-American Slaves, 14.; Baptist, The Half Has Never Been Told, 9.; Matthew Spalding, "Slave Trade," The Heritage Guide to the Constitution, accessed October 02, 2017, http://www.heritage.org/constitution/#!/articles/1/essays/60/slave-trade.

183 Michael Signer, Becoming Madison (New York: Public Affairs, 2015), 268.; United States, Charles Thomson, United States Continental Congress, and Continental Congress Broadside Collection, An ordinance for the government of the territory of the United States, North-west of the river Ohio, [New York, 1787], Library of Congress, accessed October 02, 2017, https://www.loc.gov/item/90898154.

184 Signer, Becoming Madison, 306.

185 Maier, Ratification: The People Debate the Constitution, 1787-1788, 292-300.; Library of Congress, The Federalist Papers, (accessed August 8, 2018), https://www.congress.gov/resources/display/content/The+Federalist+Papers.

186 Ambler, A History of West Virginia, 184-185.

187   David L. Pulliam, The Constitutional Conventions of Virginia from the Foundation of the Commonwealth to the Present Time, (Richmond, VA: J. T. West, 1901) 38-39, 46- 47.

188   John P. Hale, Trans-Allegheny Pioneers (Radford, VA: Roberta Ingles Steele, 1971), 278.; Atkinson, History of Kanawha County, 183-184.; Ambler, A History of West Virginia, 37, 184.; Gordon Lloyd, "Introduction to the New York Ratifying Convention," Ratification of the Constitution, accessed August 01, 2017, http://teachingamericanhistory.org/ratification/newyork/.; Pulliam, The Constitutional Conventions of Virginia from the Foundation of the Commonwealth to the Present Time, 38- 39, 46- 47.

189   Ron Chernow, Washington: A Life, 816.

190   Eric Saul, ed., "United States Abolition and Anti-Slavery Timeline," American Abolitionists and Antislavery Activists: Conscience of the Nation, accessed May 21, 2019, http://www.americanabolitionists.com/us-abolition-and-anti-slavery-timeline.html.

191   Calvin Colton, The Junius Tracts, No. V: Political Abolition (New York, NY: Greeley & McElrath, 1844), 3(67).

192   Abraham Lincoln, "Gettysburg Address." [Speech] Dedication of the Cemetery at Gettysburg, PA, Gettysburg, November 19, 1863.

193   William Henry Ruffner, "The Ruffners II: Joseph," West Virginia Historical Magazine 1, no. 3 (July 1901), 37-38.; Gerald S. Ratliff, "Clendenin Family," e-WV: The West Virginia Encyclopedia, June 20, 2012, accessed August 7, 2018, https://www.wvencyclopedia.org/articles/1303.; Cohen with Andre, Kanawha County Images: A Bicentennial History 1788- 1988, Vol. 1,14-15.

194   Hale, History of the Great Kanawha Valley, Vol. 1, 63; Gerald W. Sutphin and Richard A. Andre, Sternwheelers on the Great Kanawha River (Missoula, MT: Pictorial Histories Publishing Co., 1991), 2.

195   Hale, Trans-Allegheny Pioneers, IV, 12.

196   Hale, Trans-Allegheny Pioneers, 297.

197   Sutpin and Andre, Sternwheelers on the Great Kanawha River, 11-16.; Hale, Trans-Allegheny Pioneers, 278.; John G. Morgan and Robert J. Byers, Charleston 200 (Charleston, WV: Charleston Gazette, 1994), 10.; Atkinson, History of Kanawha County, 54.; Hale, Trans-Allegheny Pioneers, 288.

198   Virgil A. Lewis, Life and Times of Anne Bailey: The Pioneer Heroine of the Great Kanawha Valley (Point Pleasant, WV: Discovery Press, 1998[Originally published 1891]), 22.; Wayland, A History of Virginia for Boys and Girls, 263.

199   Richard Henry Lee, "Lee Resolution," an address to the Second Continental Congress, June 7, 1776, National Archives and Records Administration, accessed September 28, 2017, https://www.ourdocuments.gov/doc.php?flash=true&doc=1; "Lee Resolution (1776)," Library of Congress: Primary Documents in American History, accessed September 28, 2017, https://www.loc.gov/rr/program/bib/ourdocs/leeresolution.html.

200   Ambler and Summers, West Virginia the Mountain State, second edition, 104-105; "Robert E. Lee," The Civil War in America, Biographies: Library of Congress, accessed October 05, 2017, https://www.loc.gov/exhibits/civil-war-in-america/biographies/robert-e-lee.html.; Elizabeth Brown Pryor, "Robert E. Lee (ca. 1806-1870)," Encyclopedia Virginia, November 19, 2009, accessed October 05, 2017, https://www.encyclopediavirginia.org/Lee_Robert_Edward_1807-1870.; Clifford Dowdey, "Robert E. Lee: Confederate General," Encyclopedia Britannica, accessed October 05, 2017, https://www.britannica.com/biography/Robert-E-Lee; "Arlington House, The Robert E. Lee

Memorial," Arlington National Cemetery, October 07, 2015, accessed October 05, 2017, http://www.arlingtoncemetery.mil/Explore/History/Arlington-House.

201 Virgil Lewis, History of West Virginia, 193.; Callahan, History of West Virginia, 44.

202 Hale, Trans-Allegheny Pioneers, 278.

203 Hale, Trans-Allegheny Pioneers, 213.; Ken Burns, "Thomas Jefferson: A Film by Ken Burns."; Phil Conley, Beacon Lights of West Virginia History, 162.; Berry II, All That Makes A Man: Love and Ambition in the Civil War South, 24.

204 Flasch and Flasch, Peter Ruffner and his Descendants, Second Edition, Vol. 2, 6,9.

205 Ronald L. Lewis, Coal, Iron, and Slaves: Industrial Slavery in Maryland and Virginia, 1715-1865 (Westport, CT: Greenwood Press, Inc., 1979), 7.

206 Robert C. Whisonant, "Geology and History of the Civil War Iron Industry in the New River-Cripple Creek District of Southwestern Virginia," Virginia Minerals 44, no. 4 (1998): 31-33; Ronald L. Lewis, Coal, Iron, and Slaves, 16-17.; James M. Swank, History of The Manufacture of Iron in All Ages, and Particularly in the United States from Colonial Times to 1891 (Philadelphia, PA: The American Iron and Steel Association, 1892).

207 Ronald L. Lewis, Coal, Iron, and Slaves, 52.

208 Ronald L. Lewis, Coal, Iron, and Slaves, 52.; "George Washington Diary, January 1 - May 22, 1760." Quote in The West Virginia Heritage Encyclopedia, Vol. 5, Centennial Catalogue to Coppinger, ed. Jim Comstock (1976), 905.

209 "Old Slater Mill," National Historic Landmarks Program: National Parks Service, accessed May 3, 2019, https://web.archive.org/web/20121007141543/http://tps.cr.nps.gov/nhl/detail.cfm?ResourceId=6&ResourceType=District

210 Wilbur E. Garrett, ed., Historical Atlas of the United States (Washington D.C.: National Geographic Society, 1988), 149.

211 Kenton Beerman, "The Beginning of a Revolution: Waltham and the Boston Manufacturing Company," The Concord Review (1994): 146.

212 William Simpson and Martin Jones, Europe 1783-1914, 2nd ed (New York, NY: Routledge, 2009), 102-103.

213 Baptist, The Half Has Never Been Told, 310-325.

214 Wilbur E. Garrett, ed., Historical Atlas of the United States (Washington D.C.: National Geographic Society, 1988), 149.; Dunaway, Slavery in the American Mountain South, 118.; Beerman, "The Beginning of a Revolution: Waltham and the Boston Manufacturing Company."; "John H. Chafee Blackstone River Valley: National Heritage Corridor, MA, RI," History & Culture: Birthplace of the American Industrial Revolution, National Park Service, accessed June 12, 2019, https://www.nps.gov/blac/learn/historyculture/index.htm.; "Congress Designates Blackstone River Valley National Heritage Corridor, November 10, 1986," MassMoments: A Project of MassHumanities, accessed June 12, 2019, https://www.massmoments.org/moment-details/congress-designates-blackstone-river-valley-national-heritage-corridor.html

215 Beerman, "The Beginning of a Revolution: Waltham and the Boston Manufacturing Company," 149.

216 Gerald Ratliff "James Campbell - The First Cabin in the Kanawha Valley;"Todd A. Hanson, Campbells Creek: A Portrait of a Coal Mining Community (Charleston, WV: Pictorial Publishing Histories Company, First Printing Revised Ed. 2015) 49; William Henry Ruffner, "The Ruffners II: Joseph," 35.; D. C. Gallaher, Genealogical notes of the Miller- Quarrier- Shrewsbury- Dickinson- Dickenson Families and the Lewis, Ruffner, and Other Kindred

Branches with Historical Incidents, etc. (Charleston, WV: 1917), 90-92.

217 Hale, Trans-Allegheny Pioneers, 254.

218 William Henry Ruffner, "The Ruffners II: Joseph," 36.

219 Ruth Woods Dayton, Pioneers and Their Homes on Upper Kanawha (Charleston, WV: West Virginia Publishing Company, 1947), 97-98.; William Henry Ruffner, "The Ruffners II: Joseph," 36.; Wells, "Malden Sisters Amass Wealth of Facts About Town."

220 John E. Stealey III, The Antebellum Kanawha Salt Business and Western Markets (Lexington, KY: University Press of Kentucky, 1993), 12.; Hedrick, History of the Ruffner Family of Kanawha, 2.

221 Atkinson, History of Kanawha County, 54.

222 Flasch & Flasch ed., Peter Ruffner and his Descendants, Second Edition, Vol. 2, 11.

223 Laidley, History of Charleston and Kanawha County, West Virginia and Representative Citizens, 52; Ruffner, "The Ruffners II: Joseph,": 36, 38.; Cohen with Andre, Kanawha County Images: A Bicentennial History 1788-1988, Vol. 1,16; "Chapter VII. Scene at Fort Charleston-Ann Bailey's Ride- She Saves the Garrison from Massacre - Her Second Widowhood," Virgil A. Lewis, Life and Times of Ann Bailey: The Pioneer Heroine of the Great Kanawha Valley (Point Pleasant, WV: Discovery Press, 1998[Originally published 1891]).; Soupart, Sylvia, Stories of West Virginia For Boys and Girls, Vol. 1-2 (Charleston, WV: West Virginia University, Jarrett Printing Co., 1934), 33-34.

224 William Henry Ruffner, "The Ruffners II: Joseph," 37-38.; Laidley, History of Charleston and Kanawha County, West Virginia and Representative Citizens, 75.

225 Laidley, History of Charleston and Kanawha County, West Virginia and Representative Citizens, 75.

226 Ambler, West Virginia Stories and Biographies, 139.; Cohen with Andre, Kanawha County Images: A Bicentennial History 1788-1988, Vol. 1, 35.

227 Flasch & Flasch, Peter Ruffner and his Descendants, Second Edition, Vol. 2, 10.; De Tocqueville, Democracy in America, 50.

228 William Henry Ruffner, "The Ruffners II: Joseph," 38-41.

229 Hale. History of the Great Kanawha Valley, Vol. 1, 213.; Deed of Sale from John Dickinson to Joseph Ruffner, 1796, Kanawha County, West Virginia, Deed Book A, Page 102, Kanawha County Clerk's Office, Charleston, West Virginia; Atkinson, History of Kanawha County, 225.; John E. Stealey III, The Antebellum Kanawha Salt Business and Western Markets (Lexington, KY: University Press of Kentucky, 1993), 12.

230 Stealey, The Antebellum Kanawha Salt Business and Western Markets, 10-13.; William Henry Ruffner, "The Ruffners III: David- Second Article," West Virginia Historical Magazine 2, no. 1 (January 1902): 45- 46.

231 Peter James and Nick Thorpe, Ancient Inventions (New York: Ballantine Books, 1994), 405-406.

232 William Henry Ruffner, "The Ruffners III: David- Second Article," 48-49.

233 Carter Bruns, "The Antebellum Industrialization of the Kanawha Valley in the Virginia Backcountry," (Master's Thesis, Western Carolina University, 2013), 82.; Chemical Divisions of FMC, The Salt Industry in the Kanawha Valley (West Virginia, 1976), 9-10.; Hale, Trans-Allegheny Pioneers, 217; Rice, The Allegheny Frontier West Virginia Beginnings, 1730-1830, 311.

234 Megan Gambino, "A Salute to the Wheel," Smithsonian.com, June 17, 2009, accessed January 11, 2019, https://www.smithsonianmag.com/science-nature/a-sa-

lute-to-the-wheel-31805121/.

235 William Henry Ruffner. "The Ruffners III: David- First Article," West Virginia Historical Magazine 1, no. 4. (October 1901): 50-51.

236 William Henry Ruffner. "The Ruffners III: David- First Article," 50-51.; Stealey, The Antebellum Kanawha County Salt Business and Western Markets, 12-15.; Douglas Perry, "Lewis & Clark Expedition," National Archives, September 7, 2016[last updated], accessed September 29, 2017, https://www.archives.gov/education/lessons/lewis-clark.

237 Alistair Cooke, America (New York: Alfred A. Knopf, 1973), 158-161.; John A. Jakle, "Salt on the Ohio Valley Frontier, 1770-1820," Annals of the Association of American Geographers, Vol. 59, No. 4, December (1969), Taylor & Francis, Ltd on behalf of the Association of American Geographers, JSTOR, accessed November 26, 2018, https://www.jstor.org/stable/2561834, 687.

238 Hale, Trans-Allegheny Pioneers, 7.

239 I. C. White, West Virginia Geological Survey, Vol. 1A, Petroleum and Natural Gas Precise Levels (Morgantown, WV: The New Dominion Publishing Company, 1904), 8.

240 Stealey, The Antebellum Kanawha Salt Business and Western Markets, 11.; Atkinson, History of Kanawha County, 184.

241 Stealey, The Antebellum Kanawha Salt Business and Western Markets, 309-310.

242 William Henry Ruffner "Rev. Henry Ruffner, D. D., LL. D., and General Lewis Ruffner," The Greenbrier Independent, August 28, 1884.; Landbook: 1814, Kanawha County Clerk's Office, Charleston, West Virginia.

243 Sven Beckert, Empire of Cotton: A Global History, (NY: Alfred A. Knoff, 2014), xvii.

244 Flasch & Flasch, ed., Peter Ruffner and his Descendants, Second Edition, Vol. 2, 20.; Ambler, Sectionalism in Virginia from 1776-1861 (Morgantown, WV: West Virginia University Press, 2008), 83- 84.

245 Ambler, and Summers, West Virginia the Mountain State, second edition, 128-129; Callahan, History of West Virginia, 78-91.

246 Cicero M. Fain, III., "Presentation Forum at Horace Mann Middle School," October 11, 2011, Charleston, WV.

247 Stealey, The Antebellum Kanawha Salt Business and Western Markets, 5; Hale, History of the Great Kanawha Valley, Vol. 1, 219.

248 Hale, History of the Great Kanawha Valley, Vol. 1, 166, 217.

249 Hale, History of the Great Kanawha Valley, Vol. 1, 129-130.

250 Rice, The Allegheny Frontier West Virginia Beginnings, 1730-1830, 311.; Hale, Trans-Allegheny Pioneers, 281, 316.

251 Stealey, The Antebellum Kanawha Salt Business and Western Markets, 59-64.

252 Stealey, The Antebellum Kanawha Salt Business and Western Markets, 59-64.; Virginia Assembly, Acts passed a General Assembly of the Commonwealth of Virginia, Begun and Held at the Capitol, in the City of Richmond (Richmond, VA: Thomas Ritchie, 1833),144.

253 Hale, Trans-Allegheny Pioneers, 172; "Daniel Boone Helped Organize Kanawha County" Kanawha Valley Progress Edition of the Charleston Daily Mail (June 14, 1939).

254 Eric Saul, ed., "United States Abolition and Anti-Slavery Timeline," American Abolitionists and Antislavery Activists: Conscience of the Nation, accessed May 21, 2019, http://www.americanabolitionists.com/us-abolition-and-anti-slavery-timeline.html.; John Reuben Sheeler, The Negro in West Virginia Before 1900 [Microfilm; Kanawha County Library],

(Dissertation, West Virginia University, 1954), 126.

255 Atkinson, History of Kanawha County, 307.

256 Hale, History of the Great Kanawha Valley, Vol. 1, 219, 234.

257 Cohen with Andre, Kanawha County Images: A Bicentennial History 1788-1988, Vol.1, 35.; Lu Donnelly, "Architecture Around Us," Western Pennsylvania History: Up Front 97, no. 3 (Fall 2014): 13.; Bernard L. Allen and David Matchen, "Natural Gas and Petroleum," e-WV: West Virginia Encyclopedia, accessed June 27, 2017, https://www.wvencyclopedia.org/articles/1600.; Jim Comstock, ed., The West Virginia Heritage Encyclopedia, Vol. 6, Supplemental Series, Hardesty's Chapter 3 (Richwood, WV: 1974), 144.

258 Hale, History of the Great Kanawha Valley, Vol. 1, 166, 220.

259 Stealey, The Antebellum Kanawha Salt Business and Western Markets, 129; Cohen, with Andre, Kanawha County Images: A Bicentennial History 1788-1988, Vol. 1, 35; Gerald S. Ratliff, "Burning Spring," e-WV: West Virginia Encyclopedia [Last Revised March 25, 2014] accessed August 31, 2017, https://www.wvencyclopedia.org/articles/725; James and Thorpe, Ancient Inventions, 405-406.; M. W. Donnally, "The Van Bibber Family," The West Virginia Historical Magazine 3, no. 1 (1903): 202, 220.

260 Sellers, The Market Revolution: Jacksonian America 1815-1846, 28.

261 Hale, History of the Great Kanawha Valley, Vol. 1, 224-226.; Stealey, The Antebellum Kanawha Salt Business and Western Markets, 15-20.

262 Dunaway, Slavery in the American Mountain South, 118-119.

263 Mark Kurlansky, Salt: A World History (New York: Penguin Books, 2002), 246.; Stealey, The Antebellum Kanawha County Salt Business and Western Markets, 17-18, 42.; Callahan, History of West Virginia, 165.; Stephanie Hoover, "The history of the Pennsylvania Salt Industry," Pennsylvania Research.com, accessed November 28, 2018, http://www.pennsylvaniaresearch.com/pennsylvania-salt-industry.html.

264 Hale, History of the Great Kanawha Valley, Vol. 1, 224-226.; Stealey, The Antebellum Kanawha Salt Business and Western Markets, 124.; Gerald W. Sutphin and Richard A. Andre, Sternwheelers on the Great Kanawha River (Charleston, WV: Pictorial Histories Publishing Co.,1991), 4.; Ann Royall, Sketches of History, Life and Manners, in the United States (New Haven, 1826), 50.

265 Rice, The Allegheny Frontier West Virginia Beginnings, 1730-1830, 325.; Rody Johnson, In their Footsteps (Charleston, WV: Quarrier Press, 2005), 153; Cohen, with Andre, Kanawha County Images: A Bicentennial History 1788-1988, Vol. 1, 37; Hale, Trans-Allegheny Pioneers, 313-314.

266 Salina Lodge No. 27, History and By-Laws (Malden, West Virginia: A. F. & A. M., n.d.), 9-10, 12-19.

267 "Sketch of Ruffner Home and Wiley Children as Adults," by Nancy McCartney of Malden; copy received on April 5, 2019, in possession of author.

268 Marria Blinn, Ruffner Family: Historic Sites Guide Book (Parker, CO: Outskirts Press, Inc., 2017), 76-79.; William Henry Ruffner, "The Ruffners II: Joseph," 35-39.

269 Alexander Ruffner (Descendant) in discussion with author, December 22, 2017.; Hale, Trans-Allegheny Pioneers, 280, 321-322.; Blinn, Ruffner Family: Historic Sites Guide Book, 77.; Cohen with Andre, Kanawha County Images: A Bicentennial History 1788- 1988, Vol. 1, 43.

270 Stealey, The Antebellum Kanawha Salt Business and Western Markets, 4, 197.

271 Stealey, The Antebellum Kanawha Salt Business and Western Markets, 4, 197.

272 Stealey, The Antebellum Kanawha Salt Business and Western Markets, 4, 189-190.

273 John Edmund Stealey, III, "Salt Industry," e-WV The West Virginia Encyclopedia (October 26, 2010) accessed October 24, 2018.

274 Joseph Lovell letter to James Bream dated January 6, 1817, family document, copy in possession of author.

275 Stealey, The Antebellum Kanawha Salt Business and Western Markets, 26-27.; John E. Stealey III, Kanawha Prelude to Nineteenth-Century Monopoly in the United States: The Virginia Salt Combinations (Richmond, VA: Virginia Historical Society, 2000), 26.; Elizabeth Cometti and Festus P. Summers. The Thirty-Fifth State: A Documentary History of West Virginia (Parsons, WV: McClain Printing Company, 1968), 197-204.

276 "Articles of Agreement- Kanawha Salt Company," Charter [Original Manuscript], November 10, 1817, West Virginia Archives, ID # Ms82-10.

277 Cometti and Summers. The Thirty-Fifth State: A Documentary History of West Virginia, 201.

278 Sellers, The Market Revolution: Jacksonian America 1815-1846, 44.

279 Hale, History of the Great Kanawha Valley, Vol. 1, 225.

280 Sellers, The Market Revolution: Jacksonian America 1815-1846, 47.; Stealey, "Salt Industry."; Stealey, The Antebellum Kanawha Salt Business and Western Markets, 4, 197.

281 A. W. B. Simpson, "The Horwitz Thesis and the History of Contracts," The University of Chicago Law Review 46, no. 3 (Spring 1979): 533-535.

282 Horwitz J. Morton, "The Historical

Foundations of Modern Contract Law," Harvard Law Review 87, no. 5 (March 1974): 917-918.

283 Sellers, The Market Revolution: Jacksonian America 1815-1846, 86-88.; Stealey, The Antebellum Kanawha Salt Business and Western Markets, xvi.; William Henry Ruffner. "The Ruffners III: David-Second Article," 46-47.

284 Stealey, The Antebellum Kanawha Salt Business and Western Markets, xv, 194-197.; Schlesinger Jr., The Age of Jackson, 432-433.

285 Schlesinger Jr., The Age of Jackson, 432-433.; Stealey, The Antebellum Kanawha Salt Business and Western Markets, 194-197.

286 Bruns, "The Antebellum Industrialization of the Kanawha Valley in the Virginia Backcountry," 104-109.

287 Stealey, The Antebellum Kanawha Salt Business and Western Markets, xii, 93.

288 Stealey, The Antebellum Kanawha Salt Business and Western Markets, 18-28.

289 William Henry Ruffner. "The Ruffners III: David- First Article," 46-54.

290 William Henry Ruffner. "The Ruffners III: David-Second Article," 49.; Dunaway, Slavery in the American Mountain South, 119.; "The Salt Works of Kanawha County," Richmond Enquirer (December 4, 1846); "Malden Has Home Coming," The Charleston Gazette (June 17, 1915).; Kanawha County Land Book, 1850-1860, Kanawha County Clerk's Office, Charleston, WV.

291 "The Salt Works of Kanawha County," Richmond Enquirer (December 4, 1846); "Malden Has Home Coming," The Charleston Gazette (June 17, 1915).

292 Tim Abraham, "Setting Kanawha Valley Ablaze Again," Charleston Daily Mail, Charleston, WV, January 1, 2019.

293 Daniel Walker Howe, What Hath

God Wrought: The Transformation of America, 1815-1848 (New York: Oxford University Press, 2007), 495; Royall, Sketches of History, Life and Manners, in the United States (New Haven, 1826).

294 Hale, History of the Great Kanawha Valley, Vol. 1, 180.

295 Atkinson, History of Kanawha County, 208.; Stealey, The Antebellum Kanawha Salt Business and Western Markets, 119-20.

296 Flasch & Flasch, Peter Ruffner and his Descendants, Vol. 2, 30, 33, 35.; Dean K. Thompson, "Presbyterians," e-WV: The West Virginia Encyclopedia, October 22, 2010, accessed August 5, 2019, https://www.wvencyclopedia.org/articles/1914; "Library Archives, History," First Presbyterian Church of Charleston, accessed August 5, 2019, http://firstpresby.com/about/library-archives-history/; "Kanawha Valley celebrates 200 years of Presbyterianism," Synod of the Trinity: Featured News, June 12, 2019, accessed August 5, 2019, http://www.syntrinity.org/featured/kanawha-valley-celebrates-200-years-of-presbyterianism/

297 Stealey, The Antebellum Kanawha Salt Business and Western Markets, 25; Cohen with Andre, Kanawha County Images: A Bicentennial History 1788-1988, Vol. 1, 46.; Flasch & Flasch, Peter Ruffner and his Descendants, Vol. 2, 30, 33, 35.

298 William Henry Ruffner. "The Ruffners III: David-Second Article," 49.; Charles Hedrick, History of the Ruffner Family of Kanawha, 4; Callahan, History of West Virginia, 101.; Cohen with Andre, Kanawha County Images: A Bicentennial History 1788-1988, Vol. 1, 35.; Dayton, Pioneers and Their Homes on Upper Kanawha, 199-200.

299 Cohen with Andre, Kanawha County Images: A Bicentennial History 1788-1988, Vol. 1, 45-46.; "Abolishment of Slavery in West Virginia (Extract from proceedings of the WV House of Delegates,

Feb. 1, 1865), " West Virginia Archives & History, accessed April 7, 2019, http://www.wvculture.org/hiStory/africanamericans/slaveryabolished02.html.; Mary Lee Settle, Addie (Columbia, SC: University of South Carolina Press, 1998).; Sheeler, The Negro in West Virginia Before 1900, 126.

300 Laidley, History of Charleston and Kanawha County, West Virginia and Representative Citizens, 75.; Ambler, A History of Education in West Virginia from Early Colonial Timesto 1949, 41.

301 Olmsted, A Journey in the Seaboard Slave States, With Remarks on Their Economy, 123, 267-268.

302 Ambler, A History of Education in West Virginia from Early Colonial Times to 1949, 41.; Cohen with Andre, Kanawha County Images: A Bicentennial History 1788-1988, Vol. 1, 24; Ambler, A History of Education in West Virginia from Early Colonial Times to 1949, 19-21.

303 Olmsted, A Journey in the Seaboard Slave States, With Remarks on Their Economy, 268.; Samuel Eliot Morrison, The Oxford History of the American People (New York: Oxford University Press, 1965), 511.; Henry T. Shanks, The Secession Movement in Virginia, 1847-1861 (Richmond, VA: Garrett & Massie, Inc., 1934), 10.

304 Dayton, Pioneers and Their Homes on Upper Kanawha, 47.

305 Washington and Lee University, A Brief History, accessed August 9, 2018, https://www.wlu.edu/about-wandl/history-and-traditions/a-brief-history.

306 Rosemary Jeanne Cobb, "Alexander Campbell," e-WV: The West Virginia Encyclopedia, January 23, 2013, accessed May 8, 2019, https://www.wvencyclopedia.org/articles/901.; Phil Conley, ed., The West Virginia Encyclopedia (Charleston, WV: West Virginia Publishing Company, 1929), 59, 120.; Ambler, A History of Education in West Virginia from Early Colonial Times to 1949, 120.; Elizabeth Jill Wilson, "West

Virginia University," e-WV: West Virginia Encyclopedia, November 27, 2018, accessed August 10, 2018, https://www.wvencyclopedia.org/articles/1127.

307 Williams, Appalachia: A History, 155.; Phil Conley, West Virginia Yesterday and Today (Charleston, WV: West Virginia Review Press, 1931), 122-123.

308 "Martinsville Negro Lawyer is Admitted to University," Richmond Times-Dispatch, (September 16, 1950).; Educational Opportunities for Women in the University of Virginia (University of Virginia Special Collection, 1920), 1; Barbara Brodie, Mr. Jefferson's Nurses: The University of Virginia School of Nursing, 1901 - 2001 (Charlottesville, VA: University of Virginia, 2000), 7; Mary Whitney, Women and the University (Charlottesville, VA: University of Virginia, 1969), 133-136.; Elizabeth J. Wilson, "West Virginia University," e-WV: West Virginia Encyclopedia, November 27, 2017, accessed June 27,2018, https://www.wvencyclopedia.org/articles/1127.; West Virginia University, History, College of Law, accessed August 9, 2018, https://www.law.wvu.edu/about-us/history.

309 Jack Ewing, "Researches Who Exposed VW Gain Little Reward From Success," The New York Times, July 24, 2016, https://www.nytimes.com/2016/07/25/business/vw-wvu-diesel-volkswagen-west-virginia.html

310 Ambler, A History of Education in West Virginia from Early Colonial Times to 1949, 88-89.; Hale, History of the Great Kanawha Valley, Vol. 1, 253.; State Superintendent of Schools, History of Education in West Virginia (Charleston, WV: Tribune Printing Company, 1907), 37, 117.

311 Ambler, A History of Education in West Virginia from Early Colonial Times to 1949, 88-89.

312 Conley, West Virginia Yesterday and Today, 362-363.; Ancella R. Bickley, History of The West Virginia State Teacher's Association (Washington D.C.: National Education Association, 1979), 15-19.

313 Ambler, A History of Education in West Virginia from Early Colonial Times to 1949, 48, 56, 140; Otis K. Rice and Stephen W. Brown, West Virginia: A History, 2nd ed (The University Press of Kentucky, 1993), 56, 70-71, 140.

314 Ambler, A History of Education in West Virginia from Early Colonial Times to 1949, 48, 56, 140.

315 Blinn, Ruffner Family: Historic Sites Guide Book, 83-84.; Ambler, A History of Education in West Virginia from Early Colonial Times to 1949, 90.; Article on Kanawha Riflemen discussing supplies from Richmond, The Kanawha Valley Star, (December 5, 1859); Memorial monument to the Kanawha Rifleman by the United Daughters of the Confederacy, Ruffner Park, Charleston, WV; Flasch & Flasch, Peter Ruffner and his Descendants, Vol. 2, ,55-56.

316 Dayton, Pioneers and Their Homes on Upper Kanawha, 198.; Ambler, A History of Education in West Virginia from Early Colonial Times to 1949, 131.; New York Journal of Commerce, "Princeton College," Richmond Enquirer, October 12, 1838.; Ambler, A History of Education in West Virginia, From Early Colonial Times to 1949, 15.; Ambler, Sectionalism in Virginia from 1776-1861, 277-278.; David Walton Coffey, "William Henry Ruffner: Rave and Public Education in Post-Reconstruction Virginia," (Master's Thesis, University of North Carolina, 1972), 32-43.

317 Ambler, A History of Education in West Virginia from Early Colonial Times to 1949, 88-90.; Hale, History of the Great Kanawha Valley, Vol. 1, 253; Hale, Trans-Allegheny Pioneers, 305; Hill, History: The First Baptist Church of Charleston West Virginia, 10.

318 Hale, Trans-Allegheny Pioneers, 253-254.

319 Minnie Wayne Cooper in discussion

with author, 1990, Charleston, WV.

320 Lewis Ruffner, Cash Book [Original Receipt Book], in possession of Author.

321 Stealey, The Antebellum Kanawha Salt Business and Western Markets, 138.

322 Bill Drennen, One Kanawha Valley Bank, (Bill Drennen, 2001), 15.; Atkinson, History of Kanawha County, 320.

323 Gallaher, Genealogical notes of the Miller- Quarrier- Shrewsbury- Dickinson- Dickenson Families and the Lewis, Ruffner, and Other Kindred Branches with Historical Incidents, etc., 62.; Atkinson, History of Kanawha County, 323.; Drennen, One Kanawha Valley Bank, 13-17.

324 William Henry Ruffner. "The Ruffners III: David- First Article," 49.; Peterkin, A History and Record of the Protestant Episcopal Church in the Diocese of West Virginia and Before the Formation of the Diocese in 1878 in the Territory now Known as the State of West Virginia, 636. Stealey III, Kanawha Prelude to Nineteenth-Century Monopoly in the United States: The Virginia Salt Combinations, 40.

325 Bill Drennen, One Kanawha Valley Bank, 25-27.

326 Bill Drennen, One Kanawha Valley Bank, 17.

327 Bill Drennen, One Kanawha Valley Bank, 17-27.

328 Bill Drennen, One Kanawha Valley Bank, 17, 25-27, 19-33, 35-36.; Hale. History of the Great Kanawha Valley, Vol. 1, 211; West Virginia's Pioneer Industry: Salt Making in the Kanawha Valley," West Virginia and Regional History Collection 47, no. 1 (Spring 1991): 4.

329 Settle, Addie, 67.

330 Bill Drennen, One Kanawha Valley Bank, 37, 40-41, 77-87.

331 Martha Darneal Cole (relative descendent) in discussion with author, December, 2012 & June 2013.

332 Gallaher, Genealogical notes of the Miller- Quarrier- Shrewsbury- Dickinson- Dickenson Families and the Lewis, Ruffner, and Other Kindred Branches with Historical Incidents, etc., 70-71.

333 Peterkin, A History and Record of the Protestant Episcopal Church in the Diocese of West Virginia and Before the Formation of the Diocese in 1878 in the Territory now Known as the State of West Virginia, 633- 643.; Martha Darneal Cole in discussion with author, December, 2012 & June 2013.

334 Peterkin, A History and Record of the protestant Episcopal Church, 634-636.

335 "Give Me Liberty or Give Me Death!" Colonial Williamsburg: That the Future May Learn From the Past, accessed January 14, 2019, http://www.history.org/almanack/life/politics/giveme.cfm.

336 Jefferds, Jr., A History of St. John's Episcopal Church: Charleston, West Virginia.

337 Jefferds, Jr., A History of St. John's Episcopal Church: Charleston, West Virginia, 12-13.

338 Chris Smith, From the Shenandoah to the Kanawha: The Story of Colonel John Smith, His Descendants and Their Ancestors (Charleston, WV: Chris Smith Publishing, ND), 327.

339 Gallaher, Genealogical notes of the Miller- Quarrier- Shrewsbury- Dickinson- Dickenson Families and the Lewis, Ruffner, and Other Kindred Branches with Historical Incidents, etc., 64-65.; National Council of Jewish Women, The Gourmet Day of History #7, (October 25, 1992), 12-13.

340 Smith, From the Shenandoah to the Kanawha: The Story of Colonel John Smith, His Descendants and Their Ancestors, 328.; Joel Shrewsbury, "Last Will and Testament," Will book [1859-76] 2, page 1-6; Kanawha County Office, Charleston, WV.; "The Malden Riot," in the West Vir-

ginia Journal, ed. G. W. Atkinson (Charleston, WV, December 15, 1869).

341 "The Malden Riot," in the West Virginia Journal, ed. G. W. Atkinson (Charleston, WV, December 15, 1869).; Gallaher, Genealogical Notes of the Miller-Quarrier-Shrewsbury-Dickinson- Dickenson Families and the Lewis, Ruffner, and Other Kindred Branches with Historical Incidents, etc, 71.

342 Cook, Washington's Western Lands (Strasburg, VA: Shenandoah Publishing House, Inc., 1930), 11.; Washington, The Diaries of George Washington, 1748-1799, Vol. 2, 410.; Ron Chernow, Washington: A Life, 807-817.

343 Gallaher, Genealogical notes of the Miller- Quarrier- Shrewsbury- Dickinson- Dickenson Families and the Lewis, Ruffner, and Other Kindred Branches with Historical Incidents, etc., 60- 63.; Deed of Sale from John Dickinson to Joseph Ruffner, 1796, Kanawha County Clerk's Office, Charleston, West Virginia, Deed Book A, Page 102.

344 Prichard, A History of the Episcopal Church, 152-154.; Frances Keller Swinford and Rebecca Smith Lee, The Great Elm Tree: Heritage of The Episcopal Diocese of Lexington (Lexington, KY: Faith House Press, 1969), 272.; Ambler and Summers, West Virginia the Mountain State, second edition, 148-149.; Ambler and Summers, West Virginia the Mountain State, second edition, 290-324.

345 Larry L. Rowe, History Tour of Old Malden: Virginia and West Virginia Booker T. Washington's Formative Years (Malden, West Virginia: Larry L. Rowe Attorney at Law, 2014), 12-13.

346 Jim Comstock, The West Virginia. Heritage Encyclopedia, Vol. 19, REV - SCH (Richwood, WV: Jim Comstock, 1976), 4186-4188.; Laidley, History of Charleston and Kanawha County: West Virginia and Representative Citizens, 74-75.

347 Flasch & Flasch ed., Peter Ruffner and his Descendants, Vol. 2, 14-16; Laidley, History of Charleston and Kanawha County, West Virginia and Representative Citizens, 74-75.

348 William Henry Ruffner, "The Ruffners I: Peter," West Virginia Historical Magazine 1, no. 2. (April 1901): 34-35.; Edward L. Ayers and John C. Willis, The Edge of the South: Life in Nineteenth-Century Virginia (Charlottesville, VA: University Press of Virginia, 1991), 156.; "Virginia Tourism Revenues Reached $25 Billion in 2017," Virginia Tourism Corporation: Pressroom, 2017, https://pressroom.virginia.org/2018/05/virginia-tourism-revenues-reached-25-billion-in-2017/

349 Monroe County Historical Society, "Red Sulphur Springs," The Monroe Watchman (Union, West Virginia, January 25, 1968.; Ambler, A History of West Virginia, 202-203.

350 "About Us," City of White Sulphur Springs, WV, https://local.wv.gov/WhiteSulphurSprings/Pages/about.aspx.; Dunaway, Slavery in the American Mountain South, 82-86.; Robert S. Conte, The History of the Greenbrier: America's Resort (Charleston, WV: Pictorial Histories Publishing Co., 1989).

351 Flasch & Flasch, Peter Ruffner and his Descendants, Vol. 2, 5, 6.

352 Lewis, History of West Virginia, 193.; Callahan, History of West Virginia, 44.

353 Flasch & Flasch, Peter Ruffner and his Descendants, Vol. 2, 14.

354 Ruffner Family Bible, in possession of Author.; Flasch & Flasch, Peter Ruffner and his Descendants, Vol. 2, 120.

355 Garnett Laidlow Eskew, Salt, The Fifth Element: The Story of a Basic American Industry (Chicago, IL: J.G. Ferguson and Associates, 1948) 80.

356 Flasch & Flasch, Peter Ruffner and his Descendants, Vol. 2, 157.

357 Flasch & Flasch, Peter Ruffner and

his Descendants, Vol. 2, 202.

358 Flasch & Flasch, Peter Ruffner and his Descendants, Vol. 2, 248-254.

359 Flasch & Flasch, Peter Ruffner and his Descendants, Vol. 2, 302.; Stealey, The Antebellum Kanawha Salt Business and Western Markets, 10.

360 Rice, The Allegheny Frontier West Virginia Beginnings, 1730-1830, 310.

361 Harlan, Booker T. Washington the Making of a Black Leader 1856-1901, 42.

362 "Late Booker T. Washington, Negro Educator, Got Start in Kanawha County," Charleston Gazette (Charleston, WV), March 19, 1922.

363 William Henry Ruffner. "The Ruffners III: David- First Article," 47.; Eskew, Salt, The Fifth Element: The Story of a Basic American Industry, 14-16.; Laidley, History of Charleston and Kanawha County, West Virginia and Representative Citizens, 75.; Ruffner Family Bible, in possession of Author.

364 Sellers, The Market Revolution: Jacksonian America 1815-1846, 27-28.; Bruns, "The Antebellum Industrialization of the Kanawha Valley in the Virginia Backcountry," 82.

365 Blinn, Ruffner Family: Historic Sites Guide Book, 88-89.; Flasch & Flasch, Peter Ruffner and his Descendants, Vol. 2, 14, 62, 75.

366 William Henry Ruffner. "The Ruffners III: David-Second Article," 46, 50.; Princeton Theological Seminary, Alumni Association, "William Swan Plumer," in Necrological Report" Presented to the Alumni Association of Princeton Theological Seminary at its Annual Meeting, April 26, 1881 (Princeton Theological Seminary, 1891).

367 Flasch & Flasch, Peter Ruffner and his Descendants, Vol. 2, 26.

368 New York Journal of Commerce, "Princeton College," Richmond Enquirer,

October 12, 1838.

369 Blinn, Ruffner Family: Historic Sites Guide Book, 80-81.

370 Klaus Wust, The Virginia Germans, 127-128.; Henry Ruffner, Address to the People of West Virginia (Lexington, KY: R.C. Noel, 1847), 21-22.

371 Williams, Appalachia: A History 154.; "Honorary Degrees: 1842 to Present," Washington & Lee University: University Honors Board, accessed November 28, 2018,

https://www.wlu.edu/university-registrar/our-services/university-honors-board/honorary-degrees; Flasch & Flasch, Peter Ruffner and his Descendants, Vol. 2, 31.; William H. Maginnis, "Pioneer Academies in Kanawha Valley Trained Settlers' Youth for College," Charleston Gazette (Charleston, WV), October 30, 1949.; Dayton, Pioneers and Their Homes on Upper Kanawha, 199.; Sheeler, The Negro in West Virginia Before 1900, 171.

372 Gaius Marcus Brumbaugh, Genealogy of the Brumbach Families, (New York, NY: Fredrick H. Hitchcock, 1913), 265.; Royall, Sketches of History, Life and Manners in the United States, 57.; Letter from Henry Ruffner (Kanawha C. H., VA) to Samuel Williams (Chillicothe, OH), Typescript, February 9, 1816, in possession of author.

373 Dayton, Greenbrier Pioneers and Their Homes, 68.; Ambler, A History of Education in West Virginia from Early Colonial Times to 1949, 79.

374 Executive Circle: First Presbyterian Church, History of the Presbyterian Congregation and Other Early Churches of "Kenhawa", 1804-1900 (Charleston, WV: Executive Circle: First Presbyterian Church, 1930), 29.; Rice, The Allegheny Frontier West Virginia Beginnings, 1730-1830, 301.

375 Hale. History of the Great Kanawha Valley, Vol. 1, 180-181.

376 Cometti and Summers. The Thirty-Fifth State: A Documentary History of West Virginia, 289.

377 Hale. History of the Great Kanawha Valley, Vol. 1, 162, 166; Laidley, History of Charleston and Kanawha County, West Virginia and Representative Citizens, 52.; Flasch & Flasch, Peter Ruffner and his Descendants, Vol. 2, 33.; William Henry Ruffner. "The Ruffners III: David-First Article," 48.

378 Hale, Trans-Allegheny Pioneers, 313-314.; Gallaher, Genealogical Notes of the Miller- Quarrier- Shrewsbury- Dickinson- Dickenson Families and the Lewis, Ruffner, and Other Kindred Branches with Historical Incidents, etc., 88.; Cohen with Andre, Kanawha County Images: A Bicentennial History 1788-1988, Vol. 1, 35.; William Henry Ruffner. "The Ruffners III: David-First Article," 49.; Letter from Henry Ruffner (Kanawha C. H., VA) to Samuel Williams (Chillicothe, OH), Typescript, February 9, 1816, in possession of author.

379 Harlan, "Booker T. Washington's West Virginia Boyhood," West Virginia Archives and History Volume 32, Number 2, January 1971, accessed September 6, 2017 http://www.wvculture.org/history/journal_wvh/wvh32-1.html.63-85; George W. Summers to the Rev. R. R. Gurley, July 30, 1829, Con. 17, American Colonization Society Papers, Library of Congress.; Olmsted, A Journey in the Seaboard Slave States, With Remarks on Their Economy, 287-288.

380 Stealey, The Antebellum Kanawha Salt Business and Western Markets, 44-45, 67.

381 Flasch & Flasch, Peter Ruffner and his Descendants, Vol. 2, 25, 78.

382 Cohen with Andre, Kanawha County Images: A Bicentennial History 1788-1988, Vol. 1, 35.; Flasch & Flasch, Peter Ruffner and his Descendants, Vol. 2, 38.

383 Flasch & Flasch, Peter Ruffner and his Descendants, Vol. 2, 78.

384 Flasch & Flasch, Peter Ruffner and his Descendants, Vol. 2, 40-42, 78.

385 Harlan, Booker T. Washington the Making of a Black Leader 1859-1901, 40.; John E. Stealey III, "Slavery and the Western Virginia Salt Industry," The Journal of Negro History 59, no. 2 (1974), 116.

386 "The Malden Riot," in the West Virginia Journal, ed. G. W. Atkinson (Charleston, WV, December 15, 1869).

387 Marianne E. Julienne and the Dictionary of Virginia Biography, "William Henry Ruffner (1824- 1908)," Encyclopedia of Virginia, April 29, 2016, accessed November 14, 2017, https://www.encyclopediavirginia.org/Ruffner_William_H_1824-1908.; Wayland, A History of Virginia for Boys and Girls, 138.

388 "Honorary Degrees: 1842 to Present," Washington & Lee University: University Honors Board, accessed November 28, 2018.; Robert E. Lee, "Robert E. Lee to Col. Walter H. Taylor [Letter], February 21, 1870," transcribed by Colin Woodward, October 20 2015, Lee Family Digital Archive, accessed June 14, 2019, https://leefamilyarchive.org/9-family-papers/129-robert-e-lee-to-walter-h-taylor-1870-february-21

389 Blinn, Ruffner Family: Historic Sites Guide Book, 85.; Walter Javen Fraser, Jr., William Henry Ruffner: A Liberal in the Old and New South (Ph.D. Dissertation, University of Tennessee, March 1970).

390 Flasch & Flasch, Peter Ruffner and his Descendants, Vol. 2, 38, 42-44.; Fraser, Jr., William Henry Ruffner: A Liberal in the Old and New South, 64-65.

391 Fraser, Jr., William Henry Ruffner: A Liberal in the Old and New South.

392 "About Us," City of White Sulphur Springs, WV, https://local.wv.gov/WhiteSulphurSprings/Pages/about.aspx.

393 Flasch & Flasch, Peter Ruffner and his Descendants, Vol. 2, 54.

394 Flasch & Flasch, Peter Ruffner and

his Descendants, Vol. 2, 78.; Harlan, "Booker T. Washington's West Virginia Boyhood," 76.; Lewis Ruffner, "Valuable Salt Property for Sale," The Kanawha Republican (October 23, 1844): 4t.

395 Atkinson, History of Kanawha County, 304.; "Corresponding and Executive Commitee" The Louisville Examiner (Louisville, Ky), 10 March 1849, Chronicling America: Histotric American Newspapers, Lib. of Congress. <http://chroniclingamerica.loc.gov/lccn/sn82015050/1849-03-10/ed-1/seq-2/>.; "Bland Ballard (1819-1879)," History of the Sixth Circuit, accessed January 14, 2019, https://web.archive.org/web/20090118184446/http://www.ca6.uscourts.gov/lib_hist/Courts/district%20court/KY/KY/judges/bb-bio.html.

396 Ruffner, Union Speech of Fourth of July 1856 in the Kanawha Salines.

397 Berlin, Generations of Captivity: A History of African-American Slaves, 116-117, 186-195.; Genovese, Roll, Jordan, Roll: The World The Slaves Made, 621, 536-540.

398 Genovese, Roll, Jordan, Roll: The World The Slaves Made, 616-622.

399 Genovese, Roll, Jordan, Roll: The World The Slaves Made, 617.

400 Genovese, Roll, Jordan, Roll: The World The Slaves Made, 78-80, 144-147. Adams, A South-Side View of Slavery; or, Three Months at the South in 1854, 47.

401 Genovese, Roll, Jordan, Roll: The World The Slaves Made, 526, 533-534.

402 Kulikoff, Tobacco and Slaves: The Development of Southern Cultures in the Chesapeake, 1680-1800, 73.; Richard S. Dunn, "A Tale of Two Plantations: Slave Life at Mesopotamia in Jamaica and Mount Airy in Virginia, 1799 to 1828," The William and Mary Quarterly, Vol. 34, no. 1(January 1977), 44-46.

403 Lewis Suggs, "Book Review: The Black Family in Slavery and Freedom, 1750-1925," New Directions, vol. 4, Article 10, October 1, 1977; accessed January 21, 2019

http.//dh.howard.edu/newdirections/vol4/10.; Berlin, The Making of African America: The Four Great Migrations, 134-135.

404 Gutman, The Black Family in Slavery and Freedom 1750-1925, 431.

405 Gutman, The Black Family in Slavery and Freedom 1750-1925, 31-37, 291.

406 Gutman, The Black Family in Slavery and Freedom 1750-1925, 271-275.

407 Gutman, The Black Family in Slavery and Freedom 1750-1925, 135-233.; Berlin, Generations of Captivity: A History of African-American Slaves, 205.

408 Booker T. Washington, The Booker T, Washington Papers, vol. 1, The Autobiographical Writings, ed. Louis R. Harlan and John W. Blassingame (Chicago, Illinois: University of Illinois Press, 1972), 12.; Dunaway, Slavery in the American Mountain South, 166.

409 Gutman, The Black Family in Slavery and Freedom 1750-1925, 19.

410 Gutman, The Black Family in Slavery and Freedom 1750-1925, 226.; Ayers and Willis, The Edge of the South: Life in Nineteenth Century Virginia, 39-41.; Genovese, Roll, Jordan, Roll: The World The Slaves Made, 624.

411 Berlin, The Making of African America: The Four Great Migrations, 191.; Dunaway, Slavery in the American Mountain South, 188 -189, 246.; Genovese, Roll, Jordan, Roll: The World The Slaves Made, 621-622, 635.

412 Dunaway, Slavery in the American Mountain South, 246-247.; Baptist, The Half Has Never Been Told, 183.; Gutman, The Black Family in Slavery and Freedom 1750-1925, 146, 264-266.

413 Olmsted, A Journey in the Seaboard Slave States, With Remarks on Their Economy, 282.; Winfield H. Collins, The Do-

mestic Slave Trade of the Southern States (Port Washington, NY: Kennikat Press, Inc., 1969), 22-23.; Ruffner, Address to the People of West Virginia, 21-22, 35-36.

414   Robert William Fogel and Stanley L. Engerman, Time on the Cross: The Economics of American Negro Slavery (Boston, MA: Little, Brown and Company, 1974), 116-117. ; Robert William Fogel, Without Consent or Contract: The Rise and Fall of American Slavery (New York, NY: W. W. Norton, 1989), 121-122.

415   Olmsted, A Journey in the Seaboard Slave States, With Remarks on Their Economy, 295-296, 305.

416   Bancroft, Slave Trading in the Old South, 290, 69-71 Fogel and Engerman, Time on the Cross: The Economics of American Negro Slavery, 3-11, 115.; Olmsted, A Journey in the Seaboard Slave States, With Remarks on Their Economy, 101-112.

417   Adams, A South-Side View of Slavery; or, Three Months at the South in 1854, 81-82.; Olmsted, A Journey in the Seaboard Slave States, With Remarks on Their Economy, 98-112.

418   Berlin, Generations of Captivity: A History of African-American Slaves, 213-214.

419   Olmsted, A Journey in the Seaboard Slave States, With Remarks on Their Economy, 34-35.; Frederick Law Olmsted, The Cotton Kingdom: A Traveller's Observations on Cotton and Slavery in the American Slave States (New York, NY: Alfred A. Knopf, 1970), 595.

420   Berlin, Generations of Captivity: A History of African-American Slaves, 214.

421   Sharon Ann Murphy, "Securing Human Property: Slavery, Life Insurance, and Industrialization in the Upper South," Journal of the Early Republic 25, no. 4 (2005): 628.

422   Gutman, The Black Family in Slavery and Freedom 1750-1925, 149.

423   Gutman, The Black Family in Slavery and Freedom 1750-1925, 146.

424   Gutman, The Black Family in Slavery and Freedom 1750-1925, 146.

425   Baptist, The Half Has Never Been Told, 181-182.; Fogel and Engerman, Time on the Cross: The Economics of American Negro Slavery, 47.

426   Berlin, Generations of Captivity: A History of African-American Slaves, 167.

427   Berlin, Generations of Captivity: A History of African-American Slaves, 101-102.

428   Bancroft, Slave Trading in the Old South, 290.; Adams, A South-Side View of Slavery; or, Three Months at the South in 1854, 91, 403-406.

429   Bancroft, Slave Trading in the Old South, 198-208.; Adams, A South-Side View of Slavery; or, Three Months at the South in 1854, 66-73.; Fogel and Engerman, Time on the Cross: The Economics of American Negro Slavery, 5.; Fones-Wolf, Glass Towns: Industry, Labor, and Political Economy in Appalachia, 1890-1930s, 42.

430   Berlin, Generations of Captivity: A History of African-American Slaves, 15, 166.

431   Berlin, Generations of Captivity: A History of African-American Slaves, 215.

432   Baptist, The Half Has Never Been Told, 180.

433   Berlin, The Making of African America: The Four Great Migrations, 100-105.

434   Fogel and Engerman, Time on the Cross: The Economics of American Negro Slavery, 44-52, 78-83.; Herbert G. Gutman, Slavery and the Numbers Game: A Critique of Time On The Cross (Urbana and Chicago, IL: University of Illinois Press, 2003).

435   Stanley M. Elkins, Slavery: A Problem in American Institutional & Intellectual Life (New York, NY: Grosset & Dunlap, 1963), 236-237.

436 Fogel and Engerman, Time on the Cross: The Economics of American Negro Slavery, 44-52.; Gutman, Slavery and the Numbers Game: A Critique of Time On The Cross, 103.

437 Adams, A South-Side View of Slavery; or, Three Months at the South in 1854, 158.

438 Stampp, The Peculiar Institution: Slavery in the Ante-Bellum South, 250-262, 238.

439 Bancroft, Slave Trading in the Old South, 270, 404-405.

440 Bancroft, Slave Trading in the Old South, 397.

441 Bancroft, Slave Trading in the Old South, 69-71.

442 Bancroft, Slave Trading in the Old South, 118.

443 "CPI Inflation Calculator [Rates based on U.S. Bureau of Labor Statistics' Consumer Price Index (CPI]," Official Data.org, accessed May 20, 2019, https://www.officialdata.org/us/inflation/1850?amount=700

444 Stampp, The Peculiar Institution: Slavery in the Ante-Bellum South, 416.; Bancroft, Slave Trading in the Old South, 343. 386.

445 Bancroft, Slave Trading in the Old South, 69-71.

446 Collins, The Domestic Slave Trade of the Southern States, 61-67.

447 Ruffner, Address to the People of West Virginia, 35-36.; Olmsted, The Cotton Kingdom: A Traveller's Observations on Cotton and Slavery in the American Slave States, 17.

448 Ruffner, Address to the People of West Virginia, 35-36.

449 Olmsted, A Journey in the Seaboard Slave States, With Remarks on Their Economy, 128-129.

450 "Slavery: Virginia Historical Society,"

Virginia Museum of History & Culture, accessed March 26, 2018, https://www.virginiahistory.org/what-you-can-see/story-virginia/explore-story-virginia/18225-1861/slavery.

451 Gutman, Slavery and the Numbers Game: A Critique of Time On The Cross, 103.

452 Fogel, Without Consent or Contract: The Rise and Fall of American Slavery, 167.

453 Genovese, Roll, Jordan, Roll: The World The Slaves Made, 457.; Fogel, Without Consent or Contract: The Rise and Fall of American Slavery, 167.

454 William Loren Katz, ed., The American Negro: His History and Literature (US: Arno Press, Inc., 1968), 38.

455 Katz, ed., The American Negro: His History and Literature, 38.

456 Olmsted, A Journey in the Seaboard Slave States, With Remarks on Their Economy, 282.

457 Gutman, The Black Family in Slavery and Freedom 1750-1925, 280-282.; Berlin, Generations of Captivity: A History of African-American Slaves, 173.

458 Gutman, The Black Family in Slavery and Freedom 1750-1925, xx-xxii.

459 Dunaway, Slavery in the American Mountain South, 165-166.

460 Dunaway, Slavery in the American Mountain South, 165-166.

461 John Greenleaf Whittier, "The Farewell of a Virginia Slave Mother to her daughters, sold into Southern Bondage," Political Works, Vol. III, Anti-Slavery Poems: Songs of Labor and Reform (1886).

462 Adams, A South-Side View of Slavery; or, Three Months at the South in 1854, 79-80.

463 Baptist, The Half Has Never Been Told, 280-282.

464 Fogel and Engerman, Time on the

Cross: The Economics of American Negro Slavery, 231.; Bruce Levine "Introduction" in Gutman, Slavery and the Numbers Game: A Critique of Time On The Cross, xi-xvii.; Ballagh, A History of Slavery in Virginia, 107.; Stampp, The Peculiar Institution: Slavery in the Ante-Bellum South, 430.

465 Andrew Burstein, Madison and Jefferson (New York: Random House, 2010), 578.; Fogel and Engerman, Time on the Cross: The Economics of American Negro Slavery, 70-73, 231.

466 Fogel and Engerman, Time on the Cross: The Economics of American Negro Slavery, 70-73.; Booker T. Washington, N.B. Wood and Fannie Barrier Williams, A New Negro for a New Century (New York: Arno Press and the New York Times, 1969), 172.; Lambert, West Virginia and Its Government, 47.

467 Adams, A South-Side View of Slavery; or, Three Months at the South in 1854, 60-77.; Genovese, Roll, Jordan, Roll: The World The Slaves Made, 32, 502-507.;

468 Dunaway, Slavery in the American Mountain South, 57-60.

469 Dunaway, Slavery in the American Mountain South, 57-60, 508.; Norman R. Yetman, Voices From Slavery, 100 Authentic Slave Narratives, 56.; Washington, Up From Slavery, 11.; Genovese, Roll, Jordan, Roll: The World The Slaves Made, 551-559.

470 Genovese, Roll, Jordan, Roll: The World The Slaves Made, 507-508.; Washington, Up From Slavery, 9.

471 Thomas D. Morris, Southern Slavery and the Law, 1619-1860 (Chapel Hill, NC: The University of North Carolina Press, 1996), 190.; Genovese, Roll, Jordan, Roll: The World The Slaves Made, 35-36.

472 Stampp, The Peculiar Institution: Slavery in the Ante-Bellum South, 380-382.

473 Julius de Gruyter, The Kanawha Spectator, Vol. 2 (Charleston, WV: Jarrett Printing Company, 1953), 197.

474 Nardo, The Atlantic Slave Trade, 25, 36, 71, 84, 95; Robert Evans Jr., "The Economics of American Negro Slavery, 1830-1860," in Aspects of Labor Economics (Princeton University Press, 1962), 199.; Gerald W. Mullin, Flight and Rebellion: Slave Resistance in Eighteenth Century Virginia (New York, NY: Oxford University Press, 1972), 10.; Stampp, The Peculiar Institution: Slavery in the Ante-Bellum South, 208-211.; Olmsted, A Journey in the Seaboard Slave States, With Remarks on Their Economy, 128.; Berlin, Generations of Captivity: A History of African-American Slaves, 61.

475 Genovese, Roll, Jordan, Roll: The World The Slaves Made, 34-41.

476 Genovese, Roll, Jordan, Roll: The World The Slaves Made, 632.; Philip J. Schwarz, Twice Condemned: Slaves and the Criminal Laws of Virginia, 1705-1865 (Baton Rouge, LA: Louisiana State University Press, 1988), 12-18, 40-44.

477 Stampp, The Peculiar Institution: Slavery in the Ante-Bellum South, 209-211.

478 Mullin, Flight and Rebellion: Slave Resistance in Eighteenth-Century Virginia, 11-33.; Fogel, Without Consent or Contract: The Rise and Fall of American Slavery, 121.; Morris, Southern Slavery and the Law, 1619-1860, 306.; Schwarz, Twice Condemned: Slaves and the Criminal Laws of Virginia, 1705-1865, 14-18, 38-44.

479 Reidy, From Slavery to Agrarian Capitalism in the Cotton Plantation South: Central George, 1800-1880, 45-47.; Ayers and Willis, The Edge of the South: Life in Nineteenth-Century Virginia, 7-8.; C. Vann Woodward, The Strange Career of Jim Crow (New York, NY: Oxford University Press, 1974), 54.; Reinhold Niebuhr, Love and Justice: Selections from the Shorter Writings of Reinhold Niebuhr (Charlottes-

ville, VA: The University of Virginia Press, 1976), 147.

480 Berlin, Generations of Captivity: A History of African-American Slaves, 60-61.; Schwarz, Twice Condemned: Slaves and the Criminal Laws of Virginia, 1705-1865, 6.

481 Ballagh, A History of Slavery in Virginia, 78.; Mullin, Flight and Rebellion: Slave Resistance in Eighteenth-Century Virginia, 36-40.; Schwarz, Twice Condemned: Slaves and the Criminal Laws of Virginia, 1705-1865, 6-16.; Adams, A South-Side View of Slavery; or, Three Months at the South in 1854, 86-102.; Stampp, The Peculiar Institution: Slavery in the Ante-Bellum South, 174-182

482 Reidy, From Slavery to Agrarian Capitalism in the Cotton Plantation South: Central George, 1800-1880, 37.; Fogel and Engerman, Time on the Cross: The Economics of American Negro Slavery, 146-147.

483 Berlin, Generations of Captivity: A History of African-American Slaves, 184-190.; Reidy, From Slavery to Agrarian Capitalism in the Cotton Plantation South: Central George, 1800-1880, 183-190.; Schwarz, Twice Condemned: Slaves and the Criminal Laws of Virginia, 1705-1865, 16.

484 Reidy, From Slavery to Agrarian Capitalism in the Cotton Plantation South: Central George, 1800-1880, 184.; Schwarz, Twice Condemned: Slaves and the Criminal Laws of Virginia, 1705-1865, 18.

485 "Kanawha Salt Lick," New Bedford Gazette, January 04, 1836. Stealey, The Antebellum Kanawha Salt Business and Western Markets, 133-134.

486 Dunaway, Slavery in the American Mountain South, 166.

487 "Theresa Cozad (Gatewood), 1837-1923," History of Nebraska: Nebraska State Historical Society, accessed December 31, 2018, https://nebraskahistory.pastperfectonline.com/byperson?keyword=Cozad%2C+Theresa+%28Gatewood%29%2C+1837-1923.; Biography of Robert Henri," henrirobert.org, accessed November 30, 2017. http://www.henrirobert.org/biography.html.

488 Kathleen, 1924, Painting by Robert Henri in Huntington Museum of Art: Fifty Years of Collecting (Huntington, WV: Huntington Museum of Art, 2001), 125-126.

489 Edward Ball, "Slavery's Trail of Tears," Smithsonian Magazine, November 2015, 63.

490 Adams, A South-Side View of Slavery; or, Three Months at the South in 1854, 60-77, 113.

491 Berlin, Generations of Captivity: A History of African-American Slaves, 14-15.; Berlin, The Making of African America: The Four Great Migrations, 100.

492 Berlin, Generations of Captivity: A History of African-American Slaves, 18.

493 Berlin, Generations of Captivity: A History of African-American Slaves, 172-179.; Baptist, The Half Has Never Been Told, 108, 188.; Henry Louis Gates, "The African Americans" with Henry Louis Gates Jr., (Kumhart Mcgree Productions, 2013).

494 Baptist, The Half Has Never Been Told, 22-26, 180.; Adams, A South-Side View of Slavery; or, Three Months at the South in 1854, 77.; Bancroft, Slave Trading in the Old South, 280-285.; Berlin, The Making of African America: The Four Great Migrations, 116.

495 Berlin, Generations of Captivity: A History of African-American Slaves, 172-179.; Ball, "Slavery's Trail of Tears," Smithsonian Magazine, 64-66.

496 Ambler and Summers, West Virginia the Mountain State, second edition, 126.; Jeanette M. Rowsey, The Lose Village of Barboursville: Unsung and Vanishing

History of the "best Little Village in West Virginia (1813-2013) (Barboursville, WV: JRC Publishing, 2013), 30, 57.

497 Louise McNeill, Hill Daughter: New & Selected Poems (Pittsburgh PA: University of Pittsburgh Press, 1991), with Maggie Anderson, 77.

498 Genovese, Roll, Jordan, Roll: The World The Slaves Made, 635.

499 Bancroft, Slave Trading in the Old South, 343, 386.

500 Ball, "Slavery's Trail of Tears," Smithsonian Magazine, 63.; Calculations made using information from "Consumer Price Index," United States Department of Labor: Bureau of Labor Statistics, accessed May 22, 2019.

501 PBS, Lift Every Voice and Sing, accessed June 21,2018,

http://www.pbs.org/black-culture/explore/black-authors-spoken-word-poetry/lift-every-voiceand-sing/.; "James Weldon Johnson," Biography by A&E Television Networks, April 2, 2014, accessed January 20, 2019, https://www.biography.com/people/james-weldon-johnson-9356013.

502 David Levering Lewis, W. E. B. Du Bois: The Fight for Equality and the American Century, 1919-1963 (New York, NY: Henry Holt and Company, LLC., 2000), 21-25.

503 James Weldon Johnson, "Lift Every Voice and Sing," The Hymnal 1982 (New York: Church Pension Fund, 1985), 599.

504 Stampp, The Peculiar Institution: Slavery in the Ante-Bellum South, 44-45, 168.; Dunaway, Slavery in the American Mountain South, 62-63.

505 Ballagh, A History of Slavery in Virginia, 107.

506 Baptist, The Half Has Never Been Told, 16-165, 188, 349-350; Henry Louis Gates, Jr., ed., Classic Slave Narratives (New York, NY: New American Library, 1987), 349-350.

507 Berlin, The Making of African America: The Four Great Migrations, 128-129.

508 Berlin, The Making of African America: The Four Great Migrations, 148-149.

509 Olmsted, A Journey in the Seaboard Slave States, With Remarks on Their Economy, 239.

510 Adams, A South-Side View of Slavery; or, Three Months at the South in 1854, 211.; Baptist, The Half Has Never Been Told, 159-167.

511 The Associated Press, "Virginia Legislators Vote to Retire the State Song," The New York Times, February 18, 1997, accessed October 21, 2017, http://www.nytimes.com/1997/02/18/us/virginia-legislators-vote-to-retire-the-state-song.html.; Sellers, The Market Revolution: Jacksonian America 1815-1846, 389.

512 James Bland, Carry Me Back to Old Virginny, 1861, Notated Music, (Accessed June 15, 2017) retrieved from the Library of Congress, https://www.loc.gov/item/ihas.200000735/.

513 Kathryn Miller Haines, "Stephen Foster: The Making of Pittsburgh's Renowned Musical Export," Western Pennsylvania History: Up Front 97, no. 3 (Fall 2014), 38.; Jim O'Grady, "The Hidden Racial History of 'My Old Kentucky Home'," WNYC News May 2, 2014, accessed September 28, 2017,

http://www.wnyc.org/story/hidden-meaning-my-old-kentucky-home/.

514 Kathryn Miller Haines, "Stephen Foster: The Making of Pittsburgh's Renowned Musical Export," Western Pennsylvania History: Up Front 97, no. 3 (Fall 2014).

515 Kathryn Miller Haines, "Stephen Foster: The Making of Pittsburgh's Renowned Musical Export," Western Pennsylvania History: Up Front 97, no. 3 (Fall 2014).; Harriet Beecher Stowe, Uncle Tom's Cabin (New York: New American Library 2008), 37, 38.; Berlin, Generations of Captivity: A History of African-American Slaves, 172-

179.

516 Stephen Foster, Stephen Foster Song Book: Original Sheet Music of 40 Songs (Chelmsford, MA: Courier Corporation, 1974), 67.

517 Ellen King, West Virginia Hills, Official State Song (Publishers' Service Bureau, Washington D.C., 1913).

518 John Denver, "Take Me Home, Country Roads," Poems, Prayers and Promises (New York City, NY: RCA Records, 1971).

519 Jake Stump, "'Country Roads' Covers Uncovered," WVU Magazine, accessed February 11, 2019, https://magazine.wvu.edu/stories/2016/10/06/-country-roads-covers-uncovered.

520 Baptist, The Half Has Never Been Told, 116.

521 Beckert, "Empire of Cotton," The Atlantic, December 2014.; Baptist, The Half Has Never Been Told, 115.

522 Baptist, The Half Has Never Been Told, 2-3.; Wayland, A History of Virginia for Boys and Girls, 48.

523 Morgan, American Slavery, American Freedom, The Ordeal of Colonial Virginia, 5-6.; Baptist, The Half Has Never Been Told, 352.

524 Margaret L. Coit, The Life History of the United States, Vol. 3, The Growing Years (New York: Time-Life Books, 1963), 125, 134.; Peter Lyon, "A Tinkering People," in The American Heritage Book of the Pioneer Spirit ed. Richard M. Ketchum (American Heritage Publishing Co., Inc., 1959), 284.

525 Alan L. Olmstead and Paul W. Rhode, Creating Abundance: Biological Innovation and American Agricultural Development (Cambridge: Cambridge University Press, 2008), 129-131.; Baptist, The Half Has Never Been Told, 83.; Richard H. Stechel, "Slave Mortality: Analysis of Evidence from Plantation Records," Social Science History, Vol.3, No. 3,4(1979), 95.

526 Beckert, Empire of Cotton: A Global History (NY: Alfred A. Knoff, 2014) xviii, quoting Cotton Supply Reporter, no. 37 (March 1, 1860):33.

527 Beckert, "Empire of Cotton," The Atlantic.

528 Beckert, Empire of Cotton: A Global History (NY: Alfred A. Knoff, 2014) xiii-xix.

529 Beckert, Empire of Cotton: A Global History, (NY: Alfred A. Knoff, 2014) xviii.

530 Berlin, Generations of Captivity: A History of African-American Slaves, 162.; Adams, A South-Side View of Slavery; or, Three Months at the South in 1854, 79-80.

531 Bancroft, Slave Trading in the Old South, 290.; Adams, A South-Side View of Slavery; or, Three Months at the South in 1854, 82-87.; Charles Ball, Fifty Years in Chains (New York, NY: Dover Publications, Inc., 1970), 210-222.

532 Baptist, The Half Has Never Been Told, 103-106, 178-182.; Adams, A South-Side View of Slavery; or, Three Months at the South in 1854, 60-77.

533 Gutman, The Black Family in Slavery and Freedom 1750-1925, 291, 531-544.

534 Biography of Robert Henri," henrirobert.org, accessed November 30, 2017. http://www.henrirobert.org/biography.html; Ballagh, A History of Slavery in Virginia, 100.

535 James Truslow Adams, The March of Democracy: A History of the United States, vol. 3, Civil War and Reconstruction (New York, NY: Charles Scribner's Sons, 1933), 206-207.

536 Gutman, The Black Family in Slavery and Freedom 1750-1925, 542-544.

537 Robert Evans Jr., "The Economics of American Negro Slavery, 1830-1860," in Aspects of Labor Economics (Princeton, NJ: Princeton University Press, 1962).

538 John Moes (University of Virginia), Thomas Govan, Review of Robert Evans

Jr., "The Economics of American Negro Slavery, 1830-1860," in Aspects of Labor Economics (Princeton, NJ: Princeton University Press, 1962), 251-252.

539 Evans Jr., "The Economics of American Negro Slavery, 1830-1860," 243- 246.; Willard Cope Brinton, Graphic Presentation (New York: Brinton Associates, 1939), 191.

540 Moes and Govan, Review of Robert Evans Jr., "The Economics of American Negro Slavery, 1830-1860,", 251-252.

541 Fogel, Without Consent or Contract: The Rise and Fall of American Slavery, 121.

542 Bancroft, Slave Trading in the Old South, 290.; Adams, A South-Side View of Slavery; or, Three Months at the South in 1854, 69-71, 74.

543 Andrew Burstein, Madison and Jefferson, 578.; Yetman, Voices From Slavery, 100 Authentic Slave, 36-37.; Harlan, "Booker T. Washington's West Virginia Boyhood," 63.; Jowett, Plato's The Republic, 182-186.; Stampp, The Peculiar Institution: Slavery in the Ante-Bellum South, 350-360.; Washington, Up from Slavery, 2-3.

544 Gutman, The Black Family in Slavery and Freedom 1750-1925.

545 John Gunther, Inside Europe (Guernsey, UK: Hamish Hamilton, 1936).

546 Baptist, The Half Has Never Been Told, 321-322.; Murphy, "Securing Human Property: Slavery, Life Insurance, and Industrialization in the Upper South."

547 Baptist, The Half Has Never Been Told, 325.

548 Baptist, The Half Has Never Been Told, 114.

549 Baptist, The Half Has Never Been Told, 318-319, 324.

550 Baptist, The Half Has Never Been Told, 322.

551 Baptist, The Half Has Never Been Told, 271-272.

552 Dunaway, Slavery in the American Mountain South, 13.

553 Baptist, The Half Has Never Been Told, 119-121.

554 Stampp, The Peculiar Institution: Slavery in the Ante-Bellum South, 167-173.

555 Genovese, Roll, Jordan, Roll: The World The Slaves Made, 307.

556 Stampp, The Peculiar Institution: Slavery in the Ante-Bellum South, 174-179.

557 Fogel, Without Consent or Contract: The Rise and Fall of American Slavery, 26.

558 Stampp, The Peculiar Institution: Slavery in the Ante-Bellum South, 186, 203

559 Stampp, The Peculiar Institution: Slavery in the Ante-Bellum South, 174-182.

560 Dunaway, Slavery in the American Mountain South, 63-64.

561 Baptist, The Half Has Never Been Told, 119-121.; Fogel, Without Consent or Contract: The Rise and Fall of American Slavery, 26-29.; Joseph P. Reidy, From Slavery to Agrarian Capitalism in the Cotton Plantation South: Central George, 1800-1880 (Chapel Hill, NC: The University of North Carolina Press, 1992), 37: Citing Fogel, Without Consent or Contract: The Rise and Fall of American Slavery, "esp" 26-29.

562 Caitlin Rosenthal, "Slavery's Scientific Management: Masters and Managers," Chapter 2 of Sven Beckert and Seth Rockman, Eds, Slavery's Capitalism: A New History of American Economic Development (Philadelphia, PA: University of Pennsylvania Press, 2016), 62-86.

563 Baptist, The Half Has Never Been Told, 114-121.

564 Ball, Fifty Years in Chains, 213.

565 There are embargoed articles on line and available to review; see "Roundtable Reviews" by Murray, J., Olmstead, A., Logan, T., Pritchett, J., & Rousseau, P. (2015) of The Half Has Never Been Told: Slavery and the Making of American Capitalism. By Edward E. Baptist. New York: Basic Books, 2014. Pp. xxvii, 498, The Journal of Economic History, 75(3), 919-931. doi:10.1017/S0022050715000996, accessed January 11, 2019.

566 Olmstead and Rhode, Creating Abundance: Biological Innovation and American Agricultural Development, 98-133.

567 Olmstead and Rhode, Creating Abundance: Biological Innovation and American Agricultural Development, 132-133.; Olmstead and Rhode, Creating Abundance: Biological Innovation and American Agricultural Development, 109, quoting James L. Watkins, King Cotton: A Historical and Statistical Review, 1790 to 1908. Reprint of 1908 ed. New York: Negro Universities Press, 1969, 13.; Information on picking rates is embargoed by authors.; Ball, Fifty Years in Chains, 221-222.

568 Rosenthal, "Slavery's Scientific Management: Masters and Managers," 74.

569 Dunaway, Slavery in the American Mountain South, 12.; Citation for information has been embargoed by authors.

570 Rosenthal, "Slavery's Scientific Management: Masters and Managers," 74.

571 Ira Berlin, The Long Emancipation: The Demise of Slavery in the United States (Cambridge, MA: Harvard University Press, 2015), 1.; Pat McGeehan, Stoicism and the Statehouse: An Old Philosophy Serving a New Idea (Proctorville, OH: Wythe-North Publishing, 2017), 6.; Sven Beckert and Seth Rockman, eds., Slavery's Capitalism: A New History of American Economic Development (Philadelphia, PA: University of Pennsylvania Press, 2016), 5.

572 "Our Withdrawn Review "Blood Cotton," The Economist, September 5, 2014, accessed January 21, 2019,

https://www.economist.com/books-and-arts/2014/09/05/our-withdrawn-review-blood-cotton.; Edward E. Baptist, "How Slavery Haunts Today's America," CNN, September 8, 2014, accessed January 21, 2019,

http://www.cnn.com/2014/09/07/opinion/baptist-slavery-book-panned-economist-review/index.html.; Edward E. Baptist, "The Economist's Review of My Book Reveals How White People Still Refuse to Believe Black People About Being Black," The Guardian, September 7, 2014, accessed January 21, 2019,

https://www.theguardian.com/commentisfree/2014/sep/07/economist-review-my-book-slavery.

573 Rice, The Allegheny Frontier West Virginia Beginnings, 1730-1830, 324.

574 Stealey, The Antebellum Kanawha Salt Business and Western Markets, 133-157.

575 Stealey, The Antebellum Kanawha Salt Business and Western Markets, 133-134.; Stealey, "Slavery and the Western Virginia Salt Industry," 128.; Callahan, History of West Virginia, 56.; West Virginia Constitutional Convention, Debates, West Virginia Constitutional Convention 1861-1863, ed. Charles Ambler (Gentry Bros, 1939), 694; Hale, History of the Great Kanawha Valley, Vol. 1, 266.

576 Stealey, The Antebellum Kanawha Salt Business and Western Markets; Stealey, "Slavery and the Western Virginia Salt Industry."; "West Virginia's Pioneer Industry: Salt Making in the Kanawha Valley," West Virginia and Regional History Collection 47, no. 1 (Spring 1991): 2; Wilma A. Dunaway, Slavery in the American Mountain South, (New York: Cambridge University Press, 2003) 117.

577 Dunaway, Slavery in the American

Mountain South, 25-26.

578 Dunaway, Slavery in the American Mountain South, 25-26, 36-37, 139-140.

579 Stampp, The Peculiar Institution: Slavery in the Ante-Bellum South, 71.; Dunaway, Slavery in the American Mountain South, 74.

580 Dunaway, Slavery in the American Mountain South, 166.; Stealey, "Slavery and the Western Virginia Salt Industry," 125.; Stealey, The Antebellum Kanawha Salt Business and Western Markets, 145-46.; Joe William Trotter, Jr., River Jordan: African American Urban Life in the Ohio Valley (Lexington, KY: The University Press of Kentucky, 1998), xiii.; Article on Slave Escapes in the Kanawha Valley from the National ERA, Washington DC (May 10, 1855).

581 Sheeler, The Negro in West Virginia Before 1900 [Microfilm; Kanawha County Library], (Dissertation, West Virginia University, 1954).

582 Sheeler, The Negro in West Virginia Before 1900 [Microfilm; Kanawha County Library], (Dissertation, West Virginia University, 1954).

583 Shirley Donnelly, "Yesterday and Today: Why West Virginia Owns the Silver Bridge," Beckley-Post Herald, 1968.

584 Cohen with Andre, Kanawha County Images: A Bicentennial History 1788-1988, Vol. 1, 24.; Philip W. Strum, "Slavery in the Ohio and Kanawha Valleys: Using Local Primary Sources to Uncover the Past," presentation at West Virginian Archives and History Library, Culture Center, Charleston, WV, October 11, 2011.

585 Sheeler, The Negro in West Virginia Before 1900, viii, 1.; Sonya Rastorgi, Tallese D. Johnson, Elzabeth M. Hoeffel and Malcom P. Drewery, Jr., "The Black Population: 2010, 2010 Census Briefs," U.S. Department of Commerce: U. S. Census Bureau (September 2011), 3.

586 Stealey, The Antebellum Kanawha

Salt Business and Western Markets, 150, 154-55.

587 Stealey, The Antebellum Kanawha Salt Business and Western Markets, 154-155.; Bruns, "The Antebellum Industrialization of the Kanawha Valley in the Virginia Backcountry," 132.; Stealey, "Slavery and the Western Virginia Salt Industry," 118.; Fogel and Engerman, Time on the Cross: The Economics of American Negro Slavery, 115.; Cyrus Forman, "Disorder in the Court: The Bill Mitchell Slave Rescue of 1839 and Ohio's Antislavery Politics," Printed Source, March 8, 2017.

588 Sheeler, The Negro in West Virginia Before 1900, 126-128.

589 Woodward, The Strange Career of Jim Crow, 12.; Katz, ed., The American Negro: His History and Literature, 53.; Berlin, The Making of African America: The Four Great Migrations, 106-107.; Levering Lewis, W. E. B. Du Bois: The Fight for Equality and the American Century, 2-21

590 Berlin, Generations of Captivity: A History of African-American Slaves, 120, 239.; Kulikoff, Tobacco and Slaves: The Development of Southern Cultures in the Chesapeake, 1680-1800, 434.; Philip J. Schwarz, Migrants Against Slavery: Virginians and the Nation (Charlottesville, VA: University Press of Virginia, 2001), 13

591 Stampp, The Peculiar Institution: Slavery in the Ante-Bellum South, 400-404, 414.

592 Stealey, "Slavery and the Western Virginia Salt Industry," 129.; Dunaway, Slavery in the American Mountain South, 118.

593 Washington, Up from Slavery, 26-27.; Stealey, "Slavery and the Western Virginia Salt Industry," 123.

594 Settle, Addie, 31.; Stealey, The Antebellum Kanawha Salt Business and Western Markets, 133-134.; Lewis Ruffner, Advertisement on Runaway Slave, Kanawha

Republican (Sept. 10, 1844); Stealey, The Antebellum Kanawha Salt Business and Western Markets, 145.; Stealey III, "Slavery and the Western Virginia Salt Industry," 116.

595 Murphy, "Securing Human Property: Slavery, Life Insurance, and Industrialization in the Upper South," 616-623.

596 Murphy, "Securing Human Property: Slavery, Life Insurance, and Industrialization in the Upper South," 617-618.

597 Dunaway, Slavery in the American Mountain South, 130 131.

598 Dunaway, Slavery in the American Mountain South, 134-135.

599 Dunaway, Slavery in the American Mountain South, 165-169.

600 Gates, Jr., The Classic Slave Narratives, 365-373.; Genovese, Roll, Jordan, Roll: The World The Slaves Made, 7-10, 30-31.

601 Stealey, "Slavery and the Western Virginia Salt Industry," 109.; Rice, The Allegheny Frontier West Virginia Beginnings, 1730-1830, 186.; Rice, The Allegheny Frontier West Virginia Beginnings, 1730-1830, 186.

602 Stealey, The Antebellum Kanawha Salt Business and Western Markets, 135.

603 Reidy, From Slavery to Agrarian Capitalism in the Cotton Plantation South: Central George, 1800-1880, 61.

604 Stealey, The Antebellum Kanawha Salt Business and Western Markets, 110, 149.; Bruns, "The Antebellum Industrialization of the Kanawha Valley in the Virginia Backcountry," 119.; Cohen with Andre, Kanawha County Images: A Bicentennial History 1788-1988, Vol. 1, 134.

605 "1851- 1854 Kanawha County Lists of Taxable Peoples, Persons, etc. within the District of James A. Quarrier," Kanawha County, West Virginia.; Stealey, The Antebellum Kanawha Salt Business and Western Markets, 138.

606 Stealey, The Antebellum Kanawha Salt Business and Western Markets, 138-139.; Department of Commerce and Labor: Bureau of the Census, A Century of Population Growth: From the First Census of the United States to the Twelfth, 1790-1900 (Washington: Government Printing Office, 1909), 136.

607 Stealey, The Antebellum Kanawha Salt Business and Western Markets, 154.

608 Stealey, The Antebellum Kanawha Salt Business and Western Markets, 137-142.; Harlan, Booker T. Washington the Making of a Black Leader 1859-1901, 16-17.; Gutman, The Black Family in Slavery and Freedom 1750-1925, 271-273.

609 1870 U.S. Census, Kanawha County, West Virginia, population schedule, Malden.

610 Dunaway, Slavery in the American Mountain South, 104.

611 Granville Hall, The Rending of Virginia: A History, 49- 50.; Gruyter, The Kanawha Spectator, Vol. I, 160-163.

612 Ambler and Summers, West Virginia the Mountain State, second edition, 261.; Eric Foner, Reconstruction: America's Unfinished Revolution (New York: HarperPerennial, 2014), 1.; Settle, Addie, 34, 80.

613 Settle, Addie, 138-139.; Stealey, The Antebellum Kanawha Salt Business and Western Markets, 132- 133; Richard A. Andre, "Charleston," e-WV: The West Virginia Encyclopedia, October 29, 2014, accessed December 05, 2017, https://www.wvencyclopedia.org/articles/1089.; "Slavery: Virginia Historical Society," Virginia Museum of History & Culture.; Samuel Crane, "To The Speaker of the House of Delegates [Auditor Report]," Auditors Office, Wheeling, WV, November 8, 1863.

614 Flasch & Flasch, Peter Ruffner and his Descendants, Vol. 2, 10.

615 West Virginia Constitutional Convention, Debates, West Virginia Constitu-

tional Convention 1861-1863, ed. Charles Ambler, 668.

616 Frederick Douglass, "The Meaning of July Fourth for the Negro," Speech given at Rochester, New York, July 5, 1852, accessed October 02, 2017, http://masshumanities.org/files/programs/douglass/speech_complete.pdf.

617 Donald W. Gunter, "George William Summers (1804-1868)," Library of Virginia, accessed December 1, 2017, http://edu.lva.virginia.gov/online_classroom/union_or_secession/people/geroge_summers.

618 Ambler, Sectionalism in Virginia from 1776-1861, 198- 199.

619 Gerald S. Ratliff, "George William Summers," e-WV: West Virginia Encyclopedia, December 8, 2015, accessed December 1, 2017, https://www.wvencyclopedia.org/articles/626.; Hall, The Rending of Virginia: A History, 29.; James Miller, History of Summers County (Hinton, WV, 1908), 49.; Cometti and Summers. The Thirty-Fifth State: A Documentary History of West Virginia, 289.

620 Patricia Clark Bulla, My Dearest Husband: The Letters of Amacetta Laidley Summers to George W. Summers 1842-1843 (Charleston, WV: University of West Virginia College of Graduate Studies Foundation, Inc., 1990).

621 Nat Turner's Rebellion, 1831," The Gilder Lehrman Institute of American History, accessed December 4, 2017, https://www.gilderlehrman.org/history-by-era/slavery-and-anti-slavery/resources/nat-turners-rebellion-1831.

622 Fogel, Without Consent or Contract: The Rise and Fall of American Slavery, 95.; Robert Prichard, A History of the Episcopal Church (Harrisburg, PA: Morehouse Publishing, 1991),110-120.

623 Reidy, From Slavery to Agrarian Capitalism in the Cotton Plantation South: Central George, 1800-1880, 77-78.; Har-

lan, Booker T. Washington the Making of a Black Leader 1859-1901, 18.; Prichard, A History of the Episcopal Church, 146.; Olmsted, A Journey in the Seaboard Slave States, With Remarks on Their Economy, 198.

624 Peterkin, A History and Record of the Protestant Episcopal Church in the Diocese of West Virginia and Before the Formation of the Diocese in 1878 in the Territory now Known as the State of West Virginia, 108-109, 117-120, 526-527.

625 Ambler and Summers, West Virginia the Mountain State, second edition, 147-148.

626 Ambler and Summers, West Virginia the Mountain State, second edition, 147-148.

627 Ambler and Summers, West Virginia the Mountain State, second edition, 101.

628 Stampp, The Peculiar Institution: Slavery in the Ante-Bellum South, 211.

629 Alfred L. Brophy, "Considering William and Mary's History with Slavery: The Case of President Thomas Roderick Dew," William and Mary Bill of Rights Journal 16, no. 1091. (2008): 1135-1136.

630 Williams, Appalachia: A History, 154.

631 Calvin Colton, The Junius Tracts (New York, NY: Greeley & McElrath, 1844).

632 Stampp, The Peculiar Institution: Slavery in the Ante-Bellum South, 18-21, 423.

633 Karp, This Vast Southern Empire: Slaveholders at the Helm of American Foreign Policy, 23-25, 34-35.

634 Karp, This Vast Southern Empire: Slaveholders at the Helm of American Foreign Policy, 15.

635 Gutman, The Black Family in Slavery and Freedom 1750-1925, 165, 297.; "The Creation of 'Amazing Grace'," Library of Congress. Online Text. accessed Octo-

ber 29, 2018, https://www.loc.gov/item/ihas.200149085/.

636 Stealey, The Antebellum Kanawha Salt Business and Western Markets, ix, 153, 186-190.; Beckert, Empire of Cotton: A Global History, xvii.

637 Stealey, The Antebellum Kanawha Salt Business and Western Markets, 42.

638 Stealey, The Antebellum Kanawha Salt Business and Western Markets, 153.; John Stealey III, "Great Kanawha Salt Industry: An Overview," Goldenseal 40, no. 4 (Winter 2014): 24-25.; Stephanie Hoover, "The History of the Pennsylvania Salt Industry," Pennsylvania Research.com, accessed November 28, 2018, http://www.pennsylvaniaresearch.com/pennsylvania-salt-industry.html.; Isaac Lippincott, "The Early Salt Trade of the Ohio Valley," Journal of Political Economy, Vol. 20, No. 10, December (1912), University of Chicago Press, JSTOR, accessed November 26, 2018, https://www.jstor.org/stable/1820548.

639 Settle, Addie, 80.; "Abolishment of Slavery in West Virginia (Extract from proceedings of the WV House of Delegates, Feb. 1, 1865)," West Virginia Archives & History, accessed May 15, 2019, http://www.wvculture.org/history/africanamericans/slaveryabolished02.html.; Samuel Crane, "To The Speaker of the House of Delegates [Auditor Report]," Auditors Office, Wheeling, WV, November 8, 1863.

640 Stealey, The Antebellum Kanawha Salt Business and Western Markets, 184-190; Hale. History of the Great Kanawha Valley, Vol. 1, 211-212.

641 Dayton, Pioneers and Their Homes on Upper Kanawha, 131.

642 "Weather Event: 1861 flood in the Kanawha Valley," e-WV: The West Virginia Encyclopedia, accessed November 28, 2018, https://www.wvencyclopedia.org/weather/events/15.; Stealey, The Antebellum Kanawha Salt Business and Western Markets, 184-190; Hale. History of the

Great Kanawha Valley, Vol. 1, 211-212.

643 The Chief of Engineers, Annual Report of the U.S. Engineer Department Chief of Engineers to the Secretary of War for the Year 1877, Vol. 1 (Washington: Government Printing Office, 1877), 324.

644 Susanna Delfino and Michele Gillespie, Neither Lady nor Slave: Working Women of the Old South (Chapel Hill, NC: University of North Carolina Press, 2002), 137.; David Ruffner, "Last Will and Testament," 1843, Kanawha County Circuit Clerk's Office, Charleston, WV.; Joel Shrewsbury, "Last Will and Testament," Will book [1859-76] 2, page 1-6; Kanawha County Office, Charleston, WV.

645 Joel Shrewsbury, "Last Will and Testament," Will book [1859-76] 2, page 1-6; Kanawha County Office, Charleston, WV.; Laidley, History of Kanawha County, West Virginia and Representative Citizens, 138.; Settle, Addie, 34; The Chief of Engineers, Annual Report of the U.S. Engineer Department Chief of Engineers to the Secretary of War for the Year 1877, Vol. 1 (Washington: Government Printing Office, 1877), 324.

646 Atkinson, History of Kanawha County, 305-307.; Louis A. Coolidge, Ulysses S. Grant, (Cambridge, MA: Houghton Mifflin Company The Riverside Press Cambridge, 1922), 4.

647 Coolidge, Ulysses S. Grant, 8.; Settle, Addie, 34-35.; Richard Andre, Stan Cohen and Bill Wintz, Bullets & Steel, The Fight for the Great Kanawha Valley 1861-1865 (Charleston, WV: Pictorial Histories Publishing Company, Inc., 1995), 178.

648 Atkinson, History of Kanawha County, 306.; "Virginia's Chapel," National Register of Historic Places: United States Department of the Interior, National Park Service, October 25, 1973, Cedar Grove, County, West Virginia; Nancy Ray Adams, "Virginia's Chapel," e-WV: West Virginia Encyclopedia, January 28, 2013, accessed October 11, 2017, https://www.wvency-

clopedia.org/articles/875; H. Cummings, "The Old Brick Church," c. 1948 hymnal listed in Golden Gospel Gems; Mary Lee Settle, "Golden Gospel Gems," Beauty Mountain Studios, January 3, 2013, accessed October 11, 2017, http://www.beautymountainstudio.com/golden-gospel-gems/.

649 Atkinson, History of Kanawha County, 307.

650 Deed of Sale from Rachel M. Tompkins and Charles Hedrick (Trustee) to Charles Ferrell, 27 May 1867 (Filed 24 June 1867), Kanawha County Clerk's Office, Charleston, West Virginia, Deed Book Z, page 465.; Atkinson, History of Kanawha County, 307.; Settle, Addie, 35.

651 Ambler, West Virginia Stories and Biographies, 385-391.

652 Hale. History of the Great Kanawha Valley, Vol. 1, 225-226; Lorena Andrews Anderson, "Salt Industry of the Kanawha Valley," (Master's Thesis, Marshall College, June 1942), 29-30.; Cohen with Andre, Kanawha County Images: A Bicentennial History 1788-1988, Vol. 1, 35.

653 Dayton, Pioneers and Their Homes on Upper Kanawha, 128.; J. H. Diss Debar, The West Virginia Handbook and Immigrant's Guide (Parkersburg, WV: Gibbons Bros. 1870), 109-110; Ambler and Summers West Virginia the Mountain State, second edition, 259.; Paul Price, Charles Hare, J.B. McCue and Homer Hoskins, Salt Brines of West Virginia. Vol. 8, West Virginia Geological Survey (Morgantown, WV: Morgantown Printing & Binding Company, 1937), 12.; Hale, Trans-Allegheny Pioneers, IV-V.

654 Kurlansky, Salt: A World History, 435.

655 "John Brown," e-WV: West Virginia Encyclopedia, January 05, 2017, https://www.wvencyclopedia.org/articles/668.; Schwarz, Twice Condemned: Slaves and the Criminal Laws of Virginia, 1705-1865,

656 Oswald Garrison Villard, John Brown 1800-1859 (New York: Alfred A. Knopf, 1943), 678-687; "John Brown's Raiders," Civil War Trust, accessed September 29, 2017, https://www.civilwar.org/learn/articles/john-browns-raiders.

657 Berlin, Generations of Captivity: A History of African-American Slaves, 432.

658 Nicholas May, "Holy Rebellion: Religious Assembly Laws in Antebellum South Carolina and Virginia," The American Journal of Legal History 49, no. 3 (July 2007): 237- 238.

659 Gerald D. Swick, Historic Photos of West Virginia (Nashville TN: Turner Publishing Company, 2010), 2-5.; John Brown, "Address of John Brown to the Virginia Court, when about to receive the sentence of death, for his heroic attempt at Harper's Ferry," The Gilder Lehrman Institute of American History, Collection # GLC05508.051, Originally Written December 1859, accessed September 28, 2017,

https://www.gilderlehrman.org/collections/ed95cc2b-c74b-4394-8646-657461155140; Villard, John Brown 1800-1859, 556.

660 "John Brown's Harpers Ferry," History.com, accessed July 17, 2017, http://www.history.com/topics/harpers-ferry.

661 John Greenleaf Whittier, "Brown of Ossawatomie," Poem (1859), The Lost Museum Archive, accessed February 26, 2019, https://lostmuseum.cuny.edu/archive/brown-of-ossawatomie.

662 Mark Simpson, The Rockefeller Collection of American Art at The Fine Arts Museums of San Francisco (San Francisco, CA: Harry N. Abrams, Inc. 1994).

663 The Last Moments of John Brown, 1882-1884, Painting by Thomas Hovenden at the Metropolitan Museum of Art, Accession Number 97.5. https://www.metmuseum.org/art/collection/search/11160.

664 Villard, John Brown 1800-1859, 556.

665 Quarles, Allies for Freedom, & Black people on John Brown, 133.

666 "Civil War Music: The Battle Hymn of the Republic," Civil War Trust, accessed 17-2017, https://www.civilwar.org/learn/primary-sources/civil-war-music-battle-hymn-republic.

667 John T. L. Preston, "Letter to His Wife," Lexington (VA) Gazette (December 15, 1859).

668 Karen Hughes White and Joan Peters, compilers, "Chapter VIII: The Development of Free Compulsory Education for Negroes and Whites, Chapter XXXIX," from June Purcell Guild, LL. M's Black Laws of Virginia: A Summary of Legislative Acts of Virginia Concerning Negroes from Earliest Times to the Present, Compiled by Afro-American Historical Association of Fauquier County, 1996.; Sheeler, The Negro in West Virginia Before 1900, 122.

669 Wayland, A History of Virginia for Boys and Girls, 263.; James I. Robertson, Jr., Stonewall Jackson: The Man, The Soldier, The Legend (New York: Macmillan Publishing USA, 1997), 169.; Dunaway, Slavery in the American Mountain South, 227.; Adams, A South-Side View of Slavery; or, Three Months at the South in 1854, 105-112.; Sheeler, The Negro in West Virginia Before 1900, 122.

670 Andrew Chestnut, "The Development of a Legend: Stonewall Jackson as a Southern Hero (Master's Thesis, Liberty University, 2008), 8-10.; G. F. R. Henderson, Stonewall Jackson and The American Civil War (New York, NY: Da Capo Press, Inc., 1943), 3.; "Jacksonhole," Town of Jackson, accessed July 3,2018, https://www.jacksonhole.com/town-of-jackson.html.; "Jackson Brigade Corporation," Decedents of Edward Jackson, accessed July 3,2018. http://www.jacksonbrigade.com/descendants-of-edward-jackson/.

671 Beverly Smith, "The Last Illness and Death of General Thomas (Stonewall) Jackson" Virginia Military Institute Archives, accessed October 02, 2017, http://www.vmi.edu/media/content-assets/documents/archives/Jackson_death_article.pdf.; Jules C. Meininger, Stonewall Jackson's Last Words (Louisville, KY: McCarrell & Meininger, 1866).

672 "Fred Martin Torrey," e-WV: The West Virginia Encyclopedia, December 09, 2015. accessed August 01, 2017, https://www.wvencyclopedia.org/articles/749.

673 "West Virginia State Capitol: Walking Tour and Visitor Information," West Virginia Division of Culture and History (Charleston, WV, n.d.).; Tom Crouser, "Stonewall's Statue Should Stand," Charleston Gazette Mail (August 28, 2017).

674 Christopher B. Taylor, "John F. Kennedy Memorial," [Photo] Memorial at WV Capitol Building, taken October 13, 2018. In possession of Author.

675 "West Virginia State Capitol: Walking Tour and Visitor Information," West Virginia Division of Culture and History (Charleston, WV, n.d.).; "Robert C. Byrd Biography," Biography.com, March 18,2016, accessed November 28, 2018, https://www.biography.com/people/robert-c-byrd-579660.

676 Daniel Vorndran / DXR Photograph License link: https://creativecommons.org/licenses/by-sa/3.0/legalcode.

677 Francois Poche and Jean-Claude Rochette with translation by Ronald Corlette-Theuil, The Dome of the Invalides (Paris: Musee De L'Armee, Somogy Editions D'Art, 1995), 26.; Barbara S. Christen and Steven Flanders, Cass Gilbert, Life and Work: Architect of the Public Domain (New York: W. W. Norton & Company, 2001), 282.; "Supreme Court Building," Architect of the Capitol, April 4, 2016,accessed March 20, 2018, https://www.aoc.gov/capitol-buildings/supreme-court-building.; Legislature of West Virginia, The West Virginia Capitol: A Commemorative History (Morgantown,

WV: Morgantown Printing & Binding, 2015).

678 Scott Martelle, The Madman and the Assassin: The Strange Life of Boston Corbett, the Man Who Killed John Wilkes Booth (Chicago, IL: Chicago Review Press., 2015), 66.; William Olcott, The Greenbrier Heritage (White Sulphur Springs, WV: Arndt, Chapin, Lamb & Keen, Inc.), 30-31.; David S. Reynolds, "John Wilkes Booth and the Higher Law," The Atlantic, April 12, 2015, https://www.theatlantic.com/politics/archive/2015/04/john-wilkes-booth-and-the-higher-law/385461/

679 Eric Foner, "Abraham Lincoln: The Great Emancipator?" (Lecture as part of the Sarah Tryphene Phillips Lecture Series read at The British Academy, November 5, 2003): 160-161, accessed November 28, 2018, https://www.thebritishacademy.ac.uk/sites/default/files/pba125p149.pdf.

680 Foner, Reconstruction: America's Unfinished Revolution, 74, 223.; Woodward, The Strange Career of Jim Crow, 50-54.

681 David H. Donald, Lincoln (New York: Simon & Schuster, 1995), 588; Edward Steers, Blood on the Moon: The Assassination of Abraham Lincoln (Lexington KY: University Press of Kentucky, 2001), 91.; Foner, Reconstruction: America's Unfinished Revolution, 74.; "Preface," Claude G. Bowers, The Tragic Era: The Revolution After Lincoln (New York: Blue Ribbon Books, 1940).5-7.; John Gimbel, Origins of the Marshall Plan (Stanford, CA: Stanford University Press, 1976), 1-5.; Garrett, ed., Historical Atlas of the United States

682 Wilson, Jr., The Book of Great American Documents, 76-80.

683 Abraham Lincoln, Second Inaugural Address of Abraham Lincoln, [Original Manuscript] March 04, 1865, The Avalon Project: Library of Congress, accessed October 02, 2017, https://www.loc.gov/teachers/newsevents/events/lincoln/pdf/

avalonInaug2.pdf.

684 Gail E. Husch, Something Coming (Hanover, NH: University Press of New England, 2000), 139.

685 Villard, John Brown 1800-1859, 550.

686 John A. Williams, West Virginia: A History (Morgantown WV: West Virginia University Press, 2001) 54.

687 Stampp, The Peculiar Institution: Slavery in the Ante-Bellum South, 22-23.

688 William Waller Hening, ed, The Statutes at Large; Being a Collection of All the Laws of Virginia from the First Session of the Legislature, in the Year 1619, vol. 2 (New York: R. & W. & G. Bartow, 1823), 260.

689 Malcolm X with assistance of Alex Haley, The Autobiography of Malcolm X (New York: Ballantine Books, 33rd Printing November, 1992), 366.

690 Niebuhr, Love and Justice: Selections from the Shorter Writings of Reinhold Niebuhr, 251.; Nardo, The Creation of the U.S. Constitution, 104.

691 Nardo, The Creation of the U.S. Constitution, 106.

692 Malcolm X with assistance of Alex Haley, The Autobiography of Malcolm X, 13-14.

693 Benjamin Quarles, Allies for Freedom, & Black people on John Brown (New York City, NY: Oxford University Press, 1974), 125, 179.

694 Villard, John Brown 1800-1859, 554.

695 Reidy, From Slavery to Agrarian Capitalism in the Cotton Plantation South: Central George, 1800-1880, 442-443.

696 Ambler, Sectionalism in Virginia from 1776-1861, 217.

697 "Resolution to Call the Election of Abraham Lincoln as U.S. President a Hostile Act and to Communicate to Other Southern States South Carolina's Desire to Secede from the Union." 9 November

1860. Resolutions of the General Assembly, 1779–1879. S165018. South Carolina Department of Archives and History, Columbia, South Carolina.

698 Woodward, The Strange Career of Jim Crow, 8-12.

699 Mary DeCredico and Jaime Amanda Martinez, "Richmond during the Civil War," Encyclopedia Virginia, March 22, 2016, accessed June 17, 2019, https://www.encyclopediavirginia.org/richmond_during_the_civil_war.; Nelson D. Lankford, "Virginia Convention of 1861," Encyclopedia Virginia, June 20, 2014, accessed June 17, 2019, http://www.EncyclopediaVirginia.org/Virginia_Constitutional_Convention_of_1861.; Virginia Ordinance Secession (April 17, 1861) [Primary Source]. Encyclopedia Virginia, June 20, 2014, accessed June 17, 2019, https://www.encyclopediavirginia.org/Virginia_Ordinance_of_Secession_April_17_1861; Charles B. Dew, Apostles of Disunion: Southern Secession Commissioners and the Causes of the Civil War (University of Virginia Press: Charlottesville, VA, 2001)

700 Jon Meacham, American Lion: Andrew Jackson in the White House (New York: Random House, 2008) 229.

701 Whisonant, "Geology and History of the Civil War Iron Industry in the New River-Cripple Creek District of Southwestern Virginia," 25.; Brophy, "Considering William and Mary's History with Slavery: The Case of President Thomas Roderick Dew," 1118.

702 Iver Bernstein, The New York City Draft Riots: Their Significance for American Society and Politics in the Age of the Civil War (New York, NY: Oxford University Press, 1990).

703 Barbara Maranzani, "The Most Violent Insurrection in American History," The History Channel: History Stories, July 5, 2013, accessed March 20, 2018, https://www.history.com/news/four-days-of-fire-the-new-york-city-draft-riots.; David Hacker, "Recounting the Dead," New York Times (September 10, 2011), https://opinionator.blogs.nytimes.com/2011/09/20/recounting-the-dead/?mcubz=0; "U.S. and World Population Clock," United States Census Bureau, accessed July 18, 2017 from https://www.census.gov/popclock/; Berry II, All That Makes A Man: Love and Ambition in the Civil War South, 9.; Donald McQuade, ed., The Harper American Literature, Vol. 2 (New York: HarperCollins Publishers, Inc., 1987), 146.

704 Maggie Anderson, Years that Answer (New York: Harper & Row Publishers,1980), xi; quote from Zora Neale Hurston, Their Eyes Were Watching God (Philadelphia, PA: J.B. Lippincott,1937).

705 Hacker, "Recounting the Dead."

706 Morgan, American Slavery, American Freedom, The Ordeal of Colonial Virginia, 5-6.

707 National Park Service: U.S. Department of the Interior, "Virginia State Capitol," National Park Service, accessed March 20, 2018,

https://www.nps.gov/nr/travel/richmond/virginiastatecapitol.html.

708 Jefferson, The Declaration of Independence.

709 Ambler, A History of West Virginia, 195-196.; Ron Chernow, Alexander Hamilton (New York, NY: The Penguin Press, 2004), 650- 656, 716-722.; "'Doctor, I Despair' - The Duel and Death of Philip Hamilton," World History: American History, accessed November 28, 2018, https://worldhistory.us/american-history/doctor-i-despair-the-duel-and-death-of-philip-hamilton.php.

710 Ambler, A History of West Virginia, 195-196.

711 Catton and Kethchem, ed., The American Heritage Picture History of the Civil War, 500-505.; McQuade, Ed., The Harper American Literature, Vol. 2, 146.; Edward F. Roberts, Andersonville Journey

(Shippensburg, PA: Burd Street Press, 1998), 33.; John McElroy, Andersonville: A Story of Rebel Military Prisons (Toledo, Ohio: D. R. Locke, 1879), 302-305; R. Drisdelle, Parasites Tales of Humanity's Most Unwelcome Guests (Oakland, CA: University of California Publishers, 2010), 86.; Ovid L. Futch, History of Andersonville Prison (Gainesville, FL: University of Florida Press, 1968), 113-122.; "The Wirz Monument," The National Park Service: Andersonville, April 14, 2015, accessed October 11, 2017, https://www.nps.gov/ande/learn/historyculture/wirz-mon.htm.; Ayers and Willis, The Edge of the South: Life in Nineteenth-Century Virginia, 219-223.

712 Jeff Shaara, Jeff Shaara's Civil War Battlefields: Discovering America's Hallowed Ground (NY: Ballentine Books, 2006), 4.

713 Dr. Henry Ruffner, Union Speech of Fourth of July 1856 in the Kanawha Salines.; Ambler, A History of Education in West Virginia, From Early Colonial Times to 1949, 90.

714 Elton Trueblood, Abraham Lincoln: Theologian of American Anguish (New York: Harper & Row Publishers, 1973), 39- 40.

715 William J. Wolf, "Abraham Lincoln's Faith," The Lehrman Institute Presents: Abraham Lincoln's Classroom, accessed November 7, 2017, http://www.abraham-lincolnsclassroom.org/abraham-lincoln-in-depth/abraham-lincolns-faith/; "Nancy Hanks Lincoln," National Park Service: Lincoln Boyhood, accessed November 7, 2017, https://www.nps.gov/libo/learn/historyculture/nancy-hanks-lincoln.htm.

716 William C. Kashatus, Abraham Lincoln, the Quakers, and the Civil War: "A Trial of Principle and Faith" (Santa Barbara, California: ABC-CLIO, LLC., 2014), 46-50.; Foner, Gateway to Freedom: The Hidden History of the Underground Railroad, 32-33.; Eric Foner, The Fiery Trial: Abraham Lincoln and American Slavery

(New York, NY: W. W. Norton & Company, 2010), 210.

717 Trueblood, Abraham Lincoln: Theologian of American Anguish, 32-37.; Doris Kearns Goodwin, Leadership in Turbulent Times (New York, NY: Simon & Schuster, 2018).

718 Abraham Lincoln, "Remarks to a Delegation of Progressive Friends [June 20, 1862]," Collected Works of Abraham Lincoln, vol. 5, Roy P. Basley, ed. (New Brunswick, NJ: Rutgers University Press, 1953), 279-280.; Schlesinger Jr., The Age of Jackson, 432.

719 Gabor S. Boritt, Jakob B. Boritt, Deborah R. Huso and Peter C. Vermilyea, Of the People by the People and for the People and other Quotations by Abraham Lincoln (New York City, NY: Columbia University Press, 1996), 47.; Abraham Lincoln, The Emancipation Proclamation (Carlisle, MA: Applewood Books, originally published 1862), 11-12.; Goodwin, Leadership in Turbulent Times, 213-222.

720 Henry Steele Commager, Documents of American History, vol. 1, to 1898 (Englewood Cliffs, NJ: Prentice-Hall, 1973), 417-418.

721 Proclamation made by Lord Dunmore (November 7, 1775).; Mullin, Flight and Rebellion: Slave Resistance in Eighteenth-Century Virginia, 130.

722 Foner, Reconstruction: America's Unfinished Revolution, 1.; Howard Swint, "Saving Grace: How West (ern) Virginians Helped Save the Union., Charleston Gazette-Mail, June 16, 2019.

723 Goodwin, Leadership in Turbulent Times, 220.; National Park Service, Antietam Casualties of Battle, accessed July 3,2018, https://www.nps.gov/anti/learn/historyculture/casualties.htm.

724 Jeff Shaara, Civil War Battlefields: Discovering America's Hallowed Ground (New York, NY: Ballentine Books, 2006), 27-49, 103-106.; Bruce Catton and

Richard M. Ketchem, ed., The American Heritage Picture History of the Civil War (New York: American Heritage/Bonanza Books, 1960), 247.; Lee, Robert E. et al, The Confederate Soldier in the Civil War: The Campaigns, Battles, Sieges, Charges and Skirmishes / The Foundation and Formation of the Confederacy / The Confederate States Navy (The Fairfax Press, 1977), 159-160.

725 Abraham Lincoln, "Gettysburg Address." [Speech] Dedication of the Cemetery at Gettysburg, PA, Gettysburg, November 19, 1863.

726 Wilson, Jr., The Book of Great American Documents, 74-75.

727 Lincoln, The Emancipation Proclamation, 14.; Goodwin, Leadership in Turbulent Times, 222.

728 Lincoln, The Emancipation Proclamation, 11-12.

729 Lincoln, The Emancipation Proclamation, 11-12.

730 Boritt, Boritt, Huso and Vermilyea, Of the People by the People and for the People and other Quotations by Abraham Lincoln, 47.

731 Goodwin, Leadership in Turbulent Times, 223.

732 Abraham Lincoln, Proclamation of freedom millions! The Emancipation Proclamation (Chicago Cook Illinois United States Washington D.C, National Printing Co., Chicago, Illinois, n. d.) Photograph. https://www.loc.gov/item/scsm000906/.

733 Russell Freedman, Abraham Lincoln & Frederick Douglass: The Story behind an American Friendship (New York, NY: Clarian Books, 2012), 87-95.

734 The District of Columbia Emancipation Act," National Archives, [Last Reviewed] March 7, 2017, accessed August 01, 2017, https://www.archives.gov/historical-docs/dcemancipation-act.; Catton and Ketchem, ed., The American Heritage Picture History of the Civil War, 247.

735 Catton and Ketchem, ed., The American Heritage Picture History of the Civil War, 258.; Sheehan-Dean, Struggle for a Vast Future, 229.

736 Foner, Reconstruction: America's Unfinished Revolution, 1.

737 Katie Lange, "Meet Sgt, William Carney: The First African-American Medal of Honor Recipient," DoD News: Defense Media Activity, February 7, 2017, accessed March 20, 2018, https://www.army.mil/article/181896.

738 R. G. Grant, Slavery: Real People and Their Stories of Enslavement (London: Toucan Books, 2009), 161.

739 "Robert Gould Shaw Memorial," Encyclopedia Virginia, accessed June 28,2018. https://www.encyclopedia-virginia.org/media_player?mets_file-name=evr7553mets.xml

740 Levering Lewis, W. E. B. Du Bois: The Fight for Equality and the American Century, 14.;_ Berlin, Generations of Captivity: A History of African-American Slaves, 256-257.; Reg Grant, Slavery (London: Toucan Books, 2009), 169.; Foner, "Abraham Lincoln: The Great Emancipator?".

741 "George Briton McClellan" Dictionary of American Biography, (New York City, NY: Charles Scribner's Sons, 1936).

742 Catton and Ketchem, ed., The American Heritage Picture History of the Civil War, 247.

743 Coolidge, Ulysses S. Grant, 43-44.

744 Ken Burns, "The Civil War: A Film by Ken Burns."; Calvin Colton, The Junius Tracts (New York, NY: Greeley & McElrath, 1844), 2, 66.; The Book of Great American Documents, 29.

745 H.G. Wells, The Outline of History, 389.

746 Foner, Reconstruction: America's Unfinished Revolution, 1.

747 Ancella R. Bickley and Lynda Ann Ewen, Memphis Tennessee Garrison: The

Remarkable Story of a Black Appalachian Woman (Athens, OH: Ohio University Press, 2001), 12.

748 Ballagh, A History of Slavery in Virginia, 78.; Washington, An Autobiography: The Story of My Life and Work, 18-19.

749 Rowe, History Tour of Old Malden: Virginia and West Virginia Booker T. Washington's Formative Years, 14.

750 Jeffrey C. Stewart, 1001 Things Everyone Should Know About African American History (New York City, NY: Doubleday, 1996), 97-98.

751 Flasch & Flasch ed., Peter Ruffner and his Descendants, Vol. 2, 79.

752 Lambert, West Virginia and Its Government, 110-113.

753 Conley, West Virginia Yesterday and Today, 59; Ambler, West Virginia Stories and Biographies, 376-377.; Ambler and Summers, West Virginia the Mountain State, 270.

754 Wilson, Jr., The Book of Great American Documents, 22.

755 Lambert, West Virginia and Its Government, 113-119.; Richard Hartman, "The Rise and Fall of Reconstruction in West Virginia." (Master's Thesis, Marshall University, 2004), 1.; Howard Swint, "Saving Grace: How West (ern) Virginians Helped Save the Union., Charleston Gazette-Mail, June 16, 2019.

756 Cometti and Summers. The Thirty-Fifth State: A Documentary History of West Virginia, 337-340.;

757 Rick Steelhammer, "Kanawha Lacked 'Euphony' to Become 35th States's Name," Charleston Sunday Gazette-Mail (Charleston, WV), November 25, 2018.; Lambert, West Virginia and Its Government, 120.; Cometti and Summers. The Thirty-Fifth State: A Documentary History of West Virginia, 337-340.

758 John G. Morgan, West Virginia Governors (Charleston, WV: Charleston Newspapers, 1980), 105.

759 Lambert, West Virginia and Its Government, 119.

760 Atkinson, History of Kanawha County, 305; Flasch & Flasch ed., Peter Ruffner and his Descendants, Vol. 2, 79.; Williams, Appalachia A History, 162.

761 H. Fitzhugh, Statement from Major-General W. W. Loring to the "People of West Virginia" [original manuscript] located in The War of the Rebellion: A Compilation of the Official Records of the Union and Confederate Armies, Series 1, Vol. 19, page 1071-1072, Cornell University Library: Civil War Official Histories, accessed October 30, 2017, http://ebooks.library.cornell.edu.

762 H. Fitzhugh, Statement from Major-General W. W. Loring to the "People of West Virginia" [original manuscript] located in The War of the Rebellion: A Compilation of the Official Records of the Union and Confederate Armies, 1071-1072.

763 Letter from Major-General W. W. Loring to Hon. George W. Randolph, [original manuscript] located in The War of the Rebellion: A Compilation of the Official Records of the Union and Confederate Armies, Series 1, Vol. 19, page 1070-1071, Cornell University Library: Civil War Official Histories, accessed October 30, 2017, https://babel.hathitrust.org/cgi/pt?id=coo.31924079609610;view=1up;seq=1087

764 Richard O. Curry, A House Divided, A Study of Statehood Politics and the Copperhead Movement in West Virginia, (Pittsburgh, PA: University of Pittsburgh Press, 1964), 26.

765 John McElroy, Andersonville: A Story of Rebel Military Prisons (Toledo, Ohio: D. R. Locke, 1879), 118-121, 289, 500-501.

766 McElroy, Andersonville: A Story of Rebel Military Prisons, 639-644.

767 McElroy, Andersonville: A Story of Rebel Military Prisons, 297, 647-649.

768   Catton and Kethchem, ed., The American Heritage Picture History of the Civil War, 500-505.; McQuade, Ed., The Harper American Literature, Vol. 2, 146.; Edward F. Roberts, Andersonville Journey (Shippensburg, PA: Burd Street Press, 1998), 33.; John McElroy, Andersonville: A Story of Rebel Military Prisons (Toledo, Ohio: D. R. Locke, 1879), 302-305; R. Drisdelle, Parasites Tales of Humanity's Most Unwelcome Guests (Oakland, CA: University of California Publishers, 2010), 86.; Ovid L. Futch, History of Andersonville Prison (Gainesville, FL: University of Florida Press, 1968), 113-122.; "The Wirz Monument," The National Park Service: Andersonville, April 14, 2015, accessed October 11, 2017, https://www.nps.gov/ande/learn/historyculture/wirz-mon.htm.

769   Cometti and Summers. The Thirty-Fifth State: A Documentary History of West Virginia, 343-345.

770   Curry, A House Divided, A Study of Statehood Politics and the Copperhead Movement in West Virginia, 49, 141- 147.; Lambert, West Virginia and Its Government, 119-122.

771   U.S. Cong. Senate. West Virginia Constitutional Convention. A Certified Copy of the Constitution of the State of West Virginia: Proposed by the Convention Assembled at Wheeling on the 26th of November, 1861. 37th Cong., 2d sess. Res. 98. 1862. 1-3. Accessed July 18, 2017. http://www.wvculture.org/history/statehood/constitutionvote.html.; Stealey, West Virginia's Civil War-Era Constitution, 103-105.

772   Lambert, West Virginia and Its Government, 119-122.

773   Stealey, West Virginia's Civil War-Era Constitution, 99, 103-105.

774   Cometti and Summers. The Thirty-Fifth State: A Documentary History of West Virginia, 351.

775   Ambler and Summers, West Virginia the Mountain State, 255- 257.; "Chapter 13: Congressional Debate on the Admission of West Virginia," West Virginia Archives & History: A State of Convenience, The Creation of West Virginia, accessed July 3, 2018. http://www.wvculture.org/history/statehood/statehood13.html.; Ambler, A History of West Virginia, 330-333.

776   Ambler, A History of West Virginia, 330-333.

777   Callahan, History of West Virginia, 150-151.

778   Callahan, History of West Virginia, 150-151.; West Virginia Constitutional Convention, Debates, West Virginia Constitutional Convention 1861-1863, ed. Charles Ambler, 728.

779   West Virginia Constitutional Convention, Debates, West Virginia Constitutional Convention 1861-1863, ed. Charles Ambler, 667.

780   Deed of Lewis Ruffner [Emancipation of Slaves], 1863, Kanawha County, West Virginia, Deed Book x 17, Kanawha County Clerk's Office, Charleston, West Virginia.

781   "Debates and Proceedings of the First Constitutional Convention of West Virginia February 17, 1863," West Virginia Division of Culture and History, accessed November 7, 2017, http://www.wvculture.org/history/statehood/cc021763.html.

782   West Virginia Constitutional Convention, Debates, West Virginia Constitutional Convention 1861-1863, ed. Charles Ambler, 668.

783   West Virginia Constitutional Convention, Debates, West Virginia Constitutional Convention 1861-1863, ed. Charles Ambler, 669.

784   West Virginia Constitutional Convention, Debates, West Virginia Constitutional Convention 1861-1863, ed. Charles Ambler, 728.

785   Molly Higgins, "Juneteenth: Fact Sheet," Congressional Research Service (2017), https://fas.org/sgp/crs/misc/

R44865.pdf.; Ernest Blevins, "Commemorating the ending of slavery: After decade-slong decline, Juneteenth grows from state holiday to nationwide celebration," Charleston Gazette-Mail, June 14, 2019.

786 "Chapter 10- An ACT for the Abolishment of Slavery in this State," Acts of the Legislature of West Virginia at its Third Session, Commencing January 17th 1865, 6.; "House Bill No. 25," Journal of the House of Delegates Third Legislature of West Virginia: Regular Session 1865.

787 "Abolishment of Slavery in West Virginia (Extract from proceedings of the WV House of Delegates, Feb. 1, 1865)," West Virginia Archives & History, accessed April 7, 2019, http://www.wvculture.org/history/africanamericans/slaveryabolished02.html.

788 Settle, Addie, 80.

789 Ambler and Summers, West Virginia the Mountain State, 261.; Paul H. Smith et al, eds, "Nathan Dane to Rufus King," Letters of Delegates to Congress 1774-1789, vol. 24, November 6, 1786 – February 29, 1788 (Washington, D. C.: Library of Congress, 1976-2000), 358.

790 John Richard Dennett, The South As It Is: 1865-1866 (NY: The Viking Press, 1965), 19-20.

791 Lankford, "Virginia Convention of 1861."; Whisonant, "Geology and History of the Civil War Iron Industry in the New River-Cripple Creek District of Southwestern Virginia," 25.; Brophy, "Considering William and Mary's History with Slavery: The Case of President Thomas Roderick Dew," 1118.

792 Fogel, Without Consent or Contract: The Rise and Fall of American Slavery, 120.

793 Hale, History of the Great Kanawha Valley, Vol. 1, 266; West Virginia Constitutional Convention, Debates, West Virginia Constitutional Convention 1861-1863, ed.

Charles Ambler, 575.; Samuel Crane, "To The Speaker of the House of Delegates [Auditor Report]," Auditors Office, Wheeling, WV, November 8, 1863.

794 Samuel Crane, "To The Speaker of the House of Delegates [Auditor Report]," Auditors Office, Wheeling, WV, November 8, 1863.

795 "The Malden Riot," in the West Virginia Journal, ed. G. W. Atkinson (Charleston, WV, December 15, 1869).

796 Stealey, West Virginia's Civil War-Era Constitution, 192-193.

797 Wayland, A History of Virginia for Boys and Girls, 29.

798 Booker T. Washington, N.B. Wood and Fannie Barrier Williams, A New Negro for a New Century (New York: Arno Press and the New York Times, 1969), 173.

799 Woodward, The Strange Career of Jim Crow, 33.

800 Olmsted, A Journey in the Seaboard Slave States, With Remarks on Their Economy, 29.

801 Marie Bradby, More than Anything Else with Illustrations by Chris K Soentpiet (New York: Orchard Books, 1995), 23.

802 Booker T. Washington, Up from Slavery (NY: Dover Publications, Inc., 1995), 13.

803 Berlin, The Making of African America: The Four Great Migrations, 140-143.

804 Genovese, Roll, Jordan, Roll: The World The Slaves Made, 564-565.

805 William Henry Ruffner, A Report on Washington Territory (New York, Seattle, WA: Lake Shore and Eastern Railway, 1889).; Fraser, Jr., William Henry Ruffner: A Liberal in the Old and New South, 210-220.

806 Booker T. Washington, Up from Slavery, 14; Harlan, Booker T. Washington the Making of a Black Leader 1859-1901, 40-

42.; Emory L. Kemp, The Great Kanawha Navigation (Pittsburgh, PA: University of Pittsburgh Press, 2000), 48, 81.; Flasch & Flasch ed., Peter Ruffner and his Descendants, Vol. 2, 113-114.

807 Adams, The Epic of America.

808 Quarles, Allies for Freedom, & Black people on John Brown, 5.

809 James Baldwin, The Fire Next Time (New York: Vintage Books, 1993), 87-88. Cooke, America, 384.;_ Niebuhr, Love and Justice: Selections from the Shorter Writings of Reinhold Niebuhr, 150.

810 Reverend Ronald English, interview with author, October 21, 2018.; Dick Russell, Black Genius and the American Experience (New York: Carroll and Craf Publishers, 1999), 434.

811 Aaron Sheehan-Dean, Struggle for a Vast Future (United Kingdom: Osprey Publishing, 2006), 212.

812 Reidy, From Slavery to Agrarian Capitalism in the Cotton Plantation South: Central George, 1800-1880, 166-176.

813 Reverend Marquita Hutchens, Rector of St. John's Episcopal Church, Charleston, West Virginia, as told to the author at that church on December 23, 2018.; Woodward, The Strange Career of Jim Crow, 43-44.

814 Woodward, The Strange Career of Jim Crow, 43-44.

815 Stephen, Mansfield, Then Darkness Fled: The Liberating Wisdom of Booker T. Washington (Nashville, Tennessee: Highland Books, 1999), 129-130.

816 Foner, Reconstruction: America's Unfinished Revolution, 428.

817 Emmett J. Scott and Lyman Beecher Stowe, Booker T. Washington: Builder of a Civilization (New York: Doubleday, Page & Company, 1916), 21.

818 Eller, Miners, Millhands, and Mountaineers: Industrialization of the Appalachian South 1880-1930, 8.; Jowett, Plato's The Republic, 197, 202.

819 Gillian Brocknell, "The 1939 Concert That Changed America," for the Washington Post, printed in the Charleston Gazette-Mail, April 10, 2019.

820 Brocknell, "The 1939 Concert That Changed America."; Paul Dickson and Thomas B. Allen, Marching on History, Smithsonian Magazine February 2003, accessed July 5,2018, https://www.smithsonianmag.com/history/marching-on-history-75797769/

821 Woodward, The Strange Career of Jim Crow 8-10.; Allistair Cooke, Letter from America 1946- 2004 (New York, Alfred A. Knopf, 2004), 73.

822 Katz, ed., The American Negro: His History and Literature, 21.

823 James Baldwin and Margaret Mead, A Rap on Race (U. S. A: J. B. Lippincott Company, 1971), 206.

824 Angie Settle, CEO/Exec. Director WV Health Right, Interview with Author, June 14 & 17, 2019.; Ellen Allen, Exec. Director, Covenant House, Interview with Author, June 14, 2019. Harriett Smith Beury, Manna Meal Volunteer, Interview with Author, June 20, 2019. Tara Martinez, Manna Meal, Interview with Author, June 12 & 20, 2019.

825 Bishop Mary Adelia McLeod, Interview with Author April 14, 2010.

826 McGeehan, Stoicism and the Statehouse: An Old Philosophy Serving a New Idea, xxvi-xxvii.

827 U.S. Census Bureau, Profile America Facts for Features: National African-American (Black)History Month: February 2019, February 26, 2019.; Senator Joe Manchin, Speech for Commemoration of the Birthday of Reverend Dr. Martin Luther King, Jr., State Capitol, Charleston, West Virginia, January 15, 2018.

828 Baldwin, The Fire Next Time, 82-95.

829 U.S. Census Bureau, Profile America Facts for Features: National African-American (Black)History Month: February 2019, February 26, 2019.

830 Larry L. Rowe, "XV Landmark 2004 Legislative Session: Legislative Findings of Fact and Action on Racial Disparities," West Virginia Law Review, Vol. 107, no. 3 (Spring 2005): 657-670.

831 Maria Young, "Founding Father," Charleston Gazette-Mail, June 16, 2019.

832 U.S. Census Bureau, Profile America Facts for Features: National African-American (Black)History Month: February 2019, February 26, 2019.

Bibliography

Primary & Secondary Sources

1851- 1854 Kanawha County Lists of Taxable Peoples, Persons, etc. within the District of James A. Quarrier. Kanawha County, West Virginia.

1870 U.S. Census, Kanawha County. West Virginia. Population Schedule. Malden, West Virginia.

"Abolishment of Slavery in West Virginia (Extract from proceedings of the WV House of Delegates, Feb. 1, 1865)." West Virginia Archives & History.

"About BTW: Honors & Tributes." Booker T. Washington Society. Accessed August 11, 2017.

"About Us," City of White Sulphur Springs, WV, https://local.wv.gov/WhiteSulphur-Springs/Pages/about.aspx.

"Abraham Lincoln, Second Inaugural Address, March 4, 1865." The Abraham Lincoln Papers at the Library of Congress 3, General Correspondence 1837-1897. Accessed July 28, 2017.

Abraham Lincoln Papers: Abraham Lincoln to Horace Greeley, 1862, 1863. Manuscript/Mixed Material, Retrieved from the Library of Congress. Accessed July 3, 2018.

Abraham, Tim. "Setting Kanawha Valley Ablaze Again." Charleston Daily Mail (Charleston, WV) January 1, 2019.

Adams, James Truslow. The Epic of America. New York: Little, Brown and Company, 1931.

Adams, James Truslow. The March of Democracy: A History of the United States. Volume 3, Civil War and Reconstruction. New York, NY: Charles Scribner's Sons, 1933.

Adams, Nehemiah. A South-Side View of Slavery; or, Three Months at the South in 1854. Port Washington, NY: Kennikat Press, Inc., 1969.

Adams, Noah. Far Appalachia: Following the New River North. New York: Dell Publishing, 2001.

Adams, Nancy Ray. "Virginia's Chapel." e-WV: West Virginia Encyclopedia. January 28, 2013. Accessed October 11, 2017.

"Adventures on the Gorge: Rafting and Ziplines [Brochure]." AOTG-WV.com. n.d.

African Zion Baptist Church, Church Bulletin for Celebration, November 7 1976.

Alexander, Michelle. The New Jim Crow, Mass Incarceration in the Age of Color Blindness. New York: The New Press Rev. Edition 2011.

Allen, Bernard L. Parkersburg, A Bicentennial History. Parkersburg, WV: Parkersburg Bicentennial Committee, 1985.

Allen, Bernard L. and David Matchen. "Natural Gas and Petroleum." e-WV: West Virginia Encyclopedia. Accessed June 27, 2017.

Allen, Ellen. Executive Director for Covenant House. Interview with Author. June 14, 2019.

Allen, Mike. "Bodies From Kennedy Crash Are Found." New York Times. July 22, 1999. Accessed October 12, 2017.

Ambler, Charles H. A History of West Virginia. New York: Prentice- Hall Inc., 1933.

Ambler, Charles H. George Washington and the West. Chapel Hill, NC: University of North Carolina Press, 1936). Accessible from

Ambler, Charles H. West Virginia Stories and Biographies. New York: Rand McNally and Company, 1937.

Ambler, Charles H. and Festus P. Summers. West Virginia: The Mountain State. 2nd Edition. New Jersey: Prentice-Hall, 1940.

Ambler, Charles H. A History of Education in West Virginia from Early Colonial Times to 1949. Huntington, WV: Standard Printing and Publishing Company, 1951.

Ambler, Charles H. Sectionalism in Virginia from 1776-1861. Morgantown, WV: West Virginia University Press, 2008.

Anderson, Colleen. Discussion with Author, October 12, 2017.

Anderson, James D. The Education of Blacks in the South, 1860-1935. Chapel Hill: The University of North Carolina Press, 1988.

Anderson, Maggie. Years that Answer. New York: Harper & Row Publishers,1980. Quoting Zora Neale Hurston from Their Eyes Were Watching God. Philadelphia, PA: J.B. Lippincott,1937.

"Andersonville Prison." Civil War Trust. Accessed October 06, 2017.

Anderson, Lorena Andrews. "Salt Industry of the Kanawha Valley." Master's Thesis, Marshall College, June 1942.

Andre, Richard. Stan Cohen and Bill Wintz. Bullets & Steel, The Fight for the Great Kanawha Valley 1861-1865. Charleston, WV: Pictorial Histories Publishing Company, Inc., 1995.

Andre, Richard A. "John P. Hale." e-WV: The West Virginia Encyclopedia. November 29, 2012. Accessed October 24, 2017.

Andre, Richard A. "Charleston." e-WV: The West Virginia Encyclopedia. October 29, 2014. accessed December 05, 2017.

"Arlington House, The Robert E. Lee Memorial." Arlington National Cemetery. October 07, 2015. Accessed October 05, 2017.

Armstead, Robert. Black Days, Black Dust: The Memories of an African American Coal Miner. Knoxville, TN: The University of Tennessee Press, 2002.

"Articles of Agreement- Kanawha Salt Company." Charter [Original Manuscript]. November 10, 1817. West Virginia Archives, ID # Ms82-10.

Article on Kanawha Riflemen discussing supplies from Richmond. The Kanawha Valley Star. December 5, 1859.

Article on Slave Escapes in the Kanawha Valley. The National ERA, Washington DC. May 10, 1855.

Article on Malden Fire, 1874. Charleston Daily Courier, Charleston, WV. April 7, 1874.

The Associated Press. "Virginia legislators Vote to Retire the State Song." The New York Times. February 18, 1997.

Athey, Lou. James Kay: His Life and Work, 1849-1934. Charleston WV: The Kay Company, 2005.

Atkinson, George W. History of Kanawha County. Charleston, West Virginia: Office of the West Virginia Journal, 1876.

Ayers, Edward L. and John C. Willis, The Edge of the South: Life in Nineteenth-Century Virginia. Charlottesville, VA: University Press of Virginia, 1991.

Bailey, Kenneth R. Kanawha County Public Library, A History. Parsons, West Virginia: McClain Printing Company, n.d.

Bailey, Kenneth R. "A Judicious Mixture: Negroes and Immigrants in the West Virginia Mines, 1880- 1917." In Blacks in Appalachia. Edited by William H. Turner and Edward J. Cabbell. Lexington: University Press of Kentucky, 1985.

Bailey, Kenneth R. "The Other Brown v. Board of Education." West Virginia History 3, no. 2. (Fall 2009): 53-73.

Bailey, Rebecca J, Editor. West Virginia and Appalachia: A Series by Ronald L. Lewis, Volume 8, Matewan Before the Massacre. Morgantown, WV: West Virginia University Press, 2008.

Balandier, Georges and Jacques Maquet. Dictionary of Black African Civilization. New York: Leon Amiel, 1974.

Baldwin, James and Margaret Mead. A Rap on Race. U.S.A: J.B. Lippincott Company,1971.

Ball, Charles, Fifty Years in Chains. New York, NY: Dover Publications, Inc., 1970.

Ball, Edward. "Slavery's Trail of Tears." Smithsonian Magazine. November 2015.

Ballagh, James Curtis. A History of Slavery in Virginia. Baltimore, MD: The Johns Hopkins Press, 1902.

Baptist, Edward E. The Half Has Never Been Told: Slavery and the Making of American Capitalism. New York, NY: Basic Books, 2014.

Baptist, Edward E. "The Economist's Review of My Book Reveals How White People Still Refuse to Believe Black People About Being Black." The Guardian. September 7, 2014. Accessed January 21, 2019.

Bancroft, Frederick. Slave Trading in the Old South. New York, NY: Frederick Ungar Publishing Co., 1931.

Baptist, Edward E. "How Slavery Haunts Today's America." CNN. September 8, 2014. Accessed January 21, 2019.

Beckert, Sven and Seth Rockman, Editors. Slavery's Capitalism: A New History of American Economic Development. Philadelphia, PA: University of Pennsylvania Press, 2016.

Beckert, Sven. "Empire of Cotton." The Atlantic. Accessed November 14, 2018.

Beerman, Kenton. "The Beginning of a Revolution: Waltham and the Boston Manufacturing Company." The Concord Review, 1994.

Bellamy, Francis Rufus. "To Outlook Readers Who Order Booker T Washington's Up From Slavery In Advance of Book Publication." The Outlook 67, no. 6 (1901).

Berlin, Ira. Generations of Captivity: A History of African-American Slaves. Cambridge, MA: Harvard University Press, 2003.

Berlin, Ira. The Making of African America: The Four Great Migrations. New York, NY: Penguin Books, 2010.

Berlin, Ira. The Long Emancipation: The Demise of Slavery in the United States. Cambridge, MA: Harvard University Press, 2015.

Bernstein, Iver. The New York City Draft Riots: Their Significance for American Society and Politics in the Age of the Civil War. New York, NY: Oxford University Press, 1990.

Berry, Stephen W., II. All That Makes A Man: Love and Ambition in the Civil War South. New York: Oxford University Press, 2003.

Beury, Harriett Smith. Manna Meal Volunteer. Interview with Author. June 20, 2019.

"Biography of Robert Henri." henrirobert. org. Accessed November 30, 2017.

Bickley, Ancella R. History of The West Virginia State Teacher's Association. Washington D.C.: National Education Association, 1979.

Bickley, Ancella R. and Lynda Ann Ewen. Memphis Tennessee Garrison: The Remarkable Story of a Black Appalachian Woman. Athens: Ohio University Press, 2001.

"Birthplace of Presidents." Virginia is for Lovers: Official Tourism website of the Commonwealth of Virginia. Accessed April 2017.

Blackstone, William, Thomas McIntyre Cooley, and James De Witt Andrews. Commentaries on the Laws of England: In Four Books. 3rd ed. Whitefish, MT: Kessinger, 2010.

"Bland Ballard (1819-1879)." History of the Sixth Circuit. Accessed January 14, 2019.

Bland, James. "Carry me back to old Virginny." 1861. Notated Music. Library of Congress. Accessed June 15, 2017.

Blank, Martin. Character Building: A Musical. Adapted from talks by Booker T. Washington. New York, NY: American Ensemble Books, 2018.

Blevins, Ernest Everett. "William H. Davis – WV's First Black Candidate for Governor." West Virginia Daily Mail. February 11, 2017.

Blevins, Ernest. "Commemorating the ending of slavery: After decadeslong decline, Juneteenth grows from state holiday to nationwide celebration." Charleston Gazette-Mail. June 14, 2019.

Blinn, Marria. Ruffner Family: Historic Sites Guide Book. United States: Outskirts Press, Inc., 2017.

"Booker T. Washington." NNDB. Soylent Communications. Accessed November 2018.

"Booker T. Washington Institute: Influence on WVSU." West Virginia State University. Accessed October 25, 2017.

Borch, Fred L. "Lore of the Corps: The Trial by Military Commission of 'Mother Jones'." The Army Lawyer. (February 2012): 1-4.

Boritt, Gabor S., Jakob B. Boritt, Deborah R. Huso and Peter C. Vermilyea. Of the People by the People and for the People and other Quotations by Abraham Lincoln. New York City, NY: Columbia University Press, 1996.

Boston Manufacturing Company Records, 1813-1930. Harvard University – Baker Library. Baker Library Historical Collections, Harvard Business School.

Boven, Catherine Drinker. Miracle at Philadelphia. U.S.A: Little Brown and Company,1966.

Bowers, Claude G. The Tragic Era: The Revolution After Lincoln. New York: Blue Ribbon Books, 1940.

Bradby, Marie. More than Anything Else with Illustrations by Chris K Soentpiet. New York: Orchard Books, 1995.

Bragg, Melody. "Window to the Past: Mining man became coal baron in 13-year-span." The Fayette Tribune. September 19, 1994.

Branch, Taylor. Parting the Waters, America in the King Years 1954-63. New York,

NY: Simon & Schuster Inc., 1988.

Brinton, Willard Cope. Graphic Presentation. New York: Brinton Associates, 1939.

Brocknell, Gillian. "The 1939 Concert That Changed America." for the Washington Post, printed in the Charleston Gazette-Mail. April 10, 2019.

Brodie, Barbara. Mr. Jefferson's Nurses: The University of Virginia School of Nursing, 1901 - 2001. Charlottesville: University of Virginia, 2000.

Brophy, Alfred L. "Considering William and Mary's History with Slavery: The Case of President Thomas Roderick Dew." William and Mary Bill of Rights Journal 16, no. 1091. (2008): 1091-1139.

Brown, John. "Address of John Brown to the Virginia Court, when about to receive the sentence of death, for his heroic attempt at Harper's Ferry." The Gilder Lehrman Institute of American History, Collection # GLC05508.051. Originally Written December 1859. Accessed September 28, 2017.

Brown, Tony. What Mama Taught Me: The Seven Core Values of Life. New York: HarperCollins Publishers Inc., 2003.

Brumbaugh, Gaius Marcus. Genealogy of the Brumbach Families. New York, NY: Fredrick H. Hitchcock, 1913.

Bruns, Carter. "The Antebellum Industrialization of the Kanawha Valley in the Virginia Backcountry." Master's Thesis, Western Carolina University, 2013.

Bulla, Patricia Clark. My Dearest Husband: The Letters of Amacetta Laidley Summers to George W. Summers 1842-1843. Charleston, WV: University of West Virginia College of Graduate Studies Foundation, Inc., 1990.

Burns, Ken. "The Civil War: A Film by Ken Burns." American Documentary Inc.1990.

Burns, Ken. "Jefferson: A Film by Ken Burns." The American Experience Lives Film Project, Inc., 1996.

Burroughs, James. "Last Will and Testament." Will book 12, page 150. Franklin County Court Records, Franklin County, Virginia.

Burstein, Andrew. Madison and Jefferson. New York: Random House, 2010.

Callahan, James Morton. History of West Virginia. West Virginia: Semi-Centennial Commission, 1913.

Carroll, Greg. "Slavery and Free People of Color in Virginia." Presentation, West Virginia Archives and History Library, Charleston, West Virginia, January 6 2015.

Case, Bill. State Papers & Public Addresses of Bob Wise: Thirty-third Governor of West Virginia, 2001-2005. Central Printing Company, n.d.

Casto, James E. "J.R. Clifford had the 'Right Stuff' to Make Civil Rights History." The West Virginia Lawyer. April-June 2009.

Catton, Bruce and Richard M. Kethchem, Ed. The American Heritage Picture History of the Civil War. New York: American Heritage/Bonanza Books, 1960.

"Chapter 13: Congressional Debate on the Admission of West Virginia." West Virginia Archives & History: A State of Convenience, The Creation of West Virginia. Accessed July 3, 2018.

"Charles Hamilton Houston." In Separate is Not Equal: Brown v. Board of Education, Smithsonian National Museum of American History. Accessed August 15, 2017.

"Charleston Daily Mail, March 25, 1938." in "Obituaries for William H. Davis." West Virginia Division of Culture and History. Accessed August 31, 2017.

Charleston Civic League. Dinner Tendered to Dr. Booker T, Washington, [menu] K. Of P. Hall. December 24, 1906

Chemical Divisions of FMC. The Salt Industry in the Kanawha Valley. West Virginia, 1976.

Cherniack, Martin. The Hawk's Nest Incident. Yale University, 1985.

Chernow, Ron. Alexander Hamilton. New York, NY: Penguin Books, 2004.

Chernow, Ron. Washington: A Life. New York, NY: Penguin Books, 2010.

Chesnut, Andrew. "The Development of a Legend: Stonewall Jackson as a Southern Hero." Master's thesis, Liberty University, 2008.

Chief Logan. Chief Logan to Lord Dunmore, 1774. 1774. Manuscript/Mixed Material. Library of Congress. Accessed June 6, 2017.

The Chief of Engineers. Annual Report of the U.S. Engineer Department Chief of Engineers to the Secretary of War for the Year 1877, Vol. 1. Washington: Government Printing Office, 1877.

Chilton, Nelle. In Discussion with author, 2013.

Christen, Barbara S. and Steven Flanders. Cass Gilbert, Life and Work: Architect of the Public Domain. New York: W. W. Norton & Company, 2001.

"Civil War Music: The Battle Hymn for the Republic." Civil War Trust. Accessed July 17, 2017.

"The Closing of Prince Edward County's Schools." Virginia Historical Society. Accessed November 2, 2017.

"Coal Miners." State of West Virginia: National Coal Heritage Area & Coal Heritage Trail. Accessed November 1, 2017.

Coates, Ta-Nehisi. "Our First Black President." The Atlantic. September 12, 2011. Accessed August 15, 2017.

Cobb, Rosemary Jeanne. "Alexander Campbell." e-WV: The West Virginia Encyclopedia. January 23, 2013.

Coffey, David Walton. "William Henry Ruffner: Rave and Public Education in Post-Reconstruction Virginia." Master's Thesis, University of North Carolina, 1972.

Cohen, Sharon and Matt Sedensky. "Deadly Shootings; Outrage and Despair; Nation Tries to Process." The Charleston Gazette. Charleston, WV. July 9, 2016.

Cohen, Stan with Richard Andre. Kanawha County Images: A Bicentennial History 1788-1988. Charleston, WV: Pictorial Histories Publishing Company and Kanawha County Bicentennial, Inc., 1987.

Coit, Margaret L. The Life History of the United States. Volume 3, The Growing Years. New York: Time-Life Books, 1963.

Cole, Martha Darneal. Interview with author, in her ancestral Shrewsbury home on Georges Creek Drive, Malden, West Virginia 2009.

Cole, Martha Darneal. Relative descendent, in discussion with author. December, 2012 & June 2013.

Collins, Patricia Hill. Black Sexual Politics. Routledge, New York: Taylor & Francis, 2004.

Collins, Winfield H. The Domestic Slave Trade of the Southern States. Port Washington, NY: Kennikat Press, Inc., 1969.

"Colonial Laws." PBS, Africans in America. Accessed September 26, 2017.

Colton, Calvin. The Junius Tracts, No. I-VIII. New York, NY: Greeley & McElrath, 1844.

Commager, Henry Steele. Documents of American History. Volume 1. to 1898. Englewood Cliffs, NJ: Prentice-Hall, 1973.

Cometti, Elizabeth and Festus P. Summers. The Thirty-Fifth State: A Documentary History of West Virginia. Parsons, WV: McClain Printing Company, 1968.

Comstock, Jim. The West Virginia. Heritage Encyclopedia. Volume 19, REV - SCH. Richwood, WV: Jim Comstock, 1976.

Cone, James H. Martin & Malcolm & America: A Dream or a Nightmare. New York: Orbis Books, 1970.

"Congress Designates Blackstone River Valley National Heritage Corridor, November 10, 1986." MassMoments: A Project of MassHumanities. Accessed June 12, 2019.

Conley, Phil, Editor. The West Virginia Encyclopedia. Charleston, WV: West Virginia Publishing Company, 1929.

Conley, Phil. West Virginia Yesterday and Today. Charleston, WV: West Virginia Review Press, 1931.

Conley, Phil. Beacon Lights of West Virginia History. Charleston, WV: West Virginia Publishing Co., 1939.

The Constitution of the United States of America (Bedford: Massachusetts, ND),

"Constitution of the United States." in The World Book Encyclopedia 2000. Volume 4. Ci - Cz. Chicago, IL: World Book, Inc, 2000.

"Consumer Price Index," United States Department of Labor: Bureau of Labor Statistics, accessed May 22, 2019.

Conte, Robert S. The History of the Greenbrier: America's Resort. Charleston, WV: Pictorial Histories Publishing CO., 1989.

"Controversy Over the Inclusion of Berkeley and Jefferson Counties in the State of West Virginia." In The Congressional Globe. 39th Congress, 1st Session, Extracts, House of Representatives, December 11, 1865. West Virginia Archives and History. Accessed October 04, 2017.

Cooke, Alistair. America. New York: Alfred A. Knopf, 1973.

Cooke, Allistair. Letter from America 1946- 2004. New York, Alfred A. Knopf, 2004.

Cook, Roy Bird. Washington's Western Lands. Strasburg, VA: Shenandoah Publishing House, Inc., 1930.

Coolidge, Louis A., Ulysses S. Grant, Cambridge, MA: Houghton Mifflin Company The Riverside Press Cambridge. 1922.

Cooper, Minnie Wayne. In discussion with author, 1990. Charleston, WV.

"Corresponding and Executive Committee." The Louisville Examiner. 10 March 1849. Louisville, KY. Chronicling America: Historic American Newspapers, Lib. of Congress.

CPI Inflation Calculator [Rates based on U.S. Bureau of Labor Statistics' Consumer Price Index (CPI]." OfficialData.org.

Crackel, Theodore J. "George Washington and the Constitution." The Gilder Lehrman Institute of American History: The Constitution. Accessed October 04, 2017.

"The Creation of 'Amazing Grace.'" Library of Congress. Online Text.

Crouser, Tom. "Stonewall's statue should stand." Charleston Gazette Mail. August 28, 2017.

Cummings, H. "The Old Brick Church." c. 1948. Hymnal listed in Golden Gospel Gems.

Cunningham, Rodger. Apples on the Flood: The Southern Mountain Experience. University of Tennessee Press, 1987.

Curry, Richard O. "A House Divided, A Study of Statehood Politics and the Copperhead Movement in West Virginia." Pittsburgh, PA: University of Pittsburgh Press, 1964.

Damrosch, Leo. Tocqueville's Discovery of American. New York, NY: Farrar, Straus and Giroux, 2010.

"Daniel Boone Helped Organize Kanawha County." Kanawha Valley Progress Edition of the Charleston Daily Mail. June 14, 1939.

"Dates of Secession." University of Georgia Special Collections Libraries. Accessed October 05, 2017.

Davis, Elsie Mae. Celebrating Our Roots: Origins of Black Families in West Virginia. Dunbar, West Virginia: McKnight's Inc.

Davis, Keith. West Virginia Tough Boys:

Vote Buying, Fist Fighting and A President Named JFK, Revised Edition. Woodland Press, LLC., 2003.

Dayton, Ruth Woods. Greenbrier Pioneers and Their Homes. Charleston, WV: West Virginia Publishing Company, 1942.

Dayton, Ruth Woods. Pioneers and Their Homes on Upper Kanawha. Charleston, WV: West Virginia Publishing Company, 1947.

Deal, J. Douglas. Race and Class in Colonial Virginia. New York, NY: Garland Publishing, Inc., 1993.

Debar, J. H. Diss. The West Virginia Handbook and Immigrant's Guide. Parkersburg, WV Gibbons Bros. 1870.

"Debates and Proceedings of the First Constitutional Convention of West Virginia February 17, 1863." West Virginia Division of Culture and History. Accessed November 7, 2017.

DeCredico, Mary and Jaime Amanda Martinez. "Richmond During the Civil War." Encyclopedia Virginia. March 22, 2016. Accessed June 17, 2019.

Deed of Life Estate from Washington Ferguson to Elizabeth Ferguson, 1880. Kanawha County, West Virginia. Deed Book 35, Page 276. County Clerk's Office, Charleston, West Virginia.

Deed of Sale from John Dickinson to Joseph Ruffner, 1796. Kanawha County, West Virginia. Deed Book A, Page 102. Kanawha County Clerk's Office, Charleston, West Virginia.

Deed of Sale from Richard Putney to William Dickinson Sr., 20 May 1840. Kanawha County, West Virginia. Deed Book L, Page 346. Kanawha County Clerk's Office. Charleston, West Virginia.

Deed of Sale from Richard Putney to William Dickinson Sr., 2 October 1840. Kanawha County, West Virginia. Deed Book L, Page 370. Kanawha County Clerk's Office. Charleston, West Virginia.

Deed of Sale from Joel Shrewsbury to Alexander W. Quarrier, as Trustee for benefit of Martha Darneal Shrewsbury, dated May 29, 1858, and recorded in Deed Book U-V at page 392. County Clerk's Office, Kanawha County. Charleston, West Virginia.

Deed of Sale from Rachel M. Tompkins and Charles Hedrick (Trustee) to Charles Ferrell, 27 May 1867 (Filed 24 June 1867), Kanawha County, West Virginia, Deed Book Z, page 465. County Clerk's Office, Charleston, West Virginia.

Deed of Sale from Jacob D. Shrewsbury and Walter P. Shrewsbury to Elijah Rook & Co., 1868. Kanawha County, West Virginia. Deed Book 2, Page 353. County Clerk's Office. Charleston, West Virginia.

Deed of Sale from Jacob D. Shrewsbury to Washington Ferguson, 25 October 1869 (filed 28 June 1873). Kanawha County, West Virginia. Deed Book 29, page 272. County Clerk's Office, Charleston, West Virginia.

Deed of Sale from Charles Ferrell and wife to George Dilce, John W. Johnson, and Campbell Woodyard (Trustees of African Zion Baptist Church of Tinkersville 'near Malden'). 18 October 1872 (Filed 2 August 1873). Kanawha County, West Virginia, Deed Book 29, page 268. County Clerk's Office, Charleston, West Virginia.

Deed of Lewis Ruffner [Emancipation of Slaves]. 1863, Kanawha County, West Virginia, Deed Book x 17. Kanawha County Clerk's Office, Charleston, West Virginia

Deed of Sale from Lewis Ruffner Sr. And Viola Knapp Ruffner to Lewis Ruffner Jr. And Ernest Ruffner, 20 March 1873. Kanawha County, West Virginia, Deed Book 29, page 72. County Clerk's Office, Charleston, West Virginia.

Deed of Sale from Lewis Ruffner Jr. and Ernest Ruffner to Stephen F. Dana and Ezra Andrews, 5 April 1872 (Filed 14 June 1884). Kanawha County, West Virginia, Deed Book 41, Page 335. County Clerk's

Office, Charleston, West Virginia.

Deed of Sale from John F. Hubbard and Anastasia M. Hubbard to Trustees of Kanawha Salines Presbyterian Church, 11 September 1885. Kanawha County, West Virginia. Deed Book 43, Page 180-181. Kanawha County Clerk's Office. Charleston, West Virginia.

Deed of Elizabeth Winston to Amanda Ferguson Johnson, 25 December 1902 (filed 28 January 1903). Ohio, Deed Book 88, Page 367. County Clerk's Office, Kanawha County, West Virginia.

Delbanco, Andrew. The War Before the War: Fugitive Slaves and the Struggle for America's Soul from the Revolution to the Civil War. New York, NY: Penguin Press, 2018.

Delfino, Susanna and Michele Gillespie. Neither Lady nor Slave: Working Women of the Old South. University of North Carolina Press, 2002.

Dennett, John Richard. The South As It Is: 1865-1866. The Viking Press, 1965.

Denver, John. "Take Me Home, Country Roads." Poems, Prayers and Promises. RCA Records, 1971.

Department of Commerce and Labor: Bureau of the Census. A Century of Population Growth: From the First Census of the United States to the Twelfth, 1790-1900. Washington: Government Printing Office, 1909.

Devany, Erik. "How the Irish and the Scots Influenced American Music." London Celtic Punks Web-Zine. Accessed September 26, 2017.

Dew, Charles B. Apostles of Disunion: Southern Secession Commissioners and the Causes of the Civil War. University of Virginia Press, 2001.

Dew, Charles B. Apostles of Disunion: Southern Secession Commissioners and the Causes of the Civil War. University of Virginia Press: Charlottesville, VA, 2001.

Dickson, Paul and Thomas B. Allen, Marching on History, Smithsonian Magazine (online) February 2003.

The District of Columbia Emancipation Act." National Archives, [Last Reviewed]. March 7, 2017. Accessed August 01, 2017.

Division of Christian Education of the National Council of the Churches of Christ in the United States of America. The Holy Bible, New Revised Standard Version. New York: Oxford University Press,1989.

Dixon, Thomas W., Jr. "The Chesapeake and Ohio Railway at Hawk's Nest." The Chesapeake & Ohio Historical Society, Inc., 2000.

"'Doctor, I Despair' - The Duel and Death of Philip Hamilton." World History: American History. Accessed November 28, 2018.

Doddridge, Joseph. Logan, The Last Of The Race Of Shikellemus, Chief of the Cayuga Nation. Parsons, WV: McClain Printing Co., 1971.

Doherty, William Thomas. West Virginia Studies: Our Heritage. Charleston, WV: Education Foundation, Inc., 1984.

Donald, David H. Lincoln. New York: Simon & Schuster, 1995.

Donally, M. W. "The Van Bibber Family." The West Virginia Historical Magazine 3, no. 1. (1903): 213-225.

Donnelly, Lu. "Architecture Around Us." Western Pennsylvania History: Up Front 97, no. 3. (Fall 2014): 10-13.

Donnelly, Shirley. "Klan 'Show' Drew Throng At Union." Raleigh Register. 1968.

Donnelly, Shirley. "Yesterday and To-day: Why West Virginia Owns the Silver Bridge." Beckley-Post Herald. 1968.

Douglas, C. Winfred. "Were you there." Hymn written 1940.

Douglass, Frederick. "The Meaning of July Fourth for the Negro." Speech given at Rochester, New York, July 5, 1852. Accessed October 02, 2017.

Douglass, Frederick. The Slaveholders' Rebellion. Himrod's, New York, July 04, 1862. accessed July 31, 2017.

Dowdey, Clifford. "Robert E. Lee: Confederate General." Encyclopedia Britannica. Accessed October 05, 2017.

Drake, Robert. A History of Appalachia. Lexington, KY: The University Press of Kentucky, 2001.

Drennen, Bill. One Kanawha Valley Bank. Bill Drennen. 2001.

Drennen, William M. Jr. and Kojo Jones Jr. Red, White, Black, & Blue. Athens, Ohio: Ohio University Press, 2004.

Dressley, Muriel Miller. Appalachia My Land Charleston. WV MHC Productions: Morris Harvey College, 1973.

Drinker, Frederick E. Booker T. Washington: The Master Mind of a Child of Slavery. New York: Negro Universities Press, reprinted 1970.

Drisdelle, R. Parasites Tales of Humanity's Most Unwelcome Guests. University of California Publishers, 2010.

DuBois, W. E. B. The Souls of Black Folk. New York: Dover Publications, Inc., 1994 [Originally published by A.C. McClurg, 1903].

Dunaway, Wilma A. Slavery in the American Mountain South. New York: Cambridge University Press, 2003.

Dunn, Richard S. "A Tale of Two Plantations: Slave: Life at Mesopotamia in Jamaica and Mount Airy in Virginia, 1799 to 1828." The William and Mary Quarterly, Vol. 34, no. 1 (January 1977): 32-65.

"Early Times: Adventurers and Slavers." The National Archives (UK), Exhibitions: Black Presence. Accessed November 26, 2018.

"Early West Virginia Civil Rights Cases: Excerpt from The Negro Citizen of West

Virginia, by Thomas E. Posey, 1934." The Pioneer Press, Souvenir Edition. n.d.

Eckert, Allen W. The Frontiersmen: A Narrative. Boston, MA: Little, Brown and Company,1967.

"Educator Mordecai Johnson Influenced MLK Jr." African American Registry: A Non-Profit Education Organization. Accessed August 15, 2017.

Educational Opportunities for Women in the University of Virginia. University of Virginia Special Collection, 1920.

Edwards, Richards C., Michael Reich and Thomas E. Weisskopf. The Capitalist System: A Radical Analysis of American Society. 2nd Edition. Englewood Cliffs, NJ: Prentice-Hall, 1986.

EIA: Independent Statistics & Analysis, U.S. Energy Information Administration. Annual Coal Report 2015. Washington D.C.: U.S. Department of Energy, 2016.

Eller, Ronald D. Miners Millhands, and Mountaineers: Industrialization of the Appalachian South 1880-1930. Knoxville, TN: The University of Tennessee Press, 1982.

Elkins, Stanley M. Slavery: A Problem in American Institutional and Intellectual Life. New York, NY: Grosset & Dunlap, 1963.

Emerson, Ralph Waldo. "Concord Hymn." 1837.

Erdman, Rachel. "Project on Slavery, Racism, and Reconciliation." From the Mountain. The University of the South School of Theology (Fall 2018): 20-25.

Eskew, Garnett Laidlow. Salt, The Fifth Element: The Story of a Basic American Industry. Chicago, IL: J.G. Ferguson and Associates, 1948.

Evans, Maria-Lynn, Holly George-Warren, Robert Santelli and Tom Robertson. The Appalachians: America's First and Last Frontier. Evening Star Productions and Random House, Inc., 2004.

Evans, Robert Jr. "The Economics of American Negro Slavery, 1830-1860." in Aspects of Labor Economics. Princeton University Press, 1962.

"Event of Long Ago Recalled." The Charleston Daily Mail. Charleston, WV, April 26, 1925.

Ewing, Jack. "Researches Who Exposed VW Gain Little Reward From Success." The New York Times. July 24, 2016.

Executive Circle: First Presbyterian Church. History of the Presbyterian Congregation and Other Early Churches of "Kenhawa," 1804-1900. Charleston, WV: Executive Circle: First Presbyterian Church, 1930.

Fain, Cicero M., III. "Presentation Forum at Horace Mann Middle School." October 11, 2011, Charleston, WV.

"Famous Quotes: On Nonviolence." Washington State University: Martin Luther King Program. Accessed October 27, 2017.

Faragher, John Mark. Daniel Boone, The Life, and Legend of an American Pioneer. New York: Henry Holland Company, 1866.

Fernandez, Manny, Richard Perez-Pena and Jonah Engel Bromwich, "Five Dallas Officers Were Killed as Payback, Police Chief Says." The New York Times. July 8, 2016.

Finkelman, Paul. Slavery and the Founders: Race and Liberty in the Age of Jackson. Armonk, NY: M. E. Sharpe, 1996.

"The First Africans," Jamestown Rediscovery: Historic Jamestowne.

Fisher, David Hackett and James C. Kelly. Bound Away: Virginia and the Westward Movement. Charlottesville, VA. University Press of Virginia, 2000.

Fitzhugh, H. Statement from Major-General W. W. Loring to the "People of West Virginia" [original manuscript]. Located in The War of the Rebellion: A Compilation of the Official Records of the Union and Confederate Armies, Series 1, Volume 19. Cornell University Library: Civil War Official Histories. Accessed October 30, 2017.

Flasch, Mark & Pam, ed. Peter Ruffner and his Descendants, Second Edition. Volume 2. Ruffner Family Association, 2007.

Fogel, Robert William and Stanley L. Engerman. Time on the Cross: The Economics of American Negro Slavery. Boston, MA: Little, Brown and Company, 1974.

Fogel, Robert William. Without Consent or Contract: The Rise and Fall of American Slavery. New York, NY: W. W. Norton, 1989.

Foner, Eric. "Abraham Lincoln: The Great Emancipator?" (Lecture as part of the Sarah Tryphene Phillips Lecture Series read at The British Academy. November 5, 2003): 160-161. Accessed November 28, 2018.

Foner, Eric. The Fiery Trial: Abraham Lincoln and American Slavery. New York, NY: W. W. Norton & Company, 2010.

Foner, Eric. Reconstruction: America's Unfinished Revolution. New York: Harper-Perennial, 2014.

Foner, Eric. Gateway to Freedom: The Hidden History of the Underground Railroad. New York, NY: W. W. Norton & Company, 2015.

Fones-Wolf, Ken. Glass Towns: Industry, Labor, and Political Economy in Appalachia, 1890-1930s. Urbana and Chicago, IL: University of Illinois Press, 2007.

Forman, Cyrus. "Disorder in the Court: The Bill Mitchell Slave Rescue of 1839 and Ohio's Antislavery Politics." Printed Source, March 8, 2017.

Forster, John. The Life of Charles Dickens. Volume 2, 1847-1870. London; New York: Chapman & Hall; Charles Scribner's, 1904.

Foster, Stephen. Stephen Foster Song Book: Original Sheet Music of 40 Songs.

Courier Corporation, 1974.

Fraser, Jr., Walter Javan. William Henry Ruffner: A Liberal in the Old and New South. Ph.D. Dissertation, University of Tennessee. March 1970.

"Fred Martin Torrey." e-WV: The West Virginia Encyclopedia. December 09, 2015. Accessed August 01, 2017.

Freedman, Russell. Abraham Lincoln & Frederick Douglass: The Story behind an American Friendship. New York, NY: Clarian Books, 2012.

Frey, Robert L. "Baltimore & Ohio Railroad." e-WV: The West Virginia Encyclopedia. November 14, 2010. Accessed September 27, 2017.

Furbee, Mary Rodd. "Mary Draper Ingles." e-WV: West Virginia Encyclopedia. December 7, 2015. Accessed October 24, 2017.

Futch, Ovid L. History of Andersonville Prison. Gainesville, FL: University of Florida Press, 1968.

Gallaher, D.C. Genealogical notes of the Miller- Quarrier- Shrewsbury- Dickinson- Dickenson Families and the Lewis, Ruffner, and Other Kindred Branches with Historical Incidents, etc. Charleston, WV: 1917.

Gambino, Megan. "A Salute to the Wheel." Smithsonian.com. June 17, 2009. Accessed January 11, 2019.

Garrett, Wilbur E., Editor. Historical Atlas of the United States. Washington D.C.: National Geographic Society, 1988.

Gates, Henry Louis, Jr., Editor. The Classic Slave Narratives. New York, NY: New American Library, 1987.

Gates, Henry Louis, Jr. Colored People, A Memoir. New York: Vintage Books, 1995.

Gates, Henry Louis, Jr. In Search of Our Roots. New York: Crown Publishers, 2009.

Gates, Henry Louis, Jr. "The African Americans" with Henry Louis Gates Jr.,

(Kumhart Mcgree Productions, 2013).

Gay, Archer Bailey. A History of the Grand Chapter, Royal Arch Masons in the Commonwealth of Virginia. Highland Springs, VA: Masonic Home Press, Inc., 1958.

Genovese, Eugene D. Roll, Jordan, Roll: The World The Slaves Made. New York, NY: Pantheon Books, 1974.

"George Briton McClellan." Dictionary of American Biography. New York City, NY: Charles Scribner's Sons, 1936.

George, Carol V. R. Segregated Sabbaths: Richard Allen and the Emergence of Independent Black Churches, 1760-1840. New York, NY: Oxford University Press, 1973.

George Washington Papers, Series 4, General Correspondence: Fairfax County, Virginia, Citizens. July 18, 1774, Resolutions and Abstract. 1774. Manuscript/Mixed Material. Library of Congress. Accessed August 16, 2017.

"George Washington Diary, January 1 - May 22, 1760." Quote in The West Virginia Heritage Encyclopedia, Volume 5, Centennial Catalogue to Coppinger. Edited by Jim Comstock (1976).

Gerson, Kathleen. "Children of the Gender Revolution." Judith Lorber, Gender Inequality: Feminist Theories and Politics. Fifth Edition. NY: Oxford University Press, 2012, quoting Andrew Hacker, Two Nations: Black and White, Separate, Hostile, Unequal. NY: Scribner, 2003.

Gilchrist-Stalnaker, Joy Gregoire. "Lewis County." e-WV: West Virginia Encyclopedia. December 16, 2015. Accessed September 12, 2017.

Gilmer, Anna. In discussion with Author. August 01, 2014.

Gimbel, John. Origins of the Marshall Plan. Stanford, CA: Stanford University Press, 1976.

"Give Me Liberty Or Give Me Death!" Colonial Williamsburg: That the Future May Learn From the Past. Accessed January 14, 2019.

Goodwin, Doris Kearns. Leadership in Turbulent Times. New York, NY: Simon & Schuster, 2018.

Goudsouzian, Aram. Down to the Crossroads: Civil Rights, Black Power, and the Meredith March Against Fear. New York, NY: Farrarm Straus, and Giroux, 2014.

Gould, Lewis L. "William McKinley: Death of the President." UVA Miller Center: U.S. Presidents. Accessed September 21, 2017.

Grant, R. G. Slavery: Real people and Their Stories of Enslavement. London: Toucan Books, 2009.

Green, James. The Devil is Here in These Hills: West Virginia's Coal Miners and Their Battle for Freedom. New York: Atlantic Monthly Press, 2015.

Gries, John M. and James Ford. Negro Housing: Report of the Committee on Negro Housing. Washington D.C.: National Capital Press Inc., 1932.

Gruyter, Julius de. The Kanawha Spectator. Volume 1 & 2. Charleston, WV: Jarrett Printing Company, 1953.

Gunter, Donald W. "George William Summers (1804-1868)." Library of Virginia. Accessed December 1, 2017.

Gunther, John. Inside Europe. Guernsey, UK: Hamish Hamilton, 1936.

Gutman, Herbert G. Slavery and the Numbers Game: A Critique of Time On The Cross. Urbana and Chicago, IL: University of Illinois Press, 2003.

Gutman, Herbert G. The Black Family in Slavery and Freedom 1750-1925. New York, Random House Inc.,1976.

Hacker, David. "Recounting the Dead." New York Times. September 10, 2011. Accessed July 18, 2017.

Haines, Kathryn Miller. "Stephen Foster: The Making of Pittsburgh's Renowned

Musical Export." Western Pennsylvania History: Up Front, 97. no. 3 (Fall 2014): 34-39.

Hale, John Peter. History of the Great Kanawha Valley. Volume 1 & 2. Madison, Wisconsin: Brant, Fuller & Company, 1891.

Hale, John P. Trans-Allegheny Pioneers. Radford, VA: Roberta Ingles Steele, 1971.

Hall, Granville. The Rending of Virginia: A History. Chicago: Mayer & Miller, 1902.

Hamilton's America: A Documentary Film. Directed by Alex Horwitz. United States: PBS, 2016. Television.

Harbaugh, William H. Lawyer's Lawyer: The Life of John W. Davis. New York: Oxford University Press, 1973.

Hardy, Thomas. "The Darkling Thrush." Poetry Foundation. Accessed October 18, 2017.

Harlan, Louis R. Booker T. Washington the Making of a Black Leader 1856-1901. New York: Oxford University Press, 1972.

Harlan, Louis R. Harlan. "Booker T. Washington's West Virginia Boyhood." The West Virginia Historical Magazine 32, no. 2. (1971): 63-85.

Harlan, Louis R. Booker T. Washington: The Wizard of Tuskegee, 1901-1915. New York: Oxford University Press, 1983.

Harlan, Louis R. and Raymond W. Smock, ed. The Booker T. Washington Papers. Volume 14, Cumulative Index. Chicago, Illinois: University of Illinois Press, 1989.

Harlan, Louis R. Booker T. Washington in Perspective: Essays of Louis R. Harlan. Edited by Raymond Smock. Mississippi: University Press of Mississippi, 2006.

Harlan, Louis R. "Booker T. Washington's West Virginia Boyhood." West Virginia Archives and History. Accessed September 6, 2017.

Harris, Evelyn L. K. and Frank J. Krebs. From Humble Beginnings, West Virginia Federation of Labor, 1903-1957. Charleston WV: West Virginia Labor History Publishing Fund, 1960.

Harris, V. B. Great Kanawha - An Historical Outline. Commissioned by The Kanawha County Court. West Virginia: Kanawha County Commission, 1974.

Harris, Wess. Written in Blood: Courage and Corruption in the Appalachian War of Extraction. Gay, WV & Oakland, CA: Appalachian Community Services & PM Press, 2017.

Hartman, Richard. "The Rise and Fall of Reconstruction in West Virginia." Master's Thesis, Marshall University, 2004.

Hathaway, Rosemary V. "Hillbilly or Frontiersmen? A Brief Cultural History of the West Virginia Mountaineer." West Virginia Humanities Council. MacFarland-Hubbard House, Charleston WV: June 24,2018.

Hedrick, Charles. History of the Ruffner Family of Kanawha. 1884.

Heidler, David S. and Jeanne T. "Manifest Destiny." Encyclopedia Britannica. January 1, 2017.

Heineman, Kenneth J. Civil War Dynasty: The Ewing Family of Ohio. New York, NY: New York University Press, 2013.

Henderson, G. F. R. Stonewall Jackson and The American Civil War. New York, NY: Da Capo Press, Inc., 1943.

Henshey, Lori. "Vandalia Colony." e-WV: West Virginia Encyclopedia. July 13, 2018.

Herskovits, Melville J. The Myth of the Negro Past. Boston, MA: Beacon Press, 1958.

Hibbert, Christopher. George III: A Personal History. Great Britain: Basic Books, 1998.

Higgins, Molly. "Juneteenth: Fact Sheet." Congressional Research Service (2017).

Hill, Richard H. History of the First Baptist Church of Charleston West Virginia. Charleston, West Virginia: First Baptist

Church, 1934.

"History," African Zion Baptist Church Bulletin. West Virginia, 1976.

"History." College of Law | West Virginia University. Accessed July 27, 2017.

"History of Tuskegee University." Tuskegee University: History and Mission. Accessed December 4, 2017.

"Honorary Degrees: 1842 to Present." Washington & Lee University: University Honors Board. Accessed November 28, 2018.

Hoover, Stephanie. "The history of the Pennsylvania Salt Industry." Pennsylvania Research.com. Accessed November 28, 2018.

"How West Virginia Coal Fields Grew." Coal Trade Journal 50 no. 25. April 16, 1919. New York.

Howe, Daniel Walker. What Hath God Wrought: The Transformation of America, 1815-1848. New York: Oxford University Press, 2007.

Hriblan, John T., II. The Historic Midland Trail [Map]. 1 inch to 50 miles. Morgantown, West Virginia: Institute for the History of Technology and Industrial Archaeology, a part of West Virginia University, n. d.

Huddleston, Eugene L. Riding That New River Train: The Story of the Chesapeake & Ohio Railway through the New River Gorge of West Virginia. Clifton Forge, VA: The Chesapeake & Ohio Historical Society, Inc., n.d.

Hughes, Hillary. "First in War, First in Peace, and First in the Hearts of His Countrymen." Mountvernon.org. Accessed January 2, 2019.

Huddleston, Eugene L. Appalachian Conquest. Lynchburg, VA: TLC Publishing Inc., and the Chesapeake & Ohio Historical Society, Inc., 2002.

Husch, Gail E. Something Coming. Hanover, NH: University Press of New England, 2000.

Hussey, Maria. The Rise of the Jim Crow Era. New York: Rosen Publishing Group, 2016.

Hypes, Alice. Midland Trail National Scenic Byway, West Virginia, U.S. Route 60: Official Destination Guide. Charleston, West Virginia: Midland Trail Scenic Highway Association and QuikPage Publishing, 2002.

Imai, Shiho. "Gentlemen's Agreement." Densho Encyclopedia. https://encyclopedia.densho.org/Gentlemen's%20Agreement/. Accessed January 7, 2019.

Inscription from Booker T. Washington Monument, Malden, West Virginia.

Inscription on Monument of Joseph L. Beury at Quinnimont, WV. National Park Service: New River Gorge. Accessed October 04, 2017.

"Jacksonhole." Town of Jackson. Accessed July 3, 2018.

"Jackson Brigade Corporation." Decedents of Edward Jackson. Accessed July 3, 2018.

Jackson, Gloria Yvonne and Sarah O'Neal Rush. Timeless Treasures Reflections of God's Word In The Wisdom of Booker T Washington. Bloomington, IN: Author House, 2006.

Jakle, John A. "Salt on the Ohio Valley Frontier, 1770-1820." Annals of the Association of American Geographers. Vol. 59, No. 4, December (1969). Taylor & Francis, Ltd on behalf of the Association of American Geographers. JSTOR, Accessed November 26, 2018.

"Jamboree Overview." Summit Bechtel Reserve. Accessed November 2, 2017.

James, C.H. "African American Life in Charleston: A Personal Perspective, Part II." Speech at West Virginia Archives and History, State Cultural Center. Charleston, West Virginia. July 24, 2014.

James, Peter and Nick Thorpe. Ancient Inventions. New York: Ballantine Books, 1994.

"James Weldon Johnson." Biography by A&E Television Networks. April 2, 2014. Accessed January 20, 2019.

Jefferds, Joseph C. Jr. A History of St. John's Episcopal Church: Charleston, West Virginia. Charleston, WV, 1976.

"Jefferson Davis." Civil War Trust: Biographies. Accessed October 05, 2017.

Jefferson, Thomas. The Declaration of Independence [Original Manuscript]. 1776. Philadelphia, PA.

Jefferson, Thomas Jefferson. Notes on the State of Virginia. Edited by J. W. Randolph. Richmond, VA: J. W. Randolph, 1853.

"John Brown." e-WV: West Virginia Encyclopedia. January 05, 2017.

"John Brown's Harpers Ferry." History. com. Accessed July 17, 2017. http://www. history.com/topics/harpers-ferry

"John Brown's Raiders." Civil War Trust. Accessed September 29, 2017.

"John D. Rockefeller IV." Council on Foreign Relations. Accessed October 12, 2017.

"John H. Chafee Blackstone River Valley: National Heritage Corridor, MA, RI." History & Culture: Birthplace of the American Industrial Revolution. National Park Service. Accessed June 12, 2019.

"John Hawkins' Coat of Arms," The National Archives (UK), Exhibitions: Black Presence by permission of The college of Arms, London (1568), accessed November 26, 2018.

Johnson, James Weldon. "Lift Every Voice and Sing." The Hymnal 1982. New York: Church Pension Fund, 1985.

Johnson, Matthew. "Timeline of Events Relating to the End of Slavery." Massachusetts Historical Society, The Case for Ending Slavery. Accessed September 26, 2017.

Johnson, Rody. In their Footsteps. Charleston, WV: Quarrier Press, 2005.

"Joseph Buery." National Park Service: New River Gorge. February 26, 2016. Accessed October 31, 2017.

Jowett, B. Plato's The Republic. NY: Vintage Books, N.D.

Julienne, Marianne E. and the Dictionary of Virginia Biography. "William Henry Ruffner (1824- 1908)." Encyclopedia of Virginia. April 29, 2016. Accessed November 14, 2017.

Kanawha County Land Book. 1797. Kanawha County Clerk's Office. Charleston, West Virginia.

Kanawha County Land Book. 1814. Kanawha County Clerk's Office. Charleston, West Virginia.

Kanawha County Land Book, 1824, Kanawha County Clerk's Office, Charleston, West Virginia.

Kanawha County Land Book. 1850-1860. Kanawha County Clerk's Office. Charleston, West Virginia.

Kanawha County Land Book. 1868-71. Kanawha County Clerk's Office. Charleston, West Virginia.

Kanawha County Land Book. 1875. Kanawha County Clerk's Office. Charleston, West Virginia.

"Kanawha Valley celebrates 200 years of Presbyterianism." Synod of the Trinity: Featured News. June 12, 2019. accessed August 5, 2019.

"Kanawha Salt Lick." New Bedford Gazette. January 04, 1836.

Karp, Matthew. This Vast Southern Empire: Slaveholders at the Helm of American Foreign Policy. Harvard University Press, 2016.

Kashatus, William C. Kashatus. Abraham Lincoln, the Quakers, and the Civil War: "A Trial of Principle and Faith." Santa Barbara, California: ABC-CLIO, LLC., 2014.

Kathleen, 1924. Painting by Robert Henri in Huntington Museum of Art: Fifty Years of Collecting. Huntington, WV: Huntington Museum of Art, 2001.

Katz, William Loren, Editor. The American Negro: His History and Literature. US: Anro Press, Inc., 1968.

Katznelson, Ira. When Affirmative Action Was White: An Untold History of Racial Inequality in Twentieth-Century America. New York: W. W. Norton & Company, 2005.

Kemp, Emory L. The Great Kanawha Navigation. Pittsburgh: University of Pittsburgh Press, 2000.

Keenan, Steve. "Boyhood home of Washington being recreated at Malden." The Montgomery Herald/The Fayette Tribune. March 25-26, 1998 (WV).

Keenan, Steve. "Rowe stresses importance of preserving our history." Montgomery Herald. December 17, 2014. (WV).

Kennedy, B. "Ulster-Scots and the United States Presidents, Ulster-Scots Agency. Accessed August 25, 2017.

Kercheval, Samuel. A History of the Valley of Virginia. 4th Edition. Strasburg, VA: Shenandoah Publishing House, 1925.

Kidder, David S. and Noah D. Oppenheim. The Intellectual Devotional: American History. New York: Modern Times, 2007.

King, Coretta Scott. "On Achievement." In Nat Turner by Terry Bisson. New York & Philadelphia: Chelsea House Publishers, 1988.

King, Ellen. West Virginia Hills. Official State Song. Publishers' Service Bureau, Washington D.C., 1913.

King, Martin Luther, Jr. "I have a Dream...." Speech for "March on Washington." Washington D.C. August 28, 1963.

Kinnear, Dr. Duncan Lyle. "A Short History of Virginia Tech: Founding of the College 1872." Special Collections: University Libraries, Virginia Tech. Accessed November 11, 2017.

Kladky, William P. "Constitutional Convention." George Washington's Mount Vernon. Accessed October 04, 2017.

Klein, Christopher. The Ex-Slaves Who Fought with the British. History.com. May 24, 2016. Accessed August 10, 2018.

Klotter, James C. Henry Clay: The Man Who Would Be President. New York, NY: Oxford University Press, 2018

Kratz, Jessie. "The Compromise of 1790." National Archives. May 31, 2015. Accessed January 11, 2019.

Kulikoff, Allan. Tobacco and Slaves: The Development of Southern Cultures in the Chesapeake, 1680-1800. Chapel Hill, NC: The University of North Carolina Press, 1986.

Kurland, Philip B and Ralph Lerner, Editors. "Equality: Chapter 15, Document 28: Thomas Jefferson, Notes on the State of Virginia, Queries 14 and 18, 137-43, 162-63." The Founders' Constitution, 2000. Accessed April 12, 2018.

Kurlansky, Mark. Salt: A World History. New York: Penguin Books, 2002.

Ladle, W. S. History of Charleston and Kanawha County, West Virginia and Representative Citizens. Chicago: Richmond-Arnold Publishing Co., 1911.

Lambert, Oscar Doane. West Virginia and Its Government. Boston: D. C. Heath and Company, 1951.

Lancaster, Lucy Lee. "First Tech Coed Earned Degree in 1923: Dr. Burruss Paved Way for Women." News Messenger Centennial Edition. December 31,1969. Accessed October 12, 2017. https://spec.lib.vt.edu/archives/125th/women/coed.htm.

Lange, Katie. "Meet Sgt, William Carney: The First African-American Medal of Honor Recipient." DoD News: Defense Media Activity. February 7, 2017. Accessed March 20, 2018.

Lankford, N. D. "Virginia Convention of 1861." Encyclopedia Virginia. Virginia Foundation for the Humanities. June 20, 2014. accessed December 11, 2017.

The Last Moments of John Brown, 1882-1884. Painting by Thomas Hovenden at the Metropolitan Museum of Art. Accession Number 97.5.

"Late Booker T. Washington, Negro Educator, Got Start in Kanawha County." Charleston Gazette. Charleston, West Virginia. March 19, 1922.

Lay, Shawn. "Ku Klux Klan in the Twentieth Century." New Georgia Encyclopedia: History and Archaeology, Progressive Era to WWI, 1900-1945. July 07, 2005. Accessed October 13, 2017.

Lee, Howard B. Bloodletting in Appalachia. Morgantown WV: West Virginia University Press, 1969.

Lee, Howard B. "Bloody Mingo." In Bloodletting In Appalachia. Parsons, WV: McClain Printing Company, [reprinted] 2013.

"Lee Resolution (1776)." Library of Congress: Primary Documents in American History. Accessed September 28, 2017,

Lee, Richard Henry. "Lee Resolution." An address to the Second Continental Congress. June 7, 1776. National Archives and Records Administration. Accessed September 28, 2017.

Lee, Robert E. "Robert E. Lee to Col. Walter H. Taylor [Letter], February 21, 1870." Transcribed by Colin Woodward, October 20 2015. Lee Family Digital Archive. Accessed June 14, 2019.

Lee, Robert E., Albert S. Johnston, Joseph E. Johnston, Pierre G. T. Beauregard, Braxton Bragg, E. Kirby Smith, John B. Hood, James Longstreet, Thomas J. Jackson, Jefferson Davis, Alexander H. Stephens, Judah P. Benjamin, Franklin Buchanan, and Raphael Semmes. The Confederate Soldier in the Civil War: The Campaigns, Battles, Sieges, Charges and Skirmishes / The Foundation and Formation of the Confederacy / The Confederate States Navy. The Fairfax Press, 1977.

Legburn, James G. Scotch-Irish: A Social History. Chapel Hill, NC: The University of North Carolina Press, 1989.

Legislature of West Virginia. The West Virginia Capitol: A Commemorative History. Morgantown, WV: Morgantown Printing & Binding, 2015.

Lehr, Dick. "The Racist Legacy of Woodrow Wilson." The Atlantic. November 27, 2015. Accessed July 27, 2017.

Letter from General Henry Knox to George Washington [original manuscript] March 19, 1787. National Archives: Founders Online. Accessed October 04, 2017.

Letter from Henry Ruffner (Kanawha C. H., VA) to Samuel Williams (Chillicothe, OH., Typescript. February 9, 1816. In possession of author.

Letter from Major-General W. W. Loring to Hon. George W. Randolph, [original manuscript]. Located in The War of the Rebellion: A Compilation of the Official Records of the Union and Confederate Armies, Series 1, Volume 19. Cornell University Library: Civil War Official Histories. Accessed October 30, 2017.

Leuchtenburg, William E. The LIFE History of the United States. Volume 12, From 1945: The Age of Change. New York: Time Life Books, 1976.

Lewis, David Levering. W. E. B. DuBois: The Fight for Equality and the American Century, 1919-1963. New York, NY: Henry Holt and Company, LLC., 2000.

Lewis, Ronald L. Coal, Iron, and Slaves: Industrial Slavery in Maryland and Virginia, 1715-1865. Westport, CT: Greenwood Press, Inc., 1979.

Lewis, Ronald L. Aspiring to Greatness: West Virginia University Since World War II. Morgantown, WV: West Virginia University Press, 2013.

Lewis, Virgil A. History of West Virginia. Philadelphia: Hubbard Brothers Publishers, 1889.

Lewis, Virgil A. History of the Battle of Point Pleasant. Charleston, West Virginia: Tribune Printing Co., 1909.

Lewis, Virgil A. History and Government of West Virginia. New York: American Book Company, 1912.

Lewis, Virgil A. Life and Times of Anne Bailey: The Pioneer Heroine of the Great Kanawha Valley. Point Pleasant, WV: Discovery Press, 1998[Originally published 1891].

Lewis, Virgil A. Lewis. History of the Battle of Point Pleasant (West Virginia). Westminster, Maryland: Willow Band Books, 2005.

"Library Archives, History," First Presbyterian Church of West Virginia. accessed August 5, 2019.

Library of Congress. The Federalist Papers. Accessed August 8, 2018.

Lincoln, Abraham. The Emancipation Proclamation. Carlisle, MA: Applewood Books, Originally published 1862.

Lincoln, Abraham. "Remarks to a Delegation of Progressive Friends [June 20, 1862]." Collected Works of Abraham Lincoln. Volume 5. Roy P. Basley, Editor. New Brunswick, NJ: Rutgers University Press, 1953.

Lincoln, Abraham. "Gettysburg Address." [Speech] Dedication of the Cemetery at Gettysburg, PA, Gettysburg. November 19, 1863.

Lincoln, Abraham. Second Inaugural Address of Abraham Lincoln, [Original Manuscript] March 04, 1865. The Avalon Project: Library of Congress. Accessed October 02, 2017.

Lincoln, Abraham. Proclamation of freedom millions! The Emancipation Proclamation. Chicago, Cook, Illinois, United States, Washington D. C., National Printing Co., Chicago, Illinois, n. d.

Photograph.

"Lincoln's Cooper Institute Address: address at Cooper Institute, New York, Feb. 27, 1860." Old South Leaflets, no. 107 (Boston: Directors of the Old South Work, 1902).

Lippincott, Isaac. "The Early Salt Trade of the Ohio Valley." Journal of Political Economy. Vol. 20, No. 10, December (1912). University of Chicago Press. JSTOR. Accessed November 26, 2018.

Lloyd, Gordon. "Introduction to the New York Ratifying Convention." Ratification of the Constitution. Accessed August 01, 2017. http://teachingamericanhistory.org/ratification/newyork/.

Lockard, Duane. Coal: A Memoir and Critique. Charlottesville, VA: University Press of Virginia, 1998.

Locke, Alain. "The American Temperament." The North American Review 194, no. 669 1911): 262-270. Accessed July 7, 2017.

Lofaro, Michael A. Daniel Boone: An American Life. University Press of Kentucky, 2003.

Long, John. "The Indian Captivity Narrative of Charles Johnston." Blacksburg, Virginia: The Smithfield Review. Volume XI, 2007.

Lonn, Ella. Foreigners in the Confederacy. Chapel Hill, NC: The University of North Carolina Press, 1940.

Lovell, Joseph. Letters to James Bream dated November January 6, 1817. Family document. Copy in possession of author.

Lyon Peter. "A Tinkering People." in The American Heritage Book of the Pioneer Spirit. Edited by Richard M. Ketchum. American Heritage Publishing Co., Inc., 1959.

MacCorkle, William. The Recollections of Fifty Years of West Virginia. New York: G. P. Putnam's Sons, 1928.

Madison, James, Notes of the Debates in

the Federal Convention of 1787, Reported by James Madison. Bicentennial ed., with introduction by Adrienne KochNew York: W.W Norton and C0., p. d.

Maginnis, William H. "Pioneer Academies in Kanawha Valley Trained Settlers' Youth for College." Charleston Gazette (Charleston, WV) October 30, 1949.

Maier, Pauline. Ratification: The People Debate the Constitution, 1787-1788. New York, NY: Simon & Schuster, 2010.

Major, J. Russell (Emory University). Civilization in the Western World, Renaissance to 1815. Philadelphia, PA: J.B. Lippincott Company, 1966.

"Malden Has Home Coming." The Charleston Gazette. June 17, 1915.

"The Malden Riot." In the West Virginia Journal, Edited by G. W. Atkinson. Charleston, WV, December 15, 1869.

Mansfield, Stephen. Then Darkness Fled, The Liberating Wisdom of Booker T. Washington. Nashville, Tennessee: Highland Books, 1999.

Maranzani, Barbara. "The Most Violent Insurrection in American History." The History Channel: History Stories. July 5, 2013. Accessed March 20, 2018.

Marriage between Booker T. Washington and Fanny Norton Smith. Kanawha County. Marriage Book 1, page 192, no. 193. Kanawha County Court House. Charleston, West Virginia.

Martelle, Scot. The Madman and the Assassin: The Strange Life of Boston Corbett, the Man Who Killed John Wilkes Booth. Chicago: Chicago Review Press., 2015.

"Martinsville Negro Lawyer is Admitted to University." Richmond Times-Dispatch. September 16, 1950.

Martinez, Tara. Manna Meal. Interview with Author. June 12 & 20, 2019.

Maurice, Jack. "Malden Woman Helped Youth Early in Life," Charleston Dailey Mail. June 18, 1939.

May, Ernest R. The LIFE History of the United States, Volume 9, 1901-1917: The Progressive Era. New York: Time Life Books, 1976.

May, Ernest R. The LIFE History of the United States, Volume 10, 1917-1932 Boom and Bust. Edited by Henry F. Graff. New York: Time-Life Books, 1976.

May, Nicholas. "Holy Rebellion: Religious Assembly Laws in Antebellum South Carolina and Virginia." The American Journal of Legal History 49, no. 3. (July 2007): 237-256.

"Mayflower Compact." Encyclopedia Britannica. Encyclopedia Britannica Inc. Accessed August 25 2017.

McAlester, Virginia and Lee. A Field Guide to American Houses. New York: Alfred A. Knopf Inc., 1984.

McAllister, J.T. "The Battle of Point Pleasant." The Virginia Magazine of History and Biography, IX. 1902.

McAteer, J. Davitt. "Monongah Mine Disaster." e-WV: West Virginia Encyclopedia. December 06, 2013. Accessed October 06, 2017.

McCain, John. "Concession Speech." November 5, 2008.

McCallum, Barbara Beury. "Minnie Cooper." Hodge Podge. January -March 1991.

McElroy, John. Andersonville: A Story of Rebel Military Prisons. Toledo, Ohio: D.R. Locke, 1879.

McGeehan, Pat. Stoicism and the Statehouse: An Old Philosophy Serving a New Idea. Proctorville, OH: Wythe-North Publishing, 2017.

McGirr, Lisa. The War on Alcohol: Prohibition and the Rise of the American State. New York: W. W. Norton, 2016.

"McKendree Hospital." National Park Service. February 26, 2015. Accessed October 18, 2017.

McLaughlin, John C. Brown. History of

Kanawha Salines, The Presbytery's Oldest Church, An address at the Centennial Celebration. October, 1940.

McNeill, Louise. Hill Daughter: New and Selected Poems. Pittsburgh, PA: University of Pittsburgh Press, 1991.

McQuade, Donald, Editor. The Harper American Literature. Volume 2. New York: HarperCollins Publishers, Inc., 1987.

McWhorter, John H. Losing the Race: Self-Sabotage in Black America. New York, NY: Perennial, 2001.

Meacham, Jon. American Lion: Andrew Jackson in the White House. New York: Random House, 2008.

Meadows, Phyllius. In discussion with author. March 21, 2014.

Meininger, Jules C. Stonewall Jackson's Last Words. Louisville: McCarrell & Meininger, 1866.

Memorial monument to the Kanawha Rifleman by the United Daughters of the Confederacy. Ruffner Park. Charleston, WV.

Meyer, Simon. Editor. One Hundred Years, An Anthology- Charleston Jewry. Charleston, WV: Jones Printing Company, 1972.

Miller, James. History of Summers County. Hinton, WV, 1908.

Miller, Thurman I. Coal Bloom. Lincoln, NE: iUniverse, Inc., 2003

Miller, Kelly. Race Adjustment: Essays on the Negro in America. New York: The Neale Publishing Co., 1909.

Miller, Thomas and HU Maxwell. West Virginia and Its People. Volume 1 & 3. New York: Lewis Historical Publishing Company, 1913.

Mintz, Steven. "Childhood and Transatlantic Slavery." in Children and Youth in History, Item #57. Accessed August 8, 2017.

Moes, John (University of Virginia). Review of Robert Evans Jr. "The Economics of American Negro Slavery, 1830-1860."

in Aspects of Labor Economics. Princeton University Press, 1962.

Momodu, Samuel. "Johns, Vernon Napoleon (1892–1965)." Blackpast.org, Accessed November 9, 2017.

Monroe County Historical Society, "Red Sulphur Springs," The Monroe Watchman (Union, West Virginia, January 25, 1968.

"Mordecai Johnson." In Profiles: West Virginians Who Made a Difference. Edited by Robert J. Byers. Charleston, WV: The Charleston Gazette, 1999.

Morgan, Edmund S. American Slavery, American Freedom, The Ordeal of Colonial Virginia. New York: W.W. Norton & Company Inc., 1975.

Morgan, John G. and Robert J. Byers. Charleston 200. Charleston, WV: Charleston Gazette, 1994.

Morgan, John G. A Point in History: The Battle of Point Pleasant. Charleston, WV: Charleston Gazette, 1975.

Morgan, John G. West Virginia Governors. Charleston, WV: Charleston Newspapers, 1980.

Morris, Thomas D. Southern Slavery and the Law, 1619-1860. Chapel Hill, NC: The University of North Carolina Press, 1996.

Morrison, Samuel Eliot. The Oxford History of the American People. New York: Oxford University Press, 1965.

Mosby, Maryida W. "Salt Industry in the Kanawha Valley." Master's Thesis, University of Kentucky, 1950.

Morton, Horwitz J. "The Historical Foundations of Modern Contract Law." Harvard Law Review 87, no. 5 (March 1974): 917-956.

Moton, Robert R. "A Life of Achievement." Speech given at Memorial Meeting in Honor of Booker T. Washington. New York, NY, February 11, 1916.

Mott, Joyce. "Greenbrier County." e-WV: The West Virginia Encyclopedia. 31 May

2013.

Mullin, Gerald W. Flight and Rebellion: Slave Resistance in Eighteenth-Century Virginia. New York, NY: Oxford University Press, 1972.

Murphy, Sharon Ann. "Securing Human Property: Slavery, Life Insurance, and Industrialization in the Upper South." Journal of the Early Republic 25, no. 4 (2005): 615-52.

"Nancy Hanks Lincoln." National Park Service: Lincoln Boyhood. Accessed November 7, 2017.

Nardo, Don, Editor. The Creation of the U.S. Constitution. Detroit, MI: Thomson Gale, 2005.

Nardo, Don. The Atlantic Slave Trade. Detroit, MI: Lucent Books, 2008.

National Council of Jewish Women. The Gourmet Day of History #7. October 25, 1992.

National Park Service: U.S. Department of the Interior. "Virginia State Capitol." National Park Service. Accessed March 20, 2018.

National Park Service: U.S. Department of the Interior. "Antietam Casualties of Battle." National Park Service. Accessed July 3, 2018,

"Nat Turner's Rebellion, 1831." The Gilder Lehrman Institute of American History. Accessed December 4, 2017.

Nelson, Scott Reynolds. Steel Drivin' Man- John Henry- The Untold Story of an American Legend. Oxford, New York, Oxford University Press, 2006.

New York Journal of Commerce. "Princeton College." Richmond Enquirer. October 12, 1838.

Niebuhr, Reinhold, Love and Justice: Selections from the Shorter Writings of Reinhold Niebuhr. Charlottesville, VA: The University of Virginia Press, 1976.

Nilsson, Jeff. "The Debt and Death of Thomas Jefferson." The Saturday Evening Post (July 2, 2015). Accessed January 7, 2019.

"No title [Grand Jury Preceding's]," in The West Virginia Journal, ed. G. W. Atkinson. Charleston, WV, March 30, 1870.

Norrell, Robert J. Up From History: The Life of Booker T. Washington. Cambridge, Massachusetts: The Belknap Press of Harvard University Press, 2009.

Northrop, Henry Davenport, Joseph R. Gay and I. Garland Penn. The College of Life or Practical Self=Educator: A Manual of Self-Improvement for the Colored Race. Chicago, IL: Chicago Publication and Lithograph Co., 1895.

"Nullification Crisis: United States History [1832-1833]." Encyclopedia Britannica. December 11, 2018. Accessed January 7, 2019. https://www.britannica.com/topic/nullification-crisis.

Nyden, Paul J. "J.R. Clifford Story Helps People Understand State History in Unique Way." Charleston Gazette. Charleston, West Virginia. February 4, 2012.

Obama, Barack. Speech given at Democratic National Convention. Boston, MA. 2004.

Obergefell v. Hodges, 576 U. S. ___ (2015): 3.

Office of the Surgeon General, U.S. Department of Health and Human Services. The Health Consequences of Smoking--50 Years of Progress: A Report of the Surgeon General, Executive Summary. Rockville, MD: U.S. Department of Health and Human Services, 2014.

O'Grady, Jim. "The Hidden Racial History of 'My Old Kentucky Home'." WNYC News. May 2, 2014. Accessed September 28, 2017. http://www.wnyc.org/story/hidden-meaning-my-old-kentucky-home/

Olcott, William. The Greenbrier Heritage. White Sulphur Springs, WV: Arndt, Chapin, Lamb & Keen, Inc.

"Old Slater Mill." National Historic Landmarks Program: National Parks Service. Accessed May 3, 2019.

Olmstead, Alan L., and Paul W. Rhode. Creating Abundance: Biological Innovation and American Agricultural Development. Cambridge University Press, 2008.

Olmsted, Frederick Law, A Journey in the Seaboard Slave States, With Remarks on Their Economy. New York, NY: Dix & Edwards, 1856.

Olmsted, Frederick Law. The Cotton Kingdom: A Traveller's Observations on Cotton and Slavery in the American Slave States. New York, NY: Alfred A. Knopf, 1970.

"Opening the Door West: The Story of How the Ohio Company of Associates Began the First Organized American Settlement on the Old Northwest Territory." Reedsville OH: Shelbourne Films mmIII.

Ottenberg, Simon & Phoebe. Cultures and Societies of Africa. New York, NY: Random House, 1960.

"Our History Runs Deep," West Virginia State University, accessed April 11, 2018.

"Our Salt." J. Q. Dickinson Salt-Works. Accessed July 12, 2017.

"Our Withdrawn Review "Blood Cotton." The Economist. September 5, 2014. Accessed January 21, 2019.

The Oxford Dictionary of Quotations. 2nd Edition. New York: Oxford University Press, 1959.

"Past Presidents: Dr. William Henry Ruffner 1884-87." Longwood University: President's Office. Accessed August 31, 2017.

Palmer, R. R. and Joel Colton. History of the Modern World Since 1815. New York: Alfred A. Knopf. 1978.

PBS. Lift Every Voice and Sing. Accessed June 21,2018.

Perry, Douglas. "Lewis & Clark Expedition." National Archives. September 7,

2016[last updated]. Accessed September 29, 2017.

Perry, Huey. They'll Cut off Your Project: A Mingo County Chronicle. Morgantown, WV: West Virginia University Press, 2011.

Peterkin, George W. A History and Record of the protestant Episcopal Church in the Diocese of West Virginia and Before the Formation of the Diocese in 1878 in the Territory now Known as the State of West Virginia. Charleston, WV: The Tribune Company Printers, 1902.

Peyton, Billy Joe. "James River & Kanawha Turnpike." e-WV: The West Virginia Encyclopedia. May 29, 2012. Accessed August 01, 2017.

Pilcher, James Evelyn. The Surgeon General of the Army of the United States of America. Carlisle, PA: The Association of Military Surgeons, 1905.

Pitts, Leonard. "What War on Whites?" The Charleston Gazette. Charleston, WV. August 10, 2014.

Platania, Joseph. "Salt by The River." Wild Wonderful West Virginia. December 1993.

Poche, Francois and Jean-Claude Rochette. Translation by Ronald Corlette-Theuil. The Dome of the Invalides. Paris: Musee De L'Armee, Somogy Editions D'Art, 1995.

Ponton, Anthony W. "John F. Kennedy and West Virginia, 1960-1963." Master's Thesis, Marshall University, 2004.

"President Clinton: Celebrating America's Rivers." American Heritage Rivers. July 30, 1998. Accessed September 26, 2017.

Preston, John T. L. "Letter to his wife." Lexington (VA) Gazette. December 15, 1859.

Price, Paul, Charles Hare, J.B. McCue and Homer Hoskins. Salt Brines of West Virginia. Vol. 8, West Virginia Geological Survey. Morgantown, WV: Morgantown Printing & Binding Company, 1937.

Prichard, Robert. A History of the Episcopal Church. Harrisburg PA: Morehouse

Publishing, 1991.

Priest, Karl C. Protester Voices - The 1974 Textbook Tea Party. Poca, WV: Praying Mantis Publishing, 2010.

Prillerman, Byrd. "Booker T. And His Malden Neighbors." The West Virginia Hillbilly (West Virginia) Nov 2 1989.

Princeton Theological Seminary, Alumni Association. "William Swan Plumer." In Necrological Report Presented to the Alumni Association of Princeton Theological Seminary at its Annual Meeting, April 26, 1881. Princeton Theological Seminary, 1891.

Proclamation made by Lord Dunmore (November 7, 1775). Manuscript/Mixed Material Retrieved from University of Maryland-Baltimore County. Accessed June 06, 2017.

Pryor, Elizabeth Brown. "Robert E. Lee (ca. 1806-1870)." Encyclopedia Virginia. November 19, 2009. Accessed October 05, 2017.

Pulliam, David L. The Constitutional Conventions of Virginia from the Foundation of the Commonwealth to the Present Time. Richmond, VA: John T. West, publisher, 1901.

Purdum, Todd S. An Idea Whose Time Has Come. New York, NY: Henry Holt and Company, LLC., 2014.

Puttkammer, Charles W. and Ruth Worthy. "William Monroe Trotter." The Journal of Negro History 43, no. 4 (October, 1958): 298-316.

Quarles, Benjamin. Allies for Freedom, & Blacks on John Brown. Oxford University Press, 1974.

"Race and Voting in the Segregated South." Constitutional Rights Foundation. Accessed October 13, 2017.

Randall, James D. and Anna E. Gilmer. Black Past. 1989.

Rastogi, Sonya, Tallese D. Johnson,

Elizabeth M. Hoeffel, and Malcolm P. Drewery Jr. "The Black Population: 2010, 2010 Census Briefs." U.S. Department of Commerce: U. S. Census Bureau (September 2011).

Ratliff, Gerald S. "George William Summers." e-WV: West Virginia Encyclopedia. December 8, 2015.

Ratliff, Gerald S. "Burning Springs." e-WV: West Virginia Encyclopedia. Last Revised March 25, 2014. Accessed August 31, 2017.

Ratliff, Gerald S. "Clendenin Family." e-WV: The West Virginia Encyclopedia, June 20, 2012, accessed August 7, 2018,

Reidy, Joseph P. From Slavery to Agrarian Capitalism in the Cotton Plantation South: Central George, 1800-1880. Chapel Hill, NC: The University of North Carolina Press, 1992.

"Resolution to Call the Election of Abraham Lincoln as U.S. President a Hostile Act and to Communicate to Other Southern States South Carolina's Desire to Secede from the Union." 9 November 1860. Resolutions of the General Assembly, 1779–1879. S165018. South Carolina Department of Archives and History, Columbia, South Carolina.

"Results from the 1860 Census." The Civil War HomePage. Accessed September 26, 2017.

Reynolds, David S. "John Wilkes Booth and the Higher Law." The Atlantic. April 12, 2015.

Rhee, William and Stephen C. Scott. "Geographic Discrimination: of Place, Space, Hillbillies, and Home." West Virginia Law Review 2, Volume121 (Winter 2018): 531-611.

Rice, Otis K. The Allegheny Frontier West Virginia Beginnings, 1730-1830. Lexington: The University Press of Kentucky, 1970.

Rice, Otis K. and Wayne E. Williams. The Sheltering Arms Hospital. Charleston, WV:

West Virginia Educational Services, 1990.

Rice, Otis K. And Stephen W. Brown. West Virginia: A History. 2nd Edition. The University Press of Kentucky, 1993.

Riddle, Frank S. A Historical Atlas of West Virginia. Morgantown: West Virginia University Press, 2008.

The Riverside Church: In the City of New York. New York, NY: The Riverside Church, 2002.

"Robert C. Byrd Biography" Biography.co., March 18,2016. Accessed November 28, 2018.

"Robert E. Lee." The Civil War in America, Biographies: Library of Congress, accessed October 05, 2017.

"Robert Gould Shaw Memorial." Encyclopedia Virginia. Accessed June 28,2018.

Roberts, Edward F. Andersonville Journey. Shippensburg, PA: Burd Street Press, 1998.

Robertson, James I. Jr. Stonewall Jackson: The Man, The Soldier, The Legend. New York: Macmillan Publishing USA, 1997.

"Rockefeller, John Davison IV(Jay)." Biographical Directory of the United States Congress. Accessed October 12, 2017.

Rose, Arnold. The Negro in America. New York, NY: Harper & Row, Publishers, Inc. 1948.

Rosen, Jeffrey and David Rubenstein. "Why did Jefferson Draft the Declaration of Independence." National Constitution Center. April 13, 2015. Accessed February 7, 2019.

Rosenthal, Caitlin. "Slavery's Scientific Management: Masters and Managers." Chapter 2 of Sven Beckert and Seth Rockman, Editors, Slavery's Capitalism: A New History of American Economic Development. Philadelphia, PA: University of Pennsylvania Press, 2016.

"Rough Justice!" The West Virginia Courier VI, no. 30. Charleston, WV. January 5, 1876.

Rousseau, Caryn and Emily Wagster Pettus. "Cousin Who Saw Emmett Till Get Kidnapped Dies at Age 74." Charleston Gazette Mail. Charleston, WV. September 6, 2017.

Rothenberg, Paula S. Race, Class, and Gender in the United States: An Integrated Study. New York: St. Martin's Press, 1995.

Rowe, Larry L. "XV Landmark 2004 Legislative Session: Legislative Findings of Fact and Action on Racial Disparities." West Virginia Law Review. Volume 107, no. 3. (Spring 2005): 661- 672.

Rowe, Larry L. "Malden and the Salt Industry." Speech at West Virginia Archives and History. State Cultural Center. Charleston, West Virginia. July 5, 2012.

Rowe, Larry L. History Tour of Old Malden: Virginia and West Virginia Booker T. Washington's Formative Years. Malden, West Virginia: Larry L. Rowe attorney at law, 2014.

Rowsey, Jeanette M. The Last Village of Barboursville. Barboursville, WV: JRC Publishing, 2013.

Royall, Anne. Sketches of History, Life and Marines in the United States. U.S.A: New Haven, 1826.

Ruffner Family Bible. In possession of Author.

Ruffner, Alexander (Descendant). In discussion with author, December 22, 2017.

Ruffner, David. "Last Will and Testament." 1843. Kanawha County Circuit Clerk's Office, Charleston, West Virginia.

"Ruffner Hall." Longwood University: Campus Map. Accessed October 13, 2017.

Ruffner, Henry. Address to the People of West Virginia. Lexington, KY: R.C. Noel, 1847.

Ruffner, Henry. "Union Speech." Speech delivered at Kanawha Salines, VA on the Fourth of July, 1856. Cincinnati: Applegate & Co., Printers and Publishers, 1856.

Ruffner, Henry. "Rev. Henry Ruffner, D. D., LL. D., and General Lewis Ruffner." The Greenbrier Independent. August 28, 1884.

Ruffner, Lewis. Article on Runaway Slave. Kanawha Republican. Sept. 10, 1844.

Ruffner, Lewis. Cash Book [Original Receipt Book]. In possession of Author.

Ruffner, Lewis. "Valuable Salt Property for Sale." The Kanawha Republican. October 23, 1844.

Ruffner, Viola to Gilson Willetts, May 29, 1899, in Willetts, "Slave Boy and Leader of His Race." New Voice, XVI (June 24, 1899), 3. Cited in Louis Harlan, "Booker T. Washington's West Virginia Boyhood," West Virginia History 2, Vol. 32 (January 1971).

Ruffner, William Henry. "The Co-education of the White and Colored Race." Scriber's Monthly. Volume. 8. May 1874-October 1874. New York.

Ruffner, William Henry. A Report on Washington Territory. New York, Seattle: Lake Shore and Eastern Railway, 1889.

Ruffner, William Henry. "The Ruffners I: Peter." West Virginia Historical Magazine 1, no. 2. (April 1901): 31-38.

Ruffner, William Henry. "The Ruffners II: Joseph." West Virginia Historical Magazine 1, no. 3. (July 1901): 33-41.

Ruffner, William Henry. "The Ruffners III: David- First Article." West Virginia Historical Magazine 1, no. 4. (October 1901): 46-54.

Ruffner, William Henry. "The Ruffners III: David-Second Article." West Virginia Historical Magazine 2, no. 1. (January 1902): 45-53.

"The Salt Works of Kanawha County." Richmond Enquirer. December 4, 1846.

Sambol-Tosco, Kimberly. "Historical Overview: Legal Rights and Government." PBS, Slavery and the Making of America, The Slave Experience: Legal Rights & Government. Accessed September 26, 2017. http://www.pbs.org/wnet/slavery/experience/legal/history.html.

Salina Lodge No. 27. History and By-Laws. Malden, West Virginia: A. F. & A. M., n.d.

Salsberg, Bob and Angeliki Kastanis. "Analysis finds blacks largely left out among high-paying jobs." Sunday Gazette Mail. April 1, 2018. Charleston, WV.

Saul, Eric, Editor. "United States Abolition and Anti-Slavery Timeline." American Abolitionists and Antislavery Activists: Conscience of the Nation. Americanabolitionists.com.

Schlesinger, Arthur M., Jr. The Age of Jackson. Boston: Little Brown and Company, 1945.

Scott, Emmett J. and Lyman Beecher Stowe. Booker T. Washington: Builder of a Civilization. New York: Doubleday, Page & Company, 1916.

Schwarz, Philip J. Twice Condemned: Slaves and the Criminal Laws of Virginia, 1705-1865. Baton Rouge, LA: Louisiana State University Press, 1988.

Schwarz, Philip J. Migrants Against Slavery: Virginians and the Nation. Charlottesville, VA: University Press of Virginia, 2001.

Schweitzer, Mary M. "The Ratification Paradox in the Great Valley of the Appalachians" in Eliga H. Gould's Empire and Nation, Part II, Society, Politics, and Culture in the New Nation. Baltimore, MD: Johns Hopkins University Press, 2005.

Seaton, Carter Taylor. Hippie Homesteaders. Morgantown, WV: West Virginia University Press, 2014.

Sedensky, Matt and Sharon Cohen. "Outrage and Despair: Nation tries to process long week of tragedy." Saturday Gazette-Mail. July 19, 2016. Charleston, West Virginia.

Sellers, Charles. The Market Revolution:

Jackson America 1815-1846. New York: Oxford University Press, 1991.

Senator Joe Manchin. Speech for Commemoration of the Birthday of Reverend Dr. Martin Luther King, Jr. State Capitol, Charleston, West Virginia. January 15, 2018.

Settle, Angie. CEO/Executive Director for West Virginia Health Right. Interview with Author. June 14, 2019.

Settle, Mary Lee. Addie. Columbia, South Carolina: University of South Carolina Press, 1998.

Settle, Mary Lee. "Golden Gospel Gems." Beauty Mountain Studios. January 3, 2013. Accessed October 11, 2017.

Shaara, Jeff. Civil War Battlefields: Discovering America's Hallowed Ground. New York, NY: Ballantine Books, 2006.

Shanks, Henry T. The Secession Movement in Virginia, 1847-1861. Richmond, VA: Garrett & Massie, Inc., 1934.

"Shays's Rebellion." Encyclopedia Britannica. Accessed February 13, 2019.

Sheehan-Dean, Aaron. Struggle for a Vast Future. United Kingdom: Osprey Publishing, 2006.

Sheeler, John Reuben. The Negro in West Virginia Before 1900 [Microfilm; Kanawha County Library]. Dissertation, West Virginia University, 1954.

Shetterly, Margot Lee. "Katherine Johnson Biography." National Aeronautics and Space Administration (NASA). August 03, 2017. Accessed October 20, 2017.

Shifflett, Crandall A. Coal Towns: Life, Work, and Culture in Company Towns of Southern Appalachia, 1880-1960. Knoxville TN: The University of Tennessee Press, 1991.

Shrewsbury, Joel. "Last Will and Testament." Will book 2[1859-76], page 1-6. Kanawha County Circuit Clerk's Office, Charleston, West Virginia.

Siebert, William Henry. The Mysteries of Ohio's Underground Railroads. Columbus, OH: Long's College Book Company, 1951.

Signer, Michael. Becoming Madison. New York: Public Affairs, 2015.

Simpson, A. W. B. "The Horwitz Thesis and the History of Contracts." The University of Chicago Law Review 46, no. 3 (Spring 1979): 533-601.

Simpson, William and Martin Jones. Europe 1783-1914. 2nd Edition. New York, NY: Routledge, 2009.

Sims, Edgar B. Making a State. Charleston, WV: Matthews Printing and Lithographing Company, 1956.

Simmons, Martha and Frank A. Thomas. Preaching With Sacred Fire: An Anthology of African American Sermons, 1750 - Present. New York: W. W. Norton & Co, Inc., 2010.

Simpson, Mark. The Rockefeller Collection of American Art at The Fine Arts Museums of San Francisco. San Francisco: Harry N. Abrams, Inc., 1994.

Simpson-Poffenbarger, Livia Nye. The Battle of Point Pleasant: A Battle of the Revolution, October 10th, 1774. Point Pleasant, WV: State Gazette Publisher, 1909.

"Sketch of Ruffner Home and Wiley Children as Adults." by Nancy McCartney of Malden. Copy received on April 5, 2019. In possession of author.

"Slavery: Virginia Historical Society." Virginia Museum of History & Culture. Accessed March 26, 2018.

Smith, Beverly. "The Last Illness and Death of General Thomas (Stonewall) Jackson." Virginia Military Institute Archives. Accessed October 02, 2017.

Smith, Chris. From the Shenandoah to the Kanawha: The Story of Colonel John Smith, His Descendants and Their Ancestors. Charleston, WV: Chris Smith

Publishing, n.d.

Smith, Paul H., et al, Editors. "Nathan Dane to Rufus King." Letters of Delegates to Congress 1774-1789. Volume 24. November 6, 1786 – February 29, 1788. Washington, D. C.: Library of Congress, 1976-2000.

Sohi, Seema. "Immigration Act of 1917 and the 'Barred Zone' in Xiaojian Zhao and Edward J. W. Park. Asian Americans: An Encyclopedia of Social, Cultural, Economic, and Political History. Volume 1, A-F. ABC-CLIO, 2013.

Soupart, Sylvia. Stories of West Virginia For Boys and Girls. Volumes. 1-2. Charleston WV: West Virginia University, Jarrett Printing Co., 1934.

Spalding, Matthew. "Slave Trade." The Heritage Guide to the Constitution. Accessed October 2, 2017.

Stampp, Kenneth M. The Peculiar Institution: Slavery in the Ante-Bellum South. New York, NY: Vintage Books, 1989.

Statement by Judge Marmaduke H. Dent of Taylor County, Williams v. Board of Education of Fairfax District, Supreme Court of Appeals of West Virginia. "Williams v. Fairfax District Decided." West Virginia Archives & History. Accessed October 18, 2017.

State Superintendent of Schools. History of Education in West Virginia. Charleston, WV: Tribune Printing Company, 1904.

State Superintendent of Schools. History of Education in West Virginia. Charleston, WV: Tribune Printing Company, 1907.

Stealey, John Edmund, III. "Slavery and the Western Virginia Salt Industry." The Journal of Negro History 59, no. 2. (1974): 105-131.

Stealey, John E., III. The Antebellum Kanawha Salt Business and Western Markets. Kentucky: University Press of Kentucky, 1993.

Stealey, John E., III. Kanawha Prelude to Nineteenth-Century Monopoly in the United States: The Virginia Salt Combinations. Richmond, VA: Virginia Historical Society, 2000.

Stealey, John E., III. "Marker Dedication, Bee Line March, July 4, 2012." Good News Paper. (Fall 2012): 18-19.

Stealey, John E., III. West Virginia's Civil War-Era Constitution. Kent, Ohio: The Kent State University Press, 2013.

Stealey, John E., III. "Great Kanawha Salt Industry: An Overview." Goldenseal 40, no. 4. (Winter 2014): 24-25.

Stealey, John E., III. The Antebellum Kanawha Salt Business and Western Markets. Morgantown: West Virginity Press, 2016.

Stealey, John E., III. "Salt Industry." e-WV: The West Virginia Encyclopedia. October 26, 2010. Accessed October 24, 2018.

Stechel, Richard H. "Slave Mortality: Analysis of Evidence from Plantation Records." Social Science History, Vol.3, No. 3, 4 (1979): 86-114.

Steers, Edward. Blood on the Moon: The Assassination of Abraham Lincoln. University Press of Kentucky, 2001.

Steelhammer, Rick. "Kanawha Lacked 'Euphony' to Become 35th States's Name." Charleston Sunday Gazette-Mail (Charleston, WV). November 25, 2018.

Sterling, Dorothy. The Making of an Afro-American: Martin Robison Delany 1812-1885. Garden City, New York: Doubleday & Company, Inc., 1925.

Stewart, Jeffrey C. 1001 Things Everyone Should Know About African American History. U.S.A: Doubleday, 1996.

Stowe, Harriet Beecher. Uncle Tom's Cabin. New York: New American Library 2008.

Strum, Philip W. "Slavery in the Ohio and Kanawha Valleys: Using Local Primary Sources to Uncover the Past." Presentation at West Virginian Archives and History

Library, Culture Center. Charleston, WV, October 11, 2011.

Stump, Jake. "'Country Roads' Covers Uncovered." WVU Magazine. Accessed February 11, 2019.

Suggs, Lewis. "Book Review: The Black Family in Slavery and Freedom, 1750-1925." New Directions, Volume 4, Article 10, October 1, 1977.

Sullivan, Ken. The West Virginia Encyclopedia. Charleston, WV: West Virginia Humanities Council, 2006.

Sullivan, Ken. "Joseph Lawton Beury." e-WV: West Virginia Encyclopedia. September 25, 2012. Accessed October 31, 2017.

Sullivan, Leon H. Moving Mountains, The Principles and Purposes of Leon Sullivan. Valley Forge, PA: Judson Press, 1998.

Summers, George W. Letter to the Rev. R. R. Gurley, July 30, 1829. Con. 17. American Colonization Society Papers, Library of Congress.

Sutphin, Gerald W and Richard A. Andre. Sternwheelers on the Great Kanawha River. Missoula, MT: Pictorial Histories Publishing Co., 1991.

Sutphin, Gerald W. "Locks and Dams." e-WV: The West Virginia Encyclopedia. [Last revised] October 07, 2010. Accessed July 21, 2017.

Swank, James M. History of The Manufacture of Iron in All Ages, and Particularly in the United States from Colonial Times to 1891. Philadelphia: The American Iron and Steel Association, 1892.

Swick, Gerald D. Historic Photos of West Virginia. Nashville TN: Turner Publishing Company, 2010.

Swinford, Frances Keller and Rebecca Smith Lee. The Great Elm Tree: Heritage of The Episcopal Diocese of Lexington. Lexington, KY: Faith House Press, 1969.

Szatmary, David P. Shays' Rebellion: The Making of an Agrarian Insurrection. Am-

herst, MA: The University of Massachusetts Press, 1980.

Tackach, James. The Abolitionist Movement. Detroit, MI: Greenhaven Press, 2005.

Tams, W. P., Jr. The Smokeless Coal Fields of West Virginia. Morgantown, WV, 2001.

Tatum, Beverly Daniel. Why Are All the Black Kids Sitting Together in the Cafeteria. U.S.A., Basic Books, 1997.

Taylor, Christopher B. "John F. Kennedy Memorial," [Photo] Memorial at WV Capitol Building, Taken October 13, 2018. In possession of Author.

Tennyson, Alfred Lord. "Crossing the Bar." Poem Published 1889.

"T. G. Nutter." In Profiles: West Virginians Who Made a Difference. Edited by Robert J. Byers. Charleston, WV: The Charleston Gazette, 1999.

"Theresa Cozad (Gatewood), 1837-1923." History of Nebraska: Nebraska State Historical Society. Accessed December 31, 2018.

Thibeault, James. "Vista." e-WV: West Virginia Encyclopedia. November 5, 2010. Accessed November 2, 2017.

Thibeault, James. Discussion with author, October 12, 2017.

Thom, James Alexander. Follow the River. Random House Publishing Group, 1981.

Thomas, Cliff. "BB&T Salt Fest returning to Malden this month." Kanawha Metro, Charleston Gazette-Mail. Charleston, WV. October 10, 2018.

Thompson, Dean K. "Presbyterians." e-WV: The West Virginia Encyclopedia. October 22, 2010. accessed August 5, 2019.

Thwaits, Reuben Gold and Louise Phelps Kellogg Ed. Documentary History of Lord Dunmore's War 1774. Madison; Wisconsin Historical Society, 1905.

Tiernan, William. "Putting Booker T. Back

Together Again." The Charleston Gazette. Charleston, WV. August 16, 1979.

Tocqueville, Alexis De. Democracy in America. Edited by Richard Heffner. New York: Mentor Books, 1956.

"The Toll of Tobacco in West Virginia." Campaign for Tobacco Free Kids. Accessed August 6,2018.

Trotter, Joe William, Jr. River Jordan: African American Urban Life in the Ohio Valley. Lexington, KY: The University Press of Kentucky, 1998.

Trueblood, Elton. Abraham Lincoln: Theologian of American Anguish. New York: Harper & Row Publishers, 1973.

Tucker, Gary Jackson. Governor William E. Glasscock and Progressive Politics in West Virginia. Morgantown, West Virginia: West Virginia University Press, 2008.

"The Tuskegee Normal and Industrial Institute." The Tuskegee Student 27, no. 18. September 4, 1915. Tuskegee, Alabama.

United States, Charles Thomson, United States Continental Congress, and Continental Congress Broadside Collection, An ordinance for the government of the territory of the United States, North-west of the river Ohio, [New York, 1787], Library of Congress, accessed October 02, 2017,

"U.S. and World Population Clock." United States Census Bureau. Accessed July 18, 2017.

U.S. Census Bureau. Profile America Facts for Features: National African-American (Black)History Month: February 2019. February 26, 2019.

U.S. Cong. Senate. West Virginia Constitutional Convention. Certified Copy of the Constitution of the State of West Virginia: Proposed by the Convention Assembled at Wheeling on the 26th of November, 1861. 37th Cong., 2d sess. Res. 98. 1862. 1-3. Accessed July 18, 2017.

U. S. Supreme Court: Civil Rights Cases, 109. U. S. 3 (1883).

U. S. Supreme Court: Brown v. Board of Education of Topeka, 349 U.S. 294 (1955): P. 349 U. S. 301. Justia. Accessed November 27, 2018.

U. S. Supreme Court: Strauder v. West Virginia, 100 U.S. 303 (__).

Valentine, Fawn. West Virginia Quilts and Quiltmakers: Echoes from the Hills. Athens OH: Ohio University Press, 2000.

Velke, John A., III. The True Story of the Baldwin-Felts Detective Agency. 2004.

Villard, Oswald Garrison. John Brown 1800-1859. New York: Alfred A. Knopf, 1943.

Virginia Assembly. Acts passed a General Assembly of the Commonwealth of Virginia. Begun and Held at the Capitol, in the City of Richmond. Richmond, VA: Thomas Ritchie, 1833.

"Virginia's Chapel." National Register of Historic Places: United States Department of the Interior, National Park Service. October 25, 1973. Cedar Grove, County, West Virginia.

"Virginia News." Alexandria Gazette. January 26, 1876.

Virginia Ordinance Secession (April 17, 1861). [Primary Source]. Encyclopedia Virginia. June 20, 2014. Accessed June 17, 2019.

"Virginia Tourism Revenues Reached $25 Billion in 2017." Virginia Tourism Corporation: Pressroom. 2017.

Vollaro, Daniel R. "Lincoln, Stow, and the 'Little Woman/Great War' Story: The Making, and Breaking, of a Great American Anecdote." Journal of the Abraham Lincoln Association 30, no. 1 (2009): 18-34.

"The Voyage Made by M. John Hawkins Esquire, 1565." American Journeys Collection: Wisconsin Historical Society Digital Library and Archives. Document No. AJ-030. Accessed November 14, 2018.

Walker, Robert. Rousseau: A Very Short Introduction. Oxford University Press, 1995.

Wallace, Jim. "Moving Capital." In A

History of the West Virginia Capitol: The House of State. South Carolina: Arcadia Publishing, 2012.

Wallace, Robert M. Hawk on a Power Line. Hammond, Louisiana: Louisiana Literature Press, 2015.

Ward, Geoffrey C. The Civil War: An Illustrated History. New York: Alfred A. Knopf, 2009.

Washington and Lee University. A Brief History. Accessed August 9, 2018.

Washington, Booker T. "Address at Opening of Atlanta Exposition." Located in The Negro and the Atlanta Exposition by Alice Mabel Bacon. Baltimore: The Trustees, 1896.

Washington, Booker. Up From Slavery: An Autobiography. New York: Doubleday & Company, 1901.

Washington, Booker T. An Autobiography: The Story of My Life and Work. Toronto, ON; Naperville, ILL; Atlanta, GA: J.L. Nichols & Company, 1901.

Washington, Booker T. "Up From Slavery: An Autobiography." The Outlook, February 1901.

Washington, Booker T. Working with the Hands. New York, Doubleday, Page & Company, 1904.

Washington, Booker T., N.B. Wood and Fannie Barrier Williams. A New Negro for a New Century. New York: Arno Press and the New York Times, 1969.

Washington, Booker T. The Booker T, Washington Papers. Volume 1. The Autobiographical Writings. Edited by Louis R. Harlan and John W. Blassingame. Chicago, Illinois: University of Illinois Press, 1972.

Washington, Booker T. The Booker T, Washington Papers. Volume 2 1860-89, Edited by Louis R. Harlan, Pete Daniel, Stuart B Kaufman, Raymond W. Smock, and William M. Welty. Chicago, Illinois: University of Illinois Press, 1972.

Washington, Booker T. The Booker T, Washington Papers. Volume 4, 1895-98. Edited by Louis R. Harlan. Chicago, Illinois: University of Illinois Press, 1975.

Washington, Booker T. The Booker T, Washington Papers. Volume 13. 1914-15. Edited by Louis R. Harlan and Raymond W. Smock. Chicago, Illinois: University of Illinois Press, 1984.

Washington, Dianne. "Johnson, Mordecai Wyatt (1890-1976)." Black Past.org: Remembered & Reclaimed. Accessed August 15, 2017.

Washington, George. The Diaries of George Washington, 1748-1799. Volume 1. Boston: Houghton Mifflin Company, 1925.

Washington, George. The Diaries of George Washington, 1748-1799. Volume II. Boston: Houghton Mifflin Company, 1925.

Watts, Matthew J. "Rev. Matthew J. Watts: 13th Amendment's Legacy Lingers." Charleston Gazette (Charleston, WV) April 16, 2014.

Wayland, John W. A History of Virginia for Boys and Girls. New York, NY: The MacMillan Company, 1922.

"Weather Event: 1861 flood in the Kanawha Valley," e-WV: The West Virginia Encyclopedia, accessed November 28, 2018.

Weiner, Deborah R. Coalfield Jews: An Appalachian History. Illinois: University of Illinois Press, 2006.

Webster's Unabridged Dictionary of the English Language. New York City, NY: Random House ,1989.

Weinstein, Allen and David Rubel. The Story of America. New York: DK Publishing, 2002.

Weisberger, Bernard A. The LIFE History of the United States. Volume 7, 1877- 1890: Steel and Steam. New York: Time Life Books, 1976.

Wells, H.G. The Outline of History. Garden City Publishing Company, 1920.

Wells, Sandy. "Malden Sisters Amass Wealth of Facts About Town." The Charleston Gazette. Charleston, WV. March 07, 1991.

West Virginia Constitutional Convention. Debates, West Virginia Constitutional Convention 1861-1863. Edited by Charles Ambler. Gentry Bros, 1939.

"West Virginia Governors." West Virginia Division of Culture and History. Charleston, WV, 2019.

"West Virginia State Capitol: Walking Tour and Visitor Information," West Virginia Division of Culture and History. Charleston, WV, n.d.

"West Virginia's Pioneer Industry: Salt Making in the Kanawha Valley." West Virginia and Regional History Collection 47, no. 1. (Spring 1991): 1-4.

West Virginia University. History. College of Law. Accessed August 9, 2018.

Whisonant, Robert C. "Geology and History of the Civil War Iron Industry in the New River-Cripple Creek District of Southwestern Virginia." Virginia Minerals 44, no. 4 (1998).

White, Eugene. West Virginia Office of Miners', Health, Safety and Training: 2015 Statistical Report and Directory of Mines. Accessed November 1, 2017.

White, Karen Hughes and Joan Peters, Compilers. "Chapter VIII: The Development of Free Compulsory Education for Negroes and Whites, Chapter XXXIX." from June Purcell Guild, LL. M's Black Laws of Virginia: A Summary of Legislative Acts of Virginia Concerning Negroes from Earliest Times to the Present. Compiled by Afro-American Historical Association of Fauquier County, 1996.

White, I. C. West Virginia Geological Survey, Volume 1A, Petroleum and Natural Gas Precise Levels. Morgantown, WV: The New Dominion Publishing Company, 1904.

Whitman, Walt. "O Captain! My Captain!" Poem originally published 1865.

Whitney, Mary. Women and the University. Charlottesville: University of Virginia, 1969.

Whitten, Norman E., Jr. and John F. Szwed. Afro-American Anthropology: Contemporary Perspectives. New York, NY: The Free Press, 1970.

Whittier, John Greenleaf. "Brown of Ossawatomie." Poem (1859). The Lost Museum Archive. Accessed February 26, 2019.

Whittier, John Greenleaf. "The Farewell of a Virginia Slave Mother to her daughters, sold into Southern Bondage." Political Works. Vol. III, Anti-Slavery Poems: Songs of Labor and Reform, 1886.

Wilkinson, Todd J. "Hillbillies and Rednecks." Scottish Tartans Authority. Accessed September 26, 2017.

Williams, John Alexander. West Virginia and the Captains of Industry. Parsons WV: McClain Printing Company, 1976, reprinted 1997.

Williams, John Alexander. West Virginia A History. New York: W.W. Norton & Company, 1984.

Williams, John A. Appalachia: A History. University of North Carolina Press, 2002.

Williams, Lena. It's the Little Things, Everybody Interactions That Get Under the Skin of Blacks and Whites. Orlando, FL: Harcourt, Inc., 2000.

Williams v. Board of Education of Fairfax District. 45 W.Va. 199, 31 SE 985. 1898.

"The Wirz Monument." The National Park Service: Andersonville. April 14, 2015. Accessed October 11, 2017.

Wilson, Elizabeth Jill. "West Virginia University." e-WV: West Virginia Encyclopedia. November 27, 2018. Accessed August 10, 2018.

Wilson, Vincent, Jr. The Book of Great American Documents. Brookeville, MD: American History Research Associates, 2017.

Wilson, Vincent, Jr. The Book of the Founding Fathers. Brookeville, MD: American History Research Associates, 2018.

Wilson, Woodrow. A History of the American People. Volume IV. Critical Changes and Civil War. New York, NY: Harper & Brothers Publishers, 1902.

Withers, Alexander Scott. Chronicles of Border Warfare. Edited by Reuben Gold Thwaites. Cincinnati: Stewart & Kidd Company, 1912.

Withrow, Cheryl Wintz. The Course of History in the Kanawha Valley. Charleston WV: Charleston Blueprint, 2003.

Woodson, Carter, G. The Education of the Negro Prior to 1861. NY: Arno Press and the New York Times, 1968.

Woodson, Carter G. Woodson. "Freedom and Slavery in Appalachian America." in Blacks in Appalachia. Edited by William H. Turner and Edward J. Cabbell. Lexington: University Press of Kentucky, 1985.

Woodson, Carter G. "Early Negro Education In West Virginia." West Virginia Division of Culture and History. Accessed November 7, 2017.

Woodward, C. Vann. Reunion and Reaction: The Compromise of 1877 and the End of Reconstruction. Boston, MA: Little, Brown and Company, 1951.

Woodward, C. Vann. The Strange Career of Jim Crow. New York, NY: Oxford University Press, 1974.

Wolf, William J. "Abraham Lincoln's Faith." The Lehrman Institute Presents: Abraham Lincoln's Classroom. Accessed November 7, 2017.

Wordsworth, William. My Heart Leaps Up. 1807.

Wright, Andrew McCanse. "The Take Care Clause, Justice Department Independence, and White House Control." In West Virginia Law Review. Volume 121, Issue 2. (Winter 2018): 353-417

X, Malcolm. With assistance of Alex Haley. The Autobiography of Malcolm X. New York: Ballantine Books, 33rd Printing November, 1992.

Yetman, Norman R. Voices from Slavery, 100 Authentic Slave Narratives. Mineola, NY: Dover Publications, Inc., 1970.

Zakaria, Fareed. "The Great American Power Shift." The Charleston Gazette. Charleston, WV. January 3, 2016.

Zechmeister, Gene. "Establishment of the University of Virginia." Thomas Jefferson's Monticello. June 28, 2011. Accessed November 9, 2017.

Zinn, Howard. Writings on Disobedience and Democracy. New York: Seven Stories Press, 1997.

Index

#

12th Massachusetts Regiment 284
54ᵗʰ Massachusetts Regiment Volunteer Infantry 320

A

Abraham Lincoln Walks at Midnight 287, 338
Adams, James Truslow 236
African Zion Baptist Church 14, 17, 146, 150, 152, 153, 154, 277, 339, 350, 353, 357, 358, 371
Alderson, George 107, 175
Alma Lee 11, 12, 13, 16
Almost Heaven 227
Ambler, Charles H. 58, 60, 66, 147, 150
American Colonization Society 176
American Dream 1, 26, 29, 41, 43, 125, 146, 347, 349, 350, 354, 357, 359, 363, 369, 371
Anderson, Marian 361
Armstrong, Grant & Company 276
Articles of Agreement 135, 436, 468
Articles of Confederation 85, 88, 93, 252, 342
Atlanta Compromise 30
Auditor slave tax report 274

B

Baker, Abraham 107
Baldwin, James 355, 364
Ball, Edward 218
Ballagh, James C. 221, 235
Ballagh, James Curtis 206
Bland Ballard 181
Bancroft, Frederic 199
Baptist, Edward E. 205
Baptist, Edward E. Professor 205, 240, 241, 243, 244, 245, 246, 247, 248
Barbarians 235
Bath County 74, 158, 165
Battle of Point Pleasant 68, 77, 79, 80, 81, 83, 84, 85, 115, 161
Beckert, Sven 230, 231, 240
Bedford County 135, 155, 156, 158, 161
Beeline March to Cambridge 65
Belcher, Allen 17, 142
Berlin, Ira 92, 192, 194, 198, 217, 222, 248, 281
Beury, Joseph Lawto 73
Bill of Rights 86, 87, 98, 99
Black Hawk Hollow 146, 153
Blackstone River 108, 111
Blassingame, John W. 202
Boone, Daniel 105, 115, 123, 127, 132
Boone, Jesse 127
Booth, John Wilkes 291, 292
Bream, James 134
Brinton, Willard Cope 270
Brown, John 56, 128, 271, 277, 281, 282, 283, 284, 285, 286, 291, 293, 294, 295, 296, 297, 299, 301, 311
Brown v. Board of Education 14, 153, 355, 362
Brumbach, Henry 173
Bruns, Nancy Payne 278
Burning Spring 74, 128, 156, 277
Burr, Aaron 306
Burstein, Andrew 207
Byrd, Robert C. 289

C

Cabell, John J. 135
Cabell, Samuel L. 131
Calhoun, John C. 48, 272
Campbell, Alexander 148
Campbell, Archibald W. 148
Campbell, Archibald W. 148
Camp Union 72, 73
Carnegie, Andrew 138
Carry Me Back to Old Virginia 42, 224, 225
Cavalier 50
Cheney, Dick 26
Chief Logan 79
China 24, 121
Christian believers 14, 146, 153, 262, 350, 358
Civilization 24, 37, 69, 84, 85, 235
Civil Rights Acts 289

Clay, Henry 26, 131, 132, 157, 176, 276
Clayton, Richard 143
Clendenin, Alexander 105
Clendenin, Charles 105
Clendenin, George 105, 106, 118
Clendenin, Robert 105
Clendenin, William 105, 107
coffles 192, 198, 217, 218, 219, 220, 261
Cole, John L. 18, 115, 131
Cole, Llewellyn Shrewsbury 18, 115, 162
Cole, Martha Darneal 17, 115, 162, 439
Coleman, C. N. 131
College of William & Mary 147, 150, 198
Collins, Winfield H. 200
Colton, Calvin 27, 102, 271
Conley, Phil 79, 149
Cooke, Alistair 123, 434
Cooper, Minnie Wayne 11, 13, 14, 15, 16, 18,
    153
C & O Railway 73
Cornstalk, Chief 75, 76, 77, 79
Cotton gin 122, 229, 230, 231
Cotton States & International Exposition 30
County of Kanawha 106
Covenant 21, 53, 175, 350, 371
Covenant 365, 366
Cozad, John Jackson 216
Craik, James 66, 67, 68, 131, 160, 163
Craik family 163
Craik-Patton House 131, 164
Crane, Samuel 262, 345
Crawford, William 66, 68, 69, 72, 163
Cummings, David 163
Custis, Mary Anna Randolph 108

D

Darneal, Jacob 18, 131, 162, 172, 179
Darneal, Martha 17, 115, 161, 162, 179
Daughters of the American Revolution 361
Davis, Jefferson 308
Davis, William 353
Declaration of Independence 33, 34, 37, 79,
    89, 95, 96, 107, 264
Denver, John 227
Dew, Thomas 198, 199, 200, 207, 239, 269,

270, 271, 302, 344
Dickinson, Henry Clay 127, 131, 156, 157,
    276
Dickinson, John 74, 115, 120, 131, 155, 156,
    158, 161, 163, 258
Dickinson, John Quincy 131, 157, 158, 278
Dickinson, Joseph 155
Dickinson, Pleasant 155, 156, 159
Dickinson, Sally 155, 175
Dickinson, William Jr. 156, 157
Dickinson, William, Sr. 135, 155, 156, 157,
    159
J. Q. Dickinson 276, 278, 279
Dickinson family 76, 155, 157, 158, 169
Dickinson & Shrewsbury salt partnership
    176
Dominion 50
Donnally, Andrew Jr. 120
Donnally, Andrew Sr. 107, 120, 130, 134, 135
Douglass, Frederick 206, 264, 317, 360
Drake, Edwin 128
Draper, Dorothy 166
Dred Scott 296
Dunaway, Wilma A. 188, 198, 204, 208, 241,
    247, 250, 251

E

Eating Like Pigs 208
Elk River 67, 75, 105, 117, 160
Emerson, Ralph Waldo 77, 428
Engerman, Stanley L. 196, 207
Evans, Robert 237, 238
Exports 198, 199, 231, 240, 272, 305, 319, 343
Exposition Universelle 278

F

Factories 42, 57, 109, 110, 111, 112, 113, 114,
    120, 121, 124, 125, 126, 129, 131, 135,
    136, 137, 141, 142, 143, 156, 169, 196,
    229, 250, 256, 257, 260, 261, 263, 273,
    278, 281, 305, 345
Fairfax County Resolves 81
Fallen Timbers 77, 85, 108, 117, 118, 166
Fallen Timbers Battle 77, 85, 108, 118, 166

Father of West Virginia 149
Federal Constitution 37, 52, 80, 86, 88, 89, 90,
    91, 94, 95, 96, 97, 98, 99, 100, 101, 103,
    106, 107, 158, 229, 230, 271, 282, 292,
    296, 308, 309, 311, 323, 328, 329, 337,
    338, 341, 342
Ferguson, Jane 38, 47, 196, 294, 346, 347, 350,
    353, 359
Ferguson, Washington 38, 168, 196, 253, 260,
    261, 262, 359
First Baptist Church 28, 43, 152, 353, 362
First Presbyterian Church 171
First Wheeling Convention 328
Fleming, Col. William 73
Fogel, Robert William 196, 201, 207, 239
Fort Gower 68, 72, 80, 81
Fort Henry 68
Fort Lee 107, 117, 118, 128, 131, 175
Fort Randolph 76
Fort Sumter 173, 301, 344
Fort Wagner 320, 321
Foster, Stephen 224
Frankenberger, Moses 334
Franklin, Benjamin 64, 70, 96
Franklin & Armfield 197
French and Indian War 63, 65, 67, 79, 80
Fuqua, Moses M. 131

G

Gaines, Herbert P. 150
Gallaher, D. C. 159
Garrison, Memphis Tennessee 324, 326
Gates, Henry Louis Jr. 25, 46
Gatewood, Theresa 216
Gauley River 66, 73, 74, 105, 115
Genovese, Eugene D. 183, 184, 202, 208, 211,
    220, 352
Gilbert, Cass 291
Gilmer, Anna Evans 153, 349
Gilmer, Paul Sr., 153
Gilmer, Rev. Paul 153
Girty, Simon 69
Govan, Thomas 237
Grant, Alexander 135
Grant, Ulysses S. 57, 276, 322

Gray, Harriet Ann 179
Great Exhibition of the Works
    of Industry of All Nations 278
Greeley, Horace 312
Greenbrier County 106, 130
Greenbrier Hotel Resort 165
Gutman, Herbert G. 186, 187, 197, 239, 260

H

Hale, John P. 79, 105, 122, 123, 128, 136, 175,
    278, 330, 361
Hall, Granville 49, 261, 423, 453
Hamilton, Alexander 70, 86, 88, 89, 95, 99,
    100, 113, 306, 324
Hamilton, Philip 306
Hampton Institute 9, 38, 168, 359, 360
Harlan, Louis R. 14
Harpers Ferry 56, 97, 110, 227, 280, 281, 282,
    284, 285, 294, 300
Hatfield, Anderson "Devil Anse" 333
Hawkins, John 35
Henri, Robert 216
Henry, Patrick 70, 76, 99, 107, 160
Hewett, James 131
Hewitt, Ruffner & Company 139, 142, 176
Hillbilly 57
Holly Grove 131, 132, 167
holy nation 21, 43, 350, 358, 359, 371
House Bill No. 25 341
Howe, Julia Ward 285
Hubbard, John F. 131, 474
Huddlestone, Paddy 115

I

Industrial Revolution 39, 111, 112, 113, 114,
    123, 133, 167, 169, 229, 350, 351
Ingles, Mary Draper 105, 107, 115
inheritance 58, 59, 60, 109, 119, 175, 177, 276
Iroquois Six Nations 64

J

Jackson, Thomas "Stonewall" 152, 304
James, F. C. 152
Rev. James F. C. 152

Jamestown 25, 31, 33, 35, 52, 229, 422, 476
Jefferson, Thomas 33, 34, 35, 36, 60, 70, 74,
    79, 89, 95, 96, 98, 100, 123, 147, 165,
    199, 200, 207, 229, 265, 269, 305, 306,
    324
Jefferson County 110
Jesus of Lubek 35
Johns, Vernon 28, 362
Johnson, Amanda Ferguson 14, 18, 349
Johnson, James Weldon 220
Johnson, Mordecai Wyatt 362
Johnston, Charles 50
Jones, John 128
J. Q. Dickinson Salt Works 276
Juneteenth 341

K

Kanawha 65
Kanawha County 2, 14, 19, 68, 106, 107, 113,
    117, 124, 132, 142, 150, 152, 155, 156,
    160, 174, 250, 253, 254, 259, 262, 266,
    274, 328, 330, 341, 345, 346
Kanawha Presbyterian Church 144, 171
Kanawha Red Salt 278
Kanawha Riflemen 151, 164, 180, 287, 310
Kanawha River 46, 65, 66, 67, 68, 73, 74, 75,
    105, 106, 109, 110, 115, 117, 126, 127,
    128, 130, 143, 160, 166, 217, 257, 275,
    335, 352
Kanawha Salines 54, 107, 113, 114, 124, 125,
    127, 129, 130, 131, 142, 143, 144, 145,
    146, 150, 153, 160, 169, 171, 172, 173,
    250, 253, 254, 257, 260, 261, 274, 326,
    330
Kanawha Salines Presbyterian Church 131,
    145, 146, 153, 171, 172, 173
Kanawha Salt 115, 120, 126, 127, 133, 134,
    135, 138, 176, 181, 250, 266, 273
Kanawha Salt Company 120, 133, 134, 135,
    138, 176, 266, 436, 468
Kanawha Spectator 150, 210, 446, 453, 478
Kanawha Valley 19, 28, 37, 39, 42, 45, 47, 48,
    50, 60, 65, 67, 68, 71, 73, 74, 75, 84,
    107, 108, 109, 110, 115, 117, 118, 119,
    120, 121, 122, 124, 125, 126, 129, 130,
    134, 142, 143, 144, 155, 156, 157, 158,
    159, 161, 163, 165, 166, 168, 169, 171,
    175, 177, 180, 181, 196, 198, 210, 216,
    217, 219, 242, 249, 250, 251, 252, 253,
    254, 255, 256, 257, 259, 260, 261, 262,
    263, 275, 276, 278, 330, 332, 333, 335,
    340, 345, 346, 351, 353
Kanawha Valley Bank 157, 158
Kennedy, John F. 108, 289
Kentucky Derby 225
Kiashuta, Chief 67
King, Ellen 226, 448
King, Martin Luther Jr. 296, 356, 362
King Carter 211
King George 51, 63, 64, 165, 313, 360
Kirby, Laura J. 172
Ku Klux Klan 40, 236, 289, 347, 355

L

Laidley, Amasetta 267
Lambert, Oscar 58
Lee, Henry III 107
Lee, Robert E. 107, 108, 179, 284, 304, 322
Lewis, Ann Dickinson 157
Lewis, Colonel Charles Cameron 73, 75
Lewis, David Levering 255, 448
Lewis, General Andrew 71, 76, 77, 78, 83, 84,
    115, 128, 132, 218
Lewis, John Dickinson 131, 155, 156, 258
Lewis, Virgil 19, 83, 84
Lewis and Clark Expedition 123
Lewisburg Academy 173, 175
Lewis County 76, 152
Lift Every Voice and Sing 220, 221
Lightburn, Joseph A. J. 152
Lincoln, Abraham 69, 78, 104, 181, 220, 261,
    282, 287, 291, 292, 293, 298, 299, 301,
    309, 310, 312, 316, 321, 323, 324, 325,
    335, 336, 338, 347
Locke, John 36
Logan County 333
Longwood University 39, 179, 352
Lord Dunmore 68, 70, 71, 72, 75, 76, 77, 78,
    79, 313
Lord Fairfax 66, 165

Loring, W. W. 152, 332
Louisiana Purchase 80, 109, 255
Lovell, Joseph 131, 133, 134, 135, 136, 138, 176, 266, 269
Lowell, Francis Cabot 111
Lowell, Massachusetts 111, 169, 249
Lyle, Sarah "Sally" Montgomery 172

M

MacFarland, James 131
Mad Anne Bailey 117
Madison, James 36, 86, 87, 88, 91, 97, 98, 99, 100, 239, 286, 296, 324
Manifest Destiny 24, 37, 71
Manna Meal 365
Marion County 149, 329, 337, 340
Married Women's Property Act 276
Marshall, John 97, 148
Marshall, Thurgood 95
Mason, George 81
Mason County 67, 275
Mason-Dixon Line 148
Masonic lodge 131
Maxwell, Hu 55, 72
Mayflower Compact 51, 52, 90
McClellan, General George 322
McConaughy, William 128
McConihay, John H. 131
McLeod, Mary Adelia 366
McNeill, Louise 43, 45, 48, 219
Meade, William 55, 56, 68, 160, 254, 269
Mechanical revolution 48, 60, 61, 111, 112, 113, 114, 121, 136, 137, 167
Mercer, Charles Fenton 147, 149
Mercer Academy 138, 144, 149, 150, 151, 152, 180, 310
Metropolitan Museum of Art 283
Midland Trail Scenic Highway 73, 74, 480
Migration 54, 55, 57, 63, 70, 80, 103, 112, 166, 185, 186, 188, 189, 194, 195, 196, 197, 202, 203, 204, 205, 217, 218, 222, 223, 224, 229, 230, 232, 234, 240, 252, 273
Miller, Thomas C. 55
Mineral County 46, 310
Mingo Town 65, 67, 70, 79, 163

Minstrel 42, 364
Moes, John E. 238
Monroe, James 100, 126
Monroe County 11, 143, 165
Montesquieu 36
Morgan Morgan 329
Morris, Charles 135
Morris, John Sr. 107
Morris, Leonard 107, 135
Morris, William 107
Morrison, Agnes Westbrook 149
Mother Ruffner, Anna Brumbach Ruffner 169
Mount Vernon 89, 163, 167, 184
Mt. Airy 185
Mt. Ovis Academy 172, 173, 179
My Old Kentucky Home 42, 192, 224, 225

N

NAACP 14, 220, 221, 284, 355, 360
National Association for the Advancement of Colored People, *See NAACP*
National Council of Jewish Women 366
Newton, John 272
Northrup, Solomon 242
Northwest Ordinance 93, 94, 98, 342
Norton, James 131
Noyes, Bradford 135
Noyes, Isaac 135

O

Ohio River 50, 64, 65, 66, 67, 68, 70, 71, 72, 73, 74, 75, 76, 77, 79, 80, 93, 98, 105, 106, 109, 110, 117, 121, 123, 125, 129, 130, 166, 181, 217, 218, 225, 250, 252, 273, 274, 275, 342, 352
Old Greasy 128
Olmstead, Alan L. 246, 449
Olmsted, Frederick Law 184, 190, 191, 201, 223
O'Sullivan, John L. 37
Over The Mountain 45

P

Panic of 1819 136, 138
Parks, John 131
Patrick, Spicer H. 131
Patton, George S. 151, 164, 180
Payne, Lewis 278
Pease, Louise McNeill 43, 45, 219
Pennsylvania Canal 273
Peterkin, George W. 269
Peyton, Colonel J. L. 75
Philadelphia Convention 87, 89
Pierpont, Frances Harrison 329
Pierpont, Francis Harrison 149, 329
Pioneer Coal Company 259
Pocahontas County 63
Point Pleasant 64, 65, 67, 68, 72, 73, 74, 75,
    76, 77, 78, 79, 80, 81, 82, 83, 84, 85,
    115, 117, 132, 156, 161, 252, 275
Preliminary Emancipation Proclamation 313,
    315, 316, 317, 327, 340, 341
Presbyterian 39, 53, 54, 58, 131, 144, 145, 146,
    150, 151, 153, 170, 171, 172, 173, 179,
    180, 263, 268, 351
Preston County 63
Princeton College 55, 151, 171
Putnam County 67, 262
Putney, Richard E. 131, 141

Q

Quarrier, Alexander W. 68, 131, 269
Quarrier, Sally Burns 269
Quebec Act 80

R

Radcliff, Stephen 135
Railroad
  B & O Railroad 252, 329
    Underground 251, 335
Randolph, A. Philip 360, 361
Randolph, J. W. 34
Ratliff, Gerald 17, 43
Reformed Episcopal Church 163
Resolution to Call the Election of Abraham
    Lincoln as U. S. President a Hostile

Act 299
Reynolds, Charles 126
Reynolds, John 134, 135
Reynolds, J. W. 131
Rhode, Paul W. 246
Rice, Lewis 146, 353
Richmond Coal Basin 110
Rockefeller, John D. 14, 138, 481
Rogers, Henry 68
Roosevelt, Eleanor 361
Roosevelt, Franklin 361
Rousseau, Jean-Jacques 36, 52, 90, 91
Royall, Anne Newport 143
Royal priesthood 21, 350, 358, 362, 367, 371
Ruffin, Thomas 209
Ruffner, Abraham 119, 120, 167
Ruffner, Anna Brumbach 55, 169, 170, 173,
    177, 179, 328
Ruffner, Anna Heistand 117, 330
Ruffner, Charles 131
Ruffner, Daniel 131, 134, 135, 167
Ruffner, David Lewis 151, 180, 310
Ruffner, Elizabeth Dickinson Shrewsbury
    175
Ruffner, Ernest Howard 166, 180, 181, 352,
    353
Ruffner, Esther 117
Ruffner, Eve 117, 141, 169
Ruffner, Henry 39, 54, 122, 124, 126, 130,
    142, 144, 146, 148, 150, 151, 152, 169,
    170, 171, 172, 173, 174, 175, 178, 179,
    180, 181, 200, 263, 270, 271, 310, 330,
    351, 352
Ruffner, Joseph 75, 107, 108, 109, 110, 111,
    114, 115, 117, 118, 119, 120, 122, 123,
    124, 125, 131, 158, 161, 163, 166, 169,
    260, 263, 330
Ruffner, Joseph II 119, 120, 123, 124, 166
Ruffner, Lewis 37, 39, 40, 138, 139, 146, 151,
    152, 155, 162, 168, 172, 173, 174, 175,
    176, 177, 178, 180, 181, 216, 254, 256,
    259, 260, 262, 263, 266, 275, 278, 298,
    309, 310, 319, 327, 328, 332, 333, 337,
    339, 340, 342, 346, 351, 352
Ruffner, Mary Steinman 164

Ruffner, Peter 164, 165
Ruffner, Samuel 167
Ruffner, Stella Blanche 181
Ruffner, Tobias 121, 122, 124, 126, 135, 166
Ruffner, W. H. 39, 119, 146, 152, 165, 170,
    175, 178, 179, 180, 263, 352
Ruffner Cave 165
Ruffner family 28, 37, 38, 39, 41, 57, 116, 125,
    131, 142, 147, 151, 164, 165, 167, 168,
    170, 173, 180, 310, 327, 328, 348
Ruffner Hollow 117
Ruffner Meeting House 144
Ruffner Pamphlet 171, 179, 200
Ruffner Plan 152

S

Salina Lodge No. 27 131
Salt Aristocracy 155
Saltborough 131, 135, 141, 142, 144, 169
Salt Kings 125, 130, 131, 155, 175
Salt Lick 74, 106, 107, 115, 117, 118, 119, 121,
    141, 158, 161
Salt Rush 124
Salt works 107, 113, 128, 256, 342
Schwarz, Philip J. 212
Scrip 24, 259
Scripture 21
Second Inaugural Address 292, 293, 322
Second Middle Passage 196, 217, 218
Second Wheeling Convention 329
Settle, Mary Lee 157, 277
Shay, Daniel 89
Shay's Rebellion 89
Sherman Anti-Trust Act 139
Shrewsbury, Jacob Darneal 18, 131, 162, 179
Shrewsbury, Joel 18, 68, 74, 131, 134, 135,
    155, 156, 159, 160, 161, 162, 175, 176,
    276
Shrewsbury, John 74, 120, 135, 160
Shrewsbury, John D. 135
Shrewsbury, Juliet 160, 163
Shrewsbury, Martha Darneal 162, 179, 474
Shrewsbury, Martha Dickinson 74
Shrewsbury, Robert Peal 162
Shrewsbury, Samuel 120, 131, 135, 160, 161

Shrewsbury, William Dickinson 161, 162
Shrewsbury family 18, 158, 159, 178
Slater, Samuel 111
Slaughter, Reuben 107
Slave markets 196, 207, 225, 261
Sovereignty 36, 52, 81, 86, 88, 90, 91, 94, 95,
    98, 308, 343, 362
Stampp, Kenneth M. 47, 197, 213, 243, 255
State Superintendent of Public Instruction
    152
Stealey, John E. III 20, 133, 250, 425
Steam engines 122, 130, 175
Steele, William 134, 135
St. John's Episcopal Church 18, 68, 131, 160,
    163, 258, 265, 269, 341, 365
St. Mark's Episcopal Church 160
Stockton, Aron 135
St. Paul 55
Sullivan, Leon 28, 362, 494
Summers, George W. 151, 265, 266, 267
Summers, Lewis 265
Summers, William S. 131
Summers County 143, 266

T

The Meaning of July Fourth for the Negro
    264
The Society of Cincinnati 99
The War of 1812 95, 129
Thom, James Alexander 106
Tichenell, Moses 340
Tinkersville 40, 146, 254, 260, 347, 348
Tocqueville, Alexis de 51, 52, 59, 60, 119,
    155, 177
Tomahawk Rights 64
Tompkins, Rachel Grant 127, 262, 274, 276,
    277, 341
Tompkins, Virginia 277
Tompkins, William 128, 276, 277
Trails of tears 200, 217, 218, 220
Treasurer 35
Treaty of Paris 80
Trough 142, 209
Truman, Harry 57
Tuition 147, 151

Turner, Frederick Jackson 123
Turner, Nat 55, 176, 254, 263, 267, 268, 269, 270, 281, 282, 286, 298
Tuskegee 297, 359, 360, 361
Tuskegee Airmen 361

U

Uncle Tom 192, 197, 224, 225, 226
Underground 110, 121, 126, 129, 278
United Daughters of the Confederacy 335
University of Virginia 50, 147, 148, 149, 180, 238
U.S. Route 60 73, 132

V

Viola Ruffner 37, 38, 146, 168, 170, 173, 180, 181, 327, 328, 350, 351, 352
Virginia Military Institute 283, 285
Virginia Polytechnic Institute 179, 188
Virginia's Chapel 277
Virginia Tech 39, 179, 352
Volkswagen fraud 149

W

Waltham factory 111
Ward, Henry Dans 258
Washington, Booker T. 1, 12, 14, 18, 20, 23, 25, 26, 27, 28, 29, 37, 41, 43, 125, 138, 146, 153, 162, 168, 170, 178, 196, 208, 209, 221, 239, 287, 288, 292, 297, 300, 324, 347, 349, 350, 353, 354, 355, 357, 358, 359, 360, 361, 362, 363, 364, 368, 371
Washington, George 65, 66, 67, 68, 70, 71, 74, 81, 87, 88, 89, 97, 99, 106, 107, 108, 147, 148, 163, 164, 184, 266, 324
Washington, Martha Dandridge Custis 108
Washington College 126, 147, 148, 150, 151, 170, 171, 172, 173, 175, 179
Wayne, Caroline 14, 153
Wayne, General Anthony 77, 108, 166
Wayne, Martha 14, 32
Wells, H. G. 33, 80, 91
West Virginia Health Right 366, 365

West Virginia State University 2, 15, 17, 20, 53, 278
West Virginia University 17, 50, 58, 149, 227, 266, 287, 299
White Lion 35
White Sulphur Springs 73, 165, 180
Whitman, Walt 333
Whitney, Eli 229, 230, 231
Whittier, John Greenleaf 204, 283
Whittle, Francis M. 269
Willey, Waitman T. 337
Willey, William P. 58
Willey Amendment 275, 337, 339, 340, 341, 342
William H. Ruffner Medal 39
Wilson, James 128
Wilson, Vincent Jr. 52, 315, 424
Wirt County 128
Wirz, Henry 335
Wise, Bob 46
Wise, Governor Bob 46
Withers, Alexander Scott 85, 428
Wood, Nehemiah Jr. 117, 167
Woodson, Carter G. 53
Woodward, C. Vann 357
W. Steele and Company 135

Y

Young Booker: See Washington, Booker T 13, 20, 28, 29, 37, 38, 39, 41, 43, 47, 146, 161, 168, 173, 178, 262, 263, 347, 348, 349, 351, 353, 358, 359, 360
Young, John 107

Z

Zion 14, 17, 21, 146, 150, 152, 153, 154, 277, 339, 350, 353, 357, 358, 367, 371